INTRODUCTORY COLLEGE ACCOUNTING

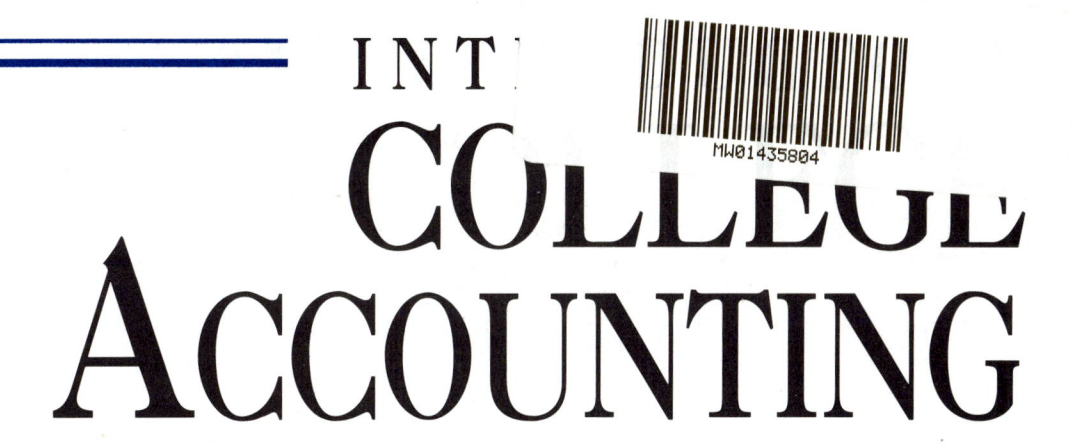

SECOND EDITION

With Microcomputer Applications

Henry J. Kaluza
University of Western Ontario

McGraw-Hill Ryerson Limited

Toronto Montreal New York Auckland Bogotá Caracas
Lisbon London Madrid Mexico Milan New Delhi
Paris San Juan Singapore Sydney Tokyo

INTRODUCTORY COLLEGE ACCOUNTING

SECOND EDITION

With Microcomputer Applications

© McGraw-Hill Ryerson Limited, 1992, 1980.
All rights reserved. No part of this publication
may be reproduced or transmitted in any form or by
any means, or stored in a database or retrieval
system, without the prior written permission of
McGraw-Hill Ryerson Limited.

1 2 3 4 5 6 7 8 9 10 RRD 1 0 9 8 7 6 5 4 3 2

Care has been taken to trace ownership of copyright
material contained in this text. However, the publishers
welcome information that enables them to rectify any
reference or credit in subsequent editions.

SPONSORING EDITOR: ANN BYFORD

PRODUCTION AND COPY EDITOR: RODNEY RAWLINGS

COVER AND TEXT DESIGN: MATTHEWS COMMUNICATIONS DESIGN

Printed and bound in the United States of America

Cover Photograph courtesy Miller Comstock/H.A.Roberts

Canadian Cataloguing in Publication Data

Kaluza, Henry J., 1930–
Introductory college accounting

2nd ed. with microcomputer applications
Includes index.
ISBN 0-07-549534-1

1. Accounting.   I. Title

HF5635.K35 1992   657'.044   C91-094324-9

CONTENTS

Preface v
Acknowledgements x

PART 1 The Framework of Accounting

Chapter 1 Introductory Accounting Concepts and Principles 3

TOPIC 1: Establishing the Accounting Model 4
TOPIC 2: Completing the Accounting Model 16

Chapter 2 Debit and Credit Concepts 31

TOPIC 1: Recording Changes in Balance Sheet Accounts 32
TOPIC 2: Recording Changes in Income Statement and Related Balance Sheet Accounts 42

Chapter 3 Accounting Cycle for a Service Firm 50

TOPIC 1: Bookkeeping Aspects 51
TOPIC 2: Six-Column Worksheet and Financial Statements 68
TOPIC 3: Completing the Accounting Cycle 73
TOPIC 4: Introducing the Electronic Spreadsheet 80

Chapter 4 Merchandising Concepts 99

TOPIC 1: Financial Statements of Merchandising Firms 100
TOPIC 2: Analyzing Merchandising Transactions 115

Chapter 5 Accounting Cycle for a Merchandising Firm 145

TOPIC 1: Bookkeeping Aspects 146
TOPIC 2: Ten-Column Worksheet 160
TOPIC 3: Completing the Accounting Cycle 183
TOPIC 4: Introducing the Microcomputer General Ledger System 192

Chapter 6 An Introduction to Partnership and Corporation Accounting 228

TOPIC 1: Partnership Accounting Concepts 229
TOPIC 2: Corporation Accounting Concepts 243

PART 2 Common Accounting Applications

Chapter 7 Accounts Receivable Application 271

TOPIC 1: Special Journals and Ledgers 272
TOPIC 2: Controlling and Accounting for Cash Receipts 289
TOPIC 3: Shortcuts in Manual Journalizing and Manual Posting 304

Chapter 8 Accounts Payable Application 327

TOPIC 1: Special Journals and Ledgers 329
TOPIC 2: Controlling and Accounting of Cash Payments 337
TOPIC 3: Applying Shortcuts in Journalizing and Posting 357

Chapter 9 Banking Applications 374

TOPIC 1: Bank Accounting Concepts 375
TOPIC 2: Preparing a Bank Reconciliation and the Statement of Cash Flows 390

Chapter 10 Payroll Application 413

TOPIC 1: Computing Gross Earnings and Deductions 414
TOPIC 2: Accounting for the Payroll 439
TOPIC 3: Accounting for Payroll Disbursements and Preparing Annual Tax Statements and Returns 453
TOPIC 4: Applying Manual Shortcuts to Payroll Accounting 463

Chapter 11 Using Microcomputer Software to Process Common Accounting Applications 477

TOPIC 1: Examining General Accounting Packages 478
TOPIC 2: Examining a Customized Accounting Package 525

Appendix Accounting for the Goods and Services Tax (GST) 545

TOPIC 1: Examining the Basics of the GST and GST Accounting 546
TOPIC 2: Analyzing Alternative Methods of Accounting for the GST 567

PREFACE

Purpose and Scope of This Text

This text, *Introductory College Accounting, Second Edition, With Microcomputer Applications*, represents a major revision of the first edition. In writing it, the following aims were kept in mind:

- To offer an introductory course for students classified as non-accounting majors at the college level
- To present a view of modern accounting principles and practices
- To give a good balance between "theory" and "accounting applications"
- To provide a foundation of learning to students who may find employment in accounting positions confined "to the end of the trial balance stage"
- To present measures of controlling cash not only from a business viewpoint, but also for personal-use applications

I have kept in mind the varying needs, abilities, and objectives of beginning accounting students, who, in the main, are preparing for careers as secretaries and accounting clerks. Consequently, the text is divided into three parts. The first six chapters, **Part 1,** teach the framework of accounting, for students who have no previous background in the fundamentals of financial accounting. **Part 2,** consisting of Chapters 7 through 11, introduces the learner to common accounting applications, with special emphasis on their use in small and medium-sized businesses. The third part consists of the **Appendix,** which provides an introduction to the complex subject of the Goods and Services Tax (GST).

The contents are so arranged that the book can be used for either a half- or a full-year program, and the material adapted for regular or more-intense study according to the student's ability.

New Features of This Edition

Application of the Microcomputer Perhaps the greatest change in accounting practice since the first edition has been the impact of the microcomputer and the various *accounting packages* (programs) available. Consequently, this second edition introduces electronic spreadsheet accounting applications (Chapter 3) and the microcomputer general ledger system (Chapter 5). Also, one entire chapter (Chapter 11) is devoted to the use of microcomputer software to process common accounting applications such as accounts receivable, accounts payable, and (Canadian) payroll.

In presenting this material, great care has been taken to simplify matters. No previous computer exposure is assumed, and the treatment of all applications is based on what students have learned about the manual system. In this way, students can make comparisons as well as gain a valuable introduction to the way accounting data is handled by microcomputers.

Many argue that students must use the computer in all accounting courses. However, this text presents the microcomputer applications as optional, and therefore some curriculum planners may choose to require only the reading of those parts of the text dealing with microcomputer accounting applications, while ignoring the computer-related accounting problems. Such omission in studying this text will not detract from its value toward the completion of a rewarding introductory course for non-accounting majors.

On the other hand, for the convenience of teachers who do require exposure of their students to microcomputer applications, the text identifies all such applications with a special icon in the left margin. In addition, McGraw-Hill Ryerson, the publisher of this text, provides supporting software materials as stated under "Supporting Materials" in this Preface.

An Introduction to Perpetual Inventory Accounting

The support of perpetual inventory accounting by leading microcomputer accounting software packages required an introduction to perpetual inventory accounting. Therefore, both the traditional, periodic inventory system and the perpetual inventory system are covered under merchandising concepts and the merchandising accounting cycle in Part 1.

Cash Flow Reporting

Since the first edition was published, much emphasis has been placed on the use of the statement of cash flows in accounting practice. Therefore, this statement is presented both as part of introducing corporation accounting concepts (Chapter 6) and in the discussion on preparing bank reconciliations and cash flow statements (Chapter 9).

Appendix on GST Accounting

An introduction to the accounting of the GST appears in the form of an appendix.

New Text Format

The wide margin to the left of the text has been used for key definitions, notes, and small illustrations. In addition, each chapter begins with a set of instructional objectives, giving readers an overview of the chapter as well as informing them as to what is expected of them on completing the chapter. All illustrations are now presented as double-numbered figures; for example, "Figure 1-1" identifies the first illustration in Chapter 1. Finally, a Chapter Summary has been included before the Chapter Questions and Accounting Case Problems sections.

Features Retained from the First Edition

Topic Problems

All chapters are divided into two or more "Topics," so that lesson planning can be facilitated. Each Topic is followed by a series of graded problem exercises in order of difficulty.

Chapter Questions Thought-provoking questions are found at the end of each chapter.

Accounting Cases Two accounting cases will be found at the end of each chapter. These are designed to challenge the student to analyze accounting problems that may be encountered in small and medium-sized business enterprises and to learn to make appropriate business decisions. These cases are ideal for promoting student-led discussions.

Equation Approach The "accounting equation" approach is used, as the best means of presenting the framework of accounting. That is, we delay discussion of the traditional implements—the general journal, general ledger, and debit-credit terminology—on the grounds that these are non-essential, and in fact may be an obstacle to grasping basic accounting concepts and principles. Through the equation approach, it is believed, students learn the *why* before the *how*.

Spiral Development The Topics are arranged to proceed from the simple to the complex, and from the known to the unknown. Part 1 features two accounting cycles: the first a simplified one in which a service firm is used without accounting adjustments, and the second one that treats a merchandising firm which employs the periodic inventory method with basic accounting adjustments. In keeping with the emphasis on avoiding complexities, only the general journal and general ledger are explained in Part 1. Special journals, subsidiary ledgers, and various bookkeeping shortcuts are dealt with in Part 2.

Introduction to GAAPs In Part 1, students are introduced to those generally accepted accounting principles that can be learned by beginners. The emphasis has been placed on an understanding of accounting principles for acceptable financial statement preparation rather than on how data is recorded into books.

Current Terminology In keeping with the updating of accounting terms generally accepted by the accounting profession, extreme care has been taken to adopt current and precise language throughout the text.

Common Applications Part 2 features the common accounting applications of accounts receivable, accounts payable, banking, and payroll. The material has been organized so that the emphasis is always on the accounting activity "to the end of the trial balance stage."

Conversion to SI For the most part, the International System of Units (SI) has been carried forward from the first edition in conformity with the recommendations of the Council of Ministers of Education's *Metric Guide*. However, two exceptions should be noted. One deals with the presentation of actual dollar amounts in current business usage. At the time of writing, dollar amounts in computer printouts of accounting data either use the comma as the traditional triad separator or dispense with any separation regardless of the number of digits; where such printouts are illustrated, no change has been made in the style of presentation of amounts.

The other exception deals with the writing of dollar amounts in numerical form on negotiable instruments such as cheques, money orders, and bank drafts. In these cases, to reflect the reality, no space is shown in the model for writing the amount on any negotiable instrument regardless of the number of digits.

Supporting Materials

Introductory College Accounting, Second Edition, With Microcomputer Applications offers the following supporting materials:

Study Guide and Working Papers

Two separate sets of working papers are published, one for Part 1 and one for Part 2 and the Appendix. These working papers allow the students to solve all Topic problems without the time-consuming task of ruling forms. Also included in each set are study guides in the form of Key Check Figures for each problem, a demonstration problem with suggested solution, and a set of multiple-choice questions with key so that students can test their final reading of each chapter.

Instructor's Manual

The separate *Instructor's Manual* is divided into two parts:

Part 1 provides the teacher with complete keys for all the problems, chapter questions, and cases in the text, and for the study guides included in the working papers.

Part 2 contains progress tests for all chapters in the text. In general, these tests are designed to be part of, but not replace, the teacher's overall testing and evaluation plan. Each test is divided into sections that closely correspond to the Topics in the chapter and are, in the main, objective in format. In addition, comprehensive tests—one for Part 1 and one for Part 2 plus the Appendix—are included to test the student's knowledge of more than one chapter. The solutions for the chapter progress tests and comprehensive tests are included in the source book.

Supporting Accounting Software

McGraw-Hill Ryerson Limited is pleased to offer the following software packages to instructors with the adoption of this textbook:

- One student edition of the electronic spreadsheet package called Quattro®, a widely used spreadsheet developed by Borland International, Inc.
- One set of Summation, Version 2.40 diskettes plus an accompanying data file diskette

Teachers are permitted to duplicate the disks and instruction material so that students can complete the suggested general ledger applications away from school laboratories.

Contact your local McGraw-Hill Ryerson representative for details.

ACKNOWLEDGEMENTS

I would like to express my appreciation to the following persons and business enterprises who provided information and supported the inclusion of some of the illustrations in the text: Abel Computers Ltd. (DYNA Dental Office Management System); Computer Associates Canada, Ltd. (AccPac Plus and AccPac Bedford); Vukusic Consulting Services Inc. (Easypay); SaltSpring Computer Systems (AccPac Bedford, Macintosh Version); Esselte Pendaflex Canada Inc. (Brownline Time Book Weekly); Dean et Fils Inc. (Dean Payroll Book and Dean Payroll Statements); Safeguard Business Systems Inc. (Safeguard one-write applications); SumWare Corporation (Summation); The Royal Bank of Canada; Bank of Montreal; Richardson Greenshields of Canada Limited; Dr. R. Wong of the Town Centre Dental Office (Mississauga, Ontario); Joan Murray of the Town Centre Dental Office (accounts receivable and payroll systems); B/J Robinson BusinessKeeping Inc. (Mardan—Safeguard Business Systems); and Stelco Inc.

I would also like to thank Michael Murk and Peter Murk of SumWare Corporation for their support in allowing their latest version of Summation to be used by students in conjunction with the microcomputer accounting applications offered as problems and illustrative material.

Henry J. Kaluza
Professor Emeritus
University of Western Ontario
London, Canada

PART 1

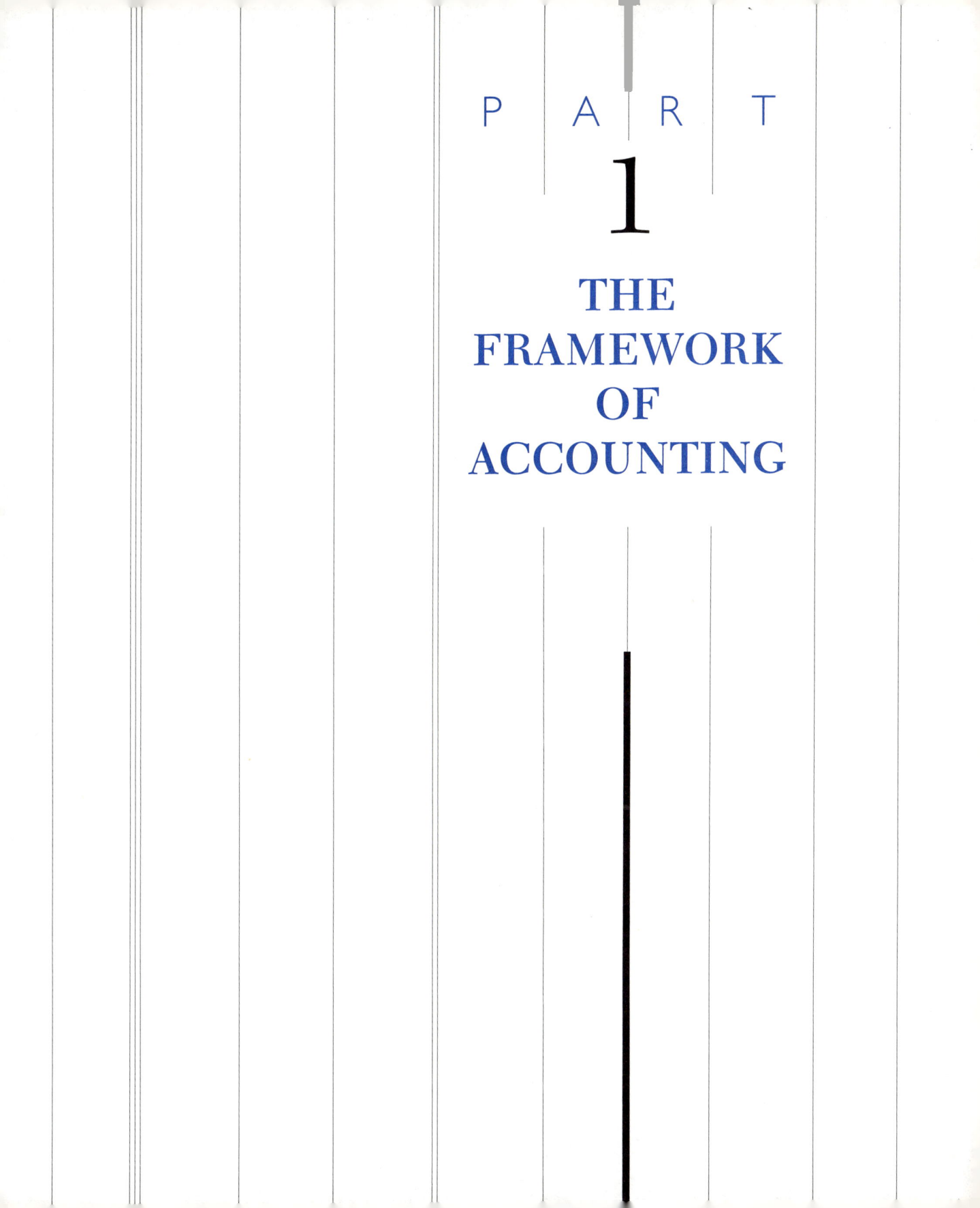

THE FRAMEWORK OF ACCOUNTING

CHAPTER 1 Introductory Accounting Concepts and Principles

After completing this chapter, you should be able to:

— Construct the basic accounting equation and define the three elements making up that equation.
— Prepare a pre-operating balance sheet from a basic accounting equation.
— Analyze revenue and expense transactions within an expanded accounting equation.
— Rearrange an expanded accounting equation to reflect the matching principle.
— Prepare an income statement and related balance sheet from the totals of an expanded accounting equation.
— Distinguish between the account form and report form of balance sheet.
— Analyze owner's withdrawals of assets for personal use on the accounting equation and report the totals of such withdrawals on a balance sheet.
— Define and apply the following accounting concepts: entity, going concern, time period, and unit of measure.
— Define and apply the following generally accepted accounting principles: cost, revenue recognition, expense recognition, and matching.
— Define the following key accounting terms presented in this chapter: assets, liabilities, owner's equity, capital, revenue, expense, drawings, net income, current assets, fixed assets, current liabilities, long-term liabilities, accounting concepts, entity concept, going-concern concept, time-period concept, unit of-measure concept, generally accepted accounting principles, cost principle, revenue principle, expense principle, and matching principle.

Language of business: the vocabulary of accounting.

The first half of this text presents the framework or structure of modern accounting. Within this framework only the basic language of accounting will be used so that you can apply it to the common accounting applications that are treated in the second half of the book. As you will learn, accounting is acknowledged as the *language of business*, because the vocabulary of accounting is largely used to communicate financial information about profit-seeking enterprises to interested persons both within and outside the business firm. Although the language of business may also

PART 1: THE FRAMEWORK OF ACCOUNTING

be applied to non-profit organizations (churches, clubs, social fraternities), this text is concerned primarily with accounting as it is practised by profit-seeking businesses.

Regardless of size, type, and form of ownership, all profit-seeking firms look to accounting to provide up-to-date financial information about all aspects of their business operations. This first chapter introduces you to some of the important accounting concepts and principles so that you can begin to understand the basic financial information that is commonly reported in the language of business.

TOPIC 1 Establishing the Accounting Model

One way to introduce the basic concepts and principles that make up the framework or structure of accounting is to examine answers to two questions: (1) What is required to begin any business? (2) How does any business acquire what is needed to commence its business operations?

The answer to the first question will vary with the type of business. Some examples of items required will include money, building, equipment, furniture, etc.; these items are called *resources*. Since these resources are scarce — in the sense that they are not free, that is, they must be produced and sold for dollars — all resources to establish any business can be acknowledged as **economic resources**.

Economic resources: scarce items which require effort to produce and to acquire which a price must be paid.

Two answers are possible for the second question. First, the owner or owners may have borrowed from a bank or other lending institution to acquire some of the needed money. In turn, the money could be used to acquire economic resources such as equipment and furniture. Or, the owner or owners may have acquired some of these economic resources directly from suppliers who agreed to grant the new business time, say 30, 60, or 90 days, to pay for the purchased economic resources. One source of acquiring economic resources, therefore, is by *borrowing* from banks and suppliers of goods. And since the banks and suppliers of goods have granted time for delayed payment, they are called **creditors** in the language of business.

Creditors: persons or firms who have granted credit (time for delayed payment).

No business can acquire all of its required economic resources by borrowing. Consequently, it is usually the case that the owner or owners have invested some of their personal savings (money) and possibly some of their own furniture, equipment, etc. to establish the business enterprise. A second important source of acquiring economic resources, therefore, is through the *investment* of the owner or owners of the business.

Establishing Important Accounting Equations

The relationship between economic resources and how they were acquired can now be presented in a form of business shorthand called

CHAPTER 1: Introductory Accounting Concepts and Principles **5**

> Accounting equations: shorthand ways of presenting accounting models.

accounting equations. Examine carefully the three equations in the illustrations which follow.

FIGURE 1-1

(1) *Economic Resources = Claims Against Economic Resources*
$100 000 = $100 000

FIGURE 1-2

(2) *Economic Resources = Claims of Creditors + Claim of Owner(s)*
$100 000 = $40 000 + $60 000

FIGURE 1-3

(3) A = L + OE
     Assets = Liabilities + Owner's Equity
     $100 000 = $40 000 + $60 000

Analysis The first equation, Figure 1-1, presents the basic idea that the total economic resources of any business enterprise must always be equal to the total claims against those economic resources. Observe that the economic resources have been placed on the left side of the equation, while the claims against the resources are identified on the right side.

The second equation, Figure 1-2, explains the relationship between economic resources and how they were acquired. Observe that the claims against the total economic resources come from two sources: the claims of creditors (resulting from borrowing by the business) and the claim of the owner or owners of the business (resulting from investment). The equals sign between the left and right sides of the equation suggests that the two sides must balance.

The third equation, Figure 1-3, translates the second one into the language of accounting. It is important to remember the following accounting concepts: economic resources are known as **assets**; the claims of creditors are known as **liabilities**; and the claim of the owner is called **owner's equity**. (The claims of several owners would be identified as *owners'* equity.)

> Assets: the economic resources of the business.
> Liabilities: the claims of creditors against the total assets.
> Owner's equity: the claim of the owner against the total assets.

Observe that the accounting equation consists of three parts or elements: *assets* (located on the left), *liabilities* (on the right), and *owner's equity* (also on the right). Observe further that the liabilities are identified before the owner's equity. This order is very important, because it is recognized under law that the claims of creditors take precedence over those of an owner (or owners). For example, if the business were to be declared bankrupt (incapable of paying its debts), then in any sale of the

Solving for One Unknown Element

You should have little difficulty in solving any accounting equation for one unknown element. For example, if A (Assets) = $100 000 and L (Liabilities) = $40 000, then OE (Owner's Equity) can be solved within the equation as shown in figure 1-4.

Illustrating the Accounting Equation

The three elements of the accounting equation can now be applied to a hypothetical business. To simplify matters at the start, a service-type firm known as Office Services will be used. Assume that this firm is owned and managed by Elizabeth LeClair. As the name suggests, Office Services will provide services such as keyboarding, copying, and duplicating for persons and other firms which require this service. To establish her sole proprietorship, assume that the following financial events occurred during September:

FIGURE 1-4

A	=	L	+	OE
$100 000	=	$40 000	+	?
OE	=	A	−	L
OE	=	$100 000	−	$40 000
OE	=	$60 000		

1. Elizabeth LeClair invested $50 000 of her personal cash savings.
2. She purchased office equipment for $35 000 cash.
3. She purchased furniture for $5 000 cash.
4. By signing a demand note at her bank, she raised $10 000 cash for the business in the form of a bank loan. (A bank demand note is a promissory note, signed by the borrower, agreeing to pay the amount of the loan whenever the bank demands payment.)

FIGURE 1-5

5. Additional office equipment costing $6 000 was acquired on 60 days' credit from a supplier of office equipment.
6. Additional furniture costing $9 000 was acquired from a furniture dealer on 30 days' credit.
7. Before using the office equipment, LeClair sold one piece — an electronic typewriter — to Lee Barnes, a real estate agent friend, at the same cost price of $1 000. LeClair gave Barnes 30 days' credit to pay for the cost of the typewriter.

CHAPTER 1: Introductory Accounting Concepts and Principles

The impact of each of the above financial transactions on the elements of the accounting equation may be analyzed in table form as illustrated in Figure 1-6. *Note:* The federal goods and services tax (GST) and the provincial sales tax (PST) have been omitted to simplify the accounting at this point. These taxes are treated in other chapters and in the Appendix of this text.

Analysis of Transaction 1 Two elements of the accounting equation are affected as a result of the owner's investment of cash in the business. Assets are established, because the business has $50 000 of cash. Since the economic resource was acquired through the owner's investment, the owner's claim against the Assets must be identified. In the language of accounting, the owner's claim against Assets through an investment is described as **capital**. And since the owner is known, the full identification is described as *E. LeClair, Capital* directly under *Owner's Equity*. Observe that the accounting equation is equal since Assets must always be equal to the claims against those Assets.

Capital: the investment of the owner or owners of a business enterprise.

FIGURE 1-6

SUMMARY TABLE

Trans-action	Assets					=	Liabilities			+	Owner's Equity
	Cash	Acct. Rec.	Office Equip.	Furni-ture	Total Assets		Bk. Loan Payable	Acct. Pay.	Total Liabilities		E. LeClair, Capital
(1)	+50 000				+50 000						+50 000
(2)	−35 000		+35 000		—						
(3)	−5 000			+5 000	—						
(4)	+10 000				+10 000		+10 000		+10 000		
(5)			+6 000		+6 000			+6 000	+6 000		
(6)				+9 000	+9 000			+9 000	+9 000		
(7)		+1 000	−1 000		—						
Totals	+20 000	+1 000	+40 000	+14 000	+75 000	= +10 000	+15 000	+25 000			+50 000

Equality Check: A   =   L   +   OE
                $75 000   = $25 000   + $50 000
                $75 000   = $75 000

Analysis of Transaction 2   Since office equipment was purchased for cash, only Assets are affected by this financial event. The business has acquired a new economic resource — Office Equipment — by decreasing another economic resource called Cash. And since one Asset amount is increased while a second one is decreased by the same dollar amount, the total Assets do not change. Finally, observe that the accounting equation is in balance; that is, the total dollar amount on the left side is equal to the total dollar amount on the right side.

Analysis of Transaction 3   Only one additional point of analysis is required, since this financial event is similar to the second one. Observe that a separate subheading, Furniture, is given under Assets to distinguish the new economic resource from Office Equipment.

Analysis of Transaction 4   A loan granted by a bank to a business results in the deposit of that loan in the firm's bank account; therefore, the business has acquired an additional economic resource in the form of Cash. In this case, however, the claim against the Asset is through borrowing. Consequently, a liability called **bank loan payable** is disclosed to show that the economic resource has been acquired by borrowing from a bank. Observe that both the left and the right side of the accounting equation have increased by the same dollar amount; therefore, the accounting equation still balances.

> Bank loan payable: the claim of a bank against the total assets of the borrowing business.

Analysis of Transaction 5   Since additional office equipment has been acquired by borrowing from suppliers on 60 days' credit, the element Liabilities must be increased. Observe that a separate creditors' identification, called **accounts payable**, is shown to distinguish borrowing from suppliers of goods as opposed to borrowing cash from a bank. And finally, note that the accounting equation must balance, because the total Assets and the total Liabilities have been increased by the same dollar amount.

> Accounts payable: amounts due to creditors (generally limited to liabilities for purchase of goods or services).

Analysis of Transaction 6   You should have no difficulty in recognizing that the analysis of this transaction is identical to that of Transaction 5. In this case, additional assets of furniture are offset by additional liabilities called Accounts Payable.

Analysis of Transaction 7   Since one piece of unused office equipment was sold for $1 000 (the original cost), the total Assets must be decreased by this dollar amount. And since the business gave 30 days' credit, a new economic resource called **accounts receivable** is shown as an increase to Assets. You can think of accounts receivable as an asset because it represents a claim against the customer's property (assets) until he or she pays the amount owed. However, the more common application of accounts receivable is the business operation of selling services to customers. The sales side of accounting will be treated later on in this chapter.

> Accounts receivable: amounts claimed against debtors usually arising from the sale of goods or services.

CHAPTER 1: Introductory Accounting Concepts and Principles

Following the final transaction, observe the equality check below the summary table. Just as the accounting equation must balance following the analysis of each financial event, so too must the equation balance when the various elements are totalled.

Reporting the Accounting Equation of Any Business

In actual practice, the items contained in the accounting equation are commonly reported in a financial statement called the **balance sheet**. In the language of business, the balance sheet is the financial statement that reports the details of assets, liabilities, and the owner's equity of a business enterprise as at a particular date. And since the owner has yet to commence actual business operations, this balance sheet is more accurately called the opening or **pre-operating balance sheet**. Let us assume that the totals of the final equation for Office Services show the financial pre-operating position of assets, liabilities, and the claim of the owner as at the end of September. The pre-operating balance sheet for the business may then be reported as illustrated in Figure 1-7.

Balance sheet: a financial statement reporting the assets, liabilities, and owner's equity of a business as at a particular date.

Pre-operating balance sheet: a balance sheet prepared before the commencement of actual business operations.

FIGURE 1-7

	Assets			=	Liabilities		+	Owner's Equity
Cash	Acct. Rec.	Office Equip.	Furni- ture		Bk. Loan Pay.	Acct. Pay.		E. LeClair, Capital
$20 000	+ $1 000	+ $40 000	+ $14 000	=	$10 000	+ $15 000	+	$50 000
	$75 000			=		$25 000	+	$50 000

Office Services
Pre-operating Balance Sheet
As at September 30, 19—

Assets			Liabilities	
Current Assets:			Current Liabilities:	
Cash............................	$20 000		Bank Loan Payable...............	$10 000
Accounts Receivable..............	1 000		Accounts Payable	15 000
Total Current Assets..............	21 000		Total Liabilities	$25 000
Fixed Assets (at cost):			Owner's Equity	
Office Equipment................	40 000		E. LeClair, Capital	50 000
Furniture.......................	14 000			
Total Fixed Assets................	54 000			
Total Assets	$75 000		Total Liabilities and Owner's Equity	$75 000

10 PART 1: THE FRAMEWORK OF ACCOUNTING

Analysis of the Heading

Three-line heading of the balance sheet reports:
(1) Who?
(2) What?
(3) When?

Separate entity concept: the idea whereby accounting views the business as having a separate existence apart from its owners; thus, all assets in the balance sheet belong only to the business, all liabilities are claims of creditors against those business assets, and the owner's equity is the claim of the owner against the total business assets.

Observe the three-line heading, properly centred, over the body of the pre-operating balance sheet. The ***first line*** reports the name of the firm; the ***second line*** identifies the financial statement; and the ***third line*** discloses the particular moment of time for reporting the firm's assets and claims against those assets.

In the pre-operating balance sheet for Office Services, the date reads "As at September 30, 19—." Keep in mind that, when the third line of the heading discloses only the particular date, the words "as at" are understood.

It is also important to remember that the first line reports the name of the firm. Therefore, only assets and claims belonging to that firm will be reported in the body below. It would be a serious error to include the personal assets of the owner such as the owner's home and contents, cottage, personal-use automobile, etc. as part of the firm's assets. Similarly, it is a serious error to report personal debts under the liabilities of the business. Accounting treats every business enterprise as being a separate entity; that is, the business is regarded as being separate, distinct, and apart from its owners. This is called the ***separate entity concept***.

Analysis of the Body

The body of the balance sheet presents the three main elements of the accounting equation. Assets are reported on the left side, while the liabilities and owner's equity appear on the right side. In this context, the arrangement of the items in the balance sheet follows the form of the accounting equation. A second form of reporting these elements will be examined in Chapter 3.

Analysis of the Assets Section

Current assets: cash and other assets which are expected to be converted into cash within one year (this is a preliminary definition only).

Fixed assets (or property, plant, and equipment, or capital assets): tangible, long-lived assets which are held for use within the firm.

Several important points are worth remembering when reporting the assets on a balance sheet.

- Centre between the left side of the form and the first money column the title "Assets" on the first line of print or writing.
- Classify assets into at least two groups: current assets and fixed assets. At this point in the introduction of ***current assets***, this new idea will consist of cash and other assets that, in the normal course of business operations, are expected to be converted into cash within one year of the date of the balance sheet. For Office Services, Accounts Receivable is placed behind Cash, because the business expects to convert the amount due from customers within 30 days. Although this "liquidity" definition for current assets is appropriate here, it is important to realize that a more complete accounting definition of the term will be introduced in Chapter 5.
- Not all assets on a balance sheet are converted into cash; therefore, a separate class called ***fixed assets*** (or property, plant, and equipment, or capital assets) will be shown, to report those tangible, long-term assets which are retained in the business to support the day-to-day

CHAPTER 1: Introductory Accounting Concepts and Principles

operations. For Office Services, two important fixed assets are revealed. Note that only the general term "Office Equipment" is used in the balance sheet. It would include such economic resources as typewriters, calculators, copiers, duplicators, computers, filing cabinets, etc. Similarly, the term "Furniture" includes such economic resources as desks, chairs, and tables. In accounting practice, it is important to group related assets into broad categories rather than to itemize each asset separately on a balance sheet.

There are many other kinds of assets. In a manufacturing enterprise, the land, plant, raw materials, tools, and machinery that the business owns are among its most important assets. In wholesale and retail merchandising firms, the goods (merchandise) that the business has on hand to sell are among its chief assets.

- Note that the total for current assets and for fixed assets should be shown on a balance sheet. Since neither one represents the final total at the bottom of its column, *each is considered a subtotal, and is completed by showing only a singled ruled line below the dollar amount*. The two subtotals will be added to calculate the total assets at the bottom of the column.

- Observe the words "at cost" shown in parentheses after "Fixed Assets." This qualification is in keeping with the accounting profession's broad guidelines, called **generally accepted accounting principles (GAAPs)**. These principles set the standards for reporting money amounts on a balance sheet and other financial statements which are prepared for readers outside the business enterprise. The GAAP that sets the standard for reporting asset amounts is known as the *cost principle*, which may be stated as shown in the side margin.

The cost principle means that accountants prefer to report assets on the basis of the dollars that have been used to acquire these economic resources. When applied to the familiar balance sheet, the cost principle recognizes that the assets reported show the cost of that asset, and not the present value or worth of that asset. When studying any balance sheet, therefore, care should be exercised to avoid reading too much into this financial statement, because a balance sheet does not show either present values of assets to the enterprise or values that might be realized in any liquidation process. The cost principle is an attempt to define the term "value" as the cost value of the assets. Therefore, always show "at cost" after "Fixed Assets" or "Property, Plant, and Equipment" in any balance sheet intended to be read by persons outside the firm.

Side margin:
Generally accepted accounting principles (GAAPs): those broad guidelines adopted by accountants for the preparation of financial statements to interested persons outside the firm.

Cost principle: as applied to assets, a GAAP that the basis for reporting assets is the cost at the date of their acquisition.

Analysis of the Liabilities Section

From earlier study of the accounting equation, you will recall that the claims of creditors — the liabilities — came before the claim of the owner. Hence, the title "Liabilities" is centred on the right side on the first line of printing or writing. Like the assets, the liabilities are classified and reported in a certain order. Since the liabilities represent debts, most accountants prefer to list the claims of creditors in the order in which they must be paid on a time basis. Two classes or groups of liabilities are shown:

- First, list the debts of the business which are expected to be paid within one year of the balance sheet date. In the language of accounting, such debts are called **current liabilities**. For Office Services, note that the bank loan payable precedes the listing of accounts payable, because the loan from the bank was transacted on a demand basis, while the accounts payable were to be paid within a normal 30- or 60-day period. Since the payment of current liabilities is expected within one year, it is logical to conclude that the payments are made from dollars shown by the current asset section of the balance sheet. Consequently, a useful analysis of the financial position of the firm may be made by comparing the current assets with the current liabilities.

> Current liabilities: debts owing which will fall due within one year of the balance sheet date.

- Second, group under a separate heading all liabilities which, in the ordinary course of business, will not be liquidated within one year of the balance sheet date. For example, in acquiring land and a building some businesses find it necessary to negotiate a loan on a long-term basis, say for 20 or 30 years. Such a long-term debt is usually supported by a document called the *mortgage*. Since the mortgage payable will not be liquidated within one year, it should be classified in the balance sheet under a heading such as **long-term liabilities.**

> Mortgage: a promise in writing which assigns property as security for the payment of debt.
>
> Long-term liabilities: debts which, in the ordinary course of business, will not be liquidated within one year.

In Figure 1-8, observe the common practice to disclose information such as the due date of the long-term debt and the assets that are pledged or assigned as security for the mortgage. Any portion of the long-term debt which is due within one year would be classified under current liabilities and excluded from the long-term amount. Note also that separate subtotals should be shown for current liabilities and long-term liabilities.

Analysis of the Owner's Equity Section

From the two illustrated balance sheets, you can observe that the claim of the owner is reported below the claims of the creditors. For a better appearance, leave one line after the liability section; then centre the title for the owner's equity section. As indicated earlier, the claim of the owner through an initial investment is described by identifying the owner's name followed by the word "Capital."

Analysis of Other Formats

Three additional points are worth recalling for the preparation of any pre-operating balance sheet:

- After the assets, liabilities, and owner's equity are entered on a balance sheet, rule a single line across each money column and total

FIGURE 1-8

National Car Rental Company
Pre-operating Balance Sheet
As at September 1, 19—

Assets			Liabilities		
Current Assets:			Current Liabilities:		
Cash	$ 16 000		Bank Loan Payable (demand)	$ 7 000	
Government Bonds	10 000		Accounts Payable	3 000	
Accounts Receivable	4 000		Principal payment on mortgage due within one year	2 000	
Total Current Assets		30 000	Total Current Liabilities		12 000
Fixed Assets (at cost):			Long-Term Liabilities:		
Land (security for mortgage)	40 000		10% Mortgage Payable, due September 1, 2008	40 000	
Building (security for mortgage)	60 000		Less: Current portion due within one year	2 000	
Automobiles	35 000				
Office Equipment	3 000				
Furniture	2 000		Total Long-Term Liabilities		38 000
Total Fixed Assets		140 000	Total Liabilities		$ ~~67 000~~ 50 000
			Owner's Equity		
			R. Pasichnyk, Capital (Owers investment)		120 000
Total Assets		$170 000	Total Liabilities and Owner's Equity		$170 000

the dollar amounts in the columns. Obviously, the total on the left side will represent the total assets, while the total on the right side will be the total of the liabilities and owner's equity. Note that the single rules are placed on the same writing line. Observe also that the totals must be equal, since a balance sheet is based on the accounting equation.

- Show dollar signs opposite the first amount and opposite the final amount in each money column. In addition, a dollar sign may be placed opposite important amounts such as that for "Total Liabilities." It is important to use the dollar sign regardless of whether the financial statement is handwritten, typewritten, typeset, or printed by a computer. Contemporary accounting practice favours the use of dollar signs in the preparation of all financial statements to "outsiders" for two reasons: (a) such financial statements are regarded as formal reports; and (b) all financial statements to those outside the firm should disclose the nature of the money unit used to report the results of economic activities of the reporting firm.

TOPIC 1 Problems

Classifying items within the accounting equation.

1.1 Each of the items below is a fundamental element of the accounting equation. Classify each item correctly by using A for assets, L for liabilities, and OE for owner's equity.
- a Cash in Bank *A*
- b L. Marcotte, Capital *E*
- c Bank Loan Payable *L*
- d Accounts Receivable *A*
- e Accounts Payable *L*
- f Office Equipment *A*
- g Delivery Equipment *A*
- h Inventory *A*
- i Machinery *A*
- j Tools *A*
- k Mortgage Payable *L*
- l Land *A*
- m Buildings *A*
- n Current Portion of Long-Term Debt *L*

Solving one unknown within accounting equations.

1.2 Solve the one unknown in each of the following equations:

	Assets	=	Liabilities	+	Owner's Equity
a	$200 000	=	$100 000	+	*100 ? 000*
b	300 000	=	*40? 00*	+	$260 000
c	*180 ? 000*	=	80 000	+	100 000
d	450 000	=	0	+	*450?000*
e	*200 ? 000*	=	0	+	200 000
f	700 000	=	*150 ? 000*	+	550 000

Calculating owner's equity; constructing an accounting equation.

1.3 On September 30 of the current year, Lenore Finnie began the practice of law under her own name. Her business's assets and liabilities on that date and before commencing operations are as follows: Cash, $1 800; Office Equipment, $30 000; Furniture, $10 000; Law Books, $3 200; Accounts Receivable (J. Newton), $500; Accounts Payable (Milton Equipment Co.), $2 000; Bank Loan (demand note), $3 500. Calculate the owner's equity; then construct an accounting equation by itemizing the three elements of the equation.

Note: Keep your answer for use in Problem 1.5.

CHAPTER 1: Introductory Accounting Concepts and Principles **15**

Calculating owner's equity; constructing an accounting equation.

1.4 Franca Zadra, owner of the Manitoba Car Rental Company, established her car rental business on this date with these economic resources and debts: Cash, $2 900; Accounts Receivable, $5 000; Land, $24 000; Buildings, $86 000; Automobiles, $40 000; Furniture, $2 400; Office Equipment, $23 800; Bank Loan (demand note), $10 000; Accounts Payable, $1 600; and Mortgage Payable, $50 000 (assume a 10% ten-year mortgage, with annual payments of principal at $5 000, with the land and buildings as assets assigned to secure the mortgage). Calculate the owner's equity; then construct the accounting equation for Franca Zadra's business by itemizing the three elements of the equation.

Note: Keep your answer for use in Problem 1.5.

Preparing pre-operating balance sheets for Problems 1.3 and 1.4.

1.5 Refer back to the accounting equations solved for Problems 1.3 and 1.4; then prepare separate pre-operating balance sheets for (a) L. Finnie, Barrister and (b) Manitoba Car Rental Company.

Analyzing pre-operating transactions within a summary table; proving the totals of the accounting equation; preparing the resulting pre-operating balance sheet.

1.6 On September 1 of the current year, Nancy Barrington formed the Barrington Advertising Agency. During the first month, her business had the following business transactions prior to the commencement of actual operations:

1. Nancy Barrington invested $75 000 of her personal cash savings.
2. She purchased furniture for $6 000 cash.
3. She purchased office equipment for $45 000 cash.
4. She signed a demand note at her bank to raise $20 000 cash for the business.
5. Additional office equipment costing $5 000 was acquired on 30 days' credit from Hay Stationery Inc.
6. Additional furniture costing $4 000 was acquired from Centre Office Furniture on 30 days' credit.
7. Before using the office equipment, Barrington sold one piece — a copier — to Alice Baker, a real estate agent friend, at the same cost price of $2 000. Barrington gave Baker 30 days' credit to pay for the cost of the typewriter.

Required

a Set up a summary table with the following column headings: Cash; Acct. Rec.; Office Equipment; Furniture; Total Assets; Bank Loan Payable; Acct. Pay.; Total Liabilities; N. Barrington, Capital.

b Analyze the effect of each of the seven transactions on the three elements of the accounting equation.

c After completing the analysis of the final transaction, total the individual columns; then show a check to prove that the equation is in balance.

d From the column totals, prepare a pre-operating balance sheet in good form as at September 30, 19—.

TOPIC 2 Completing the Accounting Model

So far, the framework of accounting has been restricted to a basic accounting equation and a basic balance sheet for a simplified business enterprise. To complete the model of accounting, it is necessary to record the activities which relate to the main reason for conducting any business enterprise. The primary reason for operating a business is to earn a profit over a period of time. As you will learn, a profit will have the effect of increasing the claim of the owner by expanding the owner's equity section within the accounting equation.

In the language of business, the financial events that are directly related to the accounting of a business profit (or loss) are known as ***revenue and expense transactions***. To illustrate the effects of such transactions, five financial events will be analyzed on the accounting equation earlier established for Office Services. It is important to realize that the transactions offered below are simplified so that you can easily analyze their effects on an expanded accounting model.

> Revenue and expense transactions: financial events that determine the profit (or loss) of a business enterprise.

8. During October, assume that Office Services received $8 000 cash from the sale of services during the month.
9. Also during October, assume that Office Services sold services to customers on 30 days' credit and that the total of such services rendered as of October 31 amounted to $12 000.
10. To obtain the total revenue for the month, assume that Office Services paid cash for the following expenses: Rent, $950; Salaries, $9 000; Telephone, $50; and Utilities, $100.
11. Assume that Office Services on October 31 received a bill for $2 000 from *The Local Press*, a daily newspaper, for running advertisements during October. Assume further that the bill allowed the business a period of 30 days in which to pay for the bill.
12. And, finally, during October, assume that Elizabeth LeClair withdrew $1 000 cash from the firm's bank account for her personal use.

The effect of each of the above transactions on the elements of the accounting equation may be analyzed in table form as illustrated in Figure 1-9. *Note*: Again, the accounting of federal and provincial sales taxes has been omitted from these transactions.

Analysis of Transaction 8   As you will recall, when a business receives cash the Assets on the left side of the accounting equation must increase; therefore, a plus sign is placed before the cash amount of $8 000. Furthermore, you have learned that once the left side of the accounting equation is increased, the right side must also be increased, because assets must always be equal to the claims against those assets. There are only two elements on the right side: Liabilities and Owner's Equity. Since the

CHAPTER 1: Introductory Accounting Concepts and Principles   17

FIGURE 1-9

SUMMARY TABLE

Trans-actions	Assets				=	Liabilities		+	Owner's Equity			
	Cash	Acct. Rec.	Office Equip.	Furni-ture		Bk. Loan Pay.	Acct. Pay.		E. LeClair, Capital	Revenue	Expenses	E. LeClair, Drawing
Balances after (7)	+20 000	+1 000	+40 000	+14 000	=	+10 000	+15 000	+	+50 000			
(8)	+8 000									+8 000		
(9)		+12 000								+12 000		
(10)	–10 100										–10 100	
(11)							+2 000				–2 000	
(12)	–1 000											–1 000
Totals	+16 900	+13 000	+40 000	+14 000	=	+10 000	+17 000	+	+50 000	+20 000	–12 100	–1 000

Equality Check: A ($83 900) = L ($27 000)   +   OE ($50 000 + $20 000 – $12 100 – $1 000)
                  A ($83 900) = L ($27 000)   +   OE $56 900
                  A ($83 900) = L + OE ($83 900)

Revenue: an inflow of cash and accounts receivable to the business enterprise that results from the sale of services (and goods) to customers.

transaction did not identify the asset as having been acquired through borrowing, Liabilities must not be affected by this financial event. The exclusion of Liabilities must mean that the claims of the owner — Owner's Equity — increase by $8 000. But, since the owner did not invest the cash, E. LeClair, Capital could not have caused the increase. What, then, caused the claim of the owner to be increased as a result of the selling of services for cash? In the language of accounting, the answer is **revenue**. Observe that Owner's Equity has been expanded on the right side of the accounting equation to reveal "Revenue" as a plus factor in affecting the claim of the owner against total assets. A quick check of the equality on both sides should prove that the equation is in balance.

Analysis of Transaction 9   As a result of sales of services on credit, the Assets are increased, because the business now has additional claims on the property of customers until their debts are paid. On the right side of the equation, the additional revenue causes a second increase to Owner's Equity. Observe that this increase is shown as a second plus factor under Revenue and that the total revenue for October is now $20 000. Since the right side of the equation has been increased by an identical amount ($12 000) of increase as shown on the left side, the equation is in balance.

The analysis of Transactions 8 and 9 offers one excellent definition of revenue, as shown in the side margin. It is important to remember that an inflow of cash does not automatically affect revenue. As you will recall, an investment by the owner causes an inflow of cash and is offset by causing an increase in Owner's Equity through the Capital (investment). Furthermore, cash may enter the business as a result of a customer's payment of his or her accounts receivable. In this case, one asset — Cash — is exchanged for another—Accounts Receivable.

One other point is worth introducing here. Notice that revenue is recognized both when a sale is made for cash and when it is made on credit. In other words, it would be a violation of generally accepted accounting principles to make a sale on credit and then recognize revenue only when the cash is received. Always remember that, according to the **revenue recognition principle,** revenue occurs as at the point of sale of goods or as at the point of rendering services.

Revenue recognition principle: the idea whereby revenue earned is recognized as at the time of the sale of goods, or as at the time of the rendering of services.

Analysis of Transaction 10 No profit-seeking business can generate amounts of revenue without incurring some expense. In this transaction, a total of $10 100 cash was used up to pay for the rent, salaries, telephone, and utilities expenses. Consequently, the Assets on the left side of the equation must decrease by this total amount. And since Liabilities on the right side are not affected by this transaction, the claim of the owner must be decreased by $10 100 to balance the accounting equation.

Observe that Owner's Equity is decreased in an expanded equation by showing the concept "Expenses" as a subelement and placing a minus sign in front of the dollar amount. This, of course, does not mean that expenses are going down; they must be interpreted as a minus factor under Owner's Equity in the accounting equation. In other words, expenses cause a *decrease* in the claim of the owner against the total assets of the business. Note that the minus sign must be correct, for otherwise the accounting equation could not balance.

Analysis of Transaction 11 Since the advertising bill was incurred for the purpose of generating revenue, the cost of advertising must be regarded as an expense. In this transaction, however, the left side of the equation is not affected, since Office Services was given 30 days to pay the bill. What remains, therefore, is a careful analysis of balancing the right side of the equation only.

First, observe that Liabilities must be increased by $2 000, because a debt has been recognized. Second, note that the claim of the owner must be decreased by the same amount, because an expense has been incurred in the process of earning revenue. In the expanded equation, this decrease is indicated by showing a second expense amount and a second minus sign opposite the amount of the expense. Once again, the minus sign does not mean that expenses have decreased; it only means that a second expense

CHAPTER 1: Introductory Accounting Concepts and Principles   19

is listed to show another decrease to Owner's Equity in the accounting equation. And, third, the owner's claim against the total assets must be lower, since the claims of creditors — the Liabilities — have been increased; otherwise, the accounting equation could not balance.

It is appropriate after Transaction 11 to give an accounting definition for **expenses**. One good definition is stated in the side margin. Since expenses represent the cost of the goods and services used up (or consumed), they may also be known as *expired costs*.

One other principle related to the accounting of expenses is important to remember. By the ***expense recognition principle***, expenses occur as at the time costs have been used up to create revenue and not necessarily when cash is paid for those expenses. You should recall these important concepts when other expense transactions are introduced in the later chapters of this text.

> Expenses: the costs of goods and services used up (consumed) in the process of generating revenue (expired costs).
>
> Expense recognition principle: the idea that expenses must be accounted for when they are incurred in the process of generating revenue.

Analysis of Transaction 12   The owner's withdrawing $1 000 cash from the business for personal use causes the left side of the equation to decrease, because the business no longer has $1 000 cash. Since the left side of the equation has decreased by $1 000, a similar amount of decrease must be recognized on the right side to balance the equation. Since Liabilities are not affected, Owner's Equity must decrease by $1 000.

But what subelement under Owner's Equity causes this decrease to OE? Not capital, for it refers to the idea of investing. Revenue has been defined as an inflow of assets resulting from the sale of goods and services. Expense could be considered; however, expenses have been defined as costs used up to generate revenue. In this case, the owner withdrew cash for personal use. Cash has been used up, but not to create revenue or support revenue-making activities. The owner withdrew the cash for needed personal expenses in order to maintain a living. Personal-use expenses must never be included in the accounting of business expenses; as you recall, the separate entity concept requires the separation of the owner's personal assets, personal liabilities, personal revenues, and personal expenses from the accounting of business assets, business liabilities, business revenues, and business expenses.

The correct analysis is to show a further expansion of the Owner's Equity section to include a subelement called ***E. LeClair, Drawing***. As the summary table shows, the withdrawal of $1 000 is shown as a minus quantity to support the concept that Owner's Equity must decrease as a result of any withdrawal of assets from the business for the personal use of the owner.

> E. LeClair, Drawing: an example of a subelement under Owner's Equity which shows amounts withdrawn from the business for the personal use of the owner.

Matching Revenues and Expenses

The final line of totals in the expanded equation may now be rearranged to relate the revenues and expenses in order to determine whether the business has made a profit or a loss for the month. In the language of

20 PART 1: THE FRAMEWORK OF ACCOUNTING

Matching: the accounting process of correlating revenues with expenses in order to determine the net income or net loss of an accounting period.

accounting, this process is called **matching** the revenues with related expenses. It may be shown as in Figure 1-10.

FIGURE 1-10

Assets	=	Liabilities	+	Owner's Equity

Cash	Acct. Rec.	Office Equip.	Furniture		Bk. Loan Pay.	Acct. Pay.		E. LeClair, Capital	+20 000 −12 100	Revenue Expenses	E. LeClair, Drawing
$16 900	+ $13 000	+ $40 000	+ $14 000	=	$10 000	+ $17 000	+	$50 000	+ $7 900 Net Income		− $1 000
	$83 900			=		$27 000	+		$56 900		

Analysis of Matching Revenues and Expenses

The matching in this accounting equation reveals an excess of revenue over related expenses. In common language, this excess of $7 900 may be termed the *net profit*, but although "profit" is an acceptable term, the majority of accountants today prefer to use the term "income." Therefore, when all revenues for a certain time period have been matched against all related expenses and the result is an excess of revenue, that result is generally known as the **net income.** (A third acceptable synonym in accounting for net income is *net earnings*. In terms of modern reporting, both "net income" and "net earnings" are used more often than "net profit.")

In the rearranged expanded equation, notice that the net income is a plus factor under Owner's Equity. Also note that the owner's drawings are shown as a minus factor under Owner's Equity. In other words, the owner's claim against the total assets now consists of three parts: the original investment, called Capital; the Net Income for the accounting period (in this case, for the month of October); and the total withdrawals — Drawing — of assets for the personal use of the owner.

It should be emphasized that the matching process does not always result in a net income. For example, if the total expenses were greater than the revenue for a definite time period, then a *net loss* will be identified in the rearranged equation, as partially illustrated in the side margin. In this case, the net loss must be a minus factor under Owner's Equity, because the excess expense amount must have decreased the owner's claim against the total assets.

Net income: the excess of revenues over related expenses for an accounting period (net earnings; net profit).

FIGURE 1-11

Owner's Equity

J. Rice, Capital	+$10 000	Revenue
	−15 000	Expense
$30 000 −	$ 5 000	Net Loss

Reporting the Results of the Expanded Accounting Equation

The results of the expanded accounting equation may now be summarized into two accounting reports: the income statement, which summarizes the revenue and related expenses to report the net income or net loss for the accounting period; and a new, related balance sheet to report the position of assets, liabilities, and the owner's equity at the end of the accounting

made to the owner in advance of accounting for such incomes. In other words, all ***owner drawings*** — personal withdrawals by the owner — are distributions of the net income paid before the net income has been reported. One can conclude that the net income becomes the connecting link between the income statement and the balance sheet at the end of the accounting period.

In the analysis of the balance sheet, two other important accounting concepts can now be introduced. One is called the ***going-concern concept***. Accounting theory assumes, on the basis of present facts, that the business entity will not wind up its operations immediately after commencing business. Therefore, the fixed assets acquired are reported in the balance sheet on the assumption that those economic resources will be used to generate revenue or assist in revenue-making activities for as long as those fixed assets have a useful life. This concept does not suggest that the business will last forever. It simply allows accountants to classify assets between current and fixed. It also permits accountants to report assets at their cost values on the assumption that the business will have a long life.

Another important accounting concept that may be applied to the study of both the income statement and the balance sheet is called the ***unit-of-measure concept*** or stable monetary unit concept. For the purpose of reporting financial statements to interested parties outside the business, accounting assumes that the purchasing power in the monetary unit being reported — in Canada, the dollar — has not changed, even though inflation may have occurred during the accounting period being reported.

In summary, the complete accounting model in its most elementary form may be related to the expanded accounting equation. From this expanded equation, two important financial statements are commonly prepared: the income statement, which reports the net income (or net loss) for a definite accounting period; and the related balance sheet, which reports in terms of historical dollars the assets, liabilities, and owner's equity as at a particular date.

period. These financial statements may be reported for Office Services as in Figures 1-12 and 1-13.

FIGURE 1-12

Office Services
Income Statement
For the Month Ended October 31, 19—

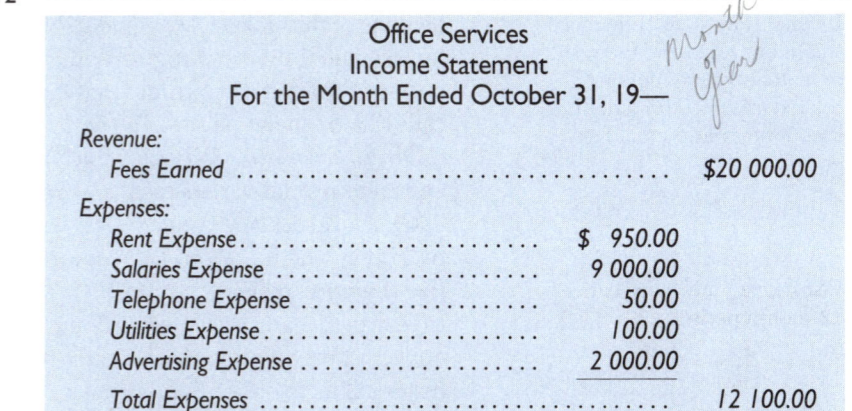

Revenue:		
Fees Earned		$20 000.00
Expenses:		
Rent Expense	$ 950.00	
Salaries Expense	9 000.00	
Telephone Expense	50.00	
Utilities Expense	100.00	
Advertising Expense	2 000.00	
Total Expenses		12 100.00
Net Income		$ 7 900.00

FIGURE 1-13

Office Services
Balance Sheet
As at October 31, 19—

Assets

Current Assets:		
Cash	$16 900.00	
Accounts Receivable	13 000.00	
Total Current Assets		$29 900.00
Fixed Assets (at cost):		
Office Equipment	$40 000.00	
Furniture	14 000.00	
Total Fixed Assets		54 000.00
Total Assets		$83 900.00

Liabilities

Current Liabilities:		
Bank Loan Payable (on demand)	$10 000.00	
Accounts Payable	17 000.00	
Total Liabilities		$27 000.00

Owner's Equity

E. LeClair, Capital		$50 000.00
Add: Net Income		7 900.00
		57 900.00
Less: Withdrawals		1 000.00
Total Owner's Equity		56 900.00
Total Liabilities and Owner's Equity		$83 900.00

TOPIC 2 Problems

1.7 On September 1 of the current year, Kathy Campling formed the Campling Word Processing Service. During the first month her business had the following business transactions:

1. Kathy Campling commenced business with the following assets and liabilities: Cash, $30 000; Accounts Receivable, $1 000; Office Equipment, $20 000; Furniture, $4 000; Bank Loan (demand note), $10 000; and Accounts Payable, $5 000.
2. Campling Word Processing Service received a cheque from Mary Graham for $1 000 in payment of her debt owing to the business.

PART 1: THE FRAMEWORK OF ACCOUNTING

Analysis of the Income Statement

Income statement: a financial statement reporting the results of matching revenues and related expenses for a definite accounting period that has ended.

Fiscal year: any consecutive 12-month period.

Time-period concept: assumes the need to divide the life of a business entity into convenient time periods.

As you can see, the basic structure of an *income statement* is based upon the Revenue and Expense subelements of the expanded portion of Owner's Equity within the accounting equation. Observe the three-line heading of this financial statement. Since the net income (or net loss) must be calculated by matching revenues with related expenses for a definite period of time, it is important that the third line of the heading communicate this financial period. In the language of business, such a period is called an *accounting period* or *fiscal period*. If the period of matching revenues with related expenses covered 12 months, the period would be known as an *accounting year* or a *fiscal year*. Although many firms use a fiscal year which ends on December 31, it is important to recognize that a ***fiscal year*** can be any consecutive 12-month period. Also, it is important to realize that any fiscal period being reported in an income statement has ended; consequently, the heading reports correctly that the figures are historical facts rather than estimates of future income.

Emphasizing the fiscal period in any income statement introduces another accounting concept called the ***time-period concept***. This concept supports the theory that business operations of an accounting entity can be divided into arbitrary time periods. Government and the business community have required the entity to have a cut-off point at which that entity must report its results from business operations. For example, Revenue Canada — Taxation requires all profit-seeking businesses to report their income on an annual basis. And, as you will learn from Chapter 6, corporation acts require the use of an *annual report to shareholders,* in which financial reports must be communicated on a comparative yearly basis.

In the body of the income statement, observe the format of identifying and explaining the revenue with related expenses for the accounting period. In interpreting the revenue for a particular business, the nature of the revenues which an enterprise earns depends upon the character of its routine operations. Consequently, retailing, wholesaling, or manufacturing businesses would probably describe their revenue as *Sales Revenue* or *Sales* because revenue is mainly derived from the sale of goods. On the other hand, many businesses are involved in the operation of earning revenue through the rendering of services. For example, a real estate broker earns revenue by charging a commission; therefore, this service firm may report its revenue as *Commissions Earned*. Similarly, many firms engaged in the professional practice of law, medicine, dentistry, accountancy, etc. will charge a fee for their services; therefore, the income statement of these firms may show revenues described as *Professional Fees Earned*. Of course, service enterprises could call their revenue simply "Sales," but it is more common to describe revenues according to the nature of the business operations.

In the preparation of the income statement, notice too that dollar signs are required before the appropriate amounts in money columns, and that the double rule is used below the net income amount to of the financial statement. Of course, if total expenses enue, the words "Net Loss" would be used to end the

Analysis of the Related Balance Sheet

From the earlier study of the expanded accounti emphasized that the income statement forms o the accounting model. In preparing the income ices, one can conclude that the net income r the amount shown in the expanded accou hand, it is important to note that this equa consist of the capital (investment) and owner withdrawals for personal use. It i this net income is the amount remair expenses have been matched for an to the inflow of assets through sale assets such as cash or the increa clude that assets and the claims at the end of the accounting creased as a result of owner changes, therefore, it will immediately after the inc

Observe carefully tw ance sheet in Figure 1 the Assets, Liabilities ported vertically, th be presented in **re** is reported in the the statement j tice, the repc handwritten form, how typesette The the ne tion bal i

Report form (of balance sheet): an arrangement of assets, liabilities, and owner's equity in a vertical format of the balance sheet.

Account form (of balance sheet): an arrangement of assets on the left side of the balance sheet, while the claims against the assets are reported on the right side.

3. Issued a cheque for $5 000 in full payment of the debt owing to Office Equipment Co., a creditor.
4. Bought additional furniture for $1 000 cash.
5. Acquired additional office equipment costing $1 500 from Office Equipment Co. on 60 days' credit.
6. Returned one piece of office equipment costing $300 because the equipment arrived in damaged condition. The creditor accepted the return of the damaged equipment.
7. Kathy Campling made an additional investment of $1 000 cash.
8. Issued a cheque for $1 000 to the bank in part payment of the demand loan.
9. Purchased $2 000 of Government of Canada bonds (a current asset) by paying cash.
10. The owner withdrew cash totalling $1 000 for her personal use.
11. As of September 30, Campling Word Processing Service has received $8 000 cash from the sale of services during September.
12. The total sales of services on credit for September amounted to $4 000.
13. Cheques were issued to pay for the following expenses incurred in September: Rent, $900; Utilities, $150; Telephone, $100; and Salaries, $4 800.
14. Received an advertising bill at the end of the month for $1 600. City Advertising Agency allowed 30 days' credit to pay the bill.

Required
a From Transaction 1, prepare a pre-operating balance sheet as at September 1 in account form.
b Set up a summary table with the following column headings: Cash; Gov't Bonds; Accounts Receivable; Office Equipment; Furniture; Total Assets; Bank Loan Payable; Acct. Pay.; Total Liabilities; K. Campling, Capital; K. Campling, Drawing; Revenue; Expense; and Total Owner's Equity.
c Analyze the effect of each of the 14 transactions on the three elements of the accounting equation.
d After completing the analysis of the final transaction, total the individual columns; then show a check to prove that the equation is in balance.
e From the expanded equation and data supplied by Transactions 11 to 14, prepare an income statement for the month ended September 30.
f Prepare a related balance sheet as at September 30 in report form.

Rearranging an expanded accounting equation to reflect the matching principle; preparing the resulting financial statements.

1.8 After having operated the Poremba Service Company for the month ended October 31, Richard Poremba reports the elements within his final equation as follows: Cash, $6 400; Government of Canada bonds (to be liquidated within one year), $25 000; Accounts Receivable,

$2 000; Equipment $12 000; Furniture, $4 600; Bank Loan (demand note), $8 000; Accounts Payable, $5 000; R. Poremba, Capital, $33 000; Fees Earned, $11 600; and Expenses (advertising, $2 000; rent, $700; salaries, $4 690; utilities, $150; telephone, $60).

Required

a Set up an expanded accounting equation to classify the financial data for this business. Use the "matching principle" form of expanded accounting equation.
b Prepare an income statement for the accounting period.
c Prepare a related balance sheet for the end of the accounting period in report form.

Preparing financial statements; identifying and explaining accounting concepts and GAAPs related to those statements.

1.9 Donna Brown owns the Stylette Beauty Salon. Information covering a three-month accounting period which ended on June 30 appears below. Note that of the $60 000 mortgage payable $3 000 is due in the next accounting period. Note also that the land and building have been pledged as collateral to secure the mortgage payable.

FIGURE 1-15

Land	$40 000
Shop equipment owned	9 000
Office equipment owned	6 000
Cash in bank	4 000
Due from customers	600
Advertising costs incurred	1 800
Paid for supplies used	2 200
Paid for telephone	50
10% mortgage payable (20-year)	60 000
Building owned	80 000
Donna Brown, capital (April 1)	77 300
Fees earned for services rendered	13 800
Owed on equipment	2 200
Salaries paid	8 900
Paid for utilities	330
Miscellaneous expense	20
Interest expense	400

Required

a Prepare an income statement for the three-month period.
b Prepare a related balance sheet in report form.
c Identify and briefly explain three accounting concepts and three GAAPs that are related to the study of the income statement.
d Identify and briefly explain four accounting concepts and one GAAP that are related to the study of the balance sheet.

Chapter Summary

The study of accounting begins with an examination of a simple accounting model, an equation stated as A = L + OE. Simply translated, this equation states that assets must be equal to the claims against those assets. In the beginning, these claims consist of amounts owing to creditors (liabilities) and the claim derived from the investment (capital) of the owner. A pre-operating balance sheet is usually reported from this beginning accounting model, with OE consisting only of Capital.

During the period of business operations, the enterprise engages in revenue and expense transactions. Therefore, the Owner's Equity section will be expanded to recognize subelements for Revenue and Expense. Hence, the expanded accounting model may be stated as A = L + C + R − E.

Also during the accounting period, the owner must sustain a living. Therefore, it is common for him or her to make personal withdrawals of cash from the business to pay household bills. These withdrawals are actually distributions of the net income paid before such net incomes are accounted for. Consequently, all withdrawals for personal use become drawings and as such must be shown under a separate subelement of Owner's Equity called Drawing. The complete accounting model, in simplified form, may now be stated as A = L + C + R − E − D.

The Owner's Equity section of the expanded accounting model may be rearranged to reflect the matching principle as A = L + C + (R − E) − D. If revenue exceeds related expenses, a Net Income results. Therefore, the accounting equation may be stated as A = L + C + NI − D. On the other hand, a net loss (NL) will result in the accounting model becoming A = L + C − NL − D.

The results of the complete accounting model at the end of an accounting period, also known as a fiscal period, are reported in two important financial statements. The first is an income statement, which is prepared from the details making up the Revenue and Expense subelements under Owner's Equity. All income statements, therefore, report the matching of revenues with related expenses for a fiscal period that has *ended*.

The second is the balance sheet, which reports the balances of all assets, liabilities, and owner's equity as at the end of the fiscal period. In this balance sheet, Owner's Equity is broken down into the owner's Capital (investment), plus the Net Income (or less the Net Loss), and less the owner's Drawing for the period. The net income is regarded as the connecting link between the income statement and balance sheet, because the amount of net income reported by the income statement must be added to owner's equity in the balance sheet.

A balance sheet may be prepared in either account or report form. In account form, the balance sheet reports the assets and claims against those assets in the form of the basic accounting equation; that is, assets are reported on the left side while liabilities and owner's equity are reported on the right side. On the other hand, in report form, a vertical arrangement reports assets first, followed by liabilities and then the owner's equity.

Chapter Questions

1. Accounting is often called the "language of business." What is meant by this expression?
2. In the accounting equation A = L + OE, why is L identified before OE?
3. Explain the meaning of the generally accepted accounting principle known as the cost principle.
4. Use examples to explain how liabilities are listed in a balance sheet.
5. Explain the meaning of the matching principle.
6. Does the matching process always result in a net income? Explain why or why not.
7. Name two other acceptable accounting synonyms for *profit*.
8. Explain the difference in reporting the dates in the headings of the balance sheet and the income statement.
9. Explain how the net income becomes the connecting link between the income statement and the balance sheet at the end of the accounting period.
10. What is meant by the term *revenue and expense transactions*?
11. Does the receipt of cash by a business indicate that revenue has been earned? Explain your answer.
12. Does the payment of cash by a business indicate that an expense has been incurred? Explain your answer.
13. Why are expenses recognized as expired costs?
14. Distinguish between the account form and the report form of balance sheet.
15. What is a pre-operating balance sheet? How would a reader of this financial statement know that it is a pre-operating balance sheet?
16. Why is it necessary to report the current portion of a mortgage payable under "Current Liabilities" on the balance sheet?
17. Why would an owner withdraw cash from his or her firm's bank account? Explain how this withdrawal would be accounted for. What is the accounting theory of such personal withdrawals?

Accounting Case Problems

CASE 1-1

Analyzing the violation of a basic GAAP.

On October 31, a junior accountant produced the year-end financial statements for the sole owner of a sporting goods firm. After examining the balance sheet, the owner called the junior accountant into her office and said, "This store is worth at least $100 000 more than your records show. Revise them to report the true value of my firm's assets." Fearful for his job, the junior accountant obeyed, adding amounts to several fixed asset accounts and adding the total of such increases ($100 000) to the owner's capital element of the accounting equation.

CHAPTER 1: Introductory Accounting Concepts and Principles

Required
a Name the accounting principle which has been violated in this case.
b Briefly explain the nature of the violation.
c Give two reasons in support of the generally accepted accounting principle affected by this case.

CASE 1-2

Analyzing errors and omissions made in reporting an income statement and related balance sheet.

The following income statement and related balance sheet, prepared by an inexperienced bookkeeper, have come to your attention. Assume that all amounts reported represent accurate totals of an expanded accounting equation for the month ended October 31, current year.

FIGURE 1-16

Income Statement
Karen Wong
As at October 31, 19—

Income:		
Professional fees earned		$10 869
Expenses:		
Dental supplies expense	$ 640	
Rent expense	1 000	
Salaries expense	2 900	
Utilities expense	190	
Telephone expense	210	
Withdrawal by owner	500	
Total expenses		5 440
Net profit		$ 5 429

FIGURE 1-17

Karen Wong, D.D.S.
Balance Sheet
For the Month Ended October 31, 19—

Assets

Cash	$ 4 422	
Accounts receivable	1 394	
Dental equipment	28 175	
Office equipment	12 940	
Total assets		$46 931

Liabilities and Owner's Equity

Accounts payable	$1 240	
Bank loan payable (on demand)	7 000	
Total liabilities		$8 240
K. Wong, capital	$33 262	
Add: Net profit for October	5 429	
Total owner's equity		38 691
Total		$46 931

Required **a** List the errors and omissions in the order in which they appear. Briefly explain each of your criticisms and the correct treatment that should have been adopted.

b Redo the financial statements in accordance with generally accepted accounting principles.

CHAPTER **2** Debit and Credit Concepts

After completing this chapter, you should be able to:
— Identify the need for a recording device called the account.
— Establish a set of T-accounts with opening balances from a given pre-operating balance sheet.
— Explain the rule for recording increases in any account.
— Explain the rule for recording decreases in any account.
— Calculate the balance remaining in a T-account showing several debit and credit recordings.
— Analyze and record changes in balance sheet accounts.
— Analyze and record changes in income statement and related balance sheet accounts.
— Define the following key accounting terms presented in this chapter: account, debit, credit, debit balance, credit balance, opening balance, ledger, general ledger, double entry bookkeeping.

In the opening chapter you were shown how to analyze business transactions on the key elements of the accounting equation. For example, when a customer remitted cash to discharge a claim held by the business, the asset Cash was increased on the left side of the equation, and the asset Accounts Receivable was decreased, also on the left side of the equation. Similarly, when the business paid cash to eliminate the claim of a creditor, the asset Cash was decreased on the left side of the equation, while the liability Accounts Payable was decreased by an identical amount, on the right side of the equation.

Now consider this problem. If the asset Cash was involved in 300 business transactions during a normal business day, would you record the increases and the decreases to Cash directly on one equation, or through a set of 300 separate accounting equations? Or would you even consider preparing a new balance sheet after each change in Cash?

Obviously, the preparation of a new equation or a new balance sheet is a most inefficient way to record the daily changes to an asset like Cash, or

FIGURE 2-1

	Assets			= Liabilities	+ Owner's Equity
Cash	+ Accounts Receivable	+ Furniture	=	Accounts Payable	+ Owner, Capital
~~$6 000~~	~~$500~~	+ ~~$1 500~~	=	~~$300~~	+ $7 700
$6 500	0			$800	
~~$6 000~~				~~$1 900~~	~~$300~~
$5 800				$2 100	$200

to any other element in the accounting equation. What is clearly needed is some device to record each increase and decrease to every item under any element within the accounting equation. In the language of business, such a device is known as the **account**.

In practice, a separate account is identified for each element or subelement in the accounting equation; therefore, an account can be established for every asset, for every liability, for the investment part of owner's equity (Capital), for the owner's withdrawal of assets for personal use, for each source of revenue, and for each expense. Topic 1 examines how changes in balance sheet accounts are recorded. Topic 2 treats the method of recording change in income statement and related balance sheet accounts.

> Account: a device for recording the effects of business transactions under one title.

TOPIC 1 Recording Changes in Balance Sheet Accounts

FIGURE 2-2

Assets	= Liabilities +	Owner's Equity

Account Title

Left Side	Right Side

Cash

E. LeClair, Capital

In practice, several different forms of accounts are in actual use. To avoid complexities at this time, a simplified form of account will be illustrated so that you can learn how to establish dollar amounts in all accounts, how to record an increase, how to record a decrease, and how to calculate the amount remaining after recording increases and decreases. Since this simplified form of account is based on the equation, that is, there is a left and a right side to the form, the account is called the **T-account**. It is usually illustrated and labelled as shown in the side margin.

Debits and Credits

> Debit: the left side of any account (*dr.* for short).
>
> Credit: the right side of any account (*cr.* for short).

A few accounting terms must be introduced before you can learn how to use accounts. In accounting language, the left side of an account is known as **debit** (*dr.* for short), while the right side of an account is called **credit** (*cr.* for short). Consequently, to debit an account simply means that one has recorded a dollar amount on the left side of the account. Similarly, to credit an account will refer to the action of recording a dollar amount on the right side of the account. It is important that one associate no other meaning to the words "debit" and "credit." Always think of debit as the left

CHAPTER 2: Debit and Credit Concepts

side of any account and credit as the right side of any account. After an account has been debited and credited, the amount remaining (the difference between the two sides) will be either a **debit balance** or a **credit balance**, as shown in Figures 2-3 and 2-4.

Debit balance: an amount remaining on the left side of an account.

Credit balance: an amount remaining on the right side of an account.

FIGURE 2-3

Account Title	
Debit side (dr.)	Credit side (cr.)

Cash	
29 000	5 000
29 000	
− 5 000	
Dr. balance 24 000	

FIGURE 2-4

Account Title	
Debit side (dr.)	Credit side (cr.)

Bank Loan Payable	
1 000	5 000
	5 000
	− 1 000
	Cr. balance 4 000

Establishing a Set of Accounts

Opening balances: beginning amounts establishing accounts; account balances are established on the side on which they originate in the accounting equation.

FIGURE 2-5

A	=	L	+	OE
X		X		X

All accounts are established by placing their beginning amounts, called *opening balances*, on the side on which the accounts originate in the accounting equation. And since the original accounting equation was summarized in more detail in the opening balance sheet, it follows that an account is opened for each asset, for each liability, and for the owner's equity. In the case of Office Services, the opening set of T-accounts would appear as illustrated in Figure 2-6.

Analysis   The following points should be related to the illustration showing how accounts are established for Office Services:

- Observe that asset accounts are established by placing the date of the pre-operating balance sheet and the opening balance on the debit side. This is logical, because assets originate on the left side of the accounting equation.
- Similarly, all liability accounts have the date of the pre-operating balance sheet and opening balances on the credit side, because the right side is the place of origin for liabilities in the accounting equation.
- There is no account called Owner's Equity as such. Instead, a Capital account is created to establish the first claim of the owner under Owner's Equity. Since Capital originates under Owner's Equity on the right side of the accounting equation, it is correct to open this account with a credit amount. Of course, this opening balance would be shown with the date of the pre-operating balance sheet.

34 PART 1: THE FRAMEWORK OF ACCOUNTING

FIGURE 2-6

Office Services
Pre-Operating Balance Sheet
As at September 30, 19-1

Assets		Liabilities	
Current Assets:		Current Liabilities:	
Cash	$20 000	Bank Loan Payable	$10 000
Accounts Receivable	1 000	Accounts Payable	15 000
Total Current Assets	21 000	Total Liabilities	$25 000
Fixed Assets (at cost):		**Owner's Equity**	
Office Equipment	40 000	E. LeClair, Capital	50 000
Furniture	14 000		
Total Fixed Assets	54 000		
Total Assets	$75 000	Total Liabilities and Owner's Equity	$75 000

Cash		Bank Loan Payable	
19-1			19-1
Sept. 30 20 000			Sept. 30 10 000

Accounts Receivable		Accounts Payable	
19-1			19-1
Sept. 30 1 000			Sept. 30 15 000

Office Equipment		E. LeClair, Capital	
19-1			19-1
Sept. 30 40 000			Sept. 30 50 000

Furniture	
19-1	
Sept. 30 14 000	

Assets ($75 000) = Liabilities ($25 000) + Owner's Equity ($50 000)

- After all accounts are opened, the total of the debit balances must equal the total of the credit balances. One can state, therefore, that the accounting equation now rests within the group of accounts established for the business. In the language of accounting, when accounts are opened for all elements and subelements, the entire group forms an accounting concept called the **ledger**. Thus, one can support the concept that the accounting equation must balance within the ledger after accounts are established for any business.

Ledger: a file or group of accounts.

The General Ledger

General ledger: the main ledger containing account balances required for the preparation of financial statements.

In practice, an accounting system will contain several ledgers. To avoid complexities, only the main or general ledger will be introduced in Part 1 of this book. As you will learn, the **general ledger** is considered the main ledger because it contains the account balances required for the preparation of future financial statements. Other ledgers will be presented in Part 2. Since only T-accounts have been used so far, we can define the main ledger as the T-account general ledger.

In the T-account general ledger established for Office Services, you should have observed that no specific customer and creditor names are identified in the general accounts "Accounts Receivable" and "Accounts Payable." Appropriately, general accounts in the general ledger will contain only the totals of specific related accounts; therefore, only the total amount owing by customers will be filed in Accounts Receivable, and the total owing to creditors of goods and services will be disclosed in Accounts Payable. As you will learn in Part 2, the individual customers and individual creditors will be maintained in subsidiary or secondary ledgers called the *accounts receivable ledger* and *accounts payable ledger* respectively. The important point to remember here is that the general ledger will contain sufficient data for the eventual preparation of financial statements.

Recording Increases in Balance Sheet Accounts

In general, an increase in an account is recorded on the side of origin—that is, on the side where the account is placed in the accounting equation. Since asset accounts originate on the left side of the equation, an increase to any asset account must be recorded on the same side, that is, the debit side. Similarly, all liability accounts must be increased on the credit side, since the element Liabilities originates on the right side of the accounting equation.

As for any increase to owner's equity, keep in mind that more than one account can cause the increase to this third element in the equation. For example, an additional investment by the owner would cause an increase to owner's equity. Since Owner's Equity originates on the right side of the accounting equation, the amount of additional investment would be recorded on the credit side of Capital — the account which caused the increase to Owner's Equity. Similarly, you have learned from Chapter 1 that revenue causes an increase to owner's equity as a result of the sale of goods or services; therefore, an inflow of revenue must be recorded as a credit in an appropriate revenue account like Sales or Fees Earned or some similar revenue account. The analysis of revenue accounts will be treated in Topic 2 of this chapter.

You will find it useful to remember the summary illustrated in Figure 2-7 when analyzing the recording of increases in balance sheet accounts.

Let us now apply the logic of recording increases in balance sheet accounts to three examples studied in Chapter 1 for Office Services. You

FIGURE 2-7

	Assets	=	Liabilities + Owner's Equity
	Asset Accounts		Liability Accounts
	Record increases on the debit side.		Record increases on the credit side.
			Owner's Equity Accounts
			Record increases to Owner's Equity on the credit side of accounts that have caused the increase.

may wish to review the effect of these transactions on the accounting equation before you translate the results in the form of debits and credits.

Transaction 1   On September 30, 19-1, Elizabeth LeClair invested $50 000 of her personal cash savings in a bank account established for Office Services. The analysis of recording the dollar results of this investment may be illustrated as shown in Figure 2-8.

FIGURE 2-8

What Happens	**Accounting Logic**	**Accounting Entry**
The asset Cash increases by $50 000.	To increase an Asset, record the amount on the side where assets originate in the accounting equation.	Debit: Cash, $50 000
Owner's Equity increases by $50 000.	To increase Owner's Equity, record the amount on the side of origin, that is, where OE originates in the accounting equation. Select an account that has caused the increase to owner's equity.	Credit: E. LeClair, Capital, $50 000

Cash	E. LeClair, Capital
19-1	19-1
Sept. 30 50 000	Sept. 30 50 000

CHAPTER 2: Debit and Credit Concepts **37**

Transaction 4   On September 30, 19-1, Elizabeth LeClair raised $10 000 cash for the business by signing a demand note at her bank. The analysis of recording the dollar results of this bank loan is shown in Figure 2-9.

FIGURE 2-9

What Happens	Accounting Logic	Accounting Entry
The asset Cash increases by $10 000.	To increase an Asset, record the amount on the side where assets originate in the accounting equation.	Debit: Cash, $10 000
The liability Bank Loan Payable increases by $10 000.	To increase a Liability, record the amount on the side where liabilities originate in the accounting equation.	Credit: Bank Loan Payable, $10 000

```
            Cash                                          Bank Loan Payable
19-1                                                                        19-1
Sept. 30   10 000                                                           Sept. 30   10 000
```

Transaction 5   On September 30, 19-1, additional office equipment costing $6 000 was acquired on 60 days' credit from a supplier of office equipment. The analysis of recording the dollar results of this transaction may be illustrated as shown in Figure 2-10.

FIGURE 2-10

What Happens	Accounting Logic	Accounting Entry
The asset Office Equipment increases by $6 000.	To increase an Asset, record the amount on the side where assets originate in the accounting equation.	Debit: Office Equipment, $6 000
The liability Accounts Payable increases by $6 000.	To increase Liability, record the amount on the side where liabilities originate in the accounting equation.	Credit: Accounts Payable, $6 000

```
       Office Equipment                                    Accounts Payable
19-1                                                                        19-1
Sept. 30   6 000                                                            Sept. 30   6 000
```

Recording Decreases in Balance Sheet Accounts

If increases in accounts are recorded on the side on which the accounts originate in the accounting equation, then it is logical to record decreases on the *opposite* side. Since assets originate on the left side, a decrease to any asset must be recorded on the opposite or right side. It follows, therefore, that decreases in all assets must be credited.

Similar logic is followed for recording decreases in liability accounts. Since liabilities originate as credits, the opposite or debit side must represent the decrease side. Consequently, decreases in all liabilities must be debited.

And the same logic is applied to the recording of decreases to owner's equity. Earlier, you learned to record an increase to owner's equity by crediting the account that caused the increase. A decrease to OE, therefore, would be recorded as a debit in any account that caused the decrease. Refer to Figure 2-11.

FIGURE 2-11

Assets = Liabilities + Owner's Equity

Asset Accounts		Liability Accounts	
Record increases on the debit side.	Record decreases on the credit side.	Record decreases on the debit side.	Record increases on the credit side.

Owner's Equity Accounts

Record decreases to Owner's Equity on the debit side of accounts that have caused the decrease.	Record increases to Owner's Equity on the credit side of accounts that have caused the increase.

Now follow closely the three examples below of selected transactions that result in the recording of increases and decreases in balance sheet accounts for Office Services.

Transaction 2 On September 30, 19-1, Elizabeth LeClair purchased furniture for $5 000 cash. The analysis of recording the dollar results of this transaction may be illustrated as shown in Figure 2-12.

Obviously, the analysis of Transaction 2 results in the recording of an increase in one account — the asset Furniture — while a second account — the asset Cash — is being decreased as a result of the same transaction.

Transaction 12 On October 31, 19-1, Elizabeth LeClair withdrew $1 000 cash from the firm's bank account for her personal use. The analysis of recording this withdrawal is illustrated in Figure 2-13.

CHAPTER 2: Debit and Credit Concepts 39

FIGURE 2-12

What Happens	Accounting Logic	Accounting Entry
The asset Furniture increases by $5 000.	To increase an Asset, record the amount on the side where assets originate in the accounting equation.	Debit: Furniture, $5 000
The asset Cash decreases by $5 000.	To decrease an Asset, record the amount on the side opposite to where assets originate in the accounting equation.	Credit: Cash, $5 000

Furniture		Cash	
19-1			19-1
Sept. 30 5 000			Sept. 30 5 000

FIGURE 2-13

What Happens	Accounting Logic	Accounting Entry
Owner's Equity decreases by $1 000.	To decrease Owner's Equity, record the amount on the debit side of the account which caused the decrease to OE.	Debit: E. LeClair, Drawing, $1 000
The asset Cash decreases by $1 000.	To decrease an Asset, record the amount on the side opposite to where assets originate in the accounting equation.	Credit: Cash, $1 000

E. LeClair, Drawing		Cash	
19-1			19-1
Oct. 31 1 000			Oct. 31 1 000

The analysis of Transaction 12 shows decreases to two elements in the accounting equation: Assets and Owner's Equity. Since the specific asset is Cash that decreases, a credit amount must be recorded in the Cash account.

The difficult part of the analysis is to know how to record the decrease to owner's equity. It is important to remember that Owner's Equity as such is not an account. It represents the total claim of the owner against assets in any accounting equation. To record any decrease to OE, you must first identify the account that decreases this element. Here, the account is E. LeClair, Drawing. Since this Drawing account causes the decreases to OE, you must record this decrease in the Drawing account

40 PART 1: THE FRAMEWORK OF ACCOUNTING

on the debit side. Why the debit side? Because that is the side opposite where OE is placed in the accounting equation. Remember the earlier point that all increases are recorded on the side where the element originates in the equation and all decreases are recorded on the opposite side.

Transaction 14 On November 1, 19-1, Elizabeth LeClair signed a cheque for $9 000 in full settlement of the account payable to City Furniture, Inc. The analysis of recording the dollar results of this transaction is illustrated in Figure 2-14.

FIGURE 2-14

What Happens	Accounting Logic	Accounting Entry
The liability Accounts Payable decreases by $9 000.	To decrease a Liability, record the amount on the side opposite to where liabilities originate in the accounting equation.	Debit: Accounts Payable, $9 000
The asset Cash decreases by $9 000.	To decrease an Asset, record the amount on the side opposite to where assets originate in the accounting equation.	Credit: Cash, $9 000

```
         Accounts Payable                              Cash
19-1                                         19-1
Nov. 1    9 000                              Nov. 1    9 000
```

Calculating the Balance in Any T-Account

It is a simple procedure to calculate the balance remaining in any T-account. Simply show a single line across the debit and credit sides below the last recording. Add the debit side and the credit side to obtain separate totals. Subtract the lesser total from the greater total and place the remaining balance amount on the greater side, as in the case of the Cash account shown in Figure 2-15. If the debit and credit totals are equal, there is no balance remaining in the account. One way to show a "no balance" or "zero balance" in a T-account is illustrated for the case of the Accounts Payable account in Figure 2-16.

FIGURE 2-15

```
              Cash
        50 000    | 35 000
        10 000    |  5 000
        60 000    | 40 000
       - 40 000   |
Balance  20 000   |
```

FIGURE 2-16

```
       Accounts Payable
       17 000  |  6 000
               |  9 000
               |  2 000
       17 000  | 17 000
              ∅
```

CHAPTER 2: Debit and Credit Concepts

TOPIC 1 Problems

Opening a T-account general ledger from a pre-operating balance sheet.

2.1 Open a T-account general ledger for each asset, liability, and owner's equity item reported on the pre-operating balance sheet of L. Finnie, Barrister (refer back to Problems 1.3 and 1.5 of Chapter 1), and enter the account balance and date. Check that the accounting equation has been transferred correctly to the ledger. *Note*: Save this T-account ledger for use in Problem 2.2.

Recording changes in balance sheet accounts in a T-account ledger.

2.2 Use the T-account general ledger set up for L. Finnie, Barrister (Problem 2.1) to record the business transactions summarized below. Following the recording of the final transaction, calculate and show the balance in each account. Finally, total the debit balances and credit balances to prove that the equation is still in balance within the general ledger. *Note:* Open new accounts as required by the transactions.

Oct. 1 Borrowed an additional $2 500 cash from the bank on a demand note. The loan amount was immediately deposited in the firm's chequing account.
   2 Received $500 cash from J. Newton in full settlement of his accounts receivable.
   6 Purchased an electronic calculator for the office. The calculator was acquired from Milton Equipment Co. on 30 days' credit for $600.
   15 Purchased additional law books for $500 cash.
   22 Issued a cheque for $2 000 to Milton Equipment Co. in payment of September's debt owing to this creditor.
   31 L. Finnie withdrew $100 cash for personal use.

Opening a T-account general ledger from a pre-operating balance sheet.

2.3 Open a T-account general ledger for each asset, liability, and owner's equity item reported on the pre-operating balance sheet of the Manitoba Car Rental Company (refer back to Problems 1.4 and 1.5 of Chapter 1), and enter the account balance and date. Check that the accounting equation has been transferred correctly to the ledger. *Note:* Save this T-account ledger for use in Problem 2.4.

Recording changes in balance sheet accounts in a T-account ledger.

2.4 Use the T-account general ledger set up for the Manitoba Car Rental Company (Problem 2.3) to record the business transactions summarized below. Following the recording of the final transaction, calculate and show the balance in each account. Finally, total the debit balances and credit balances to prove that the equation is still in balance within the general ledger. *Note:* Open new accounts as required by the transactions.

Nov. 1 Before using the office equipment, Franca Zadra sold one piece — an electronic calculator — to Betty Tustin, a dental surgeon friend, at the same cost price of $1 000. Zadra gave Tustin 30 days' credit to pay for the cost of the calculator.
   8 Returned one piece of defective office equipment to Main Office Supply, Inc. This piece was originally purchased at a cost of $600 as part of a large acquisition for $1 600. The supplier accepted the return of the defective equipment.

10 Issued a cheque for $1 000 in full payment of the amount owing to Main Office Supply, Inc., an account payable.
15 Borrowed an additional $5 000 cash from the bank on a demand note. The loan amount was immediately deposited in the firm's chequing account.
20 Received $1 000 cash from Betty Tustin in full settlement of her accounts receivable.
25 Purchased a large supply of office stationery, copy paper, and envelopes from Main Office Supply, Inc. totalling $2 000. The supplier gave 30 days' credit. (Open a new asset account called Office Supplies on Hand.)
30 Franca Zadra withdrew $1 500 cash for her personal use.

TOPIC 2 Recording Changes in Income Statement and Related Balance Sheet Accounts

In Chapter 1, you learned that revenue and expense transactions affected the third element, called Owner's Equity, within the accounting equation. As you will recall, all revenue transactions resulted in an increase to OE, while all expense transactions caused a decrease to OE within the accounting equation. In addition, revenue transactions resulted in an increase to either Cash or Accounts Receivable, while expense transactions decreased the asset Cash or increased the liability Accounts Payable. Therefore, all revenue and expense transactions affect not only accounts that will be reported in the future income statement, but also accounts on the future related balance sheet. To record changes resulting from these transactions, separate general ledger accounts must be maintained as illustrated in the four selected transactions studied in Chapter 1 for Office Services. You may wish to review the effect of these transactions on the accounting equation before you translate the results in the form of debits and credits.

Transaction 8   During October, Office Services received $8 000 cash from the sale of services during the month. Although individual cash sales during the month may be considered, the recording of the total cash received for fees earned in T-accounts as at October 31 will be as illustrated in Figure 2-17.

Observe that a revenue account called Fees Earned is used to record the revenue earned for rendering offices services for cash. The title of the revenue account is related to the main source of revenue for the business, as explained in Chapter 1 when the income statement was presented.

Transaction 9   Also during October, Office Services sold services to customers on 30 days' credit and the total of such services rendered as of October 31 amounted to $12 000. Here again, we are concerned with

CHAPTER 2: Debit and Credit Concepts   43

FIGURE 2-17

What Happens	Accounting Logic	Accounting Entry
The asset Cash increases by $8 000.	To increase an Asset, record the amount on the side where assets originate in the accounting equation.	Debit: Cash, $8 000
Owner's Equity increases by $8 000 because of an inflow of revenue.	To increase Owner's Equity, record the amount on the credit side of the account which caused the increase to OE. In this case, select an appropriate revenue account.	Credit: Fees Earned, $8 000

```
        Cash                                    Fees Earned
19-1                                     |                    19-1
Oct. 31    8 000                         |                    Oct. 31    8 000
```

the analysis of only the total credit fees earned rather than with the recording of individual fees earned on a credit basis. The analysis of recording the dollar results of this transaction may be illustrated as shown in Figure 2-18.

Transaction 10   Office Services paid cash for the following expenses: Rent, $950; Salaries, $9 000; Telephone, $50; and Utilities, $100. Although these expenses would probably have been incurred on different dates, for simplicity assume that all were incurred and paid for on

FIGURE 2-18

What Happens	Accounting Logic	Accounting Entry
The asset Accounts Receivable increases by $12 000.	To increase an Asset, record the amount on the side where assets originate in the accounting equation.	Debit: Accounts Receivable, $12 000
Owner's Equity increases by $12 000 because of an inflow of revenue.	To increase Owner's Equity, record the amount on the credit side of the account which caused the increase to OE. In this case, select an appropriate revenue account.	Credit: Fees Earned, $12 000

```
   Accounts Receivable                           Fees Earned
19-1                                     |                    19-1
Oct. 31    12 000                        |                    Oct. 31    12 000
```

44 PART 1: THE FRAMEWORK OF ACCOUNTING

FIGURE 2-19

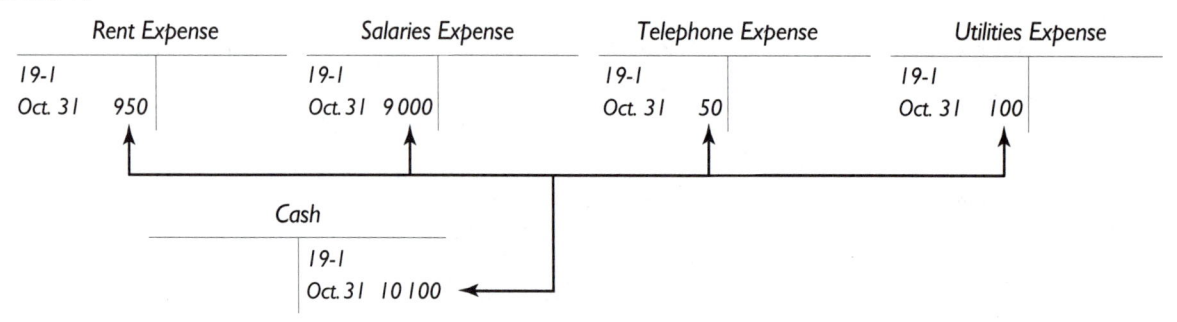

Rent Expense	Salaries Expense	Telephone Expense	Utilities Expense
19-1	19-1	19-1	19-1
Oct. 31 950	Oct. 31 9 000	Oct. 31 50	Oct. 31 100

Cash

19-1
Oct. 31   10 100

October 31. The analysis of the "compound" transaction may be analyzed and recorded in T-accounts as shown in Figure 2-19.

From the figure observe that a separate account has been used for each expense that caused the decrease to Owner's Equity. Note also that the total of the individual debit amounts (the total expenses) does equal the one amount credited to the Cash account. In this sense, the total debit or debits must always be equal to the total credit or credits following the recording of every business transaction. In the language of accounting, this important rule identifies the system called **double entry bookkeeping**.

> Double entry bookkeeping: the system of bookkeeping in which every transaction is recorded both in one or more accounts as a debit and in one or more as a credit in such a manner that the total of the debit entries equals the total of the credit entries.

Transaction 11 Office Services received a bill on October 31 for $2 000 from The Local Press for publishing advertisements during the month. The bill allowed the business a period of 30 days in which to pay the amount owing. To record this transaction, a debit for $2 000 would be recorded to Advertising Expense to recognize the decrease to Owner's Equity in the accounting equation. On the other hand, a credit entry for $2 000 would be made to Accounts Payable to record the increase to the liability as shown in the side margin illustration.

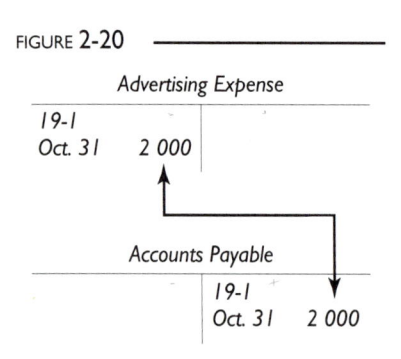

From these examples, you should be able to record increases and decreases to any account resulting from business transactions. In recording the dollar results of such transactions, it is important to avoid any memorization of rules. Instead, it is better to identify and classify the accounts affected by the business transaction; to analyze their effects on the accounting equation; and then to record the dollar results of the transaction in accordance with the accounting logic developed earlier. After the recording of any business transaction, remember to check that an equal debit amount has been recorded for an equal credit amount. This equality of debit for credit follows the same logic earlier developed for the accounting equation. As you will recall, the totals of the left and right sides of the equation must always balance immediately following the recording of every business transaction. Similarly, debits must always equal credits in account recording to support the double entry bookkeeping system.

FIGURE 2-20

Advertising Expense

19-1
Oct. 31   2 000

Accounts Payable

	19-1
	Oct. 31 2 000

TOPIC 2 Problems

Opening a T-account general ledger for a word processing service firm; recording a set of transactions for one month; calculating the balance in each T-account; proving the equality of the equation within the general ledger.

2.5 Refer back to Problem 1.7 of Chapter 1 (Campling Word Processing Service).

Required
a Open a T-account general ledger for the opening entry in Transaction 1. Assume that the date of this opening transaction is September 1.
b For Transactions 2, 3, 4, 5, 6, 7, 8, 9, and 10, assume that the transaction numbers correspond to actual dates in September. That is, Transaction 2 becomes September 2, Transaction 3 September 3, etc. Record the effects of these transactions in T-accounts. Open new T-accounts with appropriate account titles as required.
c Assume that the remaining transactions from 11 through 14 occur on September 30. Record the effects of these transactions in T-accounts. Open new T-accounts with appropriate account titles as required.
d Following the recording of the final transaction, calculate and show the balance in each account. Total the debit balances and credit balances to prove that the equation is still in balance within the general ledger.

Opening a T-account general ledger for a cleaning company; recording a set of transactions for one month; calculating the balance in each T-account; proving the equality of the equation within the general ledger; preparing an income statement for the month and a related balance sheet as at the end of that month.

2.6 On November 1 Gerald O'Neil commenced his Spot-Free Cleaners with the following assets and liabilities: Cash, $8 000; Equipment, $12 000; Store Fixtures, $2 000; Bank Loan, $3 000 (on demand); and Accounts Payable, $5 000.

Required
a Open the following T-account general ledger for the Spot-Free Cleaners: Cash; Accounts Receivable; Equipment; Store Fixtures; Truck; Bank Loan Payable; Accounts Payable; Gerald O'Neil, Capital; Gerald O'Neil, Drawing; Fees Earned; Rent Expense; Advertising Expense; Salaries Expense; Telephone Expense; Utilities Expense; and Bank Interest Expense.
b Record the opening balances in the appropriate accounts. Check the total debits and total credits of these accounts to prove that the equation is maintained in the general ledger.
c Record the following transactions for November in the T-accounts established for the Spot-Free Cleaners. Identify each transaction by date.

Nov. 2 Gerald O'Neil made an additional investment of $10 000 cash in the business.
3 Bought a new truck for $15 800 on 60 days' credit from Swan's Auto.
4 Sold services for $475 in cash.
5 Paid $600 cash for rent.
7 Sold services for $125 on credit to S. Harvey.
9 Paid $32 for telephone bill.

11 Sold services for $1 000 in cash.
12 Sold services for $225 in cash.
14 Paid $300 to King Furniture, a creditor, on account.
15 Received $50 from S. Harvey, a customer on account.
17 Sold services for $680 on credit to Eastview Garage.
19 Paid $140 for utilities.
20 Newspaper advertising was ordered at a price of $180, payment to be made within 30 days to The Daily News.
23 Sold services for $200 in cash.
28 Paid monthly salary of $1 000 each to two employees.
30 Issued a cheque for $800 to Swan's Auto, a creditor, on account.
30 Received $200 from Eastview Garage, a customer, on account.
30 Issued a cheque to the bank for $530 as follows: on the principal amount of the bank loan, $500; for bank interest, $30.
30 Gerald O'Neil withdrew $600 cash for his personal use.

d Calculate the balance of each account at the close of business on November 30; then prove the equality of the accounting equation within the general ledger by totalling all of the debit balances and the credit balances.

e From the data in the T-account ledger, prepare an income statement for the month of November and a related balance sheet in report form as of November 30.

Opening a T-account general ledger for a real estate agency; recording a set of transactions for one month; calculating the balance in each T-account; proving the equality of the equation within the general ledger; preparing an income statement for the month and a related balance sheet as at the end of that month.

2.7 After working several years for a Nova Scotia realty company, Nancy Hyland decides to establish her own real estate agency. After acquiring the appropriate licences, Nancy opens a chequing account at her bank under her firm's name, Maritime Real Estate Agency, by depositing $5 000 cash on November 1, 19-1. The following transactions occurred during her agency's first month of business operations:

Nov. 2 Issued a cheque for $800 for the rental of office space.
3 Acquired office supplies on 30 days' credit in the amount of $200 (debit Office Supplies Expense).
4 Obtained a bank loan on a demand basis for $10 000. Deposited the $10 000 in the firm's bank account.
5 Purchased an automobile for business use costing $20 000. Paid $5 000 cash and agreed to pay the remaining amount in 60 days.
7 Obtained office equipment costing $8 000 on 60 days' credit.
7 Purchased furniture costing $2 000 on 30 days' credit.
12 Received $2 500 cash commission on real estate sold.
14 Received $4 000 cash commission on real estate bought.
17 Paid telephone bill, $26.
19 Paid utility bill, $85.
21 Sold real estate resulting in commissions of $2 800 which have not yet been received. The client was given 30 days to pay the commission.
22 Nancy Hyland paid a personal bill from her firm's chequing account in the amount of $45.

CHAPTER 2: Debit and Credit Concepts

25	Paid $200 of the amount due on the office supplies purchased earlier this month.
26	Received payment on one-half of the amount due from the previous sale of real estate on November 21.
28	Paid office salaries of $1 800.
29	Received an advertising bill totalling $2 900. The bill gave 30 days' credit.
30	Issued a cheque for $185 in payment of auto gas bill received today.
30	Issued a cheque for $5 000 in part payment of the purchased automobile on November 5.
30	The proprietor withdrew $1 500 for personal use.
30	Issued a cheque to the bank for $1 000 as follows: on the principal amount of the bank loan, $900; for bank interest, $100.

Required

a Record the transactions in a T-account general ledger. Open T-accounts with appropriate account titles.

b Calculate the balance of each account at the close of business on November 30; then prove the equality of the accounting equation within the general ledger by totalling all of the debit balances and the credit balances.

c From the data in the T-account ledger, prepare an income statement for the month of November and a related balance sheet in report form as of November 30.

Chapter Summary

Recording changes to any element or subelement of the accounting equation directly on the equation, or by preparing a new equation, or by preparing a new set of financial statements immediately after any change, is most inefficient. Therefore, a device is required to record the effects of business transactions under one title. This device is known as an "account."

To keep an accurate record of every change in the accounting equation, a separate account is kept for each subelement of the equation. Thus, there will be separate accounts for each asset, for each liability, and for each subelement under Owner's Equity. Taken together, the accounts form a ledger.

In an accounting system, those accounts that give information for the future preparation of financial statements are filed in the G/L. All other ledgers will be secondary or subsidiary to the general ledger. Examples of secondary ledgers are the accounts receivable ledger (a file of all customer accounts) and the accounts payable ledger (a file of all vendor accounts).

Several different forms of accounts are used in practice. The simplest form is called the T-account. A T-account does not exist in practice; however, it is a useful device in the beginning stages of learning how to record increases and decreases in accounts.

The left side of any account is the debit side. *Dr.* is the short form for *debit* (the letter *r* comes from the old Latin and Italian translations used when bookkeeping was first explained in textbooks some 400 years ago). The right side of any account is the credit side. *Cr.* is the short form for *credit*.

Debiting an account simply refers to the action of recording an amount on the left side of the account. Crediting an account refers to the action of recording an amount on the right side of the account.

All accounts in a general ledger are established by placing their beginning amounts, called *opening balances*, on the side on which the accounts originate in the accounting equation and the pre-operating balance sheet. After opening balances are established, the accounting equation is said to rest within the general ledger.

An increase in any account is recorded on the side where the account is placed in the accounting equation. Thus, all asset accounts are increased on the debit side, because assets originate on the left side of the accounting equation. Similarly, all liabilities are increased on the credit side, because liabilities originate on the right side of the accounting equation. When Owner's Equity is increased in the accounting equation, the record of this increase is placed in an account that has caused the increase on the side on which OE originates in the equation, that is, the right side.

A decrease in any account is recorded on the side opposite to where the account is shown in the accounting equation. Thus, all asset accounts are decreased on the credit (right) side; all liability accounts are decreased on the debit (left) side; and all accounts that cause a decrease to Owner's Equity record that decrease on the debit (left) side.

After an account has been debited or credited, the amount remaining will be either a debit balance or a credit balance. At the end of any accounting period, all asset accounts will normally show a debit balance, because the category Assets originates on the left side of the accounting equation. Similarly, all liability accounts will normally show a credit balance, because Liabilities originate on the right side of the accounting equation. Since there is no general ledger account called Owner's Equity, all accounts affecting this element will show normal balances in accordance with their effects. Thus, the Capital account and all revenue accounts will normally show credit balances, because they cause an increase to OE within the accounting equation. On the other hand, the owner's Drawing account and all expense accounts cause a decrease to OE. Therefore, these accounts will normally show a debit balance at the end of any accounting period.

Chapter Questions

1. What is an account and how does it differ from a ledger?
2. What is a general ledger? Why is the G/L considered the most important ledger in an accounting system?
3. What is a T-account? Identify the three parts of any T-account.

4 Briefly explain how opening balances are established in a T-account general ledger.
5 State the accounting rule for increasing any account; then explain this rule in your own words.
6 State the accounting rule for decreasing any account; then explain this rule in your own words.
7 Does the term *debit* mean increase and the term *credit* mean decrease? Explain.
8 Explain the letter *r* in the short form for debit.
9 Explain how the balance of a T-account is calculated.
10 Explain why any expense incurred must be recorded as a debit to an appropriate expense account.
11 An inexperienced accounting clerk debited Telephone Expense in payment of the owner's home telephone bill. Did the clerk debit the correct account? Explain why or why not.
12 Explain why recording transactions in debit and credit form is called *double entry bookkeeping*.
13 An inexperienced accounting clerk calculated the balance in the Fees Earned account for March as a debit balance. Did the clerk calculate the balance correctly? Explain why or why not.

Accounting Case Problems

CASE 2-1
Calculating the amount of OE within an accounting equation at year-end; explaining the change in OE at the end of the year.

After one year of owning and operating the Lakeside Marina, Laura Muzzatti received the following data on her claim against the total assets of the business: (1) the assets of the business on January 1 amounted to $100 000; (2) the assets on December 31 of Year 1 totalled $140 000; (3) during the year, the liabilities increased by $30 000; (4) and the owner's equity at January 1 of Year 1 amounted to $80 000.

Required
a What was the amount of owner's equity as at December 31 of Year 1? Use the three elements of the accounting equation to explain the basis of your answer.
b On the assumption that the owner did not invest any additional amount during the year, explain the increase or decrease to owner's equity at the end of the year.

CASE 2-2
Analyzing the rules for debiting and crediting accounts.

In reviewing the rules for debiting and crediting accounts, Student A presented the following question: "Expenses represent decreases in the owner's equity. Decreases in liabilities and owner's equity are recorded on the debit side of the account. Yet to record an increase in an expense, you debit the account. Why is this?"

Required Why is this student having difficulty? What explanation would you give to clear up the difficulty in analyzing the debit to any expense account?

CHAPTER **3** Accounting Cycle for a Service Firm

After completing this chapter, you should be able to:

— List in correct order the eight steps of a simplified accounting cycle for a service firm.

— Identify and explain the accounting function of common source documents such as the pre-operating balance sheet, invoice, cheque record, and remittance slip.

— Record and post correctly the opening entry from given data.

— Record and post correctly a set of normal transactions from given data.

— Prepare formal and informal trial balances.

— Prepare a six-column worksheet and the financial statements that result from a correctly completed worksheet.

— Record and post correctly the year-end closing entries.

— Prepare the postclosing trial balance.

— Identify the main parts of an electronic spreadsheet and explain briefly its main uses and limitations in solving accounting applications.

— Demonstrate how a common electronic spreadsheet like Lotus 1-2-3® is used to prepare a simple income statement.

— Define the following key accounting terms presented in this chapter: accounting cycle; source documents; invoice; cheque stub; remittance slip; journal; compound entry; opening entry; posting; balance ledger form; trial balance; zero-proof trial balance; bookkeeping; worksheet; statement of owner's equity; Revenue and Expense Summary account; postclosing trial balance; permanent accounts; temporary accounts; accounting; financial (general) accounting; management (managerial) accounting; C.A.; C.M.A.; C.G.A.; electronic spreadsheet; mainframe computer; minicomputer; microcomputer; macro; operating system software.

In the opening chapter, you learned some very important concepts: how a business enterprise is established; how an accounting equation is formed; how changes are analyzed within the equation; how business transactions are recorded in a T-account ledger; and how basic financial

CHAPTER 3: Accounting Cycle for a Service Firm 51

statements are prepared. Now, while the use of accounting equations and a T-account analysis of transactions were adequate to introduce accounting concepts and principles, in actual practice an accounting system is organized to record and accumulate accounting data so that financial statements can be prepared systematically at the end of any accounting period. In the language of accounting, such an accounting system would include a series of steps or routines which form the ***accounting cycle.*** Furthermore, some of the forms and the financial statements prepared by manual means within that accounting cycle can be completed by using computer software known as the electronic spreadsheet. The electronic spreadsheet is defined in Topic 4.

> Accounting cycle: the complete sequence of accounting activities repeated in every accounting (fiscal) period.

TOPIC 1 Bookkeeping Aspects

Step 1. Originating Transaction Data

In the last chapter, you learned that accounting is concerned with the important activity of recording the dollar results of various business transactions. Up to this point, all business transactions were identified for you in brief narrative form. For example, you were told that on a particular date a financial event occurred, that is, the business sold services for a certain dollar amount either for cash or on a credit basis. It is important to understand, however, that the majority of transactions on a daily basis do not originate in narrative form. In accounting practice, most transaction data originate through the creation of business forms known as ***source documents.*** Four examples of common source documents are described below.

> Source documents: business forms that give objective evidence of business transactions.

THE FIRST BALANCE SHEET When a business is established, the assets, liabilities, and owner's equity are "captured" on the beginning or pre-operating balance sheet. This financial statement becomes the source document from which a subsequent permanent record can be made of each asset, liability, and owner's equity.

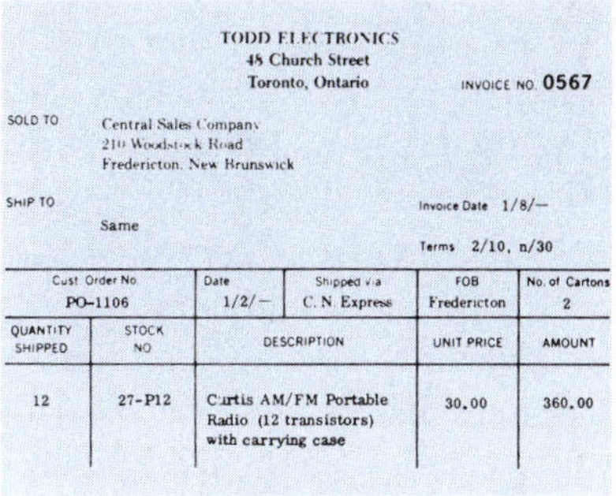

THE INVOICE When a business acquires an asset either for cash or on credit, the seller will make out a bill of sale commonly known as the sales invoice or the ***invoice***. Because invoices vary according to the type and need of each business, the bill of sale may be known as a sales slip, a sales ticket, or a cash register tape. Regardless of the name applied to the business form, the buyer will receive a copy which, in turn, becomes the source document that originates the business transaction. From the seller's viewpoint, a copy of the invoice is retained and, in turn, becomes the source document which gives evidence to the sale. Of course, the invoice can also be used to originate a sale of services. For example, an advertising bill becomes the agency's source document which originates the sales transaction for services rendered. From the buyer's viewpoint, however,

FIGURE 3-1

> Invoice: the source document giving evidence to a sale (seller's view) and to a purchase (buyer's view).

52 PART 1: THE FRAMEWORK OF ACCOUNTING

the advertising bill becomes the source of originating the expense transaction.

THE CHEQUE RECORD To give evidence of originating a cash payment, many businesses create a cheque record. This record may take the form of an actual copy of the cheque, a record of the transaction on the **cheque stub** or chequebook, or a description of the cash payment on one part of a two-part form known as the voucher.

THE REMITTANCE SLIP When a customer remits an amount owing in the form of a cheque, many businesses will require the preparation of a remittance form for every cheque received. The **remittance slip** becomes the source document to be used to record the dollar results of the business transaction. Of course, in other businesses, the document may be known as a receipt which can be included in a book of receipt forms or on one of the sales slips with a proper description of the transaction. See Figure 3-3.

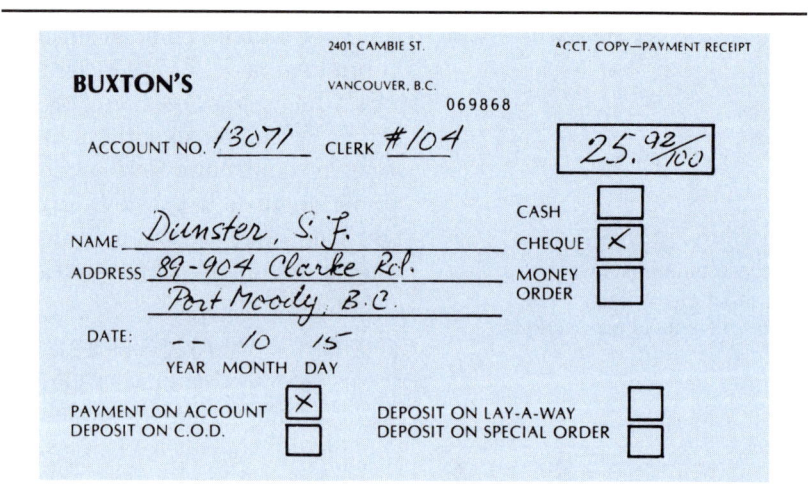

FIGURE 3-2

Cheque stub: the source document giving evidence of a cash payment.

FIGURE 3-3

Remittance slip: a source document prepared by business giving proof that a customer remitted to (paid) the business on account.

Since every accounting system starts with a transaction that is captured on some form of source document, it is important to ensure the accuracy, safety, and reliability of each document. Undiscovered errors in original data cause errors in the results of further processing based on that data. Almost without exception, errors are made by people, mainly through illegible handwriting, incorrect arithmetic, inaccurate copying, inaccurate data entry on the microcomputer keyboard, and inefficient filing. Since accuracy of source documents is so important, and since the transaction data are usually completed by persons who are not assigned to the accounting function, special steps should be taken to minimize errors. These steps would include: the use of forms registers, cash registers, and other equipment to capture the data; the design of forms to ensure their simplicity

Step 2. Journalizing Transaction Data

and uniformity; the serial-numbering of forms to detect their loss; the careful instruction and supervision of personnel so that the forms may be completed and filed correctly; and periodic inspection to check the accuracy and reliability of all source documents.

In the first chapter, you learned how to record the debits and credits for each business transaction directly into a T-account ledger. Although business transactions could be recorded directly into accounts, there are several disadvantages to showing debits and credits only in the ledger.

- The debit side of the entry will appear in one or more accounts, while the credit entry will appear in one or more different accounts. Thus, you would have to search the entire ledger just to analyze one complete business transaction.
- By itself, the account does not show a record of all the business transactions for a particular date. Once again, you would have to search through many accounts to discover the volume of business transactions on a given day.
- And, finally, if an error were made in the debit or the credit entry, this error would be more difficult to locate quickly because the double entry has been separated into two or more accounts.

To overcome these limitations, many accounting systems support the recording of transactions in a chronological record known as the ***journal*** before the debits and credits are entered in the ledger. In simple terms, the journal is like a diary; it will show for each day the debits and credits analyzed from each source document. These debits and credits can later be transferred to individual ledger accounts. Under this system, the debit and credit entry will appear for the first time in the journal; therefore, the journal in an accounting system is generally recognized as the "book of original entry."

In modern practice, there are many different types and forms of journals. One common type is a two-column form called the general journal, which may be illustrated for Office Services as in Figures 3-4 and 3-5.

Analysis   The following points are related to the entries recorded on pages 1 and 48 in the general journal for Office Services:

- Observe that each journal page is numbered in consecutive order.
- The first column receives the date of the transaction. Since the date of the transaction is supported in the majority of cases by a source document, the date in the journal is also the date of the transaction document. On the other hand, if there were no source document, the date in the journal would become the date of the transaction.
- The second column receives the account title or titles which are related to each transaction, and the explanation of the entry when

---

Journal: a chronological record of business transactions in debit and credit form; a "book of original entry," since the debits and credits analyzed in transactions are recorded first in the journal.

FIGURE 3-4

DATE 19-1	ACCOUNT TITLE AND EXPLANATION	POST. REF.	DEBIT	CREDIT
Sept 30	Cash		20 000 00	
	Accounts Receivable		1 000 00	
	Office Equipment		40 000 00	
	Furniture		14 000 00	
	Bank Loan Payable			10 000 00
	Accounts Payable			15 000 00
	E. LeClair, Capital			50 000 00
	To record the opening balance sheet into accounts.			
Oct. 31	Cash		8 000 00	
	Fees Earned			8 000 00
	Fees earned for Cash for October.			
31	Accounts Receivable		12 000 00	
	Fees Earned			12 000 00
	Fees earned on credit for October.			
31	Rent Expense		950 00	
	Salaries Expense		9 000 00	
	Telephone Expense		50 00	
	Utilities Expense		100 00	
	Cash			10 100 00
	Expenses incurred and paid in October.			
31	Advertising Expense		2 000 00	
	Accounts Payable			2 000 00
	Advertising bill from The Local Press; terms 30 days.			
31	E. LeClair, Drawing		1 000 00	
	Cash			1 000 00
	Withdrawal of cash for personal use.			

required. Observe carefully that the debit part of the transaction is shown *before* the credit side. Furthermore, observe that the credit account titles are recorded with a slight indentation so that in reading one can easily distinguish debit accounts from credit accounts. As for the explanation, note that each should be recorded as briefly as possible. In this chapter, you are asked to show an explanation for each entry that you do; however, in practice, explanations are usually shown only when the double entry is not self-explanatory.

CHAPTER 3: Accounting Cycle for a Service Firm 55

FIGURE 3-5

DATE 19-2	ACCOUNT TITLE AND EXPLANATION	POST. REF.	DEBIT	CREDIT
Sept. 5	Cash		1000 00	
	Accounts Receivable			1000 00
	Received cheque from L. Barnes in full settlement of account.			
10	Accounts Payable		2000 00	
	Cash			2000 00
	Issued Cheque 72 to Office Supply Ltd. on account.			
30	Cash		4500 00	
	Fees Earned			4500 00
	Fees earned for cash for September.			
30	Accounts Receivable		18000 00	
	Fees Earned			18000 00
	Fees earned on credit for September.			
30	Rent Expense		950 00	
	Salaries Expense		9600 00	
	Telephone Expense		40 00	
	Utilities Expense		118 00	
	Supplies Expense		60 00	
	Repairs Expense		35 00	
	Bank Interest Expense		500 00	
	Cash			11303 00
	Expenses incurred and paid in September.			
30	E. LeClair, Drawing		400 00	
	Cash			400 00
	Withdrawal of cash for personal use.			

General Journal Page 48

- The next column, labelled "Post. Ref.," will be explained under Step 3.
- The fourth and fifth columns need little explanation. Obviously, the debit column must receive the dollar amount that is related to the debit account title, and the credit column likewise must receive the amount that corresponds to the credit account title.
- Note that dollar signs are omitted from the journal money columns, because this accounting record is not a financial statement. As outlined in the last chapter, dollar signs are required in all financial reports; but they may be omitted in many financial records.

Compound entry: a journal entry in which there are more than one debit and more than one credit entry.

Opening entry: the first journal entry, which establishes the business.

- Observe that a line is left blank between transactions. This blank line separates one transaction from another for easy reading.
- On page 1 of the journal, note that one line remains at the bottom of the page. It is recommended that only complete entries be shown on every page—that entries not be broken up so that part is shown on one page and part on another.
- Observe that some of the entries contain more than one debit and more than one credit entry. For example, the first entry is not only a **compound entry**, but also an **opening entry**. By the term *opening entry*, one simply acknowledges the transaction which "opens" a set of accounting records. On the other hand, the second entry on October 31 is simply a "double entry," because only one debit and one credit account are offseting each other.
- It is very important to remember that all double entries support the logic that the equation analysis of transactions must show a balance of sides. Consequently, an excellent check within any journal is to add the debits of any entry, which, logically, must agree with the total of the credits.
- Observe the method of making a correction in the recorded amount for any transaction in a handwritten journal. As illustrated on page 48 of the journal, simply rule out with a single line the complete error amount; then rewrite neatly the correct amount in full above, and initial the change. Under this method, one can see both the error and the correction and one can know who authorized the change.

THE COMPUTERIZED GENERAL JOURNAL You may be surprised to learn that much of what you have learned about journalizing and the use of the general journal under the hand method also applies to accounting done on a microcomputer. The computerized general journal is examined in Chapter 5 after the accounting cycle under the traditional manual method has been completed.

Step 3. Posting Transaction Data

Although having a chronological record of business transactions in a journal offers definite advantages, you will recall that accounts are required to classify accounting data under one title so that a set of financial statements can be prepared at the end of any accounting period. In addition, during the accounting period management will want useful information such as how much cash is available in the bank account, how much is owing from customers on account, how much is owing to the bank or to creditors on accounts payable, how much revenue has been earned, and how much expenses have been incurred. Consequently, once the debits and credits have been recorded in the journal, it follows that these debits and credits must be transferred to the appropriate accounts that are filed

CHAPTER 3: Accounting Cycle for a Service Firm 57

Posting: transferring debits and credits to the general ledger (updating a ledger file).

in the general ledger. In the language of accounting, the process of transferring such information to the ledger file is called **posting** or, as interpreted under a computer method, *updating* a ledger file. And since the debits and credits are not processed further, that is, they are not transferred to any other recording device, the general ledger is viewed traditionally as the "book of final entry."

Before an example of posting is illustrated, it is appropriate to introduce two important concepts regarding the ledger and account forms.

CHART OF ACCOUNTS   Accounts are generally identified not only by name, but also by a specific number in a *chart of accounts*. For accounts that supply the data for the ultimate preparation of financial statements, a chart of accounts is organized around the main elements of the accounting equation as illustrated in Figure 3-7.

FIGURE 3-6

Office Services
Chart Of Accounts

Assets
101   Cash
102   Marketable Securities (bonds)
103   Accounts Receivable
110   Office Equipment
112   Furniture

Liabilities
201   Bank Loan Payabale
202   Accounts Payable

Owner's Equity
301   E. LeClair, Capital
302   E. LeClair, Drawing

Revenue
401   Fees Earned
402   Interest Earned on Investments

Expenses
501   Rent Expense
502   Salaries Expense
503   Telephone Expense
504   Utilities Expense
505   Advertising Expense
506   Supplies Expense
507   Repairs Expense
508   Bank Interest Expense

FIGURE 3-7

Office Services
Chart Of Accounts

Asset accounts:	101 through 199
Liability accounts:	201 through 299
Owner's equity accounts:	301 through 399
Revenue accounts:	401 through 499
Expense accounts:	501 through 599

It is important to realize that the various account numbers become the codes to identify not only the class of account, but also the specific account within the class. In the case of Office Services, for example, the Cash account is given the first number in a three-digit plan, because it is the first asset to be listed in the balance sheet. You should also recognize from the illustration that gaps are left in the code sequence so that other accounts can be inserted as required.

Computerized Chart of Accounts   The illustration given earlier supports a chart of accounts commonly used under a manual general ledger system.

However, when a computer accounting package is used to process the general ledger (G/L), the chart of accounts must be enlarged to identify codes not only for actual accounts but also for every heading and subheading that will be printed on financial statements. The computerized chart of accounts will be examined in Chapter 5.

FORM OF GENERAL LEDGER ACCOUNT

Earlier, you learned how to record debits and credits in T-account form. This format was selected because its simplicity facilitated the learning of the meanings of debits and credits, the logic of recording increases and decreases in various accounts, and the method of calculating and disclosing account balances. In practice, however, the simple T-account form does not exist; instead, accounting forms are designed in accordance with the specific information required from the account and with the data processing method adopted by the firm's accounting system. One form that is in widespread use under a handwritten method is the three-column type shown in Figure 3-8.

FIGURE 3-8

General Ledger

Advertising Expense — Account No. 505

DATE 19-1	EXPLANATION	POST. REF.	DEBIT	CREDIT	BALANCE
Oct. 31		J 1	200000		200000
Dec. 31		J 5	100000		300000
Feb. 28		J 12	50000		350000
May 31		J 21	100000		450000
July 31		J 30	30000		480000
Aug. 31		J 46	120000		600000

Analysis Notice that there are three money columns: the debit column, which receives the debits recorded first in the debit column of the journal; the credit column, which receives the credits recorded first in the credit column of the general journal; and an additional money column labelled "Balance." As you can see, the Balance column shows the calculation of the balance remaining in the account immediately after the debit or credit has been posted from the general journal to the general ledger. Because the current balance can be shown immediately after each posting, the three-column form is more commonly called the **balance ledger form**.

The other columns require only a brief explanation. Observe that the Date column in the ledger account must receive the date of the journal; therefore, the date of the ledger is the date of the business transaction. The next column, marked "Explanation," is for a brief explanation when

Balance ledger form: a three-column account with a "running" balance.

CHAPTER 3: Accounting Cycle for a Service Firm

one is required. Often in practice the source document is identified in this column or an unusual entry is explained. Note that an explanation is not ordinarily required for every entry, because the source of posting is acknowledged in the Post. Ref. column.

A brief comment is required to explain the difference between the Post. Ref. column of the journal and the ledger. In posting entries from the journal to the ledger under the hand method, one would first locate the appropriate account from the ledger in accordance with the number code from the chart of accounts. Then, the data would be transferred in a basic left-to-right writing order: the date; an explanation if necessary; the source of posting, that is, the initial of the journal and the related page number; the debit or credit amount, as the case may be; the calculated balance after posting; and, finally, the cross-referencing back in the journal with the account number of the account posted in the Post. Ref. column of the journal. It is important to remember that cross-referencing the Post. Ref. column in the journal is the last step of posting, because the absence of any account number in the journal would suggest that the data has not been posted. The posting to Cash from the first journal entry may be illustrated as shown in Figure 3-9.

FIGURE 3-9

account number

GENERAL JOURNAL — Page 1

DATE 19-1	ACCOUNT TITLE AND EXPLANATION	POST. REF.	DEBIT	CREDIT
Sept. 30	Cash	101	20000 00	
	Accounts Receivable		1000 00	
	Office Equipment		40000 00	
	Furniture		14000 00	
	Bank Loan Payable			10000 00
	Accounts Payable			15000 00
	E. LeClair, Capital			50000 00
	To record the opening balance sheet into accounts.			

General Ledger

Cash   Account No. 101

DATE 19-1	EXPLANATION	POST. REF.	DEBIT	CREDIT	BALANCE
Sept. 30	Opening entry	J1	20000 00		20000 00

60 PART 1: THE FRAMEWORK OF ACCOUNTING

DISCLOSING THE BALANCE IN THE BALANCE COLUMN

It is important to realize that the Balance column is an additional column only. It is not required for the recording of debits or credits in accounts. Nor is one expected to compute balances after each posting under a manual method of processing data. The Balance column, however, is convenient when monthly balances of accounts are computed for the purpose of checking the mathematical accuracy of the records, for reference purposes, and for the preparation of financial statements.

In some accounting systems that use the hand method, the running balance is shown to disclose the balance in the account immediately after each posting. In addition, accounting clerks may find it necessary to qualify every running balance as either "dr." or "cr." as shown in Figure 3-10. Or, they may simply wait until the end of the month to add the debits and credits, and then subtract one from the other to check the final balance. This final balance would then be qualified as shown in Figure 3-11.

FIGURE 3-10

FIGURE 3-11

The following procedures may be followed when solving problems in this text using the hand method of posting. Posting under a computer method is examined in Chapter 4.

- Calculate and disclose the balance immediately after each posting. This procedure permits the reader to learn what balance remains after each posting, and also eliminates the possibility of making arithmetic errors in calculating the difference between debits and credits after a lengthy posting.
- For the majority of accounts, do not qualify the balance as "cr." or "dr." unless the amount results in an abnormal balance — for example, when a customer has overpaid his or her account, in which case a credit balance would result and may be disclosed as illustrated in Figures 3-12 and 3-13.

   Observe that the resulting abnormal balance is qualified — that is, "cr." is placed opposite it. In other manual systems, the amount may be circled to show that the balance is translated as opposite to the normal balance.
- If only abnormal balances are qualified, it follows that all normal balances must be translated in relation to their position within the

CHAPTER 3: Accounting Cycle for a Service Firm   **61**

FIGURE 3-12

Accts. Rec./Tires, Inc.					Account No. 105
DATE 19--	EXPLANATION	POST. REF.	DEBIT	CREDIT	BALANCE
Oct 10	Invoice 356; n/30	J4	1 550 00		1 550 00
30		J6		1 600 00	50 00 CR.

FIGURE 3-13

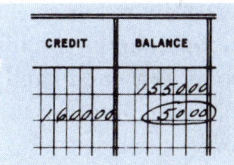

CREDIT	BALANCE
	1 550 00
1 600 00	50 00

accounting equation. Consequently, normal asset account balances must be read as debit balances; normal liability account balances must be interpreted as credit balances; the owner's Capital account will have a credit balance because it increases owner's equity; the owner's Drawing account will have normal debit balances because it decreases owner's equity; all revenue accounts must have credit balances because they increase the owner's equity in the accounting equation; and all expense accounts will read as normal debit balances because they decrease the owner's equity within the accounting equation.

- If the resulting balance is *nil* (zero) following the posting of a transaction to an account, one procedure is to show a large *cipher* (zero symbol) with a diagonal line similar to that shown in Figure 3-14.
- At the end of each month, the final account balance should be double-checked by deducting the total debits from the total credits. This procedure can easily be done with the assistance of any adding machine to ensure complete accuracy.

FIGURE 3-14

Accts. Pay./Bell Furniture Co.					Account No. 202
DATE	EXPLANATION	POST. REF.	DEBIT	CREDIT	BALANCE
Sept 30	Opening entry	J1		800 00	800 00
Oct 5		J1	800 00		

FIGURE 3-15

Cash						Account No. 101
DATE 19-2	EXPLANATION	POST. REF.	DEBIT	CREDIT	BALANCE
Sept 1	Balance forward	✓			11 480 00
4		J47	500 00		11 980 00
5		J47		72 00	11 908 00
6		J47	2 500 00		14 408 00
10		J48		2 000 00	12 408 00
30		J48	4 500 00		16 908 00
30		J48		5 578 00	11 330 00
30		J48		4 000 00	7 330 00

FIGURE 3-16

```
     0.00 *
11 480.00 +
   500.00 +
 2 500.00 +
 4 500.00 +
    72.00 −
 2 000.00 −
 5 578.00 −
 4 000.00 −
 7 330.00 *
```

Step 4. Preparing a Trial Balance

To this point, three important steps have been identified in the routine of accounting called the accounting cycle. First, business transactions were captured on source documents to originate the accounting data. Second, the dollar results of business transactions were analyzed into debits and credits and recorded in chronological order in the general journal. And third, the debits and credits in the general journal were posted to the accounts filed in the general ledger. At the end of any accounting period, therefore, it is logical to assume that the data necessary to prepare financial statements is contained in the general ledger.

Before such financial statements are prepared, however, accountants recommend the practice of taking a number of accounting proofs to ensure that the data recorded in the general ledger is accurate and that all transactions have been accounted for. One important proof has to do with the concept of proving that the general ledger is in balance.

If the debits and credits are posted correctly to the account, the general ledger must balance; that is, the concept of a balanced accounting equation within that ledger must be true. One of the best routine checks of this concept is achieved by preparing a summary of the balances of the general ledger accounts at regular intervals and especially before financial statements are drafted. This summary is known as a ***trial balance***.

In practice, two forms of the trial balance are common. One is acknowledged as the formal trial balance, while the other is an informal or quick preparation of the listing of accounts with their respective balances. As you will learn, this informal listing produces a ***zero-proof trial balance***. Examine carefully Figures 3-17 and 3-18.

> Trial balance: a list of account balances in the general ledger, usually showing the account numbers and/or names, prepared to prove that the G/L is in balance.
>
> Zero-proof trial balance: a listing of G/L account balances in one column, resulting in a zero total.

Analysis of the Formal Trial Balance   These points will help you to prepare a formal trial balance using the manual method. The computerized trial balance is examined in Chapter 5.

- Show a three-line heading. Observe that the date can be at the end of an accounting period or at any time when a formal listing of account balances is required.
- Commencing with the order of accounts which are filed in the general ledger, list only accounts that have a balance. Include account titles and the account number codes. In some formal presentations, the account codes only are shown.
- Since the trial balance is not a financial statement, the use of dollar signs in ruled money columns is optional. However, the dollar sign is usually included when the trial balance is typewritten or printed through a computer program.
- When the total debits equal the total credits, the trial balance provides an accounting proof that the ledger is in balance. This agreement would suggest that equal debits and credits have been

CHAPTER 3: Accounting Cycle for a Service Firm

FIGURE 3-17

Office Services
Trial Balance
September 30, 19-2

ACCOUNT TITLE	ACCT. NO.	DEBIT	CREDIT
Cash	101	7 330 00	
Marketable Securities	102	15 000 00	
Accounts Receivable	103	5 700 00	
Office Equipment	110	40 000 00	
Furniture	112	14 000 00	
Bank Loan Payable	201		2 000 00
Accounts Payable	202		4 000 00
E. LeClair, Capital	301		50 000 00
E. LeClair, Drawing	302	10 600 00	
Fees Earned	401		167 500 00
Interest Earned on Investments	402		1 500 00
Rent Expense	501	11 400 00	
Salaries Expense	502	110 000 00	
Telephone Expense	503	500 00	
Utilities Expense	504	1 100 00	
Advertising Expense	505	6 000 00	
Supplies Expense	506	1 300 00	
Repairs Expense	507	1 170 00	
Bank Interest Expense	508	900 00	
		225 000 00	225 000 00

FIGURE 3-18

Trial Balance
Zero Proof
Sept. 30, 19-2

```
       0•00 *
   7,330•00 *+
  15,000•00  +
   5,700•00  +
  40,000•00  +
  14,000•00  +
  10,600•00  +
  11,400•00  +
 110,000•00  +
     500•00  +
   1,100•00  +
   6,000•00  +
   1,300•00  +
   1,170•00  +
     900•00  +
   2,000•00  -
   4,000•00  -
  50,000•00  -
 167,500•00  -
   1,500•00  -
       0•00 *
```

recorded for all transactions, and that the debit or credit balances of each account have been calculated correctly.

Analysis of the Zero-Proof Trial Balance When a quick listing of account balances is required at any time, an adding-listing machine or a printing calculator may be used. Observe in the illustration of the tape printout that all accounts with debit balances have been listed with the addition or plus key, while all credit balances have been listed with the subtraction or minus key. Since the debits and credits have been listed in one column, the final result must be a zero proof of the trial balance; otherwise, the G/L is not in balance. Of course, the debits could have been listed with a separate total, followed by a separate listing of all credits also with a separate total. However, the zero-proof approach is more common.

Bookkeeping Defined

Bookkeeping: the process of classifying and recording business transactions in terms of money in the "books" of account.

FIGURE 3-19

> **BOOKKEEPER**/office administrator required for Yonge-Eglinton chartered accountant's office. Applicant should have strong bookkeeping & microcomputer/keyboard skills, as well as the knowledge of accounting & w/p software. Forward résumés to

FIGURE 3-20

> Leading educational publisher in Mississauga has an immediate opening for a:
>
> **General Accounting Clerk**
>
> Minimum 2 years' experience on a computerized accounting system. Must have good organizational and communication skills.
>
> Send resume to:

With the completion of the trial balance stage of the accounting cycle, it is appropriate to define the bookkeeping base of accounting. Briefly, the four steps of the accounting cycle discussed so far have identified the concept of **bookkeeping**. These steps are: (1) originating data on source documents; (2) journalizing; (3) posting; and (4) preparing a trial balance.

From time to time, you may hear or see advertisements requiring a person to perform tasks "to the end of the trial balance stage." Of course, such a person would be properly classified as a "bookkeeper," because that person's activities would be restricted to the recording function of accounting. Regardless of the term used, it is important to realize two points:

- Bookkeeping is only part of the overall accounting process. Bookkeeping is not a synonym for accounting. You will only be able to supply an introductory definition of accounting when the remaining steps of the accounting cycle have been covered in this chapter.

- The terms "accounting clerk" and "accounting data entry clerk" are being used by many firms instead of "bookkeeper," especially when microcomputers are being used to process accounting data.

TOPIC 1 Problems

Identifying source documents to support common business transactions.

3.1 For each of the business transactions below, name one or more appropriate source documents that provide evidence of a financial event.

    a Dorothy Curzon commenced business with the following: Cash, $40 000; Equipment, $5 000; Furniture, $5 000; Bank Loan Payable, $10 000; and D. Curzon, Capital, $40 000.

    b Acquired a new microcomputer costing $1 800 from IBM Canada Ltd. for cash.

    c Bought a new office calculator costing $800 from Monroe Canada Ltd. on 30 days' credit.

    d Sold services for $1 000 cash to Marjorie Sanderson.

    e Acquired Canada Savings Bonds costing $5 000 for cash.

    f Sold services on 30 days' credit to Ms. Madelaine Elliot, $200.

    g Issued a cheque for $15.50 to Bell Canada in payment of office telephone bill.

    h Received advertising bill for $300 from WBJK/TV for advertising. Thirty days were given to submit payment in full.

    i The owner withdrew $100 cash for personal use.

j Paid $900 to Canadian Properties Ltd. for the monthly rent of the office.
k Received cheque for $100 from Ms. M. Elliot, on account.
l Paid monthly utilities bill, $80 cash.

Journalizing common business transactions.

3.2 Return to the business transactions outlined in Problem 3.1. Use a two-column general journal beginning with Page 1 to record the dollar results of each transaction. Give a brief explanation for each journal entry. Use appropriate titles to each account, and make up suitable dates of the current month for each lettered transaction.

Preparing a chart of accounts; jounalizing common business transactions.

3.3 Return to Problem 2.6 of Chapter 2 (Spot-Free Cleaners); then perform the following tasks:

a Prepare an appropriate chart of accounts that would be related to the transactions outlined for Spot-Free Cleaners. Assume that the chart would support journalizing and posting procedures under the manual method of processing accounting data.

b Record the dollar results of all transactions for November in a "book" of original entry. Use the account titles identified in the chart of accounts established for **a**, and show a brief explanation for each journal entry.

Journalizing and posting common business transactions; preparing a formal and zero-proof trial balance.

3.4 The Brandon Parking Service was established on October 1 with the following chart of accounts:

FIGURE 3-21

Account	Number
Cash	101
Land	110
Equipment	112
Bank Loan Payable	201
Accounts Payable	202
Mortgage Payable	220
Val Mikolayenko, Capital	301
Val Mikolayenko, Drawing	302
Parking Fees Earned	401
Advertising Expense	501
Utilities Expense	502
Salaries Expense	503
Telephone Expense	504
Interest Expense	505

The business transactions for the enterprise during the first month of operation were summarized as follows:

Oct. 1 Val Mikolayenko deposited $75 000 cash in a bank current account in the name of Brandon Parking System.

2 The firm purchased land in a downtown location for $100 000. Of this total cost, $60 000 was paid in cash, while the balance was to be paid to The City Realty Co. on a ten-year 12% mortgage payable.

It was agreed that a minimum monthly payment of $900 would be made to cover both principal and interest.
3 Paid $4 200 cash for a cash register.
4 Arranged with the City Sign Co. to construct a sign which advertised the parking services of the firm. The bill for the sign amounted to $250. Credit terms of 30 days were offered in the bill. (Use Advertising Expense.)
7 Paid $100 cash for advertisement carried in the local newspaper.
10 Cash collected to date from parking customer cars totalled $1 200.
15 Paid $40 cash for telephone bill.
20 Parking receipts since October 11 totalled $2 100.
25 Electricity bill received from the Public Utilities Commission totalled $140. The bill was to be paid by November 5.
28 Borrowed $5 000 cash on a demand loan from the bank.
30 The owner withdrew $2 400 cash for personal use.
31 Issued a cheque for $1 500 to C. Hapko, the parking attendant, for services rendered for the month.
31 Parking receipts since October 20 totalled $1 900.
31 Issued cheque for $900 to The City Realty Co. in part payment on the mortgage payable. The interest on this payment amounted to $400.

Required

a Record the business transactions for October in a two-column general journal. Show an explanation for each entry.
b Post the transactions from the journal to a G/L which uses the balance ledger form.
c Prepare a formal trial balance at the end of October. If you have access to a tape-listing machine, prepare also a zero-proof trial balance on the machine tape.

Journalizing and posting common business transactions; preparing a formal and zero-proof trial balance.

3.5 Thompson's Real Estate Agency was established on September 1 with the following chart of accounts to support a manual method of processing accounting data:

FIGURE 3-22

Account	Number
Cash in Royal Bank	1003
Accounts Receivable	1011
Office Equipment	1101
Furniture	1103
Bank Loan Payable	2001
Accounts Payable	2101
Denise Thompson, Capital	3001
Denise Thompson, Drawing	3002
Commissions Earned	4001
Rent Expense	5001
Utilities Expense	5002
Telephone Expense	5003
Advertising Expense	5004
Salaries Expense	5005
Bank Interest Expense	5020

CHAPTER 3: Accounting Cycle for a Service Firm   **67**

The business transactions for the enterprise during the first month of operation were summarized as follows:

Sept. 1 Denise Thompson commenced business with the following assets and liabilities: Cash in Royal Bank, $8 000; Office Equipment, $20 000; Furniture, $7 000; and Bank Loan Payable, $5 000. *Note:* Do not forget to calculate and account for the owner's equity through her investment.
   2 Paid $800 cash for monthly rent of office.
   3 Bought additional office equipment costing $2 000 on 60 days' credit from Office Equipment Ltd.
   4 Returned one piece of defective office equipment acquired for $600 to Office Equipment Ltd.
   7 Earned a commission of $2 500 cash by selling a client's residence.
   9 Paid Office Equipment Ltd. $500 cash on account.
   11 Paid $1 000 to the bank in partial payment of the bank loan.
   15 Earned a commission of $3 000 by selling a client's residence. The sale agreement provided that the client, J. Jacks, would pay the commission in 60 days.
   16 Paid $48 cash for office telephone bill received today.
   20 Paid $80 cash for utilities bill received today.
   25 Earned a commission of $1 200 cash by buying a residence for a client.
   28 The owner instructed you to pay her *home* telephone bill, which totalled $22. A cheque was issued against the business's bank account in payment of that bill.
   30 Received from The Local Press a bill for $800 for advertisements published during September. The bill gave 30 days in which to make full payment.
   30 Paid $2 400 cash for monthly salaries to office personnel.
   30 Received a cheque for $1 000 from J. Jacks, as part payment of his debt owing on account.
   30 The owner requested you to issue a cheque to her for $1 400 as payment of her monthly salary in the business. Issued a cheque made payable to Denise Thompson, the owner.
   30 Received a memo from Royal Bank informing the business that the bank has deducted $42 for monthly interest on the bank loan.

Required
   a Record the business transactions for October in a two-column general journal. Show an explanation for each entry.
   b Post the transactions from the journal to a ledger which uses the balance ledger form.
   c Prepare a formal trial balance at the end of September. If you have access to a tape-listing machine, prepare also a zero-proof trial balance on the machine tape.

TOPIC 2 Six-Column Worksheet and Financial Statements

The second topic of this chapter treats the fifth and sixth steps of an introductory accounting cycle for a service firm.

Step 5. Preparing a Worksheet

Worksheet: an expanded trial balance for computing, classifying, and sorting accounting balances before preparing financial statements.

When a trial balance is correct and it contains only a short listing of G/L accounts, a set of financial statements can easily be prepared from it. However, in practice, some accountants prepare a columnar working paper form called a ***worksheet*** before the financial statements are reported to interested persons within the firm and outside the business. A worksheet becomes useful especially when the trial balance contains many accounts, when some accounts need updating at the end of each financial period, and when financial statements are required at the end of each month or quarter of the year.

In practice, the worksheet can contain six, eight, ten, twelve, or more columns. Figure 3-23 is a simplified six-column form. A larger worksheet is introduced in Chapter 5.

Analysis The following points should be considered in any study of the worksheet:

- The extended balances in the worksheet should not be confused with the financial statements themselves. Neither should the worksheet be considered as part of the accounting records. The worksheet is merely an aid to the accountant who may find it convenient if there are numerous adjustments at the end of a financial period; it is by no means essential to the preparation of financial statements.
- Because the worksheet is not part of the accounting records, it is usually prepared neatly in pencil.
- In the illustration, observe the heading which contains the name of the business, the identification of the form, and the date of the financial period. It is important to recognize the complete accounting period, because the connecting link between the financial statement columns is the net income (or net loss). As you will recall, the net income (or net loss) covers a financial period that has ended.
- From the body of the worksheet, you can conclude that this working paper is an extended form of trial balance. What is new is the arrangement of financial statement columns in debit and credit form.
- Observe carefully that the Income Statement columns precede the Balance Sheet statement columns. This order is logical, because the net income (or net loss) calculated by the Income Statement columns must be transferred to the Balance Sheet columns to bring about the increase (or decrease) to Owner's Equity at the end of the financial period.
- To transfer trial balance amounts, move a debit balance to the debit column of the related financial statement. Similarly, move a credit

FIGURE 3-23

Office Services
Worksheet
For the Year Ended September 30, 19-2

	Account Title	Acct. No.	TRIAL BALANCE Debit	TRIAL BALANCE Credit	INCOME STATEMENT Debit	INCOME STATEMENT Credit	BALANCE SHEET Debit	BALANCE SHEET Credit	
1	Cash........................	101	7 330				7 330		1
2	Marketable Securities..........	102	15 000				15 000		2
3	Accounts Receivable...........	103	5 700				5 700		3
4	Office Equipment.............	110	40 000				40 000		4
5	Furniture....................	112	14 000				14 000		5
6	Bank Loan Payable............	201		2 000				2 000	6
7	Accounts Payable.............	202		4 000				4 000	7
8	E. LeClair, Capital.............	301		50 000				50 000	8
9	E. LeClair, Drawing...........	302	10 600				10 600		9
10	Fees Earned.................	401		167 500		167 500			10
11	Interest Earned on Investments...	402		1 500		1 500			11
12	Rent Expense................	501	11 400		11 400				12
13	Salaries Expense..............	502	110 000		110 000				13
14	Telephone Expense...........	503	500		500				14
15	Utilities Expense..............	504	1 100		1 100				15
16	Advertising Expense...........	505	6 000		6 000				16
17	Supplies Expense.............	506	1 300		1 300				17
18	Repairs Expense..............	507	1 170		1 170				18
19	Bank Interest Expense.........	508	900		900				19
20			225 000	225 000	132 370	169 000	92 630	56 000	20
21						132 370			21
22	Net Income				36 630			36 630	22
23							92 630	92 630	23

balance to the credit column of the related financial statement. Begin with the first account and proceed to transfer all accounts to their related statement columns.

- Following the transfer of the last account balance, rule a single line across all financial statement columns and show the totals for those columns.
- In the Income Statement columns, analyze the debit and credit totals. The total debits would represent the total expenses for the financial period; the total credits would be the total revenue for the same financial period.
- Observe the method of calculating the matchup between the total revenues, and total expenses in the Income Statement columns. In

FIGURE 3-24

Calculating a Net Loss

	INCOME STATEMENT		BALANCE SHEET	
	Debit	Credit	Debit	Credit
50	37 000	35 000	101 000	103 000
51	35 000			
52	2 000 →	2 000	
53			103 000	103 000

the illustration, the total expenses are deducted from total revenue, because the revenue total is greater. Of course, the result of such a matchup is the net income for the financial period. On the other hand, if the total expenses were greater, a net loss may be calculated as illustrated in Figure 3-24.

- After the net income (or net loss) is calculated from the Income Statement columns, transfer this key figure to the Balance Sheet columns. If the result is a net income, then show this amount in the credit column to indicate that Owner's Equity has been increased within the accounting equation. On the other hand, if a net loss is reported, the figure must be entered in the debit column, because Owner's Equity can only be decreased by a debit entry.

- And, finally, observe how the worksheet shows the balancing of the two totals in the Balance Sheet columns. In this sense, the worksheet balances just like any accounting equation, because the total debits must also equal the total credits.

COMPUTERIZED WORKSHEETS When a computer is used to process accounting data, it is not necessary to use a worksheet unless adjustments are required at the end of the accounting period. When that is the case, some accounting packages do print a worksheet on which the trial balance is listed and additional columns to record by hand any final adjustments. The study of adjustments will be treated in Chapter 5.

Step 6. Preparing Financial Statements

Since the preparation of the income statement and the related balance sheet has been covered in Chapter 1, only a brief analysis is required to cover aspects not treater earlier. Observe the following four points of analysis when you examine the financial statements illustrated in Figures 3-25 and 3-26. *Note*: Computerized financial statements are treated in Chapter 5.

- The first financial statement to be prepared is the income statement. The data for this statement is found in the Income Statement columns of the worksheet.

- The related balance sheet is prepared after the income statement. The data for this statement should be found in the Balance Sheet money columns of the worksheet.

- In the balance sheet, observe that only the final figure of owner's equity is reported. Some firms prefer to report the claim of the owner by disclosing only the residual (final) figure as it is derived from the accounting equation (OE = A − L).

- When the new owner's equity only is reported, it is customary to prepare an accompanying **statement of owner's equity** (sometimes

Statement of owner's equity: a financial statement reporting the changes in owner's equity from one accounting period to the next.

CHAPTER 3: Accounting Cycle for a Service Firm

FIGURE 3-25

Financial statement

Office Services
Income Statement
For the Year Ended September 30, 19-2

Revenues:		
Fees Earned		$167 500.00
Interest Earned on Investments		1 500.00
Total Revenues		169 000.00
Expenses:		
Rent Expense	$ 11 400.00	
Salaries Expense	110 000.00	
Telephone Expense	500.00	
Utilities Expense	1 100.00	
Advertising Expense	6 000.00	
Supplies Expense	1 300.00	
Repairs Expense	1 170.00	
Bank Interest Expense	900.00	
Total Expenses		132 370.00
Net Income		$ 36 630.00

FIGURE 3-26

Office Services
Balance Sheet
As at September 30, 19-2

Assets

Current Assets:		
Cash	$ 7 330.00	
Marketable Securities	15 000.00	
Accounts Receivable	5 700.00	
Total Current Assets		$28 030.00
Fixed Assets (at cost):		
Office Equipment	$40 000.00	
Furniture	14 000.00	
Total Fixed Assets		54 000.00
Total Assets		$82 030.00

Liabilities

Current Liabilities:		
Bank Loan Payable (on demand)	$2 000.00	
Accounts Payable	4 000.00	
Total Liabilities		$ 6 000.00

Owner's Equity

E. LeClair, Capital	$76 030.00	
Total Owner's Equity		76 030.00
Total Liabilities and Owner's Equity		$82 030.00

FIGURE 3-27

```
Office Services
Statement of Owner's Equity
For Year Ended September 30, 19-2

E. LeClair, Capital,
  September 30, 19-1 ...  $50 000.00
Add: Net Income .......     36 630.00
                            86 630.00
Less: Withdrawals ......    10 600.00
E. LeClair, Capital,
  September 30, 19-2 ...  $76 030.00
```

called the *schedule of owner's equity*). Examine carefully Figure 3-27 in the margin.

Analysis In the statement of owner's equity, notice that all the details of the owner's claims against the assets are disclosed. This would include the balance of the Capital account at the beginning of the accounting period, any additional investments made during the period, the net income or loss for the accounting period, and the personal withdrawals also for the same accounting period. Of course, not all such information is readily available on the worksheet. The owner's beginning capital and any additional investments would be found in the Capital account of the general ledger.

When a separate statement of owner's equity is not provided, the details of owner's equity are usually included in the balance sheet.

TOPIC 2 Problems

Preparing a six-column worksheet from the trial balance solved for Problem 3.4.

3.6 Return to the trial balance solved for Problem 3.4 (Brandon Parking Service); then do the following for this problem:
  a Prepare a six-column worksheet for the month ended October 31.
  b From the worksheet, prepare an income statement and a related balance sheet in *report form*. Include the details of owner's equity within the balance sheet.

Preparing a six-column worksheet from the trial balance solved for Problem 3.5; preparing the financial statements from the worksheet.

3.7 Return to the trial balance solved for Problem 3.5 (Thompson's Real Estate Agency); then do the following for this problem:
  a Prepare a six-column worksheet for the month ended September 30.
  b From the worksheet, prepare an income statement and a related balance sheet in *account form*. Report the details of owner's equity in a separate statement of owner's equity.

Preparing a six-column worksheet from given data; preparing the financial statements from the worksheet.

3.8 A trial balance of the G/L for Allan's Auto Repair at the year-end of June revealed the following balances: Cash, $6 260; Accounts Receivable, $1 520; Land, $32 000; Building, $58 000; Repair Equipment, $7 580; Office Equipment, $2 400; Bank Loan Payable (demand), $6 000; Accounts Payable, $400; Property Taxes Payable, $200; Tom Allan, Capital, $96 300; Tom Allan, Drawing, $27 200; Service Revenue, $89 100; Advertising Expense, $1 900; Repair Parts Expense, $10 520; Property Taxes Expense, $2 400; Utilities Expense, $740; Wages Expense, $38 980; Office Supplies Expense, $1 900; Interest Expense, $600.

Required
  a Prepare a six-column worksheet for the year ended June 30.
  b From the worksheet, prepare an income statement and the related balance sheet in report form. Include the details of owner's equity within the balance sheet.

Preparing a six-column worksheet from given data; preparing the financial statements from the worksheet.

3.9 The general ledger accounts for Price's Music Conservatory revealed the following data at the year-end of December 31: Cash, $5 654; Marketable Securities (Government of Canada bonds), $10 000; Accounts Receivable, $825; Land, $25 000; Building, $50 000; Musical Instruments, $12 000; Office Equipment, $3 000; Bank Loan Payable (on demand), $3 000; Accounts Payable, $1 062; Property Taxes Payable, $240; Mortgage Payable, $30 000 (20-year mortgage at 12% per annum; $2 000 is due within the current financial year); Debbie Price, Capital, $112 945 (January 1, $85 000; additional investment on June 1, $27 945); Debbie Price, Drawing, $19 600; Tuition Revenue, $47 753; Interest Earned on Bonds, $1 000; Advertising Expense, $5 400; Salaries Expense, $53 600; Telephone Expense, $984; Property Taxes Expense, $3 030; Utilities Expense, $776; Supplies Expense, $1 216; and Interest Expense, $4 915.

Required
a Prepare a six-column worksheet for the year ended December 31.
b From the worksheet, prepare an income statement, a related balance sheet, and a statement of owner's equity.

TOPIC 3 Completing the Accounting Cycle

Step 7. Preparing the Year-End Closing Entries

At the end of each financial year, each revenue account and each expense account must be *closed*, that is, reduced to a zero balance. This procedure is required in order to prepare the G/L to receive the accumulation of next year's revenue and expense amounts without mixing in the previous year's.

A second objective is accomplished through the procedure of closing the G/L. From the worksheet and year-end balance sheet, you have learned that owner's equity (the claim of the owner against total assets) was updated by adding the net income to the owner's capital, and subtracting the personal withdrawals for the year. Through the process of closing, the net income and personal withdrawals are transferred to the owner's Capital account so that the balance in Capital agrees with the total Owner's Equity as disclosed by the year-end balance sheet. Thus, the procedure of closing accomplishes two things: (1) it reduces all revenue and expense accounts to a zero balance; and (2) it updates the Capital account in the G/L to make it agree with the total of Owner's Equity in the year-end balance sheet.

THE MECHANICS OF CLOSING To accomplish the two objectives in closing the general ledger, under the manual method of processing accounting data, a special clearinghouse account called **Revenue and Expense Summary** is used. (The computerized method of closing will be examined in Chapter 5.) As the title of the account suggests, this account summarizes the revenue and expense data for the calculation of the net income or net loss within the G/L.

Revenue and Expense Summary: a temporary owner's equity account used to summarize revenue and expenses for an entire accounting period.

To transfer the revenue and expense data, two sets of compound entries are made. One set debits the individual revenue accounts to reduce each to zero, and credits the Revenue and Expense Summary account with the total revenue; observe that the data for this entry can be obtained from the credit column of the Income Statement section of the worksheet. A second compound entry debits the Revenue and Expense Summary account for the total expenses, and credits the individual expense accounts to reduce each expense to zero. Again, note that the information for this entry can be obtained from the debit column of the Income Statement section of the worksheet. After these entries have been posted, the Revenue and Expense Summary account should contain the same data as disclosed by the Income Statement columns of the worksheet. If the Summary account has a credit balance, this credit amount must be interpreted as the net income. On the other hand, if the Summary account were to contain a debit balance, then the amount indicates a net loss for the accounting period.

Two final journal entries are required to complete the closing process. One double entry would close (transfer) the net income or loss to the owner's Capital account; a final entry would close (transfer) the balance

FIGURE 3-28

GENERAL JOURNAL				Page 49
DATE 19-2	ACCOUNT TITLE AND EXPLANATION	POST. REF.	DEBIT	CREDIT
Sept. 30	Fees Earned	401	16750 00	
	Interest Earned on Investments	402	1500 00	
	Revenue and Expense Summary	399		16900 00
	To close the revenue accounts.			
30	Revenue and Expense Summary	399	12370 00	
	Rent Expense	501		1400 00
	Salaries Expense	502		11000 00
	Telephone Expense	503		500 00
	Utilities Expense	504		1100 00
	Advertising Expense	505		6000 00
	Supplies Expense	506		1300 00
	Repairs Expense	507		1170 00
	Bank Interest Expense	508		900 00
	To close the expense accounts.			
30	Revenue and Expense Summary	399		
	E. LeClair, Capital	301		
	To transfer the net income.			
30	E. LeClair, Capital	301	1060 00	
	E. LeClair, Drawing	302		1060 00
	To transfer the drawing.			

CHAPTER 3: Accounting Cycle for a Service Firm

in the Drawing account to Capital. After both entries have been posted, the Capital account balance should agree with the total Owner's Equity in the year-end balance sheet. The closing entries for Office Services may be illustrated as shown in Figures 3-28 to 3-30.

FIGURE 3-29

E. LeClair, Capital Account No. 301

Date	Explanation	Post. Ref.	Debit	Credit	Balance
19-1 Sept. 30	Opening entry.	J1		40 000 00	40 000 00
19-2 Sept. 30	Net income.	J49		36 630 00	86 630 00
30	Withdrawals.	J49	10 600 00		76 030 00

FIGURE 3-30

Owner's Equity

E. LeClair, Capital	$50 000
Add: Net income	36 630
Subtotal	86 630
Less: Withdrawals	10 600
Total Owner's Equity	$76 030

Step 8. Preparing a Postclosing Trial Balance

After all closing entries have been posted, the G/L should reveal these facts: (1) all revenue and expense accounts, the Revenue and Expense Summary account, and the owner's Drawing account should have zero balances; (2) only the accounts that supply data for the year-end balance sheet should contain balances; and (3) the balance in the owner's Capital account should agree with the total of Owner's Equity in the year-end balance sheet.

To prove these facts, an after-closing trial balance called the ***postclosing trial balance*** is prepared. For Office Services, this may be prepared by hand as shown in Figure 3-31. (The computerized postclosing trial balance is examined in Chapter 5.)

From an analysis of the postclosing trial balance, you can see that the accounts listed are the balance sheet accounts. These balance sheet accounts are regarded as ***permanent accounts,*** because their balances are carried forward into the next accounting period. On the other hand, all

Postclosing trial balance: a trial balance prepared after the G/L has been closed.

Permanent accounts: balance sheet accounts carried forward into the next accounting period.

FIGURE 3-31

Office Services
Postclosing Trial Balance
September 30, 19-2

ACCOUNT TITLE	ACCT. NO.	DEBIT	CREDIT
Cash	101	7330 00	
Marketable Securities	102	1500 00	
Accounts Receivable	103	570 00	
Office Equipment	110	4000 00	
Furniture	112	1400 00	
Bank Loan Payable	201		200 00
Accounts Payable	202		400 00
E. LeClair, Capital	301		7603 00
		8203 00	8203 00

Temporary accounts: income statement accounts; the revenue and expense summary account; and the drawing account reduced to zero at the end of each financial year.

revenue and expense accounts, the Revenue and Expense Summary account, and the Drawing account are acknowledged as **temporary accounts**, because their balances are reduced to zero at the end of each business year.

DEFINING ACCOUNTING   Accounting may be defined in several ways, depending on the background of topics covered in an introductory course. With the completion of an elementary accounting cycle, accounting may be defined as follows:

The process of analyzing and systematically recording business transactions and of summarizing, reporting, and interpreting the results to interested parties both within and outside the business enterprise.

These points should be emphasized when studying the above definition:
- The accounting process includes bookkeeping. Bookkeepers (accounting clerks) analyze transactions on the basis of approved source documents into debits and credits (see "Step 1. Originating Accounting Data"). These debits and credits are recorded systematically in a journal ("Step 2. Journalizing Transaction Data") and then transferred

CHAPTER 3: Accounting Cycle for a Service Firm 77

to ledger accounts ("Step 3. Posting Transaction Data"). Later, at appropriate times, summaries of the posted debits and credits are made in prior preparation of financial statements ("Step 4. Preparing a Trial Balance").

- Usually, accountants are hired to set up the accounting system, a task which includes creating a chart of accounts for the general ledger. In addition, accountants may prepare summaries such as worksheets prior to their preparing useful financial statements ("Step 5. Preparing a Worksheet" and "Step 6. Preparing Financial Statements").

- Useful financial statements are prepared for two groups of interested parties. One group consists of interested people who are outside the firm — that is, *outsiders* such as investors or potential investors, bankers, unions, Revenue Canada — Taxation, etc. To be useful, these financial statements must be general in nature, and therefore they are prepared in accordance with generally accepted accounting principles (GAAPs). This branch of accounting is called **general or financial accounting**.

> General (financial) accounting: that branch of accounting that deals with the preparation of financial statements using GAAPs to interested parties called outsiders.

The second group, commonly known as *insiders*, consist of those who manage the business. They require financial statements and other, related financial reports on which useful business decisions can be made. Although the same financial statements prepared under GAAPs are often used, it is important to emphasize that managers usually require additional information which does not conform to GAAPs. For example, management may find useful a set of budgeted financial statements that project how much net income (or net loss) will occur over the next year or more. Budgeted financial statements can then be compared with actual, historical ones so that differences in key figures can be analyzed and appropriate action can be taken. The study of financial statements and other reports for management is usually called **management or managerial accounting**.

> Management (managerial) accounting: that branch of accounting that deals with the preparation of financial reports useful for managerial decision-making.

- Bookkeepers (accounting clerks), under the supervision of accountants, record the debits and credits to close the books ("Step 7. Preparing the Year-End Closing Entries") and prepare the after-closing trial balance ("Step 8. Preparing a Postclosing Trial Balance") to complete the accounting cycle.

- This final point is important. Bookkeepers are clerks who normally perform accounting activities to the end of the trial balance stage of the accounting process. On the other hand, accountants are professional people who have qualified to practise under one or more designations awarded by Canada's three accounting bodies: the Canadian Institute of Chartered Accountants (whose members are entitled to the professional designation **C.A.**); the Society of Management Accountants (whose members are entitled to the professional

> C.A.: chartered accountant.

TOPIC 3 Problems

Preparing a set of closing entries in the general journal for Allan's Auto Repair.

3.10 Return to the trial balance solved for Problem 3.8 (Allan's Auto Repair); then prepare the closing entries in the general journal using the information contained in the worksheet. Include the closing entry to transfer the drawings to the owner's permanent equity account. *Note*: No postings are required for this problem; however, show an explanation for each closing entry.

Preparing a set of closing entries in the general journal for Price's Music Conservatory.

3.11 Use the worksheet solved for Problem 3.9 to prepare the year-end closing entries to close all temporary accounts in the general ledger of Price's Music Conservatory. *Note*: No postings are required for this problem; however, show an explanation for each closing entry.

Preparing the six-column worksheet; preparing the year-end financial statements; recording and posting the year-end closing entries; preparing the postclosing trial balance.

3.12 M. Daeninck, D.D.S. completed his first year of professional practice. His dental firm's year-end trial balance was disclosed as shown in Figure 3-32.

FIGURE 3-32

M. Daeninck, D.D.S.
Trial Balance
December 31, 19-1

Cash	101	$ 3 600	
Marketable Securities	102	5 000	
Accounts Receivable	103	1 760	
Dental Equipment	110	25 000	
Office Equipment	112	4 840	
Bank Loan	201		$ 4 000
Accounts Payable	202		2 500
M. Daeninck, Capital	301		27 000
M. Daeninck, Drawing	302	18 000	
Professional Fees Earned	401		36 160
Rent Expense	501	4 800	
Dental Supplies Expense	502	5 600	
Telephone Expense	503	180	
Utilities Expense	504	670	
Interest Expense	505	210	
		$69 660	$69 660

CHAPTER 3: Accounting Cycle for a Service Firm 79

Required
a Prepare a six-column worksheet for the year ended December 31, 19-1.
b From the worksheet, prepare the year-end income statement and the related balance sheet in report form. Prepare a separate statement of owner's equity.
c Open a general ledger to include accounts shown in the trial balance, and an account for Revenue and Expense Summary (account number 399). For each account shown in the trial balance, indicate a "balance forward" as at December 31.
d Record the year-end closing entries in the general journal; then post these entries to the general ledger. Use "Page 20" for the general journal.
e Prepare a postclosing trial balance.

Preparing the six-column worksheet; preparing the year-end financial statements; recording and posting the year-end closing entries; preparing the postclosing trial balance.

3.13 M. Cole, owner and manager of Martha Cole Advertising Agency, completed her first year of business with the year-end trial balance shown in Figure 3-33.

FIGURE 3-33

The Martha Cole Advertising Agency
Trial Balance
June 30, 19-2

Account	No.	Debit	Credit
Cash	1010	$ 10 000	
90-Day Bank Deposit Receipts	1020	50 000	
Accounts Receivable	1030	4 500	
Land	1100	30 000	
Building	1120	70 000	
Office Equipment	1140	50 000	
Furniture	1160	25 000	
Bank Loan Payable	2010		$ 20 000
Accounts Payable	2020		5 000
10% Mortgage Payable	2200		60 000
Martha Cole, Capital (June 30, 19-1)	3010		185 000
Martha Cole, Drawing	3020	18 820	
Fees Earned	4010		70 000
Interest Earned	4020		5 000
Salaries Expense	5010	55 000	
Advertising Expense	5020	18 000	
Telephone Expense	5030	480	
Utilities Expense	5040	1 200	
Insurance Expense	5050	1 800	
Property Taxes Expense	5060	2 200	
Bank Interest Expense	5200	2 000	
Mortgage Interest Expense	5210	6 000	
		$345 000	$345 000

PART 1: THE FRAMEWORK OF ACCOUNTING

Additional Information
- The bank loan is payable on demand.
- The mortgage payable is due in ten years.
- The mortgage is secured by assigning the land and building as collateral.
- The principal payment on the mortgage, due within one year, is $5 000.

Required
a Prepare a six-column worksheet for the year ended June 30, 19-2.
b From the worksheet, prepare the year-end income statement and the related balance sheet in report form. Prepare a separate statement of owner's equity.
c Open a general ledger to include accounts shown in the trial balance, and an account for Revenue and Expense Summary (3999). For each account shown in the trial balance, indicate a "balance forward" as at June 30, 19-2.
d Record the year-end closing entries in the general journal; then post these entries to the general ledger. Use "Page 60" for the general journal.
e Prepare a postclosing trial balance.

TOPIC 4 Introducing the Electronic Spreadsheet

In previous Topics, all stages in the accounting cycle have been prepared by using the traditional hand or manual method. This Topic is a good place to introduce the electronic spreadsheet, which enables us to carry out some aspects of the accounting cycle on a computer. To keep matters simple, discussion of the technical aspects of computing will be kept to a minimum, and application examples will be made with reference only to the microcomputer.

Some Historical Background

Electronic spreadsheet: an applications program in which the computer's memory serves as a large working paper called the worksheet or spreadsheet.

An *electronic spreadsheet* may be defined as a large worksheet set up in vertical columns and horizontal rows on a computer screen. A second definition is shown in the side margin.

Accountants have prepared spreadsheets manually long before computers were invented. Typical of such spreadsheets are accounting worksheets of six or more columns and financial statements prepared on a monthly comparative basis.

When computers were introduced in the 1950s to perform common accounting applications such as payroll and the general ledger, few accountants had access to the electronic spreadsheet. During those early years, the cost of programming electronic spreadsheet software was very high on centralized, **mainframe computer** systems. Thus, the majority of accounting problems were still solved on manually prepared spreadsheets with the aid of calculators.

Mainframe computer: the largest of three computer systems: mainframe, microcomputer, and minicomputer.

CHAPTER 3: Accounting Cycle for a Service Firm   81

Microcomputer: a small computer containing a single microprocessor; also known as a desktop computer or personal computer.

However, with the introduction of the **microcomputer** in 1978, accountants found that computer data processing could be decentralized and thus be made available on their desktops. There followed development of electronic spreadsheet software for use in accounting and other applications.

The first successful electronic spreadsheet for microcomputer accounting applications was **VisiCalc**, which subsequently was acquired by Lotus Development Corporation. In turn, Lotus improved on the old VisiCalc version by creating the now-popular *Lotus 1-2-3®*.

VisiCalc: the first successful electronic spreadsheet developed for the microcomputer.

The success of VisiCalc prompted other software companies to develop spreadsheet software packages. Among the successful ones in common use are *SuperCalc®* (developed originally by Sorcim and now redeveloped and marketed by Computer Associates International, Inc.); *MultiPlan®* (developed by Microsoft Corporation); and *Quattro®* (developed by Borland International, Inc.).

A recent trend in developing electronic spreadsheets is to include them in integrated software packages. This means that the spreadsheet is combined with other software programs such as a database management package, a graphics package, and even a word processing package. This type of integrated software would convert the spreadsheet data into data tables or instant graphs and permit the user to type useful notes below such tables and graphs. Examples of such integrated software packages containing powerful spreadsheets are *Lotus 1-2-3®* (developed by Lotus for the IBM PC and compatibles); *JAZZ®* (developed by Lotus for the Apple Macintosh); *Excel* (developed by Microsoft with versions for both the IBM PC and compatibles and for the Apple Macintosh); and *Microsoft Works®* (with versions for the IBM PC and compatibles and for Apple Macintosh).

Regardless of future developments, accountants and accounting educators have agreed that the use of electronic spreadsheets will continue to increase in accounting practice. Hence, students should master the fundamentals of at least one electronic spreadsheet. Once learned, these fundamentals can easily be related to the mastery of any other electronic spreadsheet.

Common Features   Although differences are evident, the leading electronic spreadsheet programs have many design features in common, because in many ways they have been modelled after VisiCalc. All modern electronic spreadsheet programs should include these features:

- **Spreadsheet**   This consists of a number of rows down the left-hand side and a number of columns across the top of a computer screen. A typical example is the popular Lotus 1-2-3 spreadsheet screen as illustrated in Figure 3-34.

FIGURE 3-34

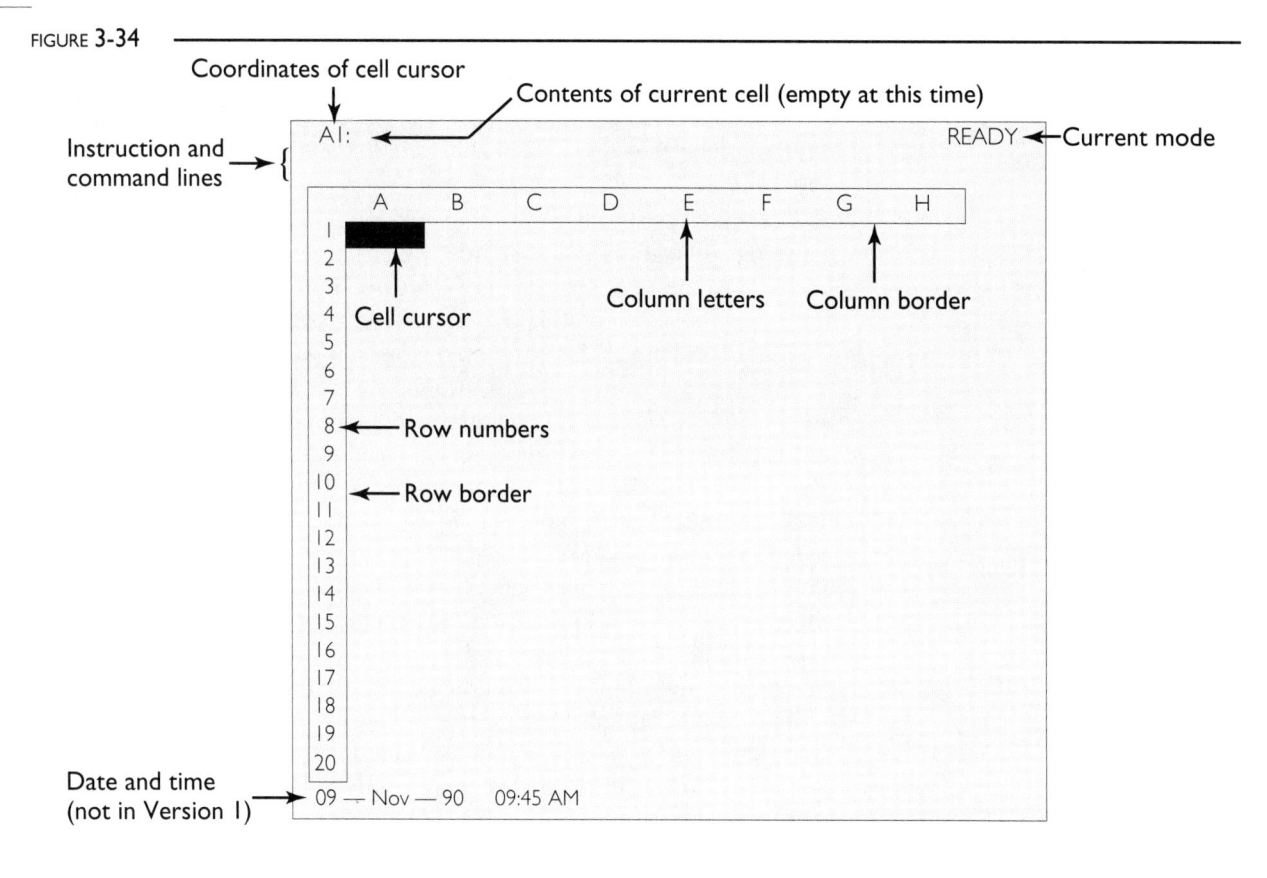

```
                    Coordinates of cell cursor
                         │          ┌─ Contents of current cell (empty at this time)
                         ↓
                    A1: ←
Instruction and                                                          READY ← Current mode
command lines
                    ─────────────────────────────────────────────────────────
                      A      B      C      D      E      F      G      H
                    1 ███
                    2       ↑
                    3
                    4       Cell cursor          Column letters    Column border
                    5
                    6
                    7
                    8 ← Row numbers
                    9
                   10 ← Row border
                   11
                   12
                   13
                   14
                   15
                   16
                   17
                   18
                   19
                   20
Date and time        09 — Nov — 90    09:45 AM
(not in Version 1)
```

- **Cells** Each cell, which is the intersection of a row and column, stores either a single value or a label.
- **Cell cursor**, usually in the form of a highlighted bar. In the illustration, the cell cursor is located at coordinates A1.
- **Cell cursor indicator** Each time the cell cursor is moved to another cell, the cell cursor indicator will identify the coordinate. In the illustration, the cell cursor indicator is located in the upper left-hand corner.
- **Cell contents indicator** Notice that the contents of the current cell, at A1, are empty because no value or label has been entered at this time.
- **Scrolling** To see more than the first 20 rows, you would tap the <downward arrow> key until you reach the 21st row or more. Similarly, to see more than the first eight columns, you would tap the <leftward arrow> arrow until you reach column I, J, K, etc. *Note:* The symbols < > will be used to indicate the names of keys in this text.
- **Built-in functions** In general, built-in functions are provided to automate calculations. For example, entering @SUM(D10. .D18) permits the user to add ("sum") the values that are located in a group of cells — in this case cells D10 through D18.

- **Commands** After the initial spreadsheet screen appears, the majority of spreadsheets offer a menu of simple commands that the user can follow. For example, Lotus 1-2-3 requires the user to press the </> key (the normal slash key) to bring out its command line as in Figure 3-35.

FIGURE 3-35

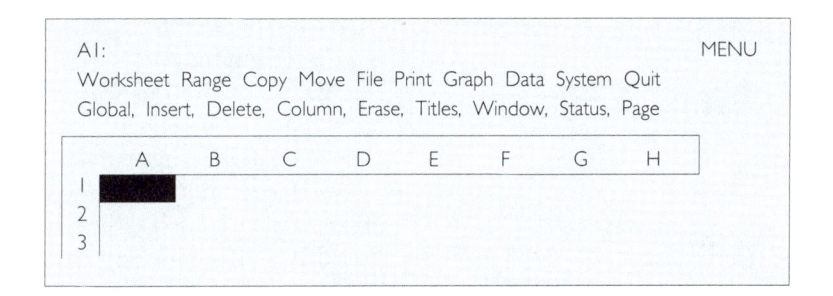

```
A1:                                                              MENU
Worksheet Range Copy Move File Print Graph Data System Quit
Global, Insert, Delete, Column, Erase, Titles, Window, Status, Page

       A        B        C        D        E        F        G        H
  1
  2
  3
```

Therefore, when the command line menu appears, the user can simply use the appropriate word to command the computer to do something. For example, by moving the cursor to Quit or by simply pressing the letter <Q> and then pressing <Enter>, the user can Quit the spreadsheet program. Commands are an important part of every electronic spreadsheet.

Macro: a string of commands placed in a column of cells on the spreadsheet.

- **Macros** In its simplest form, a ***macro*** is a way to store keystroke sequences that can be used at a later time. Suppose, for example, you wanted to get to the bottom of the spreadsheet in a hurry. You could use a single word or keyboard symbol to replace having to press the series of keys necessary to take the cell cursor to the bottom of the spreadsheet.

Key Differences Differences between leading electronic spreadsheet packages do exist. In general, they have to do with style, efficiency, speed, and the match of the various features to a user's computer preferences. Five main differences may be summarized as follows:

Operating system software: the set of programs controlling the internal operations of the computer.

- **Operating systems** All microcomputers have their own unique system program (software) so that the main processing unit can communicate with different parts of the computer system. These programs are referred to as ***operating system software***. It is important to realize that an electronic spreadsheet program must be written for a specific operating system. Consequently, Lotus 1-2-3, which is written to run under the MS-DOS (Microsoft Disk Operating System), will not run on the Macintosh, because Macintosh uses the Finder Operating System. Similarly, the same Lotus 1-2-3 written for MS-DOS will not run on IBM's new OS/2 operating system.

- **Spreadsheet sizes** Spreadsheet capacity is identified by rows and columns. Some spreadsheets offer dimensions of 9999 rows by 255 columns; others only allow 256 rows by 64 columns; and education versions are usually limited to 60 rows by 90 columns or even fewer.
- **Graphics** Most of the modern spreadsheets provide for different selections of graphs such as converting spreadsheet data into pie charts and bar graphs. However, not all spreadsheets allow for the plotting of graphs.
- **Possibility of linking spreadsheets** If several spreadsheets are developed and if changes are made to one spreadsheet, will that change be carried over (linked) to the other spreadsheets? Some programs are built so the spreadsheets act independently of each other, while others have the ability to link them together.
- **Possibility of exporting spreadsheet data** Often, users plan to incorporate their spreadsheet data and tables into their word processing programs. Unfortunately, not all spreadsheets permit this type of exporting.

A Simple Example This easy accounting problem is designed to demonstrate the power of an electronic spreadsheet package. For the purposes of this demonstration, an early version of Lotus 1-2-3 will be assumed; however, other software packages may be used, since only the basics of the electronic spreadsheet are covered. After completing this demonstration, you should be able to:

- Prepare an income statement on any electronic spreadsheet screen.
- Use your electronic spreadsheet's built-in @SUM( ) function to calculate the total revenues and the total expenses.
- Use your electronic spreadsheet's simple formula to calculate the net income for the month.
- Solve two "what if" situations.

If you are already familiar with the fundamentals of using an electronic spreadsheet, skip this whole section and go to the subtopic "Main Advantages and Limitations."

THE ACCOUNTING PROBLEM Dr. Robert Y. F. Wong operates the Town Centre Dental Office in your town/city. His general ledger showed the following data for the month of June:

FIGURE 3-36

Fees earned during June	$15 500
Interest earned on investments for June	225
Rent paid for June	1 800
Salaries paid for June	6 200
Utilities bill paid for June	178
Telephone bill paid for June	130
Supplies used for June	2 700

ANALYZING STEP-BY-STEP PROCEDURES

Step-by-step procedures with appropriate screen displays and explanations follow. Read each procedure before you use the computer. *Note*: Not all of the Lotus 1-2-3 commands and formats are introduced at this point. Only a few basic commands and formats are used to demonstrate a simple solution to the accounting problem outlined above.

LOADING YOUR SPREADSHEET PROGRAM

- Load your electronic spreadsheet program into your computer's working memory.
- Wait for the initial spreadsheet screen to appear. On some spreadsheet programs, an initial *menu* (list of choices) may appear which requests that you select and enter the spreadsheet (worksheet) from that menu.
- If you are using a floppy disk system, remove the program diskette and place it into its protective envelope.

ENTERING THE INCOME STATEMENT HEADING

- If NUM appears in the lower right corner of the spreadsheet screen, find the <Num Lock> key on the keyboard and press it to remove the number lock function. The word NUM will disappear from the screen.
- At cell A1, begin typing the name of the firm, "Town Centre Dental Office," from left to right. Check the keyboarding of this line. Make any corrections by using the <Backspace> key. Then press the <downward arrow> key to enter this line and move the cursor down to row 2. (You could have pressed <Enter> and then pressed the <downward arrow> key to move to row 2.) *Note*: Centering the statement headings will be avoided to simplify procedures.
- At A2, keyboard the name of the statement, "Income Statement". Then press the <downward arrow> key.
- At A3, keyboard the time period, "For the Month Ended June 30, 19—". Then press the <downward arrow> key.

ENTERING ACCOUNT TITLES

- At A4, press the <downward arrow> key to leave one line.
- At A5, press the <Caps Lock> key and type "REVENUES:" (you may have to hold down <Shift> to type the colon). Press <downward arrow>. Then press the <Caps Lock> key to disengage it.
- At A6, type the title, "Fees Earned". Then press the <downward arrow> key.
- At A7, type the title, "Interest Earned". Then press the <downward arrow> key.
- At A8, type the title, "Total Revenues". Then press the <downward arrow> key.

- At A9, press the <downward arrow> key to leave one line.
- At A10, press <Caps Lock> and type "EXPENSES:". Press the <downward arrow> key.
- At A11, type "Rent" and press the <downward arrow> key. (Typing the complete account title, "Rent Expense", is optional.)
- At A12, type "Salaries" and press <downward arrow>.
- At A13, type "Utilities" and press <downward arrow>.
- At A14, type "Telephone" and press <downward arrow>.
- At A15, type "Supplies Used" and press <downward arrow>.
- At A16, type "Total Expenses" and press <downward arrow> twice (to leave one line).
- At A18, type "Net Income -Net Loss" and press the <downward arrow> key. As you will discover, the final result of matching total revenues with total expenses may result in either a net income or a net loss. The net loss will be indicated with a minus sign in front of the amount. At A19, your screen will look like Figure 3-37.

FIGURE 3-37

```
A19:                                                    READY

       A        B        C        D        E        F        G        H
 1  Town Centre Dental Office
 2  Income Statement
 3  For the Month Ended June 30, 19--
 4
 5  REVENUES:
 6  Fees Earned
 7  Interest Earned
 8  Total Revenues
 9
10  EXPENSES:
11  Rent
12  Salaries
13  Utilities
14  Telephone
15  Supplies Used
16  Total Expenses
17
18  Net Income -Net Loss
19  ■
20
25 — Nov — 90   09:29 AM
```

ENTERING DOLLAR AMOUNTS   Let's continue your income statement by entering dollar amounts for all revenues and all expenses now entered on your spreadsheet. To simplify procedures in this demonstration,

CHAPTER 3: Accounting Cycle for a Service Firm

the use of dollar signs and the usual preliminary and main money columns will be omitted. Follow the steps below.

- Move the cursor to E6, opposite Fees Earned. Check to see that the coordinates of the cell cursor show " E6:" in the upper left corner.
- At E6, type "15500" (without the dollar sign and without the comma or space for the triad separator). Press the <downward arrow> key.
- At E7, type "225" and press the <downward arrow> key.
- At E8, simply press the <downward arrow> key to skip the calculation of Total Revenues at this time.
- Move the cell cursor down to the first expense, that is, at E11 for Rent. Type "1800" and press <downward arrow>.
- At E12, type "6200" and press <downward arrow>.
- At E13, type "178" and press <downward arrow>.
- At E14, type "130" and press <downward arrow>.
- At E15, type "2700" and press <downward arrow>.

ENTERING TOTALS   Your cursor is now at E16. You are now ready to enter the total for Total Expenses.

- At E16, type this command:

@SUM(

— that is, the <@> (short form for "at") key followed by SUM and the left parenthesis. Do not insert any spaces.

- Use the <upward arrow> key to move the cursor to E15, where the Supplies Used amount of "2700" is located. The top left corner shows E15: 2700 and directly below the formula is shown as:

@SUM(E15

- Press <.> (the period key) once. The formula now reads:

@SUM(E15..E15

- Use the <upward arrow> key to move up over each of the remaining expenses to E11. The screen will show the formula as:

@SUM(E15..E11

Notice too that all of the expense amounts have been highlighted.

- At E11, type the right parenthesis, <) >, once.
- The cell cursor jumps down to E16 while the complete formula is shown as:

@SUM(E15..E11)

In other words, you have instructed the computer to add ("sum") the values shown in cells ranging from E15 through E11.

- At E16, press <Enter>. Total Expenses is shown at 11008, while the coordinate line in the upper left corner shows:

E16: @SUM(E15..E11)

@SUM(: Lotus's built-in function, allowing the user to add (sum) a group of designated cells. Many other spreadsheets have identical or similar built-in functions to add a column or row of designated cells.

- Use the <upward arrow> key to move to cell E8, the row line for Total Revenues.
- Use the @SUM(function to add the two revenue cells — that is, type:

@SUM(E6..E7)

- At E8, press <Enter>. Total Revenues is 15725.

ENTERING THE NET INCOME

- Move the cell cursor down to E18. Here, you want to enter a formula that matches total revenues with total expenses.
- At E18, type the plus sign, <+>, followed by the cell containing Total Revenues, that is, E8. Next, type the minus sign followed by the cell containing the Total Expenses, E16.
- At E18, the formula is:

+E8-E16

Why start this formula with a plus sign? The answer is that the computer must be told how to distinguish a formula from an ordinary letter label like E. If you entered E8-E16, the computer would interpret E8 as simply a label and not a value.

- At E18, press <Enter>. The Net Income is 4717. Notice that the coordinates of the cell cursor shows the formula:

E18: +E8-E16

Your screen should show the completed spreadsheet as in Figure 3-38.

+E8-E16: a simple formula instructing the computer to subtract the amount in cell E16 from the amount in cell E8. Most spreadsheet programs include a formula of this type.

FIGURE 3-38

```
E18: +E8-E16                                            READY

        A              B          C          D        E        F        G        H
  1  Town Centre Dental Office
  2  Income Statement
  3  For the Month Ended June 30, 19--
  4
  5  REVENUES:
  6  Fees Earned                                    15500
  7  Interest Earned                                  225
  8  Total Revenues                                 15725
  9
 10  EXPENSES:
 11  Rent                                            1800
 12  Salaries                                        6200
 13  Utilities                                        178
 14  Telephone                                        130
 15  Supplies Used                                   2700
 16  Total Expenses                                 11008
 17
 18  Net Income -Net Loss                            4717
 19
 20
 25 — Nov — 90    09:40 AM
```

ENTERING "WHAT IF" SITUATIONS The power of any electronic spreadsheet program can be illustrated through solving two "what if" problems.

1. What if the value of Fees Earned was 12000 instead of 15500?
- Move the cell up to the cell containing Fees Earned, that is, at E6.
- Type the "what if" amount 12000 (without the dollar sign and without commas or spaces).
- Press the <Enter> key.
- Notice that the coordinates of the cell cursor now read E6: 12000, while the cell E6 shows 12000. Also note that the Net Income is now 1217. In other words, Lotus automatically made the change in the Net Income cell, because the formula +E6-E16 was executed immediately.

2. What if the value of Fees Earned was 12000 and the salaries were changed to 8200?
- Move the cell cursor to the cell containing the salaries, at E12. Here, type 8200 and press <Enter>.
- Notice that this added change results in a negative amount; therefore, a net loss can be inferred.

The income statement could have been "dressed up" (formatted) to look more like the ones you prepared for outsiders. For example, the three-line heading could have been centred, dollar signs could have been used at appropriate amounts, single and double rules could have been added, and the net loss amount could have been shown in parentheses. However, the formats used in this lesson are acceptable for use by insiders. You can add format features such as proper centring and dollar amounts by referring to your spreadsheet manual.

SAVING YOUR SPREADSHEET Your completed spreadsheet can easily be saved onto your hard disk or a properly formatted diskette by using the Save command. Most spreadsheets like Lotus 1-2-3 bring out their command line or menu by simply pressing the normal slash, key </>. See your spreadsheet manual for the use of the Save command.

QUITTING YOUR SPREADSHEET Most spreadsheet programs allow you to Quit through their command line or command menu. For example, both Lotus 1-2-3 and Borland's Quattro initiate their command structure by means of the </> key. One then presses <Q> to Quit and then <Y> to say yes.

Main Advantages and Limitations

Before you attempt the Topic problems that follow, it is useful to summarize the main advantages and limitations of electronic spreadsheets in accounting applications.

The main advantages may be summarized as follows:
- An electronic spreadsheet can be used for any accounting you might otherwise have done with a pad and pencil or a hand-held calculator.

- Electronic spreadsheets are especially suited for one of the two main branches of accounting — management accounting. As you may recall, management accounting is concerned with the preparation of special-purpose reports to meet the needs of managers. Four of the more common applications of the electronic spreadsheet in management accounting are: sales forecasting (calculating future sales for a number of months); budgeting (calculating future income statements and future balance sheets, along with their supporting schedules); costing of products (calculating how much a product will cost before it is manufactured; calculating how many units of a product need to be sold to make a reasonable profit); and financial statement analysis (calculating various ratios common to the study of balance sheets and income statements).
- Electronic spreadsheets may also be used to solve problems in financial accounting. As stated earlier, financial (general) accounting is the branch of accounting that deals with the preparation of financial statements for outsiders in accordance with GAAPs. For example, an accounting clerk may be asked to use the electronic spreadsheet to produce depreciation schedules for individual fixed assets and aged schedules for accounts receivable to determine the estimated amount of bad debts.
- Perhaps the most outstanding use of an electronic spreadsheet is to apply it to "what if" situations. What if sales revenue increases by 10% per month for the next twelve months? What if salaries and wages expenses increase by 5% for the first six months and by only 2% for the last six months? It is safe to conclude that what used to take days and weeks to calculate manually may now take only hours or minutes with an electronic spreadsheet.

The main limitations of electronic spreadsheets may be summarized as follows:

- By itself, the electronic spreadsheet is only one type of applications software. It cannot do everything in accounting. For example, you cannot record journal entries and automatically post them to appropriate ledger accounts, prepare automatically trial balances, and then produce automatically the resulting financial statements with any single electronic spreadsheet program. Consequently, you will still need separate software applications packages for the general ledger, accounts receivable, accounts payable, payroll, and inventory control.
- Although you do not have to be a programmer to run spreadsheet software, you do have to have some accounting background before you can use electronic spreadsheets to solve accounting problems. For example, if you want to produce an income statement and apply several "what if" situations, it would be essential to know how to construct the income statement.

CHAPTER 3: Accounting Cycle for a Service Firm 91

TOPIC 4 Problems

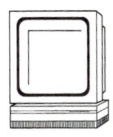

3.14 *Special Note:* This problem may be solved on a microcomputer using your school's electronic spreadsheet software or any other package to which you have access. On the other hand, the problem may also be solved using the traditional manual approach with the aid of a calculator.

Donna Brown owns the Stylette Beauty Salon. Information covering a three-month accounting period which ended on June 30 appears below. Note that of the $60 000 mortgage payable, $3 000 is due in the next accounting period. Note also that the land and building have been pledged as collateral to secure the mortgage payable.

FIGURE 3-39

Land	$40 000
Shop equipment owned	9 000
Office equipment owned	6 000
Cash in bank	4 400
Due from customers	600
Advertising costs incurred	1 800
Paid for supplies used	2 200
Paid for telephone	50
10% mortgage payable (20-year)	60 000
Building owned	80 000
Donna Brown, capital (April 1)	77 300
Sales to customers	13 800
Owed on equipment	2 200
Salaries paid	8 900
Paid for utilities	330
Miscellaneous expense	20

Required

a Prepare an income statement for the three-month period.
b Prepare a related balance sheet in report form.
c Assume that interest expense on the mortgage amounted to $1 500 for the three-month period. Prepare revised financial statements showing the effect of interest expense (paid in cash) on the income statement and related balance sheet.
d What if the bill for telephone expense for the three-month period was $150 instead of the reported $50? Prepare revised financial statements showing the effect of this "what if" statement.

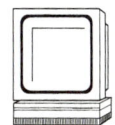

3.15 *Special Note:* This problem may be solved on a microcomputer using your school's electronic spreadsheet software or any other package to which you have access. On the other hand, the problem may also be solved using the traditional manual approach with the aid of a calculator.

Penny Thornton began a dental practice under her name on January 2, 19-1 in a newly developed suburb of a large city. After two months, her dental practice reported income statements as illustrated in Figure 3-40.

FIGURE 3-40

Penny Thornton, D.D.S.
Comparative Income Statements
For the Months Ended:

	Jan. 31, 19-1	Feb. 28, 19-1
Revenues:		
Professional Fees Earned	$10 000	$12 000
Interest Earned	100	100
Total Revenues	10 100	12 100
Expenses:		
Office Rental	1 000	1 000
Equipment Rental	6 000	6 000
Salaries	4 800	4 800
Telephone	125	125
Utilities	220	220
Office Supplies Used	100	100
Dental Supplies Used	500	500
Interest Expense	120	120
Total Expenses	12 865	12 865
Net Income (Net Loss)	($ 2 765)	($ 765)

Although the income statements reported net losses for the first two months, Dr. Thornton believes that construction of new homes will generate sufficient revenue to realize net incomes for most of the remaining months in Year 1. Accordingly, Dr. Thornton estimates that her dental practice's main source of revenue will increase as follows: by 10% of February's amount in March, April, and May; by 20% of February's amount in June, July, and August; and by 25% of February's amount for the remaining months in Year 1.

Required

a Prepare a spreadsheet showing monthly income statements as reported for January and February and the estimated net incomes (net losses) for the remaining ten months in accordance with the data provided in the case.

b What if the office rental expense for the estimated ten-month period (March through December) was increased by 5% instead of the reported amounts for January and February? Prepare revised income statements showing the effects of this "what if" statement.

3.16 *Special Note:* This problem may be solved on a microcomputer using your school's electronic spreadsheet software or any other package to which you have access. On the other hand, the problem may also be solved using the traditional manual approach with the aid of a calculator.

The following accounts and their balances have been taken from the general ledger of a dry cleaning business established under the name Hardy Cleaners. Assume that all the balance shave been checked for accuracy as at December 31, current year, the firm's year-end. Also assume that all account balances are normal — that they are credits if on the right side of the equation and debits if on the left.

FIGURE 3-41

101	Cash	$ 24 960
103	Accounts Receivable	1 600
110	Land	140 000
112	Building	160 000
114	Cleaning Equipment	12 500
116	Office Equipment	6 000
118	Delivery Equipment	24 000
201	Bank Loan Payable	10 000
202	Accounts Payable	6 000
203	Interest Payable	4 200
220	Mortgage Payable	80 000
301	Helen Hardy, Capital	259 800
302	Helen Hardy, Drawing	62 000
401	Fees Earned	190 000
501	Cleaning Supplies Expense	18 400
502	Salaries Expense	84 120
503	Building Repairs Expense	2 800
504	Utilities Expense	2 750
505	Telephone Expense	1 770
520	Bank Interest Expense	1 100
530	Mortgage Interest Expense	8 000

Required

a Prepare a formal trial balance from the above data.
b Use your spreadsheet's Repeating Label command to rule off the trial balance in the traditional manner. (Lotus 1-2-3 users should first go to the cell where the double line is to be drawn; next, type the backslash followed by the equals sign. Then press <Enter>.)
c Test the accuracy of the formal trial balance through the expanded form of the accounting equation.
d Add one column to prepare a zero-proof trial balance.
e Save the spreadsheet solution to your storage (data files) floppy diskette or hard disk using an appropriate file name.
f Solve the following two "what if" situations:
 • What if one fee bill for $118 cash was not recorded and posted?
 • What if a cheque for $100 was issued in December for Cleaning Supplies Expense and the cheque was not recorded and posted?

g Save your final spreadsheet solution to your storage (data files) diskette or hard disk.
h Print a hard copy of your final spreadsheet solution.

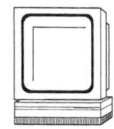

3.17 The separate problems below may be solved on a microcomputer using your school's electronic spreadsheet software or any other spreadsheet package to which you have access.

a Return to the solution prepared for Problem 3.4 (Brandon Parking Service). Use an electronic spreadsheet package to prepare a formal trial balance and a zero-proof trial balance.
b Return to the solutions solved for Problem 3.5 and 3.7 (Thompson's Real Estate Agency). Use an electronic spreadsheet package to prepare the six-column worksheet, the income statement, and the related balance sheet in report form.

Chapter Summary

A simple accounting cycle for a service firm begins with the origination of data. Source documents such as invoices and cheque records must be analyzed (broken up) into appropriate debits and credits. These are journalized (recorded) in the general journal. Under an efficient accounting system, no entry should ever be made without an appropriate source document to prove the existence of a business transaction.

After an entry is recorded correctly in the general journal, those same debits and credits are transferred to appropriate accounts in the general ledger (G/L) by a process called posting. In most G/L systems, posting occurs to accounts that use a three-column format or the balance-ledger form. Under this format, a running balance is normally kept after posting each entry from the journal to the ledger account.

Under a manual system, cross-references are required in both the general journal and the three-column ledger account. After transferring the information from the journal to the ledger, the ledger account must show in the Post. Ref. column the journal identification and page number of the journal from which the transfer was made. After obtaining the new running balance, the account number of the account posted is placed in the Post. Ref. column of the journal on the same line as that on which the account title is located in that journal. Any absence of posting references means that the account has not been posted.

At appropriate times, usually at the end of each month, a trial balance is prepared to test that the total debit balances and the total credit balances within the general ledger balance. In other words, the accounting equation, $A = L + OE$, must balance within the G/L. Two types of trial balances are common. A formal trial balance lists in order of accounts in the G/L all accounts with balances, their account numbers, and their debit or credit balances as at the date of preparing the listing. The totals of this listing must show that the total debits are equal to the total credits within the ledger. An informal listing is usually prepared on an adding machine tape. Each account debit balance is listed as a plus amount while each account credit balance is listed as minus figure in the same column. At the end, the total is obtained on the machine, which results in a zero proof of the general ledger. A zero proof indicates that the G/L is in balance.

Before financial statements are prepared at the end of any financial period, it is customary to prepare a worksheet. Worksheets are not formal statements. They are the accountant's rough working papers to summarize all data that must be reported in financial statements. The most elementary worksheet consists of six columns: the first pair list the formal trial balance; the second pair will receive income statement amounts in debit and credit form; and the final pair will receive the balance sheet figures, also in debit and credit form.

A simple procedure is followed to transfer amounts from the trial balance to the appropriate columns of the worksheet. Move a debit balance from the trial balance to the debit column of the financial statement column where that amount will be reported. Similarly, move a credit balance from the trial balance to the credit column of the related financial statement. For example, all asset account balances will be moved from the debit column of the trial balance to the debit column of the balance sheet. And all revenue account balances will be moved from the credit column of the trial balance to the credit column of the income statement.

After all account balances have been moved to appropriate columns of the worksheet, totals are obtained in all money columns. A rough income statement is prepared in the income statement columns by matching total revenues (credit column total) with total expenses (debit column total). The net result will be the net income or net loss for the accounting period. This figure is moved to the balance sheet. If a net income occurs, it will be a credit balance; therefore, it will be moved to the credit side of the balance sheet to show that the net income results in an increase to OE within any accounting equation. On the other hand, a net loss will result in a debit balance which must be moved to the debit side of the balance sheet. This debit has the effect of decreasing OE within any accounting equation. The final step is to balance the balance sheet columns on the worksheet.

With the aid of a completed worksheet, financial statements can be prepared by using the amounts located in appropriate debit and credit columns. The income statement is always prepared first. A balance sheet follows by selecting the debit and credit amounts from the debit and credit columns of the balance sheet section of the worksheet. When only one figure is reported under Owner's Equity in the balance sheet, that is, the final Capital figure as at the end of the accounting period, a separate statement of owner's equity is prepared to report the changes in owner's equity for the entire period. However, when these details are reported under OE in the balance sheet, a separate statement is not required.

Year-end closing involves transferring all revenue and expense account balances from those accounts to a Revenue and Expense Summary account. Each time a closing entry is made, a transfer is made to the Summary account as well as bringing down to zero the revenue and expense accounts when posting occurs. After all revenue and expense account balances have been transferred, the Summary account will contain a balance figure. If it is a credit balance, this means that net income results; if it is a debit, a net loss results. The balance of the Summary account is then transferred (closed) to the owner's Capital account. Finally, the owner's Drawing account debit balance is closed to the owner's Capital account.

A postclosing trial balance is taken to prove that the year-end closing procedures have been successful. This trial balance will show account balances related to the balance sheet only. They represent the permanent accounts because their account balances are not brought down to zero. On the other hand, all revenue, expenses, the Summary account, and the owner's Drawing account will not be reported with balances, because they represent temporary accounts. They exist temporarily during the accounting period to give information for the preparation of financial statements. All accounting cycles end with the postclosing trial balance.

Electronic spreadsheets may be used to computerize individual aspects of the accounting cycle. However, the chief benefit of any electronic spreadsheet is to analyze a company's operations and provide information for effective management decision-making. For example, it can be used as a management tool to measure past and current activities and as an aid to plan company strategy. The main advantage of any electronic spreadsheet is its ability to evaluate "what if" situations that involve working with numbers.

Chapter Questions

1. What purpose is served by source documents in any accounting system?
2. Explain the difference between a purchase invoice and a sales invoice.
3. State two advantages for the use of the journal in an accounting system.
4. Explain the difference between the journal and the ledger.
5. Explain the difference in use of the Post. Ref. columns in the journal and ledger.
6. Give three transactions that would require a debit to the owner's Drawing account in each case.
7. Will accounting support the practice of charging (debiting) the Salaries Expense account of the business with a monthly salary paid to the sole proprietor? Explain why or why not.
8. In simple terms, what is meant by the expression "updating a general ledger file"?
9. What main purpose is served by a chart of accounts in a manual accounting system?
10. Can the Cash account have a credit balance in its account after the posting of a transaction? Explain why or why not.

11. How are all normal balances in accounts translated? Give two examples to support your answer.
12. What is the difference between an ordinary trial balance and a postclosing trial balance?
13. What date is identified in the heading of any worksheet? Explain why this date and no other is the correct one.
14. Why do the Income Statement columns precede the Balance Sheet columns in a worksheet?
15. State two rules to support the correct transfer of trial balance amounts to the other columns of the six-column worksheet.
16. If the total debit amount exceeds the total credit column of the Income Statement section of the worksheet, what net result must be identified? Explain where this net result is treated in the Balance Sheet section of the worksheet.
17. What is a statement of owner's equity? When would such a statement be required? Explain.
18. Why are year-end closing entries required?
19. What purpose is served by the Revenue and Expense Summary account in the general ledger?
20. Identify three checks to prove that a postclosing trial balance must be correct at the end of an accounting cycle.
21. Explain the difference between the permanent and temporary accounts of a general ledger.
22. List the eight steps of the accounting cycle in correct order.
23. What is an electronic spreadsheet? Briefly identify nine features that are common on all modern spreadsheets.
24. Explain briefly five differences that may exist between leading electronic spreadsheet software packages.
25. Briefly explain four advantages and two limitations of using electronic spreadsheets in accounting applications.

Accounting Case Problems

CASE 3-1

Analyzing transactions affecting owner's equity; reconciling an incorrect net income to an amount acceptable for income tax purposes.

The owner of Krestel's Consulting Services—a single proprietorship form of business enterprise—seeks your help to prepare a year-end income statement which will be included in the owner's personal income tax return. You learn the following facts through an examination of the firm's general ledger:

- The total sales for the year amounted to $225 000.
- The total expenses charged against the business amounted to $195 000.

- Among the expenses, an account headed Owner's Salary Expense showed a debit balance of $48 000. You find that the owner paid himself a monthly salary of $4 000.
- An analysis of the Telephone Expense account revealed a debit balance of $480. Of this amount, only $240 represented the actual business expense; the remainder represented the payment of all telephone bills for the owner's home.
- One expense account, called Golf and Country Club Expense, showed a debit balance of $2 000. This amount represented the owner's yearly dues to a private club in the community.

Required

a Prepare an income statement showing the reconciliation of the net income reported by the business to the net income for income tax purposes. *Hint:* Begin with the traditional income statement reporting the matchup of revenues with related expenses in condensed form. From the net income figure make the necessary adjustments to arrive at the net income for tax purposes.

b What suggestions would you offer in the proper accounting of the owner's "personal" expenses? How would you explain your recommendations to the owner?

CASE 3-2
Discussing the pros and cons of using the electronic spreadsheet to do work within the accounting cycle.

Wright is a computer fanatic and believes that the spreadsheet will prepare financial statements that comply better with GAAPs than handwritten statements. In addition, Wright believes that ledger accounts can be included in an electronic spreadsheet along with a general journal and that posting can be completed electronically.

Required

a What comments would you make to Wright regarding his belief that the electronic spreadsheet will prepare statements that comply better with GAAPs than handwritten statements?

b Is Wright correct in his belief that it is possible to complete both journalizing and posting using an electronic spreadsheet? Explain your answer.

c Discuss the pros and cons, and then draw a conclusion as to the effective use of the electronic spreadsheet for all aspects of the accounting cycle.

CHAPTER 4 Merchandising Concepts

After completing this chapter, you should be able to:

— Distinguish between a merchandising firm and a service firm.
— Distinguish between perpetual and periodic inventory systems.
— Calculate the gross profit from sales from given data for merchandising firms.
— Identify factors affecting the sales revenue for merchandising firms.
— Identify factors affecting the cost of goods sold for merchandising firms using the periodic inventory method.
— Prepare an income statement and related balance sheet for merchandising firms using the periodic inventory method.
— Apply merchandising concepts by preparing an income statement with a percentage analysis column and a 12-month income statement projecting the gross profit from sales after applying a "what if" situation.
— Analyze the effects of common merchandising transactions on the accounting equation and by use of T-accounts and general journal entries.
— Compare common merchandising transactions between the periodic and perpetual inventory systems.
— Define the following key terms used in this chapter: merchandising firm; wholesaler, retailer; inventory; perpetual inventory; periodic inventory; cost of goods sold; gross profit (margin) from sales; net sales; operating expenses; transportation-in (freight-in); purchases returns and allowances; cost of delivered goods; purchases discounts; sales returns and allowances; inventory losses expense; the PST Payable account; sales discounts; cost of goods sold ratio; gross margin ratio; total operating expense ratio; and net sales ratio.

Merchandising firm: a business that buys finished goods and sells them at increased prices.

Wholesalers: merchandising firms which buy finished goods in large quantities from the manufacturer or producer and sell them to retailers.

The first three chapters treated the accounting concepts for a service-type firm. This chapter will take you through the basic accounting concepts as they apply to a **merchandising firm**. In general terms, a merchandising firm is a business enterprise that buys finished goods — merchandise — from one firm and sells those goods to customers at increased prices in order to make a profit. Some merchandising firms, known as ***wholesalers***, buy finished goods from the manufacturer or producer and sell them

PART 1: THE FRAMEWORK OF ACCOUNTING

Retailers: merchandising firms that buy goods, usually from wholesalers, and sell them to end-users called consumers.

to other merchandising firms known as **retailers**. In turn, retailers sell these goods at marked-up prices to consumers.

Many of the accounting concepts you have learned for a service-type business are also applicable to a merchandising firm. What this chapter will emphasize, however, are a few added concepts that are peculiar to any merchandising firm.

TOPIC 1 Financial Statements of Merchandising Firms

A good place to begin the study of merchandising ideas for accounting is to develop the concepts for the financial statements of merchandising firms. As you will recall from Chapter 1, any type of business requires economic resources, called assets, in order to commence its operations. Of course, claims against the assets will be held by creditors and the owner to indicate how these economic resources were acquired. Therefore, all firms will establish the accounting equation: *Assets are equal to Liabilities* (claims of creditors) *plus Owner's Equity* (claim of the owner). In the case of a merchandising firm, only one additional asset must be learned. That asset consists of the goods (merchandise) acquired for resale. In the language of accounting, merchandise for resale is known as merchandise inventory or, simply, **inventory**.

Inventory: merchandise or goods acquired for resale; a current asset on the balance sheet of any merchandising firm.

You learned also that all firms must match revenue earned with related expenses during an accounting period to determine whether a net income or net loss was made. A merchandising firm earns revenue by selling merchandise from its inventory. To calculate its net income (or net loss), however, any merchandising firm must deduct the **cost of goods sold** plus the operating expenses, as the condensed income statement shown in Figure 4-1 illustrates.

Cost of goods sold: an expense to be matched against sales revenue.

FIGURE 4-1

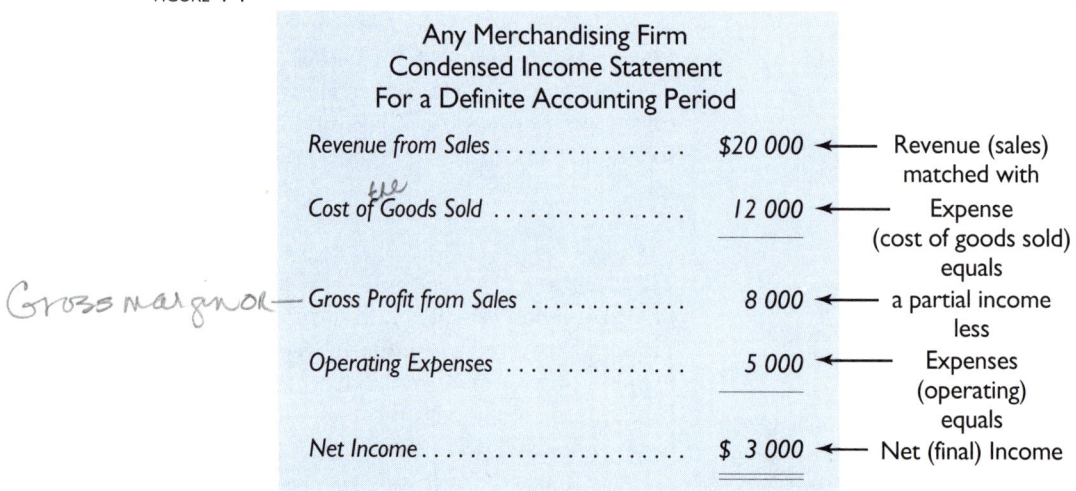

```
                Any Merchandising Firm
               Condensed Income Statement
              For a Definite Accounting Period

Revenue from Sales..............   $20 000   ←  Revenue (sales)
                                                  matched with
Cost of Goods Sold .............    12 000   ←  Expense
                                                 (cost of goods sold)
                                                 equals
Gross Profit from Sales ........     8 000   ←  a partial income
                                                  less
Operating Expenses .............     5 000   ←  Expenses
                                                 (operating)
                                                  equals
Net Income .....................   $ 3 000   ←  Net (final) Income
```

(handwritten: "Gross margin or" pointing to Gross Profit from Sales; "the" inserted before "Cost of Goods Sold")

CHAPTER 4: Merchandising Concepts

As you can observe, two important steps are required to calculate the net income of a merchandising firm: (1) the cost of goods sold must be matched against the revenue to determine the first profit known as **gross profit from sales**; and (2) the operating expenses are then matched against the gross profit from sales to determine the final profit, called net income. Some accountants prefer to use the term *gross margin on sales* to avoid any misinterpretation on the word "profit." You should easily conclude that the basic difference in determining the net income between a service firm and a merchandising firm is the important calculation of matching the cost of goods sold against the sales revenue.

<small>Gross profit from sales (gross margin on sales): a partial income resulting from the matching of sales revenue with the cost of goods sold.</small>

Calculating the Cost of Goods Sold

In some merchandising firms, determining the cost of goods sold not only is an important calculation, but also often becomes a complex procedure. For example, it is common among firms like appliance stores and automobile dealers to hire cost clerks and even to use the computer to determine the cost price of each inventory item sold. In simple terms, suppose an inventory item were sold for $1 500. To determine the cost of the good sold, then, a cost clerk (or the computer) would search the accounting records for the cost price, say $800. The difference between the sales price and the cost price can now be taken to determine the margin (difference) known as the gross profit from the sale. Now, if the firm sold hundreds of thousands of different types of merchandise at varying prices, one could easily understand why many cost clerks or an expensive computer system would be required to determine the cost of all the goods sold for an entire accounting period. In the language of accounting, merchandising firms that determine the cost price of each inventory item after it has been sold follow what is known as the **perpetual inventory method**. This method will be examined in Topic 2.

<small>Perpetual inventory method: a system of calculating the cost of each good sold and of updating the inventory item immediately after the sale of that inventory item.</small>

On the other hand, many firms like drugstores, hardware stores, bookstores, grocery stores, and similar enterprises selling low-priced items would not be able to afford the luxury of maintaining records of the cost of each inventory item sold. Consider, for example, the added expense of hiring a clerk or renting computer time to search for the cost of a tube of toothpaste immediately after every sale. Because this added expense is too great, these firms wait until the end of an accounting period to calculate at one time the cost of goods sold for an entire accounting period. In the language of accounting, such firms follow the **periodic inventory method** to determine the cost of goods sold for an accounting period. This method will now be examined through the following two examples.

<small>Periodic inventory method: a system of calculating the cost of all goods sold and of the final inventory at the end of an accounting period.</small>

Example 1 To keep matters simplified, suppose that a merchandising firm buys and sells goods called "widgets" and that the firm follows the periodic inventory method of accounting. Suppose further that the business revealed the following information from its accounting records for the month of November:

102 PART 1: THE FRAMEWORK OF ACCOUNTING

- The cost of the inventory on hand on November 1 consisted of four cartons containing 100 widgets which cost $10 each. The total cost of the beginning inventory, therefore, is $4 000 (4 cartons × $1 000 each).
- Additional widgets purchased during the month consisted of eight cartons, each carton containing 100 widgets costing $10 each. Consequently, the **total cost of November purchases** is $8 000 (8 cartons × $1 000 each).
- A *physical stocktaking (inventory)* at the close of business on November 30 reported that the cost of the inventory on hand at the end of November consisted of seven cartons containing 100 widgets which cost $10 each. The total cost of the inventory unsold on November 30, therefore, is $7 000 (7 cartons × $1 000 each).

From the above information, you could easily calculate the cost of all goods available for sale for the month. Obviously, the cost of the inventory at the beginning of the month *plus* the cost of the goods purchased during the month will give this important figure. Figure 4-2 is offered to assist you to visualize this calculation. Treat each block as one carton which holds 100 widgets at a cost of $10 each.

The important question now is: How can the cost of the goods actually sold be determined when no cost records were kept for the goods sold? The answer is simply to determine the **cost of goods unsold**, that is, the cost of the ending inventory, and then to subtract this cost from the cost of all goods available for sale. In the first example, we were told that a physical stock (inventory) count at the end of November revealed that widgets costing $7 000 were not sold during the month. Consequently, the calculation of the cost of goods sold during the month may be visualized as illustrated in Figure 4-3.

Example 2 In this example, consider the information of Marion's Book Store which also uses the periodic inventory method of accounting to report the following data for March: Cost of goods on hand at the

---

Total cost of November purchases: 8 cartons × $1 000 each = $8 000.

Physical stocktaking (inventory): the actual counting of inventory items on hand at the end of an accounting period.

Cost of goods unsold: the cost of the inventory at the end of the accounting period (the current asset to be reported on the balance sheet).

FIGURE **4-2**

Calculating the Total Cost of Goods Available for Sale

Beginning Inventory $4 000 *plus* Purchases $8 000 *equals* Total Cost of Goods Available for Sale = $12 000

FIGURE 4-3

Calculating the Cost of Goods Sold

$1 000	$1 000	$1 000	$1 000
$1 000	$1 000	$1 000	$1 000
$1 000	$1 000	$1 000	$1 000

Total Cost of Goods Available for Sale = $12 000

less

$1 000	$1 000	$1 000
$1 000	$1 000	$1 000
$1 000		

Ending Inventory $7 000

equals

$1 000	$1 000	$1 000
$1 000	$1 000	

Cost of Goods Sold $5 000

beginning of March (the beginning inventory), $4 000; cost of goods purchased during March, $8 000; cost of inventory on hand at the end of March (through a physical counting of items on hand on March 31), $7 000; sales of books, magazines, stationery, etc. during March, at retail sales prices, $10 000.

From the above information, you can easily calculate the cost of goods available for sale, the cost of goods sold during March, and the gross profit from sales for March. Examine closely Figures 4-4 to 4-6.

FIGURE 4-4

Inventory, March 1 . . .	$ 4 000
Purchases	8 000
Cost of Goods Available for Sale	$12 000

FIGURE 4-5

Cost of Goods Available for Sale	$12 000
Less: Inventory, March 31	7 000
Cost of Goods Sold . . .	$ 5 000

FIGURE 4-6

Marion's Book Store
Partial Income Statement
For the Month Ended March 31, 19—

Revenue from Sales.		$10 000
Cost of Goods Sold:		
Inventory, March 1	$ 4 000	
Purchases	8 000	
Cost of Goods Available for Sale	12 000	
Less: Inventory, March 31	7 000	
Cost of Goods Sold		5 000
Gross Profit from Sales		$ 5 000

104 PART 1: THE FRAMEWORK OF ACCOUNTING

For merchandising firms using the periodic inventory method, therefore, three important factors are required to calculate the cost of goods sold: (1) the inventory cost of merchandise available at the beginning of the accounting period; (2) the cost of all merchandise purchased during the accounting period; and (3) the inventory cost of merchandise unsold at the end of the accounting period. Factors 1 and 2 added together will give the **cost of goods available for sale** for the accounting period. And by subtracting factor 3—the ending inventory cost—one determines the important calculation of the cost of goods sold for the accounting period.

> Cost of goods available for sale: the theoretical cost of goods sold if no ending inventory exists at the end of the accounting period.

Factors Affecting Sales Revenue

For many merchandising firms, especially the wholesalers, three factors will affect the final reporting of the sales revenue for an accounting period: (1) returns of merchandise sold to customers; (2) allowances off the sales price granted to customers; and (3) sales discounts granted to customers. When analyzing the effects of each of these factors, it is customary to group the first two under the heading of Sales Returns and Allowances. Sales discounts are usually studied separately. Each of these two factors, then, will be examined briefly.

SALES RETURNS AND ALLOWANCES

In most retail and wholesale firms, management will permit customers to return any unsatisfactory goods. Such returns are called **sales returns**. In some instances, especially where the sold merchandise is slightly marked, the customer may be allowed to keep the goods and given a **sales allowance** off the sales price. In both cases, it is important to understand that sales returns and allowances will have the effect of *decreasing* the original amount of sales revenue.

> Sales returns: returns of merchandise by customers to the seller.
>
> Sales allowance: a reduction from original sales price for slightly marked goods.

SALES DISCOUNTS

To encourage credit customers to pay their bills ahead of the usual credit period, many wholesalers will offer what is known as a **sales discount**. For example, a wholesaler merchandiser may offer a retailer credit terms such as 2/10, n/30. These terms give the customer the opportunity to receive a discount of 2% off the sales amount provided that the remittance is received by the seller within 10 days of the date of the bill; otherwise, the net amount of the bill must be paid within 30 days of the invoice date. When sales discounts are taken by customers, the effect of the discount will be to *decrease* the amount of original sales revenue. The net revenue from sales, therefore, consists of the original amount of the sales, usually called gross sales, less sales returns and allowances, and less sales discounts. Both factors are commonly reported on the income statement as shown in Figure 4-7.

> Sales discount: a cash discount deducted from the sales invoice amount.

FIGURE 4-7

Revenue from Sales:		
Gross Sales		$10 980
Less:		
Sales Returns and Allowances	$75	
Sales Discounts	48	123
Net Sales		$10 857

Factors Affecting Cost of Goods Sold

Merchandising firms that use the periodic inventory method will encounter several items that affect the final calculation of cost of goods sold. These items or factors are identified as (1) transportation or freight charges required to bring the merchandise from the supplier to the place of business, (2) returns of purchases to the supplier, (3) allowances granted to the buyer of merchandise, and (4) purchase discounts taken by the buyer. As with the study of factors affecting the sales revenue, returns and allowances from the buyer's viewpoint are usually examined together.

TRANSPORTATION-IN COSTS In general, the buyer of merchandise may have to pay for the cost of transporting the goods from the seller's place of business to the buyer's store. In the language of accounting, such costs are known as ***transportation-in*** or ***freight-in*** and must be added to the purchase cost to obtain the cost of delivered goods. For example, if the buyer had to pay $200 in order to have goods costing $8 500 delivered to the place of business, then the final cost of delivered merchandise must include the amount paid to the seller plus any transportation charges paid to the transport company. On an income statement this final cost may be shown as Cost of Delivered Goods, as illustrated in Figure 4-8. It is important to remember that transportation-in charges will *increase* the cost of purchases. And, finally, it is worth noting that expenses incurred for delivering sold merchandise to customers are treated as operating expenses under a heading such as Delivery Expense, Transportation-out, or Freight-out.

PURCHASES RETURNS AND ALLOWANCES Sometimes merchandise arrives in unacceptable condition. For example, goods received may be damaged, or the quantity may be greater or less than was ordered, or the wrong merchandise may have been shipped. Consequently, the buyer will return the unacceptable amount in full expectation of *decreasing* the cost of delivered goods. Similarly, some goods may be received in slightly scratched condition and, instead of returning the goods, the buyer may request that an allowance be given off the buyer's cost of buying goods. From a combined viewpoint, therefore, it is important to remember that purchases returns and allowances have the effect of *decreasing* the original cost of purchases, as illustrated in Figure 4-9.

PURCHASES DISCOUNTS As previously analyzed under the factors that affect sales revenue, the supplier (seller) of merchandise quite often offers credit terms that include a cash discount. This practice is common in the relationship between manufacturers selling to wholesalers, and between wholesalers selling to retailers. When a discount is accepted by the buyer, it is important to remember that, from the buyer's viewpoint, the cash discount has been taken to decrease the cost of purchases. Thus, if a wholesale hardware merchant received a shipment of nails, bolts, washers, etc. from a steel manufacturer for a total purchase cost of $1 000, and the supplier offered terms of 1/15, n/60, then the buyer can send a cheque for $990 ($1 000 less $10) provided that the remittance is received within 15 days of the invoice date. In this case, the effect of the cash discount taken will decrease the buyer's original cost of purchases.

Transportation-in (freight-in): the cost of shipping purchased merchandise to the buyer's place of business.

FIGURE **4-8**

Purchases	$8 500
Add: Transportation-in	200
Cost of Delivered Goods	$8 700

FIGURE **4-9**

Cost of Delivered Goods	$8 700
Less:	
Purchases Returns and Allowances	200
Net Purchases	$8 500

FIGURE 4-10

Cost of Delivered Goods		$8 700
Less:		
Purchases Returns and Allowances	$200	
Purchases Discounts	150	350
Net Purchases		$8 350

Two factors—purchases returns and allowances and purchases discounts—will have the combined effect of decreasing the cost of delivered goods to arrive at the net purchase cost. On an income statement, the decreasing effect may be reported as illustrated in Figure 4-10.

In summary, three factors must be considered to arrive at the net purchase cost: transportation-in, which must be added to the total purchases to arrive at the cost of delivered goods; purchases returns and allowances, which must be subtracted from the cost of delivered goods; and purchases discounts, which also must be subtracted from the cost of delivered goods. The net purchase cost may now be added to the cost of beginning inventory to arrive at the cost of goods available for sale. Finally, the cost of the

FIGURE 4-11

Mississauga Wholesale Hardware Company
Income Statement
For the Year Ended December 31, 19—

Revenue from Sales:				
Sales				$91 250.00
Less:				
Sales Returns and Allowances		$640.00		
Sales Discounts		100.00	740.00	
Net Sales				$90 510.00
Cost of Goods Sold:				
Inventory, January 1			12 540.00	
Purchases		$45 630.00		
Add: Transportation-in		960.00		
Cost of Delivered Goods		46 590.00		
Less:				
Purchases Returns and Allowances	$500.00			
Purchases Discounts	160.00	660.00		
Net Purchases			45 030.00	
Cost of Goods Available for Sale			58 470.00	
Less: Inventory, December 31			13 550.00	
Cost of Goods Sold				44 920.00
Gross Profit from Sales				45 590.00
Operating Expenses:				
Advertising Expense			$ 120.00	
Salespersons' Salaries Expense			18 150.00	
Office Salaries Expense			17 100.00	
Payroll Taxes Expense			600.00	
Delivery Expense			340.00	
Store Supplies Expense			210.00	
Office Expense			270.00	
Telephone Expense			310.00	
Utilities Expense			390.00	
Legal Expense			200.00	
Total Operating Expenses				37 690.00
Net Income				$ 7 900.00

final inventory may be acquired and subtracted to calculate the cost of goods sold. The complete income statement in Figure 4-11 illustrates how all factors affecting sales revenue and cost of goods sold may be reported for a wholesale hardware merchant. This format may be used for all merchandising firms that use the periodic inventory method. The related balance sheet is also illustrated, in Figure 4-12. You should refer to these illustrations as you do the reinforcement problems for this Topic.

FIGURE 4-12

Mississauga Wholesale Hardware Company
Balance Sheet
As at December 31, 19—

Assets

Current Assets:		
Cash	$ 7 020.00	
Marketable Securities	11 500.00	
Accounts Receivable	2 000.00	
Inventory (at cost)	13 550.00	
Total Current Assets		$ 34 070.00
Fixed Assets (at cost):		
Land (pledged as security for mortgage payable)	$15 000.00	
Building (pledged as security for mortgage payable)	45 600.00	
Furniture and Fixtures	2 320.00	
Delivery Truck	15 000.00	
Total Fixed Assets		77 930.00
Total Assets		$112 000.00

Liabilities

Current Liabilities:		
Bank Loan Payable (on demand)	$ 5 000.00	
Accounts Payable	3 790.00	
Current Portion of Long-Term Debt	2 000.00	
Total Current Liabilities		$ 10 790.00
Long-Term Liabilities:		
10% Mortgage Payable, Due in Year 2005	$42 000.00	
Less: Current Portion as Reported Above	2 000.00	
Total Long-Term Liabilities		40 000.00
Total Liabilities		$ 50 790.00

Owner's Equity

T. Wong, Capital	$59 210.00	
Add: Net Income for Year	7 900.00	
Subtotal	67 110.00	
Less: Withdrawals for Year	5 900.00	
Total Owner's Equity		61 210.00
Total Liabilities and Owner's Equity		$112 000.00

Applying Merchandising Concepts

To make their financial statements more useful, management of merchandising firms add information to them. Two common methods are in use to add information to the income statement.

ADDING A PERCENTAGE COLUMN One common method is to add a percentage column to a prepared income statement. In that column, key components of the income statement would be related to the reported net sales. For example, in the case of the income statement prepared for Mississauga Wholesale Hardware Company, management might request a percentage column to report key ratios as shown in Figure 4-13.

FIGURE 4-13

Mississauga Wholesale Hardware Company
Income Statement
For the Year Ended December 31, 19—

				Percentage
Revenue from Sales:				
Sales			$91 250.00	
Less:				
Sales Returns and Allowances	$640.00			
Sales Discounts	100.00	740.00		
Net Sales			$90 510.00	100.0%
Cost of Goods Sold:				
Inventory, January 1		12 540.00		
Purchases	$45 630.00			
Add: Transportation-in	960.00			
Cost of Delivered Goods	46 590.00			
Less:				
Purchases Returns and Allowances	$500.00			
Purchases Discounts	160.00	660.00		
Net Purchases		45 030.00		
Cost of Goods Available for Sale		58 470.00		
Less: Inventory, December 31		13 550.00		
Cost of Goods Sold			44 920.00	49.6%
Gross Profit from Sales			45 590.00	50.4%
Operating Expenses:				
Advertising Expense		$ 120.00		
Salespersons' Salaries Expense		18 150.00		
Office Salaries Expense		17 100.00		
Payroll Taxes Expense		600.00		
Delivery Expense		340.00		
Store Supplies Expense		210.00		
Office Expense		270.00		
Telephone Expense		310.00		
Utilities Expense		390.00		
Legal Expense		200.00		
Total Operating Expenses			37 690.00	41.6%
Net Income			$ 7 900.00	8.7%

CHAPTER 4: Merchandising Concepts **109**

Analysis With a percentage column added, merchandise managers can focus attention on key components as they relate to the net sales.

- Notice that net sales is always made to equal 100%. Net sales is selected because that is the revenue earned from selling merchandise after returns and allowances and sales discounts have been considered.
- One key ratio is the relationship between the cost of goods sold and net sales. This **cost of goods sold ratio** is obtained by dividing the cost of goods sold amount by net sales. In the income statement for Mississauga Wholesale, the cost of goods sold ratio is 49.6% (taken to the nearest third decimal).
- Another key ratio (relationship between one component and net sales) is called the **gross margin ratio**. Obviously, this ratio is obtained by dividing amount of gross profit (margin) from sales by the net sales amount. In the illustration, the gross margin ratio is 50.4% (taken to the nearest third decimal).
- Another key ratio is the **total operating expense ratio**. In the illustration, this ratio is computed as 41.6% of net sales. (Although this is not shown, managers may request that the individual expenses also be expressed as a percentage of net sales.)
- And, finally, the "bottom line" or **net income ratio** is 8.7%.
- Observe that the calculations in the percentage column do work out. For example, the cost of goods sold ratio matched with net sales results in the correct calculation of the gross margin ratio. Similarly, the total operating expense ratio when matched with the gross margin ratio results in the correct net income ratio.

Why do merchandise managers look to the income statement with a percentage column analysis? The answer is to obtain useful information. For example, most merchandisers in competition learn that the industry standard for the gross margin ratio will be between 30 and 50%. Thus, proper action may be taken if a firm's results are below this standard.

Other merchandise managers, particularly in the retail business, look to the gross margin (profit) ratio to decide on their **markups** — the amounts added to the cost of merchandise to arrive at their selling prices. From a manager's viewpoint, this markup becomes very important in pricing the goods to be sold. For example, if the selling price of a book is $675 and its cost price is $225, then the gross margin on sale is the difference or $450. However, the retail manager will say that the $450 is the markup of the good above its cost. Knowing the markup, the merchandiser can calculate useful percentages such as the markup on cost and markup on retail (selling prices). In the calculations of Figure 4-14 and 4-15, the markup on cost is 200% — that is, management has doubled the cost price to arrive at the selling price. Based on retail, this same markup is only 66.67%; that is, management has increased the cost price by 66.67%

Cost of goods sold ratio: the ratio of cost of goods sold to net sales.

Gross margin ratio: the ratio of the gross margin (profit) on sales to net sales.

Total operating expense ratio: the ratio of total operating expenses to net sales.

Net income ratio: the ratio of net income to net sales.

Markups: amounts added to the cost of merchandise to arrive at their selling price.

FIGURE **4-14**

To find the percentage of markup on cost:

$$\frac{\text{Markup in \$}}{\text{Cost in \$}} \times 100\%$$

$$\frac{\$450}{\$225} \times 100\% = 200\%$$

FIGURE **4-15**

To find the percentage of markup on retail:

$$\frac{\text{Markup in \$}}{\text{Retail in \$}} \times 100\%$$

$$\frac{\$450}{\$675} \times 100\% = 66.7\%$$

of the selling price. Obviously, a knowledge of markups (and markdowns) helps retail managers to increase or decrease the selling prices of individual goods.

PROJECTING THE GROSS PROFIT FROM SALES Another useful tool of analysis by merchandise managers is to request accounting clerks to prepare a forecast of what happens if the gross profit from sales is projected for the remaining months in the year. For example, if the results of the current month's income statement, say in January, showed that net sales equalled $100 000 and the cost of those goods sold equalled $60 000, the gross profit (margin) on sales would be $40 000. Suppose that management decides that the net sales revenue would be increased by 10% per month for the remaining 11 months. If the cost of goods sold remained the same, what would be the resulting gross margins for the rest of the year? A worksheet or spreadsheet might be prepared as shown in Figure 4-16.

FIGURE 4-16

	A	B	C	D	E	F	G	H
1	W. Hamming Wholesale Company								
2	Projected Gross Margin on Sales								
3	For the Year Ending December 31, 19—								
4								
5				Jan.	Feb.	Mar.	Apr.	May
6	Sales			$100.00	$110.00	$121.00	$133.10	$146.41
7	Cost of Goods Sold			$60.00	$66.00	$72.60	$79.86	$87.85
8	Gross Margin on Sales			$40.00	$44.00	$48.40	$53.24	$58.56
9								
10	Verification—Gross Margin			40.00%	40.00%	40.00%	40.00%	40.00%
11								

	H	I	J	K	L	M	N	O
1								
2								
3								
4								
5	May	June	July	Aug.	Sept.	Oct.	Nov.	Dec.
6	$146.41	$161.05	$177.16	$194.87	$214.36	$235.79	$259.37	$285.31
7	$87.85	$96.63	$106.29	$116.92	$128.62	$141.48	$155.62	$171.19
8	$58.56	$64.42	$70.86	$77.95	$85.74	$94.32	$103.75	$114.12
9								
10	40.00%	40.00%	40.00%	40.00%	40.00%	40.00%	40.00%	40.00%
11								

Analysis In the 12-month spreadsheet, notice that the "thousands" of dollars have been cut off to simplify the use of numbers. In fact, by keeping only amounts in hundreds, the columns can be interpreted in terms of percentages, because net sales is equal to 100% in the first month. Obviously, by increasing each subsequent month's net sales by 10%, the gross margin increases for each of those months.

In practice, adding a percentage column to any income statement and preparing a projected 12-month gross profit from sales forecast may be done on paper with the aid of an electronic calculator. More often, however, accountants and accounting clerks have turned to the use of the microcomputer and electronic spreadsheet software to prepare such "spreadsheets" at management's request.

TOPIC I Problems

Calculating the cost of goods sold under five alternative assumptions.

4.1 During the year, the British Columbia Company purchased merchandise costing $350 000. State the cost of goods sold under each of the following alternative assumptions:
  a No beginning inventory; ending inventory, $60 000.
  b Beginning inventory, $50 000; ending inventory, $95 000.
  c Beginning inventory, $30 000; ending inventory, $65 000.
  d Beginning inventory, $100 000; no ending inventory.
  e Beginning inventory, $12 000; ending inventory, $150 000.

Calculating the cost of goods sold from basic data.

4.2 Compute the amount of cost of goods sold, given the following figures: beginning inventory, $32 000; purchases, $94 000; purchases returns and allowances, $5 400; transportation-in, $600; and ending inventory, $46 000. *Note*: Save your solution for use in Problem 4.4 in this Topic.

Calculating the cost of goods sold from complex data.

4.3 Compute the amount of cost of goods sold, given the following figures: beginning inventory, $45 000; purchases returns and allowances, $4 950; purchases, $108 035; purchases discounts, $2 780; transportation-in, $1 420; and ending inventory, $59 000. *Note*: Save your solution for use in the next problem.

Calculating the gross profit from sales from data solved in previous problems.

4.4 Assume that the sales revenue for the accounting period was reported to be $100 000. Calculate the gross profit (margin) from sales for each of the cost of goods sold obtained in Problems 4.2 and 4.3.

Calculating the gross profit from sales from given data.

4.5 Find the Gross Profit (Margin) from Sales for the month ended June 30 from the following amounts: Sales, $6 000; Inventory, June 1, $3 000; Purchases, $5 800; Inventory, June 30, $3 700.

Preparing a partial income statement for a merchandising firm.

4.6 Prepare a partial income statement for Calgary Hardware for the month of July, using the following figures: Inventory, July 1, $12 000; Inventory, July 31, $15 000; Sales, $17 380; Purchases, $16 000; Sales Returns and

112   PART 1: THE FRAMEWORK OF ACCOUNTING

Allowances, $1 150; Purchases Returns and Allowances, $1 500; Sales Discounts, $600; Purchases Discounts, $500; and Transportation-in, $1 100.

Preparing a partial income statement from given merchandising data.

4.7 Prepare a partial income statement for the Regina Book Shop for the year ended December 31, using the following figures: Sales, $178 385; Sales Returns and Allowances, $1 960; Purchases Discounts, $1 915; Sales Discounts, $1 370; Inventory, January 1, $13 145; Inventory, December 31, $14 750; Purchases, $82 480; Purchases Returns and Allowances, $1 365; and Transportation-in, $1 670.

Preparing a partial income statement from given merchandising data.

4.8 Prepare a partial income statement for the Maritime Sales Company for the year ended December 31, using the following figures: January 1, $14 540; Inventory, December 31, $16 040; Sales, $174 415; Transportation-in, $1 575; Sales Returns and Allowances, $1 315; Purchases Returns and Allowances, $1 465; Sales Discounts, $1 155; Purchases Discounts, $1 890; and Purchases, $102 230.

Preparing a complete income statement for a merchandising firm.

4.9 The items summarized below, with expenses condensed to save space, were reported for the Winnipeg Wholesale Hardware Company for the year ended December 31. From the information, prepare an income statement.

FIGURE 4-17

Inventory, January 1	$ 22 000
Inventory, December 31	19 000
Sales Revenue	170 000
Sales Returns and Allowances	1 500
Sales Discounts	1 100
Purchases Returns and Allowances	1 400
Purchases Discounts	1 900
Purchases	87 950
Transportation-in	2 890
Selling Expenses	44 970
General and Administrative Expenses	22 650

Preparing a complete income statement and a related balance sheet for a merchandising firm.

4.10 Peter Brent operates the Niagara Wholesale Company. His firm's year-end activities reported the following information: Inventory, beginning of the accounting year, $37 240; Inventory, end of the accounting year, $27 910; Sales, $229 735; Sales Returns and Allowances, $3 000; Sales Discounts, $290; Purchases, $119 930; Purchases Returns and Allowances, $2 000; Purchases Discounts, $145; Freight and Duty-in, $2 965; Salaries and Wages Expense, $57 880; Payroll Taxes Expense, $2 320; Property Taxes Expense, $1 685; Insurance Expense, $1 340; Supplies Expense, $1 200; Miscellaneous Expense, $270; P. Brent, Capital (January 1), $94 820; P. Brent, Drawing, $15 000; Cash in Bank, $18 585; Petty Cash, $100; Accounts Receivable, $24 260; Land, $31 000 (pledged

CHAPTER 4: Merchandising Concepts   113

as collateral for the mortgage payable); Building, $67 380 (pledged as collateral for the mortgage payable); Equipment, $17 435; Bank Loan Payable (on demand), $2 000; Salaries Payable, $3 140; Accounts Payable, $30 040; 10% Mortgage Payable, $40 000 (20-year due in 2010; $2 000 due within the current accounting year).

Required
a Prepare an income statement for the year ended December 31.
b Prepare a balance sheet in report form as at December 31.

Preparing percentage analysis income statements for merchandising firms.

4.11 The separate problems below may be solved on a microcomputer using your school's electronic spreadsheet software or one to which you have access.

a Return to the solution prepared for Problem 4.8 (Maritime Sales Company). Use an electronic spreadsheet package to redo the partial income statement with an added percentage column. Use appropriate formulae to compute the cost of goods sold ratio and the gross profit (margin) from sales ratio. (Calculate all ratios to the nearest second decimal.)

b Return to the solution prepared for Problem 4.9 (Winnipeg Wholesale Hardware Company). Use an electronic spreadsheet package to show the income statement with an added percentage column. Show percentages to net sales for the cost of goods sold, gross profit from sales, selling expenses, general and administrative expenses, the total operating expenses, and the "bottom line."

c Return to the solution prepared for Problem 4.10 (Niagara Wholesale Company). Use an electronic spreadsheet package to show the income statement with an added percentage column. Show percentages to net sales for the cost of goods sold, gross profit from sales, the individual operating expenses, the total operating expenses, and the "bottom line."

Preparing a projected gross margin on sales spreadsheet.

4.12 Assume that the management of the W. Hamming Wholesale Company has requested a projection of the gross margin on sales using the following criteria:

- The initial sales begins at $100 for the first month (January).
- The cost of goods sold will remain at 60% of sales for the current calendar year.

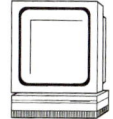

Required
a Develop a spreadsheet (worksheet) projecting the figures for sales, cost of goods sold, and the gross margin on sales for 12 months of the current year. Use the format illustrated in Figure 4-16.
- On line (row) 1, beginning at A1, enter the name of the firm.
- On line (row) 2, beginning at A2, enter "Projected Gross Margin on Sales".
- On line (row) 3, beginning at A3, enter "For the Year Ending December 31, 19—". (Notice that the word "Ending" is used correctly,

because a projected statement is forecasting what the future amounts will be. On the other hand, the word "Ended" is always used when revenues have been matched with expenses in the past.)
- Leave line (row) 4 blank.
- On line (row) 5, begin in the fourth column (column D), enter titles for the 12 months in the calendar year.
- On line (row) 6, enter the title "Sales".
- On line (row) 7, enter the title "Cost of Goods Sold".
- On line (row) 8, enter the title "Gross Margin on Sales".
- Skip the next line.
- On line (row) 10, enter the title "Verification—Gross Margin".
- The first sales amount in January is $100. (You can format the dollar sign later.)
- The cost of goods sold is 60% of sales. Use a formula to determine this figure.
- Use a formula to determine the gross margin on sales.
- Subsequent sales figures are to increase by 10% each month. Use a formula for the second month and copy (replicate) this formula for the remaining ten months.
- Copy (replicate) the formulae for the cost of goods sold and gross margins to complete the spreadsheet.
- Convert all values to integers and then to two decimal places.
- Two lines (rows) below the gross margin on sales line, verify the accuracy of each gross margin figure by writing a formula for the gross margin as a percentage of sales. *Hint*: This formula contains the sales and gross margin amounts.
- Save your spreadsheet under an appropriate file name. Print a hard copy of this first version.

b After completing the spreadsheet, solve the following "what if" situations:
- What if the January sales figure was $125 instead of $100? Save your solution under an appropriate file name. Print a hard copy of this solution.
- Return the initial sales figure to $100. What if the cost of goods sold changes from 60% to 65%? Save your solution under an appropriate file name. Print a hard copy of this solution.

Preparing a markup spreadsheet for a merchandising firm.

4.13 The following accounting problem can be solved by using your school's spreadsheet software or an electronic spreadsheet package to which you have access.

Assume that you have been provided with the following information on ten products of Cornwall Retailers.

FIGURE 4-18

Product	Cost Price	Selling Price
A	$125.00	$160.00
B	132.00	174.00
C	140.00	190.00
D	149.00	208.00
E	159.00	228.00
F	170.00	250.00
G	182.00	247.00
H	195.00	300.00
I	209.00	328.00
J	220.00	400.00

Required

a Develop a markup worksheet with the following suggested columns: Product, Cost Price, Selling Price, Markup Amount, Markup % on Cost, and Markup % on Selling.

b Apply formulae to complete columns for the markup amount, the markup percentage on cost, and the markup percentage on selling.

c What if the cost prices and selling prices for the ten products were increased by 10% and 20% respectively?

TOPIC 2   Analyzing Merchandising Transactions

As suggested earlier, much of what you have learned for the service firm also applies to the accounting of business transactions for a merchandising firm. From Chapter 2, you will recall three logical rules for understanding when to debit and when to credit accounts.

- All increases in accounts are recorded on the side on which the element originates in the accounting equation. Since the element Assets originates on the debit (left) side of the accounting equation, all increases to this element are recorded on the debit side of the appropriate asset accounts. Similarly, since the element Liabilities originates on the credit (right) side of the accounting equation, all increases to this element are recorded on the credit side of the appropriate liability accounts. And, finally, any increase to Owner's Equity must be recorded as a credit in the account that has caused the increases, simply because the element Owner's Equity originates on the credit (right) side of the accounting equation. As you know, both investments by the owner and sales revenue cause an increase to Owner's Equity in the accounting equation; therefore, the increase must be recorded as a credit in the capital account or the appropriate revenue account, as the case may be.

- All decreases in accounts are recorded on the side opposite to the one on which the element in the equation originates. Consequently, decreases to Assets must be recorded as credits in appropriate asset accounts; decreases to Liabilities must be recorded as debits to appropriate liability accounts; and decreases to Owner's Equity must be recorded as debits in accounts that caused this decrease. For example, expenses and owner's withdrawals cause decreases to Owner's Equity within the accounting equation; therefore, the decreases to owner's equity are recorded as debits in appropriate expense accounts or the owner's drawing account, as the case may be.
- Normal balances in accounts are identified on the same side as they are associated with in the elements of the equation. Consequently, asset accounts will have a normal debit balance; liability accounts will have a normal credit balance; and owner's equity accounts will have a normal balance in relationship to their increasing or decreasing effect on owner's equity. For example, the Capital and Revenue accounts will have credit balances, because they increase owner's equity; and Expense and Drawing accounts will have debit balances, because they decrease owner's equity.

Keep the above rules in mind when studying the analysis of merchandising transactions that follow. It will also be helpful to refer back to the factors that affect the revenue from sales, and, especially, to examine the various factors that affect the calculation of cost of goods sold. You will observe that all transactions are analyzed in "general journal" form to avoid the added problem of your having to learn the various special journals and ledgers common to merchandising firms. These special journals and ledgers will be examined in Part 2 of the text.

Analyzing Transactions Affecting Sales Revenue

Special Note: On January 1, 1991, the federal government's new Goods and Services Tax (GST) became law, thus replacing the former federal sales tax system with an extensive consumption tax. However, to simplify matters in this chapter, only the provincial sales tax (where applicable) will be added to sales transactions. The GST is treated in the Appendix to this textbook.

You should have little difficulty in the analysis of debits and credits for cash sales of merchandise and goods sold to customers on account. The two factors that decrease the sales revenue—sales returns and allowances and sales discounts—will require careful examination.

CASH SALES

Many merchandising firms, especially retailers, will transact their sales for cash. The double entry to record the cash sales may be analyzed as follows:

CHAPTER 4: Merchandising Concepts 117

FIGURE 4-19

```
Feb. 4   Cash ..............................    300
              Sales ...........................           300
         To record the day's cash sales.
```

CREDIT SALES   It is common practice for wholesalers to sell goods to retailers on some credit arrangement. Credit sales may be analyzed as follows:

FIGURE 4-20

```
Feb. 5   Accounts Receivable ................    500
              Sales ...........................           500
         Sold merchandise on credit to Central
         Hardware; terms 2/10, n/30.
```

FIGURE 4-21

Percentage Rates of
Provincial Sales Tax

Alberta	No tax
B.C.	6%
Saskatchewan	7%
Manitoba	7%
Ontario	8%
Quebec	9%
Nova Scotia	10%
P.E.I.	10%
New Brunswick	11%
Newfoundland	12%

Example

Cash sale	$300.00
Ontario 8% sales tax	24.00
Customer pays	$324.00

SALES WITH PROVINCIAL SALES TAXES   All provinces except Alberta require the retailer to collect and account for the provincial sales tax (PST) on the majority of merchandise sold in their respective provinces. For example, if the retailer in the case of the first Cash Sales transaction were required to collect the PST at a rate of 8%, the first step would be to calculate the amount of the tax. The compound entry to record the cash sale would show a separate current liability account to identify the sales taxes owing to the provincial government. By provincial law, the sales taxes collected by the retailer must be remitted at specified times to the provincial treasurer.

FIGURE 4-22

```
Feb. 4   Cash ..............................    324.00
              Sales ...........................          300.00
              PST Payable ....................           24.00
         To record the day's cash sales plus the
         8% PST to the provincial government.
```

SALES RETURNS AND ALLOWANCES   As explained in Topic 1 of this chapter, sales returns and allowances have the effect of decreasing revenue. Such decreases *may* be recorded on the debit side of the revenue account; however, it is customary to use the combined account Sales Returns and Allowances so that such information may be kept separate to assist management in analyzing the number, type, and frequency of returns, and thus enable management to reduce future returns. In analyzing transactions, it is important to consider two things: (1) whether the return or allowance originated from a previous cash sale or a previous credit sale; and (2) whether the sale originated from the wholesaler or retailer. Of course, a return or allowance resulting from a previous credit sale must affect the customer's accounts receivable. If the sale was made by the wholesaler, no adjustment is made to PST Payable, because only retailers collect provincial sales taxes where applicable. For example, in the case of the credit sale on February 5 recorded by a wholesaler, if the customer, Central Hardware, made a return of $25 of unsatisfactory goods on February 6, the journal entry may be analyzed as follows:

FIGURE 4-23

Feb. 6	Sales Returns and Allowances............	25.00	
	Accounts Receivable		25.00
	To record the return of $25 of unsatisfactory goods by Central Hardware.		

It is important to know how to classify the Sales Returns and Allowances account. Since the account decreases sales revenue, one can say that it is *in opposition* to that of the revenue account. In accounting language, the word used to describe an account that is in opposition to a related one is **contra**. In this case, Sales Returns and Allowances is a contra revenue account, because it has the effect of decreasing revenue and, of course, Owner's Equity within the accounting equation. Since decreases to owner's equity are recorded as debits in accounts that caused the decrease, all sales returns and allowances will be recorded as debits in the contra account.

FIGURE 4-24

Chart of Accounts

401 Sales
402 Sales Returns and Allowances

Contra: said of an account that is in opposition to or offsets another, related account.

PROVINCIAL SALES TAX ON SALES RETURNS AND ALLOWANCES

In the province in which sales taxes have to be collected on retail sales, an additional accounting problem must be considered when sales returns and allowances are involved. Consider, for example, the case in which in an earlier sales transaction a credit sale was made to a customer for goods totalling $200 in a province where a sales tax of 8% was recorded. Therefore, the 8% would have been applied to the sales invoice price plus the PST ($200 + $16 = $216).

Suppose the customer returned one part of the credit sale — a 12 mm drill — and was given full credit for the unit price of $34.95. In this case, the correct accounting entry for the return of the drill would be analyzed as follows:

FIGURE 4-25

Feb. 10	Sales Returns and Allowances............	34.95	
	PST Payable.........................	2.80	
	Accounts Receivable		37.75
	To record the credit customer's return of one drill for $34.95 and the decrease to PST Payable of $2.80.		

From the illustration, observe that the return is correctly debited for $34.95, because the original sales revenue has been decreased by the amount of the return. Notice, too, that the provincial sales tax on the original sold item is no longer payable to the provincial government; therefore, the current liability account for the PST must be decreased by the amount of the sales tax originally charged on the item. And, finally, observe that the credit to Accounts Receivable in the general ledger must be for the amount of the sales return plus the PST. Remember the point that, originally, the customer was charged not only for the sale, but also for the PST. When the compound entry is posted to the ledger, the balances of the accounts would reveal the correct amounts owing to the provincial government and to the business enterprise through accounts receivable.

FIGURE 4-26

Supporting Computations

Amount of return on invoice price	$34.95
PST: 8% of $34.95	2.80
Credit to Acct. Rec.	$37.75

SALES DISCOUNTS Consider the simple example of a credit sale made by a wholesaler on February 7 to Downtown Hardware for $1 000 on terms of 2/10, n/30. Suppose that the credit customer mails a cheque for $980 and that the remittance is received within the sales discount period of ten days. The correct analysis of the cheque received may be shown as follows:

FIGURE 4-27

Feb. 17	Cash	980.00	
	Sales Discounts	20.00	
	Accounts Receivable		1 000.00
	To record the receipt of payment for the sale of Feb. 7 to Downtown Hardware, less the 2% sales discount applied to the sales invoice only.		

Notice that the debit to Cash correctly records the exact amount of cash received. The debit to Sales Discounts ($1 000 × 2%) identifies the decrease to sales revenue and to Owner's Equity within the accounting equation. Once again, this decrease could have been recorded on the debit side of Sales; however, preference is given to recording the entry in a separate contra revenue account called Sales Discounts. This practice will avoid the mixing of figures in the revenue account and also permits the information to be reported on the income statement. And, finally, observe that the credit to Accounts Receivable must be for the *total* decrease to that asset account. It would be an error to credit the customer's Accounts Receivable with only the cheque amount when a sales discount is taken. Such an error would still reveal an amount owing in Accounts Receivable.

FIGURE 4-28

Supporting Computations

Invoice price	$1 000.00
Less: 2% discount ($1 000 × 0.02)	20.00
Amount of cheque	$ 980.00

An accounting problem must be considered in the case where a customer is sold goods on credit, returns some goods, or is granted an allowance on the sale, and subsequently sends in the cheque within a sales discount period. Consider, for example, the earlier credit sale made to Central Hardware for $500 and the subsequent sales return of $25 made on February 6. Now consider the problem of analyzing a sales discount of 2%. On what amount would the sales discount rate be applied? On the original invoice of $500, or on the original invoice of $500 less the sales return of $25? The answer is: on $475, because that is the amount owing on the original invoice. In this case, the original invoice amount of $500 was reduced by the amount of sales return, $25. Hence, the 2% cash discount will be applied to the net invoice amount of $475. The correct analysis of the cheque received may be shown as computed in Figure 4-29.

The journal entry to record the cheque received may be shown as illustrated in Figure 4-30.

FIGURE 4-29

Supporting Computations

Invoice price	$500.00
Less: Return	25.00
Amount owing	475.00
Less: 2% discount ($475 × 0.02)	9.50
Amount of cheque	$465.50

FIGURE 4-30

Feb. 15	Cash	465.50	
	Sales Discounts	9.50	
	Accounts Receivable		475.00

To record the receipt of payment for the sale of Feb. 5 to Central Hardware, less the return, and less the 2% sales discount on $475.

FIGURE 4-31

Acct. Rec./Central Hardware

Feb. 5 Inv.	500	Feb. 6 Ret.	25
		Feb. 15 Chq.	475

∅

It is useful to point out that sales discounts in merchandising accounting normally occur between wholesalers and retailers. On the other hand, sales discounts are rarely given in sales terms offered by the retailer to consumers.

To summarize the analysis of transactions affecting sales revenue, remember that both Sales Returns and Allowances and Sales Discounts are contra revenue accounts and, therefore, must show debit entries. Since both accounts are related to the revenue classification, it is customary to code these accounts in a chart of accounts immediately following the revenue account. Also remember that any PST is a current liability account that must be remitted to the provincial government at specified intervals.

FIGURE 4-32

Chart of Accounts

Revenue
401 Sales
402 Sales Returns and Allowances
403 Sales Discounts

Analyzing Transactions Affecting Cost of Goods Sold

Cost of goods sold: an expense of a merchandising business, to be matched against sales revenue.

Before examining the entries that account for the cost of goods sold, it is very important that you understand the concept of **cost of goods sold**. You have observed from Topic 1 that the cost of goods sold must be matched with the related sales revenue for an accounting period to determine the gross profit from sales. And as you know from accounting for a service firm, expenses are matched against related revenue to determine the net profit (net income) for an accounting period. For the accounting of a merchandising firm, the matchup of cost of goods sold must be regarded as one of the expenses of carrying on a merchandising business. In fact, some firms do show in their income statement the concept of cost of goods sold grouped together with all the operating expenses just to emphasize that cost of goods sold is an expense to be matched against the revenue to determine net income. (See the illustration of Stelco's income statement, Figure 4-33.) However, accountants recommend that the cost of goods sold for wholesale and retail firms be matched alone under the revenue to disclose the difference (margin) between the sale and the cost of the sale. Regardless of the approach taken, remember that the cost of goods sold is an expense to be matched against sales revenue.

FIGURE 4-33

CONSOLIDATED STATEMENT OF INCOME AND RETAINED EARNINGS

Years ended December 31
(Thousands of Dollars)

		1989	1988
REVENUE	Sales	$ 2,749,054	$ 2,711,491
	Equity income	7,569	21,824
	Income from short-term investments	3,312	5,469
		2,759,935	2,738,784
EXPENSE	Cost of sales, exclusive of the following items	2,266,482	2,253,696
	Administrative and selling	138,108	132,363
	Research and development	8,209	9,489
	Depreciation	129,570	124,604
	Interest on long-term debt	85,220	79,809
	Other interest	5,303	1,912
	Income taxes (Note 4) – current	6,816	3,661
	– deferred	26,358	34,879
		2,666,066	2,640,413
INCOME BEFORE EXTRAORDINARY ITEMS		93,869	98,371
	Extraordinary items net of income taxes (Note 3)	–	1,600
NET INCOME		93,869	96,771
RETAINED EARNINGS	Balance at beginning of year	571,452	544,069
	Premium on redemption of preferred shares (Note 10)	–	(5,750)
	Dividends (Note 10)	(50,043)	(63,638)
	Balance at end of year	$ 615,278	$ 571,452
INCOME PER COMMON SHARE (NOTE 1)	Before extraordinary items	$ 2.25	$ 2.00
	– fully diluted	$ 2.13	$ 1.96
	After extraordinary items	$ 2.25	$ 1.95
	– fully diluted	$ 2.13	$ 1.91

Note: At the time of writing, Stelco Inc. has not considered the introduction of the International System of Units (SI); consequently, the comma appears in the dollar amounts.

A careful analysis of a sales transaction and its effect within the accounting equation will support the idea that cost of goods sold must be an expense of any merchandising business. To simplify the analysis, assume a beginning equation as shown below.

FIGURE 4-34

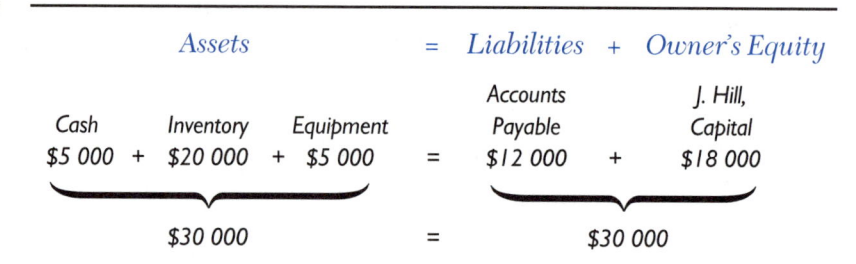

	Assets		=	Liabilities	+	Owner's Equity
Cash	Inventory	Equipment		Accounts Payable		J. Hill, Capital
$5 000 +	$20 000 +	$5 000	=	$12 000	+	$18 000

$30 000 = $30 000

Now consider the effects of selling some of the goods on hand (inventory) costing $1 000 for $4 000 cash. The inflow of cash resulting from the sale would be analyzed as shown in the following second equation:

FIGURE 4-35

Assets			=	Liabilities	+	Owner's Equity		
Cash	Inventory	Equipment		Accounts Payable		J. Hill, Capital		Revenue (Sales)
$5 000	$20 000	$5 000	=	$12 000	+	$18 000		
(1)+4 000							+	$4 000
$9 000 +	$20 000 +	$5 000	=	$12 000	+	$18 000	+	$4 000

$34 000 = $34 000

Analysis Since $1 000 cost of the inventory has been sold, it naturally follows that the firm no longer has this amount of inventory; therefore, the total assets on the left side of the equation must decrease by $1 000 because there is $1 000 less inventory on hand. And as you well know, any total decrease on the left side of the equation must be balanced by a similar amount on the right side of the equation. Since the element Liabilities is not affected, some item must cause a $1 000 decrease to Owner's Equity. And since both capital and revenue increase Owner's Equity through investment and sales respectively, an expense must have caused a $1 000 decrease to Owner's Equity. In the language of accounting, this expense is the cost of the asset Inventory used to produce the sales revenue or, in short, the cost of goods sold. The effect of the cost of the goods sold within the equation is shown in Figure 4-36.

FIGURE 4-36

	Assets					=	Liabilities	+		Owner's Equity		
	Cash		Inventory		Equipment		Accounts Payable		J. Hill, Capital		Revenue	Cost of Goods Sold (Expense)
	$9 000	+	$20 000	+	$5 000	=	$12 000	+	$18 000	+	$4 000	
(2)			− 1 000									− $1 000
	$9 000	+	$19 000	+	$5 000	=	$12 000	+	$18 000	+	$4 000	− $1 000

Assets: $33 000 = $33 000

By matching the cost of goods sold under the revenue, the equation may be rearranged to disclose the gross profit from sales, as shown in the next equation, below.

FIGURE 4-37

	Assets					=	Liabilities	+		Owner's Equity
	Cash		Inventory		Equipment		Accounts Payable		J. Hill, Capital	+4 000 Sales Revenue −1 000 Cost of Goods Sold $3 000 Gross Profit from Sales
	$9 000	+	$19 000	+	$5 000	=	$12 000	+	$18 000	

$33 000 = $33 000

Now if the various items shown in the accounting equation were replaced by account names, it should be quite easy to follow the analysis of debits and credits to account for the cost of goods sold. This step would suggest that an asset account called Inventory would be credited and an expense account called Cost of Goods Sold would be debited to account for the cost of goods sold. And these accounts are definitely used for merchandising firms that follow the perpetual inventory method, but, unfortunately, not for the firms that use the periodic inventory method. As you will recall from Topic 1, under the periodic inventory method the cost of goods sold is calculated only once — and that calculation is done at the end of the accounting period for all of the goods sold. You should refer back to the examples in Topic 1 as you study the analysis of the transactions for firms using the periodic inventory method. A comparative view using the perpetual method will follow.

INVENTORY CHANGES An asset account, Inventory, does exist under a periodic inventory method. However, under this method, accounting entries are made to the Inventory account only at the end of the accounting period. Since accounting periods follow one another, it must be true that the ending inventory of the last accounting period always will be the beginning inventory of the next accounting period. In general, the entries to update the Inventory account at the end of the accounting period under a manual system are done through the closing steps of the accounting cycle. Under a microcomputer system, these entries would be made as part of adjusting entries. The adjusting and closing entries for a merchandising firm will not be treated here, since they are examined fully in Chapter 5. What you should remember here, however, are two important points:

- For the new accounting period, the Inventory account will disclose the cost of the beginning inventory; hence, this information can be used together with the net purchases to calculate the cost of goods available for sale on the income statement of the accounting period under study. In this sense, the beginning Inventory is no longer an asset but part of the cost of goods sold at the end of the accounting period.
- At the end of the accounting period, a physical count is taken to determine the cost of the inventory unsold. This ending inventory becomes a current asset to be shown on the balance sheet as at the last date of the accounting period. Furthermore, the cost of the ending inventory is deducted from the cost of goods available for sale to calculate the cost of the goods sold. As stated earlier, under a manual system, the ending inventory cost will be recorded in the asset account through the process of closing entries.

FIGURE 4-38

Inventory
Beginning inventory is the cost of the unsold inventory carried forward from the last accounting period.

PURCHASES OF MERCHANDISE

Under a periodic inventory method, the cost of merchandise purchased for resale is accumulated in an account called Purchases. For each purchase, either for cash or on credit, the account Purchases must be debited. For example, if a wholesale merchandiser purchased goods showing an invoice amount of $1 000, the entry to record this purchase may be analyzed as shown in the following double entry:

FIGURE 4-39

Feb. 5	Purchases	1 000.00	
	Accounts Payable (or Cash)		1 000.00
	Purchased merchandise on credit terms of 2/10, n/30 (or purchased merchandise for cash).		

Three points must be analyzed for the debit entry to Purchases. First, remember that this account is used only for merchandise acquired for resale. The purchase of assets not intended for resale — equipment, truck, building, etc. — must be recorded as debits to appropriate asset accounts, but not to Purchases. Second, the Purchases account is not an inventory account. It does not indicate whether the purchased goods have been sold or are still on hand; therefore, it must not be viewed as an asset account. And, finally, since the only purpose served by the Purchases account is to reveal the total cost of purchased during the accounting period (so that the cost of goods available for sale can be calculated), the Purchases account must be regarded as part of the cost of goods sold. As you know, cost of goods sold is an expense; therefore, it is quite correct to view Purchases as an expense account under the cost of goods sold. In a chart of accounts for a merchandising firm, Purchases would be classified under the broad heading "Costs and Expenses," to acknowledge that Purchases is part of "Costs," the short form for "Cost of Goods Sold" and other expired costs (expenses).

FIGURE **4-40**

Chart of Accounts
Costs and Expenses
501 Purchases

Suppose this same wholesaler marks up the purchase of $1 000 by 40% on cost and sells the merchandise for $1 400 to a retailer. To record this sale, the wholesaler would make the following double entry:

FIGURE **4-41**

Feb. 10	Accounts Receivable...............	1 400.00	
	Sales........................		1 400.00
	Sold merchandise on credit terms of 2/10, n/30 on an invoice amount of $1 400.		

TRANSPORTATION-IN (FREIGHT-IN)   From Topic 1, you learned that freight costs must be added to the cost of purchases to determine the cost of delivered goods. Each time a transport company is paid or gives credit terms for these freight charges, an accounting entry must be made as follows:

FIGURE **4-42**

Feb. 6	Transportation-in....................	80	
	Accounts Payable (or Cash)..........		80
	To record freight charges on merchandise purchased on Feb. 5.		

FIGURE **4-43**

Chart of Accounts
Costs and Expenses
501 Purchases
502 Transportation-in

It is important to classify the account Transportation-in (or Freight-in, if you prefer) as part of the cost of goods sold. As such, Transportation-in is an *expense* under cost of goods sold. It should also be pointed out that purchased merchandise from countries outside of Canada may be charged a tax called a *duty* before such goods are allowed to cross the border. In this case, the duty would also have to be added to the cost of purchases. Although separate accounts may be used, it is common to debit only one account — Transportation-in or Transportation and Duty-in — with the cost of the duties.

PURCHASES RETURNS AND ALLOWANCES When merchandise received from suppliers is not acceptable, it may be returned or an allowance off the purchase price may be granted. In either case, the cost of the purchased goods must be decreased by the cost of the returned goods or by the allowance granted. If $100 of defective merchandise were returned, the double entry to record such a transaction may be analyzed as follows:

FIGURE 4-44

Feb. 6:	Accounts Payable (or Cash)	100	
	Purchases Returns and Allowances		100
	To record the return of $100 of defective merchandise acquired previously on Feb. 5.		

In the correct analysis of Purchases Returns and Allowances, it is important to remember that the account decreases the original cost of purchases. In theory, this decrease could have been shown as a credit to the Purchases account. In practice, however, accountants recommend the use of a separate account so that the information can be reported to management and it can also be used on the income statement to arrive at the net purchases. It is quite correct, therefore, to classify Purchases Returns and Allowances as a *contra expense account*, in the sense that the account is in opposition to its related Purchases account.

FIGURE 4-45

Chart of Accounts

Costs and Expenses

501 Purchases
502 Transportation-in
503 Purchases Returns and Allowances

PURCHASES DISCOUNTS When a supplier offers credit terms that include a cash discount, it is important that the buyer take advantage of such discounts in order to decrease the firm's cost of purchases. Consider, for example, the earlier case of accounting for purchases on February 5 on credit terms of 2/10, n/30. Under normal situations, the buyer would mail a cheque for $882 as shown in the computation in Figure 4-46. The accounting entry would be analyzed as follows.

FIGURE 4-46

Computation of Cheque

Invoice	$1 000
Less: Return	100
Net invoice	900
Less: 2%	18
Amount of cheque	$ 882

FIGURE 4-47

Feb. 5	Accounts Payable	900.00	
	Purchases Discount		18.00
	Cash		882.00
	Issued Chq. 45 in payment of Feb. 5 invoice, less return, and less cash discount.		

Observe that the purchase discount has been calculated on the net invoice price (purchase price less the return). At this point, you should have no difficulty in understanding that the account Purchases Discounts is exactly like Purchases Returns and Allowances. You should conclude, therefore, that Purchases Discounts is a contra expense account under the cost of goods sold. As contra to Purchases, the discount decreases the cost, thereby increasing owner's equity. And as you are aware, any increase to

FIGURE 4-48

Chart of Accounts

Costs and Expenses

501 Purchases
502 Transportation-in
503 Purchases Returns and Allowances
504 Purchases Discounts

CHAPTER 4: Merchandising Concepts   **127**

owner's equity must be recorded as a credit in the account that caused the increase.

Using the Perpetual Inventory Method

Not all merchandising firms wait until the end of an accounting period to update their Inventory account and to account for their cost of goods sold. Some business concerns, especially those which sell merchandise of a high unit cost value such as automobiles and expensive television sets, prefer to update their inventory accounts every time goods are bought and sold. And, in addition, these firms prefer to do a costing of the goods sold every time a sale is made.

As stated earlier, such merchandising firms use the perpetual inventory method in their accounting system. It is useful to do a short comparison of entries between the periodic and perpetual inventory methods, especially since the majority of computer systems now support only the perpetual inventory method. For the comparative study, examine carefully the following demonstration problem.

The following is information relating to the Winnipeg Wholesale Trading Company for the year ended December 31:

1. Beginning inventory, January 1: 1 000 items at a unit cost of $75. (This inventory represents the balance of inventory carried forward at the end of the last accounting period.)
2. Purchases of merchandise on credit for the year: 20 000 items at a unit cost of $75 each.
3. Returned: 500 items costing $75 each to the supplier.
4. Cheques issued during the year to suppliers in payment of purchases invoices: $1 390 000.
5. Sales of merchandise on credit for the year: 18 500 items at a unit selling price of $200 each.
6. Issued credit memos totalling $40 000 for the return of 200 stock items from credit customers. (Cost price of all 200 items is $75 each.)
7. Customers were allowed a price allowance of $5 000.
8. Cheques received during the year from credit customers in remittance of sales invoices totalled $2 100 000; sales discounts granted totalled $55 000; total accounts receivable credited amounted $2 155 000.
9. A physical count of goods on hand after store hours on December 31 showed that 1 500 items were in stock at a unit cost of $75 each.

A good comparison may be made by recording each of the above nine transactions in general journal form.

Transaction 1   This first "transaction" is not a transaction in the normal accounting sense. It merely sets the scene for the Inventory accounts under both the periodic and the perpetual inventory method. Under both methods, an Inventory account exists in the general ledger showing the beginning balance as illustrated by the T-account in Figure 4-49.

Transaction 2   This second transaction identifies the purchases of merchandise on credit for the year. Notice the difference in accounting for these purchases under the comparative journal entry shown in Figure 4-50.

FIGURE 4-49

Inventory	
Jan. 1 1 000 items @ a cost of $75 each = $75 000	

FIGURE 4-50

Periodic Inventory Method	Perpetual Inventory Method	Debit	Credit

Dr. Purchases
  Cr. Accounts Payable
To record the purchases of merchandise on credit for the year.
	Dr. Inventory
	  Cr. Accounts Payable
		1 500 000	1 500 000

Analysis   Under the perpetual inventory method, the debit is made to the current asset account, Inventory. However, under the periodic inventory method, the debit is made to the expense account called Purchases. As stated earlier, all purchases of goods for resale are expensed immediately as part of the computation for cost of goods sold.

Transaction 3   Notice in Figure 4-51 the difference in accounting when some goods purchased on credit earlier are returned to the supplier.

FIGURE 4-51

Periodic Inventory Method	Perpetual Inventory Method	Debit	Credit

Dr. Accounts Payable
  Cr. Pur. Ret. & Allow.
To record the return of 500 items costing $75 each.
	Dr. Accounts Payable
	  Cr. Inventory
		37 500	37 500

Analysis   Under both methods, the debit is to Accounts Payable, since this current liability account has to be decreased by the amount of the return. Under the perpetual inventory method, however, the current asset Inventory is credited, since goods costing $37 500 have been returned. Under the periodic inventory method, the credit is made to the contra account Purchases Returns and Allowances.

Transaction 4   The accounting of cheques issued to suppliers in payment of purchases invoices is identical under both inventory methods as shown in Figure 4-52.

FIGURE 4-52

Periodic Inventory Method	Perpetual Inventory Method	Debit	Credit

Dr. Accounts Payable
  Cr. Cash
To record the issuance of cheques on account.
	Dr. Accounts Payable
	  Cr. Cash
		1 390 000	1 390 000

Transaction 5 As Figure 4-53 shows, the accounting of revenue earned from the sale of goods on credit is essentially identical under both inventory methods. However, note the second entry, here labelled 5(b), that is required under the perpetual inventory method.

FIGURE 4-53

Periodic Inventory Method	Perpetual Inventory Method	Debit	Credit
5(a) Dr. Accounts Receivable Cr. Sales To record sales on credit for the year.	Dr. Accounts Receivable Cr. Sales	3 700 000	3 700 000
5(b) — —	Dr. Cost of Goods Sold Cr. Inventory To record the cost of goods sold for the year.	1 387 500	1 387 500

Analysis Under both methods, the entry to record revenue earned from the sale of goods on credit is identical. However, a second entry, a costing entry, is required under the perpetual inventory method. Since 18 500 items were sold, and since the cost of these items is $75 each, a debit is made to an expense account called Cost of Goods Sold. Of course, the credit is made to Inventory to record the decrease of 18 500 inventory items.

Under the periodic method, no such costing entry is made. As stated earlier, the cost of goods sold is calculated at the end of the accounting period. Also, no updating of the Inventory account is made until the end of the accounting period when closing entries are recorded.

Transaction 6 Notice that the analysis to record the issuance of credit memos to customers who have returned some goods previously sold to them on credit requires a second entry under the perpetual inventory method as shown in Figure 4-54.

FIGURE 4-54

Periodic Inventory Method	Perpetual Inventory Method	Debit	Credit
6(a) Dr. Sales Ret. & Allow. Cr. Accounts Receivable To record credit memos issued for the return of sold merchandise on credit.	Dr. Sales Ret. & Allow. Cr. Accounts Receivable	40 000	40 000
6(b) — —	Dr. Inventory Cr. Cost of Goods Sold To return to stock goods returned by credit customers.	15 000	15 000

Analysis Under both methods, the first entry is identical, since it records the decrease of sales revenue resulting from issuing credit memos to credit customers. A second entry is required under the perpetual inventory method to record the return of stock items to the Inventory account. Of course, a credit must be made to Cost of Goods Sold for the cost of the goods returned (200 items × $75 each).

Transaction 7 This transaction involving a price reduction (sales allowance) is tricky for the perpetual inventory method. Study the comparative entries that are presented in Figure 4-55.

FIGURE 4-55

Periodic Inventory Method	Perpetual Inventory Method	Debit	Credit
Dr. Sales Ret. & Allow.	Dr. Sales Ret. & Allow.	5 000	
Cr. Accounts Receivable	Cr. Accounts Receivable		5 000
To record the allowance granted to customers on earlier credit sales.			

Analysis The entry to record the sales allowance is identical under both inventory methods. Note that no costing entry is required because no goods were returned. Compare this entry with an actual return of goods in Transaction 6.

Transaction 8 This transaction involving a price reduction (sales allowance) is tricky for the perpetual inventory method. Study the comparative entries that are presented in Figure 4-56.

FIGURE 4-56

Periodic Inventory Method	Perpetual Inventory Method	Debit	Credit
Dr. Cash	Dr. Cash	2 100 000	
Dr. Sales Discounts	Dr. Sales Discounts	55 000	
Cr. Accounts Receivable	Cr. Accounts Receivable		2 155 000
To record the allowance granted to customers on earlier credit sales.			

Analysis Both inventory methods will record the identical double entry. Cash is debited for the amount of cheques received; Sales Discounts is debited to support the theory that sales revenue will be decreased by the amount of cash discounts offered; and Accounts Receivable is credited for the total decrease to customer accounts.

Transaction 9 This transaction is for information only at this time. At this stage, it is useful to compare the general ledger accounts affected by all transactions. Study carefully the T-account general ledger as illustrated in Figure 4-57. All postings are supported by transaction numbers. Balances in T-accounts are shown where more than one entry is posted.

FIGURE 4-57

General Ledger Under Periodic Inventory Method

Inventory		
(1)	75 000	

Purchases		
(2)	1 500 000	

Accounts Payable			
(3)	37 500	(2)	1 500 000
(4)	1 390 000		
		Bal.	72 500

Pur. Ret. & Allow.		
	(2)	37 500

Cash			
(8)	2 100 000	(4)	1 390 000
Bal.	710 000		

Accounts Receivable			
(5)	3 700 000	(6)	40 000
		(7)	5 000
		(8)	2 155 000
Bal.	1 500 000		

Sales		
	(5)	3 700 000

Sales Ret. & Allow.		
(6)	40 000	
(7)	5 000	
Bal.	45 000	

Sales Discounts		
(8)	55 000	

FIGURE 4-58

General Ledger Under Perpetual Inventory Method

Inventory			
(1)	75 000	(3)	37 500
(2)	1 500 000		
(6)	15 000		
Bal.	165 000		

Accounts Payable			
(3)	37 500	(2)	1 500 000
(4)	1 390 000		
		Bal.	72 500

Cash			
(8)	2 100 000	(4)	1 390 000
Bal.	710 000		

Sales		
	(5)	3 700 000

Cost of Goods Sold			
(5)	1 387 500	(6)	15 000
Bal.	372 500		

Accounts Receivable			
(5)	3 700 000	(6)	40 000
		(7)	5 000
		(8)	2 155 000
Bal.	1 500 000		

Sales Ret. & Allow.		
(6)	40 000	
(7)	5 000	
Bal.	45 000	

Sales Discounts		
(8)	55 000	

Analysis These comparative points are important:
- The following G/L accounts are identical under both inventory methods: Cash; Accounts Receivable; Accounts Payable; Sales; Sales Returns and Allowances; and Sales Discounts.
- Under the periodic inventory method, the Inventory account shows only the balance at the beginning of the accounting period. However, under the perpetual inventory method, the Inventory account shows not only the balance at the beginning of the accounting period, but

also all changes made during the accounting period and the end-of-period balance.
- Under the perpetual inventory method, the G/L shows an account called Cost of Goods Sold. Obviously, the balance of this account must be the actual cost of the goods sold during the accounting period. No such account exists under the periodic inventory method. As you learned earlier, the Cost of Goods Sold must be computed at the end of the accounting period by using the balances in these G/L accounts: Beginning Inventory, Purchases, and Purchases Returns and Allowances. Had there been accounts for Transportation-in and Purchases Discounts, the balances of these accounts would also be part of the computation for the Cost of Goods Sold. Of course, the ending inventory, determined by actual physical count, must also be considered in this calculation.
- Under the perpetual inventory method, the balance in the Inventory account at the end of the accounting period represents the amount of inventory on hand according to the entries made in the "books" of account. As you can see, this balance is $165 000. However, Transaction 9 states that an actual physical count of goods on hand after store hours on December 31 showed that 1 500 items were in stock at a unit cost of $75 each or $112 500. This means a difference of $165 000 – $112 500 = $52 500. Obviously, this difference represents a loss of inventory, caused probably by actual fraud or outright theft during the accounting period. Under the perpetual inventory method, such an inventory loss would be accounted for by the double entry shown in Figure 4-59.

FIGURE 4-59

Periodic Inventory Method	Perpetual Inventory Method	Debit	Credit
Dr. (No entry)	Dr. Inventory Loss Expense	52 500	
Cr. (No entry)	Cr. Inventory		52 500
To record the loss of inventory after a physical count was made: $165 000 – $112 500.			

Analysis This final double entry recognizes the actual loss of inventory when the balance of the Inventory account is compared with an actual physical count at the end of the accounting period. No such entry is made under the periodic inventory method, because the Inventory account shows only the beginning balance of inventory.

It is now useful to compare partial income statements under both inventory methods. Study Figures 4-60 and 4-61.

Concluding Analysis These final points will bring out a few of the important advantages and limitations of each inventory method.

FIGURE 4-60

Winnipeg Wholesale Trading Company
Partial Income Statement (Periodic Inventory Method)
For the Year Ended December 31, 19—

Revenue from Sales:			
Sales		$3 700 000	
Less:			
Sales Returns and Allowances	$45 000		
Sales Discounts	55 000	100 000	
Net Sales			$3 600 000
Cost of Goods Sold:			
Inventory, January 1		$ 75 000	
Purchases	$1 500 000		
Less: Purchases Returns and Allowances	37 5000		
Net Purchases		1 462 500	
Cost of Goods Available for Sale		1 537 500	
Less: Inventory, December 31		112 500	
Cost of Goods Sold			1 425 000
Gross Profit from Sales			2 175 000
Less: Other Expenses (nil)			000
Net Income			$2 175 000

FIGURE 4-61

Winnipeg Wholesale Trading Company
Partial Income Statement (Perpetual Inventory Method)
For the Year Ended December 31, 19—

Revenue from Sales:			
Sales		$3 700 000	
Less:			
Sales Returns and Allowances	$45 000		
Sales Discounts	55 000	100 000	
Net Sales			$3 600 000
Cost of Goods Sold			1 372 500
Gross Profit from Sales			2 227 500
Other Expenses:			
Less: Inventory Loss Expense			52 500
Net Income			$2 175 000

- Only under the perpetual inventory method will inventory losses during the accounting period be disclosed. Therefore, the perpetual method offers management a measure of control over inventory. Once an inventory shortage is discovered, management can take the

necessary steps to safeguard the actual physical state of one of its most valuable assets.
- Under the periodic inventory method such inventory losses are not disclosed, because the Inventory account is not updated during the accounting period. Instead, any losses are absorbed under the calculation for the Cost of Goods Sold as seen in the partial income statement.
- The outstanding feature of the periodic inventory method is that it is inexpensive to maintain. Therefore, it is most appropriate for low-cost items for which continual control of the inventory is not required. Obviously, the loss of a few of these low-unit-cost items would not offset the extra costs of maintaining records required under the perpetual method.
- The outstanding feature of the perpetual inventory method is *inventory control*. Obviously, management tends to support the extra accounting in the expectation that worthwhile savings will result from keeping inventory losses of high-unit-cost items to a minimum.

TOPIC 2   Problems

Analyzing basic revenue transactions in general journal form for a wholesale merchandising firm in a province without a retail sales tax.

4.14 Record the transactions below on behalf of Alberta Wholesale Hardware in "general journal" form. Show a brief explanation for each entry. *Note:* Charge all customer sales to the general ledger account Accounts Receivable. Show in parentheses the name of the credit customer.

Oct. 5 The cash sales at the end of the day totalled $400.
7 Sold merchandise on credit to Calgary Hardware; terms 2/10, n/30; invoice amount, $1 000.
8 Sold merchandise for cash, $100.
8 Granted a $20 cash refund to a customer who was sold goods for cash and who returned $20 of damaged merchandise.
15 Received a cheque from Calgary Hardware for the sale of October 7, less the sales discount.
19 Sold merchandise on credit to Edmonton Supply Co.; terms 1/15, n/60. Invoice amount, $850.
20 Granted Edmonton Supply Co. an allowance of $50 on slightly marked goods sold on October 19.
30 Received a cheque from Edmonton Supply Co. for the amount owing on the invoice of October 19, less the allowance and less the sales discount.

Analyzing basic revenue transactions in general journal form for a retail merchandising firm in a province with a retail sales tax.

4.15 Helen Bugno Flowers is located in a province that has an 8% sales tax on retail sales. During May the store accounted for the following business transactions that affected sales revenue. Record these transactions in general journal form, showing a brief explanation for each entry. Use the general ledger account Accounts Receivable for all transactions affecting credit customer accounts. Show in parentheses the name of the individual credit customer.

May 1 Sold goods on Invoice 330 to C. Barzo; terms n/30; sale amount, $100; PST, 8%.

6 Cash sales for the week totalled $2 000. The PST was added and collected over and above the $2 000.

7 Sold goods on Invoice 331 to A. Chan; terms n/30; sale amount, $78; PST, 8%.

12 Sold goods on Invoice 332 to D. Gander; terms n/30; sale amount, $60; PST, 8%.

13 Issued a credit memo to D. Gander as an adjustment for $21.60 given on the return of goods sold for $20 on Invoice 332.

13 Cash sales for the week totalled $2 500. The PST was added and collected over and above the $2 500.

15 Sold goods on Invoice 333 to A. Hart; terms n/30; sale amount, $75; PST, 8%.

18 Sold merchandise on Invoice 334 to M. Herr; terms n/30; sale amount, $115; PST, 8%.

19 Issued a credit memo to M. Herr as an adjustment of $32.40, granted on return of goods sold for $30 on Invoice 334.

20 Cash sales for the week totalled $2 200. The PST was added and collected over and above the $2 200.

25 Received a cheque from C. Barzo in full payment of Invoice 330 plus the PST payable.

25 Sold merchandise to B. Howison on Invoice 335; terms n/30; sale amount, $130; PST, 8%.

27 Cash sales for the week totalled $1 600. The PST was added and collected over and above the $1 600.

29 Received a cheque for $84.24 from A. Chan in full payment of Invoice 331 plus the amount owing for PST.

31 Received a cheque from D. Gander in full settlement of Invoice 332, less the adjustment on May 13, plus the amount owing for PST.

Analyzing basic transactions affecting the cost of goods sold in general journal form for a retail merchandising firm in a province without a retail sales tax; posting the transactions to a T-account general ledger; calculating the cost of goods sold for one month; repeating the work required assuming that the perpetual inventory method is used.

4.16 Assume that the transactions below are representative of some of the financial events for a retail merchandising firm operating under a periodic inventory method and in a province where no retail sales tax exists.

Nov. 1 The cost in the Inventory account showed a debit balance of $8 000. (No double entry required; merely show the Inventory account with the debit balance.)

3 Purchased merchandise for cash, $500.

5 Purchased merchandise on credit from Regina Supply Co.; terms 2/10, n/30; invoice amount, $1 000.

5 Paid Saskatchewan Truck Line $40 for freight charges on the foregoing shipment of merchandise.

10 Purchased merchandise on credit from Medicine Hat Mfg. Co. on terms of 1/15, n/60; invoice amount, $1 500.

12 Returned $100 of unacceptable goods received in the shipment from Medicine Hat Mfg. Co.

15 Issued cheque to Regina Supply Co. for goods purchased on November 5, less the purchase discount.
20 Purchased merchandise for cash, $2 000.
21 Received a cash refund of $500 for unsatisfactory goods returned on the cash purchase of November 20.
25 Issued cheque to Medicine Hat Mfg. Co. for the amount owing on the goods purchased on November 10, less the return and less the purchase discount.
30 Purchased merchandise on credit from Red Deer Supply Co. on terms of 2/10, n/30; invoice amount, $600.

Required

a Analyze the transactions in "general journal" form. Show a brief explanation for each entry. Use the general ledger account Accounts Payable for all transactions affecting individual accounts payable.

b Post the transactions to a T-account general ledger. Use names of accounts that have been illustrated in this chapter.

c Suppose that at the end of November a physical stocktaking disclosed that the cost of unsold goods amounted to $6 000. From the information of the problem and the T-account general ledger, show a statement calculating the cost of goods sold for the month of November.

d Repeat a, b, and c above, assuming now that the business enterprise uses the perpetual inventory method.

Analyzing basic transactions affecting the cost of goods sold in general journal form for a retail merchandising firm in a province with a retail sales tax; posting the transactions to a T-account general ledger; calculating the gross profit from sales for one month; repeating the work required, assuming that the perpetual inventory method is used.

4.17 The Peterborough Lumber Company uses the periodic inventory method of accounting. Listed below are the transactions for the month of July that affect the firm's calculation of the gross profit from sales. Note that a provincial sales tax of 8% must be collected by this retailer on all sales.

July 1 Cost of inventory on hand at the beginning of the month, $6 500. (No double entry is required; merely show the Inventory account with the debit balance.)
3 Purchased merchandise on account from Vancouver Supply Company; terms 2/10, n/30, $3 000.
3 Paid C. P. Express $200 cash for freight charges on the foregoing shipment.
5 Cash sales of merchandise totalled $4 000. The PST was added and collected.
7 Sold merchandise on credit to George Construction Company; terms 2/10, n/30; invoice amount, $4 000.
9 Cash sales of merchandise totalled $6 320. The PST was added and collected.
9 Issued a cash refund of $108 to a customer who returned unsatisfactory goods sold for cash today. (Original sale was for $100 plus the PST.)
12 Issued a cheque to Vancouver Supply Company for goods purchased on July 3, less the purchase discount.
14 Purchased merchandise on credit from Northern Lumber Company; terms 1/15, n/60, $6 000.

15 Paid freight bill on good received from Northern Lumber Company, $60.
15 Returned defective goods which cost $300 to Northern Lumber Company.
17 Received a cheque for $4 240 from George Construction Company, in payment of the sale of July 7, less the sales discount, plus the amount owing on PST.
19 Sold goods on account to Elmdale Construction Co.; terms net 30 days, $2 200 plus 8% PST.
20 Granted an allowance of $108 to Elmdale Construction Co. for slightly marked goods sold on July 19. (The original price of the goods was $100 plus the 8% PST.)
25 Cash sales of merchandise totalled $6 000, plus the 8% PST.
29 Issued a cheque to Northern Lumber Company for the purchase of goods on July 14, less the return and less the purchase discount.
30 Purchased merchandise for cash, $200.
31 Received a cheque for $600 from Elmdale Construction Co. in part payment of their account.

Required

a In "general journal" form, prepare a separate entry for each of the above transactions. Include a brief explanation for each. Use only the general accounts Accounts Receivable and Accounts Payable for all transactions affecting customer and creditor accounts.

b Post the transactions to a T-account general ledger. Use names of accounts that have been illustrated in this chapter.

c Assume that a physical inventory was taken at the end of business on July 31, and that the cost of unsold goods amounted to $5 400. From the information contained in the problem, prepare a partial income statement for the month ended July 31.

d Repeat a, b, and c above, assuming that the Peterborough Lumber Company now uses the perpetual inventory method.

Recording merchandising transactions for one month for a retail hardware store; posting the double entries to a T-account general ledger; preparing a month-end trial balance; preparing an income statement and a related balance sheet; repeating the work assuming that the perpetual inventory method is used.

4.18 Pat Kwiatkowski operates a retail hardware store that uses the periodic inventory method to calculate the cost of goods sold. Listed below are the firm's financial transactions for May. (Assume that Kwiatkowski's Hardware operates in a province where a 7% provincial sales tax exists.)

May 1 Pat Kwiatkowski commenced business with the following assets and liabilities: Cash, $10 000; Inventory, $6 000; Furniture and Fixtures, $7 000; Bank Loan (demand), $4 000; and Accounts Payable, $2 000.
2 Paid rent on building for May, $1 200.
3 Purchased merchandise on credit from Hobbs Wholesale Hardware Co.; terms 2/10, n/30. Invoice amount, $1 000.
4 Issued cheque for $1 000 to Winnipeg Supply Ltd., on account.
5 Sold merchandise on credit to E. Johnson; terms net 30 days. Invoice amount, $500 plus PST at 7%.
6 Cash sales for the week totalled $3 800, exclusive of the amount to be computed for the PST.
9 Purchased a small truck from Brandon Motors; terms n/60. Invoice amount, $12 000.

10 Sold merchandise on credit to S. Le Maitre; terms net 30 days. Invoice amount, $500 plus 7% PST.
10 Granted S. Le Maitre an allowance of $42.80 for slightly marked goods sold today for $40.
11 Cash sales for the week, exclusive of the amount for PST, totalled $3 000.
12 Received a shipment of goods costing $4 000 from American Hardware Distributors; terms 1/15, n/60.
12 Paid freight and duty totalling $200 for shipment received from American Hardware Distributors.
13 Issued cheque to Hobbs Wholesale Hardware for merchandise purchased on May 3, less the purchase discount.
14 Pat Kwiatkowski invested additional cash, $3 000.
15 Acquired an office electronic typewriter for cash. Invoice amount was $1 600.
17 Cash sales for the week, exclusive of the amount required for the PST, totalled $3 500.
18 Received a cheque from E. Johnson for $535 in full payment of sale made on May 5.
19 Issued a cheque for $78 in payment of monthly telephone bill.
21 Received a shipment of goods costing $1 000 from Regina Wholesale Hardware Canada Ltd.; terms 2/10, n/30.
21 Paid freight on goods received from Regina Wholesale Hardware, $60.
22 Received advertising bill for $175 from City Press; terms net 30 days.
26 Cash sales for the week, exclusive of PST, totalled $3 800.
27 Issued cheque to American Hardware Distributors for purchase of May 12, less the purchase discount.
28 Received a cheque for $100 from S. Le Maitre, on account.
29 Paid for gas and oil for truck, $60 (use Delivery Expense).
30 Pat Kwiatkowski withdrew $500 cash for personal use.
30 Cash sales for the week, exclusive of the PST, totalled $1 300.
31 Pat Kwiatkowski withdrew goods costing $100 for personal use. *Hint*: Do not credit the Inventory account for the withdrawal of merchandise. Instead, use the account in which the original cost of purchasing the goods was debited.
31 Issued the following cheques: to the bank for $100 in part payment of the bank loan; to Brandon Motors for $1 000 on account; to Regina Wholesale Hardware for merchandise purchased on May 21, less the purchase discount; and to Winnipeg Supply Ltd. for $500 on account.

Required

a Record the transactions above in general journal form. Show a brief explanation for each transaction.
b Post the transactions to a T-account general ledger. Use names of accounts that have been illustrated in this chapter.
c Prepare a trial balance of the ledger at the end of May.
d A physical stocktaking on May 31 showed a cost of unsold goods at $2 150. Prepare an income statement for the month of May and a related balance sheet in report form as at May 31.

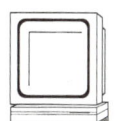

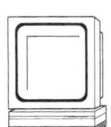

e Repeat the work in **a**, **b**, and **c** above, assuming now that Kwiatkowski's Hardware uses the perpetual inventory method.

4.19 Return to the solution prepared for Kwiatkowski's Hardware in Problem 4.18. Use an electronic spreadsheet package to show the income statement with an added percentage column. Show percentages to net sales for the cost of goods sold, gross profit from sales, the individual operating expenses, the total operating expenses, and the "bottom line."

4.20 Refer to the solutions prepared for Kwiatkowski's Hardware in Problems 4.18 and 4.19. Assume that the owner-manager has requested a projection of the gross margin on sales using the following criteria:
- The initial net sales begins with the amount solved for May. Round off any cents to the nearest dollar.
- The cost of goods sold begins with the amount solved for May. Round off any cents to the nearest dollar.
- The gross profit from sales begins with the amount solved for May. Round off any cents to the nearest dollar.

Required

a Develop a spreadsheet projecting the figures for sales, the cost of goods sold, and the gross profit from sales for the remaining seven months (June through December); that is, assume that subsequent net sales figures are to increase by 10% each month. Use the same format as followed for Problem 4.12.

b After completing the spreadsheet, ask what if the individual operating expenses were increased by 20% in each month beginning with June? Save your spreadsheet under an appropriate file name. Print a hard copy of this solution.

Chapter Summary

The financial statements of merchandising firms are similar to those prepared for service firms except for these changes: on the balance sheet, merchandising firms would report a new current asset called Merchandise Inventory at cost, or simply Inventory at cost (the cost of goods available for sale); on the income statement, merchandising firms would report a major expense called Cost of Goods Sold. This major expense would be matched against the sales revenue to report a partial income called the Gross Profit from Sales or Gross Margin from Sales. From this gross margin on sales would be deducted the operating expenses to report the final income, called the Net Income (or Net Loss).

Two types of inventory systems exist in accounting practice. One is called the perpetual inventory system, because the Inventory account is updated each time a change is made to inventory (such as through a purchase or a sale). In addition, the

FIGURE 4-62

```
           Any Merchandising Firm
            Partial Balance Sheet
                  As at —

Current assets:
    Inventory, at cost..........    $xxxxxx
```

FIGURE 4-63

```
           Any Merchandising Firm
            Partial Balance Sheet
               For Year Ended —

Sales revenue.................   $xxxxxx
Less: Cost of goods sold ........    xxxxxx
Gross profit from sales ..........    xxxxxx
Less: Total operating
       expenses ................    xxxxx
Net income (loss)..............   $ xxxxx
```

perpetual inventory system records the cost of goods sold each time a sale is made. Therefore, separate accounts exist for Inventory and Cost of Goods Sold. The perpetual inventory system is popular among firms that handle high-unit-cost items and employ computer systems to do their accounting.

On the other hand, many small businesses which handle low-unit-cost items use the periodic inventory system. Here, the Inventory account is updated only at the end of the accounting period. In addition, the expense of the cost of goods sold is calculated only at the end of the accounting period. Although an Inventory account does exist, no account for Cost of Goods Sold exists as such. Instead, separate accounts are kept to permit the accounting clerk to calculate the cost of goods sold at the end of the accounting period.

Calculating the cost of goods sold under the periodic inventory method begins with the beginning balance of the Inventory account. To this beginning balance is added the cost of all merchandise purchased during the period to give the cost of all goods available for sale for that accounting period. Thus, if the beginning Inventory balance were $10 000 and the balance in the Purchases account were $60 000, the cost of goods available for sale would be reported as $70 000. Obviously, if no inventory exists at the end of the accounting period, this $70 000 would be the cost of the goods sold. However, if a physical count showed $20 000 of current inventory, the actual cost of goods sold would be $70 000 minus the $20 000 or $50 000. In turn, the cost of goods sold would be matched against the sales revenue to report the gross profit from sales.

Intermediate computations of both the sales revenue and cost of goods sold are usually required. For example, both sales returns and allowances and sales discounts will decrease the gross revenue from sales to report the net sales revenue. Similarly, the cost of purchases will be increased by costs of transportation-in (freight-in) and any duty-in. The cost of purchases plus transportation-in will report the cost of delivered goods. Any purchase returns and allowances and purchases discounts would be deducted from the cost of delivered goods to report the net purchase cost during the accounting period. The net purchase cost would be added to the cost of the beginning inventory to report the cost of goods available for sale.

Managers of merchandising firms often request accountants to add information to their firm's financial statements. One common request is to add a percentage column

FIGURE 4-64

Beginning Inventory
plus
Purchases
equals
Cost of Goods Available for Sale
less
Ending Inventory
equals
Cost of Goods Sold

FIGURE 4-65

Gross Sales
less
Sales Returns and Allowances
less
Sales Discounts
equals
Net Sales

FIGURE 4-66

Gross Purchases
plus
Freight-in
equals
Cost of Delivered Goods
less
Purchases Returns and Allowances
less
Purchases Discounts
equals
Net Purchases

to a prepared income statement. By adding a percentage column, managers can relate key components to the reported net sales to obtain key ratios. Common key ratios on the income statement are the cost of goods sold ratio (dividing the cost of goods sold by net sales), the gross margin ratio (dividing the gross profit from sales by net sales), the operating expense ratio (total operating expenses divided by net sales), and the net income (loss) ratio (net income or loss divided by net sales).

Another common managerial request is to ask accounting clerks to prepare a forecast of what happens if the gross profit from sales is projected for several months after reporting the historical figures for one month. This projected spreadsheet could then be changed by applying several "what if" situations. For example: What if sales for the next six months were increased by 10%? What if the cost of goods sold were increased by 5%? And so on. In modern accounting practice, such a spreadsheet would be done on a microcomputer using appropriate electronic spreadsheet software.

The accounting of transactions affecting sales revenue is relatively straightforward. For example, a sale of goods for $1 000 would be analyzed as a debit to Cash or Accounts Receivable for $1 000 and a credit to Sales for $1 000. Sales is credited to recognize the fact that revenue increases OE in the accounting equation.

Sales is a revenue account.

A complication does occur when a retailer makes a sale in a province that imposes a provincial retail sales tax. For example, if the same sale of $1 000 were made in Nova Scotia, where a 10% retail sales tax exists, the debit for Cash or Accounts Receivable would be increased by $100 (10% of $1 000) and an additional credit entry would be made to PST Payable for $100.

PST Payable is a current liability account.

Sales Returns and Allowances is a contra account to sales revenue (a decreasing revenue account).

Sales Discounts is a contra account to sales revenue (a decreasing revenue account).

Further complications arise when contra transactions are made to sales revenue. For example, sales returns and allowances have the effect of decreasing sales revenue. Therefore, such amounts would be debited to a contra revenue account called Sales Returns and Allowances. Similarly, any cash discounts offered and taken by customers would decrease sales revenue. Therefore, cash discounts would be debited to a contra revenue account called Sales Discounts. It is important to remove that portion of PST Payable on sales returns and allowances. However, no cash discount is applied to any portion of the remaining PST. Sales discounts are normally offered in transactions between wholesalers and retailers.

In accounting for the cost of goods sold under the periodic inventory system, a current asset called Inventory would show on the cost of the inventory at the beginning

Beginning Inventory account balance at the end of the accounting period is an expense (part of the cost of goods sold) under the periodic inventory method.

The cost of the ending inventory becomes the current asset to be reported as inventory at cost on the balance sheet.

The Purchases account is an expense (as part of the calculated cost of goods sold at the end of the accounting period).

Transportation-in is an expense account (part of the cost of goods sold at the end of the accounting period).

Purchases Returns and Allowances is contra to Purchases (a decreasing expense account).

Purchases Discounts is contra to Purchases (a decreasing expense account).

of the accounting period. In accounting theory, this beginning inventory is deemed to have been sold under the periodic inventory method. Therefore, it is treated as part of the calculated cost of goods sold at the end of the accounting period. No accounting entries are made to the Inventory account during the accounting period. Instead, the Inventory account is updated at the end of the accounting period to receive the cost of the ending inventory. The entries to close out the old inventory and to receive the new ending inventory are made as part of closing the books. (Closing the books for merchandising firms will be covered in the next chapter.)

All purchases of merchandise (goods) during the accounting period are debited to a Purchases account. Under the periodic inventory method, the Purchases account is treated as an expense, because its balance is part of the expense called Cost of Goods Sold on the income statement. Since all expenses decrease OE in the accounting equation, always debit Purchases for the costs of buying goods during the accounting period.

All transportation-in (freight-in) costs are debited to Transportation-in or Freight-in or Transportation and Duty-in if goods are imported and subject to excise duties to cross the border. Since the balance of this account is added to Purchases on the income statement, Transportation-in must be classified as an expense (as part of the reported Cost of Goods Sold on the income statement).

All purchases returns and allowances, and all purchases discounts taken by the buyer, are contra to the cost of delivered goods on the income statement. Therefore, credit all such amounts to these accounts to reflect the theory that the original purchase costs have been decreased by purchases returns and allowances and cash discounts taken.

At the end of the accounting period, separate accounts for Inventory (showing only the beginning inventory amount), Purchases, Transportation-in, Purchases Returns and Allowances, and Purchases Discounts would show balances that would be used to calculate and report the cost of goods sold for the period. Of course, this expense would be matched against the net sales revenue to report the gross profit from sales. From this partial income would be deducted the total operating expenses to report the final income or net loss for the accounting period.

Under perpetual inventory accounting, the Inventory account is updated each time a change occurs in inventory during the accounting period. Therefore, all purchases and any transportation-in costs are debited to the current asset, Inventory. Two entries are required when a sale is made. The first entry recognizes the revenue earned from the sale. A second entry — a costing entry — is made by debiting the expense account called Cost of Goods Sold and crediting the current asset Inventory for the *cost* of the goods sold. A physical inventory is taken at the end of the accounting period so that the balance of the Inventory account can be checked against the actual physical count. Any discrepancy will be accounted for as an Inventory Loss Expense and an offsetting credit to Inventory. The main advantage of perpetual inventory accounting is its system of controlling high-unit-cost inventory items.

Chapter Questions

1. Distinguish briefly between a wholesaler and a retailer.
2. How does any merchandising firm earn its main source of revenue?
3. Summarize the two important steps required to calculate the net income of a merchandising firm.
4. What is the basic difference in determining the net income between a service firm and a merchandising firm?
5. Distinguish between a merchandising firm's use of the perpetual inventory method and its use of the periodic inventory method of determining the cost of goods sold. What is the main advantage claimed under each method?
6. Name the three important factors that are required to calculate the cost of goods sold for a firm which uses the periodic inventory method.
7. Distinguish between a sales return and a sales allowance.
8. Explain the following credit terms: (a) 2/10, n/30; (b) 1/15, n/60; (c) n/30.
9. Distinguish between the gross sales and the net sales of a merchandising firm.
10. What is the difference between transportation-in and transportation-out in accounting for the net income of a merchandising firm?
11. What calculations are required to calculate the net purchase cost of a merchandising firm which follows the periodic inventory method?
12. Distinguish between the cost of goods available for sale and the cost of goods sold.
13. What type of account is Sales Returns and Allowances? On what side of this account would a normal entry be recorded? Explain your answer.
14. Are sales discounts recorded as debits or credits? Explain your answer.
15. An accounts receivable account shows the following data: credit sale of $428 ($400 sales price plus $28 for PST) with terms of 1/10, n/30; sales return of $16.05 ($15 for the sales return plus $1.05 for the PST). For what amount should the customer send a cheque if the sales discount were taken? Show your complete calculation. Explain your answer.
16. Refer to the accounting equation to explain the concept that cost of goods sold is an accounting expense of any merchandising business.
17. Does an accounting system that follows the periodic inventory method use an expense account called Cost of Goods Sold? Explain why not.
18. How should the account Transportation-in be classified? Explain your answer.
19. Inventory at the beginning of an accounting period shows 1 000 items costing $100 each. During the accounting period, an additional 2 000 items costing $100 each were purchased on credit. Also during the accounting period, 2 250 items were sold on credit at triple their cost price. At the end of the accounting period, a physical stocktaking showed 740 items costing $100 in

stock. Compare periodic and perpetual inventory accounting by showing partial income statements under both methods. Explain any difference.

20. Which item on the income statement for merchandising firms is used as the basis for all computations of percentages? Why?

21. A retail microcomputer dealer purchases a line of microcomputers at a cost of $2 200 each. To compete, the dealer must achieve a markup of 115% on cost. At what price should this dealer sell the new line of microcomputers? Show your calculation.

22. During the current year, Woodrow Wholesale Company reported all sales of merchandise at prices in excess of cost. Will this business necessarily report a net income for the year? Explain why or why not.

Accounting Case Problems

CASE 4-1

Analyzing five entries made under the periodic inventory method.

An inexperienced accounting clerk made the following entries on behalf of the vacationing accountant. In each case, state whether the clerk made the correct entry and explain why or why not. Assume that the periodic method of inventory accounting is followed.

1. The Purchases account was debited for the purchase of a new truck.
2. Delivery Expense was debited and Cash was credited for a shipment of goods received via CN Express.
3. The Inventory account was debited for the purchase of goods.
4. The owner's Drawing account was debited and the Inventory account was credited for the personal withdrawal of merchandise by the owner.
5. The Sales account was debited for the return of merchandise earlier sold to a customer.

CASE 4-2

Calculating and explaining retail prices to support a 34% markup on cost.

As an accounting clerk employed in a clothing store, you have been asked to assist in the calculation of retail prices (selling prices) to fulfill management's request to have a 34% gross profit from the sales of all such goods purchased.

Assume that the following purchases were made: 100 blouses at $4.45 each, 100 at $4.15 each, and 200 at $3.95 each. Calculate the retail price of each blouse so that the goods will show a 34% gross profit from sales. In other words, at what one retail price should the blouses be sold in order to ensure a 34% markup on the entire lot? Explain how you arrived at your answer.

CHAPTER **5 Accounting Cycle for a Merchandising Firm**

After completing this chapter, you should be able to:
— Analyze and record business transactions for a merchandising firm in the general journal.
— Post the recorded transactions in the general ledger.
— Prepare the general ledger trial balance.
— Prepare a ten-column worksheet.
— Prepare the year-end financial statements.
— Record and post the adjusting entries.
— Record and post the year-end closing entries.
— Prepare the postclosing trial balance.
— Identify the essential characteristics of G/L packages for microcomputer accounting systems.
— Use your school's microcomputer and accompanying general ledger software or the Summation program to complete the accounting cycle of the merchandising firm illustrated in this chapter.
— Compare the accounting cycle processed under a manual method with a microcomputer general ledger package.
— Define the following key terms used in this chapter: general ledger application; Summation; credit memo; purchase order; FOB shipping point; FOB destination; purchase invoice; debit memo; adjustments; ten-column worksheet; prepaid expense; supplies on hand; prepaid insurance; current assets; normal operating cycle; marketable securities; bad debts expense; allowance for bad debts; aging accounts receivable; depreciation; straight-line method (of depreciation); accumulated depreciation; income from operations; other revenues; other expenses; multi-step income statement; single-step income statement; backup procedures; month-end close; year-end close.

The first three Topics in this chapter will examine an accounting cycle for a merchandising firm. To keep matters simple, only the general journal and general ledger will be used, and it will be used to record and classify accounting data for a merchandising firm which employs the periodic

146   PART 1: THE FRAMEWORK OF ACCOUNTING

General ledger application: the coverage of the accounting cycle when applied to a microcomputer.

inventory method of accounting. Comparisons with firms which support perpetual inventory accounting will also be made at appropriate stages. As indicated in earlier chapters, the treatment of special journals and secondary ledgers will be deferred until Part 2 of the text. Therefore, the coverage of the accounting cycle in this chapter with emphasis on the general journal and general ledger is ideally suited for the study of a ***general ledger application*** for the microcomputer in Topic 4.

TOPIC 1   Bookkeeping Aspects

As you will recall from Chapter 3, the initial steps of any accounting cycle deal with those aspects of accounting called bookkeeping. In treating the origination of data, journalizing, posting, and the trial balance, needless repetition of what has been introduced earlier will be avoided. Instead, emphasis will be placed on those bookkeeping aspects that are common to many merchandising firms.

The Need for a Chart of Accounts

Before any bookkeeping of transactions can begin, it is important to organize a chart of accounts to meet the needs of a particular merchandising firm. In practice, the creation of a well-organized chart of accounts is usually done by hiring a professional accountant. Without a properly organized chart of accounts, the correct journalizing and posting of transactions to the general ledger cannot be done. In the case of a manual accounting system, the chart may be organized using a three-digit number code as illustrated in Figure 5-1.

Analysis   These points should be emphasized when studying the chart of accounts for Scarborough Wholesale Hardware, a wholesale merchandising firm that buys large quantities of hardware goods from manufacturers and sells these goods in smaller quantities to retail hardware stores.

- Accounts have been organized around the order of accounts in the accounting equation: A = L + OE. The Owner's Equity has been subdivided into OE for Capital and Drawing, Revenue, and Expenses.
- Although a three-digit number plan has been adopted, in practice, accountants may recommend the use of four or more digits to suit the needs of a particular business.
- Account titles such as Purchases, Transportation-in, Purchases Returns and Allowances, and Purchases Discount suggest that Scarborough Wholesale Hardware prefers to use the periodic inventory system. In practice, the decision to use either the periodic or the perpetual inventory system is usually made by management in consultation with a professional accountant. Once the decision is made,

CHAPTER 5: Accounting Cycle for a Merchandising Firm

FIGURE 5-1

Scarborough Wholesale Hardware
Chart of Accounts

Assets
101 Cash in Royal Bank
103 Bank Term Deposit Receipts
104 Accounts Receivable
105 Allowance for Doubtful Accounts
106 Inventory
107 Supplies on Hand
108 Prepaid Insurance
110 Land
111 Building
112 Accumulated Depreciation
       — Building
113 Warehouse Equipment
114 Accumulated Depreciation
       — Warehouse Equipment
115 Office Equipment
115 Accumulated Depreciation
116   — Office Equipment
117 Delivery Trucks
118 Accumulated Depreciation
       — Delivery Trucks

Liabilities
201 Bank Loan Payable
202 Accounts Payable
203 Property Taxes Payable
220 Mortgage Payable

Owner's Equity
301 Tom Allan, Capital
302 Tom Allan, Drawing
399 Revenue and Expense Summary

Revenue from Sales
401 Sales
402 Sales Returns and Allowances
403 Sales Discount

Costs and Expenses
501 Purchases
502 Transportation-in
503 Purchases Returns and Allowances
504 Purchases Discount
510 Advertising Expense
511 Utilities Expense
512 Property Taxes Expense
513 Delivery Expense
514 Wages and Salaries Expense
515 Telephone Expense
516 Bad Debts Expense
517 Depreciation Expense — Building
518 Depreciation Expense — Warehouse Equipment
519 Depreciation Expense — Office Equipment
520 Depreciation Expense — Delivery Trucks

Other Revenues
601 Interest Earned

Other Expenses
701 Bank Interest Expense
702 Mortgage Interest Expense

however, the chart of accounts must support the system by including appropriate account titles and account number codes.
- If the chart were organized to support perpetual inventory accounting, accounts such as Purchases, Transportation-in, Purchases Returns and Allowances, and Purchases Discount would be replaced by one expense account called Cost of Goods Sold.
- Contra accounts such as Sales Returns and Allowances and Sales Discounts have been included and given account codes so that they can be properly related to their main account. As you will learn, contra accounts are common to any chart of accounts.

- No account for PST Payable has been included, because Scarborough Wholesale Hardware is not required to collect the provincial sales tax. Only retailers must be registered to collect the sales tax from sales to consumers. (As stated earlier, the new federal GST has also been excluded to allow for the study of this complex new sales tax in the Appendix section of this text.)
- A separate account category for "Other Revenues" has been included to avoid mixing the main source of revenue from sales. Similarly, a separate account category for "Other Expenses" has been identified to avoid mixing the accounts needed to compute the Cost of Goods Sold and Operating Expenses with other expenses like bank interest and mortgage interest.
- If a computerized system were supported, the chart would be enlarged so that the computer would recognize the nature of each account, the normal balance for that account, and where that account will be printed on designated financial statements and supporting schedules. The computerized chart of accounts is examined in Topic 4.

Step 1. Originating Transaction Data

In Chapter 3, the opening balance sheet, the invoice, the cheque record, and the remittance slip were identified as four examples of common source documents to support the idea that business transactions generally are captured through the creation of a variety of business forms. You will find reference to these documents in the general journal entries illustrated for Scarborough Wholesale Hardware in Figure 5-7. The additional examples given in Figures 5-3, 5-4, 5-5, and 5-6 may be found in the accounting practices of many merchandising firms as well as for other types of businesses.

THE CREDIT MEMO When unsatisfactory goods are returned to the seller, or when the seller agrees to grant an allowance from the invoice price because the merchandise received was in slightly marked condition, the seller prepares a source document called the "credit memorandum" or simply **credit memo**. (In some firms, the credit memo is called a "credit note" or "credit invoice.") Regardless of the name, this source document is prepared by the seller to notify the purchaser that his or her account is being reduced by a stated amount because of an allowance, return, or cancellation of the original invoice. At least one copy of the credit memo would be retained for the seller's accounting records.

The significance of the word "credit" in the document is easily understood from the accounting analysis of the seller's books. Since the effect of the transaction will reduce a customer's accounts receivable, the asset Accounts Receivable must be credited through the process of journalizing and posting the double entry. Of course, the offsetting debit will be recognized either to the contra revenue account called Sales Returns and

Credit memo: a statement granting a reduction in the invoice price for damaged or returned goods.

FIGURE 5-2

SCARBOROUGH WHOLESALE HARDWARE

330 Progress Avenue
Scarborough, Ontario M1P 2Z5

INVOICE NO. 101

SOLD TO: Eglinton Hardware Centre
1975 Eglinton Avenue East
Scarborough, Ontario M1L 2N1

INVOICE DATE: 19— 05 02
TERMS: 2/10, n/30

SHIP TO: Same

Purchase Order No. 645839	Date 19—05 01	Shipped Via Barr Transport	FOB Scarborough	No. of Packages 3

QUANTITY	STOCK NO.	DESCRIPTION	UNIT PRICE	AMOUNT
30 sets	53Y5197	Wrench Set	3.59	107.70
20 sets	53Y1883	Socket Wrench Set	6.49	129.80
30 only	53-R1755	Tool Boxes	14.89	446.70
10 only	58-4628	Heavily Insulated Pliers	2.10	21.00
10 only	57-4121	450 g Deluxe Claw Hammer	3.79	37.90
		TOTAL INVOICE PRICE		743.10

COPY 2 - ACCOUNTING

FIGURE 5-3

SCARBOROUGH WHOLESALE HARDWARE

330 Progress Avenue
Scarborough, Ontario M1P 2Z5

CREDIT MEMO
NO. **CM-01**

TO: Eglinton Hardware Centre
1975 Eglinton Avenue East
Scarborough, Ontario M1L 2N1

DATE: 19— 05 25

Your Order No. 645839	Our Invoice No. 101

We have credited your account as follows:

Return of eight No. 53Y5197 wrench sets received in damaged condition:

8 sets at $3.59 $28.72

Allowances for the invoice price of the damaged goods returned or to the Sales revenue account. Since Scarborough Wholesale Hardware's chart of accounts supports a contra account, the debit would be made to Sales Returns and Allowances. It should be clear that the credit memo has the opposite effect of the original (sales) invoice.

THE PURCHASE ORDER AND PURCHASE INVOICE To order merchandise for resale, many firms will use their own form called the ***purchase order***. In Figure 5-4, note that more than one copy of the purchase order is made out, with copy 1 being designated for the supplier. The remaining copies would be held for use with Scarborough Wholesale Hardware's system to control the activities of various departments which are involved in the ordering and receiving of the future shipment of merchandise.

Purchase order: a business document created by the buyer for the purpose of ordering goods from a supplier.

FIGURE 5-4

PURCHASE ORDER   PO-0078

SCARBOROUGH WHOLESALE HARDWARE
330 Progress Avenue
Scarborough, Ontario M1P 2Z5

Small Tools Limited
229 Kearney Street
Winnipeg, Manitoba R2M 4B5

Purchase order number must appear on all letters and packages

Date Issued 19— 05 03	Date Needed 19— 05 10	Terms 2/10, n/30
Via Inter-City Express Ltd.		FOB Winnipeg, Manitoba

QUANT. ORDERED	STOCK NO.	DESCRIPTION	UNIT PRICE
90 sets	53Y5197	Wrench Set	2.59
80 sets	53Y1883	Socket Wrench Set	4.25
50 only	53-R1650	Tool Boxes	8.75

SCARBOROUGH WHOLESALE HARDWARE

By _G. Morrison_
Purchasing Agent

Copy 1 — Supplier
Copy 2 — Requesting Department
Copy 3 — Purchasing Deparment
Copy 4 — Receiving Report: Inventory
Copy 5 — Receiving Report: Purchasing

CHAPTER 5: Accounting Cycle for a Merchandising Firm

In the illustrated purchase order form, note that the buyer has requested credit and shipping terms. Of course, the seller would have to agree to these terms. For the method of shipment, observe that the buyer requests that Inter-City Express Ltd. be used, and that the shipment be made "FOB Winnipeg" (an example of the **FOB shipping point** arrangement). In simple terms, this means that the seller is requested to deliver the merchandise "free on board" to the shipping point in Winnipeg, that is, to the office of Inter-City Express Ltd. in Winnipeg. The buyer, of course, must bear the transportation costs from that shipping point to Scarborough, the ultimate destination point. On the other hand, if the buyer had requested FOB Scarborough, Ontario (**FOB destination**), the transportation costs would be absorbed by the supplier. Of course, the seller would normally include these shipping costs in the price of the goods. In any case, no accounting entry is made of the purchase order until the supplier accepts the order and mails his or her invoice, as illustrated in Figure 5-5.

FOB shipping point: an arrangement whereby the buyer agrees to pay the shipping charges from the shipping point to his or her place of business.

FOB destination: an arrangement whereby the seller agrees to pay the carrier for all transport costs from the shipping point to the buyer's place of business.

FIGURE 5-5

Small Tools Limited
229 Kearney Sreet
Winnipeg, Manitoba R2M 4B5

Invoice No. **0387**

Sold To: Scarborough Wholesale Hardware
330 Progress Avenue
Scarborough, Ontario M1P 2Z5

Ship To: Same as above

Invoice Date: 19— 05 09
Terms: 2/10, n/30

Purchase Order No.	Date	Shipped Via	FOB	No. of Cartons
PO-0078	19— 05 03	Inter-City Express	Winnipeg	3

QUANTITY	STOCK NO.	DESCRIPTION	UNIT PRICE	AMOUNT
90 sets	53Y5197	Wrench Set	2.59	233.10
80 sets	53Y1883	Socket Wrench Set	4.25	340.00
50 only	53-R1650	Tool Boxes	8.75	437.50
		TOTAL INVOICE PRICE		1 010.60
		TOTAL PAYABLE		1 010.60

DATE 5/10/—
APPROVED
QUANTITIES RECEIVED   G Morrison
PRICES CHARGED   G Morrison
EXTENSIONS & TOTALS   S Davies
DATE PAID
CHEQUE NO.

Purchase invoice: a bill received for merchandise purchased on credit.

From Chapter 3, you will remember that the seller generally mails a sales invoice to the buyer of goods on credit just as soon as the merchandise is shipped. From the buyer's point of view, the document received becomes the **purchase invoice**. In many firms, this invoice will be checked against a copy of the *receiving report* (a completed copy of the purchase order when the shipment of the goods is received). This step is necessary before an accounting entry is made to record the dollar results of the purchase of merchandise on credit. As you will recall from Chapter 4, the account Purchases is debited and Accounts Payable is credited in the buyer's accounting records to record the dollar results of merchandise purchased on credit. If perpetual inventory accounting were used, the debit would be made to the Inventory account. Under the periodic method, the accounting entry for the purchase invoice received from Small Tools Limited is illustrated in the general journal shown in Figure 5-8.

THE DEBIT MEMO

Debit memo: a source document created by the buyer to notify the seller that the account payable has been decreased by the amount of the purchase return or the allowance requested.

Many merchandising firms do not wait for the seller's credit invoice to originate the transaction of returning damaged goods, asking for an allowance, or cancelling the original invoice of goods. Instead, these firms prepare their own source document, called "debit note," "debit memorandum," or simply **debit memo**. It is important to realize that this document is prepared by the purchaser in order to notify the seller that his or her account on the buyer's books has been reduced by a stated amount because of the return, allowance, or cancellation. As you are aware, the original purchase created a liability called Accounts Payable. To reduce this liability, a debit entry must be acknowledged; hence the significance of the word "debit" in the purchaser's source document.

FIGURE 5-6

SCARBOROUGH WHOLESALE HARDWARE

330 Progress Avenue
Scarborough, Ontario M1P 2Z5

DEBIT MEMO
NO. **DM-04**

TO: Small Tools Limited
229 Kearney Street
Winnipeg, Manitoba

DATE: 19— 05 26

WE DEBIT YOUR ACCOUNT AS FOLLOWS:

Return of merchandise. Ten only Tool Boxes No. 53-R1650 arrived badly damaged and are being returned via Inter-City Express Ltd.

10 @ $8.75 $87.50

References: Your Invoice No. 0387, dated 19— 05 09
Our Order No. PO-0078, dated 19— 05 03

G. Morrison
Purchasing Agent

Some merchandising firms may not create a debit memo; instead they may merely wait for the seller's credit memo. Where debit memos are used, however, they are treated as the source document which creates the business transaction for the purchase return or allowance. Any subsequent receipt of the seller's credit memo would merely be stapled to the debit memo for added reference.

There are other source documents which are common to specific types of businesses. Some of these will be introduced in other chapters. It is worth noting again, however, that source documents such as the invoice, debit and credit memos, the cheque record, and the remittance slip are essential for the organization of accounting transaction data. It is also important to emphasize that, in order for any document originating outside the business to be treated as a source for entry, it should carry a notation of approval by management or someone with specifically delegated authority as to receipt of goods, correctness of calculations, acceptance of the basis of adjustment, etc. In other words, accounting clerks do *not* approve source documents for data entry. It would be unfair as well as inefficient to leave this responsibility to bookkeepers. Of course, once the source documents are approved, the accounting clerks are required to analyze them correctly before the entries are made in the general journal and general ledger.

Step 2. Journalizing Transaction Data

From Chapter 3, you learned that the debits and credits resulting from the analysis of source documents are recorded in a chronological record called the journal. For this chapter, only the general journal will be used to illustrate a selection of the more important merchandising transactions for Scarborough Wholesale Hardware.

In the manually prepared illustrations in Figures 5-7, 5-8, and 5-9, note that break lines are used to indicate that many of the entries throughout the year would have been included. As for those entries that are shown, you should have little difficulty in their correct analysis, because the majority have been treated in Chapter 4.

One transaction, however, requires emphasis. In Figure 5-9, observe carefully that the entry on December 10 shows that the sole proprietor withdrew merchandise costing $110 for his personal use. From earlier work, you will recall that the debit for this transaction must be charged (debited) to the owner's Drawing account for the cost of the withdrawn merchandise. Under a periodic inventory method, the credit must be made to Purchases, because the Inventory account is not updated until the end of the accounting period. However, under perpetual inventory accounting, the credit would be made to the Inventory account, because this method supports the updating of the current asset, Inventory, whenever any change is made to Inventory. Keep in mind that the owner has the right to withdraw merchandise for his or her own use at any time, and

FIGURE 5-7

		GENERAL JOURNAL			Page 1
DATE 19-1		ACCOUNT TITLE AND EXPLANATION	POST. REF.	DEBIT	CREDIT
Jan.	1	Cash in Royal Bank		10000 00	
		Inventory		10000 00	
		Land		32000 00	
		Building		60000 00	
		Warehouse Equipment		12000 00	
		Office Equipment		7200 00	
		Delivery Trucks		44000 00	
		Accounts Payable			5200 00
		Mortgage Payable			60000 00
		Tom Allen, Capital			110000 00
		To record the beginning balance sheet of Scarborough Wholesale Hardware.			
	3	Purchases		5000 00	
		Accounts Payable			5000 00
		Acquired merchandise from Stelco Inc.; P.O.—0001; Stelco Invoice 1100; terms 2/10, n/30.			
	15	Accounts Receivable		1250 75	
		Sales			1250 75
		Issued Sales Invoice 011 to Woodbridge Hardware; terms 2/10, n/30.			

that such withdrawals will be accounted for at their *cost* rather than their retail price.

Step 3. Posting Transaction Data

From Chapter 3, you learned of the process of transferring the debits and credits from the general journal to appropriate accounts in the general ledger. You also learned that such a process was called "posting," or "updating a ledger file" when a computer is used. And, finally, you learned that all accounts in the general ledger were identified by name and account number in accordance with a chart of accounts organized for the particular business enterprise. From the illustration of the Purchases account in Figure 5-9, it should be self-evident that the balance in the account will accumulate month by month so that a final year-end balance can be included in the Cost of Goods Sold section of the year-end income statement.

CHAPTER 5: Accounting Cycle for a Merchandising Firm **155**

FIGURE **5-8**

GENERAL JOURNAL Page 85

DATE 19-1	ACCOUNT TITLE AND EXPLANATION	POST. REF.	DEBIT	CREDIT
May 2	Accounts Receivable		743 10	
	Sales			743 10
	Issued Invoice 101 to Eglinton Hardware Centre; 2/10, n/30			
10	Purchases		1010 60	
	Accounts Payable			1010 60
	Purchased merchandise from Small Tools Limited on P.O.-0078; their Invoice 0387; dated May 9; terms 2/10, n/30.			
25	Sales Returns and Allowances		28 72	
	Accounts Receivable			28 72
	Issued credit memo CM-01 to Eglinton Hardware Centre for return of damaged goods sold on Invoice 101.			
Dec 10	Tom Allan, Drawing		110 00	
	Purchases			110 00
	To record the personal withdrawal of merchandise costing $110 by the proprietor.			

FIGURE **5-9**

Purchases — Account No. 501

DATE 19-1	EXPLANATION	POST. REF.	DEBIT	CREDIT	BALANCE
Jan 3	P.O.-001	G.J. 1	5000 00		5000 00
12	P.O.-002	G.J. 1	6000 00		11000 00
23	P.O.-003	G.J. 2	1900 00		12900 00
Feb 4	P.O.-004	G.J. 2	1100 00		14000 00
Dec 8	P.O.-078	G.J. 88	4000 00		72000 00
10	Personal withdrawal	G.J. 88		110 00	71890 00
30	P.O.-079	G.J. 89	5000 00		76890 00

**Step 4.
Preparing the
Trial Balance**

From Chapter 4, you learned that a trial balance of the general ledger must be taken before the preparation of the year-end set of financial statements. In the case of Scarborough Wholesale Hardware, assume that monthly trial balances were reported accurately, and that the formal trial balance at the end of December appeared as illustrated in Figure 5-10.

Four steps of the accounting cycle have been treated for the case of Scarborough Wholesale Hardware: (1) originating transaction data; (2) recording the dollar results of transaction data (journalizing); (3) transferring debits and credits from the general journal to accounts in the general ledger (posting or updating the general ledger file); and (4) preparing the trial balance of the general ledger. Since accounting clerks (bookkeepers) are not formally involved in the origination of transaction data, it follows

FIGURE 5-10

Scarborough Wholesale Hardware
Trial Balance
December 31, 19-1

Account	No.	Debit	Credit
Cash in Royal Bank	101	$ 18 576	
Bank Term Deposit Receipts	103	20 000	
Accounts Receivable	104	21 500	
Inventory (January 1)	106	10 000	
Supplies on Hand	107	1 600	
Prepaid Insurance	108	3 600	
Land	110	32 000	
Building	111	60 000	
Warehouse Equipment	113	12 000	
Office Equipment	115	7 200	
Delivery Trucks	117	44 000	
Bank Loan Payable	201		$ 5 000
Accounts Payable	202		9 000
Property Taxes Payable	203		5 500
Mortgage Payable	220		57 000
Tom Allan, Capital	301		110 000
Tom Allan, Drawing	302	38 110	
Sales	401		246 686
Sales Returns and Allowances	402	2 640	
Sales Discount	403	1 740	
Purchases	501	76 890	
Transportation-in	502	1 800	
Purchases Returns and Allowances	503		2 520
Purchases Discount	504		1 920
Advertising Expense	510	2 220	
Utilities Expense	511	720	
Property Taxes Expense	512	7 100	
Delivery Texpense	513	2 160	
Wages and Salaries Expense	514	67 700	
Telephone Expense	515	420	
Bank Interest Expense	701	450	
Mortgage Interest Expense	702	5 200	
		$ 437 626	$ 437 626

that the bookkeeping part of accounting consists of journalizing, posting, and preparing trial balances.

The next Topic will treat the need for an accountant's expanded working paper, called the "ten-column worksheet."

TOPIC 1

Problems

5.1 Journalizing, posting, and preparing a trial balance of common transactions for a wholesale merchandiser operating as a sole proprietorship.

Linda Martin, owner and manager of the Welland Wholesale Supply Co., completed her first 11 months of business with the trial balance shown in Figure 5-11.

FIGURE 5-11

Welland Wholesale Hardware
Trial Balance
November 30, 19-1

Account	No.	Debit	Credit
Cash in Bank of Montreal	101	$ 30 750	
Accounts Receivable	104	5 980	
Inventory (January 1)	106	12 000	
Supplies on Hand	107	2 460	
Prepaid Insurance	108	1 320	
Land	110	20 000	
Building	111	45 000	
Warehouse Equipment	113	12 000	
Office Equipment	115	10 200	
Bank Loan Payable	201		$ 6 000
Accounts Payable	202		4 800
Property Taxes Payable	203		10 358
Mortgage Payable	220		40 927
Linda Martin, Capital	301		53 000
Linda Martin, Drawing	302	23 200	
Sales	401		233 575
Sales Returns and Allowances	402	1 600	
Sales Discount	403	1 200	
Purchases	501	85 400	
Transportation-in	502	1 900	
Purchases Returns and Allowances	503		2 395
Purchases Discount	504		2 460
Property Taxes Expense	510	2 400	
Advertising Expense	511	1 875	
Utilities Expense	512	1 640	
Delivery Expense	513	2 700	
Wages and Salaries Expense	514	86 200	
Telephone Expense	515	1 380	
Bank Interest Expense	701	110	
Mortgage Interest Expense	702	4 200	
		$353 515	$353 515

The business transactions for December were summarized as follows:

Dec. 1 Obtained one truck from Welland Motors at a cost of $18 000. A cash down payment of $5 000 was made, the balance to be paid by the end of the next month in the form of two equal monthly installments. (Use the account Delivery Truck, No. 117.)

3 Purchased merchandise on credit from Toronto Mfg. Co. Ltd., $11 000. Terms 2/10, n/30.
4 Issued cheque to City Transport for $100 for delivery of goods purchased from Toronto Mfg. Co. Ltd.
5 Issued the following sales invoices: No. 850 to Swain Retailers, $3 000; No. 851 to Larry's Supply, $2 000; and No. 852 to E. Hawkes Co., $2 000. All customers were given credit terms of 2/10, n/30.
8 Issued a credit invoice to E. Hawkes for return of $200 of damaged goods on Invoice 852.
8 Received a cheque for $4 000 from Harris Supply Co. in full payment of Sales Invoice 843.
9 The owner withdrew merchandise costing $500 for her personal use. *Note:* The owner uses the periodic inventory method of accounting.
10 Issued cheque to National Advertisers for $535 in payment of advertising bill received today.
10 Issued cheque for telephone bill showing telephone charges of $100.
11 Received a purchase invoice of goods from Oshawa Mfg. Co. Ltd., $15 000. Terms 2/10, n/30.
11 Paid $2 800 to Brantford Mfg. Co. in full settlement of purchase invoice of November 18.
12 Returned merchandise costing $1 000 to Oshawa Mfg. Co. Ltd. because the goods received were not as ordered.
12 Borrowed $20 000 on a demand note from the bank.
12 Issued cheque for $10 780 to Toronto Mfg. Co. Ltd. in payment of invoice of goods on December 3, less the 2% purchase discount.
15 Received $2 940 cash from Swain Retailers in full settlement of Sales Invoice 850 ($3 000 less 2% sales discount).
16 Issued the following sales invoices: No. 853 to Niagara Retailers, $4 000; No. 854 to Grimsby Supply, $2 000; and No. 855 to St. Catharines Retail, $6 000. All invoices give credit terms of 2/10, n/30.
21 Issued cheque for $13 720 to Oshawa Mfg. Co. Ltd. in full settlement of merchandise purchased on December 11, less the return on December 12, less the 2% purchase discount.
22 Received the following cheques: from Larry's Supply for $2 000 in full settlement of Invoice 851; from Niagara Retailers for $3 920 in full settlement of Invoice 853; and from St. Catharines Retail for $5 880 in full settlement of Invoice 855.
22 Issued cheque to bank for $1 000 in part payment of bank loans.
23 Paid final property tax installment of $400, due today.
24 Issued cheque for $137 in payment of utility bill showing electricity charges of $100 and water consumption of $37.
27 Issued cheque for $500 to Linda Martin, the owner, for her personal use.
30 Paid monthly wages and salaries of $8 000.
30 Paid gas and oil bill for delivery truck, $120. (Charge to Delivery Expense account.)
31 Issued cheque for $645 to Canada Trust in payment of monthly mortgage as follows: mortgage interest, $400; mortgage principal, $245.

31 The bank notified Linda Martin that her business bank account was decreased by $130 for monthly bank interest on the bank loans. (Use Bank Interest Expense account.)

31 Received a cheque for $1 000 from E. Hawkes Co. in part payment of Invoice 852.

31 Issued cheque to Welland Motors for $6 500, as payment of the first installment under the terms outlined on December 1.

31 Issued the following sales invoices: No. 856 to Swain Retailers, $2 500; and No. 857 to Hamilton Supply, $1 800. All customers were given credit terms of 2/10, n/30.

Required

a Record the dollar results of the transactions for December in the general journal, commencing with Page 101.

b Open general ledger accounts for all accounts shown in the trial balance of November 30; then post the December transactions from the general journal to the general ledger.

c Prepare a trial balance of the general ledger as at December 31.

Note: Save the solutions in **b** and **c** for use in Problem 5.11 in this chapter.

Analyzing trial balance errors; preparing a corrected trial balance.

5.2 For the trial balance summarized for Brantford Wholesale Supply Co. in Figure 5-12, assume that the balance of each ledger account has been

FIGURE 5-12

Brantford Wholesale Hardware Supply Co.
Trial Balance
December 31, 19-1

Account	No.	Debit	Credit
Cash in Bank of Nova Scotia	101	$ 18 500	
Government of Canada Bonds	102	20 000	
Accounts Receivable	103	8 710	
Inventory	106	8 500	
Supplies on Hand	107	4 210	
Prepaid Insurance	108	960	
Warehouse Equipment	113	8 000	
Office Equipment	115		$ 6 000
Bank Loan Payable	201		4 000
Accounts Payable	202		6 500
Wages and Salaries Payable	203		6 000
D. Ciotti, Capital	301	100 000	
D. Ciotti, Drawing	302	12 000	
Sales	401		154 420
Sales Returns and Allowances	402	1 900	
Sales Discount	403		1 480
Cost of Goods Sold	501	72 445	
Rent Expense	510	6 000	
Advertising Expense	511	1 500	
Utilities Expense	512	600	
Delivery Texpense	513	5 800	
Wages and Salaries Expense	514	95 400	
Telephone Expense	515	450	
Interest Revenue	610		1 600
Bank Interest Expense	710	65	
		$365 040	$180 000

verified and that all the journal entries have been posted correctly. The error or errors must then be in the trial balance. Note that management supports the *perpetual* inventory method of accounting.

Instructions Analyze each account carefully; correct any errors; then prepare a new trial balance.

Note: Save the corrected trial balance for use in Problem 5.12.

TOPIC 2   Ten-Column Worksheet

From Chapter 3, you learned that Step 5 of the accounting cycle involved the preparation of a worksheet. In that chapter, a six-column worksheet was used to avoid complexities in order to present the concept of an accountant's use of working papers in prior preparation of the financial statements. In the real world of accounting, however, an accountant faces the problem of treating what are known as **adjustments** in order to resolve mismatches between revenues and expenses which are identified at the end of any accounting period. Consequently, a larger worksheet is often used to include not only the columns in the six-column worksheet, but also columns to record necessary adjustments and their effects on year-end trial balance accounts. Before examining the preparation of the ten-column worksheet as used in this chapter, consider first the concept of accounting adjustments.

Adjustments: entries made before closing the books for the period, to apportion amounts of revenue or expense to accounting periods.

What Are Adjustments?

In the opening chapter, you learned the generally accepted accounting principle for matching. As you will recall, revenues of one time period must be matched with the expenses incurred in securing that revenue for the same time period in order to calculate fairly the net income (or net loss) of a business for that period.

To avoid any problems with the identification of this matchup, the earlier chapters presented illustrations and exercise material that gave a fair matchup; that is, <u>all revenue</u> and all <u>expenses</u> related to generate that revenue for the same time period were assumed to have been disclosed by the trial balance. In accounting practice, it seldom occurs that the trial balance of the general ledger shows all the revenue and expenses recorded for a given accounting period. For example, some revenue may have been earned at the end of the accounting period but, because of timing, the revenue has not been posted to the appropriate account in the general ledger. Similarly, an expense may have been incurred during the accounting period but not as yet recorded in appropriate accounts of the general ledger at the end of the accounting period. Of course, such unrecorded revenue earned and such unrecorded expenses incurred will cause a mismatch; that is, a fair calculation of net income (or net loss) cannot be presented until adjustments are made at the end of the accounting period to record such unrecorded earned revenue and unrecorded incurred expenses.

In addition to the problem of unrecorded earned revenue and unrecorded incurred expenses, there is also the opposite problem. Revenue may have been recorded during the accounting period but not as yet completely earned until a future accounting period. For example, a landlord may have received cash for six months' rent of office space. At the end of one month, it is logical to identify only revenue earned for the proper matchup. This matching would require only revenue earned for one month and, yet, the revenue account in the trial balance may show the amount for six months. Similarly, an insurance premium may have been paid for insurance expense covering twelve months. At the end of one month, a fair matchup should show the insurance expense for one month and not for twelve. Such recorded revenues and recorded expenses covering more than the accounting period under the matchup must also be adjusted; otherwise, a fair presentation of the calculation of net income (or loss) cannot be given.

In this text, adjustments will be treated for what are known as prepaid expenses; the adjustment of bad debts expense; the adjustment of depreciation expense; the adjustment for unrecorded bank interest and mortgage interest expense; and the adjustment for unrecorded interest earned. These adjustments will be treated in the steps that follow in the preparation of the ten-column worksheet.

Step 5. Preparing the Ten-Column Worksheet

The actual mechanics of preparing the ten-column worksheet may be learned through a series of orderly sequences. Analyze closely the steps that follow.

STEP 1. COMPLETE THE HEADING SECTION As you will recall from Chapter 3, the heading answered the questions *who* (name of the business), *what* (the worksheet), and *when* (the accounting period). For Scarborough Wholesale Hardware, the accounting period of one accounting year is used to take advantage of the trial balance illustrated in Topic 1.

STEP 2. COMPLETE THE TRIAL BALANCE SECTION As you will recall, the initial step in the preparation of the body of the worksheet is to transfer the general ledger trial balance at the end of the accounting period to the first pair of columns on the worksheet. For Scarborough Wholesale Hardware, the trial balance on the worksheet is illustrated in Figure 5-25. As you analyze the preparation of this worksheet, keep in mind that the worksheet is not part of the records of an accounting system; consequently, it is usually prepared in pencil so that errors may be easily erased and corrected.

STEP 3. COMPLETE THE ADJUSTMENTS SECTION Since the trial balance does not disclose the information for the adjustments, additional data would have to be obtained at the end of the accounting period. For example, a physical count would be made of all supplies on hand at the close of business on the final day of the accounting period. Similarly, the used portion of insurance premiums would be calculated on that final day. For Scarborough Wholesale Hardware, assume that the following additional information has been identified at the close of business on December 31, 19-1:

a. A physical count of office and warehouse supplies on December 31 showed an amount on hand of $75.

b. A fire and theft insurance policy on the building and contents was negotiated on June 30 of this year. The premium of $3 600 was paid to give one complete year of protection from the date of purchase.

c. An aged accounts receivable was prepared at the close of business on December 31. The loss from uncollectible accounts was estimated at $1 095.

d. The useful life of the building was estimated at 30 years with no disposal value. The straight-line method of depreciation is used.

e. The useful life of the warehouse equipment was estimated at 10 years with no disposal value. The straight-line method of depreciation is used.

f. The useful life of the office equipment was estimated at 5 years with a disposal value of $1 200. The straight-line method of depreciation is used.

g. The useful life of the delivery trucks was estimated at 5 years with an estimated disposal value of $3 000 for each truck. (Total of $6 000 for two trucks.)

h. A physical inventory of the merchandise on hand was taken at the close of business on December 31. This count showed merchandise on hand at a cost of $8 000.

i. The mortgage payable is to cover another 19 years, with $3 000 payable in the next accounting year. Both the land and the building have been assigned as collateral to secure the mortgage payable. The interest on the mortgage for Year 19-1 has been paid and is reflected in the Mortgage Interest Expense account.

j. The bank loan payable was negotiated on December 1 on a demand basis. No interest on this demand loan has been recorded. Information received from the Royal Bank indicates that interest at 12% for December will be charged on December 31.

k. A bank memo received from the Royal Bank stated that interest was earned on the 90-day term deposit in the amount of $530. This interest was deposited in the business's chequing account on December 30 at the Royal Bank. However, this interest has not been recorded in the books of account and, therefore, does not appear in the preliminary year-end trial balance.

The adjustments will now be treated in the order given in the additional data.

Adjustment for Supplies Used The additional data states that the physical count of office and warehouse supplies on hand on December 31 showed a cost of $75 still to be used. Since the trial balance indicates a cost of $1 600 unused at the beginning of the accounting period, an adjustment is required to record the expired cost for the period and to reduce the unexpired portion to the correct balance. In the language of accounting, this adjustment is made by debiting Supplies Expense and crediting Supplies on Hand for $1 525 ($1 600 less $75). Before treating the adjustment on the worksheet, it is useful to analyze the double entry in the form of T-accounts, as illustrated in Figure 5-13.

FIGURE 5-13

	Supplies Expense	517		Supplies on Hand	106
(a)	1 525			1 600 (a)	1 525

Analysis Notice that the credit entry has the effect of decreasing the asset account by the amount of the supplies used. Of course, the balance in this asset account ($75) should show the amount of supplies unused. This unused or unexpired cost would be disclosed on the balance sheet as the current asset carried forward into the next accounting period. On the other hand, the debit entry would record the amount of used supplies for the accounting period. This amount must be the correct expense to be matched against the related revenue on the firm's income statement. With such an adjusting entry, the financial statements would report the accurate amounts for the current asset and the expense.

You may well ask this question: Why was an expense account like Supplies Expense not used, since the supplies were acquired for the purpose of supporting revenue-making activities during the year? In practice, an expense account may be used; however, since the expenditure was made to benefit more than one accounting period, the amount is more commonly debited to the asset account. In the language of accounting, this asset is known as a ***prepaid expense***, because more than one accounting period will benefit from the expenditure. At the end of each accounting period that benefits from the expenditure, an adjustment must be made to transfer the used portion from the asset account to an appropriate expense account. Keep in mind that the accounting period may be one month, two months, six months, and even one year.

Now turn to Figure 5-25a to examine how the prepaid adjustment is recorded on the worksheet. Notice that the credit has been placed in the

> Prepaid expense: an expense payment made in advance to benefit more than one accounting period.

credit column of the Adjustments section opposite the account Supplies on Hand. Since an account for the debit entry does not exist in the trial balance, the account name Supplies Expense is shown on the first available line *below* the trial balance. And notice that the label "(a)" has been placed in front of both the debit amount and the credit amount. Alphabetic-letter labels are used for each adjustment to ensure, for example, that an equal (a) debit is offset against an equal (a) credit. Furthermore, the letter codes will serve as a useful reference source later when formal adjusting entries must be recorded in the general journal. Three steps, therefore, must be remembered when entering adjustments on any worksheet:

- First, analyze the complete double entry. As suggested earlier, a T-account analysis is often helpful.
- Second, enter the amounts opposite the account name if the account affected is in the trial balance. If the account does not appear in the trial balance, enter the account name or both account names, as the case may be, on the first available line below the trial balance.
- Third, letter-code all adjustments, beginning with "(a)" for the first adjustment, opposite both the debit and credit amounts.

By the way, no specific order of entering these adjustments is used. What is important, however, is that all adjustments must be identified and included in the Adjustments section of the worksheet.

Adjustment for Expired Insurance The additional information states that a fire and theft insurance policy on the building and contents was taken, and that the premium of $3 600 was paid on June 30 to give one complete year's protection from the date of purchase. Since the premium of $3 600 provides fire-theft coverage for more than one month (the minimum length of an accounting period), the expenditure is definitely paid in advance; therefore, the premium becomes a prepaid expense. Back on June 30, the accounting entry would have recorded a debit to a current asset like Prepaid Insurance or Unexpired Insurance, and a credit to Cash in Royal Bank.

On December 31, however, the amount of unexpired insurance is no longer $3 600, because six months of insurance protection had been used to support revenue-making activities from June 30 to December 31. An adjusting entry, therefore, is required to transfer the expired (used) portion from the asset to the expense account. The analysis of this double entry may be shown in T-account form as in Figure 5-14.

Since this is the second adjustment, the letter code "(b)" is positioned in front of each amount on the worksheet. Notice that the name of the debit account appears on the next available line below the trial balance, because this account had not been recorded in the general ledger.

Other Prepaid Expenses A business may encounter other prepaid expenses in addition to supplies on hand and prepaid insurance. For example, a business may rent office space and have prepaid the rent expense for

FIGURE 5-14

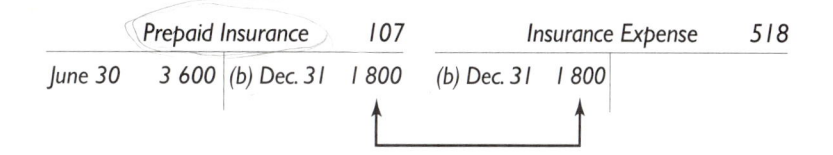

```
      Prepaid Insurance      107           Insurance Expense      518
June 30    3 600 │ (b) Dec. 31   1 800    (b) Dec. 31   1 800
```

several months. Similarly, a business may have prepaid the advertising expense for several months. Regardless of the type of prepaid expense, it is important to remember that adjustments will be required at the end of each accounting period to match fairly the used (expired) portion of these expenses against the revenue for the same accounting period.

Current Assets Redefined It is appropriate to redefine **current assets** at this time. As you may recall from the opening chapter, current assets were defined as cash and other assets that are expected to be converted into cash within one year of the date of the balance sheet. With the introduction of prepaid expenses, however, this definition must be expanded as shown in the side margin.

> Current assets (redefined): cash and other economic resources which are reasonably expected to be realized in cash or sold or consumed during the normal operating cycle of the business.

Note that two distinct types of assets are included in this new definition. One group identifies assets like accounts receivable and inventory that are intended to be converted into cash during the **normal operating cycle** of the business. In most cases, this normal operating cycle for a merchandising firm would be one year (or less) from the date of the balance sheet. In a stricter sense, the operating cycle is the average time period between the purchase of merchandise and the conversion of this merchandise back into cash.

> Normal operating cycle: the average time period between the purchase of merchandise and the conversion of this merchandise back into cash.

The other group of current assets are to be "consumed during the normal operating cycle of the business." These assets are identified as prepaid expenses. As you now know, prepaid expenses are unexpired costs (current assets) when they are acquired. In most cases, they are expected to be consumed, that is, their costs are to be expired (used up) within one year of the date of the balance sheet. You have also learned that the expired cost of such prepaid expenses must be transferred to expense accounts by preparing adjusting entries.

In presenting the current asset section on any balance sheet, it is customary to place those assets that are to be realized in cash ahead of those assets that will expire their costs in the process of being used to support revenue-making activities. For example, a 90-day certificate of deposit with a bank would be listed qualify as a short-term investment because the business can expect to receive cash in 90 days. In Figure 5-15, note that the liquidity order is shown ahead of the listing of all prepaid expenses. Also note that the term **marketable securities** would include investments in bonds and stocks which management has decided to liquidate within one year of the balance sheet date. Any bonds and stocks held for a longer period would not be classified as current. Instead, they would be reported under a separate heading, Long-Term Investments.

> Marketable securities: any securities such as bonds and stocks that can be readily converted into cash.

166   PART 1: THE FRAMEWORK OF ACCOUNTING

FIGURE 5-15

Oshawa Wholesale Dry Goods
Partial Balance Sheet
As at December 31, 19—

Current Assets:		
Cash in Royal Bank		$18 746
Bank Certificates of Deposit		10 000
Marketable Securities (at cost)		50 000
Accounts Receivable	$7 000	
Less: Allowance for Bad Debts	600	6 400
Inventory (at cost)		5 600
Prepaid Expenses:		
Supplies on Hand	$ 400	
Prepaid Insurance	600	1 000
Total Current Assets		$91 746

Adjustment for Bad Debts Expense   In all profit-seeking businesses, the seller grants credit to generate sales revenue. Of course, this credit will be granted to customers who are expected to pay their debts. Regardless of how thoroughly the seller investigates the credit reliability of prospective customers, all businesses selling on a credit basis will encounter some accounts receivable which will be uncollectible. In the language of accounting, the total cost of granting credit to an uncollectible accounts receivable is known as a ***bad debts expense***. As you will learn, an adjusting entry is required at the end of each accounting period to match the cost of uncollectible accounts receivable against the revenue; otherwise, both the revenue and the accounts receivable will be overstated for that accounting period.

The accounting method of making a correction of the assumed overstatement of sales and accounts receivable, as of each year-end, is to make an adjusting entry to record an allowance for the estimated amount of the overstatement. This estimate is called an ***allowance for bad debts***. Note carefully that, at the point of establishing an allowance, management does not know which accounts receivable will prove uncollectible; all management can do is accept the fact that *some* amount will not be collected.

In accounting practice, management bases the estimates on known facts. One common calculation, and the one that will be treated in this text, is known as ***aging the accounts receivable***. Briefly, management can estimate the cost of bad debts by analyzing the entry list of outstanding accounts receivable as to the percentage of balances overdue and the length of time involved. A typical schedule of accounts receivable by age may appear as in Figure 5-16.

Now that the percentages have been estimated for each age group, they can be applied to calculate the estimated bad debts expense for the

---

Bad debts expense: the cost of granting credit to an uncollectible accounts receivable.

Allowance for bad debts: a contra to the current asset accounts receivable.

Aging the accounts receivable: the process of analyzing accounts receivable by classifying the amounts according to the length of time they have been outstanding or for which they have been due.

FIGURE 5-16

Scarborough Wholesale Hardware
Schedule of Accounts Receivable by Age
December 31, 19-1

Account With:	Balance	Not Past Due	1–30	31–60	61–90	Over 90
Anderson Hardware	$ 600	$ 600				
Eglinton Hardware Centre	900	400	$ 500			
Hyland Hardware	700			$ 700		
Reid Home Hardware	300				$ 100	$200
Summers Hardware Limited	1 000	900	100			
Thornhill Home Hardware	200	200				
Young Hardware Centre	100					100
Totals	$21 500	$12 000	$5 000	$2 500	$1 500	$500

FIGURE 5-17

Percentage of Probable Losses

Over 90 days	50%
61–90 days	25%
31–60 days	10%
1–30 days	2%
Not past due	1%

Age Group (in days)	Total	Estimated Percentage	Estimated Loss
Over 90	$ 500	50%	$ 250
61–90	1 500	25%	375
31–60	2 500	10%	250
1–30	5 000	2%	100
0	12 000	1%	120
	$21 500		$1 095

accounting period. This calculation can be taken in relation either to the individual customer accounts or to the individual totals obtained through the Schedule of Accounts Receivable by Age. In the case of Scarborough Wholesale Hardware, assume that the total method is used in the table illustrated in Figure 5-17.

The adjusting entry to record the expense from estimated uncollectible accounts can now be analyzed. A debit is required to Bad Debts Expense, and a credit to Allowance for Bad Debts. In the case of Scarborough Wholesale Hardware, the analysis may be illustrated in T-account form as in Figure 5-18.

On the ten-column worksheet under the Adjustments section, Figure 5-25, note that both accounts are shown below the trial balance because neither account was listed in the original trial balance. And notice that the adjusting entry has been letter-coded "(c)," since it is the third adjustment to be identified.

Six Additional Points to Remember

1. At year-end, the Bad Debts Expense account would be reported in the Income Statement together with all of the other operating expenses.

FIGURE 5-18

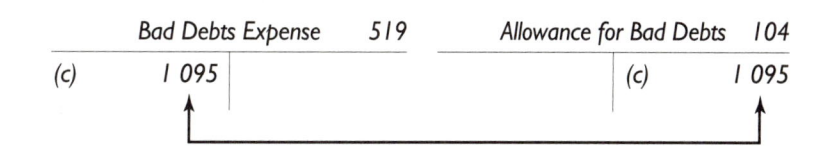

Bad Debts Expense 519	Allowance for Bad Debts 104
(c) 1 095	(c) 1 095

PART 1: THE FRAMEWORK OF ACCOUNTING

FIGURE 5-19

Partial Income Statement

Operating expenses:
    Bad debts expense ...... $xxxxx

Partial Balance Sheet

Current assets:
    Accounts receivable ...... $xxxx
    Less: Allowance for
        bad debts xxxx
Net realizable value .... $xxxx

FIGURE 5-21

Case 1
Allowance for Bad Debts

No balance	No balance

Adjustment: $1 095.

Case 2
Allowance for Bad Debts

	Balance	100

Adjustment: $1 095 − $100 = $995.

Case 3
Allowance for Bad Debts

Balance	155	

Adjustment: $1 095 + $155 = $1 250.

2. Also at year-end, the Allowance for Bad Debts would be included in the Current Assets section of the balance sheet as a deduction from Accounts Receivable. The net amount, therefore, would be translated as the amount of cash expected from the collection of accounts receivable within the next operating cycle. In this context, it is correct to state that the Allowance for Bad Debts account is contra to the current asset Accounts Receivable.

3. Whenever management learns that the amount receivable from a particular customer cannot be collected — for example, when the customer is bankrupt — the appropriate accounting procedure is to write the account off as a bad debt in the general journal as follows:

FIGURE 5-20

(Date)	Dr. Allowance for Bad Debts....................	100	
	Cr. Accounts Receivable		100
	To write off X Limited's account as uncollectible.		

The above journal entry writing off the accounts receivable achieves these results:

a. The appropriate amount is cancelled out of the asset accounts receivable. In this case, we assumed an earlier sale of $100. Therefore, the $100 debit balance in the customer's account is credited to eliminate the balance.

b. The amount of accounts receivable that is cancelled is debited to the Allowance for Bad Debts account that was established for this purpose theoretically at the point of sale. Note that the Bad Debts Expense account is not used in any write-off, because it was used in the adjusting entry to create the Allowance account.

4. If the Allowance for Bad debts account at the end of the accounting period has no balance, show the dollar amount calculated by the aging method. In the example for Scarborough Wholesale Hardware, the credit entry would be $1 095.

5. If the Allowance account at year-end had a credit balance, say $100, then deduct the credit balance from the dollar amount calculated by the aged percentage of probable losses. For example, Scarborough Wholesale Hardware would show a credit entry for only $995 so that the final balance in the Allowance account would be $1 095 after the adjusting entry is posted.

6. If the Allowance account at year-end had a debit balance of, say, $155, add this amount to the one required by the aging process. For Scarborough Wholesale Hardware, such an adjustment would show a credit entry of $1 250 ($1 095 + $155) so that the final credit balance would be $1 095. It is important to remember that, under the aging method, the calculated estimate is based on the relationship between bad debts expense and accounts receivable. The final balance in the

Allowance account must reveal the new total estimated bad debts for that period based on the aging of all accounts receivable at the end of the accounting period.

Adjustment for Depreciation Expense   Before adjusting entries are examined for depreciation expense, it is important that the accounting meaning of depreciation be understood. Briefly, all profit-seeking businesses acquire fixed assets such as buildings, machinery, delivery trucks, etc. to generate revenue or support revenue-making activities. Since all of these fixed assets will generate revenue or support revenue-making activities for more than one accounting year, it is only fair that the original cost of such assets be spread over the useful lives of such assets. For example, the building purchased by Scarborough Wholesale Hardware at a cost of $60 000 is estimated to have a useful life of 30 years. The purpose of the $60 000 expenditure was to provide a place in which to carry on business, that is, to obtain revenue. It is fair to conclude, therefore, that the original cost of the building is an expense of earning revenues during the entire length of this 30-year period. In the language of accounting, the process of allocating (spreading) the cost of the fixed asset over its useful life is known as **depreciation**.

> Depreciation: a process of allocating the cost of a fixed asset over its estimated useful life. It should be emphasized that depreciation is *not* a process of evaluation.

Note carefully that, in accounting, depreciation has nothing to do with calculating the decrease in the value of the fixed asset. That meaning is reserved for use in the study of topics in marketing and economics. In accounting, depreciation takes on a very special meaning and, unless this meaning is understood, the reader of financial statements cannot interpret fairly the results of reporting depreciation. Let us now apply the meaning of depreciation to the various fixed assets as disclosed by Scarborough Wholesale Hardware.

Land   This fixed asset appears in the trial balance at a cost of $32 000. It is important to realize that land does not depreciate, that is, its cost must not be matched against revenue of any accounting period. This is for two reasons. First, land is acquired solely with the idea of serving as a site on which the depreciable building will be constructed. And second, land is regarded as having unlimited life, because its cost can be recovered once the building is eliminated. On any balance sheet, therefore, land is placed under Fixed Assets as its original cost, but there will be no accounting of depreciation. For this reason, Land must be separated from Buildings on a balance sheet.

Building   As indicated earlier, Scarborough Wholesale Hardware acquired a building at an original cost of $60 000. In the additional information reported at year-end, we are told that management had estimated the useful life of the building to be 30 years. How management came up with the estimated life of 30 years is of no concern here. However, it is correct to conclude that factors such as wear-and-tear and obsolescence will influence management to come up with the estimate of useful life for

Straight-line depreciation: a method whereby the debit to depreciation expense is computed by dividing the depreciation base by the estimated number of periods of useful life.

every depreciable asset. Also in the additional information, we are told that no disposal value (scrap value) is estimated for the building after 30 years. Consequently, after 30 years of use the building is assumed to be worthless. If we assume that each year's operations should bear an equal share of the total cost (**straight-line depreciation**), the annual depreciation expense will amount to 1/30 of $60 000, or $2 000. There are alternative methods of spreading the cost of a depreciable asset over its useful life acceptable under accounting theory and practice. Also, there is quite a different method when the fixed asset is depreciated for income tax reporting. However, only the straight-line method will be treated in this text. In T-account form the year-end adjusting entry may be analyzed as shown in Figure 5-22.

FIGURE 5-22

Depreciation Expense — Building		Accumulated Depreciation — Building	
	520		112
(d) 2 000		(d) 2 000	

From this entry it is self-evident that Depreciation Expense — Building is an expense that will be matched against this year's revenue on the income statement. On the other hand, the credit to Accumulated Depreciation — Building has the effect of receiving the amount of the building cost which has been used up (expired) after one year's use. On the balance sheet, this accumulated depreciation will be deducted from the original cost of the building to report the unexpired cost (book value) of the building. In this context, the accumulated depreciation is a contra fixed asset account which will receive, year by year, the expired costs of the building. At the end of 30 years, therefore, the accumulated depreciation account should receive 30 years of expired costs so that the balance in the account will show the asset used up completely. Now turn to Figure 5-25a to analyze this adjusting entry on the ten-column worksheet.

Warehouse Equipment The additional information tells us that the useful life of warehouse equipment is estimated at ten years with no disposal value. Since the original cost of $12 000 is to be allocated over ten years, the annual depreciation expense on warehouse equipment must be $1 200. Now turn to Figure 5-25a to check the adjusting entry, which is coded (e).

Office Equipment Management has estimated a useful life of five years for the office equipment originally acquired at a cost of $7 200. In addition, management estimates that the office equipment will have a disposal value of $1 200 when the fixed asset is sold, traded, or scrapped after five years. Consequently, this disposal value must be *subtracted* from the original cost on the fixed asset *before* calculating the yearly depreciation, as shown in Figure 5-24.

FIGURE 5-23

Partial Income Statement

Operating expenses:
  Depreciation expense
    — building $2 000

Partial Balance Sheet

Fixed assets (at cost):
  Building $60 000
  Less: Accumulated
    depreciation 2 000
  Unexpired cost (book value) $58 000

FIGURE 5-24

Original cost: $7 200
Less: estimated disposal
  value 1 200
Amount subject to
  depreciation (the
  depreciation base) $6 000

Estimated useful life . . . . . . 5 years
Yearly depreciation: $6 000 ÷ 5 = $1 200

Of course, the year-end depreciation adjustment will record a debit to Depreciation Expense — Office Equipment for $1 200, and a credit to Accumulated Depreciation — Office Equipment also for $1 200. At the end of five years, the Accumulated Depreciation account will report the accumulation (addition) of five years of expired costs, or $6 000. To simplify matters, the added problem of accounting for the disposal of fixed assets is avoided in this text. Now turn to Figure 5-25a to analyze the adjusting entry, which is coded (f).

Delivery Trucks   From the additional data, we are told that the two delivery trucks were acquired at an original cost totalling $44 000. In addition, we are told that management has estimated the useful life of these trucks to be five years, with an estimated disposal value of $3 000 for each truck. Under the straight-line method of depreciation accounting, therefore, the yearly depreciation would be $7 600 as shown in the Figure 5-26 calculation. The adjusting entry is coded (g) on the illustrated ten-column worksheet for Scarborough Wholesale Hardware.

Unrecorded Bank Interest Expense   Under additional data (j), we are told of information received from the Royal Bank on interest charged for one month on the bank loan payable on demand. According to the information received, the Royal Bank has decreased our chequing account with interest at 12% on $5 000 for one month. The result is that a debit must be recorded to Bank Interest Expense for $50. Of course, the credit will be made to Cash in Royal Bank for $50. See the adjusting entry coded as (h) on the illustrated ten-column worksheet.

Unrecorded Interest Earned   Additional information (k) states that the Royal Bank has deposited $530 as interest earned on the 90-day term deposit. It is common practice for businesses to invest excess cash amounts in short-term investments like certificates of deposits with their banks. These bank term deposits are usually taken out for short periods like 30, 60, or 90 days. Since this interest has been earned but not as yet recorded, an adjusting entry is required to debit Cash in Royal Bank and credit Interest Earned for $530. See the adjusting entry coded as (i) on the worksheet.

Other Additional Data   We are told that a physical inventory of merchandise on hand was taken at the close of business on December 31, and that this count was a cost of $8 000. In some accounting systems, an adjusting entry is made to record the new inventory amount. Under a periodic method using the manual method, however, it is customary to avoid the adjustment method in favour of updating the Inventory account as part of the closing entries. In this text, only the closing method will be treated; therefore, no adjusting entry for the final inventory appears in the ten-column worksheet. As you will see, the beginning and ending inventories will be moved to appropriate financial statement columns after all adjustments have been entered.

FIGURE **5-26**

Original cost	$44 000
Less: Estimated disposal value	6 000
Depreciation base	$38 000
Estimated useful life	5 years
Yearly depreciation ($38 000 ÷ 5)	$7 600

FIGURE **5-27**

Computation of Unrecorded Bank Interest Expense

Demand loan	$5 000
Interest rate	12% per annum
Interest period	1 mo. (Dec.)
Interest expense ($5 000 × 0.12 × 1/12) . .	$50

FIGURE 5-25a

Scarborough Wholesale Hardware
Worksheet
For the Year Ended December 31, 19-1

	Account Title	Acct. No.	Trial Balance Debit	Trial Balance Credit	Adjustments Debit	Adjustments Credit	Adjusted Trial Balance Debit	Adjusted Trial Balance Credit	
1	Cash in Royal Bank	101	18 576		(i) 530	(h) 50	19 056		1
2	Bank Term Deposit Receipts	103	20 000				20 000		2
3	Accounts Receivable	104	21 500				21 500		3
4	Merchandise Inventory (Jan. 1)	106	10 000				10 000		4
5	Supplies on Hand	107	1 600			(a) 1 525	75		5
6	Prepaid Insurance	108	3 600			(b) 1 800	1 800		6
7	Land	110	32 000				32 000		7
8	Building	111	60 000				60 000		8
9	Warehouse Equipment	113	12 000				12 000		9
10	Office Equipment	115	7 200				7 200		10
11	Delivery Trucks	117	44 000				44 000		11
12	Bank Loan Payable	201		5 000				5 000	12
13	Accounts Payable	202		9 000				9 000	13
14	Property Taxes Payable	203		5 500				5 500	14
15	Mortgage Payable	220		57 000				57 000	15
16	Tom Allan, Capital	301		110 000				110 000	16
17	Tom Allan, Drawing	302	38 110				38 110		17
18	Sales	401		246 686				246 686	18
19	Sales Returns and Allowances	402	2 640				2 640		19
20	Sales Discount	403	1 740				1 740		20
21	Purchases	501	76 890				76 890		21
22	Transportation-in	502	1 800				1 800		22
23	Purchases Returns and Allowances	503		2 520				2 520	23
24	Purchases Discount	504		1 920				1 920	24
25	Advertising Expense	510	2 220				2 220		25
26	Utilities Expense	511	720				720		26
27	Property Taxes Expense	512	7 100				7 100		27
28	Delivery Expense	513	2 160				2 160		28
29	Wages and Salaries Expense	514	67 700				67 700		29
30	Telephone Expense	515	420				420		30
31	Bank Interest Expense	701	450		(h) 50		500		31
32	Mortgage Interest Expense	702	5 200				5 200		32
33			437 626	437 626					33
34	Supplies Expense	517			(a) 1 525		1 525		34
35	Insurance Expense	518			(b) 1 800		1 800		35
36	Bad Debts Expense	519			(c) 1 095		1 095		36
37	Allowance for Bad Debts	104				(c) 1 095		1 095	37
38	Depreciation Expense—Building	520			(d) 2 000		2 000		38
39	Accumulated Depreciation—Building	112				(d) 2 000		2 000	39
40	Depreciation Expense—Warehouse Equip.	521			(e) 1 200		1 200		40
41	Accumulated Depreciation—Warehouse Equip.	114				(e) 1 200		1 200	41
42	Depreciation Expense—Office Equip.	522			(f) 1 200		1 200		42
43	Accumulated Depreciation—Office Equip.	116				(f) 1 200		1 200	43
44	Depreciation Expense—Delivery Trucks	523			(g) 7 600		7 600		44
45	Accumulated Depreciation—Delivery Trucks	118				(g) 7 600		7 600	45
46	Interest Earned	601				(i) 530		530	46
47					17 000	17 000	451 251	451 251	47

FIGURE 5-25b

Scarborough Wholesale Hardware
Worksheet
For the Year Ended December 31, 19-1

	Account Title	Acct. No.	Adjusted Trial Balance Debit	Adjusted Trial Balance Credit	Income Statement Debit	Income Statement Credit	Balance Sheet Debit	Balance Sheet Credit	
1	Cash in Royal Bank	101	19 056				19 056		1
2	Bank Term Deposit Receipts	103	20 000				20 000		2
3	Accounts Receivable	104	21 500				21 500		3
4	Merchandise Inventory (Jan. 1)	106	10 000		10 000				4
5	Supplies on Hand	107	75				75		5
6	Prepaid Insurance	108	1 800				1 800		6
7	Land	110	32 000				32 000		7
8	Building	111	60 000				60 000		8
9	Warehouse Equipment	113	12 000				12 000		9
10	Office Equipment	115	7 200				7 200		10
11	Delivery Trucks	117	44 000				44 000		11
12	Bank Loan Payable	201		5 000				5 000	12
13	Accounts Payable	202		9 000				9 000	13
14	Property Taxes Payable	203		5 500				5 500	14
15	Mortgage Payable	220		57 000				57 000	15
16	Tom Allan, Capital	301		110 000				110 000	16
17	Tom Allan, Drawing	302	38 110				38 110		17
18	Sales	401		246 686		246 686			18
19	Sales Returns and Allowances	402	2 640		2 640				19
20	Sales Discount	403	1 740		1 740				20
21	Purchases	501	76 890		76 890				21
22	Transportation-in	502	1 800		1 800				22
23	Purchases Returns and Allowances	503		2 520		2 520			23
24	Purchases Discount	504		1 920		1 920			24
25	Advertising Expense	510	2 220		2 220				25
26	Utilities Expense	511	720		720				26
27	Property Taxes Expense	512	7 100		7 100				27
28	Delivery Expense	513	2 160		2 160				28
29	Wages and Salaries Expense	514	67 700		67 700				29
30	Telephone Expense	515	420		420				30
31	Bank Interest Expense	701	500		500				31
32	Mortgage Interest Expense	702	5 200		5 200				32
33									33
34	Supplies Expense	517	1 525		1 525				34
35	Insurance Expense	518	1 800		1 800				35
36	Bad Debts Expense	519	1 095		1 095				36
37	Allowance for Bad Debts	104		1 095				1 095	37
38	Depreciation Expense—Building	520	2 000		2 000				38
39	Accumulated Depreciation—Building	112		2 000				2 000	39
40	Depreciation Expense—Warehouse Equip.	521	1 200		1 200				40
41	Accumulated Depreciation—Warehouse Equip.	114		1 200				1 200	41
42	Depreciation Expense—Office Equip.	522	1 200		1 200				42
43	Accumulated Depreciation—Office Equip.	116		1 200				1 200	43
44	Depreciation Expense—Delivery Trucks	523	7 600		7 600				44
45	Accumulated Depreciation—Delivery Trucks	118		7 600				7 600	45
46	Interest Earned	601		530		530			46
47			430 721	430 721					47
48	Inventory (Dec. 31)	106				8 000	8 000		48

The remaining item — information on mortgage payable — does not require an adjustment. The additional information has been given for the future preparation of the year-end balance sheet, which is treated in Topic 3 of this chapter.

Since all of the adjustments have now been treated on the worksheet, the final step in completing the Adjustments section is to test the equality of the totals. If the total debits are equal to the total credits in this section, one can move to the next pair of columns on the worksheet.

STEP 4. COMPLETE THE ADJUSTED TRIAL BALANCE SECTION

After all of the adjustments have been recorded in the Adjustments section of the worksheet, a new trial balance must be taken to ensure that the original trial balance figures are brought up to date. This updating is done simply by combining each account balance in the Trial Balance section with any related adjustment. The new balance is then extended to the appropriate column of the Adjusted Trial Balance section. Examine this procedure closely as it is presented on the worksheet in Figure 5-25a.

In the Adjusted Trial Balance section, notice that each account balance is a new balance after any adjustment occurs. For example, the original debit balance of $1 600 for Supplies on Hand has been combined with the credit adjustment of $1 525 to give the new debit balance of $75 — the amount of the physical count of office and warehouse supplies on hand on December 31. Similarly, every other adjustment is carried through, including the ones identified below the original trial balance. After all account balances have been entered in the Adjusted Trial Balance section, a new total must be taken to prove that the total debits are equal to the total credits. When such is the case, the next step in completing the worksheet may be taken.

STEP 5. MOVE THE ADJUSTED TRIAL BALANCE AMOUNTS TO THE STATEMENT COLUMNS

After the Adjusted Trial Balance columns have been proved to be correct, the individual amounts are moved to one column of either the Income Statement section or the Balance Sheet section. See Figure 5-25b. Here are two rules that will help you to move an amount to the correct location:

1. If the amount is a debit in the Adjusted Trial Balance, move the amount to the debit column of the Statement section to which the account is related.
2. If the amount is a credit in the Adjusted Trial Balance, move the amount to the credit column of the Statement section to which the account is related.

Observe that these two rules simply reinforce the idea that a debit in the Adjusted Trial Balance must become a debit elsewhere, and a credit in the Adjusted Trial Balance must become a credit in a related Statement section. These rules merely help you to move to a correct location. They do not, however, explain why the figure must be a debit or a credit under a Statement section. Look closely at the next section of the worksheet illustrated in Figure 5-29; then study the important points of analysis that follow.

Analysis From the illustration, it is important to conclude that each account balance in the Adjusted Trial Balance section must be extended into either the debit or the credit column of its related Statement section. Obviously, assets, liabilities, and the owner's equity capital and drawing accounts must be moved to the Balance Sheet columns. Similarly, revenue, contra revenue, costs (cost of goods sold), expense, and contra expense accounts must be extended to the correct Income Statement columns.

One group of accounts requires careful analysis. From earlier work, you will recall that a merchandising firm using a periodic inventory method does not calculate the cost of each good sold as the sale is made; consequently, no account for Cost of Goods Sold will be found in either the trial balance or the adjusted trial balance. Instead, a group of "costs" is used to make an indirect calculation of the cost of goods sold. From Figure 5-28, you will remember these accounts as the Inventory (showing the beginning amount only), Purchases, Transportation-in, Purchases Returns and Allowances, and Purchases Discount. In addition, the figure of the final inventory is needed to calculate the cost of goods sold. Analyze carefully how each one is identified on the worksheet.

FIGURE **5-28**

Inventory (January 1)		$10 000
Purchases		$76 890
Add:		
Transportation-in	1 800	
Cost of Delivered Goods	78 690	
Less:		
Purchases Returns and Allowances	$2 520	
Purchases Discounts	1 920	4 440
Net Purchases		74 250
Cost of Goods Available for Sale		84 250
Less: Inventory (December 31)		8 000
Cost of Goods Sold		$76 250

i. The beginning inventory is shown in the Adjusted Trial Balance section. It is shown as a debit figure; therefore, it must be extended to the debit column of the Income Statement section. As a debit here, the balance is treated as part of the cost of goods sold. In other words, the effect of the debit is to decrease owner's equity in any accounting equation, since the beginning goods on hand are assumed to have been completely sold.

ii. The amount of Purchases is a debit balance in the Adjusted Trial Balance section. As a debit, it must be extended to the debit side of the Income statement section. Here, the balance must be considered part of the cost of goods sold. In theory, under a periodic inventory system, these purchases are assumed to have been completely sold; consequently, the debit indicates the effect of decreasing owner's equity in any accounting equation.

iii. Transportation-in is directly related to Purchases in order to calculate the cost of delivered goods. The account balance is a debit; therefore, it must be extended to the debit side of the Income Statement section. Since transportation-in adds to the cost of goods sold, and since the cost of goods sold decreases the Owner's Equity in any accounting equation, the figure is correctly analyzed as a debit to the Income Statement section.

iv. Purchases Returns and Allowances and Purchases Discount are both contra accounts to Purchases. Both have credit balances. Since both accounts have the effect of decreasing the cost of purchases, both must decrease the cost of goods sold. Another way to express this idea is that both must increase Owner's Equity in any accounting equation; consequently, both must be credits in any Income Statement analysis. At this stage of the analysis, you should conclude that the Income Statement section on the worksheet is simply a method of calculating the net income (or loss) through a process of debits and credits.

v. The ending inventory must be considered the critical part of this analysis. Under a periodic method, the final inventory balance is not shown in the Trial Balance section or the Adjusted Trial Balance section. At the end of the accounting period a physical stocktaking must occur to determine this cost figure. For our illustration, we are told that the amount of final inventory as at December 31 is costed at $8 000. Three points of analysis must be made for this final inventory:

- First, the final inventory must be acknowledged on the next available line below the trial balance. Notice that the account code remains the same. You will learn how to update this account by a series of closing entries which will be treated in the third Topic of this chapter.

- Second, the final inventory is an asset; therefore, the amount must be entered in the debit side of the Balance Sheet section.

- Third, the final figure is entered as a credit in the Income Statement section. As a credit here, the figure is correctly analyzed as a contra to the "costs" entered in the debit column. To remember this point, check the illustration of the partial income statement in Figure 5-28. Review the method of calculating indirectly the cost of goods sold for a firm using a periodic inventory method. It may help you to remember that the final inventory is entered on the ten-column worksheet as a double entry: a debit to the Balance Sheet section to indicate the correct asset amount as at the end of the accounting period, and a credit to the Income Statement section to indicate the effect of being contra to the cost of goods available for sale.

STEP 6. CALCULATE THE NET INCOME (OR LOSS) AND COMPLETE THE WORKSHEET

After all amounts including the final inventory have been entered correctly to the Statement sections, the totals of all Statement sections are found. Examine closely the sectional view of this worksheet in Figure 5-29. In particular, notice how the worksheet is completed.

FIGURE 5-29

Scarborough Wholesale Hardware
Worksheet
For the Year Ended December 31, 19-1

	Account Title	Acct. No.	ADJUSTED TRIAL BALANCE Debit	ADJUSTED TRIAL BALANCE Credit	INCOME STATEMENT Debit	INCOME STATEMENT Credit	BALANCE SHEET Debit	BALANCE SHEET Credit	
1	Cash in Royal Bank	101	19 056				19 056		1
2	Bank Term Deposit Receipts	103	20 000				20 000		2
3	Accounts Receivable	104	21 500				21 500		3
4	Merchandise Inventory (Jan. 1)	106	10 000		10 000				4
5	Supplies on Hand	107	75				75		5
6	Prepaid Insurance	108	1 800				1 800		6
7	Land	110	32 000				32 000		7
8	Building	111	60 000				60 000		8
43	Accumulated Depreciation—Office Equip.	116		1 200				1 200	43
44	Depreciation Expense—Delivery Trucks	523	7 600		7 600				44
45	Accumulated Depreciation—Delivery Trucks	118		7 600				7 600	45
46	Interest Earned	601		530		530			46
47			430 721	430 721					47
48	Inventory (Dec. 31)	106				8 000	8 000		48
49					195 510	259 656	263 741	199 595	49
50						195 510			50
51	Net Income				64 146			64 146	51
52							263 741	263 741	52

To calculate the net income or loss on the worksheet, the total debit column (expenses and contra revenues) must be matched against the total credit column (revenue and contra expenses). Notice how this matching is done on the illustrated worksheet. Obviously, if the total of the credit column exceeds the total of the debit column, a net income must be identified. On the other hand, if the total exceeds the total credits, there would be a net loss for the accounting period.

To complete the worksheet, observe that the net result from operations — the net income in this case — must be extended to the Balance Sheet section. As you know from the accounting equation, a net income increases owner's equity; therefore, the amount must be entered in the credit column, because Owner's Equity is increased in the accounting equation only on the credit side. If a net loss were calculated, however, this result would decrease owner's equity; therefore, a net loss would be entered in the debit column of the Balance Sheet section as shown in Figure 5-30.

The final step in completing the worksheet is to prove the equality of the Balance Sheet columns. If the net income (or loss) is calculated correctly,

FIGURE 5-30

	INCOME STATEMENT Debit	INCOME STATEMENT Credit	BALANCE SHEET Debit	BALANCE SHEET Credit
50	37 000	35 000	101 000	103 000
51	35 000			
52	2 000		2 000	
53			103 000	103 000

TOPIC 2 Problems

Preparing simple adjusting entries for supplies and prepaid insurance.

5.3 From the following date prepare adjusting entries in a general journal on May 31. (Show explanations for each adjusting entry.)
  a Supplies on hand at beginning of the accounting period, $310. Supplies on hand at the end of the period, $190.
  b Supplies on hand at beginning of the accounting period, $200. Supplies on hand at the end of the period, none.
  c Unexpired cost of prepaid insurance at the beginning of the accounting period, $720. Unexpired cost of prepaid insurance at end of period, $660.
  d Prepaid insurance at the beginning of the period, $480. Insurance that expired during the period, $80.

Preparing the adjusting entry for office supplies on hand.

5.4 Office supplies on hand in the Farlow Company amounted to $395 at the beginning of the year. During the year additional office supplies were purchased at a cost of $1 000 and charged to the Office Supplies on Hand account. At the end of the year a physical count showed that supplies on hand amounted to $470. Prepare the adjusting entry required at December 31.

Preparing adjusting entries for prepaid rent on a monthly basis and at year-end only.

5.5 The Zarnowski Investors' Advisory Service was organized on June 1 to provide investment counselling to investors in securities. On June 1, the firm signed an agreement to rent office space from L. Martin Company for a period of one year commencing June 1 at a rental rate of $1 200 per month. Helen Zarnowski, the owner, signed a cheque for $7 200 in payment of six months' rent in advance.
  a In general journal form, show the double entry to record the dollar results of the transaction on June 1.
  b Assume that the company's accounts are adjusted and closed each month. Prepare the adjusting entry required on June 30.
  c Assume that the company's accounts are adjusted and closed only at year-end, October 31. Prepare the adjusting entry required on October 31.

Preparing adjusting entries for bad debts expense using the aging of accounts receivable method.

5.6 Make the general journal entries to record the following adjustments related to bad debts expense. Assume that management prefers to use the method of aging accounts receivable to estimate the bad debts expense in each case below.

CHAPTER 5: Accounting Cycle for a Merchandising Firm **179**

a The aged accounts receivable at the end of December shows that $500 is estimated to be uncollectible. The Allowance for Bad Debts account has no balance.

b The aged accounts receivable at the end of June shows that $600 is estimated to be uncollectible. The Allowance for Bad Debts account has a credit balance of $200.

c The aged accounts receivable at the end of October shows that $800 is estimated to be uncollectible. The Allowance for Bad Debts account has a debit balance of $150.

5.7 A summary of customer accounts in business with Philip's Van Lines Limited shows the following data on December 31, 19-1.

Preparing a schedule of accounts receivable by age; computing the estimated loss based on a table of percentage of probable losses; and recording the required adjusting entry on the basis of aging the accounts receivable.

FIGURE 5-31

Name of Customer	Invoice Date (terms n/30)	Amount
Bell's Wholesale Hardware	July 10, 19-1	$ 300.00
Dabbs Contractors Ltd.	June 29, 19-1	100.00
Giacomelli Steel Products Ltd.	December 1, 19-1	450.00
Gilchrist Sales Limited	March 15, 19-1	500.00
G. McCallum Limited	November 8, 19-1	210.00
H. Orr & Sons	September 20, 19-1	480.00
H. Orr & Sons	November 10, 19-1	120.00
Regal Furniture Co.	October 15, 19-1	600.00
Stockwell Distributors	August 14, 19-1	325.00
Watson's Dry Goods	November 30, 19-1	580.00
Zimmerman Rug Co.	November 2, 19-1	230.00
Others (total)	December 10, 19-1	11 000.00

The general ledger showed a $275 credit balance in the Allowance for Bad Debts account before the year-end adjustment was made.

a Prepare a Schedule of Accounts Receivable by Age, as illustrated in Figure 5-16.

b Refer to Figure 5-17 for the table showing the Percentage of Probable Losses. On a form similar to that illustrated, compute the estimated loss for the accounting period.

c Record the required adjusting entry based on aging the accounts receivable.

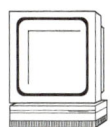

d Use your school's electronic spreadsheet software, or spreadsheet software to which you have access, to redo parts **a** and **b** above. Arrange the table showing the Percentage of Probable Losses below the Schedule of Accounts Receivable by Age. Apply appropriate formulae to calculate the percentage of probable losses.

Calculating the yearly and monthly depreciation expense on a building; recording the adjusting entry; illustrating a partial balance sheet reporting the fixed asset at the end of the first and second years.

5.8 The Gleeson River Company acquired a building at a cost of $180 000. Management estimated the useful life of the building to be 30 years. Furthermore, no disposal value is estimated at the end of the useful life of the asset. Finally, the straight-line method of depreciation is used.

180 PART 1: THE FRAMEWORK OF ACCOUNTING

a Calculate the amount of depreciation expense per year and per month.
b Give the adjusting entry to record depreciation on the building at the end of the first and second years.
c Illustrate how the accounts involved would appear in partial financial statements at the end of the first and second years.

Calculating the yearly and monthly depreciation expense on an electronic typewriter; recording the first month's depreciation; illustrating the effects of depreciation on partial financial statements prepared at the end of the first and twelfth months.

5.9 A business acquires an electronic typewriter at a cost of $1 900. Management has estimated a useful life of six years and a disposal value of $100. The straight-line method of calculating depreciation is used by the accounting system.

a Calculate the amount of depreciation expense per year and per month.
b Give the adjusting entry to record depreciation on the office equipment at the end of the first month.
c Illustrate how the accounts involved would appear in partial financial statements at the end of the first month.
d Illustrate how the accounts involved would appear in partial financial statements at the end of the 12th month.

Preparing adjusting entries for interest earned and interest expense; illustrating the effects of interest earned and interest expense on a partial income statement.

5.10 The preliminary trial balance of S. Wonnacot Company at December 31, 19-5 shows an account called Bank Certificates of Deposit with a debit balance of $50 000. However, no interest revenue from these deposits is listed in this trial balance.

A call to the Royal Bank provided the following information: (i) As at December 31, 19-5, interest has been credited in S. Wonnacot Company's chequing account for 90 days at an interest rate of 10.75% per annum. (ii) As at December 31, 19-5, interest in the amount of $350 has been charged against the business's chequing account for one month's interest on the bank loan payable on demand.

Required

a Calculate the amount of interet earned on the 90-day bank certificate of deposit. Show an appropriate adjusting entry to recordthe interest earned.
b Give the adjusting entry to record the interest charged by the bank on the bank loan payable.
c Illustrate how the accounts involved in both adjusting entries would appear in a partial income statement for the year ended December 31, 19-5.

Preparing a ten-column worksheet for Welland Wholesale Supply Co.

5.11 From the trial balance solved for Problem 5.1, and from the additional information below, prepare a ten-column worksheet for the Welland Wholesale Supply Co. for the year ended December 31, 19-1.

Additional Information

1. A physical count of office and warehouse supplies on December 31 showed an amount on hand of $670.
2. A fire and theft insurance policy on the building and contents was purchased on June 1 of this year. The premium of $1 320 was paid to give one year's protection from the date of purchase.

3. An aged accounts receivable was prepared at the close of business on December 31. The loss from uncollectible accounts was estimated at $500.
4. The useful life of the building was estimated at 20 years with no disposal value. The straight-line method of depreciation is used. Assume that the building was put to use on January 2, 19-1.
5. The useful life of the warehouse equipment was estimated at 10 years with no disposal value. The straight-line method of depreciation is used. Assume that the warehouse equipment was acquired and put to use on January 2, 19-1.
6. The useful life of the office equipment was estimated at five years with a disposal value of $1 000. Assume that the office equipment was acquired on January 2, 19-1. The straight-line method of depreciation is used.
7. One delivery truck was acquired on December 1 at a cost of $18 000. Management estimated a useful life of five years and a disposal value of $3 000. The straight-line method of depreciation is used.
8. A physical inventory of the merchandise on hand was taken at the close of business on December 31. This stocktaking showed merchandise on hand at a cost of $8 400.
9. The mortgage payable is to cover another 19 years, with $1 500 payable against the principal in the next accounting year. Both the land and building have been pledged as collateral to secure the mortgage payable. Mortgage interest expense for the complete year is reflected correctly for the current year.
10. The bank loan was negotiated on a demand basis. One month's interest in the amount of $60 has been charged by the bank but as yet has not been recorded by the business at year-end.

Note: Save this worksheet for use in Problem 5.14 in this chapter.

Preparing a ten-column worksheet for Brantford Wholesale Supply Co.

5.12 From the trial balance solved for Problem 5.2, and from the additional information below, prepare a ten-column worksheet for the Brantford Wholesale Supply Co. for the year ended December 31, 19-1.

Additional Information

1. Supplies on hand on December 31 amounted to $310.
2. A fire and theft insurance policy on the inventory and other assets was purchased on June 30 of this year. The premium of $960 was paid to give one year's protection from the date of purchase.
3. An aged accounts receivable was prepared at the close of business on December 31. The loss from uncollectible accounts was estimated at $800.
4. The useful life of the warehouse equipment, acquired on January 2, was estimated at ten years. The straight-line method of depreciation is used.
5. The useful life of the office equipment, acquired on January 2, was estimated at five years with a disposal value of $1 000. The straight-line method of depreciation accounting is used.

6. A physical stocktaking at the close of business on December 31 showed merchandise inventory on hand at a cost of $8 000. The difference between the "book" figure and the actual physical count is attributed to pilferage of inventory during the period.
7. The bank loan was negotiated on a demand basis. The interest expense on the loan, as at December 31, is stated correctly in the trial balance.
8. The interest earned on Government of Canada bonds, as at year-end, is correctly stated in the Interest Revenue account. The bonds are held as a short-term investment.

Note: Save this worksheet for use in Problem 5.15 in this chapter.

Preparing a ten-column worksheet for a service firm.

5.13 James Miller operates Miller's TV Repair Service. The firm's trial balance taken at June 30, shown in Figure 5-32, represents a summary of account balances after one month's operations.

FIGURE 5-32

Miller's TV Repair Service
Trial Balance
June 30, 19—

Account	No.	Debit	Credit
Cash	101	$20 000	
Prepaid Rent	105	1 800	
Prepaid Insurance	106	480	
Prepaid Advertising	107	865	
Supplies on Hand	108	630	
Equipment	110	12 740	
Bank Loan Payable	201		$ 8 000
Accounts Payable	202		3 250
James Miller, Capital	301		15 000
James Miller, Drawing	302	1 500	
Revenue from Services	401		19 675
Salaries Expense	501	6 300	
Truck Rental Expense	502	1 500	
Miscellaneous Expense	510	40	
Interest Expense	550	70	
		$45 925	$45 925

Additional Information

1. The monthly rent expense is $600.
2. The insurance premium expires each month at a rate of $30.
3. Advertising expense for the month totalled $300.
4. Cost of supplies on hand, based on a physical count on June 30, was $390.
5. Depreciation expense on equipment is estimated at $200 per month. No depreciation has been recorded to date.
6. Salaries earned by employees on June 30, but not as yet paid until July 3, totalled $375. *Hint*: This portion of Salaries Expense has not

CHAPTER 5: Accounting Cycle for a Merchandising Firm

been recorded; therefore, the amount is not included in the trial balance.

Required
a Enter the trial balance on a ten-column worksheet.
b Adjust and complete the worksheet for the month of June. (Note that no merchandise inventory has been identified because Miller's TV Repair Service is a service firm.)

Note: Save this worksheet for use in Problem 5.16 in this chapter.

TOPIC 3 Completing the Accounting Cycle

To this point, the following steps have been covered in the treatment of the accounting cycle for a merchandising firm employing the manual method: (1) originating transaction data; (2) journalizing transaction data; (3) posting transaction data; (4) preparing the trial balance; and (5) preparing the ten-column worksheet. This Topic will treat the remaining stages of the accounting cycle.

Step 6. Preparing the Financial Statements

Since the preparation of the income statement and the related balance sheet has been covered in earlier parts of this textbook, only a brief analysis is required to cover aspects not treated earlier. Observe the following points of analysis when you examine the financial statements illustrated in Figures 5-33, 5-34, and 5-36.

1. The first financial statement to be prepared is the year-end income statement. Obviously, the necessary data is found in the Income Statement section of the ten-column worksheet.

2. In the income statement, observe the feature of reporting **Income from Operations**. Briefly, some firms prefer to separate operating items from non-operating items — Mortgage Interest Expense and Bank Interest Expense — and treat them in a separate section following the Income from Operations. If the business reported secondary sources of revenue, say interest earned on Government of Canada bonds, this secondary revenue is also treated after Income from Operations under a separate section called **Other Revenues**. Secondary expenses might be reported under **Other Expenses**. It should be noted, however, that many firms prefer to simplify their reporting by grouping all sources of revenue under Revenue, and all sources of expenses under Expenses or Costs and Expenses. When such practice is followed, the income statement becomes a single-step income statement — as opposed to a multi-step income statement, which reports key figures such as gross profit from sales (gross margin) and the income from operations.

3. In some income statements, only the key figure for the Cost of Goods Sold is reported. When such is the case, it is customary to

Income from Operations: the result of matching the Gross Profit from Sales with Total Operating Expenses.

Other Revenues: secondary sources of revenue such as interest earned from bonds, and from dividends from holding shares of corporations.

Other Expenses: expenses other than the cost of goods sold and operating items. Examples would include interest expense.

FIGURE 5-33

Scarborough Wholesale Hardware
Income Statement
For the Year Ended December 31, 19-1

Revenue from Sales:			
Sales		$246 686.00	
Less:			
Sales Returns and Allowances	$ 2 640.00		
Sales Discount	1 740.00	4 380.00	
Net Sales			$242 306.00
Cost of Goods Sold:			
Inventory, January 1		$ 10 000.00	
Purchases	$76 890.00		
Add:			
Transportation-in	1 800.00		
Cost of Delivered Goods	78 690.00		
Less:			
Purchases Returns and Allowances	$2 520.00		
Purchase Discounts	1 920.00	4 440.00	
Net Purchases		74 250.00	
Cost of Goods Available for Sales		84 250.00	
Less: Inventory, December 31		8 000.00	
Cost of Goods Sold			76 250.00
Gross Profit from Sales			166 056.00
Operating Expenses:			
Advertising Expense		$ 2 220.00	
Utilities Expense		720.00	
Property Taxes Expense		7 100.00	
Delivery Expense		2 160.00	
Wages and Salaries Expense		67 700.00	
Telephone Expense		420.00	
Supplies Expense		1 525.00	
Insurance Expense		1 800.00	
Bad Debts Expense		1 095.00	
Depreciation Expense—Building		2 000.00	
Depreciation Expense—Warehouse Equipment		1 200.00	
Depreciation Expense—Office Equipment		1 200.00	
Depreciation Expense—Delivery Trucks		7 600.00	
Total Operating—Expenses			96 740.00
Income from Operations			69 316.00
Other Expenses:			
Mortgage Interest Expense	$ 5 200.00		
Bank Interest Expense	500.00		
Total Other Expenses		$ 5 700.00	
Other Revenue:			
Interest Earned		530.00	5 170.00
Net Income			$ 64 146.00

Multi-step income statement. Contains groupings of items in order to report intermediate balances such as Gross Profit from Sales and Income from Operations.

FIGURE 5-34

Scarborough Wholesale Hardware
Income Statement
For the Year Ended December 31, 19-1

Revenues:		
Net Sales..................................		$242 306.00
Interest Earned		530.00
Total Revenues.......................		242 836.00
Expenses:		
Cost of Goods Sold (see schedule)	$76 250.00	
Advertising...............................	2 220.00	
Utilities	720.00	
Property Taxes...........................	7 100.00	
Delivery Expense	2 160.00	
Wages and Salaries.......................	67 700.00	
Telephone	420.00	
Supplies Used	1 525.00	
Expired Insurance	1 800.00	
Bad Debts Expense	1 095.00	
Depreciation Expense on Building............	2 000.00	
Depreciation Expense on Warehouse Equipment	1 200.00	
Depreciation Expense on Office Equipment	1 200.00	
Depreciation Expense on Delivery Trucks	7 600.00	
Mortgage Interest	5 200.00	
Bank Interest.............................	500.00	
Total Expenses......................		178 690.00
Net Income		$ 64 146.00

Single-step income statement. All items of revenue are grouped under Revenues and extended in one total, as are all items of expenses, the latter being deducted from the former to arrive at a single figure of net income (or net loss).

FIGURE 5-35

Scarborough Wholesale Hardware
Income Statement
For the Year Ended December 31, 19-1

Income from Operations		$69 316.00
Other Revenue and (Expenses):		
Interest Earned	$ 530.00	
Mortgage Interest Expense	(5 200.00)	
Bank Interest Expense	(500.00)	(5 170.00)
Net Income...................		$64 164.00

prepare a separate schedule showing the calculation of the Cost of Goods Sold.

4. As an alternative to the reporting of Other Expenses and Other Revenue in the multi-step income statement, some accountants may prefer to report these items under a common heading such as Other Revenue and (Expenses), as illustrated in Figure 5-35. When one subheading is used, note that the other expense amounts are shown in parentheses to show a distinction between an expense and other revenue. Obviously, when other expenses are greater than other revenue, the resulting figure must be treated as a deduction from the amount of Income from Operations.

5. After completing the income statement, the related balance sheet can be prepared from the appropriate columns of the worksheet. As you know, one of two forms of the balance sheet may be used: the account form or the report form. The report form is used to illustrate the balance sheet for Scarborough Wholesale Hardware in Figure 5-36. In today's accounting practice, more firms use the report form.

FIGURE 5-36

Scarborough Wholesale Hardware
Balance Sheet
As at December 31, 19-1

Assets

Current Assets:
Cash in Royal Bank		$19 056.00	
Bank Term Deposit Receipts		20 000.00	
Accounts Receivable	$21 500.00		
Less: Allowance for Bad Debts	1 095.00	20 405.00	
Inventory (at cost)		8 000.00	
Prepaid Expenses:			
Supplies on Hand	$ 75.00		
Prepaid Insurance	1 800.00	1 875.00	
Total Current Assets			$ 69 336.00

Fixed Assets (at cost):
Land (security for the mortgage payable)		$32 000.00	
Building (security for the mortgage payable)	$60 000.00		
Less: Accumulated Depreciation	2 000.00	58 000.00	
Warehouse Equipment	$12 000.00		
Less: Accumulated Depreciation	1 200.00	10 800.00	
Office Equipment	$ 7 200.00		
Less: Accumulated Depreciation	1 200.00	6 000.00	
Delivery Trucks	$44 000.00		
Less: Accumulated Depreciation	7 600.00	36 400.00	
Total Fixed Assets			143 200.00
Total Assets			$212 536.00

Liabilities

Current Liabilities:
Bank Loan Payable (on demand)	$ 5 000.00	
Accounts Payable	9 000.00	
Property Taxes Payable	5 500.00	
Current Portion of Long-Term Debt	3 000.00	
Total Current Liabilities		$ 22 500.00

Long-Term Liabilities:
9% Mortgage Payable, due 19-19	$57 000.00	
Less: Current Portion Due Within the Year	3 000.00	
Total Long-Term Liabilities		54 000.00
Total Liabilities		$ 76 500.00

Owner's Equity

Tom Allan, Capital	136 036.00
Total Liabilities and Owner's Equity	$212 536.00

FIGURE 5-37

Scarborough Wholesale Hardware
Statement of Owner's Equity
For the Year Ended December 31, 19-1

Capital, January 1		$110 000.00
Add:		
Net Income for the Year	$64 146.00	
Less:		
Withdrawals During the Year	38 110.00	
Increase in Capital During the Year		26 036.00
Capital, December 31		$136 036.00

6. When the Owner's Equity section of the balance sheet is supported only by the final Capital amount, the explanatory details are given in a separate Statement of Owner's Equity, as shown in Figure 5-37.

Step 7.
Journalizing and Posting the Adjusting Entries

Under a manual system, only the worksheet and financial statements to this point reflect a proper matchup of revenues and expenses for a particular accounting period. Therefore, it is essential that the general ledger file be similarly updated.

As you will recall, all mismatches were entered on the worksheet in the form of letter-coded adjusting entries so that an equal debit for an equal credit adjustment could easily be recognized. It is important to remember that these adjusting entries must be recorded in the general journal, because posting must occur to the general ledger accounts. And it is equally important to remember that such journalizing and such posting must take place before closing the books for the financial period. In Figure 5-38, adjusting entries are shown for Scarborough Wholesale Hardware in the order of their being letter-coded in the Adjustments section of the worksheet. To save space, no postings will be illustrated. Remember, however, that posting would occur immediately after the recording of all adjusting entries.

Step 8.
Journalizing and Posting the Closing Entries

If you have forgotten the important aspects of closing the ledger, you may wish to go back to review Topic 3 of Chapter 3. As you will recall, the process of closing not only updates the general ledger with the amounts disclosed by the financial statements, but also prepares the accounts to receive transactions for the next accounting period. To accomplish these objectives, all revenues, contra revenues, expenses, and contra expenses for the accounting period must first be transferred by closing entries in the general journal to a clearinghouse account known as Revenue and Expense Summary; then the balance of this Summary account is transferred to the Capital account; and finally, the balance of the Drawing account is transferred to the Capital account.

When a worksheet is used, the closing entries to transfer all revenues, contra revenues, expenses, and contra expenses to R. & E. Summary may be taken from the Income Statement section. When such practice is followed, one large compound entry would debit R. & E. Summary for the total of the Income Statement debit column, and individual credits would be made for each account listed in this debit column. A second compound entry would be

FIGURE 5-38

GENERAL JOURNAL
Page 88

Date	Account Title and Explanation	Post. Ref.	Debit	Credit
19-1 Dec. 31	Supplies Expense	517	1 525 00	
	Supplies on Hand	106		1 525 00
	To record the amount of supplies used.			
31	Insurance Expense	518	1 800 00	
	Prepaid Insurance	107		1 800 00
	To record the amount of expired insurance.			
31	Bad Debts Expense	519	1 095 00	
	Allowance for Bad Debts	104		1 095 00
	To record estimated loss from doubtful accounts.			
31	Depreciation Expense—Building	520	2 000 00	
	Accumulated Depreciation—Building	112		2 000 00
	To record depreciation for one year on building.			
31	Depreciation Expense—Warehouse Equipment	521	1 200 00	
	Accumulated Depreciation—Warehouse Equipment	114		1 200 00
	To record depreciation for one year on warehouse equipment.			
31	Depreciation Expense—Office Equipment	522	1 200 00	
	Accumulated Depreciation—Office Equipment	116		1 200 00
	To record depreciation for one year on office equipment.			
31	Depreciation Expense—Delivery Trucks	523	7 600 00	
	Accumulated Depreciation—Delivery Trucks	118		7 600 00
	To record depreciation for one year on delivery trucks.			
31	Bank Interest Expense	701	50 00	
	Cash in Royal Bank	101		50 00
	To record one month's bank interest on demand loan.			
31	Cash in Royal Bank	101	530 00	
	Interest Earned	601		530 00
	To record interest earned for 90 days on bank deposit receipts.			

CHAPTER 5: Accounting Cycle for a Merchandising Firm   **189**

made by crediting the R. & E. Summary for the total of the Income Statement credit column, while individual debits would be made for each account listed in this credit column. After postings are made for both compound entries, all temporary accounts would be closed and the Summary account would contain the information of the Income Statement columns of the worksheet.

FIGURE 5-39

GENERAL JOURNAL Page 89

Date		Account Title and Explanation	Post. Ref.	Debit	Credit
19-1 Dec.	31	Revenue and Expense Summary	399	195 510 00	
		Inventory	106		10 000 00
		Sales Returns and Allowances	402		2 640 00
		Sales Discount	403		1 740 00
		Purchases	501		76 890 00
		Transportation-in	502		1 800 00
		Advertising Expense	510		2 220 00
		Utilities Expense	511		720 00
		Property Taxes Expense	512		7 100 00
		Delivery Expense	513		~~67 700 00~~
		Wages and Salaries Expense	514		~~73 200 00~~
		Telephone Expense	515		420 00
		Supplies Expense	517		1 525 00
		Insurance Expense	518		1 800 00
		Bad Debts Expense	519		1 095 00
		Depreciation Expense—Building	520		2 000 00
		Depreciation Expense—Warehouse Equipment	521		1 200 00
		Depreciation Expense—Office Equipment	522		1 200 00
		Depreciation Expense—Delivery Trucks	523		7 600 00
		Bank Interest Expense	701		500 00
		Mortgage Interest Expense	702		5 200 00
		To close expense and contra revenue accounts to R. & E. Summary.			
	31	Sales	401	246 686 00	
		Interest Earned	601	530 00	
		Purchases Returns and Allowances	503	2 520 00	
		Purchases Discount	504	1 920 00	
		Inventory	106	8 000 00	
		Revenue and Expense Summary	399		259 656 00
		To close revenue and contra expense accounts to R. & E. Summary.			
	31	Revenue and Expense Summary	399	64 146 00	
		Tom Allan, Capital	301		64 156 00
		To close the net income to owner's Capital account.			
	31	Tom Allan, Capital	301	~~38 110 00~~ 64 146 00	
		Tom Allan, Drawing	302		38 110 00
		To close balance of Drawing account to owner's Capital account.			

Handwritten annotations: 2160.00 ; 67700.00

From both compound closing entries, observe carefully that the Inventory account is updated to reflect the balance on hand at the end of the accounting year. Obviously, this updating is achieved by transferring the debit amount of the beginning inventory to the debit side of R. & E. Summary account. At this point, one can think of the Inventory account as being "closed" to zero. When the final inventory figure is recorded to the credit side of R. & E. Summary (by the second compound entry), then the Inventory account receives the new balance which will be carried forward on the balance sheet as the current asset. Of course, the credit to R. & E. Summary provides the effect of a contra account in the calculation of the Cost of Goods Sold.

Step 9.
Preparing a
Postclosing
Trial Balance

The final step in any closing routine is to check the accuracy of the general ledger. As you know from earlier work, a postclosing trial balance is often taken after all temporary accounts have been closed. The postclosing trial balance for Scarborough Wholesale Hardware, prepared manually, is shown in Figure 5-40.

FIGURE 5-40

Scarborough Wholesale Hardware
Postclosing Trial Balance
December 31, 19-1

Account Title	Acct. No.	Debit	Credit
Cash in Royal Bank	101	19 056 00	
Bank Term Deposit Receipts	103	20 000 00	
Accounts Receivable	104	21 500 00	
Allowance for Bad Debts	105		1 095 00
Inventory	106	8 000 00	
Supplies on Hand	107	75 00	
Prepaid Insurance	108	1 800 00	
Land	110	32 000 00	
Building	111	60 000 00	
Accumulated Depreciation—Building	112		2 000 00
Warehouse Equipment	113	12 000 00	
Accumulated Depreciation—Whse. Equip.	114		1 200 00
Office Equipment	115	7 200 00	
Accumulated Depreciation—Office Equip.	116		1 200 00
Delivery Trucks	117	44 000 00	
Accumulated Depreciation—Del. Trucks	118		7 600 00
Bank Loan Payable	201		5 000 00
Accounts Payable	202		9 000 00
Property Taxes Payable	203		5 500 00
Mortgage Payable	220		57 000 00
Tom Allan, Capital	301		136 036 00
		225 631 00	225 631 00

Balance Sheet
As at December 31, 19-1

Owner's Equity

Tom Allan, Capital... $136 036.00

Three checks may be made to prove the accuracy of this trial balance: first, the totals of the postclosing trial balance must agree; second, only permanent (real) accounts must be listed in this trial balance; and third, the balance shown by the Capital account must be identical to the figure of the new owner's equity as disclosed on the balance sheet and statement of owner's equity. In fact, you can say that a correct postclosing trial balance has the same information as the balance sheet, since the permanent accounts are balance sheet accounts. In this context, the postclosing trial balance is a balance sheet in debit and credit form.

Nine separate steps have now been identified in a complete accounting cycle of activities performed under a manual accounting system: (1) originating transaction data; (2) journalizing transaction data; (3) posting transaction data; (4) preparing the trial balance; (5) preparing the ten-column worksheet; (6) preparing the financial statements; (7) journalizing and posting the adjusting entries; (8) journalizing and posting the closing entries; and (9) preparing a postclosing trial balance.

TOPIC 3 Problems

Preparing financial statements for the Welland Wholesale Supply Co.

5.14 From the worksheet solved for Problem 5.11, prepare financial statements as directed below for the Welland Wholesale Supply Co.

    a Prepare an income statement in the multi-step form.

    b Prepare a statement of owner's equity and a classified balance sheet in report form. Assume that no additional investments were made during the year.

    Note: Save your worksheet and financial statements for use in Problem 5.17.

Preparing financial statements for the Brantford Wholesale Supply Co.

5.15 From the worksheet solved for Problem 5.12, prepare the financial statements as directed below for the Brantford Wholesale Supply Co.

    a Prepare an income statement in the single-step form ~~with a separate schedule of cost of goods sold~~.

    b Prepare a second income statement in the multi-step form ~~and without the separate schedule of cost of goods sold~~.

    c Prepare a statement of owner's equity and a classified balance sheet in report form. (Of the $100 000 disclosed in D. Ciotti, Capital, assume that $90 000 represented the opening balance on January 1, and that the remaining $10 000 was an additional investment made during the year.)

    Note: Save the worksheet and financial statements for use in Problem 5.18.

Preparing financial statements for Miller's TV Repair Service.

5.16 From the worksheet solved for Problem 5.13, prepare financial statements as directed below for Miller's TV Repair Service.

a Prepare an income statement in the single-step form.
b Prepare a classified balance sheet in report form. Do not provide for a separate statement of owner's equity. Assume that no additional investments were made during the accounting period.
Note: Save your worksheet and financial statements for use in Problem 5.19.

Completing the accounting cycle for Welland Wholesale Supply Co.

5.17 Complete these items using the data in the worksheet and financial statements prepared for the Welland Wholesale Supply Co. in Problems 5.11 and 5.14.
a Journalize the adjusting and closing entries.
b Show how the following accounts would appear after the closing entries have been posted: Revenue and Expense Summary; Linda Martin, Capital; and Linda Martin, Drawing. *Note*: If desired, the entire general ledger solved for Problem 5.1 could also be used.
c Show how the postclosing trial balance would appear after the closing entries have been posted.

Completing the accounting cycle for Brantford Wholesale Supply Co.

5.18 Complete these items using the data in the worksheet and financial statements prepared for the Brantford Wholesale Supply Co. in Problems 5.12 and 5.15.
a Journalize the adjusting and closing entries.
b Show how the following accounts would appear after the closing entries have been posted: Revenue and Expense Summary; D. Ciotti, Capital; and D. Ciotti, Drawing.
c Show how the postclosing trial balance would appear after the closing entries have been posted.

Completing the accounting cycle for Miller's TV Repair Service.

5.19 Complete these items using the data in the worksheet and financial statements prepared for Miller's TV Repair Service in Problems 5.13 and 5.16.
a Journalize the adjusting and closing entries.
b Show how the following accounts would appear after the closing entries have been posted: Revenue and Expense Summary; Jim Miller, Capital; and Jim Miller, Drawing.
c Show how the postclosing trial balance would appear after the closing entries have been posted.

TOPIC 4 Introducing the Microcomputer General Ledger System

The success of electronic spreadsheet software for use with microcomputers in the early 1980s encouraged software businesses to develop programs to do all of the steps in the traditional accounting cycle. Since the general ledger is essential in covering the steps in the accounting cycle, the electronic accounting programs were identified by labels such as General Ledger System Software, General Ledger Package, General Ledger Program, and General Ledger Module. Some of the general ledger packages in Canadian use are listed in Figure 5-41.

CHAPTER 5: Accounting Cycle for a Merchandising Firm   **193**

Identifying Essential Characteristics

FIGURE 5-41

Ten General Ledger Packages

- *Abacus*® *(Comsoft Inc.)*
- *AccPac Bedford Accounting*® *(Computer Associates International)*
- *AccPac BPI Accounting*® *(Computer Associates International)*
- *AccPac Plus*® *(Computer Associates International)*
- *Classic*® *(Classic Software Corporation)*
- *DacEasy Accounting*® *(Dac Software)*
- *Great Plains Accounting Series*® *(Great Plains Software)*
- *NewViews*® *(Q. W. Page Associates Inc.)*
- *RealWorld*® *(RealWorld Corporation)*
- *Summation*® *(SumWare Corporation)*

General accounting packages (off-shelf accounting packages): electronic accounting programs that are general in nature to suit a variety of businesses.

Real-time accounting: a type of computerized accounting system under which individual transactions, once entered, update financial statement information immediately; thus, there is no delay in printing financial statements.

Batch processing: a type of computerized accounting system under which individual transactions are first added to a transaction (batch) file that contains other, similar transactions during a period; later, usually at the end of the month, the batch file is posted to the G/L so that financial statements can be printed.

Before examining how a G/L package is used to process the traditional accounting cycle, it is useful to outline some of the main characteristics found in the majority of electronic general ledger systems.

- In the majority of cases, the G/L package is only one of several accounting programs available under a software's registered name. For example, *Abacus*, *AccPac Bedford*, *AccPac Plus*, and the other names listed in Figure 5-41, contain not only the general ledger package, but also individual programs to run (process) other common accounting applications like accounts receivable and accounts payable. Therefore, it is more accurate to call these packages as **general accounting packages** or "off-shelf accounting packages," since they include separate programs to run the general ledger, accounts receivable, accounts payable, and other specialized accounting areas like payroll, inventory, and invoicing. The word "general" in accounting packages bought from the shelves of retailers simply means that the packages are each intended to suit a variety of businesses and not necessarily a single business which requires customized software such as a dental practice.

- Some accounting software is written to run only under a specific operating system. For example, Bedford, written to run under MS-DOS (Microsoft Disk Operating System), will not run on the Macintosh Finder Operating System. Similarly, an accounting package written for IBM's new OS/2 (Operating System 2) will not run under Unix (a powerful, multi-tasking operating system originally developed by American Telephone & Telegraph).

- All accounting packages begin with a version called "1.0." Any slight changes would then be labelled as "1.1." However, major revisions to add features to the program will be marketed under a higher number such as "2.0," "3.0," etc. In general, the higher the version number, the more features the program will have. Of course, the latest version will be more expensive than earlier versions.

- Not all general accounting packages include the same accounting modules. For example, while all may offer the general ledger, accounts receivable, and accounts payable, only a few may offer a Canadian payroll module. And those that do offer a such a module may offer the program only by interfacing a widely developed Canadian program such as *EasyPay*® (Oakville, Ontario). For example, AccPac Plus, *NewViews*, and *Summation* allow their accounting packages to be interfaced with EasyPay so that their users may process a Canadian payroll and post the results to their general ledgers.

- In general, microcomputer accounting packages may be classified into two groups: (1) those that support **real-time accounting** and (2) those that support **batch processing**. For example, AccPac Plus supports batch processing, while NewViews supports real-time accounting. Although the side margin notes show a simple distinction, the difference

between real-time accounting and batch processing will be explained in Chapter 11.
- Not all of the accounting packages process the steps of the accounting cycle in the same way. For example, AccPac Plus and Summation require a G/L chart of accounts to be set up before transactions can be journalized and posted to those accounts. On the other hand, NewViews offers the option of eliminating the chart of accounts in favour of updating a predesigned set of financial statements. Similarly, NewViews does not require the use of trial balances and closing entries, while packages like Summation offer the traditional coverage of the accounting cycle with electronic features.

To simplify matters, only Summation's General Ledger System will be used in this chapter to illustrate how accounting software for a microcomputer can be used to process all of the steps in the traditional accounting cycle. Brief accounts of AccPac Bedford and AccPac Plus will be provided in Topic 1 of Chapter 11.

Step 1. Creating the Computerized Chart of Accounts

Summation: a Canadian real-time accounting package developed for the microcomputer using the Microsoft Disk Operating System (MS-DOS).

When a computerized accounting package like Summation is used to run the general ledger application, it is essential to enlarge the chart of accounts so that the computer will recognize the nature of each account, the normal balance for that account, and where that account is positioned in designated financial statements. Suppose, for example, the owner of Scarborough Wholesale Hardware decided to use **Summation** to process its general ledger. Before any transaction may be "journalized," a chart of accounts may be organized as illustrated in Figure 5-42.

Analysis   Note the following points when studying the partial computerized chart of accounts for Scarborough Wholesale Hardware:
- Although the same three-digit account codes shown for the manual method could be followed, a four-digit number code has been used to allow for more flexibility in distinguishing between headings, subheadings, and account titles.
- Account codes must clearly identify whether word groups are headings, subheadings, or regular account titles. For example, on the future printout of the balance sheet, the computer is guided by the decision that "1000 ASSETS" is merely a heading, while "1155 Inventory at Cost" is a regular account that will print a dollar amount. Similarly, the computer will interpret "5000 Cost of Goods Sold" as a heading on the future printout of the income statement, while "5005 Inventory Start of Period" will be a regular account under the Cost of Goods Sold section.
- The creation of regular accounts must indicate whether the normal balance will be a debit or a credit. Obviously, normal balances will be identified as to the account position within the expanded accounting equation.

CHAPTER 5: Accounting Cycle for a Merchandising Firm   **195**

FIGURE 5-42

Scarborough Wholesale Hardware
91.01.01   Page 1

Chart of Accounts

Account Code	Description	Total Level	Account Type	Normal Balance	Report Type	Extra Lines
1000	ASSETS	8	Heading	Debit	All Statements	1 Line
1100	Current Assets	5	Heading	Debit	All Statements	1 Line
1105	Cash on Hand	3	Heading	Debit	All Statements	No lines
1110	Petty Cash	1	Regular	Debit	All Statements	No lines
1115	Cash in Royal Bank	1	Regular	Debit	All Statements	No lines
1125	Total - Cash on Hand	3	Total	Debit	All Statements	2 Lines
1135	Accounts Receivable	3	Heading	Debit	All Statements	1 Line
1140	Accounts Receivable - Trade	1	Regular	Debit	All Statements	No lines
1145	Allowance - Bad Debts	1	Regular	Debit	All Statements	No lines
1150	Net Realizable Value	3	Total	Debit	All Statements	2 Lines
1155	Inventory at Cost	3	Regular	Debit	All Statements	1 Line
1160	Prepaid Expenses	3	Heading	Debit	All Statements	No lines
1165	Supplies on Hand	1	Regular	Debit	All Statements	No lines
1170	Prepaid Insurance	1	Regular	Debit	All Statements	No lines
1180	Total - Prepaid Expenses	3	Total	Debit	All Statements	2 Lines
1190	Total - Current Assets	5	Total	Debit	All Statements	2 Lines
5000	Cost of Goods Sold	7	Heading	Debit	All Statements	No lines
5005	Inventory at Start of Period	6	Regular	Debit	All Statements	No lines
5010	Purchases	6	Regular	Debit	All Statements	No lines
5020	Transportation-in	6	Regular	Debit	All Statements	No lines
5030	Purchases Returns and Allow.	6	Regular	Credit	All Statements	No lines
5040	Purchases Discount	6	Regular	Credit	All Statements	No lines
5050	Less - Ending Inventory	6	Regular	Credit	All Statements	No lines
5060	Total - Cost of Goods Sold	7	Total	Debit	All Statements	3 Lines
5900	Gross Margin on Sales	8	Total	Credit	All Statements	Page

- The creation of regular accounts must also indicate the total level of the amount to be printed on the future financial statement. Thus, if you want to show the Prepaid Insurance account balance under Prepaid Expenses as being reported in the same money column as Supplies on Hand, it is important to designate that level, as shown in the grid in Figure 5-43.

FIGURE 5-43

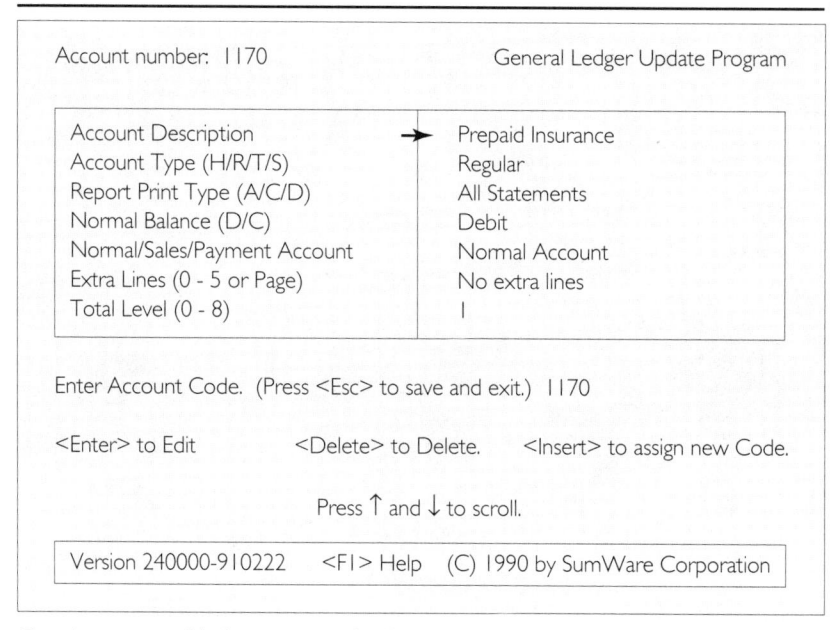

```
Account number: 1170                    General Ledger Update Program

    Account Description      →    Prepaid Insurance
    Account Type (H/R/T/S)        Regular
    Report Print Type (A/C/D)     All Statements
    Normal Balance (D/C)          Debit
    Normal/Sales/Payment Account  Normal Account
    Extra Lines (0 - 5 or Page)   No extra lines
    Total Level (0 - 8)           1

Enter Account Code. (Press <Esc> to save and exit.)  1170

<Enter> to Edit      <Delete> to Delete.     <Insert> to assign new Code.

              Press ↑ and ↓ to scroll.

    Version 240000-910222   <F1> Help   (C) 1990 by SumWare Corporation
```

Creating a general ledger account for Prepaid Insurance through Summation.

- Notice that separate account titles with separate account codes are essential to distinguish accounts for financial statement reporting. For example, the beginning inventory is no longer an asset at the end of the financial accounting period. It is considered part of the cost of goods sold; therefore, an account code such as "5005 Inventory at Start of Period" is given, to ensure that the account title and balance will be reported on the income statement under Cost of Goods Sold. Similarly, the ending inventory is both a current asset on the balance sheet and a contra to the cost of goods available for sale on the income statement. A distinct account title like "Inventory at Cost" with account number 1155 is given, to ensure that the account title and amount is reported on the balance sheet. Also, a distinct account title like "5050 Less - Ending Inventory" with a different account code is given, to ensure that the account title and amount is reported on the income statement. Without these differences, the computer cannot possibly know how to distinguish accounts and where to report their balances. (Of course, some human with accounting knowledge must set up these account codes for any microcomputer general ledger package.)

- Under any microcomputer G/L system, it is recommended that the user print a "dummy" set of financial statements so that details within the chart of accounts can be double-checked. As the partial illustration in Figure 5-44 shows, a dummy set of financial statements is the printout of the requested statement with zero dollar amounts. With these printouts, the user can double-check heading and subheading positions as well as subtotal and total levels. Changes can then be made before actual accounting transactions are journalized and posted through the accounting cycle.

FIGURE 5-44

```
91.01.01           Scarborough Wholesale Hardware              Page 1
                           Balance Sheet
                         As at January, 1991

ASSETS

  Current Assets

     Cash on Hand
        Petty Cash                         $      0.00
        Cash in Royal Bank                        0.00

     Total - Cash on Hand                              $      0.00

     Accounts Receivable
        Accounts Receivable - Trade               0.00
        Allowance - Bad Debts                     0.00

     Net Realizable Value                             $       0.00

     Inventory at Cost                                        0.00

     Prepaid Expenses
        Supplies on Hand                          0.00
        Prepaid Insurance                         0.00

     Total - Prepaid Expenses                         $       0.00

   Total - Current Assets                                             $     0.00

Assets continued on page 2
```

Step 2. Journalizing and Posting Transaction Data

Under the majority of microcomputer G/L systems using real-time accounting, the steps of journalizing and posting transactions to the general ledger are combined. For example, if Summation were used, and assuming that the computerized chart of accounts was prepared, the opening entry for Scarborough Wholesale Hardware would be journalized and posted as follows.

From Summation's Master System Menu, shown in Figure 5-45, the accounting clerk would press <3> to "Run the General Ledger System."

FIGURE 5-45

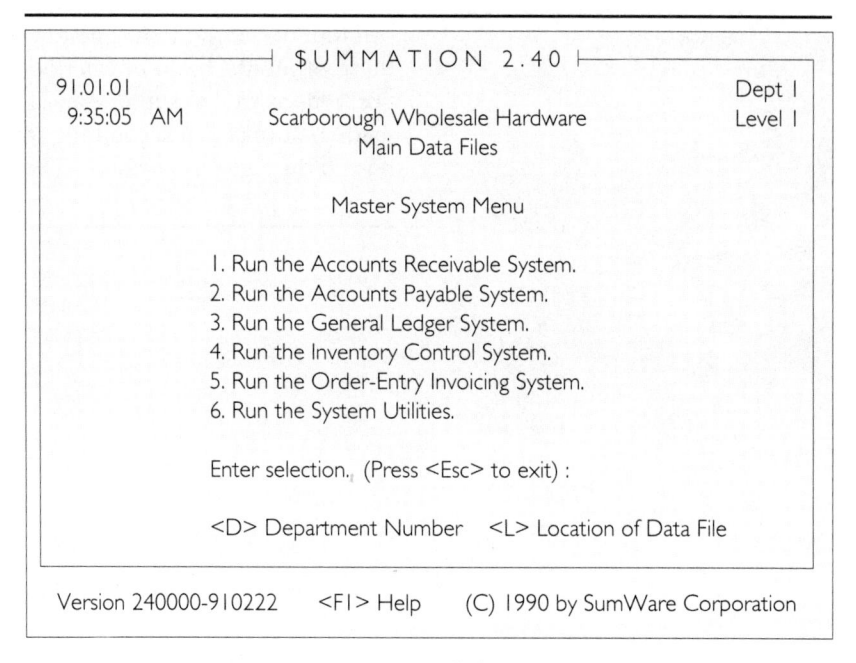

```
┤ $UMMATION 2.40 ├
91.01.01                                                    Dept 1
 9:35:05  AM      Scarborough Wholesale Hardware            Level 1
                         Main Data Files

                       Master System Menu

                 1. Run the Accounts Receivable System.
                 2. Run the Accounts Payable System.
                 3. Run the General Ledger System.
                 4. Run the Inventory Control System.
                 5. Run the Order-Entry Invoicing System.
                 6. Run the System Utilities.

                 Enter selection.  (Press <Esc> to exit) :

                 <D> Department Number    <L> Location of Data File


Version 240000-910222    <F1> Help    (C) 1990 by SumWare Corporation
```

Summation's G/L program responds by presenting the user-friendly General Ledger Master Menu shown in Figure 5-46.

FIGURE 5-46

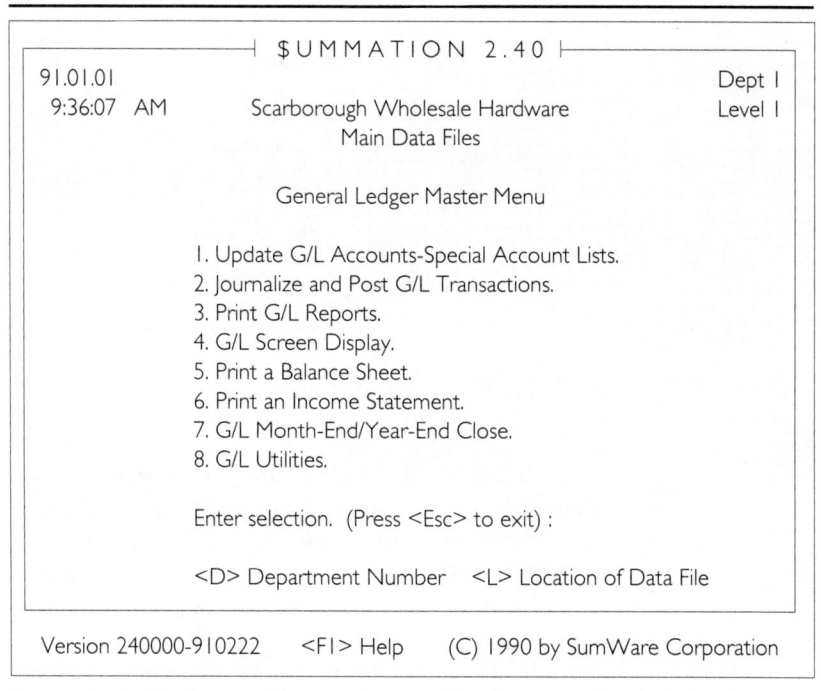

```
┤ $UMMATION 2.40 ├
91.01.01                                                    Dept 1
 9:36:07  AM      Scarborough Wholesale Hardware            Level 1
                         Main Data Files

                    General Ledger Master Menu

                 1. Update G/L Accounts-Special Account Lists.
                 2. Journalize and Post G/L Transactions.
                 3. Print G/L Reports.
                 4. G/L Screen Display.
                 5. Print a Balance Sheet.
                 6. Print an Income Statement.
                 7. G/L Month-End/Year-End Close.
                 8. G/L Utilities.

                 Enter selection.  (Press <Esc> to exit) :

                 <D> Department Number    <L> Location of Data File


Version 240000-910222    <F1> Help    (C) 1990 by SumWare Corporation
```

Summation's G/L System. Observe the user-friendly menu. The clerk simply presses <2> to run the program to "Journalize and Post G/L Transactions."

CHAPTER 5: Accounting Cycle for a Merchandising Firm **199**

Obviously, the accounting clerk would press <2> to initiate the program to journalize transactions affecting the general ledger. Once <2> has been pressed, a General Ledger Transaction Entry Grid appears as in Figure 5-47.

FIGURE **5-47**

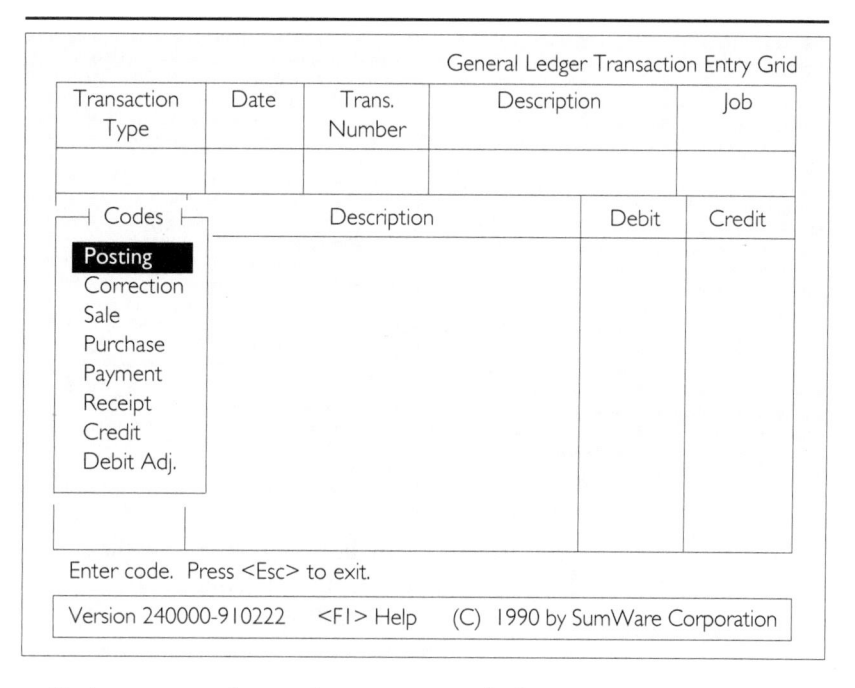

```
                                    General Ledger Transaction Entry Grid
┌─────────────┬──────┬─────────┬─────────────────────┬─────────┐
│ Transaction │ Date │ Trans.  │ Description         │ Job     │
│ Type        │      │ Number  │                     │         │
├─────────────┴──────┴─────────┴─────────────────────┴─────────┤
│ ┌─ Codes ─┐         Description          │ Debit  │ Credit  │
│ │ Posting │                              │        │         │
│ │ Correction                             │        │         │
│ │ Sale                                   │        │         │
│ │ Purchase                               │        │         │
│ │ Payment                                │        │         │
│ │ Receipt                                │        │         │
│ │ Credit                                 │        │         │
│ │ Debit Adj.                             │        │         │
│ └─────────┘                                                  │
│                                                              │
│ Enter code. Press <Esc> to exit.                             │
│ Version 240000-910222   <F1> Help   (C) 1990 by SumWare Corporation │
└──────────────────────────────────────────────────────────────┘
```

FIGURE **5-48**

To begin journalizing, the accounting clerk must enter an appropriate transaction-type entry code. In the majority of cases, this code will simply be "Posting," as shown in the figure. Notice that the code is highlighted on the screen. All that is required, then, is to press the <Enter> key on the keyboard. On the other hand, if the code for "Correction" were required, the clerk would use the <downward arrow> key to select the code, and then press <Enter>. After pressing <Enter>, the word "Posting" and the current date appear in the upper left boxes as shown in Figure 5-49.

Notice that in the Date column, immediately after the date, a cursor appears, which in the display would be flashing. If the wrong date had been entered when the initial program was run, the clerk could use the <Backspace> key to move the cursor back, deleting the old date, and then key in the correct transaction date. Here, we assume that the opening entry will be journalized and posted at the beginning of the calendar year. Therefore, the clerk would simply press <Enter> to move the cursor to the "Trans. Number" box.

Automatic numbers, in numerical sequence, will appear in the "Trans. Number" box. In this case, since no previous transactions have been entered, "1" will appear. Also, a large rectangular cursor will be shown in the Description box — which may also be referred to as "the Description field."

FIGURE 5-49

	General Ledger Transaction Entry Grid					
Transaction Type	Date	Trans. Number	Description		Job	
Posting	91.01.01					
GL Code		Description		Debit		Credit

Version 240000-910222   <F1> Help   (C) 1990 by SumWare Corporation

In the Description field, the accounting clerk would type a short description for the entry. Since this is the first entry, "Opening Entry" would be an appropriate description. If the description has been typed correctly (and any typing errors made in the description can easily be corrected by using the <Backspace> key and then making the appropriate corrections), the clerk would press <Enter> to put the description into the computer's memory. A partial view showing the General Ledger Transaction Entry Grid completed to the end of the Description field is illustrated in Figure 5-50. Notice that the (flashing) cursor and a set of stars appear in the next field, the Job field.

Since no job costing is required for this entry, the clerk would press <Enter> to skip the Job field. The cursor with a set of six stars appears on the first line immediately below the GL Code column. The clerk must now begin the formal part of journalizing the opening entry — that is, entering the debits and credits that make up the opening entry.

Of course, the accounting clerk would be authorized to enter the accounts and correct amounts from some approved source document. Some businesses use a document called a ***journal voucher***, as shown in Figure 5-51. Other businesses might simply refer to the opening (pre-operating) balance sheet to identify the accounts for the opening entry. Regardless of the business, sound accounting procedures require the use of some source document to support every transaction. Here, let's assume that the pre-operating balance sheet has been approved for the clerk's use to journalize the opening entry similar to the one illustrated under the manual system in Figure 5-7.

Journal voucher: a source document supporting an entry in a journal.

CHAPTER 5: Accounting Cycle for a Merchandising Firm   **201**

FIGURE 5-50

General Ledger Transaction Entry Grid

Transaction Type	Date	Trans. Number	Description	Job
Posting	91.01.01	1	Opening Entry	▌********

GL Code	Description	Debit	Credit

Version 240000-910222   <F1> Help   (C) 1990 by SumWare Corporation

FIGURE 5-51

JOURNAL VOUCHER   No. 01

Account Name	Account No.	Debit	Credit
Cash in Royal Bank	1115	10 000 00	
Inventory at Cost	1155	10 000 00	
Land	1210	32 000 00	
Building	1220	60 000 00	
Warehouse Equipment	1230	12 000 00	
Office Equipment	1240	7 200 00	
Delivery Trucks	1250	44 000 00	
Accounts Payable	2120		5 200 00
Mortgage Payable	2510		60 000 00
Tom Allan, Capital	3010		110 000 00
TOTALS		175 200 00	175 200 00

Particulars

To record the opening entry.

PREPARED BY: APPROVALS: DATE:
A., G/L Clerk   A.T., Gen. Acct. Mgr.   JAN. 1, 1991
                     Tom Allan

Under many G/L packages, the clerk must first key in the account code of the first account title to be entered. To do this, he or she could look up a printed chart of accounts for all account numbers. However, the Summation package provides an excellent shortcut, allowing the clerk to call up a chart of accounts window on top of the journal grid. This window is activated by simultaneously pressing <Ctrl> and <D> — that is, the control key and the key for the letter D (which then stands for Display). When these keys are pressed, a window showing the chart of accounts for the general ledger appears, as illustrated in Figure 5-52. The clerk can now select any desired account code and related account title that has been created in the official chart of accounts.

Clearly, it is most important to create this chart before any journalizing and posting occurs. In a computerized general ledger system, the chart of accounts is used to organize the future printout of financial statements and to provide the account codes and account titles for computer journalizing.

FIGURE 5-52

```
                                           General Ledger Transaction Entry Grid
 Transaction    Date      Trans.        Description              Job
   Type                   Number
                          | G/L Regular Accounts |
 Posting                  1105  Petty Cash
                          1115  Cash in Royal Bank        ebit      Credit
   GL Code                1140  Accounts Receivable - Trade
   ******                 1145  Allowance - Bad Debts
                          1155  Inventory at Cost
                          1165  Supplies on Hand
                          1170  Prepaid Insurance
                          1210  Land
                          1220  Building
                          1225  Accumulated Depreciation
                          1230  Warehouse Equipment
                          1235  Accumulated Depreciation
                          1240  Office Equipment
                          1245  Accumulated Depreciation
                                                          0.00      0.00

 Press <Del> to erase line, <Page Up> for details, <Esc> when finished.
 Version 240000-910222    <F1> Help    (C) 1990 by SumWare Corporation
```

Since the first account code and its related account title are highlighted for Cash in Royal Bank, the clerk can simply press <Enter>. Other accounts can also be selected, by using the <downward arrow> and <upward arrow> keys on the keyboard to highlight the account and pressing <Enter>. The computer responds by showing the correct account number in the G/L Code column. Pressing <Enter> a second time will

FIGURE 5-53

Transaction Type	Date	Trans. Number	Description	Job
Posting	91.01.01	1	Opening Entry	

General Ledger Transaction Entry Grid

GL Code	Description	Debit	Credit
1115	Cash in Royal Bank	*********	

Account balance is $0.00 dr   0.00   0.00
Enter <D> for debit, <C> for credit

Version 240000-910222   <F1> Help   (C) 1990 by SumWare Corporation

show the correct account title and cursor in the Debit money column as illustrated in Figure 5-53.

How does the computer know to place the cursor in the Debit column opposite the account title? The answer is that a human being has indicated the normal balances for all regular accounts in the organization and creation of the chart of accounts. In other words, the computer only does what it has been "programmed" to do by some human. Once again, it is clear that someone with a knowledge of general ledger accounting theory is vital to the future success of a computerized accounting system.

Notice that below the G/L Transaction Entry Grid, opposite the two money columns, the message "Account balance is $0.00 dr" appears. In this manner Summation gives the account balance of every account entered in the journal grid; in this case there is no balance for Cash in Royal Bank, and therefore the balance is zero.

The opening balance for Cash in Royal Bank would be typed in the Debit money column, any typing error being easily corrected by using the <Backspace> key. Even-dollar amounts do not require typing of "00" cents. The clerk would simply press <Enter> at that point to enter the correct dollar amount; the cursor then jumps to the second line, where the next account code would be entered. Again, the clerk would press <Ctrl> + <D> to display the chart of accounts window and then select the correct account code and title. Pressing <Enter> enters the account code; pressing <Enter> a second time enters the correct account title and the

FIGURE 5-54

		General Ledger Transaction Entry Grid		
Transaction Type	Date	Trans. Number	Description	Job
Posting	91.01.01	1	Opening Entry	

GL Code	Description	Debit	Credit
1115	Cash in Royal Bank	10000.00	
1155	Inventory at Cost	10000.00	
1210	Land	32000.00	
1220	Building	60000.00	
1230	Warehouse Equipment	12000.00	
1240	Office Equipment	7200.00	
1250	Delivery Trucks	44000.00	
2120	Accounts Payable		5200.00
2510	Mortgage Payable		60000.00
3010	Tom Allan, Capital		110000.00
		175200.00	175200.00

Press <Del> to erase line, <Page Up> for details, <Esc> when finished.

Version 240000-910222   <F1> Help   (C) 1990 by SumWare Corporation

cursor in the correct money column. This entire procedure would be repeated until the complete double entry is displayed as illustrated in Figure 5-54.

Observe that the G/L Transaction Entry Grid displays the totals for the Debit and Credit money columns. Summation will not permit any journal entry to be posted unless the debits equal the credits for every journal entry. In this case, the totals agree. Therefore, the clerk simply presses the <Esc> key to tell the computer that the entry is complete. At this point, a final message appears: "Post this transaction? (Y/n)." This message is a precaution just in case the clerk does not want to post the entry. In our case, the clerk would press <Enter> or <Y> to automatically post the opening entry to the general ledger.

The printout of the general journal is produced automatically by the clerk's running the appropriate program from the General Ledger Master Menu. For example, from Summation's G/L Master Menu, the clerk simply uses program "3. Print G/L Reports" to gain access to the General Ledger Report Generator as illustrated in Figure 5-55.

From the General Ledger Report Generator, one would simply press <2> to print the desired transactions entered via the G/L Transaction Entry Grid. For example, Figure 5-56 shows what the printout would look like for the opening entry.

In the general journal printout, observe that the totals are included for the all debits and credits of the entry, something that would not appear in

FIGURE 5-55

```
┤ $ U M M A T I O N   2.40 ├

        General Ledger Report Generator

        1. Print the General Ledger Detail Report.
        2. Print the General Ledger Journal.
        3. Print the General Ledger Account Worksheet.
        4. Print the Chart of Accounts.
        5. Print a Combined G/L Detail Report.

        Enter selection.  (Press <Esc> to exit) :
```

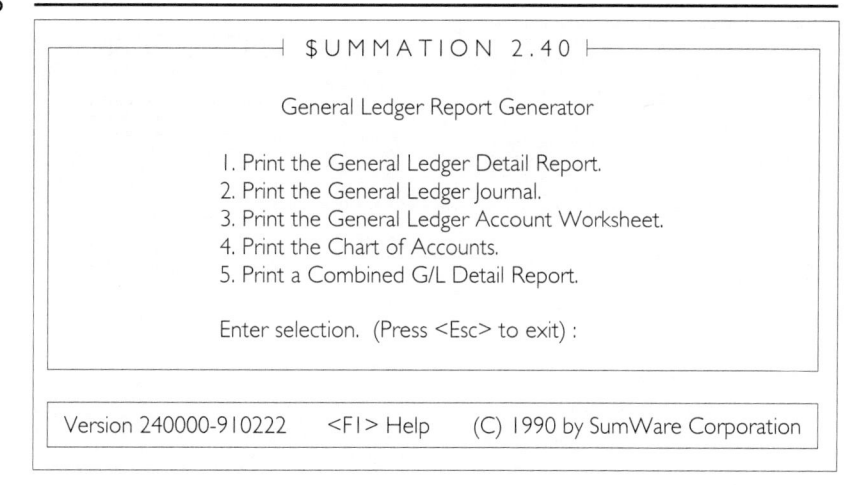

Version 240000-910222   <F1> Help   (C) 1990 by SumWare Corporation

FIGURE 5-56

Scarborough Wholesale Hardware
91.01.01
                                                                            Page   1
                            General Ledger Journal

Trans. Date	Source	Trans. Number	Trans. Type	Transaction Description	G/L Account		Debit	Credit
91.01.01	G/L	1	Posting	Opening Entry	1115	Cash in Royal Bank	10,000.00	
					1155	Inventory at Cost	10,000.00	
					1210	Land	32,000.00	
					1220	Building	60,000.00	
					1230	Warehouse Equipment	12,000.00	
					1240	Office Equipment	7,200.00	
					1250	Delivery Trucks	44,000.00	
					2120	Accounts Payable		5,200.00
					2510	Mortgage Payable		60,000.00
					3010	Tom Allan, Capital		110,000.00
							175,200.00	175,200.00

Note: At the time of writing, the majority of computer printouts did not follow the suggested use of the blank space as the triad separator in dollar amounts. Instead, the traditional comma was very much in majority usage.

a handwritten general journal. These totals are automatically produced in the computer printout to show the reader that the double entry is in balance, which is to say that the accounting equation would be in balance if the same entry were done through the accounting equation.

The clerk can also process the printout of any general ledger account by simply returning to the General Ledger Report Generator. For example, by pressing <1> to "Print the General Ledger Detail Report," the clerk can print the details of posting to an account like Cash in Royal Bank. A simulated printout of this account is illustrated in Figure 5-57.

FIGURE 5-57

Scarborough Wholesale Hardware
91.01.01   Page   1
                              General Ledger Detail Report

Starting date: 91.01.01   Ending date: 91.01.01

Trans. Date	Trans. Number	Source	Trans. Code	Transaction Description	Debit	Credit	Balance
				1115 - Cash in Royal Bank			
91.01.01	1	G/L	Posting	Opening Entry	10,000.00		10,000.00 dr

Obviously, the analysis of posting under a microcomputer system will be different from that of procedures under a manual system. It is important to recognize these differences:

- All postings were done automatically immediately after a journal entry was entered via the G/L Transaction Entry Grid.
- Since all postings were automated, there was no need for posting references through Post. Ref. columns.
- The format of the account includes not only the traditional three money columns for Debit, Credit, and Balance, but also extra columns to identify Transaction Date, Transaction Number, and Source (the particular accounting module where the original entry was journalized).
- If the original debits and credits were entered correctly, one can assume that all subsequent postings are error-free. This is a decided advantage of any computerized accounting system.

Step 3. Printing the Trial Balance

Under a manual accounting system, the formal trial balance would be prepared in handwritten or typewritten format. However, no extra time is required to do a formal trial balance under a microcomputer G/L package. For example, in Summation, the accounting clerk would use the General Ledger Report Generator, illustrated in Figure 5-55, pressing <3> to "Print the General Ledger Account Worksheet" on which is listed the entire set of general ledger accounts with their respective balances as at any designated year-end. The printout is quite similar to that prepared under the manual system.

In addition, however, most G/L packages provide a second trial balance of the general ledger. For example, in printing the Detail Report of the entire general ledger, say to the end of December 19-1, Summation displays a zero proof after the listing of the final G/L account. Under a manual system, such a zero proof can only be performed by listing the debit and credit account balances as pluses and minuses on an adding machine tape.

FIGURE 5-58

```
Scarborough Wholesale Hardware
91.12.31                                                                          Page  1
                              General Ledger Detail Report

Starting date: 91.01.01                                                    Ending date: 91.12.31

  Trans.      Trans.     Source    Trans.    Transaction           Debit       Credit      Balance
  Date        Number               Code      Description

1110 - Petty Cash
  91.12.31                                                          0.00        0.00        0.00 dr

1115 - Cash in Royal Bank
  91.01.01      1         G/L      Posting   Opening Entry       10,000.00                10,000.00 dr

  91.12.31    175         G/L      Posting   Cheque 451                        6,100.00   18,576.00 dr

7220 - Bank Interest Expense
  91.07.31     86         G/L      Posting   Monthly charge         75.00                    75.00 dr
  91.08.31    103         G/L      Posting   Monthly charge         75.00                   150.00 dr
  91.09.30    118         G/L      Posting   Monthly charge         75.00                   225.00 dr
  91.10.31    131         G/L      Posting   Monthly charge         75.00                   300.00 dr
  91.11.30    144         G/L      Posting   Monthly charge         75.00                   375.00 dr
  91.12.31    170         G/L      Posting   Monthly charge         75.00                   450.00 dr

                                                                                           $0.00
```

The total of all account debit balances, plus the total of all credit balances, as at the year-end, will produce a *zero proof* of the general ledger.

Step 4. Printing the Worksheet

Some microcomputer G/L packages include programs to print a special worksheet to allow the accountant or general ledger accounting clerk to record all year-end adjustments before those adjustments are journalized through the computer. For example, if Summation were used in the case of Scarborough Wholesale Hardware, the clerk would follow these steps:

- From the Master System Menu, press <3> to "Run the General Ledger System." (See Figure 5-45.)
- From the General Ledger Master Menu, press <3> to "Print G/L Reports." (See Figure 5-46.)

- From the General Ledger Report Generator, press <3> to "Print the General Ledger Account Worksheet." (See Figure 5-55.)
- After the instructions to print this worksheet are followed, the printout in sectional form would appear as shown in Figure 5-59.

FIGURE 5-59

Scarborough Wholesale Hardware
91.12.31
Page 1

General Ledger Worksheet
Year-to-Date Trial Balance   December, 1991

Account Code	Description	Opening Balance Debit	Opening Balance Credit	Adjustments Debit	Adjustments Credit	Closing Balance Debit	Closing Balance Credit
1110	- Petty Cash	0.00					
1115	- Cash in Royal Bank	18576.00					
1130	- Bank Term Deposit Receipts	20000.00					
1140	- Accounts Receivable - Trade	21500.00					
1145	- Allowance - Bad Debts		0.00				
1155	- Inventory at Cost	10000.00					

Page 2

5005	- Inventory at Start of Period	0.00					
5010	- Purchases	76890.00					
5020	- Transportation-in	1800.00					
5030	- Purchases Ret. and Allow.		2520.00				
5040	- Purchases Discount		1920.00				
5050	- Less - Ending Inventory		0.00				

Page 3

7210	- Bank Interest Expense	450.00					
7220	- Mortgage Interest Expense	5200.00					
	Total	437626.00	437626.00				

Analysis   Examine the following points as you study the illustrated printout of Summation's worksheet.
- The computerized worksheet contains only six money columns as follows: the first pair, called Opening Balance; a second pair, called Adjustments; and a final pair, called Closing Balance.
- The Opening Balance columns represent the year-end trial balance before adjustments are entered.

- The Adjustments section will receive all year-end adjustments similarly to the worksheet under a manual system.
- The final section, Closing Balance, is just another name for the adjusted trial balance. Even under a computer system, many accountants prefer to see this trial balance before any adjustments are entered into the computer.

It is useful to reemphasize three points made earlier about a computerized G/L accounting system:

- It is common to organize a chart of accounts with account codes of four or more digits.
- Under a periodic inventory system, it is crucial to distinguish between accounts that will be printed on the income statement and accounts that will be printed on the balance sheet. For example, "1155 Inventory at Cost" is the only account that will be recognized by the computer to print the balance of this account on the balance sheet. Similarly, "5005 Inventory at Start of Period" and "5050 Less - Ending Inventory" will be the only accounts recognized by the computer to print their account balances under the Cost of Goods Sold section of the income statement.
- From the Opening (trial) Balance section of the worksheet, "1155 Inventory at Cost" reports $10 000 as the beginning inventory balance. As you will learn, we must update this account with a series of adjustments so that the computer can recognize the correct amounts to be printed on both the income statement and the balance sheet.

Step 5. Completing the Worksheet

All of the year-end adjustments, prepared earlier under the manual system, would also be entered on the computerized worksheet in the same manner. However, the following additional adjustments are required to instruct the computer exactly how to handle complexities such as the beginning and ending inventories. As you recall, the last adjusting entry made under the manual system for Scarborough Wholesale Hardware was (i). (See Figure 5-25.) For the computerized worksheet, let's assume that the first additional adjustment will be (j) as described below.

(J) TRANSFERRING THE BEGINNING INVENTORY ACCOUNT BALANCE

Under a manual system, no adjustment was necessary. A clerk simply moved the beginning inventory account balance, $10 000, from the Adjusted Trial Balance debit column to the debit side of the Income Statement section of the worksheet. A computer, however, cannot think like a human. It must be instructed to transfer this beginning inventory balance from the current asset account to an account that will be printed under the Cost of Goods Sold section of the future income statement. Study closely the T-account entry in Figure 5-60.

FIGURE 5-60

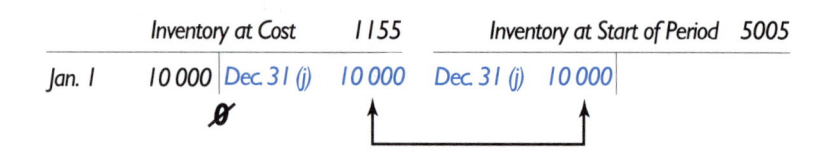

```
              Inventory at Cost      1155           Inventory at Start of Period  5005
      Jan. 1    10 000 | Dec. 31 (j)  10 000         Dec. 31 (j)  10 000
                         ∅
```

The above double entry would be entered as adjustment (j) on the computerized worksheet. Eventually, after an accounting clerk enters and posts this entry, the beginning inventory no longer exists in the current asset account. It has been transferred to "5005 Inventory at Start of Period." Since this account is organized on the chart of accounts as part of the Cost of Goods Sold, the computer will recognize it as part of the expense to compute the Cost of Goods Sold on the income statement.

(K) ADJUSTING FOR THE CURRENT INVENTORY ACCOUNT BALANCE

Another adjusting entry is required to account for the final inventory balance of $8 000. Study the T-account analysis in Figure 5-61.

FIGURE 5-61

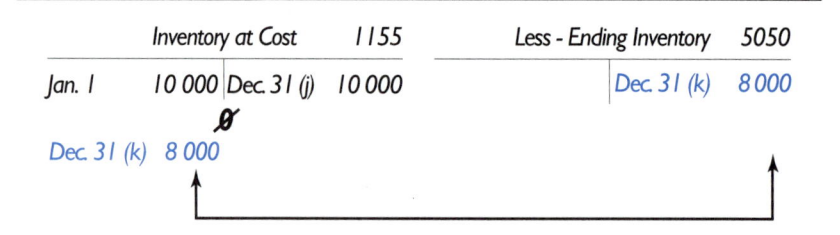

```
              Inventory at Cost      1155           Less - Ending Inventory  5050
      Jan. 1    10 000 | Dec. 31 (j)  10 000                     Dec. 31 (k)  8 000
                         ∅
      Dec. 31 (k)  8 000
```

Adjustment (k) would be entered on the computerized worksheet in the normal way. Obviously, the debit entry, once posted, will update the current asset account as at the year-end. In printing the future balance sheet, the computer will recognize the $8 000 as the only balance in that account.

The credit entry, once posted, will be received by an account that will deduct its balance in the Cost of Goods Sold section of the future income statement. Under a manual system, the accounting clerk simply performed this procedure without any adjusting entry. However, since a computer can't think, it must be directed to subtract $8 000 on the future income statement. It should become clear that additional information on the chart of accounts and adjusting entries will always be required in a computerized accounting system, to compensate for the computer's limitations.

(L) TRANSFERRING THE CURRENT PORTION OF THE LONG-TERM DEBT

The additional information given for Scarborough Wholesale Hardware states that $3 000 of the principal part of the mortgage is payable in the next accounting year. Under a manual system, no adjusting entry is required. An accounting clerk simply transfers this amount from the Long-Term Liability to the Current Liability section of the balance sheet. Under a computer system, however, an adjusting entry is required as in Figure 5-62.

FIGURE **5-62**

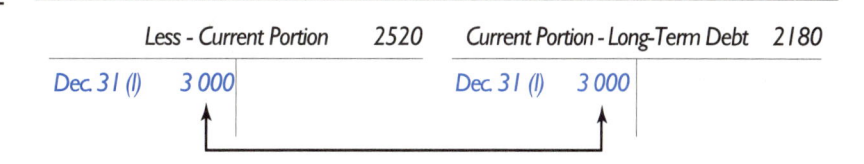

Less - Current Portion	2520	Current Portion - Long-Term Debt	2180
Dec. 31 (I) 3 000		Dec. 31 (I) 3 000	

Once this adjusting entry is posted, the computer will be able to print a balance sheet showing $3 000 as the current portion of long-term debt under Current Liabilities and $3 000 as the deduction from Mortgage Payable under Long-Term Liabilities.

This is the last the additional adjustments required for Scarborough Wholesale Hardware under a microcomputer system. Obviously, the totals of the Adjustments and Adjusted Trial Balance sections will be different from the ones prepared earlier under the manual system.

Step 6. Printing the Financial Statements

One of the outstanding features of all microcomputer G/L packages is their automated feature to print a set of detailed financial statements. Of course, the computer cannot print these statements until two conditions are met: (1) the G/L chart of accounts is organized to identify correctly all account headings, subheadings, regular account titles and their normal balances, subtotal levels, and total levels; and (2) the adjustments treated in the previous steps are entered and posted.

In the case of the Summation package, each lettered adjustment identified in the Adjustments section of the worksheet would be entered and posted via the General Ledger Transaction Entry Grid. Once all adjustments have been posted, a set of financial statements can be printed using Summation's General Ledger Master Menu. As you may recall, this menu permits the user to print an income statement and a balance sheet.

PRINTING THE INCOME STATEMENT   From the G/L Master Menu, the accounting clerk would press <6> to start the program to "Print an Income Statement." The clerk merely follows the user-friendly prompts to print the desired income statement.

Briefly, Summation's program allows the user to obtain an income statement for any period or on a quarterly basis. The most common request would be every month and every quarter for management purposes, and on a yearly basis for use by both management and other interested parties. Year-to-date figures are included in both the periodic and the quarterly report. For this the income statement prints two columns, and the user selects what will print in each. This allows the user to compare a

FIGURE **5-63**

General Ledger Master Menu
1. Update G/L Accounts - Special Account Lists.
2. Journalize and Post G/L Transactions.
3. Print G/L Reports.
4. G/L Screen Display.
5. Print a Balance Sheet.
6. Print an Income Statement.
7. G/L Month-End/Year-End Close.
8. G/L Utilities.

period from the current year with the same period from the previous year. A sectional view of the income statement prepared on a yearly basis is illustrated in Figure 5-65.

PRINTING THE BALANCE SHEET   All G/L accounting packages contain a separate program to print the balance sheet. In the case of Summation, the clerk would simply press <5> to begin the program. A special menu then appears permitting the user to print either of two types of balance sheets: (1) the Periodic Change in Account Balances Report, which facilitates the preparation of the firm's Application of Funds Statement, if management so prefers; and (2) the traditional Balance Sheet as at specified date.

The traditional balance sheet prints a report showing all year-to-date balances up to the end of the selected period. Both the Periodic Change in Account Balances Report and the year-to-date Balance Sheet Report may be run at any time, and as often as desired, without affecting any accounts or transactions in the general ledger system. A partial view of the balance sheet printout for Scarborough Wholesale Hardware, together with the schedule to support a separate statement of owner's equity, are illustrated in Figure 5-66.

Obviously, a G/L package to prepare the income statement and balance sheet offers advantages. Among them are these:

- If the debits and credits of transactions affecting the G/L have been entered and posted correctly, the printed income statement, balance sheet, and statement of owner's equity will be error-free.
- No human intervention is required. Thus, valuable time is saved in comparison with any manual system.
- The income statement can be printed at any time and covering any period. Management usually requires such printouts on a monthly basis as well as quarterly and yearly.
- Added information available on the income statement, such as a comparison of the current period with the previous period, is valuable for management analysis.
- A percentage analysis of all components is usually available on the income statement. For example, Summation's printout shows a percentage of all components related to the net sales figure — that is, the net sales figure will always be taken as 100. In this way, management can obtain key ratios such as for Cost of Goods Sold, the Gross Profit from Sales, and the Net Income.
- Both the income statement and the balance sheet reports may be run as often as desired by simply calling in the correct program. Both can be run without affecting any accounts or transactions in the general ledger system.

FIGURE 5-64

General Ledger Master Menu
1. Update G/L Accounts - Special Account Lists.
2. Journalize and Post G/L Transactions.
3. Print G/L Reports.
4. G/L Screen Display.
5. Print a Balance Sheet.
6. Print an Income Statement.
7. G/L Month-End/Year-End Close.
8. G/L Utilities.

FIGURE 5-65

91.12.31	Scarborough Wholesale Hardware Income Statement			Page 1	
Amount		Year-to-Date to December, 1991		Year-to-Date to December, 1991	
Sales - Scarborough Wholesale Hardware					
Sales		246,686.00	101.81%	246,686.00	101.81%
Less - Sales Returns and Allowances		2,640.00	1.09%	2,640.00	1.09%
Less - Sales Discount		1,740.00	0.72%	1,740.00	0.72%
Total - Net Sales		$242,306.00	100.00%	$242,306.00	100.00%
Cost of Goods Sold					
Inventory at Start of Period		10,000.00	4.13%	10,000.00	4.13%
Purchases		76,890.00	31.73%	76,890.00	31.73%
Transportation-in		1,800.00	0.74%	1,800.00	0.74%
Less - Purchases Ret. and Allow.		2,520.00	1.04%	2,520.00	1.04%
Less - Purchases Discount		1,920.00	0.79%	1,920.00	0.79%
Less - Ending Inventory		8,000.00	3.30%	8,000.00	3.30%
Total - Cost of Goods Sold		$ 76,250.00	31.47%	$ 76,250.00	34.47%

	Operating Expenses			Page 2	
Advertising		2,220.00	0.92%	2,220.00	0.92%
Utilities		720.00	0.30%	720.00	0.30%
Total - Operating Expense		$ 96,740.00	39.92%	$ 96,740.00	39.92%
Operating Income (Loss)		$ 69,316.00	28.61%	$ 69,316.00	28.61%
Other Revenue and Expense					
Interest (Earned)		(530.00)	0.22%	(530.00)	0.22%
Bank Interest Expense		500.00	0.21%	500.00	0.21%
Mortgage Interest Expense		5,200.00	2.15%	5,200.00	2.15%
Total - Other (Revenue) Expense		$ 5,170.00	2.13%	$ 5,170.00	2.13%
Net Income or (Loss)		$ 64,146.00	26.47%	$ 64,146.00	26.47%

FIGURE 5-66

91.12.31	Scarborough Wholesale Hardware Balance Sheet As at December, 1991			Page 1

ASSETS

Current Assets

    Cash on Hand
        Petty Cash   0.00
        Cash in Royal Bank   19,056.00

        Total - Cash on Hand $ 19,056.00
    Bank Term Deposit Receipts $ 20,000.00

    Accounts Receivable
    Accounts Receivable - Trade   21,500.00
        Less - Allowance for Bad Debts   1,905.00
    Net Realizable Value $ 20,405.00

Total - Current Assets $ 69,336.00

Assets continued on page 2

Page 2

Total - Assets $212,536.00

LIABILITIES   Page 3

    Current Liabilities
        Bank Loan Payable (on demand)   5,000.00
        Accounts Payable   9,000.00
        Property Taxes Payable   5,500.00
        Current Portion of Long-Term Debt   3,000.00

    Total - Current Liabilities $ 22,500.00

    Total - Liabilities $ 76,500.00

OWNER'S EQUITY

Tom Hall, Capital
    Total - Owner's Equity   136,036.00
    (see Schedule #1)

Total - Liabilities and Owner's Equity $212,536.00

CHAPTER 5: Accounting Cycle for a Merchandising Firm **215**

FIGURE 5-67

```
91.12.13                    Scarborough Wholesale Hardware                        Page 4
                                  Supporting Schedule

              SCHEDULE #1

Tom Hall, Capital                   $110,000.00
Past Earnings                              0.00

Add:  Net Income (Net Loss)           64,146.00
                                    _____
                                    $174,146.00

Less:  Tom Hall, Drawing              38,110.00
                                    _____

Total - Owner's Equity              $136,036.00
                                    ===========
```

Under the computer method, the accounting cycle so far consists of: (1) creating the computerized chart of accounts; (2) journalizing and posting transaction data (both are done at the same time); (3) printing the trial balance; (4) printing the worksheet; (5) completing the worksheet; (6) printing the financial statements.

Step 7. Closing the Books

Businesses using a manual G/L system normally close their books once a year. This is because it would be time-consuming and most awkward to close revenue and expense accounts on a monthly basis. Picture the attempt to bring down to zero all revenues and expenses each month and then to recalculate the balances forward for each subsequent month!

However, many microcomputer G/L packages are programmed to offer both a month-end close and a year-end close. How can a computer accomplish this? Without getting too technical, computers contain separate registers (or files) to store the results of accounting of all G/L accounts on a monthly basis. Thus, 12 registers may be programmed to keep track of monthly revenue and expense transactions. A 13th register can then be programmed to accumulate each month's results to give a year-to-date accounting of revenues and expenses. Some packages even offer the accounting of 14 periods, so that the previous year's year-to-date is always available. In this way, the computer user can print trial balances, worksheets, and financial statements for each month as well as a year-to-date accumulation of two or more months.

Before any closing procedure is considered, it is essential to do a backup of all G/L accounting files (normally called "accounting data files" or simply "data files"). **Backup procedures** vary in practice. However, it

Backup procedures: preparing a copy of the latest data files to one or more disks and/or tape.

is important to do at least one backup of the latest data files on disk and/ or tape. Once a month-end close is performed, the transaction detail is removed and posted as a balance forward. And, even more critically, once a year-end close is performed, all previous month-end balances are removed. Consequently, in some practices, clerks may be instructed to maintain a backup system of all data files using a rotation of three disks.

This extra precaution often proves invaluable should one of the disks be lost or become defective. In general, all computer users have learned, some the hard way, that it is cost-effective to follow strict backup procedures rather than to face the consequence of having to reenter accounting transactions for any time period.

FIGURE 5-68

General Ledger Master Menu
1. Update G/L Accounts - Special Account Lists.
2. Journalize and Post G/L Transactions.
3. Print G/L Reports.
4. G/L Screen Display.
5. Print a Balance Sheet.
6. Print an Income Statement.
7. G/L Month-End/Year-End Close.
8. G/L Utilities.

MONTH-END CLOSE Ideally, a month-end close should be run on the last day of the month following the close of business. This allows the year-to-date accumulator to receive the balances forward of G/L accounts on the "current" date. The mechanics of closing vary from one accounting package to another but are usually easy to follow. In the case of running Summation, for example, the accounting clerk simply presses <7> from the G/L Master Menu. A screen showing the General Ledger Period Closing menu appears as shown in Figure 5-69.

FIGURE 5-69

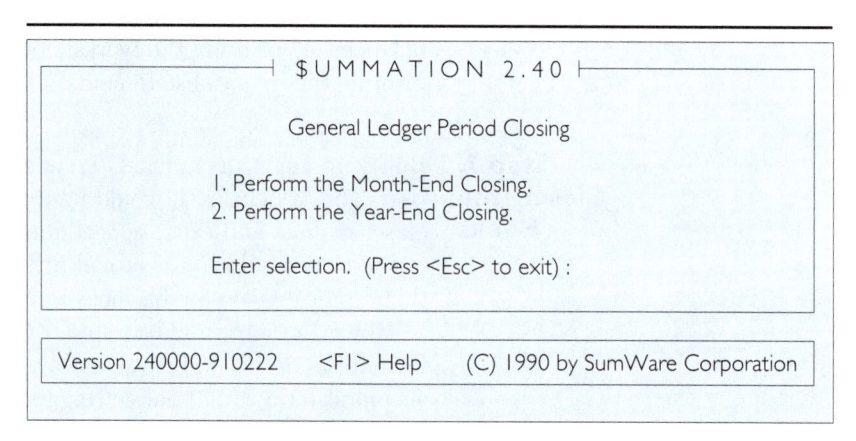

```
┤ $UMMATION 2.40 ├

General Ledger Period Closing

1. Perform the Month-End Closing.
2. Perform the Year-End Closing.

Enter selection.  (Press <Esc> to exit) :


Version 240000-910222    <F1> Help    (C) 1990 by SumWare Corporation
```

As you can see, you would press <1> to begin the month-end close program. A follow-up screen appears in Figure 5-70. The explanation is self-evident.

When a month-end close is performed, no G/L ledger account balances are changed in any way. No Revenue and Expense Summary account is required. Instead, the month-end close program makes a "dummy" posting to an equity account. This dummy posting will appear on the subsequent printout of the general journal but is *not* actually posted to the equity account. (An illustration of the general journal printout is shown in Figure 5-72.)

FIGURE 5-70

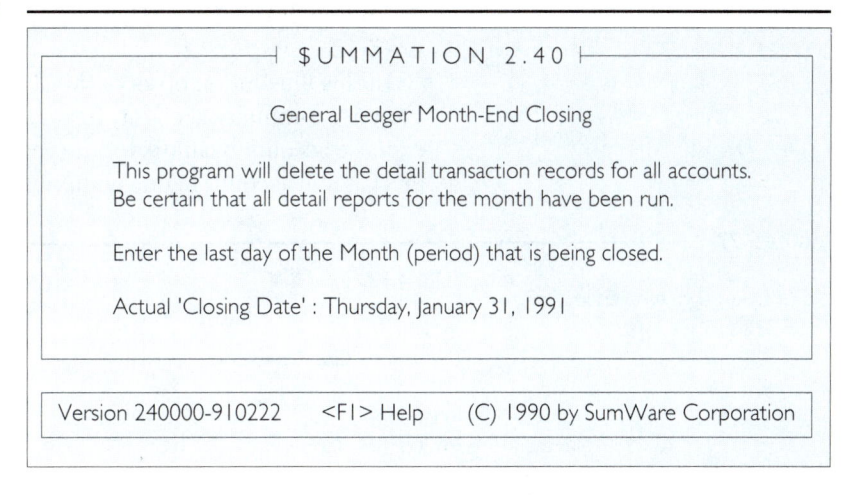

```
┤ $UMMATION 2.40 ├

        General Ledger Month-End Closing

This program will delete the detail transaction records for all accounts.
Be certain that all detail reports for the month have been run.

Enter the last day of the Month (period) that is being closed.

Actual 'Closing Date' : Thursday, January 31, 1991
```

```
Version 240000-910222    <F1> Help    (C) 1990 by SumWare Corporation
```

YEAR-END CLOSE   When a year-end close is performed, the closing will actually accumulate the revenue and expense figures from the year-to-date accumulator register and post the result of matching revenues and expenses for 12 months to the designated equity account. In the case of a sole proprietorship, the designated equity account would be the owner's Capital account; in partnership accounting, to separate partners' Capital accounts; and in a business corporation, to a special equity account called Retained Earnings. (An introduction to partnership and corporation accounting is presented in the next chapter.)

Again, the mechanics of performing a year-end close will vary with each G/L package. In the case of Summation, the clerk simply presses <7> from the G/L Master Menu and <2> from the General Ledger Period Closing menu. Two screens offer the warning messages shown in Figure 5-71.

FIGURE 5-71

```
Make sure that current BACKUPs of these data files exist prior to continuing.
There should be an INTERNAL backup on the Hard Disk and a FLOPPY Disk
Archive.
Press any key to continue.
```

```
The G/L must be closed 11 times prior to performing a Year-End Close. Read
HELP on Year-End Close.
Press any key to continue.
```

What this second message simply means is that month-end closings must have occurred 11 times before a year-end close is possible. If 11 previous month-end closings were performed, the year-end close program begins and ends with a printout of the closing entry. In the case of

218 PART 1: THE FRAMEWORK OF ACCOUNTING

Scarborough Wholesale Hardware, this printout would appear as in Figure 5-72.

In this illustration observe the absence of the traditional Revenue and Expense Summary account. Instead, the result of matching revenue and expense account balances for the year is "closed" immediately to the owner's Capital account in one compound entry. In the illustration, an equity

FIGURE 5-72

Scarborough Wholesale Tire
91.12.31   Page   1
                                    G/L Transaction Journal

                Trans.   Transaction   GL   G/L Account   Debit   Credit
                Number   Description   Code

91.12.31 Posting 1040   Closing Entry 3017   Add: Net Income (Net Loss)   64,146.00
                                         4010   Sales   246,686.00
                                         4020   Sales Ret. and Allow.   2,640.00
                                         4030   Sales Discount   1,740.00
                                         5005   Inventory at Start of Period   10,000.00
                                         5010   Purchases   76,890.00
                                         5020   Transporation-in   1,800.00
                                         5030   Purchases Ret. and Allow.   2,520.00
                                         5040   Purchases Discount   1,920.00
                                         5050   Less - Ending Inventory   8,000.00
                                         6010   Advertising   2,220.00
                                         6020   Utilities Expense   720.00
                                         6030   Property Taxes   7,100.00
                                         6040   Delivery Expense   2,160.00
                                         6050   Wages and Salaries   67,700.00
                                         6060   Telephone   420.00
                                         6070   Supplies Expense   1,525.00
                                         6080   Insurance Expense   1,800.00
                                         6090   Bad Debts Expense   1,095.00
                                         6100   Depreciation - Building   2,000.00
                                         6110   Depreciation - Warehouse Equip   1,200.00
                                         6120   Depreciation - Office Equipment   1,200.00
                                         6130   Depreciation - Delivery Trucks   7,600.00
                                         7050   Interest Earned   530.00
                                         7110   Bank Interest Expense   500.00
                                         7120   Mortgage Interest Expense   5,200.00

                                                                                  $259,656.00 $259,656.00

                                         — End of Transaction Entries —

account called "3017 Add: Net Income (Net Loss)" is used to facilitate the actual addition of the net income (or deduction of the net loss) to the Capital account in the statement of owner's equity. With this printout, you can be assured that all revenue accounts and all expense accounts for the year have been brought down to zero, because automatic posting has occurred within the year-end close program. You can also be assured that the Capital account has the latest balance.

Step 8. Preparing the Postclosing Trial Balance

Under a microcomputer system, a clerk simply initiates the correct keyboard commands to order the printout of the traditional trial balance. Since the "books" have been closed, the trial balance printout will show account balances only for those permanent (real) accounts that are related to the balance sheet. Of course, the Capital account figure will also be identical to the figure of the new owner's equity as disclosed on the balance sheet and statement of owner's equity.

For the manual system, nine separate steps were identified in a complete accounting cycle of activities performed. Under a computer system, however, as we see, only eight need be identified. Keep in mind that, except for originating transaction data and except for entering daily transactions and month-end adjustments, all steps are automated.

It is useful to end this discussion by acknowledging that, under computer accounting, the accounting cycle is better known as the "general ledger system" or "general ledger application." The term "accounting cycle" is usually reserved for discussions of a manual system.

TOPIC 4 Problems

Important Note: The problems below are intended to be solved on a G/L package of your choice. Time permitting, it would be useful to solve the problems twice: once on a package that supports batch processing and once on a package that supports real-time accounting. The problems are organized so that the entire cycle for Scarborough Wholesale Hardware illustrated in this chapter is completed through a G/L package.

If you use a package other than Summation, you must create a general ledger chart of accounts similar to the four-digit plan illustrated in this chapter. If you use the Summation disks which accompany this text, see your instructor for a copy of the program, the data files to support the chart of accounts, and the supplementary notes that provide step-by-step procedures to solve all of the problems outlined below.

If you have experience in running G/L packages, try solving the problems below twice: once with a batch processing package like AccPac Plus and a second time with a real-time accounting package like AccPac Bedford or Summation. On the other hand, if this is your first attempt at solving general ledger application problems, use only one type of software. You can consider making a comparison after you complete Chapter 11.

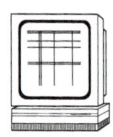

5.20 Simulate the accounting of Scarborough Wholesale Hardware illustrated in this chapter by following the suggested opening step-by-step procedures as follows:

a Create a G/L chart of accounts similar to the four-digit plan illustrated in this text for Scarborough Wholesale Hardware. (The data files in support of the Summation package already contain the chart of accounts for Scarborough Wholesale Hardware. See your instructor for instructions on loading these data files into the proper directory of your computer's system.)

b Use your software to change the company name to your name, as, for example, "Singh Wholesale Hardware." (Summation users will use the System Utilities from the Master System Menu to change the company name.)

c Print a hard copy of the entire chart of accounts.

d Print a dummy set of financial statements.

e Use your software's general journal to journalize the trial balance for Scarborough Wholesale Hardware, December 31, 19-1, illustrated in Figure 5-10. For a description, use "Balance forward." (Summation users will use the General Ledger Transaction Entry Grid under program 2 of the General Ledger Master Menu.)

f Print a hard copy of the general journal showing the correct journalizing of **e** above.

g Print a hard copy of the general ledger trial balance.

Note: Save all printouts in a filing folder for use in the subsequent problems.

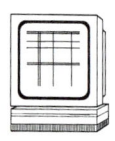

5.21 This problem is a continuation of Problem 5.20. Suggested step-by-step procedures are as follows:

a Use the data files created for Problem 5.20 to print a worksheet. (If your G/L package does not contain the program to print a trial balance with an accompanying worksheet, draw one up similar to the one illustrated for Summation in this chapter.)

b Complete all adjustments illustrated for Scarborough Wholesale Hardware. Do not forget to include adjustments (i), (j), and (k) as illustrated in this chapter. Total the Adjustments column.

c Complete the Adjusted Trial Balance section of your worksheet.

Note: Save this completed worksheet in a filing folder for use in the next problem.

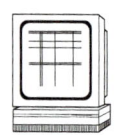

5.22 This problem is a continuation of Problem 5.21. Suggested step-by-step procedures are as follows:

a   Use the data files created for Problems 5.20 and 5.21. From the worksheet completed for Problem 5.21, enter and post all adjustments. Prepare a backup copy of your data files at this point. Suggested backup title is "5.22a."
b   Print an income statement for the year.
c   Print a balance sheet as at the end of the current year.
d   Print a supporting schedule (statement) of owner's equity showing the changes in owner's equity for the current year.
e   Do a year-end close. Prepare a second backup of your data files on a separate diskette at this point. Suggested backup title is "5.22b."
f   Print a postclosing trial balance.

Preparing an essay to compare the coverage of a computerized G/L system with the accounting cycle of the manual system.

5.23   Write an essay of approximately 500 words comparing the computerized G/L system used to solve Problems 5.20 through 5.22 with the manual system you learned from this and other, previously studied accounting textbooks. Build your essay around the following suggested outline:
- A short introduction
- Comparison of the computerized and manual G/L Systems, including similarities and main differences
- A summary of the main limitations of the microcomputer system, with reference to some of the difficulties you experienced
- A concluding paragraph

Note: If possible, use your microcomputer and an appropriate word processing package to do your essay.

Chapter Summary

Before any transactions can be journalized and posted, it is important to create a chart of accounts suitable to meet the needs of a particular merchandising business. Under a manual system, this chart may be developed around a system of three-digit number codes.

All accounting cycles begin with the origination of data. For merchandising businesses, the data may be captured on common source documents such as the sales invoice, credit and debit memos, the purchase order, and the related purchase invoice. Each document is analyzed carefully so that the resulting debits and credits of the transaction may be recorded in the general journal.

At convenient times, but no later than at the end of each month, the debits and credits recorded in the general journal are posted to appropriate accounts in the general ledger. At month-end, a trial balance is prepared to check the equality of the accounting equation within the general ledger. In theory, if the general ledger balances, a set of financial statements may be prepared from the account balances.

In practice, however, it seldom occurs that the account balances reflect correct balances at the end of any accounting period. This is due to mismatches between revenues and expenses recorded during the accounting period. For example, some revenue may have been earned during the accounting period but not have been recorded. Similarly, some expenses may have been incurred but the amounts not yet have been recorded in expense accounts. Obviously, if such unrecorded revenues and expenses were not treated, the income statement would not show a matchup of revenues with related expenses to report a fair net income or net loss for the accounting period.

All mismatches of revenue and expense accounts are resolved by making adjustments at the end of each accounting period. One group of adjustments involves accounts known as prepaid expenses. For example, the Office Supplies on Hand account balance may contain the correct current asset amount as well as the expired (used-up) portion of supplies during the period. An adjustment is required by transferring the used (expired) portion to an expense account. The accounting entry would be made by debiting Office Supplies Expense and crediting Office Supplies on Hand by the amount of supplies used during the accounting period. A similar adjusting entry would be made for other prepaid expenses such as prepaid insurance and prepaid rent.

Another important adjustment is related to the balance reported in the Accounts Receivable account. In theory, this balance should represent what management will collect from customers on account in the next accounting period. In practice, however, some of the customer accounts may go "bad" — that is, some customers may not pay their balances on account. Since it is impossible to identify specifically which customer accounts will go bad, accounting theory requires an adjusting entry to record the estimated amount that may not be collected. This amount may be obtained either by using the aging of accounts receivable method or by using a percentage of net sales. When the estimated amount is obtained, an adjusting entry is made by debiting an expense account like Bad Debts Expense and crediting a contra account to Accounts Receivable like Allowance for Bad Debts. On the future balance sheet, the amount in the Allowance for Bad Debts is always deducted from the balance reported for Accounts Receivable to report the net realizable value of accounts receivable as at the end of the accounting period. Of course, the balance of bad debts expense would be reported in the income statement along with other expenses.

Another group of adjustments is related to the depreciation of fixed assets. It is important to understand that *depreciation* in accounting has nothing to do with an attempt to calculate the so-called true or market value of any fixed asset. Rather, depreciation is a process of allocating (spreading) the cost of all fixed assets (except Land) over their estimated useful lives. Land does not depreciate, because its life is usually unlimited and its original cost is most always recovered at the end of any business venture.

A depreciation adjusting entry always shows a debit to an expense account with some such title as "Depreciation Expense — Building" and a corresponding credit to a contra fixed asset account such as "Accumulated Depreciation — Building." Of course, the amount of depreciation expense is always reported in the income statement. However, the balance in the accumulated depreciation account is reported in the balance sheet as a deduction from the original cost of the fixed asset. The remaining amount is always interpreted as the "book value" of the fixed asset as at the date of the balance sheet.

There are usually other adjustments required, especially if revenue at the end of the accounting period is actually unearned and if expenses have accrued and have yet to be recorded. These and other adjustments are best delayed for study at a more advanced level of accounting.

All adjustments should be recorded first on a ten-column worksheet to ensure that all adjustments have been accounted for and that balances reflected by such adjustments have been made correctly. Therefore, a ten-column worksheet would show columns for Adjustments (Debit and Credit) and an Adjusted Trial Balance. If the Adjusted Trial Balance balances, one could complete the worksheet by procedures similar to those used for the six-column worksheet.

Completing the accounting cycle for any merchandising firm involves the preparation of financial statements, the journalizing and posting of all adjusting entries made on the worksheet, the journalizing and posting of closing entries, and the preparation of the postclosing trial balance.

In preparing income statements for merchandising firms, it is customary to report revenues and expenses in *multiples* (groupings). One useful multiple combines all elements of sales revenue with the cost of the goods sold to report the gross profit (margin) from sales. A second combines all operating expenses so that the total operating expenses may be deducted from the gross profit from sales to report the operating income for the period. A third multiple reports Other Expenses such as interest expenses and Other Revenue such as interest revenue (earned). Once Other Expenses and Other Revenue items are reported, the final result of reporting the net income (or net loss) may be made.

In the balance sheet for the merchandising firm, it is customary to report only the final Capital amount under Owner's Equity. When the Capital amount represents the total owner's equity, it is important to create a separate schedule or statement of owner's equity to report the details of arriving at the final Capital amount.

The final Topic in this chapter presented an introduction to the microcomputer general ledger system. In simple terms, all such systems contain programs to permit the user to maintain an accurate accounting of general ledger accounts so that useful financial statements can be reported when they are required.

In practice, programs written for processing the general ledger are identified under different names such as "G/L System," "G/L Package," and "G/L Module." In addition, the G/L package is often combined with other programs to run specialized applications for accounts receivable, accounts payable, and payroll.

Of course, specific general ledger programs will be different as to their method of covering the traditional accounting cycle. One main difference is related to whether one believes in the batch processing of transactions versus the processing of those transactions on a real-time basis. Another difference involves special features. For example, one package may offer the attraction of a printout for a worksheet, while another may use the shortcut of avoiding closing entries.

Regardless of the G/L package adopted, the user will find many advantages in using the automated features of a microcomputer general ledger system. For example, once the debits and credits of all transactions have been entered accurately, the computer's program will post those transactions accurately and produce accurate financial statements without human intervention. The time-saving and accuracy of reporting financial statements normally results in valuable cost savings for businesses that require a fair volume of transactions to be processed during any accounting period.

Chapter Questions

1. Explain the difference between the debit memo and the credit memo as they are created and used by a merchandising firm.
2. Do accounting clerks approve source documents for data entry? Explain why or why not.
3. No adjustment was made to transfer $50 from the Prepaid Insurance account to the Insurance Expense account. What is the effect on net income? On total assets? On owner's equity?
4. What procedure is followed to record the purchase of a prepaid expense? When and how is the expense recorded?
5. Which of the following statements is most correct under accounting theory?
   a Adjusting entries affect income statement accounts only.
   b Adjusting entries affect balance sheet accounts only.
   c An adjusting entry cannot affect both a balance sheet account and an income statement account.
   d Every adjusting entry affects both a balance sheet account and an income statement account.
6. Office Supplies on Hand in the McKinley Company amounted to $890 at the beginning of the accounting year. During the financial period additional office supplies were acquired at a cost of $2 000 and debited to Office Supplies on Hand. At the end of the accounting year a physical count showed that supplies on hand amounted to $615. Give the adjusting entry required at year-end.
7. Explain how advertising expense may be classified as a prepaid expense during an accounting period.
8. Describe the procedure to be followed in aging the accounts receivable.
9. No adjustment was made for a bad debt loss for the Livingstone Shop. What effect does this have on assets? On net income? On owner's equity?

10. Why is the amount of bad debts credited to a contra account rather than to the accounts receivable in the general ledger?
11. What is meant by the accounting principle of "matching revenue and expenses"?
12. What is depreciation? Why must the amount of depreciation of fixed assets be shown on the financial statements?
13. What is the effect upon owner's equity if no adjustment is made for depreciation?
14. Why is the amount of depreciation credited to a contra account rather than to the fixed asset account?
15. What three items are needed in order to estimate the annual depreciation on a fixed asset when the straight-line method is used?
16. What does the credit balance in the accumulated depreciation account represent?
17. What are the similarities and differences between the accumulated depreciation account on a fixed asset and the Allowance for Bad Debts account?
18. Briefly explain why land does not depreciate in the accounting sense.
19. Why does the total of the debits not equal the total of the credits in the Income Statement section of the ten-column worksheet? In the Balance Sheet section?
20. Describe the sequence that is followed in preparing a ten-column worksheet.
21. Why are adjustments "keyed" on the worksheet?
22. Why must two separate lines be used for recording inventories on a ten-column worksheet?
23. How is the ending inventory recorded on the ten-column worksheet?
24. What one figure is most important on a ten-column worksheet? Explain why this figure is so important.
25. If the total debit of the Income Statement section of the worksheet is greater than the total credit, is the difference a net income or net loss? Explain your answer.
26. If the total debit of the Balance Sheet section of the worksheet is greater than the total credit, is the difference a net income or net loss? Explain your answer.
27. What is a separate cost of goods sold schedule? Why would such a schedule be prepared?
28. Is "Income from Operations" the same as "Net Income"? Explain why or why not.
29. When would a separate statement of owner's equity be prepared? Why would such a statement be prepared?
30. Why must adjusting entries be recorded before the closing entries?
31. Explain how the Inventory account is updated under a merchandising firm that uses the periodic inventory method of accounting.
32. List the three checks to prove the accuracy of the postclosing trial balance.
33. List and briefly explain three differences between the general ledger chart of accounts created for a microcomputer system and one that is used for the traditional, manual system.

PART 1: THE FRAMEWORK OF ACCOUNTING

34. Briefly explain the steps involved in journalizing and posting the opening entry when using a microcomputer general ledger package like Summation.
35. Briefly explain two types of trial balances that are available under a microcomputer general ledger package.
36. Does a ten-column worksheet exist under a microcomputer general ledger accounting system? Explain why or why not.
37. Explain the difference in handling the beginning and ending inventory amounts on worksheets under a microcomputer general ledger system and the traditional, manual method.
38. Explain the difference between a month-end close and a year-end close using a microcomputer general ledger package.
39. Identify and briefly explain a general ledger example to prove that computers cannot think like humans.
40. Does an accounting cycle exist under a microcomputer general ledger accounting system? Explain your answer.

Accounting Case Problems

CASE 5-1

Recording end-of-period adjustments for prepaid expenses from given data; explaining the effect of each adjusting entry on financial statements.

Kathy Bratina, a friend of yours who owns Bratina Supply Company, seeks your advice on how to record the end-of-period adjustment for prepaid expenses. The owner provides the following information:

1. Under the firm's accountant, now on a two-month overseas business trip, all prepaid expenses were recorded in current asset accounts.
2. A trial balance taken of the general ledger reported the following balances in current asset accounts: Supplies on Hand, $2 800; Prepaid Insurance, $480; and Prepaid Advertising, $6 000.
3. At the end of the accounting period, in this case at the end of March, a physical count showed a cost of supplies on hand amounting to $600.
4. The insurance premium of $480 was paid on March 1 and covers a period of 12 months.
5. The Prepaid Advertising was paid to National Advertising Co., which agreed to handle advertisements for six months commencing March 1.

Required

a Assume that it is March 31 of the current year. Prepare the required general journal entries to record each adjustment.

b Assume that the owner has no accounting background. Give an explanation to the owner in written form showing the effect of each adjusting entry on the firm's financial statements.

c Explain how these adjustments would be handled at the end of the next month's accounting period. Assume that the supplies on hand on April 30 shows an amount of unused supplies amounting to $100.

CASE 5-2 The accounting system of the McLaughlin Company presented the following yearly report to the advertising manager:

FIGURE 5-73

Calculating the amount of prepaid advertising at the beginning of the current year from given accounting data.

(1)	Advertising expense for the current year	$75 580
(2)	Prepaid advertising for the current year	7 310
(3)	Cash payments for advertising during the year	~~75 580~~ 78 580
(4)	Advertising expense reported in the annual income statement	75 580

After studying the report, the advertising manager asks you to calculate the amount, if any, of prepaid advertising at the beginning of the current year. The manager wishes this information in order to make a comparison of this amount with last year's reported figure.

From the information provided in the advertising report, calculate the amount of prepaid advertising at the beginning of the current year. Show your calculations.

CHAPTER

6 An Introduction to Partnership and Corporation Accounting

After completing this chapter, you should be able to:
— List at least eight main characteristics of a partnership form of business organization.
— Record the opening entries for the formation of partnerships from given cases and the resulting pre-operating balance sheet.
— Prepare a ten-column worksheet for a partnership from given data.
— Prepare the year-end financial statements for a partnership.
— Complete the accounting cycle for a partnership.
— Distribute profits (or losses) to partners under varying profit-sharing arrangements.
— Record the opening entries for the formation of corporations from simple cases and prepare the resulting pre-operating corporate balance sheet.
— Prepare a statement of shareholders' equity from given data.
— Record the declaration and subsequent payment of a cash dividend.
— Prepare an income statement and a statement of retained earnings from given information.
— Prepare a simple statement of cash flows using the direct method only.
— Define the following key terms used in this chapter: partnership; business corporation; partners' equity; shareholders' equity; unlimited liability; statement of partners' equity; legal entity; shareholders; share certificate; limited liability; board of directors; dividend; bond; authorized capital; issued share capital; outstanding shares; par value stock; no-par-value stock; common share; preferred share; retained earnings; deficit; date of declaration; date of record; ex-dividend share; annual report; generally accepted accounting principles; *CICA Handbook*; notes to financial statements; statement of changes in financial position; operating activities; financing activities; investing activities; accrual accounting; cash basis of accounting.

It is appropriate to end Part 1 of this text with an elementary study of accounting concepts related to two other common forms of business organization: the partnership and the business corporation. As you may

CHAPTER 6: An Introduction to Partnership and Corporation Accounting   **229**

Partners' equity: the claims of partners against the assets of a partnership.

Shareholders' equity: the claims of shareholders against the assets of a business corporation.

correctly infer, a partnership business is one wherein two or more persons agree to carry on a business enterprise; consequently, the claims of partners against the assets of a partnership are usually known as ***partners' equity***. On the other hand, in a business corporation there are usually more owners than in a partnership — generally hundreds or even thousands of them. As you will learn, the residual claim of these *shareholders*, as they are called, against the assets of the corporation is usually acknowledged as ***shareholders' equity***. *Important note:* Only an introductory view of concepts will be presented here. Any in-depth study of partnership accounting and corporation accounting, therefore, is reserved for your interest in more-advanced courses.

TOPIC 1 Partnership Accounting Concepts

The chief characteristics of the partnership form of business organization may be summarized as follows:

1. As suggested earlier, under a partnership form of business organization, ownership is divided between two or more persons who agree to carry on, as co-owners, a business enterprise for profit.

2. In Canada, the formation of partnerships is controlled by provincial legislation. For example, British Columbia has a Partnership Act while Ontario has three — a Partnership Act, a Partnership Registration Act, and a Limited Partnership Act. In general, these provincial acts require that a partnership be registered to prove the existence of the business.

3. In Canada, a few partnerships may be found in the fields of mining, manufacturing, wholesaling, and the retail trade. The greatest number, however, occur in the professions, such as law, medicine, accounting, architecture, and engineering.

4. As of 1989, the laws of most Canadian provinces still prohibit members of many of the professions from forming business corporations; consequently, a partnership is a more appropriate way to provide the services of several professionally qualified people — accountants or lawyers, for example — than a sole proprietorship is. It should be noted, however, that the laws of some of the provinces seem to be in the process of changing to allow these professional groups to form business corporations.

5. In a partnership, each partner acts as an agent of the firm. Thus, the accountant is obliged to record every transaction in which any one of the partners contracts for the purchase and sale of goods and services.

6. Each partner is personally responsible for all the debts of the firm. There is no ceiling on the liability of a partner; thus, his or her

Unlimited liability: status of an owner who is personally liable for debts of the business.

personal property (home, car, etc.) can legally be taken, if necessary, to pay these debts. In the language of business, partners have **unlimited liability.**

7. Most people who plan to go into partnership approach a lawyer, who prepares a *declaration of partnership*. Once properly signed and witnessed, the declaration becomes the partnership agreement or legal contract, which binds the partners on the method of running the business and on the method of distributing the profits (or losses).

8. In the absence of an oral or written agreement, all profits which the firm makes are shared among the partners on an *equal* basis. Also, in the absence of any agreement all losses which the firm suffers are shared on the same equal basis. Most partners who contribute a larger share, however, protect their interests by stipulating in a written agreement the ratio of sharing profits and losses.

9. A partnership may cease at any time by the death, insanity, or withdrawal of any member of the firm, by the admission of a new partner or partners, or by bankruptcy of the firm. In any of these cases, the existing partnership is legally dissolved, and a new partnership must be formed. In this context, partnerships are said to have *limited life*. Many partnerships, however, protect the continuity of their operations by stating in their written contract the terms of a new agreement which would come into existence the instant the old firm expired.

10. A partnership, unlike a corporation, is not a separate entity in itself but merely a voluntary association of individuals. Because a partnership is not a legal entity, the accounting student must remember that partners (like sole proprietors) cannot draw a business salary to be charged against their firm's day-to-day profits. As in sole proprietorship accounting, any such salaries paid to partners must be distributed from *year-end* profits. Of course, for their personal needs, partners are allowed periodic withdrawals in anticipation of the firm's making a profit.

11. As a firm, the partnership does not pay an income tax; instead, the share of the firm's profit with which individual partners are credited must be shown as part of their income on their individual tax returns.

Partnership Accounts and Statements

The accounting treatment of routine transactions such as buying, selling, processing payrolls, etc. is the same in a partnership as in a single proprietorship. But certain transactions are peculiar to the partnership form of business organization: formation of the partnership, admission of new partners, distribution of profits (or losses) to the partners, dissolution of the partnership because of the death or withdrawal of a partner, and the liquidation of the business because of bankruptcy. To avoid complexities, this text covers only an introduction to simple cases of forming partnerships, and an elementary accounting of the distribution of profits (or losses).

You should have little difficulty in learning the basic accounts as they are applied to the preparation of partnership financial statements. Except for the equity accounts, the accounts used in a partnership are the same as those used in a single proprietorship; as for the equity section, clearly a separate capital account and a separate drawing account for each partner must be provided.

Opening Entries for Formation of a Partnership

In presenting the elementary cases that follow, the capital contributions of the partners will take the form of tangible items only. Examine each case carefully.

Case 1. Investment in Cash Henry Doe and Hugh Ray agree on June 30 to form a partnership under the name of Doe and Ray Sporting Goods. Doe invests $60 000 cash, while Ray invests $40 000. The opening entry to record their investments is made in the general journal as shown in Figure 6-1.

FIGURE 6-1

Date	Account Title and Explanation	Post. Ref.	Debit	Credit
19-1 June 30	Cash	101	100 000 00	
	Henry Doe, Capital	301		60 000 00
	Hugh Ray, Capital	303		40 000 00
	To record the initial investments in the partnership of Doe and Ray Sporting Goods.			

GENERAL JOURNAL — Page 1

Case 2. Investment in Cash — Three Partners E. Anderson, G. Bobesich, and J. Levitt agree to form a legal firm on July 10. Each contributes cash as follows: Anderson, $50 000; Bobesich, $30 000; and Levitt, $20 000. These investments are credited to the three capital accounts as shown by the journal entry in Figure 6-2.

Case 3. Investment in Cash and Assets Friends Donna Field and Mary Parker enter into a partnership on September 1. Mary contributes $40 000 cash, but her friend contributes assets of a small business which she hitherto operated. For simplicity, we shall assume these assets to be merchandise and store equipment.

FIGURE 6-2

		GENERAL JOURNAL			Page 1
Date		Account Title and Explanation	Post. Ref.	Debit	Credit
19-1 July	10	Cash	101	100 000 00	
		E. Anderson, Capital	310		50 000 00
		G. Bobesich, Capital	320		30 000 00
		J. Levitt, Capital	330		20 000 00
		To record the initial investments in the partnership of Anderson, Bobesich, and Levitt.			

When a partner contributes assets other than cash, a question always arises as to their value. In partnership accounting, two steps are necessary in order to record the formation of the firm:

- All partners must agree on the dollar value of the non-cash assets. In general, their valuations should be at *fair market values* at the date of transfer to the partnership firm. In this case, let us assume that both partners have agreed to value Donna Field's non-cash assets as follows: Inventory of Merchandise, $35 000; and Store Equipment, $25 000.
- Once all partners have agreed on the value of the contributions, a separate journal entry is made to record the investment of each partner. For Field and Parker, the opening entries may be illustrated as shown in Figure 6-3.

When non-cash items are invested in a new business, it is customary to prepare the opening balance sheet of the partnership before the firm

FIGURE 6-3

		GENERAL JOURNAL			Page 1
Date		Account Title and Explanation	Post. Ref.	Debit	Credit
19-1 Sept.	1	Inventory of Merchandise	113	35 000 00	
		Store Equipment	126	25 000 00	
		Donna Field, Capital	301		60 000 00
		To record merchandise and equipment contributed by Donna Field at agreed valuation.			
	1	Cash	101	40 000 00	
		Mary Parker, Capital	303		40 000 00
		To record the cash investment of Mary Parker in the firm of Field and Parker.			

CHAPTER 6: An Introduction to Partnership and Corporation Accounting   **233**

commences business operations. The balance sheet of Field and Parker may be illustrated as in Figure 6-4.

FIGURE **6-4**

Field and Parker
Opening Balance Sheet
As at September 1, 19—

Assets			Liabilities		
Current Assets:			None.		
Cash	$40 000.00				
Inventory (cost to partnership)	35 000.00		**Partners' Equity**		
Total Current Assets	75 000.00		Donna Field, Capital	$60 000.00	
Fixed Assets:			Donna Field, Capital	40 000.00	
Store Equipment (cost to partnership)	25 000.00		Total Partners' Equity		$100 000.00
Total Assets	$100 000.00		Total Liabilities and Partners' Equity		$100 000.00

Case 4. Combining Two Sole Proprietorships   For this case, let us assume that Ronka and Weisman operate similar legal offices and that they decide to combine their sole proprietorships under their surnames. In their respective balance sheets, illustrated in Figures 6-5 and 6-6, assume that the assets of both businesses were revalued by an accountant and that the accumulated depreciation accounts were written off. Assume also that, by agreement, the capital contributions of both partners to the new firm are to be equal.

FIGURE **6-5**

E. Ronka
Balance Sheet
As at March 31, 19—

Assets

Cash	$16 000.00	
Accounts Receivable	2 000.00	
Office Supplies on Hand	500.00	
Office Equipment (at cost)	5 500.00	
Total Assets		$24 000.00

Liabilities

Bank Loan Payable	$ 1 000.00	
Accounts Payable	2 000.00	
Total Liabilities		$ 3 000.00

Owner's Equity

E. Ronka, Capital		21 000.00
Total Liabilities and Owner's Equity		$24 000.00

FIGURE 6-6

J. Weisman
Balance Sheet
As at March 31, 19—

Assets

Cash	$10 000.00
Accounts Receivable	3 000.00
Office Supplies on Hand	700.00
Office Equipment (at cost)	6 300.00
Total Assets	$20 000.00

Liabilities

Accounts Payable	$ 3 000.00
Total Liabilities	$ 3 000.00

Owner's Equity

J. Weisman, Capital	19 000.00
Total Liabilities and Owner's Equity	$20 000.00

As in the other cases, there will be two separate entries in the general journal of the new partnership business to record the capital contributions of each partner, as shown in Figure 6-7. Note that Weisman must deposit an extra $2 000 in the firm's bank account to qualify as an equal partner.

FIGURE 6-7

GENERAL JOURNAL — Page 1

Date	Account Title and Explanation	Post. Ref.	Debit	Credit
19— April 1	Cash	101	16 000 00	
	Accounts Receivable	111	2 000 00	
	Office Supplies on Hand	115	500 00	
	Office Equipment	124	5 500 00	
	Bank Loan Payable	201		1 000 00
	Accounts Payable	202		2 000 00
	E. Ronka, Capital	301		21 000 00
	To record the investment of E. Ronka.			
1	Cash	101	10 000 00	
	Accounts Receivable	111	3 000 00	
	Office Supplies on Hand	115	700 00	
	Office Equipment	124	6 300 00	
	Accounts Payable	202		1 000 00
	J. Weisman, Capital	303		19 000 00
	To record the investment of J. Weisman.			
1	Cash	101	2 000 00	
	J. Weisman, Capital	303		2 000 00
	To record the additional investment of J. Weisman.			

The opening balance sheet for the new firm will now show, at cost to the partnership, the economic resources acquired and the debts assumed from the former separate businesses. See Figure 6-8.

FIGURE 6-8

Ronka & Weisman
Opening Balance Sheet
As at April 1, 19—

Assets			Liabilities		
Current Assets:			Current Liabilities:		
Cash	$ 28 000.00		Bank Loan Payable		$ 1 000.00
Accounts Receivable	5 000.00		Accounts Payable		3 000.00
Office Supplies	1 200.00		Total Liabilities		4 000.00
Total Current Assets		34 200.00			
			Partners' Equity		
Fixed Assets (at cost):			E. Ronka, Capital	$21 000.00	
Office Equipment		11 800.00	J. Weisman, Capital	21 000.00	
			Total Partners' Equity		42 000.00
Total Assets		$ 46 000.00	Total Liabilities and Partners' Equity		$ 46 000.00

Distributing Profits (or Losses)

Having examined a few elementary transactions for forming a partnership, let us now consider several specialized transactions that may occur during the operating cycle of the firm. These will be primarily to record transactions throughout the year and to divide the year-end profits among the partners. Of course, when the year's expenses exceed revenues, net loss must similarly be shared.

The accounting activities for a partnership at the end of the accounting period are very similar to those you learned for a sole proprietorship. Briefly, a worksheet may be used to obtain all the information necessary to prepare the partnership's financial statements and to record the adjusting and closing entries. Of course, the figure that is most important to the partners is the amount of the net income. Since the net income has to be distributed to the partners, the worksheet usually provides for columns to show the income distribution to each of them. In Figure 6-9, the worksheet is shown as beginning with the adjusted trial balance only; but under a manual system, the actual worksheet would include columns for the year-end trial balance and a pair of columns to handle the year-end adjustments. In the case of a microcomputer G/L package, additional adjustments, similar to those treated in the last chapter, would be made.

From the special columns for each partner, notice how the capital position of the partner is summarized for an entire accounting period. For example, Henry Doe's pair of columns reveals the amount of his original investment (plus any additional investments during the period), the total

FIGURE 6-9

Doe and Ray Sporting Goods
Worksheet
For the Year Ended June 30, 19—

	Account Title	Adjusted Trial Balance Debit	Adjusted Trial Balance Credit	Income Statement Debit	Income Statement Credit	Henry Doe, Capital Debit	Henry Doe, Capital Credit	Hugh Ray, Capital Debit	Hugh Ray, Capital Credit	Balance Sheet Debit	Balance Sheet Credit	
1	Cash	20 000								20 000		1
2	Accounts Receivable	50 000								50 000		2
3	Allowance for Bad Debts		1 000								1 000	3
4	Inventory, July 1	66 000		66 000								4
5	Land	20 000								20 000		5
6	Building	40 000								40 000		6
7	Accumulated Dep.—Bldg.		2 000								2 000	7
8	Bank Loan Payable		20 000								20 000	8
9	Accounts Payable		45 000								45 000	9
10	Mortgage Payable		25 000								25 000	10
11	Henry Doe, Capital		60 000				60 000					11
12	Henry Doe, Drawing	8 400				8 400						12
13	Hugh Ray, Capital		40 000						40 000			13
14	Hugh Ray, Drawing	8 000						8 000				14
15	Sales		260 000		260 000							15
16	Purchases	130 000		130 000								16
17	Selling Expenses	75 000		75 000								17
18	Gen. & Admin. Expenses	35 600		35 600								18
19		453 000	453 000									19
20	Inventory, June 30				81 600					81 600		20
21				306 600	341 600							21
22	Net Income, Divided 3:2			35 000			21 000		14 000			22
23				341 600	341 600	8 400	81 000	8 000	54 000			23
24	Capitals at End of Year:											24
25	Doe, Capital					72 600					72 600	25
26	Ray, Capital							46 000			46 000	26
27						81 000	81 000	54 000	54 000	211 600	211 600	27

drawings for the period, the amount of his share of the profits according to the partnership agreement (3/5 of $35 000), and finally, the amount of his capital at the end of the accounting period. Note how the ending capital amounts for each partner are extended into the credit column of the balance sheet in order to balance the final totals.

Once the worksheet is complete, the financial statements for the partnership may be prepared. Let us examine the income statement first. See Figure 6-10.

The income statement for the partnership is the same as the one generally used by a sole proprietorship, except for an added section. This added section shows the distribution of the net income to the partners in accordance with their agreement. Obviously, under a G/L software pack-

FIGURE 6-10

Doe and Ray Sporting Goods
Income Statement
For the Year Ended June 30, 19—

Revenue from Sales:			
Sales			$260 000 00
Cost of Goods Sold:			
Inventory, July 1	$ 66 000 00		
Purchases	130 000 00		
Cost of Goods Available for Sale	$196 000 00		
Less: Inventory, June 30	81 600 00		
Cost of Goods Sold		114 400 00	
Gross Margin		145 600 00	
Operating Expenses:			
Selling Expenses	75 000 00		
Gen. & Admin. Expenses	35 600 00		
Total Operating Expenses		110 600 00	
Net Income		$ 35 000 00	
Distribution of Net Income:			
To Henry Doe (60%)	21 000 00		
To Hugh Ray (40%)	14 000 00		
Total Net Income		$ 35 000 00	

Statement of partners' equity: a breakdown of each partner's capital position.

age, a formula would be programmed to show this distribution below the income statement.

The balance sheet may now be prepared as illustrated in Figure 6-11. Notice that the Partners' Equity section contains only each partner's total capital. This figure should match the one calculated in the Balance Sheet columns of the worksheet. A supplementary schedule called a ***statement of partners' equity***, illustrated in Figure 6-12, generally follows the balance sheet, showing a complete breakdown of each partner's capital. Again, under a G/L software package, a formula would be programmed to show the distribution of net incomes within the separate statement (schedule) of partners' equity.

After completion of the financial statements, there remain the important journal entries to bring the ledger accounts into agreement with the amounts contained in the worksheet and financial statements. These entries would begin with the adjusting entries, followed by a set of closing entries to clear the revenue and expense accounts into Revenue and Expense Summary. Those entries are the same as for a sole proprietorship. What differs now is the final set of journal entries to record the distribution of partnership profits. These may be shown for Doe and Ray Sporting Goods as in Figure 6-13.

Once the journal entries have been posted, the partners' capital accounts should reflect the exact position shown by the worksheet and the

FIGURE 6-11

Doe and Ray Sporting Goods
Balance Sheet
As at June 30, 19—

Assets

Current Assets:
Cash		$ 20 000 00	
Accounts Receivable	$ 50 000 00		
Less: Allowance for Bad Debts	1 000 00	49 000 00	
Merchandise Inventory (at cost)		81 600 00	
Total Current Assets			$ 150 600 00

Fixed Assets (at cost):
Land (security for mortgage payable)		20 000 00	
Building (security for mortgage payable)	$ 40 000 00		
Less: Accumulated Depreciation	2 000 00	38 000 00	
Total Fixed Assets			58 000 00
Total Assets			$ 208 600 00

Liabilities

Current Liabilities:
Bank Loan Payable		$ 20 000 00	
Accounts Payable		45 000 00	
Current Portion of Long-Term Debt		1 250 00	
Total Current Liabilities			66 250 00

Long-Term Liabilities:
12% Mortgage Payable, Due 2010		$ 25 000 00	
Less: Current Portion Due Within Year		1 250 00	
Total Long-Term Liabilities			23 750 00
Total Liabilities			90 000 00

Partners' Equity

Henry Doe, Capital		$ 72 600 00	
Hugh Ray, Capital		46 000 00	
Total Partners' Equity			118 600 00
Total Liabilities and Partners' Equity			$ 208 600 00

FIGURE 6-12

Doe and Ray Sporting Goods
Statement of Partners' Equity
For the Year Ended June 30, 19—

	Doe	Ray	Total
Balance, Capital Accounts, July 1, 19—	$60 000 00	$40 000 00	$100 000 00
Net Income for the Year	21 000 00	14 000 00	35 000 00
Totals	81 000 00	54 000 00	135 000 00
Deduct: Withdrawals	8 400 00	8 000 00	16 400 00
Balance, Capital Accounts, June 30, 19—	$72 600 00	$46 000 00	$118 600 00

CHAPTER 6: An Introduction to Partnership and Corporation Accounting

FIGURE 6-13

19—					
June	30	Revenue & Expense Summary	399	35 000 00	
		Henry Doe, Capital	301		21 000 00
		Hugh Ray, Captial	303		14 000 00
		To distribute net income for the year in accordance with partnership agreement to share profits in the ratio of 3:2.			
	30	Henry Doe, Capital	301	8 400 00	
		Hugh Ray, Capital	303	8 000 00	
		Henry Doe, Drawing	302		8 400 00
		Hugh Ray, Drawing	304		8 000 00
		To transfer debit balances in partners' drawing accounts to their respective capital accounts.			

balance sheet. To complete the accounting cycle, a postclosing trial balance is taken to test the accuracy of the general ledger after the closing entries and distribution entries have been posted. If these have been done correctly, the postclosing trial balance will show only balance sheet accounts. See Figure 6-14.

FIGURE 6-14

Doe and Ray Sporting Goods
Postclosing Trial Balance
June 30, 19—

Account Title	Acct. No.	Debit	Credit
Cash	101	20 000 00	
Accounts Receivable	111	50 000 00	
Allowance for Bad Debts	112		1 000 00
Inventory	113	81 600 00	
Land	121	20 000 00	
Building	122	40 000 00	
Accumulated Depreciation—Building	123		2 000 00
Bank Loan Payable	201		20 000 00
Accounts Payable	202		45 000 00
Mortgage Payable	221		25 000 00
Henry Doe, Capital	301		72 600 00
Hugh Ray, Capital	303		46 000 00
		211 600 00	211 600 00

Henry Doe, Capital		301	
June 30	8 400	July 1	60 000
		June 30	21 000

Hugh Ray, Capital		303	
June 30	8 000	July 1	40 000
		June 30	14 000

TOPIC 1 Problems

Recording the opening entries to form simple partnership agreements.

6.1 Make the opening entries for the following two cases in the general journal.
  a On December 1, M. Seles and S. Graf decide to form a partnership, contributing $60 000 cash each.
  b K. Gruber, J. Olerud, and D. Stieb agree to form a partnership on April 1. The cash contributions are as follows: Gruber, $50 000; Olerud, $30 000; and Stieb, $30 000.

Recording the opening entries to form a partnership; preparing the pre-operating balance sheet.

6.2 H. Irwin and D. Barr enter into a partnership on June 30 under the firm name Maple Leaf Photographic Company. Irwin contributes $60 000 cash. Barr contributes non-cash assets at agreed values of $40 000 for merchandise inventory, and $30 000 for store equipment.
  a Record the initial investment of each partner in a general journal.
  b Prepare the opening balance sheet of the firm prior to the commencement of its business operations.

Accounting for a partnership whereby one partner invests an existing business while a second invests cash only.

6.3 B. Daniel operates a successful bookstore. To expand her business, she persuades A. Okamoto to enter into a partnership agreement. A. Okamoto has agreed to contribute cash equal to Daniel's new owner's equity amount after an appraisal is made of the business. The balance sheet of Daniel Books on July 31, before the assets have been revalued, is shown in Figure 6-15.

FIGURE 6-15

Daniel Books
Balance Sheet
As at July 31, 19—

Assets			
Current Assets:			
Cash		$ 38 200.00	
Accounts Receivable		3 800.00	
Merchandise Inventory (at cost)		37 200.00	
Prepaid Insurance		300.00	
Supplies on Hand		1 200.00	
Total Current Assets			$ 80 700.00
Fixed Assets (at cost):			
Land		15 000.00	
Building	$26 000.00		
Less: Accumulated Depreciation	12 000.00	14 000.00	
Office Equipment	$1 400.00		
Less: Accumulated Depreciation	400.00	1 000.00	
Store Equipment	$10 000.00		
Less: Accumulated Depreciation	1 000.00	9 000.00	
Total Fixed Assets			39 000.00
Total Assets			$ 119 700.00
Liabilities			
Current Liabilities:			
Bank Loan Payable		$ 3 000.00	
Accounts Payable		1 700.00	
Total Liabilities			$ 4 700.00
Owner's Equity			
B. Daniel, Capital		$ 115 000.00	
Total Owner's Equity			115 000.00
Total Liabilities and Partners' Equity			$ 119 700.00

Assume that the partners agree:
i. That $100 be provided for the estimated amount of uncollectible accounts receivable
ii. That assets be revalued at the following amounts: Merchandise Inventory, $36 000; Land, $30 000; Building, $36 500; Office Equipment, $1 000; and Store Equipment, $8 500

Required

a Prepare an adjusted balance sheet, showing the new owner's equity amount for Daniel. *Hint:* Each adjustment will increase or decrease Daniel's original Capital amount as each individual adjustment is treated.
b How much cash is Okamoto required to invest?
c Record the initial investment of each partner in a general journal.

Preparing a partnership worksheet; preparing partnership financial statements; recording entries to distribute the profit (or loss).

6.4 M. Chang and J. Berger own and operate World of Sports. According to their partnership agreement, the two partners are to share profits and losses equally. At the end of the accounting year, their firm's adjusted trial balance appears as shown in Figure 6-16.

FIGURE **6-16**

World of Sports
Adjusted Trial Balance
June 30, 19-2

Cash	$ 47 050	
Accounts Receivable	40 000	
Allowance for Bad Debts		$ 1 100
Merchandise Inventory, July 1, 19-1	38 000	
Prepaid Insurance	1 016	
Supplies on Hand	1 634	
Land	20 000	
Building	40 000	
Accumulated Depreciation—Building		1 400
Office Equipment	2 000	
Accumulated Depreciation—Office Equipment		400
Store Equipment	17 000	
Accumulated Depreciation—Store Equipment		3 400
Bank Loan Payable		2 000
Accounts Payable		4 000
M. Chang, Capital		91 700
M. Chang, Drawing	9 800	
J. Berger, Capital		91 700
J. Berger, Drawing	9 200	
Sales		210 000
Purchases	100 000	
Selling Expenses	56 000	
General and Administrative Expenses	24 000	
	$405 700	$405 700

a Prepare a worksheet showing the distribution of profits (or losses) and the partners' capitals at the end of the year. Use a worksheet form similar to the one illustrated in this chapter.
Note: The inventory of goods on hand at the year-end is costed at $58 000.

b Prepare the year-end financial statements for the partnership. Show a separate statement of partners' equity.
c In a general journal, record the required entries to distribute the net income or loss, and to transfer the debit balances of the partners' drawing accounts.

Preparing a partnership worksheet; preparing partnership financial statements; recording entries to distribute the profit (or loss).

6.5 S. Logan and A. Miles own and operate the Beauty Boutique. According to their partnership agreement they are to share profits and losses in the ratio of 3:2. At the end of the accounting year, their firm's adjusted trial balance appears as shown in Figure 6-17.

FIGURE 6-17

The Beauty Boutique
Adjusted Trial Balance
December 31, 19—

Cash	$ 2 000	
Accounts Receivable	3 000	
Allowance for Bad Debts		$ 100
Prepaid Insurance	180	
Supplies on Hand	5 620	
Equipment	12 500	
Accumulated Depreciation—Equipment		2 500
Bank Loan Payable		6 500
Accounts Payable		5 000
Shelly Logan, Capital		15 000
Shelly Logan, Drawing	6 000	
Allison Miles, Capital		10 000
Allison Miles, Drawing	5 200	
Sales		65 400
Selling Expenses	22 000	
General and Administrative Expenses	48 000	
	$104 500	$104 500

Required
a Prepare a worksheet similar to the one illustrated in this chapter, showing the distribution of profits (or losses) and the partners' capitals at the end of the year.
b Prepare the year-end financial statements for the firm, with a separate statement of partners' equity.
c In a general journal, make the necessary entries to distribute the net income or loss, and to transfer the debit balances of the partners' drawing accounts.

Distributing a net income and a net loss to three partners under different profit-sharing ratios.

6.6 Bach, Bartok, and Beethoven are partners, sharing profits or losses on the basis of their respective beginning capitals in the firm. Their beginning investments are as follows: Bach, $40 000; Bartok, $40 000; and Beethoven, $20 000. At year-end the worksheet shows a net income of $30 000.

Required
a Prepare a table showing the net income distribution among the partners.

b Show the journal entry to record the distribution.
c Assume that a net loss of $6 000 was made. Show the required journal entry to distribute that loss.
d Assume that the partners had omitted any profit-sharing ratio from their agreement. What entries would be made to record the net income of $30 000? The net loss of $6 000?

TOPIC 2   Corporation Accounting Concepts

Main Characteristics

In Canada, almost 75% of our production of goods and services comes from business firms organized as business corporations. Since they provide the majority of jobs and consequently a major source of personal money income, and since they supply most of the goods and services we buy with that money income, it follows logically that all educated students should have a basic knowledge of this important form of business organization. The main characteristics of the business corporation may be summarized as follows:

1. In simple terms, a business ***corporation*** may be defined as an artificial person, created by law to operate business under a federal and/or provincial government charter.

2. Each corporation is given by law a ***legal entity*** or personality. Like a person, a corporate entity can buy and sell merchandise in its own name, it can deal with business property in its own name, and it can hire its own employees and officers.

3. Both Canada (the federal government) and the provinces possess and use legal power to incorporate business corporations. Each formal grant of incorporation is made by a government department under the authority of a statute, that is, the federal Canada Business Corporations Act or a similar statute of one of the provinces.

4. Under the federal act and some of the provincial acts, one person may apply for incorporation; in other provincial acts, a minimum of three applicants is needed. For specialized fields like banking, insurance, and nationwide transportation, an application for a special charter must be made only to the federal government.

5. A new corporation obtains its initial resources of money or other property from the contributions of its first owners, called ***shareholders*** or ***stockholders***. These contributions to buy shares in the business do not have to be equal. For example, one shareholder might buy 100 shares at $100 each, making a contribution of $10 000 to the corporation, while another buys 10 such shares, contributing only $1 000.

Corporation: a form of business organization that may have many owners, each owner being liable only for the amount of his or her investment in the business. An artificial person created by provincial or federal law.

Legal entity: a corporation possessing a separate existence under statutory authority.

Shareholders/stockholders: owners of a business corporation.

Share certificates: documents providing evidence of share ownership in a business corporation. One certificate may represent any number of shares.

Certificates indicating the number of shares owned are issued to each initial shareholder. **Share certificates** are also issued later, if and when additional share capital contributions are formally accepted by the corporation. Figure 6-18 shows a typical share certificate.

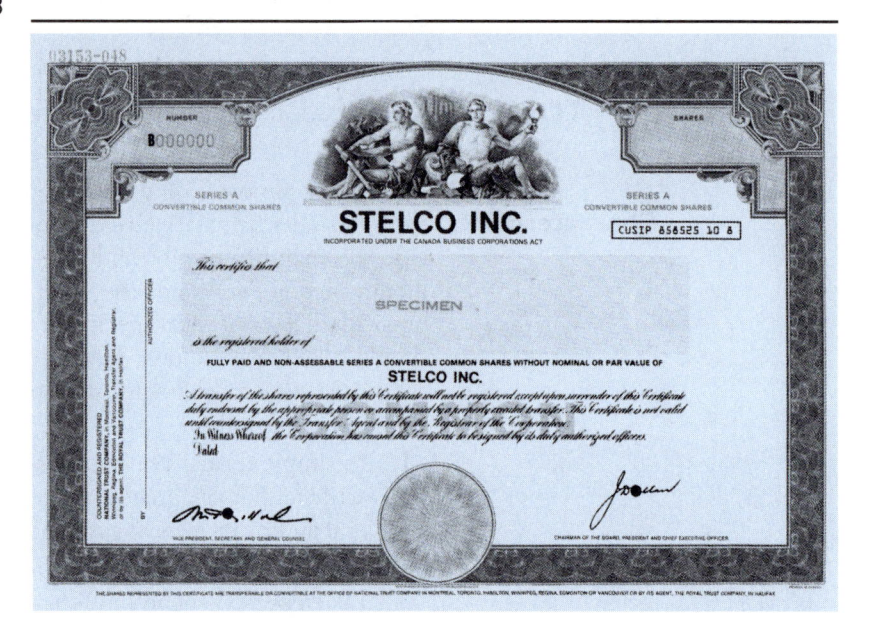

FIGURE 6-18

Limited liability: status of owners who are not personally liable for the debts of the corporation, their liability being limited to the amount of capital invested in the business.

6. The law of corporations limits the personal liability of shareholders of those corporations in which they hold shares. In the language of business, therefore, the shareholders will have **limited liability**. What this means is simply that a shareholder is not personally liable for the debts of the corporation (that is, the personal property of the shareholder cannot be sold to pay those debts). Hence, if the corporation fails, the shareholder's loss is limited to the amount of his or her investment. For example, if you acquired 100 shares costing $10 a share, the most you could lose would be $1 000. This limited liability feature is the main reason why business corporations are able to obtain sufficient capital to operate on a large scale. Because of this feature, corporations are also known as *limited companies*.

7. Under the majority of provincial acts and the Canada Business Corporations Act, the word "Limited," "Incorporated," or "Corporation," or the abbreviations "Ltd.," "Inc.," or "Corp.," must be the last word of the name of every business corporation. The purpose of this requirement is to warn other persons or corporations that they are dealing with a corporation whose owners have limited

CHAPTER 6: An Introduction to Partnership and Corporation Accounting 245

liability and whose members are not obligated as individuals by debts or contracts of the corporate entity as such.

8. A business corporation is said to have *perpetual existence*. In simple terms, this means that the capital contributions to a corporation are permanent. Shareholders wishing to discontinue their investment cannot withdraw their contribution from the corporation; instead, they have to look around for buyers to whom they can sell their holdings. New shareholders may replace the original shareholders by buying the shares, inheriting the shares, or in some cases receiving the shares as gifts.

9. The law of corporations requires every corporation to arrange a meeting of shareholders at least once a year, although more frequent meetings of shareholders can be held if desired. The voting power of each shareholder is based on the number of shares he or she holds and, in general, one vote is given for each share. As you will read later, shareholders must approve the annual report which contains the latest set of financial statements.

   Another important task of each annual meeting is the election of a **board of directors**. They form the governing body of the corporation for the next year. For this and other purposes, control usually rests in the hands of any shareholders, or group of shareholders, who can mobilize more than 50% of the votes cast at the shareholders' meeting. For example, a shareholder owning 51% of the voting shares then issued is positively assured of his or her ability to have those candidates whom he or she favours elected to the next board of directors. In cases where representation at annual meetings is smaller than 100% of the voting shares outstanding, voting can often be controlled by shareholdings smaller than 51%. If only 72% of the voting shares were represented at a meeting, effective control of the company could be achieved with 37% of the outstanding shares.

10. If a limited company's year-end profits are favourable, the board of directors may decide to distribute part or all of the profits to shareholders in the form of a **dividend**. Until then, the accumulated earnings (profits) of a limited company are represented by assets that are the property of the corporation and not of its shareholders.

11. One of the advantages of a business corporation is that it is permitted by law to borrow funds by issuing its own bonds. A **bond** is simply evidence of a long-term debt. Because bonds are issued with a repayment period of several years, you can expect to find Bonds Payable under the classification of long-term liabilities in the corporation balance sheet. Of course, the interest paid to bondholders represents an expense and must, therefore, appear in

---

Board of directors: the committee of persons elected by shareholders to be responsible for the top-level management of the corporation.

Dividend: an amount of earnings declared by the board of directors for distribution to the shareholders of a corporation in proportion to their holdings.

Bond: a certificate of indebtedness issued by a business corporation, generally for a period longer than ten years.

the income statement. See Figure 6-19 for an example of a bond certificate.

FIGURE 6-19

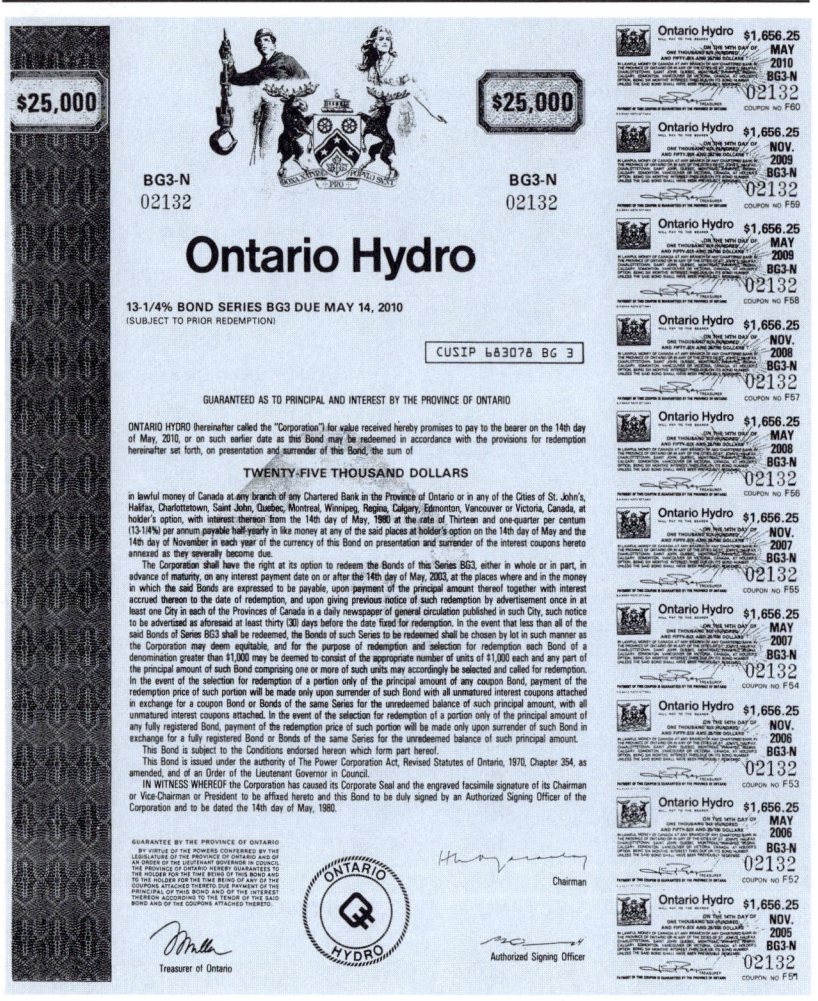

Source: Reproduced courtesy of Richardson Greenshields of Canada Limited.

12. Canadian income tax is levied by the federal and provincial governments on any legal person who earns taxable income. At the time of writing, a business enterprise is not a taxpayer unless it is incorporated. Individual owners of sole proprietorships are taxed on their income from all sources, one of which is any profit attributed on the books of the business. Individual partners are taxed on their income from all sources including any allocation of profit attributed to each on the books of the partnership. For example, if Jane McKay received $28 000 a year as an employee of General Motors but also owns a small dry cleaning business which earns her a profit of $20 000 a year, the government does not tax her

business profits separately for income tax purposes. She is taxed on her combined annual income of $48 000, and the amount of tax applicable to the profits of her business cannot be treated as an expense of its operations.

On the other hand, a business corporation is given legal status; therefore, it is treated as a separate taxpayer subject to the payment of a corporation income tax. As you will learn, a major distinction between limited companies and other forms of business organization is the fact that corporations show their income tax as one of the business expenses of the enterprise. The "income" of a corporation, for income tax purposes, is the difference between total revenues and total expenses. The net income which a corporation reports to its shareholders is the amount of income after taxes. For this reason, the ending of the published income statement usually appears as shown in Figure 6-20.

Shareholders, unlike the owners of sole proprietorships and partnerships, are not taxed directly for any profits earned by their company. Instead, shareholders are only taxed on salaries earned (if they are hired by their corporation) and on that part of the company's profit which is distributed to them as dividends.

FIGURE 6-20

Income Statement	
Income (or Earnings) Before Income Taxes	$95 000.00
Deduct: Corporate Income Taxes	38 000.00
Net Income (or Net Earnings) for Year	$57 000.00

Par Value Versus No-Par-Value Shares

Authorized capital: total amount of share capital which may be raised, because it is approved by government charter.

Issued share capital: amount obtained from sale of shares.

Outstanding shares: shares actually issued and in the hands of shareholders.

Par value: the nominal or face value of a share as specified in the company charter.

In preparing draft *articles of incorporation* or other forms of application for incorporation, the original members apply for authority to issue an unlimited number or a certain number of shares. This authority, for which a fee is paid, creates **authorized capital**. Unless the number is unlimited, the number of shares authorized may not lawfully be exceeded unless the articles or other grant of incorporation are amended on the basis of a new application and payment of an additional fee. To avoid the extra paperwork and additional fees, many of the larger corporations apply for authorized capital with an unlimited number of shares.

The actual capital — the **issued share capital** — of a corporation is not the amount authorized, but the amount from those shares actually issued and paid for. In the language of accounting, shares which have been issued and are in the hands of shareholders are **outstanding shares**.

Traditionally, and still in most provincial acts, authorized shares may possess a **par value**, that is, a minimum dollar amount to be paid in by shareholders to whom shares are issued. Note that par value is the amount

No-par-value stock: shares of capital stock that have no nominal or par value.

FIGURE **6-21a**

Jurisdictions Supporting Only Non-Par-Value Stock

Canada
Alberta
Manitoba
Newfoundland
Ontario

FIGURE **6-21b**

Jurisdictions Supporting Both Par Value and No-Par-Value Stock

British Columbia
New Brunswick
Northwest Territories
Nova Scotia
Prince Edward Island
Quebec
Saskatchewan

Common Versus Preferred Shares

Common shares/common stock: ordinary stock, which carries a vote but no preference as to dividends and distribution of assets.

Preferred shares: shares that guarantee first claim on assets if corporation is dissolved, and specify a fixed dividend.

recorded in a Share Capital account. Thus, if 10 000 shares were issued at a par value of $10, the amount in the Share Capital account would be $100 000. It is important to realize that *par value does not denote market value* of the shares once they are issued. In practice, the market value of shares usually fluctuates on stock exchanges according to investors' views concerning success or lack of success of the corporation.

In recent years, a viewpoint has become dominant that par value is so likely to mislead that corporations should only issue **no-par-value** stock. For example, the Canada Business Corporations Act, and the acts of the provinces listed in Figure 6-21a, now stipulate that companies which are incorporated under them shall be without par value. On the other hand, companies that prefer to incorporate under a provincial charter may apply to issue shares at a stated par value or without par value. Many accountants believe that, in time, all the provinces will amend their acts to follow the restriction listed in the federal act. In this text, only the accounting of no-par-value shares will be treated.

A limited company that issues only one kind of stock issues **common shares**, or **common stock**. The owners of common stock are entitled to share in the management of the company indirectly by voting at shareholders' meetings, to purchase a portion of any shares of common stock subsequently issued, and, if the company is dissolved or liquidated, to share in any assets remaining after creditors are paid. They are neither guaranteed nor entitled to any *dividend* — a fixed portion of the net income granted at regular intervals. They may receive dividends only if and when the board of directors *declares a dividend* on the common stock.

However, to appeal to as many investors as possible, a limited company may be allowed by its charter to issue not only common but also **preferred shares**. In general, a preferred share contains some features designed to attract a particular type of investor who might not be interested in investing in common shares of a company. The owners of preferred shares are usually not entitled to vote at shareholders' meetings, but they are entitled to certain rights denied to owners of common shares; these generally revolve around a preference as to dividends, and a preference as to asset distribution. In simple terms, the first preference identifies the legal measure to allow preferred shareholders to received fixed dividends, when declared by the board of directors, at regular intervals, before any dividends are declared on common stock. In the second preference, if the corporation is liquidated, all preferred shareholders are usually entitled to repayments of the full amounts of their capital investments before any payments can be made to common shareholders. For this reason, it is customary to show preferred shares before common shares on any corporation balance sheet.

FIGURE 6-22

Shareholder's Equity
Share Capital:
 Preferred, $2.25 cumulative shares
  of no par value, authorized
  and issued 100 000 shares .. $1 000 000
 Common, of no par value,
  authorized 100 000 shares;
  issued and outstanding,
  80 000 shares 800 000

In Figure 6-22, observe that the preferred share carries a fixed dividend at $2.25 per share. In practice, a preferred share dividend may be a certain percentage of the par value of the share. Under a no-par-value system, however, the dividend is expressed in a dollar amount.

Opening Entries for Formation of a Corporation

To keep matters simple, the following cases assume that the company will issue only common shares of no par value. Examine each case carefully.

Case 1. Shares Issued for Cash The simplest situation to illustrate is one in which shares are issued for cash. Assuming that 5 000 shares of no par value are issued at $10 each, the entry shown in Figure 6-23 would be made in the company's books.

FIGURE 6-23

GENERAL JOURNAL — Page 1

Date		Account Title and Explanation	Post. Ref.	Debit	Credit
19-1 Jan.	2	Cash .... Share Capital .... Issued 5 000 common shares of no par value at $10 each.	101 301	50 000 00	50 000 00

Case 2. Shares Issued for Assets Other Than Cash When a corporation issues shares in direct exchange for such assets as land, buildings, merchandise inventory, receivables, and other business assets, this logically involves two transactions:

1. A sale of property to the corporation by the previous owners at agreed values
2. An issue of shares as purchase consideration for the property bought

When more than one investor is interested in the corporation, fair treatment requires that property be acquired at a cost figure which approximates fair market value and that the amount credited to the Share Capital account be recorded at that figure.

The journal entry shown in Figure 6-24 illustrates a transaction by which a corporation acquires property valued at $150 000 in exchange for fully paid shares.

It is assumed here that the issued price of $10 per share is also the generally accepted value of that share in the marketplace, and thus, the value

FIGURE 6-24

		GENERAL JOURNAL			Page 1
Date		Account Title and Explanation	Post. Ref.	Debit	Credit
19-1 Jan.	3	Merchandise Inventory Land Building Share Capital Issued 15 000 common shares of no par value at $10 each, in exchange for assets.	110 120 121 301	70 000 00 20 000 00 60 000 00	150 000 00

of the three newly acquired assets represents their market value at the time of acquisition. Once the market value of shares moves away from the issued price, the problem of how many shares to exchange for a stated amount of money or property becomes more involved, since that market value may be constantly fluctuating. In this text we shall not venture further into the difficult areas of asset valuation or share valuation.

Case 3. Shares Issued for Services Rendered Shares may also be issued in payment for services performed by such persons as accountants, lawyers, promoters, geologists, and prospectors. Once the value of those services is agreed upon, shares are issued. Assume then that an engineer has done testing and development work valued at $20 000 on some newly acquired land. As payment for his or her services the board of directors authorizes an issue of 2 000 previously unissued common shares at $10 each. The journal entry may be viewed as in Figure 6-25.

In the example shown above, the asset Land increases in value, because any costs of bringing it into service are directly related to its value. Therefore, under the cost principle, the cost of the Land is the original cost, $20 000, plus the additional $20 000 cost for engineering services.

FIGURE 6-25

		GENERAL JOURNAL			Page 1
Date		Account Title and Explanation	Post. Ref.	Debit	Credit
19-1 Jan.	4	Land Share Capital Issue of 2 000 common shares of no par value at $10 each, in exchange for engineering services to the development of newly acquired land.	120 301	20 000 00	20 000 00

Pre-operating Balance Sheet

After the preliminary organization is complete and before the routine business transactions begin, a pre-operating balance sheet for the new corporation can be drawn up. Rules relating to share capital disclosure on financial statements have been established by the various corporation acts of the federal and provincial governments. In particular, the law requires that a balance sheet disclose the number of shares authorized, the number issued, and their par value or lack thereof as the case may be. Using our examples in the three cases just presented, Figure 6-26 discloses how many shares were authorized, how many were issued in the year, the issued price, and the consideration received, whether in the form of cash, other property, or past services.

FIGURE 6-26

Canadian Products Company Limited
(incorporated under the Canada Business Corporations Act)
Balance Sheet
As at January 31, 19—
(prior to the commencement of operations)

Assets

Current Assets:
Cash	$50 000	
Merchandise Inventory (at cost)	70 000	
Total Current Assets		$120 000

Fixed Assets:
Land (at cost)	40 000	
Building (at cost)	60 000	
Total Fixed Assets		100 000
Total Assets		**$220 000**

Liabilities

None.

Shareholders' Equity

Share Capital:
  Authorized 30 000 common shares of no par value.
  Issued and Fully Paid:
    22 000 shares issued for $10 each,
    payment received as follows:

In Cash		$ 50 000	
And For:			
Merchandise Inventory	70 000		
Land	40 000		
Building	60 000		
Total		$220 000	$220 000

Total Liabilities and Shareholders' Equity	$220 000

Approved on behalf of board:
Signed *J. A. Galt* Director
         Ann Leopold Director

Accounting for Earnings of Corporations

The accounting activities for a business corporation at year-end are very similar to those you learned for sole proprietorships and partnerships. There is, however, one major difference. In a limited company, regardless of whether there is one principal shareholder or numerous shareholders, the yearly profit or loss, after deducting a calculation for income tax expense, is transferred to a separate shareholders' equity account called **Retained Earnings**, as illustrated in Figure 6-27.

Retained Earnings: an account wherein net income held back from distribution to shareholders is reported.

FIGURE 6-27

GENERAL JOURNAL				Page 43
Date	Account Title and Explanation	Post. Ref.	Debit	Credit
19— Dec. 31	Revenue and Expense Summary .... Retained Earnings .... To transfer profit to Retained Earnings.	600 331	50 000 00	50 000 00

FIGURE 6-28

Shareholders' Equity
Share Capital:
  Authorized: 30 000 common shares
    of no par value
  Issued: 22 000 shares at $10 .. $220 000
  Retained Earnings 50 000
  Total Shareholders' Equity $270 000

FIGURE 6-29

Shareholders' Equity
Share Capital:
  Authorized: 30 000 common shares
    of no par value
  Issued: 22 000 shares at $10 .. $220 000
  Less: Deficit in Retained Earnings . 10 000
  Total Shareholders' Equity $210 000

It is important to learn that retained earnings represent part of the shareholders' equity in the business. Assuming continuous and successful (profitable) operations, the major source for financing business growth is the net income transferred to Retained Earnings. In other words, profits or earnings may be wholly or partially retained instead of being completely distributed to shareholders in the form of dividends. On the balance sheet, a credit balance in Retained Earnings is added to the balance of share capital to determine the total shareholders' equity. On the other hand, a debit balance in Retained Earnings represents a net loss; therefore, a decrease would be required from share capital when calculating the total shareholders' equity. If such is the case, accountants use the term ***deficit*** to show that a debit balance has occurred in the Retained Earnings account.

Accounting for Distribution of Earnings

Deficit: a debit balance in Retained Earnings.

If a limited company's Retained Earnings account has a credit balance, and provided the corporation has sufficient cash, the board of directors may decide to distribute part or all of this pool of undivided profits to shareholders in the form of dividends. If such is the case, the board of directors will pass a resolution *declaring a dividend*. Distribution of a dividend involves three significant dates: (1) date of declaration; (2) date of record; and (3) date of payment.

1. **Date of declaration** On the day on which the dividend is declared by the board of directors (***date of declaration***), the amount declared immediately becomes a liability of the company.

Date of declaration: the date a dividend is declared.

The entry to record the declaration of a dividend consists of a debit to Retained Earnings and a credit to a current liability account called Dividends Payable for the total amount of the dividend. If a limited company has more than one class of shares, a separate liability account is set up for dividend declarations on each kind.

2. **Date of record** Although a company knows the amount it will pay when a dividend is declared, it must also at that time establish a date for determining which shareholders are entitled to receive dividends. Since ownership of shares is transferable at any time in a corporation whose shares are widely owned, it is necessary to freeze the corporation's record of its shareholders in a special ledger (shareholders' ledger) as of a particular date. This becomes the ***date of record*** for the purpose of preparing dividend lists and cheques. The date of record is later than the date of declaration, so that parties to stock transfers will have time to have their share transactions properly recorded.

    It is customary for shares to go ***ex-dividend*** from three business days before the date of record to the date of payment. Once a share sells ex-dividend it loses the right to receive the latest declared dividend.

3. **Date of payment** The declaration of a dividend always includes announcement of the date of payment. This usually follows the date of record by two to four weeks to enable share records to be balanced to date, and the dividend list and cheques to be prepared. Of course, the payment cancels the liability created by the previous declaration of the dividend.

To illustrate the dividend distribution process, suppose the board of directors of Canadian Products Company Limited on January 15, 19-2 declared a dividend of $2 for each common share. In the declaration shown in Figure 6-30, the date of record is January 31, Year 2, and payment will be made on February 28, also of Year 2. The entry shown in Figure 6-31 is made to record the declaration of the dividend.

Date of record: the date used to determine which stockholders receive the dividend.

Ex-dividend: status of a share in which the share is not entitled to the latest declared dividend.

FIGURE 6-30

Dividend Notice

Notice is hereby given that a dividend of $2 on each Common share of Canadian Products Company Limited has been declared payable on February 28, 19-2 to shareholders on record at the close of business on January 31, 19-2.

K. L. Wong, President
January 15, 19-2

FIGURE 6-31

GENERAL JOURNAL				Page 44
Date	Account Title and Explanation	Post. Ref.	Debit	Credit
19-2 Jan. 15	Retained Earnings .... Dividends Payable .... Dividends declared on common shares at $2 per share; payable to shareholders of record as of January 31.	331 241	10 000 00	10 000 00

The individual amounts and actual shareholders to whom those dividend amounts will be paid will not be established until January 31, the date of record.

On February 28, the date of payment, Canadian Products Company Limited pays the dividend. The entry may be analyzed as shown in Figure 6-32.

FIGURE 6-32

Date	Account Title and Explanation	Post. Ref.	Debit	Credit
19–2 Feb. 28	Dividends Payable　　Cash　　To record the payment of the dividend declared on January 15, to shareholders of record on January 31.	241 101	10 000 00	10 000 00

GENERAL JOURNAL — Page 50

Statement of Retained Earnings

FIGURE 6-33

Canadian Products Company Limited
Statement of Retained Earnings
For the Year Ended December 31, 19-2

Retained Earnings,
　December 31, 19-1 .... $ 50 000
Add: Net Income for 19-2 .... 　60 000
　　　　　　　　　　　　　　　110 000
Deduct: Dividends Declared and
　Paid on Common Shares ... 　10 000
Retained Earnings,
　December 31, 19-2 .... $100 000

In corporation accounting, it is customary to produce a statement of retained earnings. Like the statement of owner's equity, the statement of retained earnings may be separate or included in the balance sheet. Some corporations even combine their income statement with the statement of retained earnings. By definition, this statement summarizes the pattern of entries which are made in the Retained Earnings account. Thus, the net income earned by a limited company is added to the balance that was in the Retained Earnings account at the beginning of the year. Any amounts that have been declared or distributed as dividends during that year are subtracted. At the end of the accounting year, the final balances in the Retained Earnings account and on the statement should agree.

The Corporate Annual Report

Annual report: document containing information provided annually by the board of directors of a corporation to the shareholders.

In Canada, federal and provincial laws stipulate the financial information that a business corporation must provide its shareholders. Under the various business corporation acts, the board of directors shall place before the shareholders at every annual meeting: (a) a set of financial statements in two-year comparative form; (b) the report of the auditor to the shareholders; and (c) such other information related to the financial position of the company as is required by the corporation's charter or bylaws. To meet this legal obligation, the board of directors will include the reporting of financial statements and other information in the company's annual report. A typical **annual report** will generally include the following contents:

1. The corporate profile
2. The president's letter to the shareholders
3. Textual material describing the business, reviewing the operations, and outlining financial objectives
4. Financial highlights depicted in charts, tables, and graphs; generally,

there is a five-year comparative income statement, or a longer period may be covered
5. A list of the directors and officers making up the corporate directory
6. The financial statements, accompanied by a statement of management's responsibility for the preparation of the financial statements and the auditor's report

Under the various corporation acts, the financial statements must include at least the following: (a) an income statement; (b) a statement of retained earnings; (c) a balance sheet; and (d) a statement of changes in financial position.

Moreover, the acts stipulate that these financial statements must be prepared in accordance with the recommendations of the Canadian Institute of Chartered Accountants as set out in the *CICA Handbook*. In general, the *Handbook* contains the guidelines, called **generally accepted accounting principles (GAAPs)**, that must be followed in financial-statement reporting to shareholders and to other interested parties outside of the business corporation. A study of the *Handbook* is well beyond the scope of this text. In the following short sections, however, an introductory treatment is given, to suggest how the majority of Canadian corporations report the four important financial statements mentioned above.

> Generally accepted accounting principles (GAAPs): guidelines set out in the *CICA Handbook* for the preparation of financial statements to shareholders and to other parties outside the firm.

INCOME STATEMENT

The majority of Canadian corporations report the income statement as a separate financial statement. At the time of writing, the two most commonly used titles to describe this statement are "Earnings Statement" and "Income Statement." It is interesting to note that very few corporations in Canada still use "Profit and Loss Statement." Furthermore, the majority of corporations follow the single-step form of reporting the income statement along the lines suggested in Figure 6-34.

FIGURE 6-34

Name of Business Corporation
Income Statement
(in thousands of dollars)

	FOR THE YEAR ENDED:	
	December 31, 19-2	December 31, 19-1
Revenue:		
Sales (net)	$xxx xxx	$xxx xxx
Interest and Dividends Earned	x xxx	x xxx
	xxx xxx	xxx xxx
Costs and Expenses:		
Cost of Sales	xxx xxx	xxx xxx
Depreciation (note 1)	xx xxx	xx xxx
Interest on Long-Term Debt	xx xxx	xx xxx
Bank and Other Interest Expense	x xxx	x xxx
Other Expenses (related expired costs matched against the year's revenue)	x xxx	x xxx
	xxx xxx	xxx xxx
Income Before Income Taxes	xxx xxx	xxx xxx
Provision for Income Taxes	xx xxx	xx xxx
Net Income	$ xx xxx	$ xx xxx

Note: The accompanying notes are an integral part of the financial statements.

FIGURE 6-35

From Paragraph 1500.08 of the CICA Handbook
To eliminate unnecessary detail it is desirable to express all amounts shown in the financial statements to the nearest dollar or, depending upon the magnitude of the amounts involved, to the nearest thousand dollars.

Notes to financial statements: explanatory or supplementary information appended to and forming an integral part of financial statements.

Two features should be noted from the illustrated income statement. First, note the use of amounts in thousands of dollars. This follows the *CICA Handbook*, which in paragraph 1500.08 offers the generally accepted accounting procedure displayed in Figure 6-35. Today, all Canadian corporations eliminate cents in financial statements reported in their annual reports. Approximately one-half of the corporations round off amounts to the nearest dollar; and approximately half report amounts to the nearest thousand dollars.

The second important point to recognize is the fact that Canadian accountants generally recognize that **notes to financial statements** provide an effective way to offer clarification or further explanation of certain items in the financial statements. For example, "note 1" next to "Depreciation" refers the reader to a note that explains the details of depreciable assets, the method of depreciation used, and the year-end calculations. As suggested by the footnote under the illustrated income statement, any accompanying notes have the same significance as if the information or explanations were set forth in the body of the statement itself.

STATEMENT OF RETAINED EARNINGS

As suggested earlier, a separate statement of retained earnings continues to be the most popular method of reporting changes in retained earnings. The condensed pattern is presented in Figure 6-36.

FIGURE 6-36

Name of Business Corporation
Statement of Retained Earnings
(in thousands of dollars)

	FOR THE YEAR ENDED: December 31, 19-2	December 31, 19-1
Balance Carried Forward—Beginning of Year (per last year's balance sheet)	$xxx xxx	$xxx xxx
Add: Net Income for Year (or Deduct: Net Loss for Year)	xx xxx	xx xxx
	xxx xxx	xxx xxx
Deduct: Dividends Declared (if any)	xx xxx	xx xxx
Balance Forward—End of Year (as shown on year-end balance sheet)	$xxx xxx	$xxx xxx

BALANCE SHEET

Canadian corporations use one of three formats in reporting the balance sheet: account form, report form, or financial position form. As you will recall, the account form reports the balance sheet in the traditional accounting equation order: assets on the left side, liabilities and shareholders' equity on the right side. In the report form, the liabilities are deducted from the assets to report the shareholders' equity as the balance. In the financial position form, the vertical alignment of the report form is used; however, the current liabilities are deducted from the current assets to report a concept called "Working Capital" (excess of current assets over current liabilities); then, the other liabilities are deducted from other assets to show net assets equivalent to shareholders' equity.

At the time of writing, approximately 50% of Canadian corporations use the report form, 35% use the account form, and the remaining 15% use the financial position form. With very minor exceptions, the balance sheets set out items of a similar nature under descriptive headings with totals or subtotals for current assets, fixed assets, intangible assets (other assets), current liabilities, long-term liabilities (debts), and shareholders' equity. For most manufacturing, retail, and wholesale corporations, the condensed pattern of a balance sheet is as illustrated in Figure 6-37.

FIGURE 6-37

Name of Business Corporation
Balance Sheet

Assets (in thousands of dollars)	As at December 31: 19-2	19-1	Liabilities (in thousands of dollars)	As at December 31: 19-2	19-1
Current Assets	$x xxx	$x xxx	Current Liabilities	$x xxx	$x xxx
Fixed Assets	x xxx	x xxx	Long-Term Liabilities	x xxx	x xxx
Intangible Assets (if any)	x xxx	x xxx	Total Liabilities	$x xxx	x xxx
			Shareholders' Equity:		
			Share Capital	$x xxx	$x xxx
			Retained Earnings	x xxx	x xxx
			Total Shareholders' Equity	$x xxx	$x xxx
Total Assets	$x xxx	$x xxx	Total Liabilities and Shareholders' Equity	$x xxx	$x xxx

Statement of changes in financial position (SCFP): a statement reporting the inflows and outflows of cash for a period that has ended; hence, a cash flow statement.

STATEMENT OF CHANGES IN FINANCIAL POSITION For many years, the ***statement of changes in financial position (SCFP)*** reported to shareholders the changes in working capital, that is, the changes of current assets over current liabilities. This statement was supposed to measure the ability of the business to pay its short-term debts and to finance current operations. Unfortunately, many businesses were able to report an increasing working capital position but not an ability to pay off their debts in cash.

To illustrate, suppose Corporation X reported current assets and current liabilities as illustrated in Figure 6-38. It would appear that the corporation has $2 of current assets to pay off any $1 of current debts.

FIGURE 6-38

X Corporation's Working Capital (WC)

Current Assets (CA):
- Cash .... $ 6 000
- Accounts Receivable (net) 20 000
- Inventories 50 000
- Prepaid Expenses 4 000
- Total CA $80 000

Current Liabilities (CL):
- Bank Loan Payable $10 000
- Accounts Payable 15 000
- Salaries Payable 8 000
- GST Payable 2 000
- Income Tax Payable 5 000
- Total CL $40 000

CA − CL = WC
$80 000 − $40 000 = $40 000

While it may appear that Corporation X has a healthy working capital position, this does not mean much unless the working capital can be turned into cash easily when required. The illustration shows immediate cash available equal to $6 000, while an additional $20 000 may be obtained within 30 days from accounts receivable. If one disregards the prepaid expense amount (since prepaid expenses are not normally liquidated), the business must rely on the large stockpile of inventories to pay off its current debts. As most merchandising businesses have learned, there is no guarantee that the amount of inventory can be realized into cash within a short time.

To meet the criticisms of using a working capital approach to the statement of changes in financial position, Section 1540 of the *CICA Handbook* was revised substantially in late 1985. Today, the *Handbook* supports the use of a cash approach only. A well-prepared SCFP should explain how and why the cash position of a business has changed during the period. In other words, the main objective of the statement of changes in financial position is now to report information about the operating, financing, and investing activities of an enterprise and the effects of those activities on cash resources. A typical pattern of presenting this statement may be illustrated as in Figure 6-39.

FIGURE 6-39

Name of Business Corporation
Statement of Changes in Financial Position
Year Ended December 31
(in thousands of dollars)

	19-2	19-1
Cash Provided By (Used In) Operating Activities:		
Net Income	$xxx xxx	$xxx xxx
Add (Deduct) Non-Cash Items:		
Add: Depreciation Expense	x xxx	x xxx
Deduct: Increase in Accounts Receivable	(xxx)	(xxx)
Deduct: Increase in Inventory	(xxx)	(xxx)
Add: Increase in Accounts Payable	x xxx	x xxx
Deduct: Increase in Prepaid Insurance	(xxx)	(xxx)
Cash Provided by Operating Activities	xx xxx	xx xxx
Cash Provided By (Used In) Financing Activities:		
Issuance of Common Shares	xxx xxx	xxx xxx
Cash Dividends	(xxx)	(xxx)
Cash Provided by Financing Activities	xxx xxx	xx xxx
Cash Provided By (Used In) Investing Activities:		
Purchase of Equipment	(xx xxx)	—
Proceeds on Sale of Investments	—	xx xxx
Cash Provided By (Used In) Investing Activities	(xx xxx)	xx xxx
Increase in Cash During the Year	xx xxx	xx xxx
Cash at Beginning of Year	xx xxx	xx xxx
Cash at End of Year	$ xx xxx	$ xx xxx

CHAPTER 6: An Introduction to Partnership and Corporation Accounting

A closer analysis of the above objective would suggest that the statement, in its most basic form, is a statement reporting the inflow of cash and the outflow of cash during an accounting period. Since that is the case, the *Handbook* permits the use of alternative titles for the statement such as "Cash Flow Statement," "Statement of Cash Flows," "Statement of Changes in Cash Resources," and "Statement of Operating, Financing, and Investing Activities." Note that, although at present the most commonly used title for this statement is the "Statement of Changes in Financial Position," there is a decided trend among corporations to use "Statement of Cash Flows."

In its simplest form, the SCFP may be prepared by tracking the cash inflows and cash outflows under three headings: Operating Activities, Financing Activities, and Investing Activities. In general, **operating activities** include all items measured by the income statement on a cash basis. Inflows of cash from operations would include sales of merchandise for cash, the collection of accounts receivable, and the receipt of cash from holding investments such as bonds and stocks. All of these transactions increase the amount of cash and, therefore, are sources (inflows) of cash. Outflows of cash in operating activities would include the purchase of merchandise for cash, the payment of accounts payable and operating expenses for cash, and the payment of interest on bank loans, mortgages payable, and bonds payable. Note that all of these items would appear on the income statement and, therefore, are considered operating activities for purposes of preparing the SCFP.

Financing activities involve transactions that are related to the method used to acquire cash through long-term debts. For example, cash proceeds from the sale of corporation stock and corporation bonds result in cash inflows. These are financing activities, because the business has entered into transactions to finance (acquire needed cash). On the other hand, repayments of principal amounts borrowed (bank loans, principal part of mortgages payable, and the face of the bond) result in cash outflows through financing activities. Similarly, cash dividends to shareholders are outflows of cash through financing activities. However, note that interest payments on long-term debts are not related to financing activities, because they are expenses reported on the income statement. For the purpose of preparing the SCFP, any item appearing on the income statement is classified as an operating activity.

In general, cash flows arising from the purchase and sale of noncurrent assets are identified as **investing activities**. For example, purchases of fixed assets represent an investment in the business, because these noncurrent assets will be used to generate revenue or support revenue-making activities now and in the future. Common examples of cash inflows resulting from investing activities include cash receipts from selling fixed assets and investments. On the other hand, cash outflows

---

Operating activities: any activities (transactions) related to items reported on the income statement.

Financing activities: transactions related to long-term debts (bonds and mortgage payables) and share capital.

Investing activities: transactions related to the purchase and sale of noncurrent assets (investing in fixed assets, long-term investments).

resulting from investing activities would include cash payments made to acquire fixed assets and investments. Cash would also flow out when a loan is made.

Although a SCFP could be prepared directly from a detailed analysis of the corporation's Cash account, it is almost impossible to prepare the statement by examining the Cash records of the majority of Canadian corporations. The reason is due to the large volume of cash transactions that are related especially to operating activities. As an alternative, most corporations prefer the indirect method supported by Section 1540 of the *Handbook*. Refer back to the earlier illustration of the SCFP, Figure 6-39, showing the pattern of cash flows. The illustration assumes the indirect method, which begins with the corporation's net income and then shows the adjustments required to convert the net income accounted on an **accrual basis** to a **cash basis**. For example, depreciation is added back to net income, because depreciation expense does not result in a cash outflow. (Think back to the double entry.) Since many of these adjustments of removing the accrual aspects of net income require an in-depth knowledge of financial accounting, the actual preparation of this statement using the indirect method is omitted and left for study in more advanced courses. Instead, any reinforcement problem on preparing the SCFP will be limited to the direct method, whereby you will be given information on inflows and outflows of cash for a specific accounting period.

Accrual basis (of accounting): used when one records revenue and expense transactions in the period in which they have been earned and incurred respectively, whether or not such transactions have been settled finally by the receipt or payment of cash.

Cash basis (of accounting): used when one records revenue and expenses only when cash is received and cash is paid.

TOPIC 2 Problems

Recording the opening entries to form a business corporation; preparing the pre-operating balance sheet in accordance with GAAPs.

6.7 Paulite Products Co. Ltd. was given a charter under the Canada Business Corporations Act and authorized to issue 100 000 common shares of no par value. The following transactions took place during August:

Aug. 1 Issued for cash 10 000 common shares for $10 per share.
12 The following assets and liabilities were appraised and then acquired from Mr. Jenkins, whose business was acquired in exchange for 24 000 common shares: Land, $50 000; Buildings, $140 000; Accounts Receivable, $30 000; Inventories, $40 000; Equipment, $80 000; and 8% Mortgage Payable, Due in 2001, $100 000.
31 Received an engineer's bill for $3 200 covering surveying services in connection with the development of the land. In lieu of payment, the engineer agreed to accept 200 common shares.

Required
a Prepare general journal entries, with narratives, to record the above transactions.
b Post the entries to appropriate T-accounts.
c Prepare a pre-operating balance sheet in accordance with prescribed minimum standards of financial reporting.

Preparing the shareholders' equity section of the pre-operating balance sheet from varying cases.

6.8 Each of the cases described below is independent of the others. Assume that all corporations were incorporated under the Canada Business

CHAPTER 6: An Introduction to Partnership and Corporation Accounting

Corporations Act. For each of the cases described, prepare the shareholders' equity section of the pre-operating balance sheet.

a Bacheid Industries Ltd. was organized in September of this year and was authorized to issue 1 million shares of no-par-value common stock, and 100 000 shares of $5 cumulative preferred stock of no par value. The entire issue was sold by the end of September as follows: common stock issued at $5 per share; preferred stock issued at $100 per share.

b Fournier Operations Ltd. was organized in October of this year and was authorized to issue 8 000 shares of $5 cumulative preferred stock of no par value, and 1 000 000 shares of no-par-value common stock. By the end of October, 8 000 shares of preferred stock were sold for $100 per share, and 600 000 common stock were issued at $5 per share.

c Guidoccio Industries Ltd. was organized in November of this year and was authorized to issue an unlimited number of common shares without par value. During the month, stock was issued at varying prices as follows: 10 500 shares at $4.50 per share; 3 000 shares at $4.85 per share; 5 000 shares at $5.85 per share; 1 500 shares at $6.55 per share; 500 shares at $7.45 per share; and 7 200 shares at $7.65 per share.

Preparing the shareholders' equity section of the pre-operating balance sheet immediately after the sale of common and preferred stock.

6.9 The Niagara Corporation Ltd. was incorporated under the Canada Business Corporations Act on June 1, 19-1. The corporation was authorized to issue 10 000 shares of no par value, $10 cumulated preferred stock, and 100 000 shares of no-par-value common stock. Assume that the preferred stock was issued at $100 and 60 000 shares of the common stock were sold at $20 per share.

Required Prepare a statement of shareholders' equity for Niagara Corporation Ltd. immediately after the sale of securities but prior to the operation of the limited company.

Recording journal entries for the declaration and payment of a cash dividend on common shares; preparing the statement of retained earnings.

6.10 Bolton Company Limited had a credit balance of $60 000 in its Retained Earnings account at the beginning of its business year, last October 1. Net income for the following year amounted to $120 000. At this year-end the board of directors declared a dividend for the year on common shares, totalling $50 000. The dividend is to be paid to shareholders on record as of October 15, 19-2 on October 31, 19-2.

Required a Prepare journal entries for the above transactions.
b Prepare a statement of retained earnings for the year ended September 30, 19-2.

Converting an existing partnership into a corporation; preparing the pre-operating corporate balance sheet; preparing the year-end balance sheet and statement of retained earnings from given data.

6.11 The three partners of ABC Company agreed on December 31, 19-1 to incorporate their business. The balance sheet of the partnership on this date is shown as follows:

FIGURE 6-40

Assets	
Total Assets	$500 000
Liabilities and Partners' Equity	
Accounts Payable	$125 000
A, Capital	$188 000
B, Capital	112 000
C, Capital	75 000
Total Partners' Equity	375 000
Total Liabilities and Partners' Equity	$500 000

The partners applied for and received a charter under the Canada Business Corporations Act. The charter authorized 100 000 common shares of no par value, and 10 000 shares of no-par-value $8 cumulative preferred stock. On January 2, 19-2, the corporation was formed, and each partner was issued common stock for one-half of his or her capital interest, and preferred stock for the remaining half. The preferred stock is to be issued at $100 per share and the common stock at $10.

During the year 19-2, the corporation earned $125 000 before income taxes. Accounts payable increased by $24 800 during 19-2; the only other liability at year-end was income taxes payable. Assume that income taxes are 40% of the income before taxes. Regular quarterly dividends were paid on preferred stock, and a dividend of $1.50 per share was paid on common stock.

Required

a Prepare the balance sheet of ABC Company Limited as of December 31, 19-2.
b Show a schedule supporting how you arrived at the amount of stock issued.
c Show a statement of retained earnings for the year ended December 31, 19-2.

Preparing a corporate income statement in multi-step form and single-step form from given data.

6.12 Assume that you are to prepare the year-end income statement for the annual report of Scott Paper Company, Limited. The Company is chartered under the Canada Business Corporations Act, and its year-end is December 31. From the results of operations summarized below, carry out the following:

a Prepare a multi-step form of income statement, expressing all amounts to the nearest dollar.
b Prepare a single-step form of income statement, expressing all amounts to the nearest thousand dollars by showing three zeros.
c Prepare a single-step form, but with the corporation income taxes shown in a separate section. Express all amounts to the nearest thousand dollars and omit the three zeros.

The information in Figure 6-41 represents the amounts taken from the income statement section of the worksheet.

CHAPTER 6: An Introduction to Partnership and Corporation Accounting

FIGURE 6-41

	19-2	19-1
Net sales	$287 000 008.70	$255 587 973.80
Cost of products sold	217 781 665.10	193 155 724.95
Provision for depreciation	15 254 971.00	14 698 905.00
Selling, general, and research expenses	20 691 798.75	17 574 055.10
Employees' pension plan expenses	3 116 740.35	2 856 260.40
Interest on bank indebtedness	791 579.90	797 778.20
Interest on long-term debt	6 393 332.20	5 714 660.30
Interest and other revenue earned	2 298 931.85	1 695 622.45
Income taxes	12 307 000.00	11 490 000.00

Completing an accounting cycle for one month for a corporation using simple data; preparing financial statements including the statement of cash flows using the direct method only.

6.13 H. Black Inc. was formed under the Canada Business Corporations Act on May 31, current year, with share capital issued for cash totalling $100 000. Transactions for the June, current year, were summarized as follows:

1. Purchased equipment for cash, $40 000.
2. Purchased merchandise on account, $50 000. (Assume a periodic inventory system. No previous balance exists in the Inventory account. This transaction represents the first purchase of goods for resale.)
3. Sold 60% of the merchandise on hand on account for $90 000.
4. Cheques issued to creditors, $40 000.
5. Cheques received from customers, $75 000.
6. Cheques issued to pay operating expenses other than depreciation, $20 000.
7. Depreciation, $1 000 per month.
8. Issued additional share capital for cash, $60 000.
9. Declared a cash dividend of $5 000.
10. Paid the dividend declared in transaction 9.
11. A physical inventory taken on June 30 following the close of business showed inventory on hand costing $20 000.
12. Transferred the net income (net loss) reported by the income statement to Retained Earnings.

Required
a Use T-accounts to record the opening entry on May 31. Show the words "Opening Entry" in both T-accounts.
b Use appropriately titled T-accounts to analyze and record transactions 1 through 10. In place of the date, use the transaction number. For example, show in the Equipment account "(1)" on the debit side for $40 000, and in the Cash account "(1)" on the credit side for $40 000.
c Show balances for each account in the T-account general ledger.
d Prepare a trial balance of the general ledger as of June 30.
e From the trial balance, prepare a condensed income statement. You will need the information given in transaction 11 to complete this statement.

f Transfer the net income (net loss) reported by the income statement to a T-account for Retained Earnings. (See transaction 12 above.)

g Prepare a condensed balance sheet using all available information. Report the net income (net loss) as Retained Earnings.

h From the postings shown by your Cash T-account, prepare a statement of cash flows showing these subheadings: (1) Cash Provided By (Used In) Operating Activities; (2) Cash Provided By (Used In) Financing Activities; (3) Cash Provided By (Used In) Investing Activities; (4) Net Increase (Decrease) in Cash for June; (5) Add: Beginning Balance of Cash (May 31); (6) Cash at June 30, 19—.

Note: The final line of this statement must show a cash balance that agrees with the balance in the Cash T-account.

Chapter Summary

In Part 1 of this text, accounting concepts have been presented for three forms of business organizations: single or sole proprietorship, partnership, and business corporation. This chapter introduced concepts for partnership and the business corporation.

A partnership is an organization in which two or more persons agree to carry on a business; therefore, the balance sheet of any partnership will report the claims of partners against the total business assets under the heading Partners' Equity.

One of the crucial characteristics of any partnership to recognize is that each partner has unlimited liability — that is, each is personally responsible for *all* of the debts of the business.

In the absence of any agreement, all profits (or all losses) must be shared among the partners on an equal basis. In practice, however, partners usually sign a written agreement stating the ratio of their sharing of business profits and losses.

Most of the accounting transactions presented in earlier chapters are common to the accounting of partnerships. For example, any withdrawal of assets by a partner for his or her personal use will be debited to the partner's drawing account similarly to what was done for a single proprietorship.

However, certain transactions are peculiar to partnerships. These include the formation of partnerships, admission of new partners, the distribution of profits (or losses) to the partners, dissolution of the partnership because of the death or withdrawal of a partner, and the liquidation of the business because of bankruptcy. This chapter discussed with simple cases dealing with the formation the partnership and the distribution of profits or losses.

Of the three common forms of business organization, the business corporation dominates in producing goods and services and in the volume of transactions. In simple terms, a business corporation may be regarded as an artificial person created by law to carry on business under a federal and/or provincial government charter.

As an artificial person, the corporation is given a legal entity. Therefore, it can enter into business transactions in its own name. As a legal entity, however, it is subject to a corporation income tax and is required to add "Limited" or "Incorporated" as the last word in its name.

Although a business corporation may be owned by one shareholder, most corporations have several shareholders. Some of Canada's largest corporations have thousands of shareholders.

One of the outstanding features of a business corporation is limited liability. This means that shareholders are limited in their liability for debts incurred by the corporation to the extent of amounts they have invested.

As evidence of their investment, shareholders receive share certificates. All business corporations must issue common shares; however, many corporations also issue preferred shares, to attract more share capital into the business.

Under the Canada Business Corporations Act, all shares must be issued without a par value. This means that the price of each share will be determined when it is issued and not earlier.

One of the accounting differences between the business corporation and sole proprietorship or partnership is the use of the idea of retained earnings. For example, the yearly net income or net loss must be transferred to a Retained Earnings account rather than to the owner's capital account. Any debit balance in this account will be regarded as a deficit. Similarly, any distribution of income earned must first be declared by a board of directors, which may declare a cash dividend. All such dividends must be debited to the Retained Earnings account.

Under all corporation acts, as well as under generally accepted accounting principles, corporations are required to present an annual report to their shareholders. In that report there must be an audited set of financial statements that include the income statement, the balance sheet, the statement of retained earnings, and the statement of changes in financial position. The new feature in the corporate income statement is the recognition of an income tax expense. The corporate balance sheet will include the reporting of new liabilities such as income tax payable and dividends payable, and a shareholders' equity section broken down between Share Capital and Retained Earnings. The statement of retained earnings is a detailed reporting of the Retained Earnings account. The statement of changes in financial position reports the flows of cash coming in and going out for a financial period.

Chapter Questions

1. Give two reasons why people engaged in professions such as law and accounting form partnerships.
2. Use one example to explain the meaning of "unlimited liability" as the term is applied to partnerships.

3. How are profits and losses shared among partners in the absence of an oral or written agreement?
4. Explain the "limited life" characteristic of partnerships.
5. Does a partnership pay an income tax as such on the net income reported by the business? Explain why or why not.
6. In what respects would the balance sheet and the income statement of a partnership differ from those of a single proprietorship?
7. What accounts would be debited and credited for a partner's withdrawal of merchandise from the firm's stock of goods? (Assume the use of the periodic inventory method.) Explain your answer.
8. What is the practical meaning of the word "limited" as applied to a company?
9. How could one individual gain control of a business corporation? What would be the practical effect?
10. What are the major sources of shareholders' equity?
11. How may authorized share capital differ from issued capital?
12. How do preferred shares ordinarily differ from common shares?
13. How does the recording of net income and losses in a limited company compare with that in a partnership?
14. How are retained earnings distributed to shareholders?
15. How do the financial statements of a corporation differ from those of a single proprietorship?
16. Name the main parts of the annual report which is presented to the annual meeting of shareholders.
17. What financial statements are required by law in the annual report of a business corporation?
18. Explain the meaning of "deficit" as it applies to corporation accounting.
19. Is a partnership a legal entity? Explain why or why not.
20. Outline the main advantages of forming a corporation instead of a sole proprietorship or partnership.
21. Distinguish between the statement of financial position and the statement of changes in financial position.
22. What form of balance sheet is currently most commonly used in corporation annual reports?
23. What alternative name best describes the statement of changes in financial position? Why is this alternative name appropriate?
24. Briefly explain why the Canadian Institute of Chartered Accountants decided to replace working capital flows with cash flows in the statement of changes in financial position.
25. Give one example to distinguish clearly items reported under Operating Activities, Financing Activities, and Investing Activities in the statement of changes in financial position.

Accounting Case Problems

CASE 6-1

Analyzing the admission of a new partner to an existing partnership.

Peal, Warwick, and Satchell operate a successful accounting firm on an "equal" profit-sharing arrangement. They agree to admit Bell, a competent young accountant, on the basis (i) that she be admitted without making any initial capital contribution; (ii) that the existing partners retain an equal profit-sharing arrangement; (iii) that Bell's share in the profits be a smaller fraction than those of the existing partners; (iv) that Bell be given junior partner status, but that her name not appear in the title of the new firm; and (v) that the agreement continue for two years, commencing June 1.

    a Are accounting entries required for the formation of the new partnership? Why or why not?

    b In terms of fractions, show a new profit-sharing arrangement giving the existing partners equal shares and the new partner junior status.

    c Suggest a name for the new partnership.

CASE 6-2

Analyzing the potential of expanding an existing single proprietorship between the owner and two employees.

Harold Stoyles has invested $100 000 in a bookstore which is conveniently located near the campus of a large university. Mr. Stoyles operates his business as the owner-manager, but he has hired two regular employees, Gerald Butler and Janice Fischer.

    The last six monthly income statements have shown a steady rate of increase in profits; consequently, Mr. Stoyles is considering the idea of expanding his business by opening similar bookstores in two other university towns. He would place Mr. Butler in charge of one store and Ms. Fischer in charge of the other. After having surveyed the situation carefully, Mr. Stoyles concludes that the new bookstores would be successful forming the partnership with both of his present employees. Although Mr. Butler and Ms. Fischer do not have any cash to invest and neither owns any property, each knows the book business and each is reliable and honest. Mr. Stoyles believes that as partners the two employees would take a much greater interest in seeing that the new stores are successful.

    a Does Mr. Stoyles' plan of forming a partnership with his two employees seem to be a good one? Explain your answer.

    b Who would lose the most if the venture should not be profitable and the stores lose money?

    c What form of business organization would limit Mr. Stoyles' responsibility to his investment?

    d Would there be any advantages or disadvantages if the owner expanded his business as a single proprietorship?

    e Do you believe that Mr. Stoyles should consider the idea of incorporating his business? Explain your answer.

PART 2

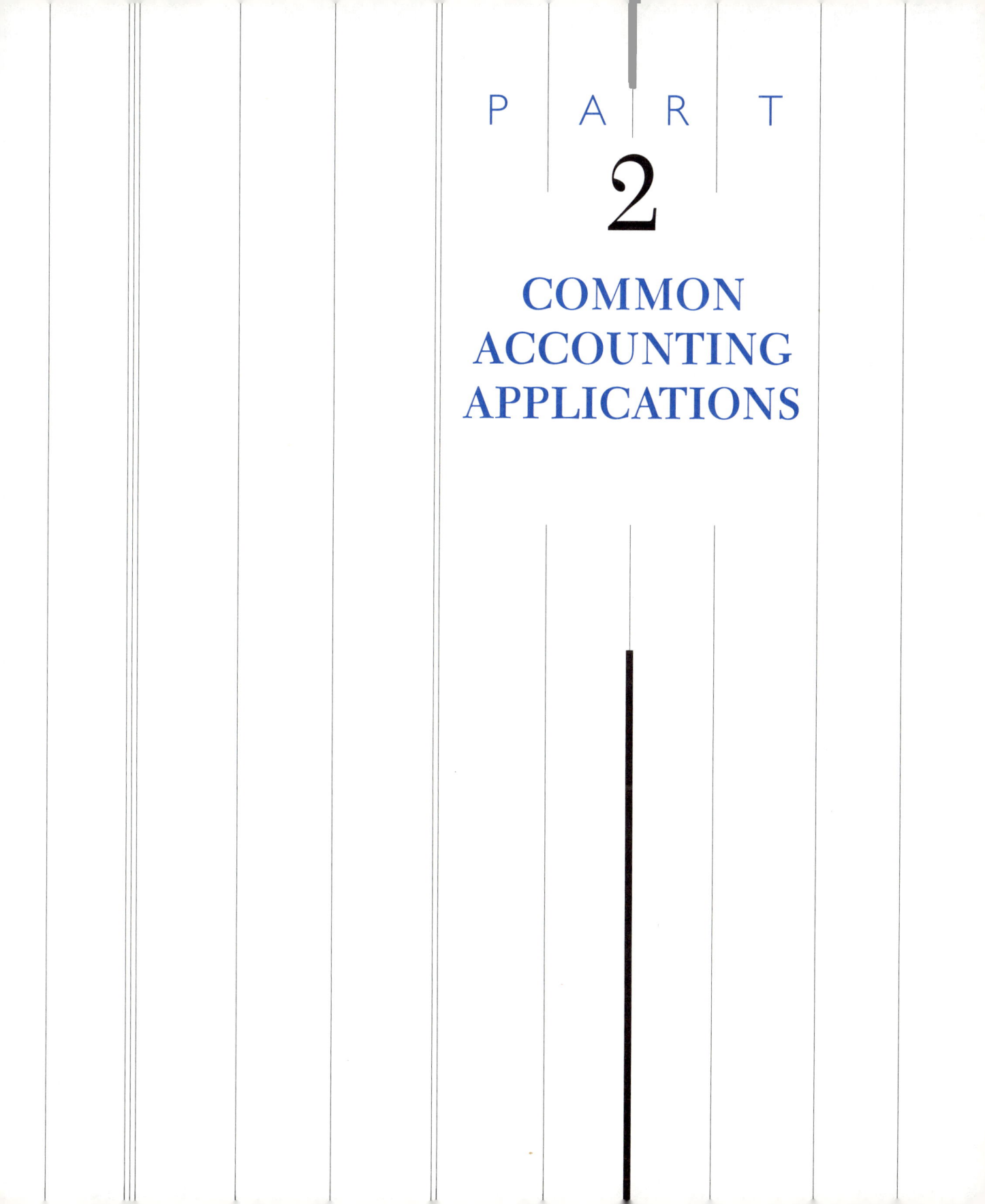

COMMON ACCOUNTING APPLICATIONS

CHAPTER **7** Accounts Receivable Application

After completing this chapter, you should be able to:
— Distinguish between the general ledger application and the accounts receivable application.
— Record selected invoices for a merchandising firm in a one-column and a three-column sales journal; post the entries to the subsidiary and general ledgers; and prepare a schedule of accounts receivable.
— List ten measures to control the cash receipts of businesses in general.
— Record selected transactions in a multi-column cash receipts journal; total and prove this special journal at month-end; and post the recorded entries and totals to appropriate ledger accounts.
— Record retail cash sales transactions in a cash receipts journal with distribution columns for credit card sales.
— Prepare a descriptive statement of account from given information on one customer.
— Prepare an aged accounts receivable statement from given data.
— Answer selected questions on journalizing batch totals, direct posting, journalless bookkeeping, and ledgerless bookkeeping.
— Answer questions on one-write applications for accounts receivable.
— Apply basic transactions to a one-write accounts receivable application for a small dental practice.
— Define the following key terms used in this chapter: general ledger application; accounts receivable application; sales journal; accounts receivable ledger; general ledger; direct posting; credit memo; double-posting; schedule of accounts receivable; cash receipts journal; bank debit card; statement of account; cycle billing; batch of invoices; direct posting; journalless bookkeeping; ledgerless bookkeeping; open-item accounts receivable system; balance-forward accounts receivable system; one-write system; collating; one-write principle.

Accounting is divided into specialized areas referred to as *applications* [or moduals]. In its most simplified form, the accounts receivable application consists of the details related to the accounting of two related transactions: the sale of goods or services on credit and the receipt of cash from credit customers

271

in payment of their accounts receivable. Of course, some firms sell goods or services for cash only; consequently, their "accounts receivable application" would naturally be confined to the accounting of cash receipts.

In Part 1, you learned that the general ledger application of the above transactions consisted of the following entries: a debit to Accounts Receivable and a credit to Sales (or another appropriate revenue account) to account for the credit sale of goods or services; a debit to Cash and a credit to Accounts Receivable to record the credit customer's remittance; and a debit to Cash and a credit to Sales (or another appropriate revenue account) to record the sale of goods or services to cash customers. At the end of an accounting period, therefore, the general ledger supplied the information for reporting the balance of Cash and Accounts Receivable in the balance sheet, and the Sales revenue in the income statement.

In treating the accounts receivable application, however, accounting is concerned mainly with the specific details related to individual customers and individual cash receipts from such customers. In practice, profit-seeking enterprises will design accounts receivable systems and procedures in keeping with their needs and costs. For example, large firms usually organize a separate department called the Accounts Receivable Department just to handle the accounting of accounts receivable. Within such a department, accounting will employ specialized accountants and clerks, specialized source documents, specialized journals and ledgers, specialized trial balances, and probably an electronic computer to control and process the firm's individual accounts receivable and cash receipts. On the other hand, a smaller firm would probably not have a separate department; would probably use fewer specialized forms; and would probably employ a general clerk who may take shortcuts under the manual method to account for individual customer transactions. Since an entire text of considerable length could easily be filled to present the details of processing accounts receivable applications for large and small firms, this chapter limits the study to those basic concepts that may be applied to all profit-seeking businesses.

TOPIC 1 Special Journals and Ledgers

In accounting for specific details related to credit sales and cash sales, many firms use special journals and ledgers. This Topic will examine the journalizing and posting procedures for credit sales only; cash sales are better treated under the procedures for journalizing and posting of cash receipts (Topic 2 of this chapter). To illustrate the accounts receivable application related to credit sales only, consider the four cases that follow.

Accounts Receivable Application for Credit Sales

Case 1. A Wholesale Hardware Firm   From earlier work, you learned that credit sales in wholesale merchandising firms are first captured on a source document known as the sales invoice. Since such credit

CHAPTER 7: Accounts Receivable Application

Sales journal: a chronological record of credit sales.

sales are quite numerous during any month, many wholesale firms will record the dollar results of their sales invoices in a special journal known as the **sales journal**. It is important to remember that this journal would include an accounting record of merchandise sales *only on credit*. A simplified one-column sales journal commonly used under the manual system for a wholesaler may be illustrated as in Figure 7-1.

FIGURE 7-1

SALES JOURNAL					Page 1
Date	Invoice No.	Account Debited	Terms	Post. Ref.	Amount
19—					
May 2	101	Eglinton Hardware Centre	2/10, n/30		743 10
5	102	Plaza Home Hardware	2/10, n/30		642 80
9	103	Woodbridge Hardware	1/20, n/30		975 30
14	104	Summers Hardware Limited	1/15, n/60		1 439 25
17	105	Markham Home Hardware	2/10, n/30		832 15
24	106	Eglinton Hardware Centre	2/10, n/30		534 40
27	107	Hyland Hardware	1/20, n/30		890 17
30	108	Thornhill Home Hardware	2/10, n/30		738 29

INVOICE NO. 101
Sale amount .. $743.10
Total owing ... $743.10
Copy 2 — Accounting

Analysis These points should be recalled as you analyze the illustrated sales journal:
- In actual practice, the form of the sales journal will depend upon the nature of the business and the method used to process the credit sales. In the case of Scarborough Wholesale Hardware, a simplified, one-column format is used, so that you can learn the concept—that is, there will be a debit to Accounts Receivable for the amount of the sale and a corresponding credit to Sales.
- Like all other special journals, the name of the special journal and the page number are identified at the top of the form.
- Note that the sales journal contains special columns for recording the important aspects of the sales transaction. Of course, these important aspects are taken from the accounting copy of the invoice.
- Only sales on credit are entered in the sales journal.
- Observe that the date recorded in the sales journal is the date of the sales invoices.
- Since this sales journal contains only one money column, each single amount must be analyzed as follows: the customer's account is shown as a debit while a Sales credit has to be understood.
- As you will discover, postings do not occur from this special journal to the general ledger until the end of the month. At this time, the Amount column can be totalled so that the total credit sales for the month can be posted to the Accounts Receivable and Sales accounts in the G/L.

THE NEED FOR AN ACCOUNTS RECEIVABLE LEDGER

In Part 1, all transactions involving accounts receivable were posted to one account only—Accounts Receivable. Although this general account served a useful purpose in supplying year-end data for the balance sheet, it did not, of course, provide information on the balance owing by each customer. Since all businesses which sell goods on credit would normally have a large number of individual customers, it follows logically that the accounting system would have to be organized so that information is available not only for the balance sheet, but also on the amount owing by each individual customer's accounts receivable.

In practice, the majority of accounting systems will provide for individual customer accounts which would be accounted for in a separate ledger known as the ***accounts receivable ledger*** (or the *customers' ledger*). Similarly, if the business had many creditors, the individual creditor accounts would be accounted for in a separate file known as the *accounts payable ledger*. The analysis of the creditors' ledger will be examined in the next chapter.

When individual customer accounts are maintained in a separate ledger, it is important to remember that the general account known as Accounts Receivable must still be used to provide information for the balance sheet. Of course, this general account would be filed in a separate ledger known as the ***general ledger***. Thus, two ledgers are needed, as illustrated in Figure 7-2.

Analysis Keep the following points in mind when breaking down the fine points in Figure 7-2:

Accounts receivable ledger: a subsidiary ledger containing only individual customer accounts.

General ledger: the main ledger containing accounts whose balances are used to prepare financial statements.

FIGURE 7-2

Accounting System with General and Subsidiary Ledgers

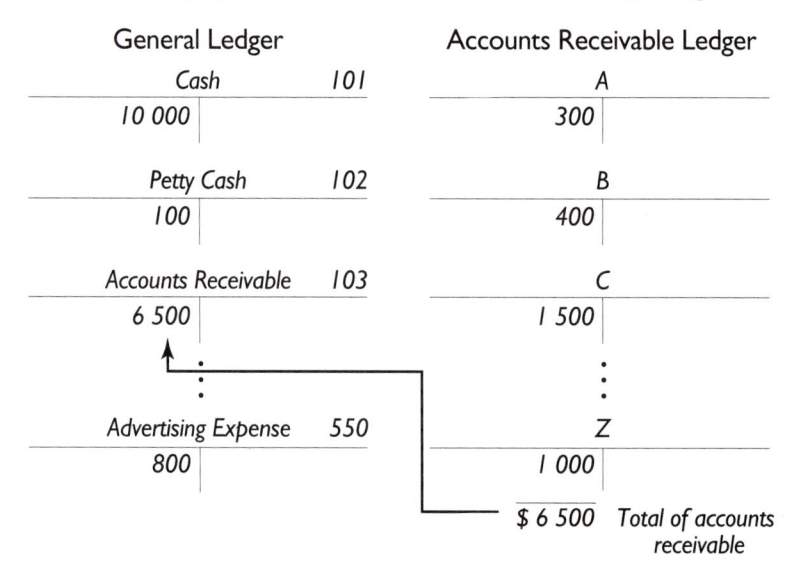

General Ledger		Accounts Receivable Ledger
Cash 101		A
10 000		300
Petty Cash 102		B
100		400
Accounts Receivable 103		C
6 500		1 500
⋮		⋮
Advertising Expense 550		Z
800		1 000

$ 6 500 Total of accounts receivable

- From the illustration, observe that there are now two ledgers: the accounts receivable ledger containing the individual customer accounts; and the main ledger, the general ledger, which now contains the general account called Accounts Receivable.
- Notice that the Accounts Receivable account contains the total amount owing by the individual customers. In the language of accounting, this account is said to "control" the individual customer accounts in total form; therefore, the account may be identified as "Accounts Receivable Control." In practice, however, the word "Control" is usually dropped from the name because it is understood.
- Since the general ledger is the main ledger, in the sense that it contains all of the information in order to prepare the financial statements, the accounts receivable ledger is a secondary or *subsidiary ledger*. This means simply that the ledger does not contain all of the accounts of the business; it contains the details of all the accounts of only *one* class of account. In a large accounting system, there will always be one general ledger and one or more subsidiary ledgers. Two other common subsidiary ledgers will be examined in the remaining chapters of this text.
- Note that the accounts stored in the subsidiary ledger are coded differently from the accounts filed in the general ledger. In the illustration, the accounts in the accounts receivable ledger are kept in alphabetical order. On the other hand, the accounts in the general ledger are filed numerically.
- In practice, a business with very few credit customers could store the individual accounts receivable in the general ledger. Consider, however, the following problems with using only one ledger when numerous customer accounts are present:
  i. The ledger would become quite crowded with the inclusion of, say, 2 000 individual customer accounts.
  ii. The ledger would be cumbersome and unwieldy.
  iii. Only one person could work on the posting at any one time.
  iv. The trial balance of such a ledger would take up several pages.
  v. If the trial balance should not balance, it would be very difficult to find the error within a reasonable time.
  vi. The current assets section of the balance sheet would be extremely long.
- One final point is worth remembering. With an accounting system that uses a general ledger and one or more subsidiary ledgers, it becomes most efficient to hire accounting clerks who may work full-time in a department that is given the responsibility for a particular ledger. For example, clerks who do the posting to individual customer accounts will work in the accounts receivable department and

FIGURE 7-3

A successful, fast-growing, centrally located art publishing company has openings for two full time positions.

ACCOUNTS RECEIVABLE CLERK

PC literate accounting clerk experienced on ACC PAC - A/R O/E I/C packages and spread sheets, good typing skills. A strong accounts receivable background preferred.

ADMINISTRATIVE ASSISTANT

Self-motivated individual to assist in the general administration of a very active customer conscious organization.

The successful applicant will be capable of conceptualizing and producing high quality correspondence, possess excellent telephone manners and have a professional appearance. Extensive 'hands on' computer experience a must. We need a team player; someone who can adapt, and fill most office functions.

Please forward resume stating salary requirements to the attention of

FIGURE 7-4

ACCOUNTS RECEIVABLE
Experienced in credit and collections with good communication skills. Knowledge of ACCPAC/A/R an asset. Salary commensurate with experience. Full or part time employment negotiable. Send or fax resume to:

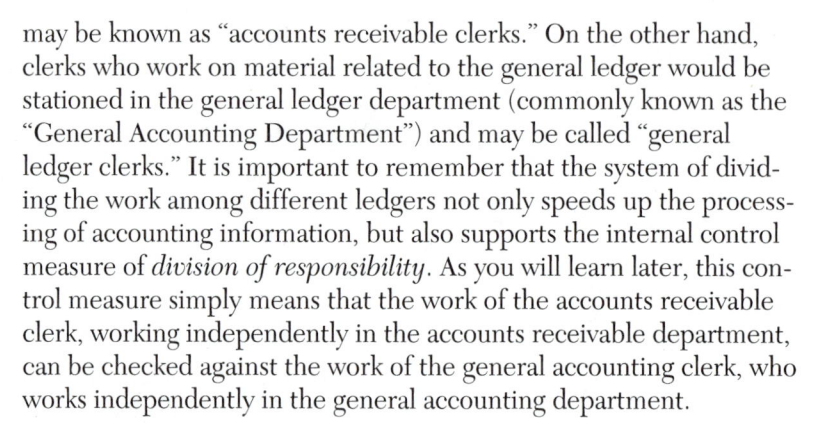

may be known as "accounts receivable clerks." On the other hand, clerks who work on material related to the general ledger would be stationed in the general ledger department (commonly known as the "General Accounting Department") and may be called "general ledger clerks." It is important to remember that the system of dividing the work among different ledgers not only speeds up the processing of accounting information, but also supports the internal control measure of *division of responsibility*. As you will learn later, this control measure simply means that the work of the accounts receivable clerk, working independently in the accounts receivable department, can be checked against the work of the general accounting clerk, who works independently in the general accounting department.

POSTING CREDIT SALES   When a general ledger and an accounts receivable ledger form part of the total accounting system, the posting of credit sales is done in two stages: first to the accounts receivable ledger on a daily basis and then to the general ledger at the end of the month.

It is important to remember that the individual credit sales are posted to the customer accounts filed in the accounts receivable ledger on the same days on which the sales occur. Posting daily to individual customer accounts is necessary because the manager or even the customer may request information on the balance owing by the customer. In some accounting systems, posting to the accounts receivable ledger may be done from the sales journal. Since the individual accounts in the subsidiary ledger are filed in alphabetical order and not in numerical code, a check mark is placed in the Post. Ref. column in the sales journal to indicate that the transfer of information has occurred from the special journal to the customer's account.

Notice from Figure 7-5 that a customer's account in the accounts receivable ledger often contains important information such as the customer's complete address, the telephone number, and the credit limit approved by the business. Observe also that the Explanation column contains a record of the invoice number and the credit terms. This additional data is usually recorded so that a check can be made on the accuracy of any future sales discount taken by the customer. Furthermore, a check can be made to see by how many days any invoice is overdue.

It is worth mentioning that, in some accounting systems, posting to the accounts receivable ledger may be done directly from the source document to the individual customer's account. Where such a system of direct posting exists, two accounting copies of the invoice are usually provided. One copy would go to the accounts receivable department, where a clerk would post directly to the customer's account. A second copy would be directed to general accounting, so that a summary of the monthly credit sales may be made and the total can be posted to the general ledger accounts. The details of the **direct posting** system are treated more fully in Topic 3 of this chapter.

Direct posting: transferring information from the source document directly to the subsidiary ledger.

CHAPTER 7: Accounts Receivable Application **277**

FIGURE **7-5**

SALES JOURNAL Page 1

Date	Invoice No.	Account Debited	Terms	Post. Ref.	Amount
19—					
May 2	101	Eglinton Hardware Centre	2/10, n/30	√	743 10
5	102	Plaza Home Hardware	2/10, n/30	√	642 80
9	103	Woodbridge Hardware	1/20, n/30	√	975 30
14	104	Summers Hardware Limited	1/15, n/60	√	1 439 25
17	105	Markham Home Hardware	2/10, n/30	√	832 15
24	106	Eglinton Hardware Centre	2/10, n/30	√	534 40
27	107	Hyland Hardware	1/20, n/30	√	890 17
30	108	Thornhill Home Hardware	2/10, n/30	√	738 29
31		Accounts Receivable Debit/Sales Credit			6 795 46

Accounts Receivable Ledger

Name Eglinton Hardware Centre **Credit Limit** $2 000
Address 1975 Eglinton Ave. E., Scarborough, Ont. M1L 2N1 **Telephone** 293-1810

Date	Explanation	Post. Ref.	Debit	Credit	Balance
19—					
May 2	Inv. 101; 2/10, n/30	S1	743 10		743 10
24	Inv. 106; 2/10, n/30	S1	534 40		1 277 50

Regardless of whether posting is done from the sales journal or directly from the invoice copy to the accounts receivable ledger, it is most important to remember the second stage of posting credit sales. At the end of the month, the sales journal is totalled to determine the amount to be posted to the general ledger. In Figure 7-6, note that the total must be in the form of a complete double entry. A debit must be acknowledged to the Accounts Receivable controlling account, while a credit is shown to the Sales account. Note also how the Post. Ref. column of the sales journal is divided with a diagonal line (slash) so that the two account numbers can be distinguished. And, finally, observe how the sales journal is ruled off to show completeness of the month's journalizing of credit sales.

RECORDING SALES RETURNS AND ALLOWANCES As explained in Chapter 5, credit customers sometimes receive shipped merchandise in unacceptable condition. In this situation, the customers may return the unsatisfactory goods with a request for an adjustment; or they may keep the goods but ask for an adjustment in the form of an allowance off the invoice price. Whenever such customers' claims have been found to be in order, the seller will issue a source document known as a credit memorandum or, for short, ***credit memo***. One copy will be

Credit memo: a source document, prepared by the seller, notifying the buyer that his or her accounts receivable has been credited by the amount indicated on the credit memo.

FIGURE 7-6

SALES JOURNAL						Page 1
Date	Invoice No.	Account Debited	Terms	Post. Ref.	Amount	
19— May 2	101	Eglinton Hardware Centre	2/10, n/30	√	743	10
31		Accounts Receivable Debit/Sales Credit		103/401	6 795	46

General Ledger

Accounts Receivable — Account No. 103

Date	Explanation	Post. Ref.	Debit	Credit	Balance
19— May 31		S1	6 795 46		6 795 46

Sales — Account No. 401

Date	Explanation	Post. Ref.	Debit	Credit	Balance
19— May 31		S1		6 795 46	6 795 46

mailed to the customer, while at least one copy will be retained as the source document for the accounting entry to record the dollar results of the adjustment as illustrated in Figures 7-7 and 7-8.

FIGURE 7-7

GENERAL JOURNAL				Page 3
Date	Account Title and Explanation	Post. Ref.	Debit	Credit
19— May 25	Sales Returns and Allowances	402	28 50	
	Accounts Receivable/Eglinton Hardware Centre	103/√		28 50
	Credit Memo CM-01.			

FIGURE 7-8

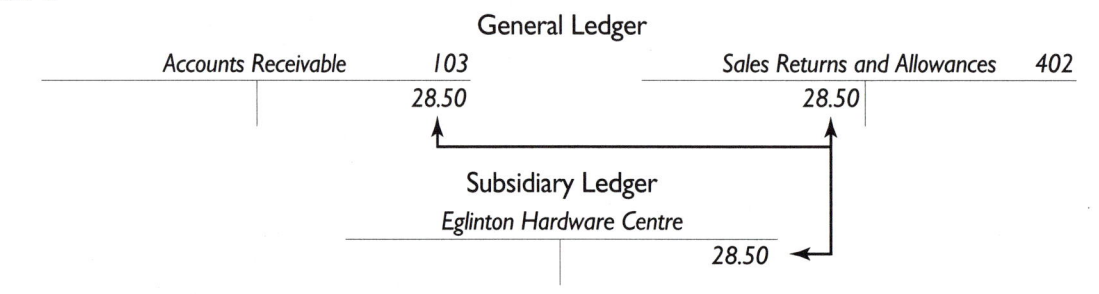

General Ledger

Accounts Receivable   103   Sales Returns and Allowances   402
                28.50   28.50

Subsidiary Ledger
Eglinton Hardware Centre
        28.50

You learned also that a contra revenue account, Sales Returns and Allowances, would be debited and the customer's accounts receivable would be credited to record the adjustment. If the merchandising firm experiences many such adjustments, the accounting system may use a special journal to record all credit memos. In practice, however, such adjustments are not as repetitive as transactions for sales, purchases, cash receipts, and cash payments; therefore, many firms do not provide for a special journal to record the dollar results of sales returns and allowances. Instead, it is common practice to use the general journal to record all entries that do not belong to a special journal. In this text, credit memos will be shown as being recorded in the general journal, as illustrated in Figure 7-7.

The debit entry in the general journal should cause little difficulty. As illustrated, the first debit of $28.50 to Sales Returns and Allowances has been posted to Account 402 in the general ledger. The credit side of the entry requires more analysis. Observe that the credit entry must be ***double-posted***: once to the Accounts Receivable controlling account in the general ledger and once to the customer's account in the subsidiary ledger. Of course, the update of the customer's account in the accounts receivable ledger could be posted directly from the source document. In any case, remember that two postings are required for the credit entry; otherwise, the general ledger would not balance with the information contained in the accounts receivable ledger.

> **Double-posted:** posted to the controlling account in the general ledger and also to the individual account in the subsidiary ledger.

When the general journal is used to double-post the credit entry, notice how the Post. Ref. column of the journal is completed. One half of the space is given to insert the general ledger account number, while the other half may be used to place a check mark (√) to indicate that the information has been transferred to the customer's account.

PREPARING MONTHLY TRIAL BALANCES

In Part 1, you learned that at the end of each month a trial balance is prepared to prove that the total of the debit balances of accounts agreed with the total of the various credit balances of accounts in the ledger. When a general ledger and one or more subsidiary ledgers are used in the accounting system, however, it is important that a trial balance be taken at the end of the month for each ledger. Consider, for example, how the trial balances are used when accounting proofs are required of the general ledger and of the accounts receivable ledger.

1. General Ledger Trial Balance   Preparation of a general ledger trial balance is no different from that of the trial balance you studied in earlier chapters. In general, all accounts with balances in the G/L would be listed in the order in which they appear in the ledger. The only point to remember here, however, is the fact that the balance reported for Accounts Receivable represents the total of all the individual customer accounts. In the case of Scarborough Wholesale Hardware, the monthly general ledger trial balance would include account balances as shown in Figure 7-9.

FIGURE 7-9

Scarborough Wholesale Hardware
Trial Balance
May 31, 19—

Account Title	Acct. No.	Debit	Credit
Accounts Receivable	103	6 766 96	
Sales	401		6 795 46
Sales Returns and Allowances	402	28 50	
		15 900 80	15 900 80

Observe that the heading merely shows the title "Trial Balance." To emphasize that this trial balance is an accounting proof of the general ledger, one could, of course, show the entire heading, "General Ledger Trial Balance." In practice, however, qualifying the trial balance is unnecessary, because a glance at the accounts listed would reveal that only general ledger accounts are listed.

2. Accounts Receivable Trial Balance   As you will recall, posting to the various customer accounts in the accounts receivable ledger was done on a daily basis. To check on the accuracy of this posting for the whole month, the balances of all the accounts in the accounts receivable ledger at the end of the month are listed on a form called the **schedule of accounts receivable**, as in Figure 7-10.

Observe that the total of the schedule of accounts receivable at the end of the month must agree with the balance of the Accounts Receivable controlling account in the G/L. In this sense, a type of "trial balance" has been made to prove that the subsidiary ledger agrees with the related controlling account in the general ledger. Notice also that the term "Schedule of Accounts Receivable" has been used. In practice, "Accounts Receivable Trial Balance" may be used, but, to avoid confusion with the trial balance of the G/L, in this text "Schedule of Accounts Receivable" will be used from now on.

If the two figures match, that is, if the total of the schedule of accounts receivable agrees with the balance in the Accounts Receivable controlling account, their agreement is treated as proof that the posting done in the subsidiary ledger has been mathematically accurate. On the other hand, if the figures are not identical and the G/L trial balance has been proved, errors must be assumed to have occurred in the subsidiary ledger. Of course, the error or errors must be located and corrected before any financial statements are considered.

> Schedule of accounts receivable: a list of all customer account balances, the total of which must agree with the controlling account balance.

FIGURE 7-10

Scarborough Wholesale Hardware
Schedule of Accounts Receivable
May 31, 19—

Eglinton Hardware Centre	$1 249.00
Hyland Hardware	890.17
Markham Home Hardware	832.15
Plaza Home Hardware	642.80
Summers Hardware Limited	1 439.25
Thornhill Home Hardware	738.29
Woodbridge Hardware	975.30
Total of Accounts Receivable	$6 766.96

General Ledger

Accounts Receivable   103

6 795.46	28.50
Balance 6 766.96	

Accounts Receivable Ledger

Eglinton Hardware Centre

743.10	28.50
534.40	
Bal. 1 249.00	

Hyland Hardware
890.17

Markham Home Hardware
832.15

Plaza Home Hardware
642.80

Summers Hardware Limited
1 439.25

Thornhill Home Hardware
738.29

Woodbridge Hardware
975.30

In preparing both trial balances for a large firm, keep in mind that each would be taken independently of the other. For example, a clerk in the accounts receivable department may be asked to prepare the schedule of accounts receivable, while a different clerk in general accounting may be required to prepare the G/L trial balance. By separating the preparation of the trial balances, and by requiring agreement of the controlling account with the total of the subsidiary ledger, the accounting system is assured of an important internal control measure at the end of each month.

Case 2. A Retail Hardware Firm In Case 1 a wholesale merchandising firm was selected to avoid the added problem of accounting for the provincial sales tax (PST). However, at the time of writing, all provinces except Alberta levy retail sales taxes at rates ranging from 6% to 12%. (See Chapter 4, Topic 2 for a summary of provincial rates.)

Briefly, retail sales taxes are levied on the final purchaser or user (the consumer) and are collected by the retailer. By provincial law, the PST collected must be reported on the books of the retail merchant in a current liability account and the money kept intact must be remitted at specified times to the provincial treasurer.

Suppose a large retail hardware and appliance store located in Vancouver, B.C. sold goods on credit and for cash. To record the credit sales with the current 6% provincial sales tax, the sales journal may be designed along the lines of Figure 7-11.

Observe carefully the analysis of each double entry in the columnar sales journal. A debit to Accounts Receivable must be entered for the total sale plus the PST. Separate credits are then identified for the exact amount of the PST and the sales revenue. In the illustration, the sales journal also includes special columns to distribute the revenue along product lines. It is important to emphasize that the total amount of the bill of sale (the sale and PST) will be charged to the customer's account. This calculation must be identical to the breakdown shown on the accounting copy of the source document (the sales slip or invoice). You should check this calculation for yourself by examining the illustration of the bill of sale to the first customer named in the sales journal, Figure 7-12.

At this point, you should have little difficulty in the correct analysis of posting from a columnar sales journal to both the subsidiary ledger and the general ledger. What should be remembered is the new current liability account in the general ledger called PST Payable. When a cheque is subsequently issued to the provincial treasurer, the liability to the provincial government will be discharged through a double entry recorded in a special journal known as the "cash payments journal." This special journal will be treated in the next chapter.

RECORDING SALES TAXES ON SALES RETURNS AND ALLOWANCES

In the provinces where sales taxes have to be collected for the PST, an additional accounting problem must be considered when sales returns and allowances are involved. Consider, for example, the sales transaction of January 4 for Vancouver Hardware & Appliance, where a credit sale was made for $200 and PST for $12 were recorded. (A PST of 6% is assumed.) Suppose the customer, D. Bailey, returned one

FIGURE 7-11

SALES JOURNAL (Vancouver Hardware & Appliance) — Page 1

Date	Invoice No.	Account Debited	Terms	Post. Ref.	Acct. Rec. Dr.	PST Pay. Cr.	Appliance Sales Cr.	Hardware Sales Cr.
19—								
Jan. 4	001	D. Bailey	n/30	√	212 00	12 00	43 65	156 35
8	002	N. Bassilly	n/30	√	79 50	4 50	75 00	
14	003	P. Catenacci	n/30	√	147 45	8 35	139 10	
19	004	J. Elcombe	n/30	√	93 17	5 27		87 90
25	005	B. Knox	n/30	√	202 44	11 46		190 98
30	006	S. Dubois	n/30	√	58 09	3 29	54 80	
31		Totals			792 65	44 87	312 55	435 23
					(103)	(204)	(401)	(402)

CHAPTER 7: Accounts Receivable Application **283**

FIGURE 7-12

Vancouver Hardware & Appliance				No. 001	
2250 Fraser Street Vancouver, B.C. V5T 3T8 Tel. 604-821-1498				Date: *19— 01 04* Credit Terms: *Net 30 days*	
SOLD TO: *D. Bailey*					
ADDRESS: *303 Cambie St., Vancouver V6B 2N4*					
Quantity	Description			Unit Price	Amount
1 only	*960 cu Aluminum Ladder*			*62.50*	*62.50*
2 only	*12 mm Drill*			*34.95*	*69.90*
1 set	*No. 58-8573 Metric Tool Set*			*23.95*	*23.95*
1 only	*No. 43-2154 Mixmaster*			*43.65*	*43.65*
CLERK: *a.L.*				Subtotal	*200.00*
				PST at 6%	*12.00*
Cash	C.O.D.	Charge √	On Acct.	Mdse. Ret'd TOTAL	*212.00*

12 mm drill and was given a full credit for the unit sales price of $34.95. In this case, the correct accounting entry would be recorded in the general journal as shown in Figure 7-13.

From the illustration, observe that the return is correctly debited for $34.95 to Sales Returns and Allowances, because the original sales revenue

FIGURE 7-13

GENERAL JOURNAL Page 2

Date	Account Title and Explanation	Post. Ref.	Debit	Credit
19— Jan. 5	Hardware Sales Returns and Allowances .... PST Payable .... Accounts Receivable/D. Bailey .... Credit Memo CM-03.	403 204 103/√	34 95 2 10	37 05

has been decreased by the amount of the return. Notice, too, that the PST on the original sold item is no longer payable to the provincial government; therefore, the PST Payable account must be decreased (debited) by the amount of the sales tax charged on the item (6% PST x $34.95 = $2.10). And, finally, observe that the credit to Accounts Receivable in the general ledger and similarly to the subsidiary ledger must be for the amount of the sales return plus the amounts for PST. Remember the point that, originally, the customer was charged not only for the sale but also for the retail sales tax. When the compound entry is posted to the ledgers, the balances of the accounts should reveal the correct amounts owing to the provincial government and to the business enterprise through accounts receivable. Check these balances out by analyzing the T-account ledger forms shown in Figures 7-14 and 7-15.

FIGURE 7-14

General Ledger

Accounts Receivable 103		PST Payable 204	
212.00	37.05	2.10	12.00

Appliance Sales 401		Hardware Sales 402		Hardware Sales Returns and Allowances 403	
	43.65		156.35	34.95	

FIGURE 7-15

Accounts Receivable Ledger

D. Bailey	
212.00	37.05

Case 3. A Service Firm Cases 1 and 2 used merchandising firms to illustrate the concepts of recording credit sales in the sales journal, posting from the sales journal to the accounts receivable ledger and the general ledger, and preparing monthly trial balances of both ledgers. These concepts also apply in the case of many service firms. For example, a large legal firm earns revenue by charging fees for services rendered. To record the revenue earned, the accounting system may employ a "fees earned journal" (sometimes called a "fees earned register") as illustrated in Figure 7-16.

From the illustration, you should conclude that all fees, when billed, would be entered in the fees earned journal. Of course, postings would be made from this special journal to the client's ledger sheet stored in the accounts receivable ledger file.

Notice that the special journal has a section called "Distribution." As stated earlier, firms design special journals to meet their own business needs. In this case, a large legal firm would have several lawyers. Consequently, a memo is usually placed on the office copy of the bill showing the name of the associate who worked on the case. In recording the "credit sale," therefore, the amount of the fee can be recorded not only in the fees earned Cr. column, but also in the appropriate lawyer's name in

CHAPTER 7: Accounts Receivable Application   **285**

FIGURE 7-16

FEES EARNED JOURNAL — Page 14

Date	Invoice No.	Case No.	Client	Post. Ref.	Amount	Distribution A	Distribution B	Distribution C	Distribution D
19—									
Sept. 2	1701	00-G-101	Highfield Hardware	√	189 10			189 10	
3	1702	00-G-102	Gibson Realty Co.	√	1 275 80	1 275 80			
5	1703	00-G-112	Moncton Plumbing	√	640 00		640 00		
9	1704	00-G-104	Fredericton TV	√	2 180 75				2 180 75
22	1728	00-G-200	T. A. George	√	75 50			75 50	
24	1729	00-G-180	H. R. Estey	√	185 50		185 50		
25	1730	00-G-210	Edmunston Repair Co.	√	485 70	485 70			
28	1731	00-G-212	Newcastle Electric	√	1 560 00				1 560 00
30			Accounts Receivable Dr./Fees Earned Cr.	103/401	10 785 50	2 587 50	1 008 50	985 75	6 203 75

the Distribution column. At the end of the month, associate lawyers can then be paid in accordance with some prior agreement in relation to a percentage of fees earned.

Also, at the end of the month, the totals of the three special account money columns can be proved to support the double entry rule (total debits must equal total credits) and posted to appropriate accounts in the general ledger. Of course, postings to individual accounts receivable would have been done on a daily basis during the month. And, finally, a schedule of accounts receivable would be taken at month-end to prove the accuracy of the Accounts Receivable controlling account in the general ledger.

TOPIC 1   Problems

Recording selected invoices in a one-column sales journal for a wholesale hardware firm; posting entries to both the subsidiary and the general ledgers; preparing a schedule of accounts receivable.

7.1 The Ottawa Wholesale Hardware issued the following sales invoices during February:

Feb. 2   To Bells Corners Hardware; Invoice 210; terms 2/10, n/30; sale amount, $390.50.
   10   To Checkers Road Hardware; Invoice 211; terms 1/15, n/30; sale amount, $460.90.
   14   To Elmsmere Home Hardware; Invoice 212; terms n/30; sale amount, $198.10.
   15   To B. Moodie Home Hardware; Invoice 213; terms 2/10, n/30; sale amount, $689.25.
   23   To Kinburn Home Hardware; Invoice 214; terms 1/15, n/30; sale amount, $895.40.
   28   To Checkers Road Hardware; Invoice 215; terms 1/15, n/30; sale amount, $570.80.

Required **a** Open general ledger accounts for Accounts Receivable (No. 103) and Sales (No. 401). Allow two lines each for these accounts. Open subsidiary ledger accounts for the customers. Show these accounts filed in alphabetical order, and allow four lines for each account.

b Record the above sales transactions in a ~~three~~ one -column sales journal (Page 4).

c Post the daily entries to the subsidiary ledger.

d Total the sales journal at the end of the month. Record the double entry for this total; then post the double entry to the general ledger. Rule the sales journal at month-end.

e Prepare a schedule of accounts receivable; then prove the total of accounts receivable with the controlling account in the G/L.

Recording selected invoices in a one-column sales journal for a wholesale auto parts firm; posting entries to both the subsidiary and the general ledgers; preparing a schedule of accounts receivable.

7.2 Winnipeg Automotive Co. Ltd. is a wholesale distributor of automotive parts and equipment. The firm issued sales invoices during March to various retail outlets as summarized below:

Mar. 1 Anderson Auto Radio Service; Invoice 151; terms net 30 days; sale amount, $78.85.
4 Art's Auto Service; Invoice 152; terms 1/15, n/60; sale amount, $395.00.
7 Art Quigg's Esso Service; Invoice 153; terms 2/10, n/30; sale amount, $784.87.
12 Bob's Esso; Invoice 154; terms 2/10, n/30; sale amount, $590.85.
14 Blake's Garage; Invoice 155; terms 1/15, n/60; sale amount, $1 895.60.
16 Anderson Auto Radio Service; Invoice 156; terms net 30 days; sale amount, $56.75.
18 Carter's Esso Service; Invoice 157; terms net 60 days; sale amount, $390.00.
24 Don's Gulf Service; Invoice 158; terms 1/15, n/60; sale amount, $887.40.
25 Art's Auto Service; Invoice 159; terms 1/15, n/60; sale amount, $360.24.
27 Blake's Garage; Invoice 160; terms 1/15, n/60; sale amount, $495.70.
29 Byron's Shell Service Centre; Invoice 161; terms 2/10, n/30; sale amount, $329.05.
30 Gerry Travis Petro-Canada Service; Invoice 162; terms net 30 days; sale amount, $48.75.

Required

a Open general ledger accounts for Accounts Receivable (No. 104) and Sales (No. 401). Allow two lines each for these accounts. Open subsidiary ledger accounts for the customers. Show these accounts filed in alphabetical order, and allow four lines for each account.

b Record the above sales transactions in a ~~three~~ one -column sales journal (Page 2).

c Post the daily entries to the subsidiary ledger.

d Total the sales journal at the end of the month. Record the double entry for this total in the sales journal; then post the double entry to the general ledger. Rule the sales journal at the end of the month.

CHAPTER 7: Accounts Receivable Application

e Prepare a schedule of accounts receivable; then prove the total of accounts receivable with the controlling account in the general ledger.

7.3 Edna McInnis Flowers is located in British Columbia, where 6% is levied on retail sales. During May the store issued the following documents that affected the firm's revenue:

Recording selected invoices in a three-column sales journal for a retail firm required to collect the PST; computing PST; recording sales returns in the general journal; posting entries to both the subsidiary and the general ledgers; preparing a schedule of accounts receivable.

May 1 Invoice 330; to S. Bahry; terms n/30; sale amount, $50.
    7 Invoice 331; to M. Bayrak; terms n/30; sale amount, $18.
   12 Invoice 332; to S. Chappell; terms n/30; sale amount, $60.
   13 Credit Memo No. CM-041; to S. Chappell; adjustment of $21.20 given on return of goods sold for $20 on Invoice 332.
   15 Invoice 333; to S. Kuxhouse; terms n/30; sale amount, $75.
   18 Invoice 334; to L. Madill; terms n/30; sale amount, $115.
   19 Credit Memo No. CM-042; to L. Madill; adjustment of $31.80 granted on return of goods sold for $30 on Invoice 334.
   24 Invoice 335; to S. Bahry; terms n/30; sale amount, $30.
   27 Invoice 336; to K. Hardy; terms n/30; sale amount, $160.
   29 Credit Memo No. CM-043; to K. Hardy; adjustment of $42.40 granted on return of goods sold for $40 on Invoice 336.

Required
a Open general ledger accounts for Accounts Receivable, PST Payable, Sales, and Sales Returns and Allowances. (Show appropriate account codes for each account and allow three lines for each account.) Open subsidiary ledger accounts for the customers. Show these accounts filed in alphabetical order, and allow four lines for each account.
b Record the above transactions in a three-column sales journal (Accounts Receivable Dr., PST Payable Cr., and Sales) and a general journal.
c Post the daily entries from both journals to the subsidiary ledger.
d Prove the sales journal at the end of the month (total of the Accounts Receivable debit column must equal the two credit columns); prove the totals to support the double entry rule; post the totals to appropriate accounts in the G/L. Also, post from the general journal all double entries that affect the general ledger.
e Prepare a schedule of accounts receivable.

7.4 R. Campbell operates a retail business under the name of Campbell's Carpet & Tile in a province that has an 8% sales tax. During June the store issued the following source documents that affected the firm's revenue. Assume that all sales amounts are subject to the 8% PST.

Recording transactions for a retail carpet and tile business in a special sales journal and the general journal; computing the 8% PST; posting daily to the subsidiary ledger; posting at month-end to the G/L; preparing month-end trial balances.

June 1 Invoice 660; to A. Adams; terms n/30; sales amount, $150. (Entire sales amount is to be credited to Carpet Sales.)
     3 Invoice 661; to S. Bateman; terms n/30; carpet sale, $85; tile sale, $40.
     4 Invoice 662; to E. DeLong; terms n/30; carpet sale, $350.
     6 Credit Memo No. CM-48; to E. DeLong; allowance of $50 granted on Invoice 662 (slightly marked carpet). (The allowance does not include adjustments for the PST, which has to be computed.)

	9	Invoice 663; to G. Folkins; terms n/30; carpet sale, $90; tile sale, $50.
	12	Invoice 664; to B. Fraser; terms n/30; tile sale, $115.
	14	Credit Memo No. CM-49; to B. Fraser; adjustment of $32.40 granted on return of tiles sold for $30 on Invoice 664.
	16	Invoice 665; to A. Adams; terms n/30; tile sale, $55.
	20	Invoice 666; to M. MacEar; terms n/30; carpet sale, $250.
	25	Invoice 667; to B. Scott; terms n/30; carpet sale, $170.40; tile sale, $150.
	27	Credit Memo No. CM-50; to B. Scott, allowance of $40 granted on slightly marked carpet sold on Invoice 667 (adjustment requires calculation for PST).
	29	Invoice 668; to W. Trail; terms n/30; tile sale, $100.

Required

a Open general ledger accounts for Accounts Receivable (103), PST Payable (204), Carpet Sales (401), Tile Sales (402), Carpet Sales Returns and Allowances (403), Tile Sales Returns and Allowances (404). Allow three lines for each G/L account. Open subsidiary ledger accounts for the accounts receivable ledger, allowing four lines for each customer account.

b Record the above transactions in a sales journal (Page 6) with special columns for Accounts Receivable, PST Payable, Carpet Sales, and Tile Sales. Use a general journal (Page 3) for appropriate entries that cannot be recorded in the special journal.

c Post the daily entries to the subsidiary ledger. (Do not forget to post the daily entries from the general journal.)

d Prove the totals in the sales journal; then post the totals to appropriate accounts in the G/L. Also post any G/L information from the general journal.

e Prepare a schedule of accounts receivable.

f Prepare a general ledger trial balance from the accounts used for the general ledger.

Recording transactions for a legal firm in a fees earned journal; posting the daily entries to the subsidiary ledger; proving the special journal and posting the totals to the G/L; preparing a trial balance of the subsidiary ledger.

7.5 The legal firm of Arnold, Brown, Cherniak, and Forbes is located in Saskatchewan. During October the firm issued the following documents that affected the firm's revenue. The policy of the legal firm is to bill all clients on terms of 30 days from the date of the invoice.

Oct. 1 Case 00-G-500, handled by Cherniak; Invoice 4560; to Central Ave. TV, Prince Albert; fee amount, $1 250.80.

5 Case 00-G-512, handled by Arnold; Invoice 4561; to T. A. Park of Prince Albert; fee amount, $645.10.

12 Case 00-G-480, handled by Brown; Invoice 4562; to Moose Jaw Hardware; fee amount, $1 050.75.

13 Case 00-G-490, handled by Forbes; Invoice 4563; to J. Kohaly of Estevan; fee amount, $135.

15 Case 00-G-514, handled by Forbes; Invoice 4564; to Moose Jaw Realty; fee amount, $2 495.15.

18 Case 00-G-520, handled by Cherniak; Invoice 4565; to N. Costeau of Moose Jaw; fee amount, $65.

19 Case 00-G-522, handled by Arnold; Invoice 4566; to T. A. Walker of North Battleford; fee amount, $170.
24 Case 00-G-590, handled by Brown; Invoice 4567; to Cowan Hardware of Prince Albert; fee amount, $680.75.
25 Case 00-G-595, handled by Cherniak; Invoice 4568; to Regina Motors; fee amount, $2 785.
27 Case 00-G-496, handled by Forbes; Invoice 4569; to A. C. Carmichael of Reginal; fee amount, $215.50.
29 Case 00-G-614, handled by Brown; Invoice 4570; to Saskatoon Cleaners; fee amount, $490.

Required

a Open general ledger accounts for Accounts Receivable (103) and Fees Earned (401). Also open subsidiary ledger accounts for the clients. Leave three lines for all accounts.
b Record the above transactions in a fees earned journal similar to the one illustrated in this chapter. Use "Page 28" to identify the journal page.
c Post the daily entries to the subsidiary ledger.
d Prove the special journal at the end of the month (the total of the Fees Earned column must agree with the total of the distribution columns); total and rule off the special journal for the month; and post the totals to appropriate accounts in the G/L.
e Prepare a schedule of accounts receivable to take the work to the end of the trial balance stage.

TOPIC 2 Controlling and Accounting for Cash Receipts

Regardless of size and type of business operation, it is a fact that the flow of cash is the lifestream of an enterprise, since few transactions do not begin or end with cash. In merchandising businesses, for example, you have learned that cash is used directly or indirectly to acquire merchandise for resale (inventory), which in turn is sold to customers who, in the end, must return cash to the business. For service enterprises, you have learned also that every sale leads to a cash receipt and the majority of expenses lead to a cash payment. In addition, you have learned that cash is used to acquire other assets for the firm and to pay creditors. In short, it is safe to conclude that cash transactions are probably the most frequently recurring type entered into by all forms and sizes of business.

Since the volume of cash transactions will be great for all businesses, it should be apparent that a real danger exists for any business which does not take steps to control the proper handling and recording of this valuable asset. As you probably are aware, cash is the asset most easily concealed and transported and, unfortunately, most often the object of human temptation. It should go without saying, therefore, that cash must be protected against fraud and outright theft. Accordingly let us now examine the basic principles for controlling the inflow of cash. (The measures for controlling cash payments are treated in the next chapter.)

Internal Control Measures for Cash Receipts

In general, a business may receive cash in two ways. First, customers may appear in person to buy goods or services, or to pay all or some of their account debts to the business. These customers may pay cash in the form of money currency (paper money and coins), negotiable instruments (cheques, money orders, etc.), or, where acceptable, a recognized credit card or "bank debit card." (See later.) Second, credit customers may pay their account debts by mailing their remittances in the form of cheques or money orders. Regardless of the form of "cash," every business will design a system to control the handling and accounting of their cash receipts. In your study of the points summarized below, keep in mind that individual firms will adopt control measures to suit their particular needs.

1. Prepare a source document for each cash receipt item, whether by person or by mail. In general, when a customer presents (1) cash in person—that is, money, (2) a negotiable instrument, or (3) an acceptable credit card or debit card, accounting requires a source document such as a sales slip, cash register tape, or receipt. On the other hand, if a customer sends a remittance through the mail (cheque, money order), correct accounting procedures require the creation of a remittance slip (often known as a receipt) to give evidence of this cash receipts transaction.
2. All cash register documents should be controlled by a ***system of locked-in tapes***, which become the responsibility of someone other than the cash register clerk. Obviously, the locked-in tapes must be the responsibility of accounting.
3. All other source documents, such as sales slips and remittance forms, should be prenumbered, and they should all be accounted for. Examples of remittance forms are given in Figures 7-17 and 7-18.

System of locked-in tapes: often called the "credit tape" system. Provides a separate listing of all transactions processed through the cash register. Clerks are prevented from gaining access to this tape by its being housed in a locked section of the cash register.

FIGURE 7-17

Buxton's 2401 Cambie St. Vancouver, B.C.

ACCT. COPY—PAYMENT RECEIPT

069868 25.92

Account No. 13071 Clerk #104

NAME Dunster, S. F.

ADDRESS 89 — 904 Clarke Rd.
Port Moody, B.C.

Date — Year 10 Month 15 Day

CASH ☐
CHEQUE ☒
MONEY ORDER ☐
CREDIT CARD VISA ☐ M/C ☐

Payment on Account ☒
Deposit on C.O.D. ☐
Deposit on Layaway ☐
Deposit on Special Order ☐

FIGURE 7-18

KELLY'S OFFICE SERVICES

Remittance Slip No. **RS-24**

Name June Cooper

Amount	Cheque Number	Cheque Date
$50.00	191	Feb. 21, 19-

Explanation
Received on account

Date Feb 25, 19 Received By B.H.

4. One copy of each source document becomes the source medium for the eventual accounting entry to record the debit to Cash and the credit to Sales (or some other revenue account) and the credit to PST Payable (when applicable); or to the customer's Accounts Receivable account when the remittance is a payment on account.
5. Prepare a cash proof for each source of cash receipt. Ideally, the person who supervises the cash proof should accompany all source documents when these are forwarded to accounting. Figures 7-19 and 7-20 give two examples of cash proofs. The first is an example of a proof of the cash register tape; the other, of a proof of individual sales slips which subsequently are listed on an adding machine tape.
6. Ideally, all cash received, once proved against the created source documents, should be prepared for bank deposit by responsible personnel in a separate cashier's or treasurer's office.
7. Endorse all cash in the form of negotiable instruments with the *restrictive endorsement* "For Deposit Only." This means that every cheque and every money order received must be marked this way on the back. Why? As you may have learned from the study of banking practice in other courses, every negotiable instrument must be endorsed before it can be deposited. Therefore, to prevent cashing or transfer of the endorsed instrument to someone else, the endorsement is restricted. Generally, since a great many negotiable

FIGURE 7-19

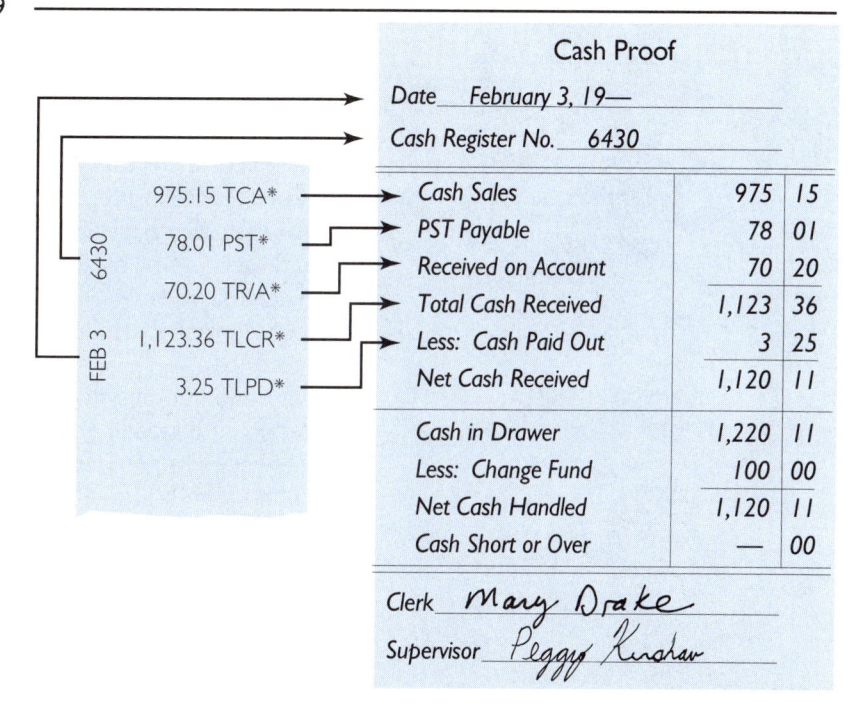

Cash Proof

Date February 3, 19—

Cash Register No. 6430

Cash Sales	975	15
PST Payable	78	01
Received on Account	70	20
Total Cash Received	1,123	36
Less: Cash Paid Out	3	25
Net Cash Received	1,120	11
Cash in Drawer	1,220	11
Less: Change Fund	100	00
Net Cash Handled	1,120	11
Cash Short or Over	—	00

Clerk *Mary Drake*

Supervisor *Peggy Kinshaw*

Tape markings (FEB 3, 6430):
- 975.15 TCA*
- 78.01 PST*
- 70.20 TR/A*
- 1,123.36 TLCR*
- 3.25 TLPD*

FIGURE 7-20

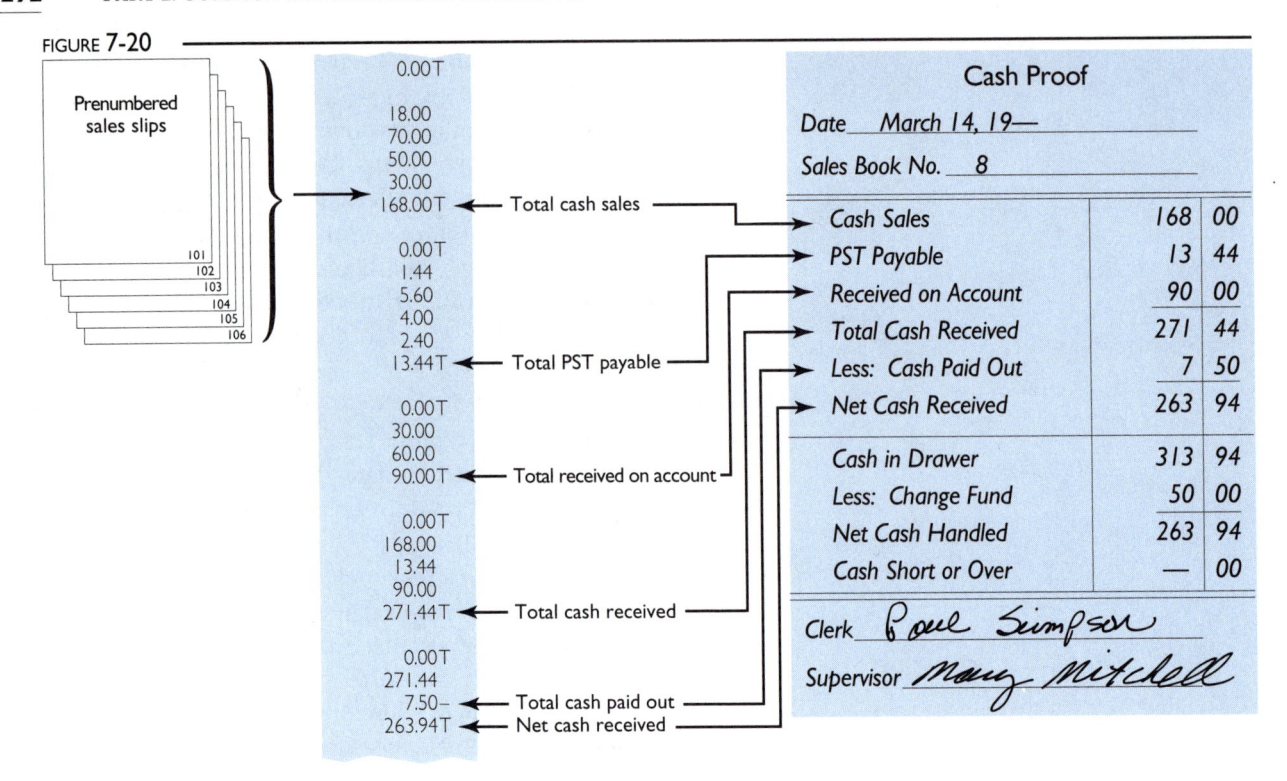

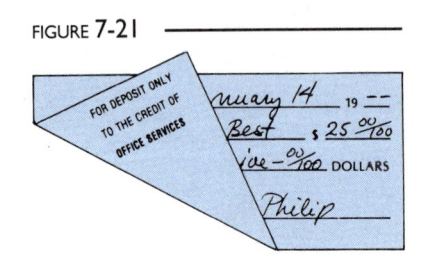

```
                    0.00T
                   18.00
                   70.00
                   50.00
                   30.00
                  168.00T  ← Total cash sales

                    0.00T
                    1.44
                    5.60
                    4.00
                    2.40
                   13.44T  ← Total PST payable

                    0.00T
                   30.00
                   60.00
                   90.00T  ← Total received on account

                    0.00T
                  168.00
                   13.44
                   90.00
                  271.44T  ← Total cash received

                    0.00T
                  271.44
                    7.50−  ← Total cash paid out
                  263.94T  ← Net cash received
```

Cash Proof		
Date __March 14, 19—__		
Sales Book No. __8__		
Cash Sales	168	00
PST Payable	13	44
Received on Account	90	00
Total Cash Received	271	44
Less: Cash Paid Out	7	50
Net Cash Received	263	94
Cash in Drawer	313	94
Less: Change Fund	50	00
Net Cash Handled	263	94
Cash Short or Over	—	00

Clerk _Paul Simpson_
Supervisor _Mary Mitchell_

FIGURE 7-21

instruments must be prepared every day for deposit, the banks allow a depositing firm to use an approved rubber stamp for the restrictive endorsement. One example of a rubber-stamp endorsement on the back of a cheque is illustrated in the side margin.

8. Deposit all cash receipts *intact* in the firm's current account (chequing account)—that is, deposit the total of cash received *to the last penny*. Depositing cash intact in the bank not only protects the asset physically, but also enables the business to receive an outside accounting of its cash receipts and cash payments. *Note*: The area of bank accounting is so important to the overall system of internal control that it is given an entire chapter of study (Chapter 9).

   It is worth mentioning that the above internal control measure does not preclude making payments in cash. As you will learn in the next chapter, a petty cash fund may be set up to take care of small (petty) expenditures.

9. Deposit all cash receipts as soon as possible, preferably on a daily basis. Many banks offer night depository service to support this control measure.

10. Prepare all deposit slips in duplicate so that one copy can be receipted by the bank teller. This receipted copy, illustrated in Figure 7-22,

CHAPTER 7: Accounts Receivable Application   **293**

should then be used to check that the total cash receipts deposited agrees with the total cash debited in the accounting records.

11. Divide the responsibility among personnel so that the persons who handle the cash are separated from the persons responsible for recording the eventual accounting entries.

12. Ideally, a special journal, known as the **cash receipts journal**, should be used to record all cash receipts transactions.

==Cash receipts journal: a special journal in which only cash receipts are recorded.==

FIGURE **7-22**

[Figure 7-22: Royal Bank Current Account Deposit Slip dated Oct. 25, 19--, for Byron Sports Centre, Acct. #110-134-4, London, Ont. Visa voucher total 195.50; Cheques from S. Buck 30.90, J. Huang 170.80, Don Tourby 45.70, Cheques Total 247.40; Details: 18×1=18.00, 12×2=24.00, 5×5=25.00, 7×10=70.00, 2×20=40.00, Coins 38.67, Canadian Cash Total 215.67, Visa & Chqs Forwarded 442.90; Net Deposit 658.57]

Cash Receipts Journal Illustrated

Record daily

The name "cash receipts journal" suggests that a chronological record of all incoming cash transactions is maintained; hence, this journal should contain a special column entitled =="Cash Dr."== In the language of accounting, it is important to remember that "Cash" would include the daily total of currency, money orders, and cheques received. Furthermore, it is important to emphasize that the daily total of all cash receipts must be deposited intact in the firm's bank current account; therefore, one should be able to check the daily debits recorded in the cash receipts journal against the certified copy of bank deposit slips. A typical form of cash receipts journal, for the firm Winnipeg Hardware & Appliance, may be illustrated as in Figure 7-23.

From the design of this special journal, it is obvious that the retail merchant must collect the sales tax from cash sales; therefore, a special money column is included to collect data on the individual sales taxes owing to the federal and provincial governments. (In Manitoba, the 7% PST is computed on the sales amount only.) Once again, it is important to analyze the line-by-line double entry. As in all journals, every double entry must balance not only in individual entries, but also in the analysis of the various column totals. You may find it helpful to analyze the double entry of each transaction before recording the various amounts in the individual money columns, just to be sure that Cash must always be debited and that the credit half agrees in total form.

In connection with the design of the cash receipts journal, it is useful to observe the trend in many retail establishments to the wide acceptance of

FIGURE 7-23

CASH RECEIPTS JOURNAL (Winnipeg Hardware & Appliance) — Page 1

Date	Account Credited	Explanation	Post. Ref.	General Ledger Cr.	Accounts Receivable Cr.	SALES Hardware Cr.	SALES Appliance Cr.	PST Payable Cr.	Cash Dr.
19—									
Jan. 6	Sales	Cash sales for week				200 00	800 00	70 00	1 070 00
10	J. Meyers	For Invoice 0001			321 00				321 00
12	Sales	Cash sales for week				250 00	550 00	56 00	856 00
14	M. Daeninck, Capital	Additional investment		1 000 00					1 000 00
19	Sales	Cash sales for week				160 00	940 00	77 00	1 177 00
23	B. Pearce	On account			100 00				100 00
26	Sales	Cash sales for week				310 00	990 00	91 00	1 391 00
28	S. Ozembloski	For Invoice 0003			417 30				417 30
30	Bank Loan Payable	Royal Bank demand note		3 600 00					3 600 00
31	Sales	Cash sales for week				175 00	487 50	46 38	708 88
31	Totals			4 600 00	815 53	1 095 00	3 767 50	340 38	10 641 18
					838 30				

FIGURE 7-24a

Source: Royal Bank of Canada, registered user of trademark.

FIGURE 7-24b

Source: Courtesy of Bank of Montreal MasterCard.

Bank debit cards: bank identification cards which transfer cash from the depositor's bank account to the store's bank account.

bank credit cards such as Visa and MasterCard. As you may be aware, these retailers endorse the use of such bank credit cards in order to eliminate the accounting of accounts receivable on their books. Hence, these credit card or "plastic money" transactions actually mean the receipt of immediate cash, because the various sales slips of any given card are deposited at the bank which supports that card. For the most part, the banker accepts these sales receipts intact and credits the depositor's current account with the total of "Bank Credit Card Sales Slips," less a special commission for providing "cash" in advance of the credit card due date. This commission becomes an expense which may be accounted for by debiting an expense account such as "Credit Card Commissions Expense," and crediting Cash. Of course, the banker will have to wait until the credit period lapses in order to collect the amount due from the credit card holder.

Since the retailer would want information on each bank's credit card sales, and the monthly total of such deposits, the cash receipts journal may be designed to include one or more distribution columns immediately after the main, Cash Dr. column. For example, if a retail clothier honours both Visa and MasterCard, the cash receipts journal may be designed as illustrated in Figure 7-25.

Briefly, there is a growing trend by customers to use their bank identification cards instead of credit cards or cheques to pay for goods and services. Where point-of-sale transfer systems exist, the store clerk inserts the card into the store's computer, which links up with the bank's computer, to transfer immediately the amount of the sale from the customer's bank account to the store's account. Because these cards debit (decrease) the customer's account at the bank, they are usually called **bank debit cards**. (See Figure 7-26.) Accounting source documents for such point-of-sale transfers are immediately

CHAPTER 7: Accounts Receivable Application   **295**

FIGURE 7-25

			CASH RECEIPTS JOURNAL (Toronto Men's Shop)			Page 10	
						DISTRIBUTION TO BANK CREDIT CARDS	
Date		Explanation	Sales Cr.	PST Payable Cr.	Cash Dr.	Visa	Master-Card
19—							
May	2	Cash sale	200 00	16 00	216 00	118 80	97 20
	3	Cash sale	300 00	24 00	324 00	178 20	145 80
	4	Cash sale	250 00	20 00	270 00	148 50	121 50
	4	Cash sale	100 00	8 00	108 00	59 40	48 60
	31	Totals	5 700 00	456 00	6 156 00	3 385 80	2 770 20

available, because these transactions appear on the monthly bank statements for both the customer and the store, as well as occurring in the form of useful printouts by the store's computer for daily cash receipts deposited.

Obviously, these bank transfers would not be recorded in the traditional cash receipts journal.

Posting from the Cash Receipts Journal

During the month, posting from the cash receipts journal is very similar to the posting procedure explained for the sales journal. In the case of the cash receipts journal illustrated earlier for Winnipeg Hardware & Appliance, each amount recorded in the general ledger credit column would be posted individually to the appropriate account in the general ledger. For example, the additional investment on January 14 by the proprietor would be posted as a credit to M. Daeninck, Capital. After posting this entry, the code number for the Capital account would be placed in the Post. Ref. column of the journal to show that this credit entry was posted.

FIGURE 7-26

ROYAL BANK   BANQUE ROYALE
CLIENT CARD   CARTE DU CLIENT

4519 02 10247329 52

V - 006   02
NAME OF CLIENT

Each amount recorded in the Accounts Receivable credit column would be posted individually to the appropriate customer's account in the accounts receivable ledger. Since customer accounts are usually filed in alphabetical order, a check mark would be placed in the Post. Ref. column to indicate that the amount has been posted to the subsidiary ledger. It is important to remember that the amount shown in this column is the correct amount to be posted to the credit of the customer's account. For example, a wholesale merchandising firm would probably have a special money column to record the Sales Discount debit for cash receipts from credit customers. Obviously, it would be a serious error to use the amount shown in the Net Cash debit column, since the cheque amount may have been based on a calculation for the sales discount. Examine Figure 7-27 to check out this important point.

FIGURE 7-27

	CASH RECEIPTS JOURNAL						Page 3
Date	Account Credited	Explanation	Post. Ref.	General Ledger Credit	Accounts Receivable Credit	Sales Discount Debit	Net Cash Debit
19— June 8	Thornhill Home Hardware	For Invoice 108.	√		738 29	14 77	723 52

It is important to remember that none of the items in the special money columns for Sales credit, PST Payable credit, the Sales Discount debit (when this column is used), or the Cash debit column are posted during the month. Since these columns are headed by actual account names, the totals of these columns would be posted at the end of the month to the general ledger. Before such postings occur, however, all money columns must be first verified to prove that the total debits are equal to the total credits. Such a journal proof may be done by listing the column totals on an adding-machine tape to obtain a zero proof. Notice in Figure 7-28 that the debit totals have been entered with the plus key, while the credit totals have been registered as minuses. If the total debits are equal to the total credits, then the tape must show a zero proof.

After the equality of the debits and credits has been proved, the journal is totalled and ruled off for the month as shown in the illustration.

In this illustration, observe that the total of the general ledger credit column is not posted, because the various amounts have been posted individually to accounts in the general ledger during the month. Consequently, a check mark is placed in the amount column immediately below the double lines to indicate that the total is not to be posted.

Notice that the total of the Accounts Receivable credit column is shown as having been posted to Account 103, the accounts receivable controlling account in the general ledger. Obviously, this total must be

FIGURE 7-28

Cash Receipts Journal
Zero Proof
June 30, 19—

```
       0.00 T

   4 394.00 −
   3 530.81 −
      43.85
   7 880.96

       0.00 T
```

	CASH RECEIPTS JOURNAL						Page 3
Date	Account Credited	Explanation	Post. Ref.	General Ledger Credit	Accounts Receivable Credit	Sales Discount Debit	Net Cash Debit
19— June 30	Bank Loan	Royal Bank demand note.	201	1 000 00			1 000 00
30	Totals			4 394 00	3 530 81	43 85	7 880 96
				(√)	(103)	(403)	(101)

transferred to the credit of the controlling account to record the total decrease to the asset Accounts Receivable during the month. If the total were not posted, the controlling account could not possibly agree with the total of the individual customer balances in the subsidiary ledger. Remember that the individual amounts in this column have already been posted to the subsidiary ledger during the month.

Finally, the illustration shows that the totals for the last two columns have been posted to related accounts in the general ledger. The Sales Discount debit total must be posted to the debit of the contra revenue account and the Net Cash debit total must be posted to the debit of Cash; otherwise, a monthly trial balance of the general ledger could not be prepared.

Preparing Monthly Statements to Credit Customers

Statement of account: a transcript of an account, usually prepared by the creditor, summarizing the customer's transactions for a stated period of time.

In many firms, especially at the large retail department store level, a *statement of account* may be mailed once a month instead of, or in addition to, the invoice. In simple terms, the statement of account is a summary of the data shown by the customer's account stored in the accounts receivable ledger. Such statements may be prepared either in *non-descriptive form*, that is, without particulars of the transactions, or in *descriptive form*. Regardless of the form, all statements usually show the previous balance receivable as at the date of the last statement, the individual charges (debits) during the current month, and the new balance owing on the account. The majority of these statement forms have a tear-off portion which is to be completed by the customer and returned along with the remittance. An example of a descriptive monthly statement of account for a department store is shown in Figure 7-29.

When the customer receives the monthly statement from the seller, he or she should make a detailed comparison of the items shown on the statement with the corresponding entries in his or her own accounts payable records. Of course, any differences in the invoiced amounts, payments, or balance owed should be analyzed. If errors have been discovered, these should be reported to the seller's accounts receivable department immediately.

Cycle billing: billing according to alphabetical sequence of last names at designated dates during the month.

It is worth noting that large department stores and other retailers with a large number of accounts receivable may use what is known as **cycle billing**. Briefly, cycle billing means that the accounts receivable have been divided into alphabetical groups. Instead of statements being prepared at the end of the month for all groups, each group is billed on a given day of the month. For example, accounts receivable whose names fall within A–K might be billed on the first of the month, those in the L–M group on the tenth, those in the N–S group on the fifteenth, and those in the T–Z group on the twentieth. By billing according to a cycle, the accounting system spreads the work of preparing customers' statements more evenly, avoiding heavy concentration of work at the end of each month.

It is also interesting to observe that some of the larger manufacturing firms, wholesale merchandisers, and service firms now issue monthly

FIGURE 7-29

SCARBOROUGH WHOLESALE HARDWARE
330 Progress Avenue
Scarborough, Ontario M1P 2Z5

STATEMENT
OF
ACCOUNT

Date: 19— 06 30

To: Thornhill Home Hardware
67 Grandview Avenue
Thornhill, Ontario L3T 1H3

Please return this stub with your cheque.

Amount Enclosed $ _____

Date	Reference	Charges	Credit	Balance
Balance Forwarded: 19— 05 30				738.29
June 8	RS-75		738.29	0.00
25	120	1 000.00		1 000.00
27	CM-80		100.00	900.00

statements in the form of an aged accounts receivable statement. As you will recall from previous work, the aging of accounts receivable simply refers to the procedure of classifying invoice amounts in columns according to the number of days each is overdue. For example, a large express line company may prepare an aged accounts receivable along the lines shown in Figure 7-30.

When the customer receives the aged statement, he or she can take the necessary steps to pay those invoice items which are past due longer than others. By showing an aged statement, the seller not only controls more efficiently its accounts receivable, but also speeds up remittances from tardy customers.

FIGURE 7-30

CANADA EXPRESS LINES LTD.
P.O. Box 500, Yourtown, Canada

YR.	MO.	DAY	ACCOUNT NO.
19-1	06	30	425-127-511

Canada Products Limited
350 Central Ave
Yourtown, Canada N6G 4H9

THIS IS A DETAILED LISTING OF YOUR ACCOUNT. COPIES OF THESE BILLS ARE ATTACHED TO THIS STATEMENT. PLEASE RETURN THIS NOTICE WITH YOUR CHEQUE.

OUR INVOICE NO.	1–30 DAYS	31–60 DAYS	61–90 DAYS	OVER 90 DAYS	NOTE
801367			127.50		Please pay this amount ↓
811760		150.75			
833765	225.70				
848766	180.40				
Terms 10 days	$406.10	$150.75	$127.50		$684.35

TOPIC 2   Problems

Recording retail hardware and appliance transactions in a multi-column sales journal, multi-column cash receipts journal, and general journal; posting to appropriate accounts; preparing a trial balance of the subsidiary ledger; preparing a descriptive statement of account for one customer.

7.6 Helen Bugno operates a retail store called London Hardware & Appliance. The firm's transactions affecting sales and cash receipts for the month of August are outlined below. Perform the following operations to process those transactions.

a Open a general ledger file and assign appropriate account codes for Cash ($6 875.50); Accounts Receivable ($4 380.75); PST Payable; Helen Bugno, Capital ($45 000); Hardware Sales; Appliance Sales; and Sales Returns and Allowances. The dollar amounts shown in parentheses represent beginning month balances as at August 1. Provide five writing lines for each account.

b Open Accounts Receivable Ledger accounts for the following London, Ontario residents: H. Beatty, 589 Middlewood Ave., N6G 1W7 ($1 040); V. Czyzewski, 56 Clinton Cr., N6G 3V8; S. Demaray, R.R. #5, N7G 3H6 ($260); D. F. Galpin, 906 Whitton Ave., N6A 4H5; C. Gibbons, 152 Old Post Road, N6A 2T4 ($480.25); H. L. Henderson, 308 Cromwell St., N6A 1Z6; P. Park, 1665 Kathryn Dr., N6G 2R8 ($1 400.50); B. J. Shapiro, 971 Colborne St., N6A 4A7 ($1 200); N. H. Stevenson, 496 Lawson Rd., N6G 1Y2; and M. Sykes, 94 Monmore Road, N6G 2W6. The dollar amounts shown in parentheses for some of the customers represent beginning month balances as at August 1. Note that the maximum credit limit for all customers is $1 500. Allow six lines for each account in the subsidiary ledger.

c Record each of the following transactions in a four-column sales journal (Accounts Receivable Dr., PST Payable Cr., Hardware Sales Cr., and Appliance Sales Cr.); a six-column cash receipts journal (General Ledger Cr., Accounts Receivable Cr., Hardware Sales Cr., Appliance Sales Cr., PST Payable Cr., Cash Dr.); or a general journal.

Aug. 1 Sales Invoice 1001 to V. Czyzewski: Hardware Sales, $200; Appliance Sales, $110. Note that Ontario residents, at the time of writing, were charged a 8% provincial sales tax on all items sold in this store.

2 Received a cheque for $260 from S. Demaray in full settlement of account.

4 Received a cheque for $1 040 from H. Beatty in full settlement of account.

6 Cash sales for the week were summarized from the cash register tape as follows: Hardware Sales, $390.50; Appliance Sales, $2 700.25; PST Payable, $247.26; total cash received, $3 338.01.

9 Sales Invoice 1002 to D. F. Galpin: Hardware Sales, $300; Appliance Sales, $1 000; plus PST, 8%.

10 Issued Credit Memo CM-101 to D. F. Galpin for return of hardware goods sold for $70 plus 8% PST ($5.60).

11 Sales Invoice 1003 to H. Beatty: Appliance Sales, $385.10 plus 8% PST.

12 Received a cheque from $700 from P. Park on account.

13 Received a cheque for $1 200 from B. J. Shapiro in full settlement of account.
13 Cash sales for the week were summarized from the cash register tape as follows: Hardware Sales $490; Appliance Sales, $3 800; PST Payable, $343.20; total cash received, $4 633.20.
16 Sales Invoice 1004 to N. H. Stevenson: Hardware Sales, $58.70 plus 8% PST.
17 Sales Invoice 1005 to M. Sykes: Appliance Sales, $895.10 plus 8% PST.
17 Helen Bugno, the owner, invested additional cash of $10 000 in her firm's bank account.
18 Received a cheque for $200 from C. Gibbons on account.
19 Sales Invoice 1006 to H. L. Henderson: Appliance Sales, $195.80 plus 8% PST.
20 Sales Invoice 1007 to H. Beatty: Hardware Sales, $195.80 plus 8% PST.
20 Issued Credit Memo CM-102 to H. Beatty for $20 plus 8% PST ($1.60) as an allowance on slightly marked goods sold on Invoice 1007.
20 Cash sales for the week were summarized from the cash register tape as follows: Hardware Sales, $1 590.50; Appliance Sales, $2 600.10; PST Payable, $335.25; total cash received, $4 525.85.
23 Sales Invoice 1008 to B. J. Shapiro: Hardware Sales, $375 plus 8% PST.
24 Sales Invoice 1009 to H. Beatty: Hardware Sales, $375 plus 8% PST.
25 Received a cheque from P. Park for $300 on account.
26 Received a cheque from H. Beatty for $415.91 in full settlement of Invoice 1003.
27 Cash sales for the week were summarized as follows: Hardware Sales, $1 480.90; Appliance Sales, $2 975.15; PST Payable, $356.48; total cash received, $4 812.53.
30 Received a money order from V. Czyzewski for $334.80 in full settlement of Invoice 1001.
30 Sales Invoice 1010 to H. Beatty: Hardware Sales, $137.50 plus 8% PST.
31 Cash sales for the two days at month-end were cleared from the cash register as follows: Hardware Sales, $189.30; Appliance Sales, $1 375.80; PST Payable, $125.21; total cash received, $1 690.31.

d Prove the totals, and rule the two special journals at month-end.
e Post the entries from the journals to the ledgers.
f Prepare a schedule of accounts receivable. Compare the total with the controlling account balance in the general ledger.
g Prepare a descriptive statement of account for H. Beatty. Use a form similar to the one illustrated in this chapter.

Recording transactions for a wholesale company in a multi-column sales journal, multi-column cash receipts journal, and general journal; posting to appropriate accounts; preparing a trial balance of the subsidiary ledger; preparing a descriptive statement of account for one customer.

7.7 A. Jenkins operates the Maritime Wholesale Company. The firm's transactions affecting sales and cash receipts for the month of April are outlined below. Perform the following operations to process those transactions.

a Open a general ledger file and assign appropriate account codes for Cash; Accounts Receivable; Bank Loan Payable; A. Jenkins, Capital; Sales; Sales Returns and Allowances; and Sales Discount. Open accounts receivable ledger accounts for Mary Carter, R.R. #2, Winsloe, P.E.I.; Barbara Casey, 6553 Berline Street, Halifax, N.S.; June Cooper, P.O. Box 9052, St. John's, Nfld.; and Harriet Rutledge,

225 Woodbridge, Fredericton, N.B. Allow eight lines for accounts receivable in the general ledger, and six lines for all other accounts.

b Record each of the following transactions in a one-column sales journal; a five-column cash receipts journal (General Ledger Cr., Accounts Receivable Cr., Sales Cr., Sales Discount Dr., Net Cash Dr.); or a general journal.

Apr. 1 The balance of Cash and A. Jenkins, Capital is $8 490.75.
  2 Sold merchandise for $510 to Mary Carter on Invoice 430; terms 2/10, n/30.
  4 Sold merchandise for $330 to Barbara Casey on Invoice 431; terms 1/10, n/30.
  5 A. Jenkins invested an additional $2 000 cash in the business.
  6 Cash sales for the week, $400.
  8 Sold merchandise for $320 to June Cooper on Invoice 432; terms 2/10, n/30.
  11 Received a cheque for $499.80 from Mary Carter in payment of invoice 430 of April 2, less the discount.
  12 Cash sales for the week, $1 000.
  13 Sold merchandise for $270 to June Cooper on Invoice 433; terms 1/10, n/30.
  14 Issued Credit Memo CM-18 to June Cooper for $50 as the adjustment of the return of damaged goods sold on Invoice 433.
  15 Received cheque from Barbara Casey for $100; payment on account for Invoice 431.
  16 Received cheque for $313.60 from June Cooper in payment of Invoice 432 of April 8, less the discount.
  17 Sold merchandise for $185 to Harriet Rutledge on Invoice 434; terms 1/15, n/60.
  18 Issued Credit Memo CM-19 to Harriet Rutledge for $20 as an allowance on slightly marked goods sold on Invoice 434.
  19 Cash sales for week, $1 310.
  22 Received cheque for $217.80 from June Cooper in payment of Invoice 433 of April 13, less the credit memo of April 14, less the cash discount.
  23 Sold merchandise for $370 to June Cooper on Invoice 435; terms 1/10, n/30.
  26 Sold merchandise for $300 to Mary Carter on Invoice 436; terms 2/10, n/30.

c Prove the totals, and rule the special journals.
d Post the entries from the journals to the ledgers.
e Prepare a schedule of accounts receivable.
f Prepare a trial balance of the general ledger.
g Prepare a descriptive statement of account for June Cooper.

Note: Save your working papers for use in Problem 7.8.

Completion of Problem 7.7.

7.8 Using the working papers from Problem 7.7, perform the following operations.

a Record these transactions in the sales journal, the cash receipts journal, or the general journal.

May 2 Received a cheque for $163.35 from Harriet Rutledge in payment of Invoice 434 of April 17, less Credit Memo CM-19, less the sales discount.
   3 Received a cheque for $330 [230] from Barbara Casey in full settlement of Invoice 431 (April 4).
   5 Sold merchandise to Harriet Rutledge for $500 on Invoice 437; terms 1/15, n/60.
   6 Issued Credit Memo CM-20 to Harriet Rutledge for $100 as the adjustment to damaged goods sold on Invoice 437.
   6 Cash sales for week, $1 120.
   8 Received a cheque for $100 from Mary Carter in part payment of Invoice 436.
   10 Borrowed on a demand note $2 000 from the Bank of Montreal. The amount of the loan was deposited to the credit of the firm's current account.
   11 Sold merchandise to Barbara Casey for $420 on Invoice 438; terms 2/10, n/30.
   12 Cash sales for week, $1 200.
   19 Received cheque for $396 from Harriet Rutledge in payment of Invoice 437 of May 5, less Credit Memo CM-20, less the sales discount.
   20 The proprietor made an additional investment of $1 000 cash.
   21 Sold merchandise to Harriet Rutledge for $200 on Invoice 439; terms 1/15, n/60.
   22 Received a cheque for $100 from Mary Carter in part payment of Invoice 436.
   24 Sold merchandise for $300 to Barbara Casey on Invoice 440; terms 2/10, n/30.
   26 Cash sales for two weeks, $1 580.
   28 Received a cheque for $420 from Barbara Casey in full settlement of Invoice 438 (April [May] 11).
   29 Sold merchandise for $200 to June Cooper on Invoice 441; terms 2/10, n/30.
   30 Issued credit memo for $10 to June Cooper (CM-21); allowance granted on Invoice 441.

  b Prove the totals, and rule the special journals for the month-end.
  c Post the journal entries to the ledgers.
  d Prepare a schedule of accounts receivable.
  e Prepare a trial balance of the general ledger.
  f Prepare a descriptive statement of account for Harriet Rutledge.

7.9 Ms. Mary Wassill owns and operates the Regina Fashion Clothiers. In selling clothing merchandise, the owner has adopted the policy of offering credit for 30 days and of accepting Visa and MasterCard credit cards. To record the dollar results of cash receipts transactions, Ms. Wassill uses a cash receipts journal with the following special money columns: General Ledger Cr., Accounts Receivable Cr., Sales Cr., PST Payable Cr., Cash Dr., and distribution columns to record cash sales based on Visa and MasterCard cards. All cash receipts transactions for

Recording retail cash sales transactions in a cash receipts journal with distribution columns for credit card sales; proving the column totals at month-end; analyzing required postings.

the business enterprise for the month of May are summarized below.

Note: At the time of writing, Saskatchewan had a 7% provincial retail sales tax.

May 2 Sold clothing merchandise to Donna Fluce, $120. The customer used Visa to pay for the goods and charges for PST.
   3 Received a cheque for $157.50 from Mrs. Jeanette Friskie in full settlement of her account.
   4 The owner invested additional cash of $5 000 in the business.
   5 Cash receipts for today were as follows: $42.80 ($40 sale plus PST) from a customer who paid money currency; $107 ($100 plus PST) from Brian Cooke who paid for his goods with MasterCard; and $193.14 ($180.50 plus PST) from Joan Wilkes who paid for her merchandise with Visa.
   6 Received a cheque for $214 from Mrs. Margaret Parker in full settlement of her account.
   9 Cash sales for today totalled $331.70, plus the 7% PST.
   11 Received a cheque for $365.94 from Larry Allemeersch, who was sold clothing earlier on 30 days' credit.
   12 Visa sale to Steve Harasymuk for $390.80 plus the 7% PST.
   15 Cash receipts today consisted of: $89.40 cash sales plus the 7% PST; Visa sale to Mrs. Pat Rydzik for $98.75 plus the 7% PST; MasterCard sale to Ms. Lois Odling for $174.80 plus the 7% PST; and a cheque for $219.46 from Miss Edna Larson in full settlement of her 30-day charge.
   18 The owner negotiated a demand loan at the bank for $5 000. The full amount of the loan was deposited in the name of the firm.
   20 Cash receipts today were as follows: $170.90 cash sales plus the 7% PST; Visa sale to Ms. Jeanne Kaye for $65.80 plus the 7% PST; and a MasterCard sale to Brian Cooke for $48.90 plus the 7% PST.
   23 Received a cheque for $109.14 from Jean Nutting in full payment of her 30-day charge account.
   26 Cash receipts for today were as follows: $378.40 cash sales plus 7% PST; Visa card sales to Lynn Tycholiz for $70 plus the 7% PST and to Ted Forrest for $67.80 plus the 7% PST; and a MasterCard sale to Shelley Ferguson for $110.70 plus the 7% PST.
   29 Received a cheque for $80.25 from Beth McDermid in full settlement of her 30-day credit account.
   31 Cash receipts for today were as follows: $475.80 cash sales plus 7% PST; Visa credit card sale to Jack Handel for $130.70 plus 7% PST; and a MasterCard credit card sale to Norma Ash for $190.00 plus 7% PST.

Required
a Record the above transactions in the cash receipts journal.
b Prove the equality of the debit and credit totals; then rule the special journal at month-end.
c Show how postings would be made by placing ledger account numbers and check marks in the appropriate columns of the journal.

Preparing an aged accounts receivable statement of account.

7.10 Canada Express Lines Ltd. uses the aging method to prepare a monthly statement of account to its customers. From the information below, prepare an aged statement of accounts receivable in a form similar to the one illustrated in this chapter.

- Customer: Central Dry Goods, 485 Main Street, Yourtown, Canada
- Account No.: 695-840-119
- Date: April 30, 19-9
- Invoice 4978, dated January 5, 19-9, $185.50
- Invoice 4990, dated February 14, 19-9, $330
- Invoice 5210, dated March 10, 19-9, $485.10
- Invoice 6110, dated April 1, 19-9, $366.90
- Terms given to remit full amount: 10 days from the date of the statement

TOPIC 3 Shortcuts in Manual Journalizing and Manual Posting

In some manual accounting systems, a number of shortcuts can be employed for processing the accounts receivable application. Common examples are journalizing batch totals for general ledger posting, direct posting to individual accounts receivable, journalless bookkeeping (eliminating the use of the journal), ledgerless bookkeeping (eliminating use of the subsidiary ledger), and use of the one-write system.

Journalizing Batch Totals and Direct Posting to Accounts Receivable

The concept of journalizing batch totals generally applies to any accounting system that reduces the amount of journalizing formerly done through conventional bookkeeping. For example, in the conventional procedure for recording the sales of merchandise on credit, the amount of each sales invoice is recorded in a sales journal. Thus, if a business processes an average of 200 sales invoices a week, the sales journal will contain 200 entries for each week, or approximately 800 to 1 000 entries for the month. In a batching system, however, the sales invoices are allowed to accumulate in groups or **batches**. The total of the batch of invoices is calculated, and only this batch total is journalized.

Batches: groups of totalled invoices.

To follow the processing of these sales in a conventional system, the entries in the sales journal would be posted at regular intervals to the individual customers' accounts in the subsidiary ledger. In a batching system, however, the amount of each credit sale is posted directly from the source document (the sales invoice) to the customer's account in the accounts receivable ledger. Because information entered in subsidiary ledger accounts is taken directly from source documents rather than from journal entries, this procedure has been given a special name, **direct posting**.

Direct posting: posting from the source document.

A batch of invoices may consist of those approved for a part of a day, for one day, for one week, or for any other period, depending on the number of invoices to be processed. For example, let us consider a business that makes several hundred sales on account daily. For processing these sales, let us assume that the accounting system has an accounts

CHAPTER 7: Accounts Receivable Application **305**

receivable controlling account in the general ledger, a subsidiary customer ledger to support the controlling account, a batching system to journalize the total of groups of invoices, and some kind of adding-listing machine, such as an electronic ten-key calculator, to assist in journalizing batch totals. Let us now examine the three procedures that are necessary to process the accounts receivable for management control and reporting. Refer to Figure 7-31 as you read the following sections "Preparation of Invoice Copies" and "Journalization of Batch Totals."

PREPARATION OF INVOICE COPIES At least three copies of each sales invoice are prepared. The original is sent to the customer; copy 2 is for processing the sales invoices in batches; and copy 3 is for posting direct to the subsidiary ledger accounts.

JOURNALIZATION OF BATCH TOTALS This is the procedure when invoices are processed in daily batches:

1. The accounting clerk sorts all second copies of the sales invoices in numerical order to account for each invoice.

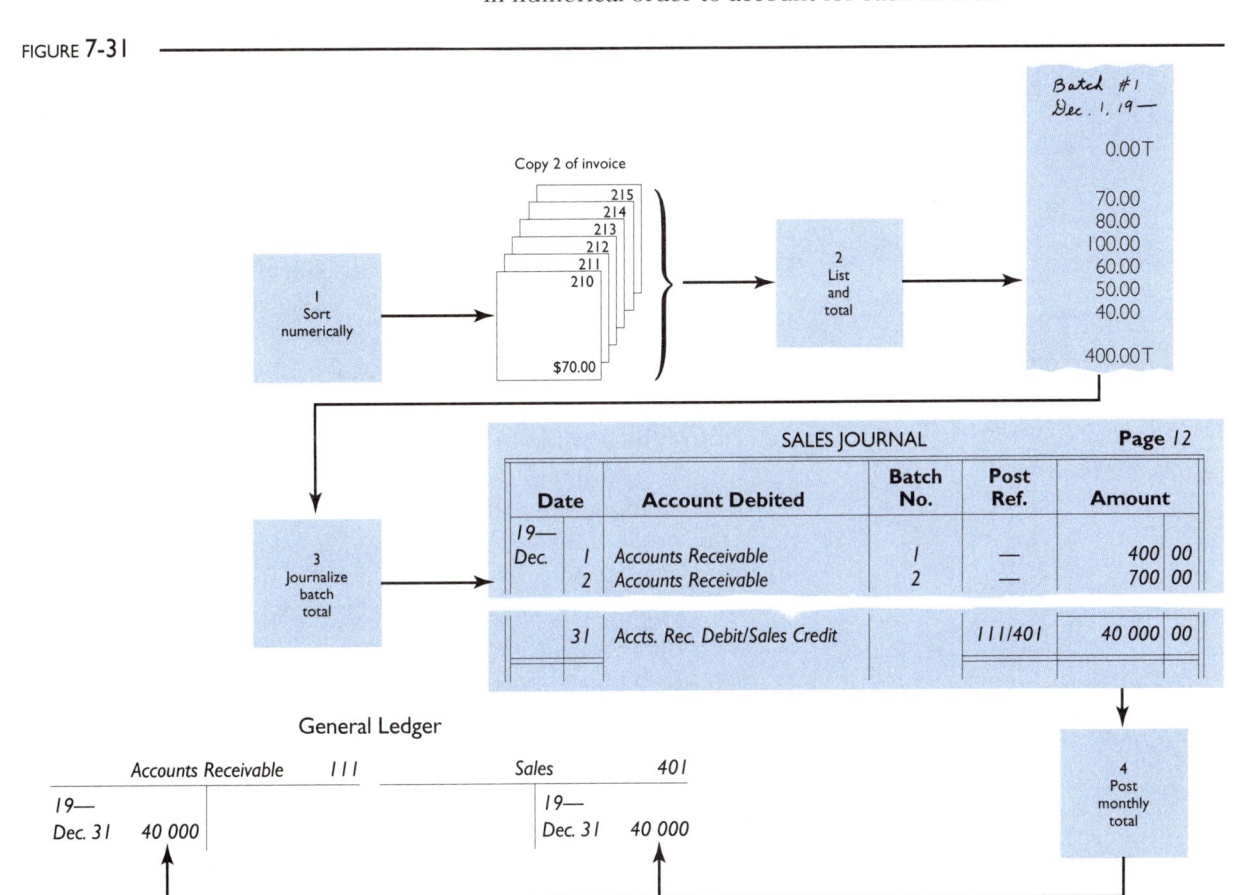

FIGURE **7-31**

2. The amount of each invoice is listed on an adding-machine tape, and the total of the credit sales is obtained. (The tape is an important control document, for it is the only independent record at this point of the number of invoices in the daily batch and the amount of each.)
3. The batch total is entered in the sales journal. At this point, the traditional double entry of Accounts Receivable debit, Sales credit, and PST Payable credit (if applicable) is recognized for the batch total only. The batch of invoices is now stored for reference in case anyone wishes to trace the batch total back to the specific invoices. In addition, these batches provide a numerical record of all sales invoices used. Note that no posting to the general ledger takes place until the end of the month, at which time the two general ledger accounts receive the normal total of credit sales for the month.

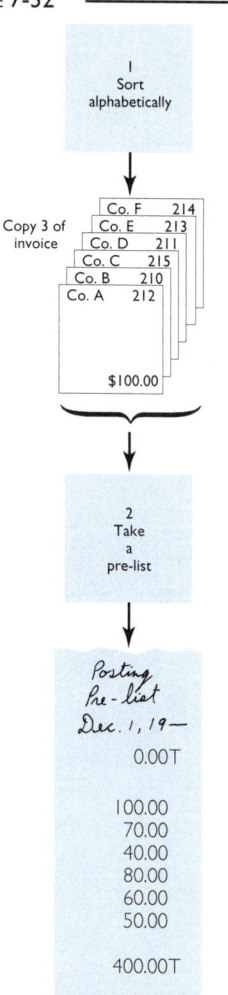

FIGURE 7-32

DIRECT POSTING FROM SOURCE DOCUMENTS

Refer to Figure 7-32 in the side margin as you analyze this section. Copy 3 of each sales invoice is used for posting the amounts of the invoices in batches directly to subsidiary ledger accounts. Here is one procedure that can be used successfully:

1. Another clerk alphabetizes the source documents by customer name.
2. A *pre-list* of the day's invoices is taken before posting occurs. This is merely a listing of all invoices to be posted on an adding-machine tape. The pre-list will be used later to check the accuracy of posting amounts to each individual customer's account.
3. The accounting clerk then posts the amount of each invoice to the appropriate customer's account in the subsidiary ledger. (See Figure 7-33.) Some form of check mark, together with the clerk's initials, is entered on the invoice to indicate that it has been posted.
4. As a check on the accuracy of the posting, a *proof tape* is generally taken of the postings to the accounts. In a manual system, this tape may be taken by listing each amount posted in each account on an adding-machine tape. Note that the invoice copy is not used in this proof. If the total of the proof tape does not agree with the total of the pre-list, errors must be located by comparing the proof tape with the sorted invoices, item by item.
5. When the totals of the two tapes agree, all third invoice copies are placed in filing folders by customer name. These folders are filed alphabetically in the accounts receivable filing cabinet.

EVALUATION OF THE JOURNALIZATION OF BATCH TOTALS

In summary, an accounting system that journalizes batch totals for its accounts receivable has provided management with the information it needs, as follows: (1) the additions to and the balance of the Accounts Receivable controlling account; (2) the amount of sales revenue for each time period,

FIGURE 7-33

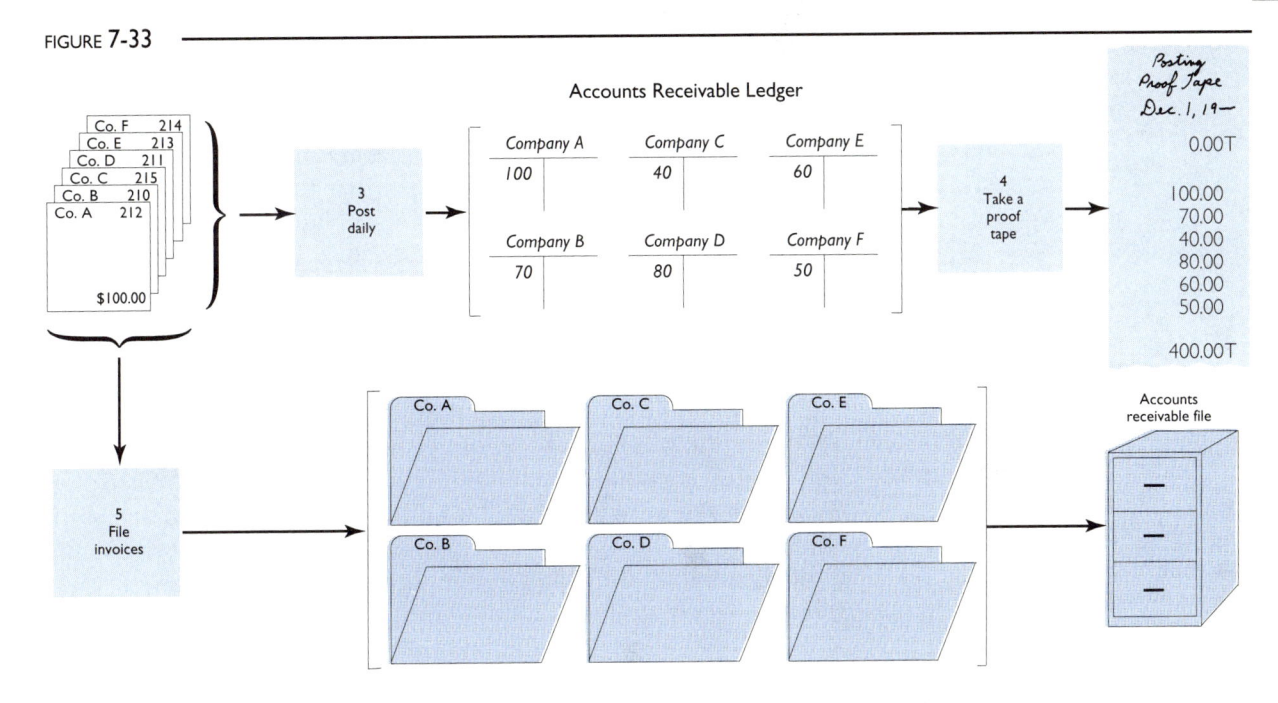

such as a day; and (3) the changes in and the balance of each customer's account. The first two types of information were provided by adding the individual sales invoices for the day and journalizing only their batch total in the sales journal. This is much faster than recording in the sales journal the date, customer's name, amount, and other data for each sales invoice. Moreover, the system of direct posting from copies of the sales invoices to individual customer accounts can be done by a separate clerk, which expedites for management an up-to-date picture of its accounts receivable. A third advantage of batch processing source documents is that it lends itself ideally to some computer systems of data processing, such as AccPac Plus®. This popular microcomputer accounting package will be examined in Chapter 11.

Variations in the batching system will certainly be found. For example, a business may file a batch total of sales invoices in a binder file instead of using a sales journal. At the end of a designated period—a week or a month—the individual batch totals may be accumulated and journalized in final-total form in a general journal. This final total can then be posted to the two general ledger accounts. As outlined earlier, posting to the individual customer accounts cannot be made from the journal, because it contains a record of the credit sales transactions only in summary form. These individual postings will be made directly from copies of the source documents, usually daily.

One final point should be noted in analyzing any firm's batching system. Work in journalizing can be reduced in a similar manner whenever subsidiary ledger accounts are affected frequently by some *single* type of transaction. Thus, any number of possibilities may be considered. The processing of cash receipts from customers may be done by journalizing only the batch totals of collections on account in the cash receipts journal. Individual credits to customers' accounts in the subsidiary ledger may then be posted directly from duplicate copies of the receipts or from other source documents which report the collections. These changes in procedure and the increasing use of direct posting from source documents point up the fact that accounting records and systems must be designed to meet the needs of the particular business firm.

Journalless Bookkeeping

Journalless bookkeeping: a system that omits use of a formal journal.

The term ***journalless bookkeeping*** is used in this textbook to refer to any accounting system that eliminates the use of a formal journal to process accounts receivable and accounts payable. In these cases, some form of batching system is usually employed. As an example, we shall examine a batching system for processing credit sales without a sales journal or general journal.

As in the procedure just outlined for journalizing batch totals, three copies of each sales invoice are generally prepared. They are handled as follows:

- **Copy 1** This original invoice is sent to the customer.
- **Copy 2** The duplicate copies of a group of invoices are sorted in numerical order to form a batch; then a batch total is prepared with the aid of an adding-machine. Instead of recording the total of the batch in a journal, the accounting clerk simply places each batch of invoices, with its own adding-machine tape attached, in a *sales invoice binder*. (See Figure 7-34.) The accounting clerk simply totals the individual batch figures on an adding machine to obtain a monthly total of credit sales. Using this new adding-machine tape as the source document medium, the accounting clerk posts the monthly batch total as a debit to Accounts Receivable and a credit to Sales (and a credit to PST Payable if appropriate) in the general ledger.
- **Copy 3** There is no change in the procedure for processing the third copy of the invoices; they are first sorted alphabetically. Then, after taking a pre-list, the accounting clerk posts the amount of each invoice to the appropriate customer's account in the accounts receivable ledger. Once this posting is verified by a proof tape, the source documents are placed in alphabetical filing folders, which are stored in a filing cabinet.

EVALUATION OF THE JOURNALLESS SYSTEM

It should be obvious that the binder containing the sales invoices takes the place of the sales journal. Each invoice is posted separately to the subsidiary ledger,

FIGURE 7-34

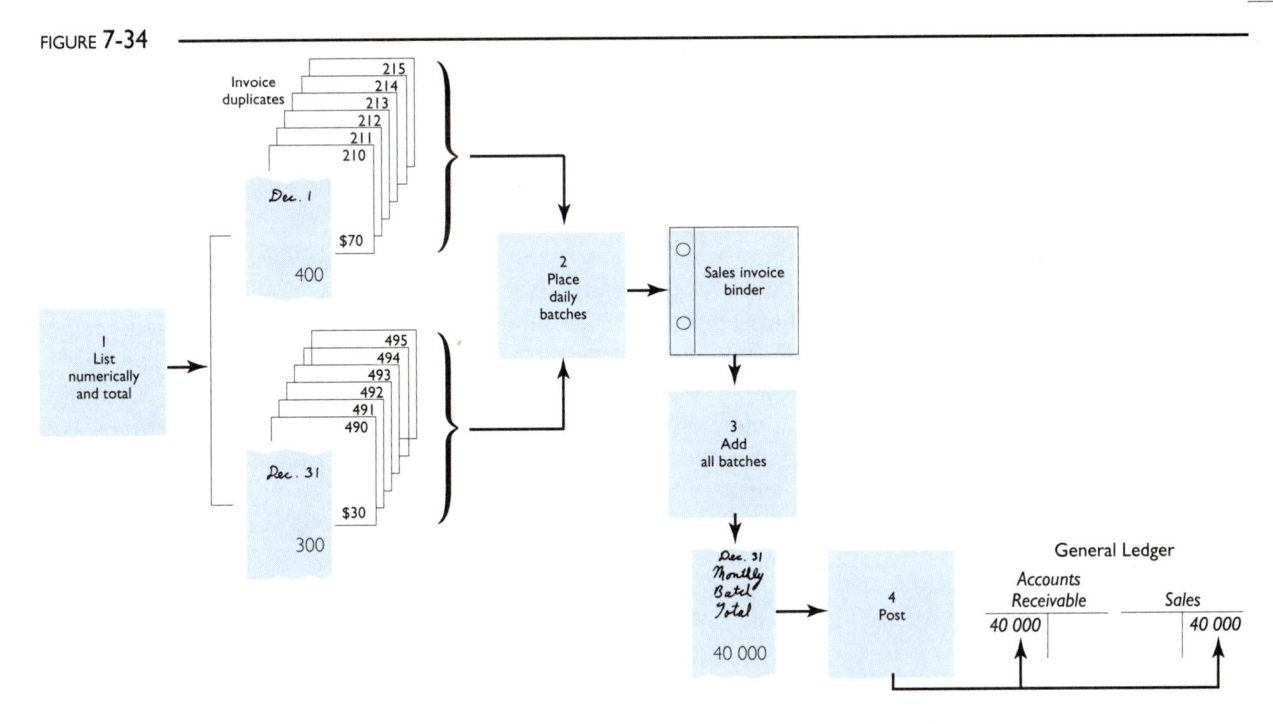

and the total of all invoices for the month is posted to the G/L. Although no journal has been used, it is important to stress that the principle of journalizing still remains. There is no change in the double entry to the G/L, nor in the daily posting of debits to each individual customer's account. What has changed, however, is that the traditional journal form has been bypassed.

The elimination of a formal journal is a further refinement in speeding up the accounting system for processing credit sales. Here are the main advantages of a journalless bookkeeping system for processing accounts receivable:

- The use of sales invoices as a sales journal may effect a substantial saving in bookkeeping expense, particularly when there is a large volume of transactions.
- Direct posting eliminates the chance of error in recording the information from the source document to a journal.
- The necessity of copying the name of the customer and other details commonly found in the journal is eliminated, thus saving considerable time.
- Time-saving by division of labour is possible. For example, invoices can be divided into a number of alphabetical batches and assigned to several posting clerks.

Although many accountants support the practice of journalizing batch totals and direct posting to subsidiary ledger accounts to save time, they do not all favour bypassing the use of a journal as well. Here are their main arguments for still retaining some form of journal:

- The journalizing of batch totals for later posting to the G/L provides a greater degree of security than the use of a binder alone, so that any transaction can be accurately and quickly traced back if a source document, or a batch of documents, is lost.
- Eliminating the journal for posting to the G/L also eliminates a valuable check on the accuracy of the complete double entry. If transactions are recorded directly in the G/L, there is a danger of omitting the debit or the credit side of the entry, or of making two debit or two credit entries.
- Eliminating the journal also eliminates the real advantage to the use of special columns in a special journal. For example, how does one calculate efficiently and quickly for posting the total PST payable to a provincial government? Or the total federal sales tax payable to the federal government? Or both forms of sales taxes? And how does one provide for the management of, say, eight different sales departments with their individual total credit sales for the month from just the sales invoices? Obviously, a form of columnar sales journal to accumulate monthly totals provides all this information very efficiently under a manual system.

Ledgerless Bookkeeping

The most radical of shortcuts under a manual accounting system in processing a firm's accounts receivable is to eliminate subsidiary ledger accounts for customers. Instead of a formal account, a filing folder is established for each customer; and instead of posting the entries from either a formal journal or source document media, the source documents are placed in a customer's folder. These folders are then filed in closed or open cabinets to make up the accounts receivable file. The complete file takes the place of the subsidiary ledger; the individual folders containing the source documents take the place of the formal customers' accounts. Because an actual subsidiary ledger is not used in the accounting system, this method is frequently referred to as **ledgerless bookkeeping**. And since the source documents, or copies thereof, replace the subsidiary accounts, another popular name for this system is the *documentary ledger system*.

Ledgerless bookkeeping: a filing system of source documents instead of accounts.

Since very few firms use ledgerless bookkeeping under a manual system, no details will be given here. Where ledgerless bookkeeping is used, it is usually the case that customers pay each invoice on an individual basis. Because a separate record of each unpaid invoice is maintained in an open file, the method is generally defined as an **open-item system** of maintaining accounts receivable records. This is different from the balance-forward approach, in which a record of the customer's total outstanding balance is maintained and payments are applied against the

Open-item system: an accounts receivable system which accounts for each unpaid invoice in an open file.

CHAPTER 7: Accounts Receivable Application   **311**

balance rather than individual invoices. Although there are exceptions, the open-item accounts receivable system is widely used by businesses which sell to other businesses (manufacturers and wholesalers), because they prefer to pay invoices on an individual basis. On the other hand, the ***balance-forward system*** will more usually be found in businesses which deal with consumers as individuals (department stores, specialty shops, oil companies, dental practices, etc.), because their customers prefer to pay the amount owing on the balance due in their accounts.

> Balance-forward system: an accounts receivable system accounting for the balance of a customer's account rather than for individual sales invoices.

The few advantages claimed under this system include its simplicity and the considerable saving of time and costs when the accounts receivable ledger is eliminated.

On the other hand, some of the obvious weaknesses are: errors can easily be made; there is lack of accounting control, especially when an error is made in the accounts receivable file; there is no running balance of individual customer accounts; inefficient coverage of payments occurs when a customer pays only part of an invoice amount; there is no customer credit history; and no detailed customer statements are possible.

The One-Write System

> One-write system: a shortcut manual bookkeeping system in which several records, including source documents, are produced simultaneously with the aid of NCR or carbon paper and a flat board on which the forms are properly aligned.

Perhaps the most successful manual shortcut in combining the bookkeeping stages of common accounting applications such as accounts receivable, accounts payable, and payroll is the ***one-write system***. In this system, as applied to accounts receivable, the accounting clerk uses an accounting pegboard on which are collated (assembled) the essential forms required to process an accounts receivable transaction. For example, the sales invoice of fee bill can be collated with the customer's subsidiary ledger card and the sales or fees earned journal. Once the forms are aligned correctly, the clerk, in one writing, originates the transaction data (sales invoice or fee bill), journalizes the transaction, and posts the transaction to the customer's account accounts receivable ledger.

In spite of the increasing trend to computerize common accounting applications, the one-write system remains popular, especially in small professional practices such as medical, dental, accounting, and legal offices. In this chapter, only the accounts receivable application for a small dental office will be examined. Once the basics are learned for this application, they can be applied to any accounts receivable application that uses the one-write system.

COMMON TRANSACTIONS FOR A DENTAL OFFICE

As you may be aware, a patient makes an appointment for dental service such as an examination, extraction, cleaning, filling, bridge, etc. After the service is rendered, one of four possible transactions may occur.

- The patient may arrange to charge the service either under a dental insurance plan or without such a plan. Hence, a statement (bill) is usually issued for the amount owing. Under conventional accounting theory, the patient's Accounts Receivable would be debited, and a revenue account such as Fees Earned would also be credited for the same amount. And, under conventional bookkeeping procedures, such a transaction would normally be recorded in a fees earned journal. Posting would then follow either directly from the source document (the statement) or from the journal to the patient's account in the accounts receivable ledger book. If a remittance is not received by the end of the month, a statement of account is usually prepared and mailed to the patient for the total amount owing as at month-end.

- When the future remittance is received, Cash would be debited and the patient's Accounts Receivable would be credited for the amount received. Under conventional bookkeeping procedures, this entry would be recorded in the cash receipts journal, after which posting would be made to credit the patient's account in the accounts receivable ledger. A cash receipt would also be prepared for the amount received and given to the patient.

- On the other hand, the patient may pay cash immediately for services rendered by signing a cheque or an acceptable credit card. In the majority of dental practices, this transaction would first be recorded "on account"—that is, the patient's Accounts Receivable would be debited and Fees Earned would be credited in the traditional fees earned journal. Then, a second entry would be made in the cash receipts journal to account for the cash received. The reason for recording the transaction initially on account is to keep a complete record of the patient's dental history on an accounts receivable patient's ledger card. Of course, a receipt would also be prepared and given to the patient for the amount of cash received.

- One other common transaction is possible. The patient may pay for only part of the amount shown for services rendered, thus charging the remaining amount as an accounts receivable. Under conventional accounting procedures, the entire amount of the service is usually recorded in the fees earned journal as an Accounts Receivable debit and Fees Earned credit. Then the part payment is recorded in the cash receipts journal as a debit to Cash and a credit to Accounts Receivable for the actual amount of cash received. Posting would then follow to the patient's account to show the results of both transactions, leaving a balance owing on account. Of course, a statement and receipt would be prepared and given to the patient to support both transactions. In addition, a monthly statement of account is usually prepared and mailed indicating the amount owing as at month-end.

APPLYING THE ONE-WRITE SYSTEM

Although several firms have developed excellent one-write systems, one enterprise called Safeguard Business Systems Inc. produces accounting boards and accompanying forms for a wide range of businesses in North America. As you will learn, the

CHAPTER 7: Accounts Receivable Application **313**

Safeguard system supports the accounts receivable application for professional practices such as dental offices by creating a combination journal in which the traditional fees earned journal and the cash receipts journal are combined on one sheet. In addition, Safeguard permits the creation of the source document, the journalizing of the transaction, and the posting of the transaction to the patient's account all in one writing. Figure 7-35 illustrates the assembly of the accounts receivable one-write system which Safeguard creates for a professional dental office. Refer to this illustration as you study the following points.

FIGURE **7-35**

- **The pegboard (accounting board)** As the name suggests, the pegboard is a flat board containing a series of pegs at the left margin. In general, the board provides a flat writing surface and receives the forms that are required for the accounting of the various accounts receivable transactions. Of course, the pegs permit the forms to be collated so that the one-write principle can be achieved.
- **The Record of Charges and Receipts (Day Sheet)** Translated into accounting language, this sheet actually becomes a combination journal which permits the journalizing of all transactions related to accounts receivable. Consequently, the journal combines the features of the traditional fees earned journal and the cash receipts journal. In addition, this journal sheet contains sections for preparing the daily proof of postings to individual accounts receivable, for proving the Accounts Receivable controlling account, and for proving the daily cash. One journal sheet is used for each day's set of accounts receivable and related transactions.

- **The carbon sheet**   A high-quality carbon sheet is fused on top of the Day Sheet and covers all columns of the Day Sheet from left to the end of the Balance column. Obviously, the carbon sheet allows the one-writing of transactions to the journal sheet.
- **The patient's ledger card**   In dental practice, it is customary to identify the accounts receivable ledger card for the principal member of the family, that is, the person who pays the family bills. In addition, the other members of the family would be listed in the top right corner of the card. Consequently, the accounts receivable card (more commonly called the patient's ledger card) will become the family financial profile which identifies services rendered for individual members of the family as well as the total amount owing by the family.

  As illustrated, the family or patient's ledger card includes the traditional three-money column format: the left-hand (debit) column to record the charge; the middle column (credit) to record the payment; and the far right column to record the current balance.
- **The patient transaction slip**   This final form is perforated to divide into two sections: the receipt/statement section and the stub section. Observe that the patient transaction slips for professional offices like dentistry come "shingled" on a sheet so that they are sequentially numbered.

  As illustrated, the two-part form consists of: (1) the left side, which becomes the receipt when cash is paid, or the statement (fee bill) when a charge is transacted, and (2) the right side, which is a perforated section known as the *travelling stub*. Briefly, in some practices, this stub is detached and "travels" to the doctor's operatory where the dentist can identify what services were rendered. The stub is then returned to the front office and serves as the source document for the dental transaction to be recorded on the one-write board. It should be noted that the top edge of the reverse side of the patient transaction slip (receipt and stub sections) contains a layer of carbon to allow the transfer of what will be written on the top line of the statement and stub to appear on the ledger card and journal forms.
- **The ballpoint pen**   Although pencil may be used, an extra-fine ballpoint pen using repro black (carbon) ink is recommended. Pencil is discouraged for two main reasons: pencil dulls down quickly, and pencil writings will fade over time. The use of a carbon black extra-fine ballpoint will ensure high-quality permanent recordings. Of course, the clerk must take care to write neatly and legibly.

COLLATING AND ASSEMBLING THE ACCOUNTS RECEIVABLE FORMS

In general, the individual parts of the accounts receivable application are put together on the Safeguard pegboard in the following order:

1. First, the Record of Charges and Receipts (Day Sheet), that is, the combination journal, is placed on top of the board. Since the side holes of the journal sheet fit over the pegs in only one position, no error can be made as to correct placement as long as the holes are positioned over all of the pegs.

    Since the carbon sheet is fused to the top of the journal sheet, there is no need to adjust it. It is placed correctly to receive and transfer the future one-writing of accounts receivable transactions.

2. Next, the shingled patient transaction slips are placed on top of the carbon so that the top line of the receipt form is lined up against the first writing line on the journal. Again, the side holes of the receipt form ensure correct positioning of the receipt over the pegs. As one is completed, the next can be used and so on.

    It is essential to remember that the patient's ledger card is not placed in position until the first four steps have been completed. In other words, always place on the Safeguard board first the journal, and then the shingled set of receipt forms.

3. And, finally, to make an entry on a family or individual patient ledger card as the case may be, one would simply slide the ledger card underneath the first receipt. Care must be taken to line up the vertical lines on the ledger card with those on the receipt form as well as to line up the column headings of the card over the journal form. With a little patience and practice, one should be able to line up the ledger card underneath the receipt form and over the journal form so that the correct writing line is automatically viewed. See Figure 7-36.

With the above knowledge of how the forms are collated and assembled, you are now ready to analyze the accounts receivable transactions that follow.

COMMON TRANSACTIONS ANALYZED To illustrate the analysis of two common accounts receivable transactions for a dental practice, a hypothetical family by the name of Howard, of Any Street and Any Town, Canada, will be used. First, assume that a patient's ledger card has been prepared for Mr. M. Howard and his family. In practice, the card would be printed, handwritten, or typewritten in the main identification section of the card. Of course, other information may be entered on the card such as the family's home telephone number, and their dental insurance policy and certificate numbers if such are applicable.

Transaction 1. Entering the Zero Balance for a New Patient Suppose Mrs. Howard arrived at Dr. Wong's office in response to an earlier dental appointment. Suppose further that Mrs. Howard is the first member

FIGURE 7-36

FIGURE 7-37

of the Howard family to be treated. Since Mrs. Howard is a new patient, the first entry which must be made by the front office person, usually the receptionist, is to record a zero balance on the stub portion of the receipt form. Assume, first of all, that the receptionist has collated correctly the one-write forms at the beginning of the day. At the beginning of the new day, therefore, a new journal sheet is positioned over the board, then a new set of shingled receipt forms. The patient's ledger card is not used to enter the zero balance; consequently, the ledger card is not inserted between the top receipt form and carbon sheet at this time. Only the stub portion of the receipt form is used to enter the zero balance as illustrated in Figure 7-37.

In some practices, the stub would be detached from the main portion of the receipt form and inserted into a pouch which also contains a dental treatment chart. The stub, together with the treatment chart, is taken to the operatory where the dentist is located. Here, the travelling stub now becomes the communication document between the front office and the operatory. Briefly, the dentist can see who is responsible for the bill, whom he is seeing today, and how much is outstanding before proceeding with additional treatment. One of the advantages of the stub can now be identified. If the stub shows a large amount above "Previous Balance," the doctor can discuss the patient's financial problem with the patient without involving the front office person.

A second advantage is the ability to use the stub as the source document from which the future accounting entry can be made. Briefly, after completing the treatment, the doctor records the services rendered and fees charged opposite the appropriate sections of the stub. In addition, the doctor can indicate approximately the time period for the next appointment. The completed stub can then be returned to the front office person for the accounts receivable entry. In the case of Mrs. Howard's treatment, the completed stub for X-rays, examination, and cleaning would look as shown in Figure 7-37.

Three points must be emphasized in the examination of the travelling stub. First, the receipt form and the detachable stub contain the same serial number. Obviously, the number of the stub must always match the main receipt (bill) form in any subsequent one-write application. Furthermore, the use of prenumbered documents supports the basic measure of controlling all cash receipt transactions. As you will recall, all firms, regardless of type, ownership, and size, should create prenumbered source documents to account for all cash transactions.

Second, note that whatever was printed at the top of the stub would also appear on the journal sheet. As you will recall, the receipt and stub form contains a top layer of carbon on the back to allow the transfer of carbon printing to the journal sheet.

And, finally, it is recognized that the travelling stub may not be detached from the main receipt (bill) form in some dental practices. Briefly, about 60% of dentists prefer to use the travelling stub concept, while 40% do not. When the stub is not detached, it remains with the main receipt form to be completed after the doctor communicates the services rendered. Obviously, dentists will modify the use of their accounts receivable application to suit their particular needs.

Transaction 2. Recording a Charge and Part Payment   In the case of Mrs. Howard, assume that the dentist has completed the stub portion as illustrated earlier. Suppose further that the stub is totalled for $70 and that the next appointment is indicated as "6 M," which means six months. (Three weeks might be written "3 WK.")

The completed stub is submitted to the front office person for proper recording. As stated earlier, the travelling stub is used as a communication document—the doctor does not have to run up to the front office to tell the receptionist how much to charge and the time of the next appointment. In addition, the stub becomes the approved source document for the accounting entry.

At the front office, the receptionist-clerk first examines the number on the travelling stub with the number on the main portion of the receipt or statement form. This check is important, because patients would necessarily return to the front office in the same order as they were admitted.

After checking the matching of numbers, the patient's ledger card is inserted under the correct receipt form and lined up with the line containing the zero balance entry. Before entering the total charge, however, the receptionist should always ask the patient: "Your bill comes to $70. Will that be cash, credit card, or cheque?" The reason for this polite request is to avoid questions which receive a negative reply. For example, if the clerk asked: "Would you like to pay your bill now?" the probable answer would be no. From the viewpoint of the dentist, some payment now is better than untimely delays which can lead to a large and troublsome outstanding amount in the future.

Suppose Mrs. Howard replies that she will pay $50 now and the balance at the end of the month. In this case, the receptionist records the entry from left to right as follows: the receipt number in the "Receipt Number" section; the current date in the "Date" column; the description code as interpreted from the standard dental codes in the receipt form section in the left side of the "Description Code" section; "Mrs." in the right side of the "Description Code" section to identify the patient; "$70" in the "Charge" column; "$50" in the "Payment" column; and "$20" in the "Current Balance" column. Figure 7-39 illustrates this entry.

The following two points should be learned in the correct analysis of the accounting entry:

- Since the one-write principle is used, it is important to be very deliberate in the writing of the complete entry, especially in the case of dollar amounts. Keep in mind that three steps are performed in one writing: the receipt or statement form, the patient's ledger card, and the combination journal. Therefore, it is essential to print legibly and large enough to see every letter and number clearly.

- An important shortcut has occurred in the correct analysis of the double entry, one that can be viewed in two separate but related entries as follows:
  - By entering the $70 in the Charge column, one acknowledges the accounting theory of debiting Accounts Receivable and crediting a revenue account such as Fees Earned. In short, the "Charge" column of the journal may be considered as the traditional revenue (fees earned) journal.
  - By entering the $50 in the Payment column, one acknowledges the accounting theory of debiting Cash and crediting Accounts Receivable. The Payment column on the journal, therefore, may be considered as replacing the traditional cash receipts journal. The payment entry may be analyzed in T-account form as shown in Figure 7-40.
  - By entering the $20 in the Current Balance column, one acknowledges the accounting theory of calculating the balance of the Accounts Receivable account. In this case, Accounts Receivable has received a debit for $70 and a credit for $50. Since no previous

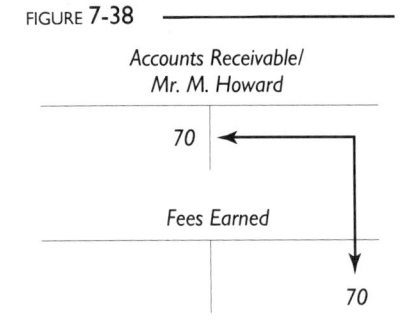

FIGURE 7-38

Accounts Receivable/
Mr. M. Howard

70

Fees Earned

70

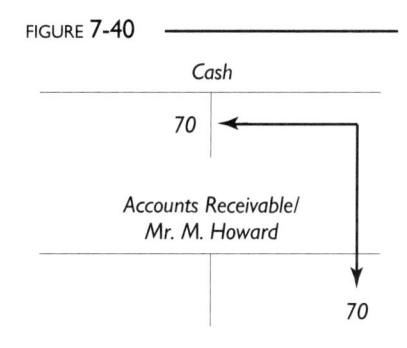

CHAPTER 7: Accounts Receivable Application

FIGURE 7-39

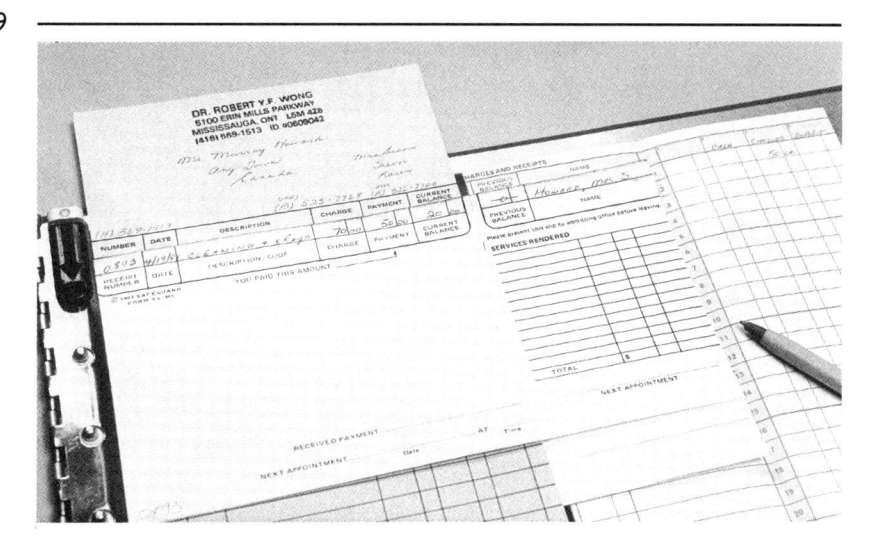

FIGURE 7-40

Cash	
70	

Accounts Receivable/ Mr. M. Howard	
	70

FIGURE 7-41

Accounts Receivable/ Mr. M. Howard			
Prev. bal.	0	Payment	50
Charge	70		
Cur. Bal.	20		

balance existed in the patient's account, it follows that the correct account balance must be the $20 recorded in the Current Balance column.

To complete the transaction with Mrs. Howard, the receipt/statement form is detached once the entry is recorded to the end of the Current Balance column. Then, with the receipt/statement form removed from the board, the receptionist records the next appointment as instructed by the doctor on the travelling stub. In this case, the appointment would be for six months from today. In addition, the surname, "Howard," is written, to identify the form for tax receipt purposes. And, finally, the clerk's initials are placed opposite "Received Payment."

The completed receipt/statement form may then be inserted into a self-addressed envelope which becomes a convenient method of returning the balance owing. Of course, the receipt/statement form shows not only what was paid, but also what is still owing on account. Consequently, by issuing both the receipt/statement form and envelope, the receptionist can emphasize that it is the policy of the office to avoid mailing duplicate statements of account at month-end. In this way, the dentist saves time and mailing costs, and also gains a positive measure of controlling accounts receivable. By giving the "customer" a statement and a self-addressed envelope, the dentist is assured, for the most part, an early remittance.

Space limitations in this edition of this text prevent the analysis of other common transactions such as recording only a charge, or a payment; uncommon transactions such as accounting for patient overpayments, NSF cheques, a write-off entry, or a bad debt recovered; end-of-day procedures such as the daily balancing and proof of posting, proving the accounts receivable control, and proving the daily cash; and monthly procedures such as reconciling accounts receivable control and aging the accounts receivable. However, with the introduction given here, you should now be aware of the following four advantages of the one-write system when applied to dental practices:

- The accounting clerk, in one writing, creates the receipt or statement form, the posting to the Accounts Receivable subsidiary ledger account (the patient's card), and the journal entry on the combination journal.
- Posting is performed automatically to the patient's account. Provided that the entry is recorded correctly, no possible error can occur on the ledger card. This feature is contrasted with the traditional bookkeeping method of posting from the journal or source document to the customer's account. As you may recall, errors are always possible when copying information from one source to another.
- The use of the family ledger card concept contains the financial profile of the family. As suggested earlier, the ledger card contains information not only on each individual family member's services, but also on the balance owing by the total family. In this way, both the doctor and the responsible family head know at a glance how much is owing in total rather than having to refer to several individual cards.
- The use of the combination journal eliminates the need for recording separate entries in a fees earned journal and cash receipts journal. As you will recall, an entry in the Charges column supports the theory of recording accounts receivable and fees earned; therefore, the Charges column in the journal may be regarded as the theoretical revenue journal. Similarly, an entry in the Payments column supports the theory of recording cash and accounts receivable; therefore, the Payments column in the journal may be regarded as the theoretical cash receipts journal.

TOPIC 3 Problems

Answering questions on journalizing batch totals and direct posting to accounts receivables.

7.11 Answer the following questions about the procedure for processing credit sales when a system of journalized batch totals and direct posting are used. (Refer to Figures 7-31 to 7-34.)

    a How many copies of each sales invoice are required for this system?
    b What is done with the original copy of the invoice?
    c What is a batch of sales invoices?
    d Why are the second copies sorted in numerical order?
    e Why are the batched invoices listed and totalled on an adding machine tape?
    f Briefly explain the procedure in journalizing the batch total in the sales journal.
    g What amount is posted to the general ledger?

h What is done with copy 3 of each sales invoice?
i What is a pre-list, and why is one prepared?
j Briefly explain the procedure for posting source documents directly to the accounts receivable ledger.
k What is a proof tape, and why is one prepared?
l What is done with copy 3 of the sales invoices after direct posting has been completed?

Answering questions on journalless bookkeeping.

7.12 Answer the following questions about the procedure for processing credit sales without the use of a formal journal. (Refer to Figure 7-34.)
   a How many copies of the sales invoice are required under this system of journalless bookkeeping?
   b What is done with copy 1 of the invoice?
   c Explain the procedure for processing copy 2 of the invoice.
   d In a journalless bookkeeping system for processing credit sales, what takes the place of the sales journal?
   e What is the source document medium for posting the monthly credit sales to the general ledger?
   f Explain the procedure for processing copy 3 of the invoice.

Answering questions on ledgerless bookkeeping.

7.13 Answer the following questions about the procedure for processing credit sales without the use of a formal accounts receivable ledger.
   a What is meant by ledgerless bookkeeping when it is used by businesses to process their accounts receivable?
   b Is the general ledger eliminated in a ledgerless system? Explain why or why not.
   c Distinguish between the open-item system and the balance-forward system of accounting for individual customer accounts. Which is used in a ledgerless bookkeeping system? Explain your answer.
   d Briefly explain two advantages claimed under a ledgerless bookkeeping system.
   e Briefly explain five weaknesses that may be identified under a system of ledgerless bookkeeping.

Answering questions on one-write bookkeeping.

7.14 Answer the following questions about the processing of accounts receivable on the Safeguard one-write system.
   a In what order should the accounting forms that comprise the accounting set for processing a dental fee be placed on the writing board?
   b Is the patient's ledger card placed on the accounting board at the time the stub portion of the receipt/statement form is prepared? Explain why or why not.
   c Briefly explain how the one-write principle is applied on the Safeguard one-write board.

Applying basic transactions to a one-write accounts receivable application for a dental practice.

7.15 Assume that you have been engaged as the receptionist-clerk for the dental office of Penny Thornton, D.D.S., of your town/city and province. Assume further that the dental office uses the Safeguard one-write system. The transactions below are related to a new patient's family, Mr. D. Gray. Perform activities that are offered for each.

- **a** From the following data, set up a new patient's family ledger card: principal family member, Mr. D. Gray; address, your town/city and province; telephone number, 471-4113; other family members, Mrs. and a daughter, Barbara.
- **b** Assume that Mrs. Gray arrived at Dr. Thornton's office on May 1, current year, in response to an earlier dental appointment. Set up a zero balance on the stub portion of a receipt/statement form similar to the one illustrated in this chapter.
- **c** Assume that the dentist has entered the following information on the travelling stub: examination, $18; X-rays, $30; cleaning, $30; next appointment, 6 M. Assume further that you have placed the required forms in their correct writing position on the Safeguard one-write board, and that Mrs. Gray will pay half of the bill today. Record the dollar results of the transaction on the receipt/statement form used in **b** above.
- **d** Assume that the receipt/statement form has been removed from the Safeguard one-write board. Show how the receipt/statement form would be receipted, and indicate the next appointment for a date in accordance with the dentist's requests.
- **e** Show how the entry would appear on the ledger card used in **a** above.
- **f** Analyze the entry made in **e** above in T-account form.

Note: Save your solutions for use in the next problem.

Completing Problem 7.15.

7.16 Use the solutions for Problem 7.15 to continue the dental transactions as they affect the Gray family to the end of May.

- **May 12** Assume that Barbara Gray received the following dental treatment: examination, $18; filling, $54. Next appointment, 3 WK. No payment is received.
- **May 25** Assume that Mr. Gray received the following services: X-rays, $30; examination, $18; cleaning, $30. Next appointment, 2 WK 1/2; Mr. Gray stated that he would mail a cheque at the end of the month for the total amount owing on his family's account.
- **May 31** Received a cheque for $159 from Mr. D. Gray in full payment of his family's account.

Required
- **a** Record the dollar results of each transaction on separate receipt/statement/stub forms. Where applicable, show how the travelling stub would appear as having been completed by the doctor in the operatory.
- **b** Show how the ledger card would appear posted for all transactions to the end of May. What balance should appear in the account as of May 31? How would this balance be indicated?

Chapter Summary

In practice, accounting is divided into specialized areas called *applications*. Common accounting applications are the general ledger, accounts receivable, accounts payable, and payroll. The accounts receivable application involves all activities related to the accounting of customer accounts.

All accounts receivable applications begin with the origination of source documents. Common source documents are bills of sale (invoice), credit memos to acknowledge customer returns and other adjustments, and receipts or similar documents to acknowledge customer remittances.

Under the traditional manual system, sales invoices are usually recorded in a book of original entry called the "sales journal." In practice, this special journal contains special money columns to facilitate the future posting of monthly totals to the general ledger. For example, a three-column sales journal may contain money columns as follows: Accounts Receivable debit, Provincial Sales Tax Payable credit, and Sales credit.

Merchandising firms will design sales journals to suit their particular needs for accounting information. For service firms, the traditional sales journal would be called the "fees earned journal." Again, special money columns would be used to meet the needs of different service firms.

Posting from the sales journal occurs at two time intervals. First, posting to individual customer accounts, filed in a subsidiary ledger called the "Accounts Receivable Ledger," is done on a daily basis. At month-end, the money columns are totalled, proved as to their equality for debits and credits, and posted to appropriate accounts in the general ledger.

Also, at month-end, two trial balances are usually prepared. One is the familiar trial balance of general ledger accounts. The second is a schedule listing all individual customer accounts with month-end balances. The total of the schedule of accounts receivable must agree with the balance reported by the Accounts Receivable controlling account in the general ledger.

A second important aspect of any accounts receivable application is the control and accounting of cash receipts. In general, all well-managed businesses adopt measures to control cash flowing into the business. One important internal control measure is to prepare a source document for every cash receipt item. A second measure is to deposit all cash receipts *intact* into the firm's chequing (current) account at the bank.

Under a manual system, cash receipts are usually recorded in a special journal called the "cash receipts journal." Again, special money columns may be used to account for the most frequent aspects of cash receipts transactions. Postings from this special journal occur at time intervals similar to those described for the sales journal.

Businesses with numerous accounts receivable usually mail out monthly statements of account. One type of statement is *non-descriptive*, simply reporting the balance owing on account. Another is *descriptive*, showing the details of each transaction for the month. A third type, known as the *aged statement*, reports amounts owing according to groupings or categories such as current, past due from 1 to 30 days, past due from 31 to 60 days, etc. Businesses with large numbers of customer accounts prepare customer statements under a cycle billing system, whereby customers are put in alphabetical groups each of which is billed on a certain day of the month.

Businesses using a manual accounting system for their accounts receivable application may adopt a number of shortcuts. Among those in common usage are the journalizing of batch totals and direct postings to accounts receivable, journalless bookkeeping, ledgerless bookkeeping, and the one-write system. Of these, the one-write system is considered to be the most successful, because it offers advantages such as reducing record-keeping time and cost by up to 75%, eliminating errors in transferring figures, and keeping all records up to date and in balance.

Chapter Questions

1. What is the underlying principle in the design of any special journal? What advantages are offered by the use of special journals?
2. List and explain the advantages of a special sales journal. Describe the procedure in posting from the sales journal.
3. Use an example to explain how a controlling account actually "controls."
4. Briefly describe what duties may be performed by an accounts receivable clerk in the accounts receivable department of a large firm.
5. Explain how an accounting system is assured of an important internal control measure by the preparation of separate trial balances of the general ledger and the accounts receivable ledger at the end of each month.
6. A sale on credit to the Jay Stores was journalized correctly as $89. The amount, however, was posted as $98 in the customer's account. When should this error be discovered? How might the customer detect the error?
7. When a retail sales tax is collected from a customer, why is it credited to a current liability account?
8. At what point in the growth of a business must an owner-manager introduce a strong system of controlling cash? Explain your answer.
9. Mention five measures to be observed by a business in establishing a strong system of controlling cash receipts.
10. Give five reasons why businesses use a bank current account.
11. What is meant by the internal control principle, "all cash receipts should be deposited intact"?

12. Why should all cash receipts be deposited intact on the day of receipt?
13. Explain why the function of handling an asset should be separated from the function of recording it in most businesses.
14. How may cash be received by a business?
15. Name three forms of accounting documents that may be used by a business to capture the transaction of receiving cash in person.
16. Name two measures that should be used to control cash received by mail.
17. Why are prenumbered source documents used to record cash receipts?
18. Name six measures to control all cash receipts for bank deposits.
19. Explain the ways in which the use of a cash receipts journal simplifies the journalizing and posting of cash receipts.
20. Describe the procedure followed in posting the individual amounts and the totals in a four-column cash receipts journal.
21. What are the main advantages of journalizing batch totals and direct posting to customer accounts in the accounts receivable application?
22. To what types of business is a ledgerless bookkeeping system suited? Unsuited? Why?
23. Give the main advantages and disadvantages of a journalless bookkeeping system.
24. State the main advantages and disadvantages of a ledgerless bookkeeping system.
25. List the components that make up the accounts receivable one-write system treated in this chapter; then offer a brief explanation of the main function of each.
26. Explain briefly what is meant by the one-write principle.
27. Is a pencil recommended for use in recording transactions in one-write applications like accounts receivable? Explain why or why not.
28. Why are accounting one-write boards also called pegboards?
29. As compared with conventional manual bookkeeping procedures, identify the shortcuts in the Safeguard one-write application for accounts receivable.
30. Explain the use of the "travelling stub" concept in the accounts receivable application for a dental practice.
31. The text stated that the record of charges and receipts sheet used in dental practices is actually a combination journal. Use two examples to explain how this sheet becomes a combination journal.
32. Why is a family ledger card to be preferred to the individual ledger card in dental practices?
33. Outline four advantages of the one-write system as it may be applied to a variety of small businesses. Are there any disadvantages? Explain your answer.

Accounting Case Problems

CASE 7-1

Analyzing a simple case of "lapping" accounts receivable.

A cashier in a large enterprise is also permitted to post information to various accounts receivable accounts. A customer named Charlie Brown sends in a remittance of $100 to be credited to his account. However, the funds are cashed by the cashier and wrongfully diverted—in other words, the cashier keeps the $100 instead of crediting the account.

The cashier receives a second $100 remittance later from a customer named Charles Sanderson. To overcome the discrepancy in Brown's account, the cashier posts the $100 credit to Brown and not to Sanderson. Still later, a third customer's remittance is posted to Sanderson's account. Once again, the credit to the proper account is not made but, in fact, delayed. The cashier feels quite safe in following this "lapping" practice, because the majority of customers do not pay very strict attention to their accounts.

    a In simple terms, what has the cashier done?

    b Suggest at least two measures that would help to control this practice.

CASE 7-2

Analyzing one dental clerk's method of charging a patient for services rendered and of recording the charge.

Mary X is employed as a receptionist-clerk in the Town Centre Dental Office. Among other duties, Mary is required to bill patients and to record accounts receivable transactions on a one-write system.

On one particular morning, a new patient, John Blinkhorn, was treated for a checkup and cleaning. After the dental service, Mary X received the "Services Rendered" portion of the stub, initialled by the doctor, with the following information: examination, $18; X-rays, $34; cleaning, $30. Mary then approached the new patient as follows:

"Your total bill comes to $72. Will that be cash, credit card, or charge?"

Mr. Blinkhorn replied: "I'm sorry, but all I have is $20. Can I pay you at the end of the next month?"

Mary smiled and then answered: "Yes, that's fine. I'll write out the receipt for a complete charge."

With that reply, Mary entered a receipt number, the date, description codes, and, in the Charge column, "$72." She then removed the main receipt portion and handed it to the patient with this final statement: "Here is your bill. Please send a cheque by the end of next month. Goodbye for now."

    a Did the clerk record the dollar results of the transaction correctly? Explain why or why not.

    b Given the same situation, how would you have handled the delicate part of billing the patient? Give reasons for your views.

CHAPTER **8 Accounts Payable Application**

After completing this chapter, you should be able to:

— Record selected transactions in a one-column purchases journal; post to appropriate ledger accounts; and prepare a schedule of accounts payable and the G/L trial balance.

— Record selected accounts payable transactions in a multi-column purchases journal and general journal; post the recorded entries to appropriate ledgers; and prepare appropriate trial balances for the accounts payable application.

— Record petty cash and non–petty cash expenditures in the petty cash book and general journal.

— Record selected account payable transactions in a one-column purchases journal, a four-column cash payments journal or a general journal; post the recorded entries to the ledgers; prepare month-end trial balances; and report the cash position in a partial balance sheet.

— Answer selected questions on the journalizing of batch totals and direct postings in an accounts payable application.

— Answer selected questions on journalless bookkeeping in an accounts payable application.

— Answer selected questions on the combination journal.

— Answer selected questions on the one-write system to process the accounts payable application.

— Define the following key terms used in this chapter: purchases journal; accounts payable ledger; schedule of accounts payable; drawer (of cheque); payee (of cheque); cash payments journal; cash short and over account; petty cash system; petty cash voucher; replenishing petty cash; imprest system of petty cash; combination (synoptic) journal; cash disbursements journal.

As one would expect, the accounts payable application in its most simplified form supports the details pertaining to the accounting of two related transactions: the purchase of assets or services on credit and the cash payment to creditors to eliminate the accounts payable. In practice, many firms do transact their "purchases" on credit; however, where businesses acquire assets or services by paying cash, it follows that their "accounts payable application" would naturally be confined to the accounting of cash payments.

From Part 1, you learned that the general ledger application of the above transactions consisted of a variety of entries. For example, a purchase of merchandise on credit was accounted for by debiting Purchases (under a periodic inventory method) or Inventory (under a perpetual inventory method) and crediting Accounts Payable. If the purchase was made to acquire a fixed asset such as a typewriter, then an account like Office Equipment was debited, and Accounts Payable was credited. On the other hand, if the firm purchased services on credit, as for example by receiving a bill for advertising to be paid within 30 days, then a debit was made to Advertising Expense, while a credit was identified to Accounts Payable. In all of these credit transactions, the liability was eliminated by the future cash payment which debited Accounts Payable and credited Cash.

Of course, when the purchase of assets or services was made for cash, an appropriate account was debited while Cash was credited. At the end of the accounting period, therefore, the general ledger supplied the information for reporting the balance of Cash, other assets acquired, and Accounts Payable in the balance sheet. Similarly, the general ledger provided the data to report Purchases (as part of Cost of Goods Sold) and other expenses in the income statement.

In treating the accounts payable application, however, accounting is concerned mainly with specific details related to individual creditors and individual cash payments to such creditors. As would be expected, profit-seeking businesses in practice will design accounts payable systems and procedures in keeping with their needs and costs. For example, large firms commonly organize a separate department called the "Accounts Payable Department" just to handle the accounting of accounts payable. Within such a department, accounting will use specialized accountants and clerks, specialized source documents, specialized journals and ledgers, specialized trial balances, and probably large computer systems to process the firm's individual accounts payable and cash payments. On the other hand, a small business would probably not have a separate accounts payable department; would probably use fewer specialized forms; and would probably employ a general clerk who might take advantage of shortcuts under the manual method, or a microcomputer system with appropriate software to account for individual creditor transactions. Since an entire text of considerable length could be written to present the details of accounts payable applications for large and small firms, this chapter limits the study to those basic concepts that may be applied to all profit-seeking enterprises. To simplify the presentation, only the manual method will be presented. Using microcomputer software to process the accounts payable application will be examined in Chapter 11.

TOPIC 1 Special Journals and Ledgers

In accounting for specific details related to accounts payable and cash payments, many firms use special journal and special ledgers to account for such transactions. This Topic will examine the traditional journalizing and posting procedures for credit "purchases" only; cash "purchases" and other cash disbursements are better treated under the procedures for journalizing and posting of cash payments (Topic 2 of this chapter). Also, the new federal GST has been eliminated from transactions, since it is treated in the Appendix section of the text. To illustrate the accounts payable application related to credit "purchases" only, consider the use of the special journals and special ledger in the two cases that follow.

Case 1. The One-Column Purchases Journal

At this stage in your learning of accounting, you should have little difficulty in understanding the need for a special journal to record a highly repetitive transaction such as purchasing, on credit, merchandise for resale. Obviously, a **purchases journal** is no different from ones earlier presented to credit sales and cash receipts.

Purchases journal: a chronological record of purchases on credit.

In practice, an accounting system for a merchandising business will design a purchases journal to suit the particular needs of that firm. To simplify the presentation of a basic purchases journal and its posting for a business using the periodic inventory system, Figure 8-1 shows only a few credit purchases recorded in a one-column purchases journal. Examine the figure closely. Observe that the one-column purchases journal is very similar to the one-column sales journal introduced in the last chapter, and that the two journals operate in the same manner.

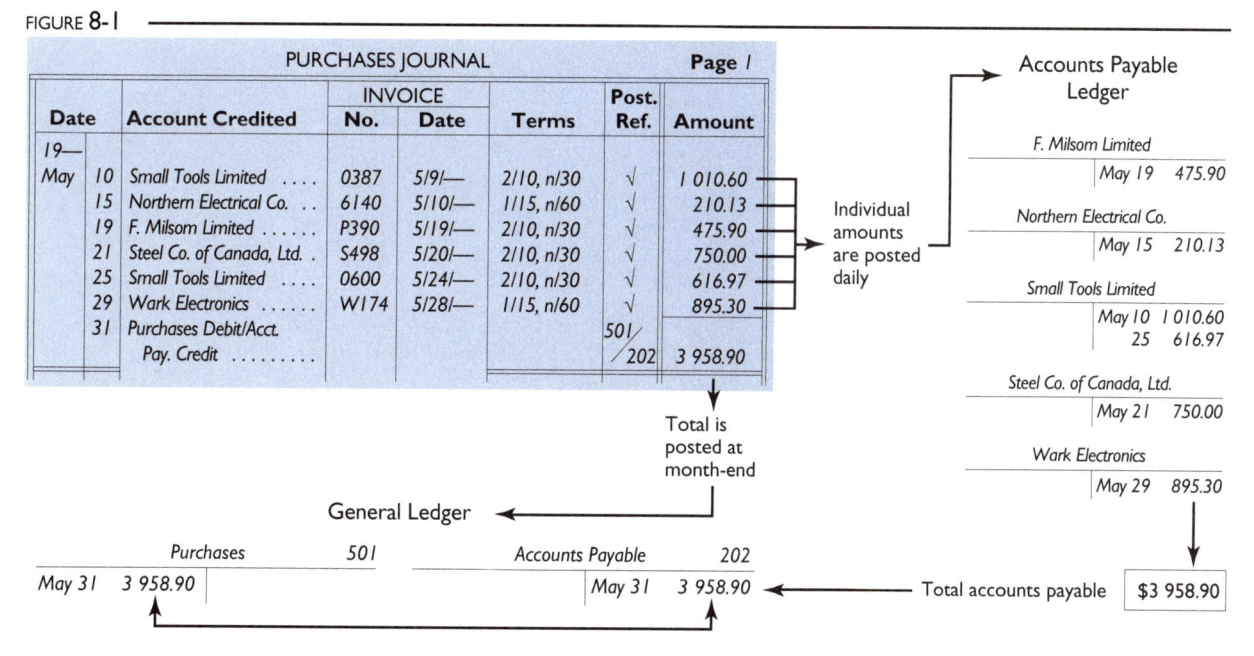

FIGURE 8-1

PURCHASES JOURNAL						Page 1
		INVOICE			Post.	
Date	Account Credited	No.	Date	Terms	Ref.	Amount
19—						
May 10	Small Tools Limited	0387	5/9/—	2/10, n/30	✓	1 010.60
15	Northern Electrical Co.	6140	5/10/—	1/15, n/60	✓	210.13
19	F. Milsom Limited	P390	5/19/—	2/10, n/30	✓	475.90
21	Steel Co. of Canada, Ltd.	S498	5/20/—	2/10, n/30	✓	750.00
25	Small Tools Limited	0600	5/24/—	2/10, n/30	✓	616.97
29	Wark Electronics	W174	5/28/—	1/15, n/60	✓	895.30
31	Purchases Debit/Acct. Pay. Credit				501/ 202	3 958.90

Individual amounts are posted daily

Total is posted at month-end

Accounts Payable Ledger

F. Milsom Limited
| May 19 | 475.90 |

Northern Electrical Co.
| May 15 | 210.13 |

Small Tools Limited
| May 10 | 1 010.60 |
| 25 | 616.97 |

Steel Co. of Canada, Ltd.
| May 21 | 750.00 |

Wark Electronics
| May 29 | 895.30 |

General Ledger

Purchases	501
May 31 3 958.90	

Accounts Payable	202
	May 31 3 958.90

Total accounts payable $3 958.90

Analysis The following points should be recalled as you analyze the illustrated purchases journal and its related posting.

- In the one-column purchases journal, notice that only purchases of merchandise on credit are recorded. Consider now this question: In what journal would one record the purchase (acquisition) on credit of assets such as a delivery truck or an office desk? The answer must be the general journal, because, under a one-column purchases journal, the total of the one money column must be posted to the debit of the Purchases account and not to an account like Delivery Truck or any other asset account.
- Observe that the purchases journal contains two Date columns. The first records the date on which the accounting department receives the approved purchase invoice from the purchasing department or appropriate officer. Check Figure 8-2, which shows the approved purchase invoice from Small Tools Limited. Notice that the approved purchase invoice date is the same as the one used for the

FIGURE 8-2

Small Tools Limited
229 Kearney Sreet
Winnipeg, Manitoba R2M 4B5   Invoice No. **0387**

Sold To: Scarborough Wholesale Hardware
         330 Progress Avenue
         Scarborough, Ontario M1P 2Z5

Ship To: Same as above   Invoice Date: 19— 05 09
                                          Terms: 2/10, n/30

Purchase Order No. PO-0078	Date 19— 05 03	Shipped Via Inter-City Express	FOB Winnipeg	No. of Cartons 3
QUANTITY	STOCK NO.	DESCRIPTION	UNIT PRICE	AMOUNT
90 sets	53Y5197	Wrench Set	2.59	233.10
80 sets	53Y1883	Socket Wrench Set	4.25	340.00
50 only	53-R1650	Tool Boxes	8.75	437.50
		TOTAL AMOUNT PAYABLE		1 010.60

APPROVED DATE 5/10
QUANTITIES RECEIVED G Morrison
PRICES CHARGED G Morrison
EXTENSIONS & TOTALS S Davies
DATE PAID
CHEQUE NO.

transaction date in the purchases journal. The second Date column, which appears under the heading "Invoice," shows the actual date of the purchase invoice.

- As with accounts receivable, notice that the individual amounts are posted daily to a subsidiary ledger. In this case, the subsidiary ledger consists of individual creditor (vendor) accounts; therefore, the subsidiary ledger is called, appropriately, the **accounts payable ledger**. Of course, a controlling account known as Accounts Payable must be filed in the general ledger in order to receive in total form all dollar amounts posted to the individual creditor accounts.

- When posting is performed to individual creditor (vendor) accounts, it is common practice to record the purchase invoice number in addition to the usual information. The reason is simply to provide more information about the nature of the liability incurred by the business. For example, the individual account for Small Tools Limited would disclose two invoices as shown in Figure 8-3.

Accounts payable ledger: the file of all individual creditor (vendor) accounts.

FIGURE 8-3

| Name | Small Tools Limited |
| Address | 229 Kearney Street, Winnipeg, Manitoba R2M 4B5 |

Date	Explanation	Post. Ref.	Debit	Credit	Balance
19—					
May 10	Inv. 0387	P1		1 010 60	1 010 60
25	Inv. 0600	P1		616 97	1 627 57

- As Figure 8-1 clearly shows, the total of the one-money-column journal is posted at the end of the month to the general ledger as a double entry: the debit goes to the Purchases account (assuming that the periodic inventory method is used), while the credit must be shown in the Accounts Payable controlling account. Do not forget that the general ledger supplies the data for the subsequent preparation of the financial statements. As explained in earlier chapters, the Purchases account is used to determine the cost of goods sold in the income statement. Of course, the Accounts Payable controlling account will supply the data for the current liability in the balance sheet.

- And finally, notice that the total of the individual creditor accounts at the end of the month must agree with the balance shown by the Accounts Payable controlling account in the general ledger. This concept would suggest that an accounts payable clerk would prepare at the end of each month a **schedule of accounts payable** similar to the one explained previously for accounts receivable. Of course, preparing such a schedule must be considered an important internal

Schedule of accounts payable: a list of all creditor (vendor) account balances, the total of which must agree with the controlling account balance in the G/L.

control procedure, for the total of the schedule must agree with the controlling account balance in the G/L. In this sense, preparing a schedule of accounts payable is a form of trial balance. If no further entries were recorded for the various creditors listed in the illustrated purchases journal, the schedule of accounts payable would appear as shown in Figure 8-4.

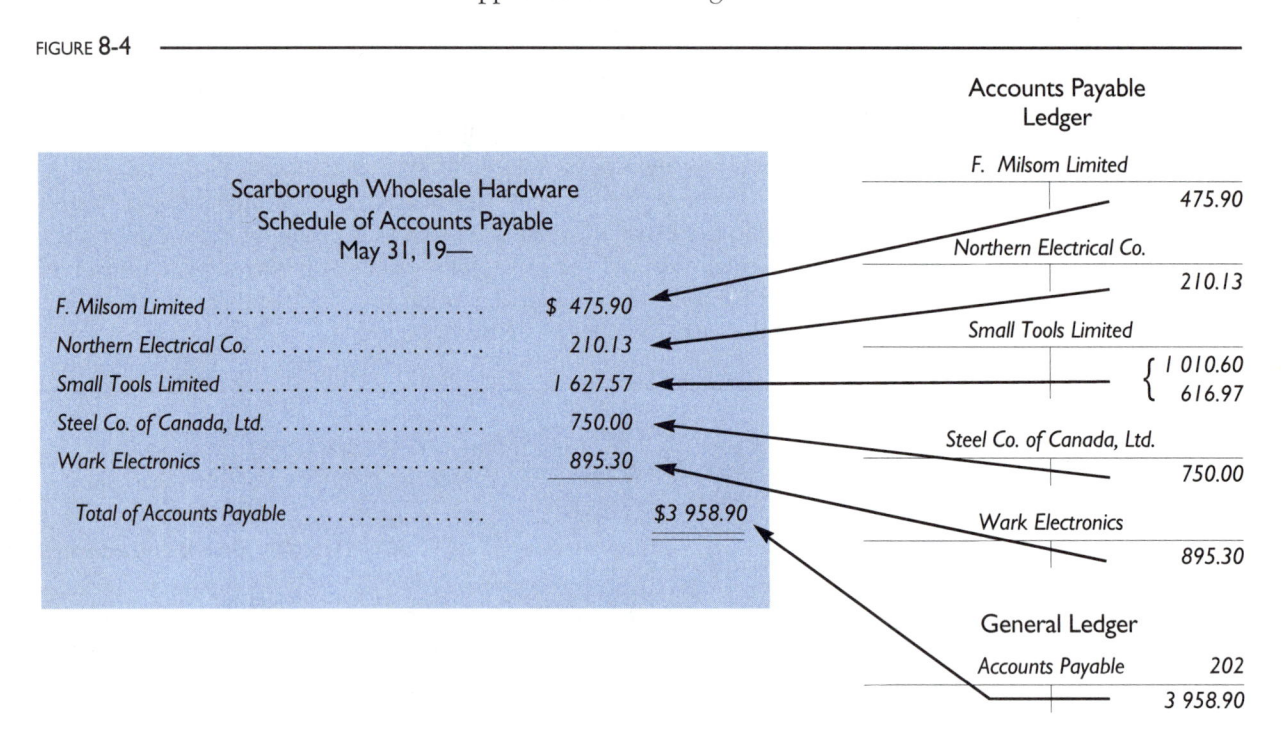

FIGURE 8-4

Scarborough Wholesale Hardware
Schedule of Accounts Payable
May 31, 19—

F. Milsom Limited	$ 475.90
Northern Electrical Co.	210.13
Small Tools Limited	1 627.57
Steel Co. of Canada, Ltd.	750.00
Wark Electronics	895.30
Total of Accounts Payable	$3 958.90

Accounts Payable Ledger

F. Milsom Limited
475.90

Northern Electrical Co.
210.13

Small Tools Limited
{ 1 010.60
  616.97

Steel Co. of Canada, Ltd.
750.00

Wark Electronics
895.30

General Ledger

Accounts Payable   202
                     3 958.90

Case 2.
The Multi-Column
Purchases Journal

As in the case of the one-column sales journal, a one-column purchases journal rarely exists in modern accounting practice. Some business managers insist on having the costs of purchases broken down for each main class of merchandise. In addition, many of the costs and expenses incurred by a merchandising firm (and other types of firms) affect accounts payable. For these reasons, a multi-column (columnar) purchases journal similar to the one illustrated for Scarborough Wholesale Hardware in Figure 8-5 has been found useful by many merchandising firms.

Analysis   From the illustration, notice that all recorded transactions have one thing in common: they affect one account—a credit to Accounts Payable. A columnar purchases journal, therefore, may be regarded as a special journal to record all transactions that affect accounts payable. In this context, therefore, the multi-column purchases journal is really an accounts payable journal.

FIGURE 8-5

COLUMNAR PURCHASES JOURNAL — Page 1

Date	Account Credited	Invoice No.	Invoice Date	Terms	Post. Ref.	Accounts Payable Cr.	Purchases Hardware Dr.	Purchases Electrical Dr.	Account Debited	Post. Ref.	Amount Dr.
19— May 2	Bell Canada	81390	5/1/—	Net 30 days	✓	17 05			Telephone Expense	515	17 05
10	Small Tools Limited	0387	5/9/—	2/10, n/30	✓	1 010 60	1 010 60				
10	Inter-City Express Ltd.	4187	5/10/—	Net 30 days	✓	24 15			Hardware Transp.-in	503	24 15
15	Northern Electrical Co.	6140	5/10/—	1/15, n/60	✓	210 13		210 13			
16	Public Utilities Co.	4X20	5/16/—	Net 10 days	✓	45 80			Utilities Expense	516	45 80
19	F. Milsom Limited	P390	5/19/—	2/10, n/30	✓	475 90	200 00	275 90			
21	Steel Co. of Canada, Ltd.	S498	5/20/—	2/10, n/30	✓	750 00	750 00				
25	Small Tools Limited	0600	5/24/—	2/10, n/30	✓	616 97	616 97				
29	Wark Electronics	W174	5/28/—	1/15, n/60	✓	895 30		895 30			
30	Craig Motors, Ltd.	X200	5/28/—	Net 60 days	✓	5 000 00			Delivery Equipment	112	5 000 00
31	Totals					9 045 90	2 577 57	1 381 33			5 087 00
						(202)	(501)	(502)			(✓)

FIGURE 8-6

Columnar Purchases Journal Proof

Hardware Purchases Dr. $2 577.57
Electrical Purchases Dr. 1 381.33
Sundries Dr. 5 087.00
Accounts Payable Cr. $9 045.90

When a multi-column purchases journal is used, observe that the individual debit money columns must add up to the total of the Accounts Payable credit money column as shown in the side margin. This proof of the debit and credit money columns must be made before the totals are posted to the G/L. And, finally, notice that the additional money columns allow the accounting system to provide management with a breakdown of purchases according to the merchandising departments established by the business.

Recording Purchases Returns and Allowances

As explained in Chapters 4 and 5, the buyer of merchandise may find it necessary to return goods because some were of the wrong kind or damaged. In some cases, the buyer may keep the damaged goods but ask for an allowance off the purchase price. Or, when verifying the receipt of the purchase invoice, a mathematical error charging the buyer too much may be discovered. And, finally, a shortage of goods received may be noted when a comparison is made with the purchase order and the invoice. As you will recall, in such cases many merchandising firms ask for an adjustment by sending a debit memo to the seller. Check back to Topic 1 of Chapter 5 for a review and illustration of a debit memo.

At least two copies of the debit memo would ordinarily be prepared. The original is mailed to the seller, while a copy goes to accounting to record the dollar results of the transaction. Since a special journal is hardly justified for the few returns and allowances that occur during the month, the double entry may be recorded in the general journal as shown in Figure 8-7.

It should be evident that double-posting is required for the debit entry, since two ledgers are affected by the transaction. Also, the seller, on receiving the buyer's debit memo, will issue a credit memo to inform the

FIGURE 8-7

		GENERAL JOURNAL			Page 2
Date		Account Title and Explanation	Post. Ref.	Debit	Credit
19—May	26	Acct. Pay./Small Tools Limited .... Purchases Returns and Allowances .... Issued DM-14 for return of damaged goods.	202/√ 503	87 50	87 50

Contra accounts — Offsets

purchaser that an adjustment has been made on the seller's books. As you know from the last chapter, a credit memo on the seller's books has the effect of decreasing the accounts receivable. When an accounting entry has been made on the issued debit memo, any subsequent credit memo received is merely attached to the debit memo for verification. No additional entry is required for the credit memo.

Some firms do not issue debit memos for a return or an allowance off a purchase. Instead, these firms merely wait for the seller's copy of the credit memo to record the purchase return or allowance. Regardless of what document is used, however, the buyer's books must be adjusted to decrease the original cost of the goods.

TOPIC 1   Problems

Journalizing selected transactions in a one-column purchases journal; posting to ledger accounts; preparing a schedule of accounts payable.

8.1 The accounting department of Central Hardware Store has received the approved invoices listed below for merchandise purchased for resale. Assume that the business follows the periodic inventory method of accounting.

a Open general ledger accounts for Accounts Payable and Purchases. Assign an appropriate number to each account. Also open subsidiary ledger accounts for the following creditors: Bezaire Hardware Supply, K. S. Conrad Ltd., and Northern Electrical Supply. Allow four lines for each account.

b Journalize the following approved purchase invoices in a one-column Purchases Journal:

Sept. 3 Invoice 4876, dated August 31; from Bezaire Hardware Supply; terms 2/10, n/30; $310.

18~~10~~ Invoice 240, dated September 17; from Northern Electrical Supply; terms 1/15, n/60; $640.

22 Invoice C1098, dated September 20; from K. S. Conrad Ltd.; terms n/30; $525.

28 Invoice 4901, dated September 26; from Bezaire Hardware Supply; terms 1/10, n/30; $220.

c Check the addition, and rule the purchases journal for September.
d Post the entries from the purchases journal to the ledger accounts.
e Prepare a schedule of accounts payable.

CHAPTER 8: Accounts Payable Application **335**

Note: Save the journal and ledgers for use in Problem 8.2.

Completing Problem 8.1.

8.2 Use the purchases journal, general ledger, and accounts payable ledger from Problem 8.1 to perform the following activities.

  a Journalize the following approved purchase invoices:

  Oct. 4 Invoice 260, dated October 1; from Northern Electrical Supply; terms 1/15, n/60; $750.
   10 Invoice C1100, dated October 8; from K. S. Conrad Ltd.; terms n/30; $125.
   15 Invoice 4980, dated October 12; from Bezaire Hardware Supply; terms 1/10, n/30; $400.
   24 Invoice 300, dated October 21; from Northern Electrical Supply; terms 1/15, n/360; $320.
   26 Invoice C1170, dated October 25; from K. S. Conrad Ltd.; terms n/30; $295.
   30 Invoice 5001, dated October 28; from Bezaire Hardware Supply; terms 1/10, n/30; $398.

  b Check the addition, and rule the purchases journal for October.
  c Post the entries from the purchases journal to the ledger accounts.
  d Prepare a schedule of accounts payable.

Recording selected accounts payable transactions in a one-column purchases journal and general journal; posting entries to the ledgers; preparing trial balances.

8.3 During April the Maple Leaf Grocery Store received and issued source documents listed below.

  a Open general ledger accounts and assign appropriate numbers for Furniture, Accounts Payable, Purchases, Transportation-in, and Purchases Returns and Allowances. In the subsidiary ledger, open accounts for B. Cayen Company, CP Express, Howe's Furniture Co., J. D. Little, and Southwestern Company. Allow four lines for all accounts.

  b Record the source documents summarized below in a one-column purchases journal and a general journal.

  Apr. 2 Purchased merchandise for $1 000 from B. Cayen Company on Invoice 478, dated April 1; terms FOB destination, 1/10, n/30.
   3 Issued Debit Memo DM-10 to B. Cayen Company for $50 to cover damaged merchandise returned on Invoice 478.
   5 Purchased $1 000 merchandise from J. D. Little on Invoice L490, dated April 4; terms FOB shipping point, 2/10, n/30.
   6 Received an approved bill from CP Express for freight charges of $75 on goods received from J. D. Little. The invoice (C-620) offered terms of n/30.
   10 Purchased new office furniture for $1 400 from Howe's Furniture on Invoice 82H400, dated April 9; terms FOB destination, n/30.
   14 Purchased merchandise for $890 from Southwestern Company on Invoice 5001, dated April 12; terms FOB shipping point, 2/10, n/30.
   14 Approved Invoice CP-689 from CP Express for $58 for transportation charges on goods received from Southwestern Company; terms n/30.
   15 Issued Debit Memo DM-11 to Southwestern Company for $50 to cover damaged merchandise returned on Invoice 5001.

16 Received credit memo from Southwestern Company for $50 confirming the debit memo issued on April 15.

19 Purchased merchandise for $1 300 from B. Cayen Company on Invoice 510, dated April 18; terms FOB destination, 1/10, n/30.

22 Purchased merchandise for $1 600 from J. D. Little on Invoice L560, dated April 21; terms FOB shipping point, 2/10, n/30.

22 Approved freight bill CP-722 from CP Express for $68 for transportation charges on goods received from J. D. Little; terms n/30.

29 Purchased furniture costing $800 from Howe's Furniture on Invoice 82H450, dated April 28; terms FOB destination, n/30.

c Check the accuracy of the journals; then rule the special journal for the end of the month.

d Post the entries from the journals to the ledgers.

e Prepare a schedule of accounts payable.

f Take a trial balance of the general ledger.

Recording selected accounts payable transactions in a multi-column purchases journal and general journal; posting entries to the ledgers; preparing trial balances.

8.4 During June, Campbell's Carpet & Tile received and issued source documents listed below.

a Open general ledger accounts and assign appropriate numbers for Delivery Truck, Accounts Payable, Carpet Purchases, Tile Purchases, Carpet Transportation-in, Tile Transportation-in, Carpet Purchases Returns and Allowances, Tile Purchases Returns and Allowances, and Advertising Expense. In the subsidiary ledger, open accounts for Canadian Carpet Mills Ltd., CN Express, Celanese Carpets Limited, City Motors Limited, The Daily Herald, Harding Carpets Limited, Peerless Tile Limited, and Potter Tile Company. Allow four lines for all accounts.

b Record the source documents summarized below in a multi-column (columnar) purchases journal similar to the one illustrated in this chapter. Show special columns for Carpet Purchases and Tile Purchases. *Note*: Record all credits to accounts payable in this all-purpose purchases journal. Any other entries should be recorded in the general journal.

June 3 Received approved invoice from Canadian Carpet Mills Ltd. Invoice No. 6789, dated June 1; total cost of carpets, $1 200; terms FOB destination, 1/15, n/60.

4 Purchased tile from Peerless Tile Limited on their approved Invoice No. 74P67, dated June 2; ~~total cost of tile, $600~~; total cost of tile, $600; terms FOB shipping point, 2/10, n/30.

4 Approved freight bill from CN Express (CN-400), dated June 4, for delivery of tile shipped from Peerless Tile Limited. Total freight cost was $75; terms n/30 days.

7 Acquired delivery truck from City Motors Limited on their Invoice No. 2109, dated June 7, for $14 800. Terms net 30 days.

11 Purchased carpets costing $2 400 from Harding Carpets Limited. Approved their Invoice No. H-4398, dated June 9, with terms FOB shipping point, 2/10, n/30.

CHAPTER 8: Accounts Payable Application **337**

11 Invoice No. CN-415 from CN Express, dated June 11, approved for $140 for delivery of carpet shipment from Harding Carpets Limited. Terms given were net 30 days.
12 Issued Debit Memo DM-30 to Harding Carpets Limited for $150 to cover return of wrong quality of carpet roll received on Invoice No. H-4398.
14 Received credit memo from Harding Carpets Limited for $150 in confirmation of the debit memo issued on June 12.
18 Purchased tile from Potter Tile Company on their approved Invoice No. 432, dated June 17. Total cost of tile, $760. Terms FOB destination, 1/15, n/60.
19 Issued Debit Memo DM-31 to Potter Tile Company for $50 to cover return of damaged tile received on Invoice No. 432.
20 Received invoice from The Daily Herald, Invoice DH-1070, dated June 19, for advertisements carried for three days. Total cost, $670. *[Terms of net 30 days]*
22 Received credit memo from Potter Tile Company for $50 in confirmation of the debit memo issued on June 19.
28 Received approved Invoice CC-7789, dated June 26, from Celanese Carpets. Total approved bill, $1 870. Terms FOB shipping point, 2/10, n/30.
29 Received approved Invoice CN-480 from CN Express, dated June 28, for $125 for delivery of carpet shipment from Celanese Carpets Limited on Invoice CC-7789. Terms net 30 days.

c Check the accuracy of the multi-column purchases journal; then rule the special journal for the month-end.
d Post the entries from the journals to the ledgers.
e Prepare a schedule of accounts payable.
f Prepare a trial balance of the general ledger.

Restating the transactions in Problem 8.4 for the perpetual inventory method of accounting.

8.5 Return to **b** of Problem 8.4.
a Using a general journal only, journalize all transactions on the assumption that Campbell's Carpet & Tile supports the perpetual inventory method of accounting.
b Show the column headings that would be suitable for Campbell's Carpet & Tile when a perpetual inventory method is followed to record all "purchases" on credit in a columnar purchases journal.

TOPIC 2 Controlling and Accounting of Cash Payments

All businesses will require an efficient system for controlling the outflow of cash. In general, such a system must include measures for controlling the handling of cash payments as well as controlling the recording of cash payments. And, in addition, many successful enterprises will provide for special measures to control minor or petty cash expenditures. This Topic examines these areas in the separate sections that follow.

Internal Control Measures for Cash Payments

In the study of the control measures given below, keep in mind that individual firms will modify or even enlarge on the procedures to suit their particular needs.

1. VERIFY AND APPROVE ALL INVOICES FOR PAYMENT

No bill (invoice) should be paid until it has been checked for two measures: (1) that the goods or services identified on the bill were actually ordered and received; and (2) that the amount of the bill has been computed accurately. To make sure that the above measure is carried out, large businesses generally require that all bills first be forwarded to their purchasing department, where the bills are checked against original purchase orders and against warehouse receiving reports to ensure that the goods ordered had arrived. Of course, in smaller businesses a general office clerk or secretary may be given this responsibility. The point to stress here is that all invoices must be verified and approved before a cash payment is made.

2. ISSUE CHEQUES FOR ALL PAYMENTS OF MATERIAL AMOUNTS

Observe that this internal control measure suggests that cheques be used for all payments of *material* amounts. In general, this means that the majority of cash payments will be made by cheque. For small amounts (minor or petty amounts) businesses use a petty cash system, but only after cheques have been issued to create and replenish the fund. Since petty cash expenditures are controlled by cheque payments, one can conclude that all cash disbursements will be made by cheque. The petty cash system is discussed later on in this Topic.

From a business viewpoint, three advantages of paying by cheque must be emphasized, of which you may already be well aware:

- Paying by cheque eliminates the need to keep large amounts of money on the business site.
- Paying by cheque provides proof of every disbursement, because the bank returns each cancelled cheque to the **drawer**.
- Paying by cheque through a bank current account automatically provides an independent accounting of every payment, because the bank furnishes a monthly bank statement on which all cheque transactions are listed.

Drawer: the person signing a cheque.

3. USE ONLY SERIALLY PRENUMBERED CHEQUES, TO PERMIT THEIR FULL ACCOUNTABILITY

Observe carefully the expression "their full accountability." This ideally means that all cheques have been specially printed and designed for the use of the business. In actual practice, banks will print a cheque form to suit the individual needs of each firm. In general, however, these cheques will be serially prenumbered and will show the name of the firm.

4. PREPARE A CHEQUE RECORD FOR EVERY ISSUED CHEQUE

This cheque record is an important accounting document, for it supplies the information upon which an accounting entry is made for every cash payment. In many enterprises, a perforated stub, known as the *cheque stub*, is used to make a permanent record of each cheque issued and to make the subsequent accounting entry to record the cash payment. In addition, the cheque stub is used by the person preparing the cheques to record amounts deposited, thus making available a running balance of cash in the bank.

FIGURE 8-8

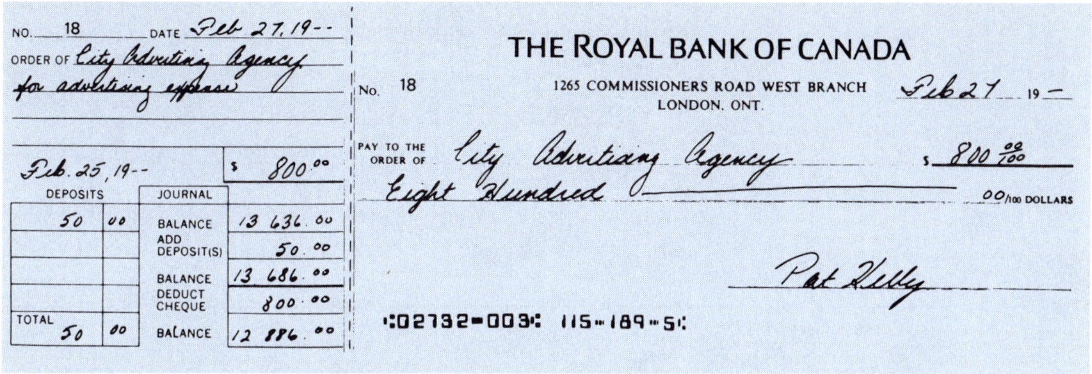
NO. 18 DATE Feb 27, 19--
ORDER OF City Advertising Agency
for advertising expense

Feb. 25, 19-- $ 800.00

DEPOSITS		JOURNAL	
50	00	BALANCE	13 636.00
		ADD DEPOSIT(S)	50.00
		BALANCE	13 686.00
		DEDUCT CHEQUE	800.00
TOTAL 50	00	BALANCE	12 886.00

THE ROYAL BANK OF CANADA
No. 18
1265 COMMISSIONERS ROAD WEST BRANCH
LONDON, ONT.
Feb 27 19--
PAY TO THE ORDER OF City Advertising Agency $ 800 00/100
Eight Hundred 00/100 DOLLARS
Pat Kelly
⑆02732⁃003⑆ 115⑈189⑈5⑆

When using a standard cheque book with a stub, it is important that the stub section be completed first; otherwise, the stub may be overlooked later and, consequently, no record of the cheque will exist once it is signed and mailed. In addition, the practice of completing the stub or cheque record first not only decreases errors when writing the cheque proper, but also allows for a cash proof before the cheque is issued.

On the other hand, some large businesses use a special cheque form, known as a *voucher cheque*. The most common type of voucher cheque has a perforated rider attached, which is removed by the recipient before the cheque is presented for payment. A typical voucher cheque is illustrated in Figure 8-9.

FIGURE 8-9

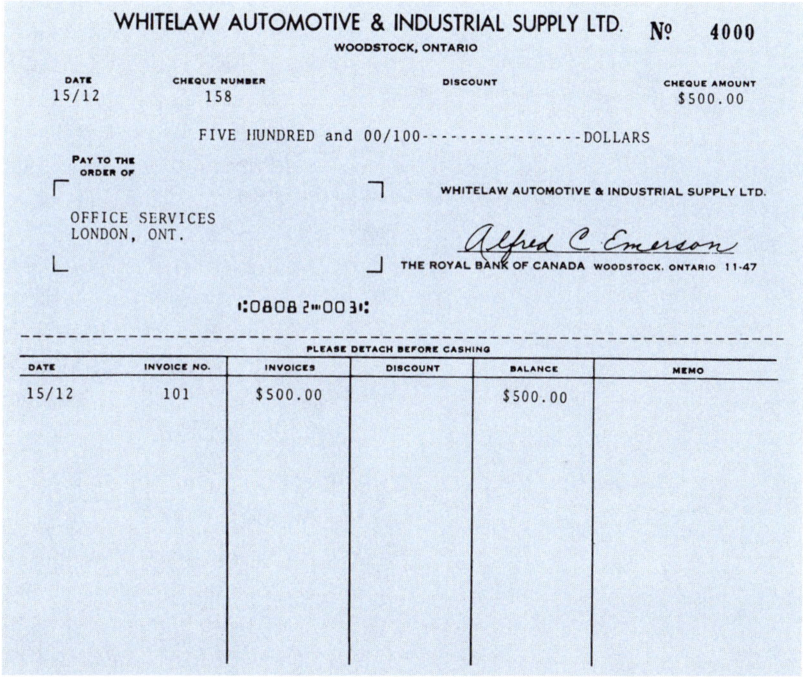
WHITELAW AUTOMOTIVE & INDUSTRIAL SUPPLY LTD. № 4000
WOODSTOCK, ONTARIO

DATE	CHEQUE NUMBER	DISCOUNT	CHEQUE AMOUNT
15/12	158		$500.00

FIVE HUNDRED and 00/100----------------DOLLARS

PAY TO THE ORDER OF
OFFICE SERVICES
LONDON, ONT.

WHITELAW AUTOMOTIVE & INDUSTRIAL SUPPLY LTD.
Alfred C. Emerson
THE ROYAL BANK OF CANADA WOODSTOCK, ONTARIO 11-47

⑆08082⑈003⑆

PLEASE DETACH BEFORE CASHING

DATE	INVOICE NO.	INVOICES	DISCOUNT	BALANCE	MEMO
15/12	101	$500.00		$500.00	

When a voucher cheque is used, it is common to make a carbon copy of the cheque and voucher. Of course, the copy will be retained for use by accounting personnel to record the dollar results of the cash payment.

5. VOID AND RETAIN ALL SPOILED CHEQUES If for some reason the cheque is spoiled, it is important to void both the cheque record and the cheque proper, as illustrated in Figure 8-10. In using serially prenumbered cheques, even spoiled cheques must be carefully voided and kept on file, because every number must be accounted for.

FIGURE 8-10

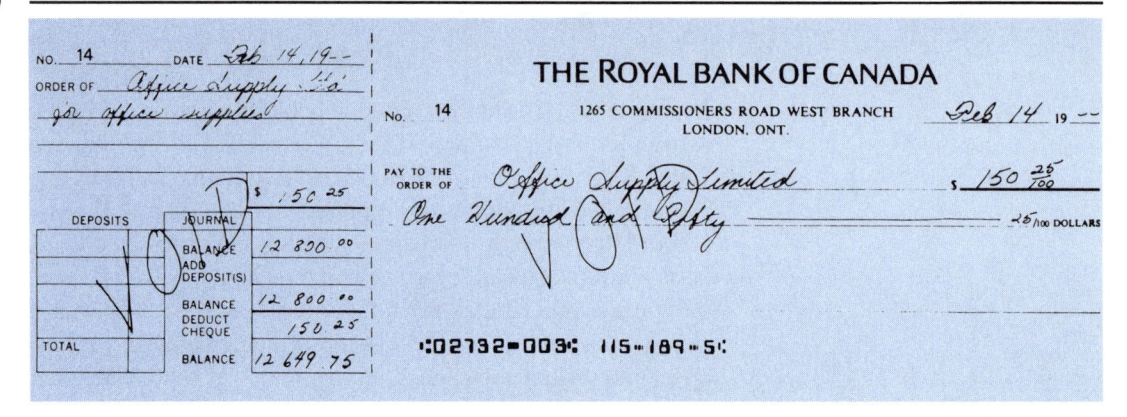

6. PREPARE CHEQUES WITH CARE TO PREVENT THEIR FRAUDULENT ALTERATION This means that each cheque is drawn in the precise name of the business concern which supplied the goods or services (the payee). If this practice is followed, the future endorsement of the cheque provides legal proof of payment. Cheques, of course, should never be drawn payable either to "Cash" or to "Bearer." In addition, no space should be left which would permit the insertion of either figures or written amounts to increase the amount of a cheque above that for which it was drawn by the issuer.

For greater control, many businesses will use a cheque protector, which imprints the amount on the cheque so that it cannot be altered in any way. Although accountants prefer no alteration on a cheque, some small firms do permit corrections. The error is crossed out neatly, the correction is made, and the change is initialled. Of course, erasures are not permitted on any cheque.

7. SUBMIT ALL CHEQUES FOR AUTHORIZED SIGNATURE In a large enterprise, an accounts payable clerk would generally prepare a cheque for signature. It is important to emphasize that only authorized persons sign cheques. In many large businesses, the treasurer or assistant treasurer will be the responsible signing officer. In other large businesses, cheques must be *countersigned* to improve internal control. This would mean that a second responsible official, perhaps the controller or chief accounting officer, signs to certify that the payment is proper.

In a small business, the owner-manager would normally sign all cheques. Of course, no cheque should be signed unless it is accompanied by its supporting data (verified and approved invoice and other documents).

It is useful to observe that, in the very large enterprises, cheques may be signed by machine. Where a cheque-signing machine is used, it is assumed that the process of cheque signing is under the careful control of, and used only in the presence of, an official authorized to sign. In all cases, it is also assumed that the bank will have specimen signatures of all individuals who are authorized to sign cheques on behalf of the enterprise.

8. CANCEL ALL BILLS PAID BY CHEQUE

An important control measure is to cancel the bill and all supporting documents at the time cheques are signed. Many firms require the cancellation of bills (invoices and other supporting documents) by rubber-stamping "Paid" or perforating the documents to prevent duplication. In smaller firms, a clerk or secretary may simply write "Paid," together with the date, the cheque number, and his or her initials on the face of the document. Regardless of the method employed, this cancellation should be done by or under the direction of the signing official, especially before the documents are returned for filing in the department or office in which the cheques originated.

9. MAIL A REMITTANCE ADVICE WITH THE CHEQUE

Many businesses enclose a remittance advice, which is simply a statement advising the *payee* of the item or items covered by the cheque. As suggested earlier, some firms may use a voucher cheque which provides the payee with the remittance advice in the form of the perforated rider attached to the cheque.

> Payee: the party to whom a cheque is made out.

10. DIVIDE THE RESPONSIBILITY WHERE POSSIBLE

When two or more employees are engaged in the business enterprise, it is important to organize their functions to ensure that no employee has responsibility for more than a part of the cash disbursements function. In particular, the responsibility for handling the cheques and recording the payments should be divided, so that the work of one employee can be checked against that of another. There are several ways and areas of applying this measure of division of responsibility. The more common are:

- Use specialized departments. Ideally, duties should be separated so that the work of one employee, without duplicating the work of another, offers a control check at different points along the systems flow of controlling the disbursements. In large businesses, these duties are well defined and clerks are placed in specialized departments to ensure that separation of functions does occur. In small firms, however, it is recognized that one clerk would perform several or all of the functions normally divided among employees of a large enterprise.

- Assign someone who looks after the bills to be paid—an accounts payable clerk perhaps—to initiate the step to have the bill paid. In actual practice, the request for a cash disbursement may also originate from those charged with payroll responsibilities and from those who request petty cash. As indicated earlier, the system of petty cash will be treated later on in this Topic; the payroll accounting application is examined in Chapter 10.
- Divide the responsibility for verifying and approving invoices. The purchasing clerk checks the bill; the head of purchasing approves the bill; the accounting clerk double-checks the same bill before making an accounting entry. On the other hand, the purchasing clerk does not finally approve the bill; nor does the accounting clerk order the goods in the first place. Of course, in small firms, management may assign some of these duties to a clerk-typist or a secretary, while the owner-manager will order the goods and approve the bill.
- Once the invoice is approved, the accounts payable clerk prepares the cheque for signature; however, some other person authorized does the actual signing. Of course, those authorized to sign cheques should not be those who prepare the cheques or who maintain accounting records for cash receipts and cash payment.
- When cancelling bills, the cancellation should be done by or under the direction of the signing official.

11. WHERE POSSIBLE, USE A TICKLER FILE SYSTEM To take advantage of the discount period, an accounts payable clerk may be assigned the important job of maintaining a tickler file system in order to keep track of when each invoice should be paid. In simple terms, a *tickler file* is a method of filing invoices according to the dates on which they must be considered for payment. As shown in Figure 8-11, notice that a file folder is established for each day of the month. After a purchase invoice has been approved by the purchasing department and recorded by Accounts Payable, the accounting clerk can file the purchase invoice under the day that it must be paid in order to take advantage of the cash discount. On that day, the accounts payable clerk can present the invoice for payment. If a responsible person decides to pay the invoice, a cheque is made out for the amount owing on the invoice, less the cash discount. On the other hand, the person may not wish to pay the invoice on the discount date. In this case, the clerk will refile the unpaid bill under the day that marks the end of the credit period.

FIGURE 8-11

Cash payments journal: a special journal in which only cash payments are recorded.

12. IDEALLY, A SPECIAL JOURNAL SHOULD BE USED TO RECORD ALL CASH PAYMENTS TRANSACTIONS In the language of accounting, this special journal is known as the **cash payments journal** or cash disbursements journal.

CHAPTER 8: Accounts Payable Application **343**

Cash Payments Journal Illustrated

By definition, the cash payments journal will receive double entries that must analyze an outflow of cash; therefore, a Cash Cr. column is essential in the design of this special journal. The criteria for determining the remaining special columns would be, of course, the same as for the other journals illustrated earlier—namely, the nature of the transactions to be recorded and the repetitiveness of their occurrence. In the cash payments journal for Scarborough Wholesale Hardware illustrated in Figure 8-12, special columns for Accounts Payable Dr. and Purchases Discount Cr. are included, because payments to creditors on account and purchases discounts taken occur frequently enough to justify special money columns. If payments for one or more of the other accounts debited were sufficiently numerous, other special columns could be added so that only the monthly total can be posted to the appropriate account.

FIGURE 8-12

CASH PAYMENTS JOURNAL — Page 3

Date	Account Debited	Explanation	Cheque No.	Post. Ref.	General Ledger Debit	Accounts Payable Debit	Purchases Discount Credit	Net Cash Credit
19— June 1	Mortgage Payable	June mortgage.	612	220	250 00			250 00
4	Small Tools Limited	Invoice 0600.	613	✓		559 47	11 19	548 28
5	Office Equipment	Typewriter.	614	115	600 00			600 00
7	Transportation-in	Reimer Transport.	615	402	40 00			40 00
12	Wark Electronics	Invoice W174.	616	✓		895 30	8 95	886 35
16	Telephone Expense	June bill.	617	518	18 95			18 95
18	R. Stone Limited	On account.	618	✓		100 00		100 00
20	Advertising Expense	City Press.	619	519	175 00			175 00
23	Northern Electrical Co.	Invoice 6270.	620	✓		750 90	7 51	743 39
26	Utilities Expense	Gas & electricity.	621	520	38 50			38 50
28	J. Thompson Ltd.	Invoice A25K30.	622	✓		800 00	16 00	784 00
30	Howard Capes, Drawing	Personal withdrawal.	623	302	100 00			100 00
30	Totals				1 222 45	3 105 67	43 65	4 284 47
					(✓)	(202)	(504)	(101)

Analysis You should have little difficulty understanding the points that follow. Keep in mind that the same principles of posting are maintained for the cash payments journal as for the cash receipts journal.

- When a cheque is issued in payment of an invoice with a cash discount, it becomes important that the cheque record (the cheque stub or cheque voucher) be analyzed correctly before the dollar results of the transaction are recorded in the cash payments journal. From earlier work you learned that a debit must be acknowledged to Accounts Payable for the entire amount owing on the invoice; that a credit must be shown to Purchases Discount for the cash discount;

and that a credit to Cash will be identified for the exact amount of the cheque. In the cash payments journal, therefore, the one debit amount must be equal to the total of the two credit amounts.

- One important feature is characteristic of the cash payments journal. Since proper accounting procedures call for all payments to be made by cheque, it follows that every Cash credit recorded in this special journal must mean a reduction in the amount of balance in the current account held by the depositor's bank. Since every cash payment affects the firm's bank account, it is important to account for the issuance of each cheque; hence, a special Cheque No. column is included to account by number for every cheque issued, including any spoiled cheques which are voided. And, in addition, the name of the payee should be identified in the Explanation column.

- The posting of the cash payments journal falls into two phases: daily posting and month-end posting. Obviously, daily posting must occur from the amounts recorded in the accounts payable ledger. Notice that check marks are entered in the Post. Ref. column opposite each creditor's name to indicate that the posting has been made.

- Daily posting also occurs for the amounts recorded in the General Ledger Debit column, because no special money column was provided for accounts affected by these amounts. Since the amounts have been posted during the month, the total of this column must not be posted at the end of the month; therefore, a check mark is placed beneath the column total to indicate this concept.

FIGURE 8-13

Cash Payment Journal
Zero Proof
June 30, 19—

    0.00 *
1 222.45 *+
3 105.67 +
   43.65 −
4 284.47 −
    0.00 *

- As with the cash receipts journal, the second part of posting is performed at the end of the month. But, before the totals of the cash payments journal are transferred to appropriate ledger accounts, it is important to remember the control measure of verifying the column totals in order to prove that the total debits recorded are equal to the total credits recorded. This journal proof may be obtained quite easily on an adding-machine tape, as illustrated in the side margin.

- Once the column totals have been verified, posting of these totals may occur to appropriate general ledger accounts. From Figure 8-12, you should easily conclude that three column totals have been posted to the general ledger: the total of Accounts Payable has been transferred to the debit of the controlling account; the total of Purchases Discount has been transferred to the credit of that contra expense account; and the total of the Net Cash has been posted to the credit side of Cash.

Cash Short and Over Transactions

You will recall from the last chapter that, as part of handing cash receipts, differences may occur when a cash proof is prepared. For example, a cash proof of a cash register system may show that the amount of cash in the drawer is less than the amount shown on the locked-in tape. Similarly, a

CHAPTER 8: Accounts Payable Application

FIGURE 8-14

CASH PROOF

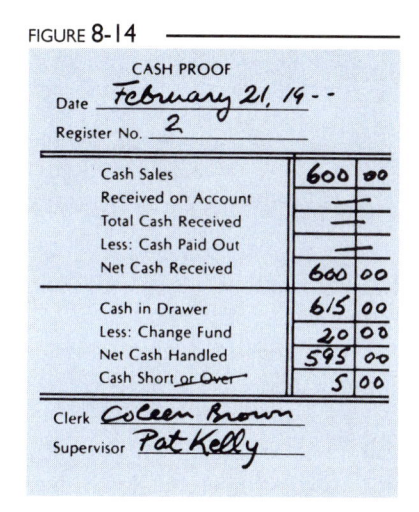

Date February 21, 19--
Register No. 2

Cash Sales	600	00
Received on Account	—	
Total Cash Received	—	
Less: Cash Paid Out	—	
Net Cash Received	600	00
Cash in Drawer	615	00
Less: Change Fund	20	00
Net Cash Handled	595	00
Cash Short or Over	5	00

Clerk Coleen Brown
Supervisor Pat Kelly

cash proof of sales slips may show a recording of a cash amount greater or less than the actual count of cash handled. In either case, when the reason for the cash difference cannot be identified, it is assumed that the discrepancy was caused by a human error in the act of making change. In most businesses, therefore, the supervisor will authorize a cash proof form with a cash shortage or overage, as the case may be.

ANALYZING CASH SHORTAGES

If the cash proof shows less cash in the drawer than there should be, the cash is said to be *short*. For example, the cash proof illustrated in the side margin on February 21 shows that the net cash received is $600 while the net amount of cash counted in the drawer after the change fund is deducted is only $595. Assuming that the difference cannot be located, accounting personnel will use the authorized cash proof as a source document to record the shortage of $5.

To understand why a special account called Cash Short and Over is debited in the cash payments journal for the shortage, it is first helpful to review the cash receipts transaction.

FIGURE 8-15

Cash	101		Sales	401
600				600

As the T-account analysis in Figure 8-15 shows, Cash must be debited for $600 and Sales must be credited for $600 to record the revenue from cash sales. Obviously, this transaction will be recorded in the cash receipts journal, since all cash sales are recorded in this special journal.

Since there is a cash shortage approved by the supervisor, an expense of operating the business is recognized. This expense, therefore, would appear as a debit to a special account called Cash Short and Over, as the second T-account analysis reveals in Figure 8-16.

FIGURE 8-16

Cash Short and Over	515		Cash	101
5				5

Since a debit to Cash is always recorded in the cash receipts journal, the credit or decrease to Cash must be recorded in the cash payments journal. Obviously, no cheque would be issued for this "cash payment"; therefore, the Cheque No. column would merely show a stroke to indicate that no cheque was issued. Notice that two steps are required when a cash shortage is recognized: first, record the debit entry to Cash in the cash receipts journal to recognize the full inflow of revenue; and second, record the credit entry to Cash in the cash payments journal to recognize the expense of the cash shortage. After postings occur at month-end, the balance in the Cash account will reflect the correct net amount of cash handled.

FIGURE 8-17

Cash	101		Cash Short and Over	515		Sales	401
595			5				600
(Net cash handled)			(Expense)				(Revenue)

Instead of recording the cash shortage in a two-step procedure, some accounting systems prefer to combine the sales and the expense transaction as analyzed in the T-account illustration of Figure 8-17.

When a one-step procedure is used, the cash receipts journal must be expanded to include a special money column called Cash Short and Over Debit, as shown in Figure 8-18.

Notice that the two debits, a Cash debit for $595 and a Cash Short and Over debit for $5, add up to the one credit of Sales for $600. Obviously, a special column for Cash Short and Over Debit would be used only when cash shortages are numerous during a monthly accounting of cash sales transactions.

FIGURE 8-18

CASH RECEIPTS JOURNAL — Page 3

Date	Account Credited	Explanation	Post. Ref.	General Ledger Credit	Cash Short/Over Debit	Net Cash Debit
19-1 Mar. 10	Sales	Daily sales.	401	600 00	5 00	595 00

ANALYZING CASH OVERAGES If the cash proof shows more cash in the drawer than there should be, then obviously the cash is said to be *over*. Although there is less likelihood of an overage appearing on a daily basis, such a calculation is possible. When such an overage is authorized by the supervisor, the correct accounting analysis requires that the excess amount of cash be credited to the Cash Short and Over account. Suppose, for example, that the actual cash counted on say March 12 is $499, but the register tape (or sales slips totalled) shows cash sales of $497. In this case, the entry in T-account form would be analyzed as in Figure 8-19.

FIGURE 8-19

Cash	101		Cash Short and Over	515		Sales	401
499				2			497
(Net cash handled)				(Miscellaneous or other revenue)			(Sales revenue)

CHAPTER 8: Accounts Payable Application 347

It should be obvious that, to record the above T-account analysis in special journals, the cash receipts journal must be used, because there is an inflow of Cash. And, unless there are special columns for both debits and credits to Cash Short and Over, the entry would require two separate lines, as illustrated in Figure 8-20.

FIGURE 8-20

		CASH RECEIPTS JOURNAL			Page 3
Date	Account Credited	Explanation	Post. Ref.	General Ledger Credit	Net Cash Debit
19-1 Mar. 12	Sales	Daily sales.	401	497 00	497 00
12	Cash Short and Over	Cash overage.	515	2 00	2 00

ANALYZING THE BALANCE After all cash shortages and overages are posted to the Cash Short and Over account, the balance in the account will be identified as either an expense balance or a revenue balance. Now, if a $5 cash shortage had also been recorded in March, there would then be a debit balance of $3; consequently, the net effect of cash difference for the month is an expense, which may appear on the income statement under a subheading such as "Other Expenses" or "Other Revenues and Expenses." Or, if the amount is small as is the case here, it may be combined with other miscellaneous expenses and reported as part of the total for Miscellaneous Expenses.

On the other hand, if the monthly balance in the account is greater on the credit side, then the balance must be identified as a source of revenue. On the income statement, the credit balance figure should not be included in the sales amount, but as a separate item reported under Other Revenue as "Miscellaneous Revenue."

Over a period of time, many accountants believe that cash shortages will be greater than the amounts of cash overage; therefore, the account Cash Short and Over is generally given an account code in the chart of accounts under "Expenses." It should be emphasized, however, that this special account is used only when differences in cash cannot be traced back to actual errors. Remember that a supervisor, or at least someone other than the clerk receiving the cash, must authorize all cash shortages.

FIGURE 8-21

Cash Short and Over	515
Mar. 3 CP3 5	Mar. 12 CR3 2
(Misc. expense)	(Misc. revenue)

FIGURE 8-22

Kelly's Office Services
Chart of Accounts

Expenses
515 Cash Short and Over

Controlling Petty Cash Expenditures

As has been emphasized, making payments by cheque helps to ensure that the outflow of cash is properly controlled. However, some businesses have learned from experience that to issue cheques for many small payments is quite costly and time-consuming. Consider, for example, the time and cost involved in verifying, approving, issuing, and recording

Petty cash system: a system for controlling minor expenditures of a business.

cheques for the payment of postage due on incoming mail or for a small freight bill on incoming goods. To take care of these and other minor expenditures, many firms will set up a ***petty cash system***. The chief features of this system may be analyzed through the flowchart in Figure 8-23.

A petty cash system, like any cash system, follows the internal control measure of dividing the responsibility between the handling and the recording of cash. In addition, as the figure shows, the petty cash system can be analyzed into three parts: (1) establishing the petty cash fund; (2) making petty cash disbursements; and (3) replenishing the petty cash fund.

1. ESTABLISHING THE PETTY CASH FUND

To establish the petty cash fund, a cheque is issued for a sufficient amount to make minor

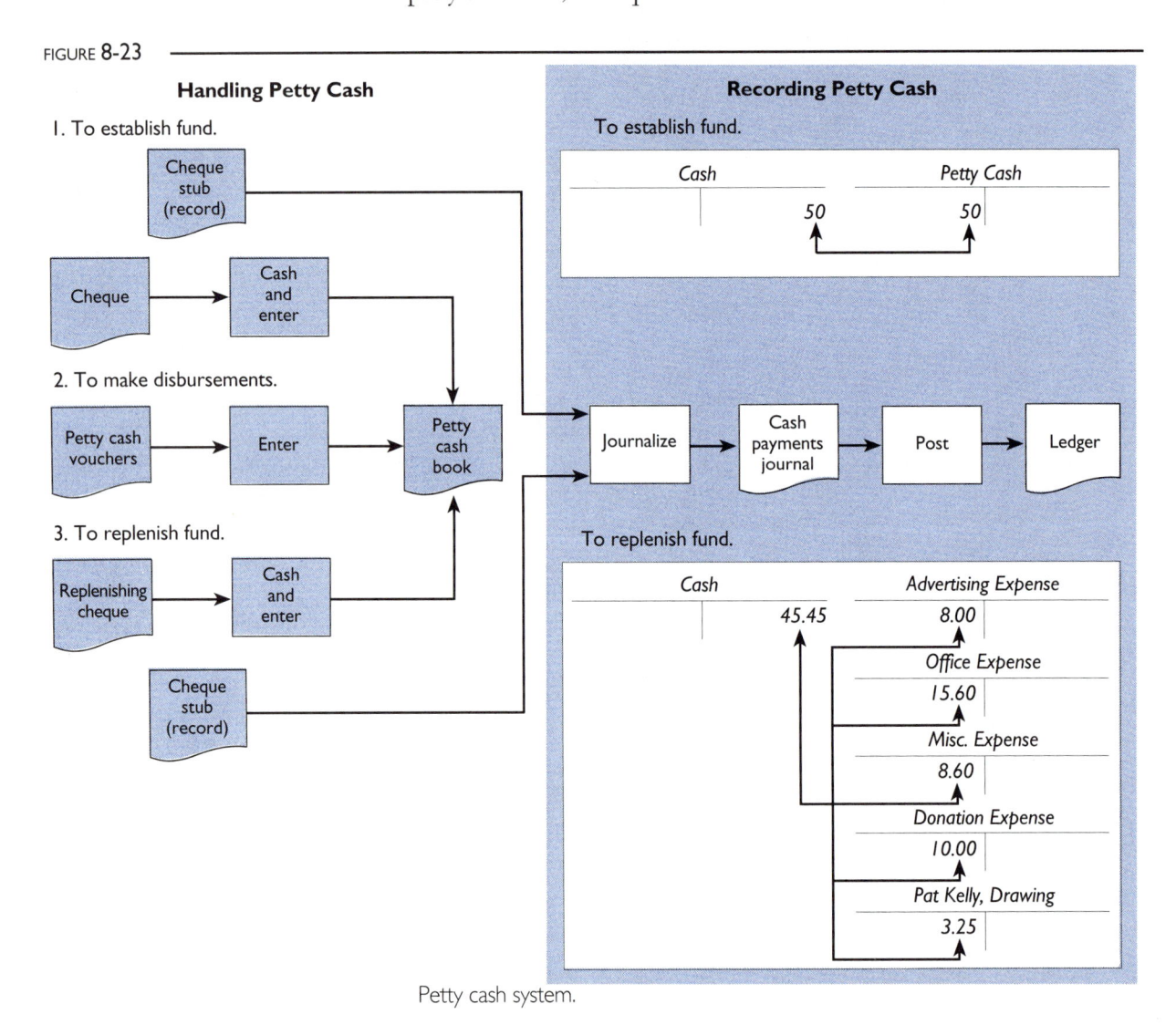

FIGURE 8-23

Handling Petty Cash

1. To establish fund.
2. To make disbursements.
3. To replenish fund.

Recording Petty Cash

To establish fund.

Cash	Petty Cash
50	50

To replenish fund.

Cash	
	45.45

Advertising Expense	
8.00	

Office Expense	
15.60	

Misc. Expense	
8.60	

Donation Expense	
10.00	

Pat Kelly, Drawing	
3.25	

Petty cash system.

payments for a week or two, and usually not for more than one month. It is important to remember these points:

- That the amount of the petty cash fund is determined by management and that this amount is some constant "round" number. For example, management may decide that $50, $75, $100, or some other amount be established. In the flowchart, the amount used is $50.
- That the cheque is issued to one individual employee—the petty cashier—who is appointed sole custodian of the fund. (From earlier work on the control of issuing cheques, you should know why this cheque should not be issued to "Cash" or "Petty Cash.")
- That the petty cashier cashes the cheque, obtains the $50 in money currency, and enters the amount of the fund in the *petty cash book*. Of course, the money currency should be kept in a locked box or drawer.
- That the petty cash book becomes a convenient record of entries, but only for the use of the petty cashier. It is very important to understand that the petty cash book is not the accounting book of original entry. As the flowchart suggests, the person who handles the asset—the petty cashier—must not be the same person who makes the accounting entry to establish the fund; consequently, a second person—an accounting clerk—will record the accounting entry in the cash payments journal.
- And, finally, that the cheque record is used to record the establishment of the fund in the accounting records. Note that the effect of the recording creates a current asset called "Petty Cash" and that the balance of this account normally never changes in any way. Two changes, however, may occur: (1) When the total of the fund must be increased, a second cheque is issued to record the extra amount. (2) When the fund must be closed, the amount is deposited in the bank and the accounting records show a reversing entry to debit Cash and credit Petty Cash.

FIGURE 8-24

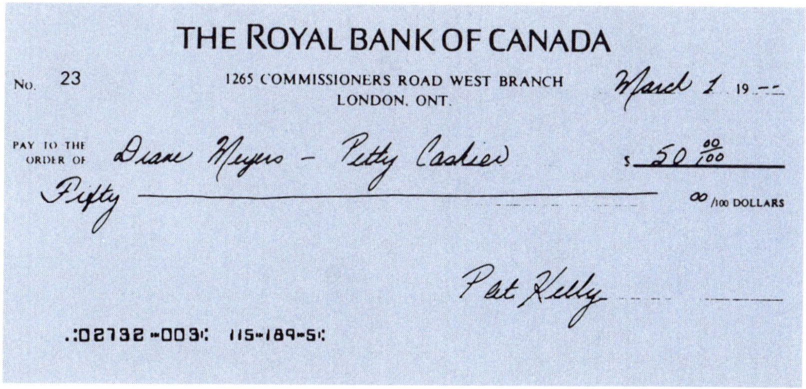

2. MAKING PETTY CASH DISBURSEMENTS

It is important to remember that individual petty cash payments do not go through the accounting records. As the flowchart clearly shows, petty cash vouchers must be issued for all disbursements and a record of these vouchers is made only in the petty cash book.

Look closely at the example of a petty cash voucher illustrated in the side margin. Notice that this voucher is prenumbered and that two signatures appear. One signature identifies the person who received the petty cash—therefore, the petty cash voucher is in fact a petty cash receipt—the other signature identifies the person who approved the payment.

Since the voucher is prenumbered and contains two signatures, it naturally follows that this voucher becomes a control document. At any time, the total of petty cash payments approved on the vouchers and remaining cash in the petty cash box must equal the established amount of the fund; consequently, as each payment is made, an approved voucher must be placed in the petty cash box or drawer. In effect, the petty cashier is required to substitute the receipted and approved voucher for the cash disbursed. As the name suggests, the document "vouches" (gives evidence) for the petty cash payment. The flowchart shows that each paid voucher is entered in the petty cash book. Notice in Figure 8-26 that all voucher numbers must be accounted for; consequently, all spoiled vouchers must be kept on file.

FIGURE 8-25

No. 1   Amount $1.85

PETTY CASH VOUCHER
Date March 4, 19—
Paid to C.P. Telecommunications
For Collect telegram
Charge to Misc. Expense

KELLY'S OFFICE SERVICES

Approved by   Received by
Pat Kelly   J.C. Forest

3. REPLENISHING THE PETTY CASH FUND

After a certain period of making petty cash disbursements, the balance of the petty cash fund will become low. The petty cashier then usually summarizes the expenditures on a *petty cash requisition*, which becomes the form that requests that the fund

FIGURE 8-26

PETTY CASH BOOK Page 1

Date	Explanation	Vo. No.	PETTY CASH FUND Received	Paid Out	Adv. Expense	Office Expense	Misc. Expense	Name of Other Account	Amount
19— Mar. 1	Cheque 23 to establish fund.	—	50 00						
4	Collect telegram.	1		1 85			1 85		
5	Ad in City Record.	2		4 00	4 00				
6	Window washing.	3		4 50			4 50		
7	Postage stamps.	4		1 60		1 60			
8	United Way.	5		10 00				Donation Expense	10 00
11	Repair of typewriter.	6		7 50		7 50			
12	Paper clips.	7		75		75			
13	Ad in City Record.	8		4 00	4 00				
14	Proprietor's lunch.	9		3 25				Pat Kelly, Drawing	3 25
15	Envelopes.	10		5 75		5 75			
15	Messenger service.	11		2 25			2 25		

CHAPTER 8: Accounts Payable Application 351

FIGURE 8-27

```
       KELLY'S OFFICE SERVICES
       PETTY CASH REQUISITION

REQUEST TO REPLENISH PETTY CASH
FOR PERIOD: March 1 to March 15, 19—

Petty Cash Summary:
Advertising Expense .............    $ 8.00
Office Expense ..................     15.60
Miscellaneous Expense ...........      8.60
Donation Expense ................     10.00
Pat Kelly, Drawing ..............      3.25
    Total Disbursements .........    $45.45
    Cash on Hand ................      4.55
    Amount of Petty Cash Fund ...    $50.00

              Nancy McLay
              (Petty Cashier)
```

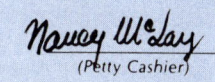

be replenished. In simple terms, this means that the petty cashier wants to build the fund up to the original amount. While the exact procedure will vary from firm to firm, the following steps are common.

- The petty cashier totals the amount of the paid vouchers in his or her custody.
- The petty cashier proves the cash; that is, the totals of the vouchers plus the balance of cash in the box or drawer must equal the original amount of the fund.
- The petty cashier prepares a petty cash requisition for a cheque made out in the precise total of the paid vouchers.
- The petty cash requisition and paid vouchers are submitted to a person responsible for issuing the replenishing cheque. Once the cheque is issued to the petty cashier and approved, the vouchers must be approved so that they cannot be used again. To cancel a voucher, a rubber stamp may be used, to imprint "Paid" and the date of cheque issued.
- On receipt of the reimbursing cheque the petty cashier will cash it, place the money currency in the petty cash box or drawer, and enter a record of the replenishment in the petty cash book.

After the replenishing cheque has been issued, the cheque record and accompanying documents (petty cash requisition and paid vouchers) serve as the source of information to record the replenishment in the accounting records. As the flowchart shows, the entry is recorded in the cash payments journal. The petty cash system, therefore, delays the actual journalizing of the petty cash payments until a replenishing cheque is issued. Observe from Figure 8-28 that the various debits identify the actual ledger accounts which have been summarized on the petty cash requisition. Since actual ledger accounts are affected only when the replenishing stage is reached, it is important to remember that the petty cash must be reimbursed at the end of each accounting period as well as when the fund is low.

FIGURE 8-28

CASH PAYMENTS JOURNAL — Page 3

Date	Account Debited	Explanation	Cheque No.	Post. Ref.	General Ledger Debit	Net Cash Credit
19-1 Mar. 1	Petty Cash	To establish petty cash fund.	23		50 00	50 00
15	Advertising Expense	⎫			8 00	
	Office Expense	⎬ To replenish petty cash			15 60	
	Miscellaneous Expense	⎬ for a total disbursement			8 60	
	Donation Expense	⎬ of $45.45.			10 00	
	Pat Kelly, Drawing	⎭	30		3 25	45 45

The Petty Cash Book

As indicated earlier, the petty cash book is for the use of the petty cashier. It serves simply as a convenient way of recording the individual petty cash transactions for the person who handles the cash. It is important to repeat that this book is not the book of original entry, that is, the journal to record the accounting entries. In fact, in actual practice, some firms do not use a petty cash book. Instead, they rely on the use of prenumbered vouchers, a petty cash box or drawer, and a responsible petty cashier who prepares a summary of petty cash payments each time a replenishment is requested. Those firms, however, that do use a petty cash book may use one designed along the lines of the one shown below in Figure 8-29.

FIGURE 8-29

PETTY CASH BOOK — Page 1

Date		Explanation	Vo. No.	Petty Cash Fund Received	Paid Out	Adv. Expense	Office Expense	Misc. Expense	Name of Other Account	Amount
19— Mar.	1	Cheque 23 to establish fund.	—	50 00						
	4	Collect telegram.	1		1 85			1 85		
	5	Ad in City Record.	2		4 00	4 00				
	6	Window washing.	3		4 50			4 50		
	7	Postage stamps.	4		1 60		1 60			
	8	United Way.	5		10 00				Donation Expense	10 00
	11	Repair of typewriter.	6		7 50			7 50		
	12	Paper clips.	7		75			75		
	13	Ad in City Record.	8		4 00	4 00				
	14	Proprietor's lunch.	9		3 25				Pat Kelly, Drawing	3 25
	15	Envelopes.	10		5 75		5 75			
	15	Messenger service.	11		2 25			2 25		
		Totals		50 00 / 50 00	45 45 / 45 45	8 00 / 8 00	15 60 / 15 60	8 60 / 8 60		13 25 / 13 25
	15	Cash on hand			4 55					
				50 00	50 00					
Mar.	15	Cash on hand	—	4 55						
	15	Cheque 30 to replenish fund.	—	45 45						

Analysis The analysis of transactions recorded in the illustration should cause few problems. Keep in mind that this "book" is not a journal; therefore, no attempt is shown to provide for double entries. The key point to remember is that this book must contain a record of each voucher. Notice too that the record identifies the various names of ledger accounts so that these accounts may be easily summarized on the petty cash requisition.

Notice how the petty cash book is totalled, balanced, and ruled off for a petty cash period. At the time of replenishing the petty cash, the various money columns may be *pencil-footed* (provided with small pencilled totals)

CHAPTER 8: Accounts Payable Application **353**

FIGURE 8-30

Proof of Petty Cash Book

Advertising Expense	$ 8.00
Office Expense	15.60
Miscellaneous Expense	8.60
Other accounts	13.25
Total paid out	$45.45
Cash on hand	4.55
Amount of fund	$50.00

to facilitate a proof of the petty cash book. This proof must show that the total petty cash paid out plus the cash on hand is equal to the amount of the fund. Notice, too, that the total of the various columns under "Distribution of Payments" must equal the total obtained in the "Paid Out" column. Of course, the entire process of checking the footings can be speeded up with the aid of an adding machine.

Your final observation of the illustrated petty cash book should be directed to the method of ruling off the various columns. Remember that the double line is required to show that one petty cash period has been completed. Notice how the next petty cash period is identified: the cash on hand is first brought down on the first available line below the double line; then, on the next line below, the replenishing cheque is recorded so that the combination of the cash on hand plus the replenishing cheque equals the original amount of the petty cash fund.

The Petty Cash System: An Imprest System

As indicated earlier, the Petty Cash account is a current asset. On a balance sheet, the amount of the petty cash fund is usually combined with the balance of Cash (in the bank) to report the Total Cash on Hand or simply Cash. The reason for combining the amount of petty cash with the Cash in Bank is to support the accountant's definition of Cash as any amount that can be deposited in the firm's current account at the bank. Since the fixed sum of petty cash was created from the cash in the bank, and since it can be redeposited any time, accountants have called this system of lending money the **imprest system of petty cash**, as the term "imprest" refers to an advance or loan. From a cash control viewpoint, remember that this system is controlled both by a cheque payment to create the fund and by a cheque payment to replenish the fund.

Imprest system of petty cash: a petty cash system established by a loan or advance of money from the main Cash (chequing) account.

TOPIC 2 Problems

Recording petty cash and non–petty cash expenditures.

8.6 a Record the following transactions in the general journal and petty cash book. Assume that the general journal is the only book of original entry. For the Distribution of Payments section, use columns similar to the ones illustrated for the petty cash book in this chapter. As a measure of cash control, assume that all expenditures *over* $10 must be paid by cheque.

Nov. 1	Issued Cheque 78 for $50 to establish the petty cash fund.
3	Paid $6.40 for stationery.
5	~~Paid~~ $27.50 for advertisement in the local newspaper. *(Issued Cheque 79 for)*
8	Paid $8.25 for messenger service.
9	Issued Cheque ~~79~~ 80 for $800 to pay the November rent.
9	Paid $4.50 for electronic typewriter correction tape.
10	Paid $8 for tickets to community church fair.
11	Paid $9.30 for cleaning the office window.
12	Issued Cheque ~~80~~ 81 for $170 to J. P. Cutsey on account.

15 The proprietor, Ben Bernath, signed a petty cash voucher and took $2 from the petty cash fund for coffee money.
16 Paid $3.75 for pencils.
19 Paid $7.35 for delivery service of a parcel.

b When all entries have been made, pencil-foot, check the additions in, and rule the petty cash book. Show a proof of the petty cash book on a form similar to the one illustrated in this chapter. (There is $0.05 in the petty cash box at this point.)

c Show a petty cash requisition form similar to the one illustrated in this chapter.

d Issue Cheque 82 to replenish the petty cash fund and make the necessary entries in the journal and the petty cash book.

Note: Save the journal and ledgers for use in Problem 8.7.

8.7 *Completing Problem 8.6 by recording petty cash and non–petty cash expenditures.*

a Using the petty cash book and the journal from Problem 8.6, record the following transactions:

Nov. 22 Paid $5.85 for cleaning office door.
23 Paid $5.28 for messenger service.
24 Issued Cheque 83 for $19.25 to pay telephone bill.
25 Paid $9 for advertisement in community directory.
26 Paid $4.50 for one 3.5 inch computer diskette.
26 Paid $10 as a contribution to the Boy Scouts.
29 Issued Cheque 84 for $450 to purchase office equipment.
29 Paid $8.75 for advertisement in school play program.
30 Purchased postage stamps, $1.20.
30 Issued Cheque 85 for Paid $18.25 for repairs to office typewriter.

b When all entries have been made, pencil-foot, check the additions in, and rule the petty cash book. Show a proof of the petty cash book on a form similar to the one illustrated in this chapter. (A proof of petty cash shows that the petty cash box contains 1 two-dollar bill, 3 one-dollar coins, 1 quarter, 1 dime, 1 nickel, and 2 pennies.)

c Show a petty cash requisition form similar to the one illustrated in this chapter.

d Issue Cheque 86 to replenish the petty cash fund and make the necessary entries in the journal and the petty cash book.

8.8 *Recording selected accounts payable transactions in a one-column purchases journal, a four-column cash payments journal, or the general journal; posting entries to the ledgers; preparing trial balances; reporting the cash position in a partial balance sheet.*

Lois Jenkins operates the Alberta Garden Centre. The firm's transactions affecting purchases and cash payments for May are outlined below. Perform the following operations to process those transactions:

a Open general ledger accounts and record May 1 balances for Cash (debit balance of $56 500); Petty Cash; Equipment; Delivery Truck; Accounts Payable; Lois Jenkins, Capital (credit balance of $56 500); Lois Jenkins, Drawing; Purchases; Transportation-in; Purchases Returns and Allowances; Purchases Discount; Rent Expense; Office Expense; Advertising Expense; Cash Short and Over; and Delivery Expense. Assign an appropriate account code for each general ledger account. Allow four lines for all accounts in this ledger.

b Open a subsidiary ledger for Accounts Payable for R. Beere Company, Box 1226, Pincher Creek, Alberta; Richard Bittle, 14 McBride Crescent, Red Deer, Alberta; CN Express, 470 Lansdowne Dr., Edmonton, Alberta; Humphries Supply Co., 14432—137 Street, Edmonton, Alberta; Neon Sign Display, 79 Patricia Dr., Edmonton, Alberta; and E. Parry Co., 39 Governor Drive S.W., Calgary, Alberta. Allow five lines for each account in the subsidiary ledger.

c Record each of the following transactions in a one-column purchases journal, a four-column cash payments journal, or a general journal. Assume that a petty cash book has been used to record all petty cash expenditures. Petty cash may be used for any expenditure under $20.

May 1 Issued Cheque 88 for $100 to establish a petty cash fund.
    1 Issued Cheque 89 for $750 for May rent.
    3 Purchased merchandise costing $500 from R. Beere Company on Invoice B1740, dated May 1; terms 2/10, n/30, FOB shipping point.
    3 Issued Cheque 90 to Alberta Transport Co., $40, for delivery of goods shipped from R. Beere Company.
    5 Purchased merchandise for $400 from Richard Bittle on Invoice RB-112, dated May 3; terms 2/10, n/30, FOB destination.
    8 Issued Cheque 91 for $475 for equipment.
    10 Issued Cheque 92 to R. Beere Company in full settlement of Invoice B1740, less the purchase discount.
    11 Purchased merchandise for $600 from Humphries Supply Co. on Invoice HU-2418, dated May 10; terms 1/15, n/60, FOB shipping point.
    11 Issued Cheque 93 for $47.50 in payment of freight charges on shipment received from Humphries Supply Co.
    12 Issued Cheque 94 to Richard Bittle in full settlement of Invoice RB-112, less the purchase discount.
    12 The petty cashier submitted a petty cash requisition form together with accompanying vouchers to replenish the petty cash fund. The summary of petty cash vouchers showed the following breakdown: Transportation-in, $22.60; Advertising Expense, $35.80; and Office Expense, $38.75. Issued Cheque 95 to replenish the fund.
    14 Issued Cheque 96 for $19 000 for a new delivery truck.
    15 Purchased merchandise for $900 from E. Parry Co. on Invoice P-1210, dated May 15; terms 1/10, n/30, FOB destination.
    15 The cash proof of the cash register showed a shortage of $11.85.
    16 Issued Debit Memo DM-09 to E. Parry Co. claiming a $50 adjustment for damaged goods received on Invoice P-1210. Returned damaged goods via City Transport, collect.
    18 Received a credit memo for $50 from E. Parry Co. granting the adjustment on damaged goods returned on Invoice P-1210.
    22 Purchased merchandise for $400 from R. Beere Company on Invoice B1770, dated May 20; terms, 2/10, n/30, FOB shipping point.
    22 Issued Cheque 97 to Alberta Transport Co., $45, for delivery of goods shipped from R. Beere Company.
    25 Issued Cheque 98 to E. Parry Co. in full settlement of amount owing on Invoice P-1210, less purchase return and less cash discount.

25 The petty cashier submitted a petty cash requisition together with accompanying vouchers to replenish the petty cash fund. Issued Cheque 99 to replenish the petty cash with the following summary: Transportation-in, $18.50; Advertising Expense, $20.50; Office Expense, $34.50; and Lois Jenkins, Drawing, $15.

26 Issued Cheque 100 for $175 for advertisement which appeared in the newspaper today.

27 Issued Cheque 101 for $100 to Humphries Supply Co. in part payment of Invoice HU-2418.

29 Issued Cheque 102 for $156.75 in payment of gas and oil used for the delivery truck.

30 Purchased merchandise for $300 from Richard Bittle on Invoice RB-176, dated May 29; terms 2/10, n/30, FOB destination.

31 The proprietor withdrew $500 cash for personal use. Issued Cheque 103 in payment.

31 Purchased merchandise for $700 from E. Parry Co. on Invoice P-1400, dated May 30; terms 2/10, n/30, FOB destination.

d Prove the equality of the debit and credit totals; then rule the special journals at month-end.

e Post the journal entries to the ledgers.

f Prepare a schedule of accounts payable.

g Take a trial balance of the general ledger.

h Prepare a partial balance sheet showing how the Alberta Garden Centre would report its cash position as at May 31.

Note: Save the journals and ledgers for use in Problem 8.9.

Completing Problem 8.8.

8.9 Using the journals and ledgers prepared in Problem 8.8, complete the following assignments.

a Record the dollar results of the following transactions.

June 1 Issued Cheque 104 for $750 for June rent.

2 Issued Cheque 105 for $500 to Humphries Supply Co. in full settlement of account. Cheque 106 was issued as Void

4 The petty cashier submitted a petty cash requisition together with accompanying vouchers analyzed as follows: Transportation-in, $19.25; Office Expense, $68.40. Issued Cheque 107 to replenish the fund.

6 Issued Cheque 108 to Richard Bittle in full settlement of Invoice RB-176, less purchase discount.

8 Issued Cheque 109 to E. Parry Co. in full settlement of Invoice P-1400, less purchase discount.

10 Purchased merchandise costing $1 000 from Humphries Supply Co. on Invoice HU-2570, dated June 9; terms 1/15, n/60, FOB shipping point.

11 Approved CN Express freight bill CN-897-301 for $80 charges on delivery of goods shipped from Humphries Supply Co. Terms net 30 days.

14 Issued Cheque 110 to R. Beere Company in full settlement of Invoice B-1770.

16 Purchased merchandise costing $800 from E. Parry Co. on Invoice P-1520, dated June 15; terms 2/20, n/30 FOB destination.

17 Issued Debit Memo DM-10 to E. Parry Co. claiming a $30 adjustment for slightly marked goods received on Invoice P-1520.

17 The petty cashier submitted a petty cash requisition together with accompanying vouchers analyzed as follows: Office Expense, $67.50; Lois Jenkins, Drawing, $28.75. Issued Cheque 111 to replenish the fund.

19 Received a credit memo for $30 from E. Parry Co. approving the allowance for slightly marked goods on Invoice P-1520.

19 The cash proof of the cash register showed a shortage of $8.67.

20 The proprietor withdrew goods costing $175 for personal use. The goods withdrawn were part of the shipment received from E. Parry Co. on Invoice P-1520. *Hint:* A periodic inventory system is followed.

24 Issued Cheque 112 to Humphries Supply Co. in full settlement of Invoice HU-2570.

26 Purchased merchandise costing $400 from Richard Bittle on Invoice RB-201, dated June 25; terms 2/10, n/30, FOB destination.

28 Issued Cheque 113 for $167.70 in payment of gas and oil used for delivery truck.

29 Received advertising Invoice 68-72-40, dated June 28, from Neon Sign Display, $275; terms net 30 days.

30 Purchased merchandise costing $350 from R. Beere Company on Invoice B-1840, dated June 29; terms 2/10, n/30, FOB shipping point.

30 Issued Cheque 114 to Alberta Transport Co., $40, for delivery of goods shipped from R. Beere Company.

30 The petty cashier submitted a petty cash requisition together with accompanying vouchers analyzed as follows: Office Expense, $62.70; Lois Jenkins, Drawing, $22.50. Issued Cheque 115 to replenish the fund.

30 The cash proof of the cash register showed an overage of $4.80. (Use the general journal to record this overage.)

b Check the equality of the debit and credit totals; then rule the special journals for the month-end.
c Post the entries from the journals to the ledgers.
d Prepare a schedule of accounts payable.
e Prepare a trial balance of the general ledger.
f Prepare a partial balance sheet to report the cash on hand.

TOPIC 3 Applying Shortcuts in Journalizing and Posting

In the last chapter, several shortcuts were introduced for processing the accounts receivable application: the journalizing of batch totals for posting to the general ledger, direct posting to the subsidiary ledger, journalless and ledgerless bookkeeping, and the one-write system. These shortcuts, together with the combination journal, work equally well for the processing of the accounts payable application.

Journalizing Batch Totals and Direct Posting to Accounts Payable

As stated in the last chapter, some accounting systems prefer to post to the subsidiary ledger directly from the source document. This system would also apply in the case of a large firm that had numerous creditor accounts and separate departments for accounts payable and general accounting.

When direct posting and the batching method are used, it is customary to request the seller to mail two copies of the invoice. After approval of the purchasing department, the copies would go to accounts payable where clerks would process the copies. No procedures will be outlined, since they will vary from business to business, especially when a computer system is used.

Journalless Bookkeeping

In Topic 3 of the previous chapter, you learned that the journalless method can be used to eliminate the formal journal in processing an accounts receivable application. A similar procedure may be used to record the purchases of merchandise on credit without the use of the traditional purchases journal.

In general, two copies of each purchase invoice are needed. Copy 1 of the invoice is filed according to the due date in the tickler file (unpaid invoice file). Copy 2 of each purchase invoice is posted directly to each creditor's account only after the invoices are alphabetized to form a batch and a pre-list is taken on an adding-machine tape. After all postings have occurred, a posting proof tape is prepared to check the total against the total of the pre-list.

Under the journalless method to account for credit purchases, a purchases invoice binder replaces the traditional purchases journal. This binder stores the daily batch of invoices. At the end of the month, the accounting clerk lists the daily batch totals on an adding-machine tape to arrive at the monthly total of credit purchases of merchandise for resale. Under the periodic method, this total is posted to the general ledger as a debit to Purchases and as a credit to the Accounts Payable controlling account.

Note that under any "journalless" method, only the traditional purchases journal and sales journal would be eliminated from the accounts payable and accounts receivable applications respectively. One would still require the traditional cash receipts journal, the cash payments journal, and the general journal to record cash receipts, cash payments, and transactions such as error corrections and adjusting and closing entries.

Ledgerless Bookkeeping

A further refinement in processing a firm's accounts payable is to eliminate the accounts payable ledger. Instead of setting up individual creditor accounts, the firm sets up a filing folder for each creditor; and instead of posting the entries from either a formal journal or a source document, the invoices received from the creditor are placed in this folder. The folders are filed in an accounts payable file, which replaces the traditional accounts payable ledger. When an invoice is paid, it is removed from the folder. Of course, the paid invoice is properly cancelled before it is filed in a separate "Paid Invoices" file.

It is essential to repeat an earlier idea that while the source documents have replaced the subsidiary ledger, they have not eliminated the need for a controlling account and other accounts in the general ledger. Furthermore, while the shortcuts offer advantages, it is important to remember that they do not eliminate the accounting theory of debiting Purchases (or Inventory under the perpetual method) and crediting Accounts Payable each time an invoice of goods is received. Similarly, the shortcuts have not eliminated the need for general ledger accounts, which must be used to provide information for the eventual preparation of financial statements.

Using a Combination Journal

Combination journal: a journal combining the general journal and one or more special journals into one book of original entry.

When there are only a few transactions to be recorded on a monthly basis, as is the case in many sole proprietorships, the general journal and all the special journals may be combined into what is commonly called the **combination journal**. This single book of original entry is also known as a *synoptic journal*, since in it all the separate journals may be viewed together.

The combination journal system must be regarded as a simplified accounting system. Generally, it is most useful when, as in a small business, the financial events that occur are within the personal knowledge and direct control of the owner, who is usually sole manager and bookkeeper.

DESIGNING A COMBINATION JOURNAL

The number of columns and the column headings in a combination journal depend upon the size of the business and the types of transactions that most frequently occur. For example, a small merchandising business would likely have special columns for highly repetitive tasks such as Purchases, Sales, and PST Payable. Regardless of the number of special columns, general columns must always be included to take care of the infrequent debits and credits to accounts for which no special columns are provided. For practical purposes, however, the number of money columns in any combination journal should be kept to a reasonable limit.

The combination journal illustrated in Figures 8-32 and 8-34 (combined) represent part of the simplified accounting system for Helen Wilkinson, owner-manager of a retail sporting goods store in a province that has a provincial sales tax. The analysis of the entries should be self-evident, since only common transactions have been recorded.

PROVING THE COMBINATION JOURNAL

It is established procedure to prove the mathematical accuracy of all journals at frequent intervals, usually by testing the accuracy of the double entries. At any given time, the total of all the debit money columns should be equal to the total of all the credit money columns. Because of the greater number of columns involved in a combination journal, a proof is considered essential at least at the end of each journal page and at the end of the month.

POSTING PROCEDURES

Posting from the combination journal is similar to the procedure for the special journals. In general, entries that affect the customer and creditor accounts in subsidiary ledgers are posted

FIGURE 8-31

	Debits	Credits
General Ledger	$ 501.37	$ 375.03
Accounts Receivable	1 502.25	986.12
Accounts Payable	1 200.00	1 675.25
Purchases	1 675.25	
Purchases Discount		27.90
Sales		2 300.50
PST Payable		126.77
Cash	2 285.75	1 673.05
Totals	$7 164.62	$7 164.62

FIGURE 8-32

Combination Journal

	Date		Account Title and Explanation	Post. Ref.	GENERAL LEDGER Debit	GENERAL LEDGER Credit	ACCOUNTS RECEIVABLE Debit	ACCOUNTS RECEIVABLE Credit
	19—							
1	Oct.	1	Cash balance, $2 480.	—				
2		2	Cash sales for week.	—				
3		4	John Bald — Sales Slip 1626.	√			94 50	
4		5	Spalding (Canada) Ltd. — Inv. 413;					
5			terms 2/10, n/30.	√				
6		6	Jennifer Bryant.	√				57 50
7		7	Sales Ret. & Allow./John Bald.	402/√	43 75			47 25
8			PST Payable.	203	3 50			
9		8	Canada Cycle Ltd. — Inv. 1280.	√				
10		9	R. Wilkinson, Drawing.	302	90 00			
32		21	Carried forward		501 37 501 37	375 03 375 03	1 502 25 1 502 25	986 12 986 12

End of page

Posting reference numbers placed in column when individual amounts are posted

during the month. This same daily posting routine also applies to individual items entered in the General Ledger columns, because no special money columns were provided for them. However, the columnar totals that affect general ledger accounts are posted in total form at the end of the month only after the combination journal has been proved.

FIGURE 8-33

Combination Journal

	Date		Account Title and Explanation		Post. Ref.	GENERAL LEDGER Debit	GENERAL LEDGER Credit	ACCOUNTS RECEIVABLE Debit	ACCOUNTS RECEIVABLE Credit
	19—								
1	Oct.	21	Totals brought forward		—	501 37	375 03	1 502 25	986 12
2		22	Office Expense	} To replenish petty cash.	514	18 20			
3			R. Wilkinson, Drawing		302	5 00			
4			Transportation-in		502	14 50			
5			Miscellaneous Expense		513	3 25			
19		31	Utilities Expense		515	48 50			
20		31	Totals			890 50 890 50	765 03 765 03	2 586 52 2 586 52	1 985 25 1 985 25
						(√)	(√)	(111)	(111)

CHAPTER 8: Accounts Payable Application   361

FIGURE 8-34

For the Month of October, 19—   Page 11

| ACCOUNTS PAYABLE || Purchases Debit | Purchases Discount Credit | Sales Credit | PST Payable Credit | CASH || Chq. No. |
Debit	Credit					Debit	Credit	
								1
				500 00	40 00	540 00		2
				87 50	7 00			3
	575 00	575 00						4
								5
						57 50		6
								7
								8
470 00			9 40				460 60	411	9
							90 00	412	10

| 1 200 00 | 1 675 25 | 1 675 25 | 27 90 | 2 300 50 | 126 77 | 2 285 75 | 1 673 05 | |
| 1 200 00 | 1 675 25 | 1 675 25 | 27 90 | 2 300 50 | 126 77 | 2 285 75 | 1 673 05 | 32 |

Using the One-Write System

The majority of firms which have developed one-write systems to account for and process the accounts receivable application also supply one-write applications for accounts payable. For illustrative purposes, the forms and systems developed by Safeguard Business Systems Inc. have again been selected for use in this text, because the Safeguard one-write application for accounts payable has been adopted by many small businesses that prefer this efficient manual accounting system. Since the one-write principle has been treated in depth in the case of accounts receivable, it will be sufficient in this chapter

FIGURE 8-35

For the Month of October, 19—   Page 12

| ACCOUNTS PAYABLE || Purchases Debit | Purchases Discount Credit | Sales Credit | PST Payable Credit | CASH || Chq. No. |
Debit	Credit					Debit	Credit	
1 200 00	1 675 25	1 675 25	27 90	2 300 50	144 88	2 285 75	1 673 05	1
								2
								3
								4
							40 95	439	5

							48 50	450	19
1 900 00	2 375 25	2 425 25	67 90	4 300 50	301 04	4 775 75	2 783 05	
1 900 00	2 375 25	2 425 25	67 90	4 300 50	301 04	4 775 75	2 783 05	20
(202)	(202)	(501)	(503)	(401)	(203)	(101)	(101)	

merely to highlight it as it applies to accounts payable. It is worth noting again that, in practice, modifications will be made to the system to suit the needs of each particular business.

ACCOUNTS PAYABLE LAYOUTS

The Safeguard application to treat accounts payable actually consists of two accounting boards with separate layouts as follows:

- A Purchase Register board on which is recorded all types of purchases on credit.
- A Cash Disbursements Journal board on which is recorded all types of cash payments made by cheque.

Both boards, showing the relationship between purchases and disbursements, are illustrated in Figure 8-36. Refer to this illustration when reviewing the analysis below.

Recording Credit Purchases   The first part of the accounts payable system is to record each day's credit purchases on the Purchase Register board. As the illustration shows, the Purchase Register sheet with carbon or NCR (no carbon required) overlay is placed on the board. Then the appropriate accounts payable account (often called the vendor's ledger card) is correctly aligned on top of the Purchase Register sheet. Obviously, the accounts payable ledger card and Purchase Register sheet are held in alignment by a clamp-locking device at the left side.

A six-step procedure is recommended to record a credit purchase, as follows:

1. Position the individual vendor ledger card correctly on the board.
2. Refer to the Balance column of the ledger card to determine the amount of any existing balance (the last amount in the column).
3. Enter this amount in the Previous Balance column on the journal sheet. (Enter "0" if no amount appears.)
4. On the vendor ledger card, (a) make entries in the Date, Vendor, and Detail columns; (b) enter the amount of the invoice in the Credit column; and (c) enter the new balance (previous balance + invoice amount) in the Balance column.
5. On the journal sheet, distribute the invoice amount to appropriate columns.
6. When the journal sheet becomes full, the journal totals are proved by adding the Previous Balance total to the Credit column total and subtracting the Debit total. The result should give a New Balance total. Also, the Credit total minus the Debit total will be equal to the grand total of all Distribution columns. Of course, all totals would be carried forward to the top line of the next Purchase Register sheet.

CHAPTER 8: Accounts Payable Application   **363**

FIGURE **8-36**

Purchases
To use the accounts payable system, each day's purchases are recorded on the purchase register and the appropriate vendors' ledgers. The accounts payable ledger and purchase register are held in alignment on Safeguard's folding accounting board, so that all entries are recorded in one writing. Since there is no chance for transposition errors, proving the journal forgoes the necessity of proving the ledger entries. Ample columns are provided for distribution.

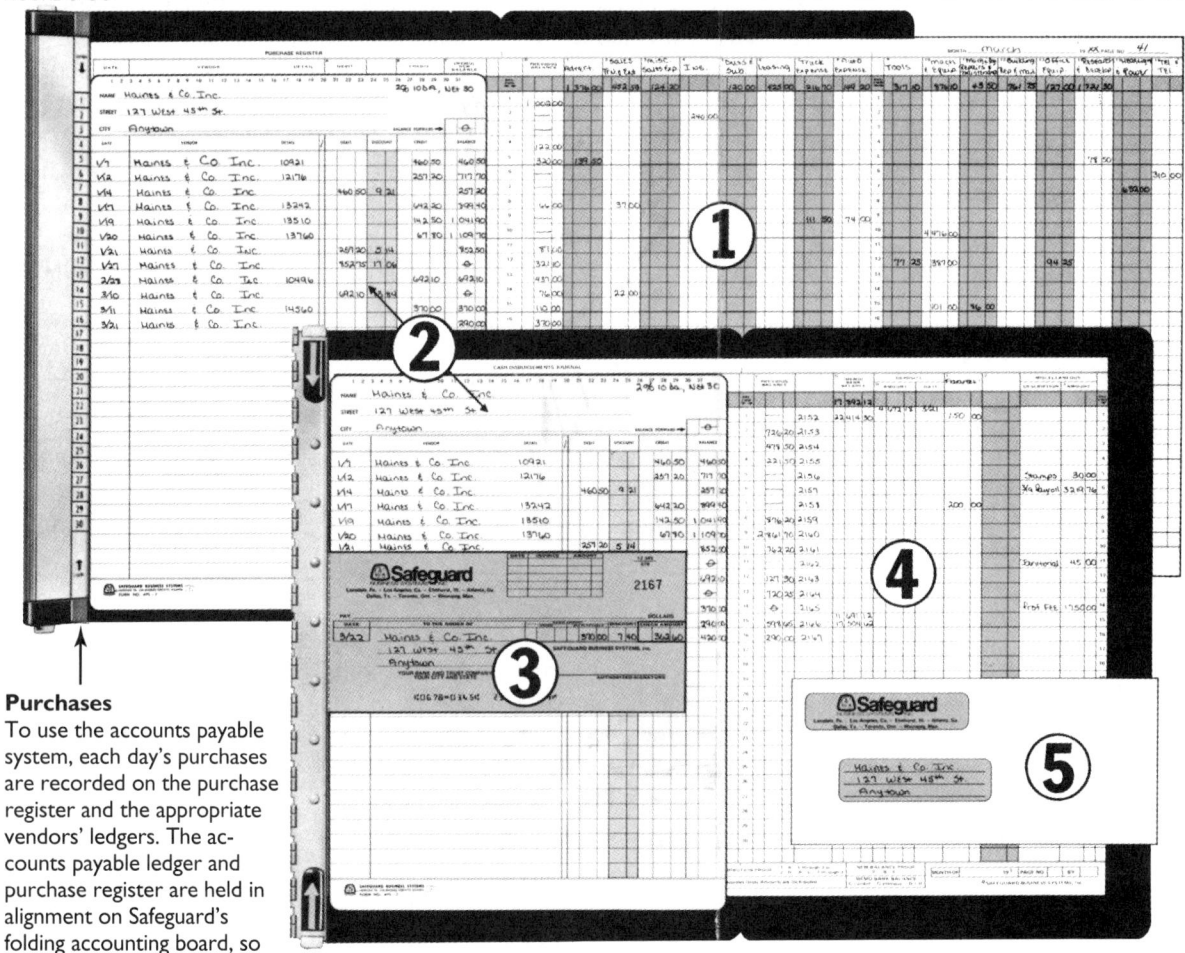

Disbursements
Cheque, ledger, and journal are completed in one writing. Accounts payable ledger registers perfectly with cheque and cash disbursements journal. Bank balance and deposit section aid in cash control. Double-window envelopes eliminate addressing.

① Purchase register
② Vendor's ledger
③ Disbursement cheque
④ Disbursements journal
⑤ Double-window envelope

Because the one-write system offers shortcuts, the accounting theory in recording the double entry must be analyzed as follows:

- The amount of the invoice recorded in the Credit column recognizes a credit to the individual vendor's account filed in the accounts payable ledger. Of course, under the one-write system, this entry is recorded and posted in one writing.

- Also, the amount of the invoice recorded in the Credit column is, in theory, a credit to the Accounts Payable controlling account in the general ledger. Of course, only the total of this column would be posted (to an Accounts Payable Control Card) at the end of each month when trial balances are prepared.
- The invoice amount distributed on the Purchase Register (journal sheet) recognizes a debit to an appropriate general ledger account (expense, fixed asset, inventory, prepaid expense, etc.). Of course, posting to these G/L accounts would be made by total at the end of each month before trial balances are prepared.

Recording Returns and Credits from Vendors The Purchase Register accounting board is used to record "purchases" returns and credits received from vendors. A five-step procedure is used, as follows:

1. The clerk positions the vendor's ledger card on the accounting board.
2. The clerk checks the Balance column on the vendor's ledger card to determine the amount of existing balance (the last amount in the column).
3. The clerk enters this amount in the Previous Balance column on the journal sheet. (A "0" is entered if no amount appears.)
4. On the ledger card, the clerk (a) makes entries under Date, Vendor, and Detail; (b) enters the amount of the return or credit in the Debit column; and (c) enters the new balance (previous balance minus the Debit amount) in the Balance column.
5. On the journal sheet, the clerk enters the amount in the appropriate distribution column. If general distribution columns are used, brackets are shown around the figure to indicate a negative amount. However, a special distribution column can be used for this amount.

Try analyzing the recording and posting of returns and credits from vendors. This analysis should conform to accounting theory that you have learned from earlier "purchases" returns and allowances transactions.

Recording Cash Payments (Disbursements) The second part of the accounts payable system is to record each day's cash payments on the Cash Disbursements board. Refer back to Figure 8-36 for the illustration of the assembly. As the figure shows, the cheque, vendor's ledger card, and cash payments journal are completed in one writing.

A ten-step procedure is recommended to record a cheque in payment of a vendor's accounts payable:

1. The vendor's ledger card is inserted beneath a cheque form, with the left edge of the card aligned with perforations along the left side of cheques and with the carbon strip of the cheque covering the first blank line of the card.

2. Reference would be made to the Balance column of the ledger card to determine the amount of existing balance (last amount in the column).
3. Any previous balance would be entered in the Previous Balance column on the journal sheet.
4. Entries would be made in boxes appropriate to the headings printed on the cheque form—that is, the Date, the name of the Payee, the gross amount of the invoice in the Accts. Payable block (shown as the Debit column on the ledger card), the amount of any discount in the Discount column, and the cheque amount in the Check Amount block (shown as the Credit column on the ledger card).
5. The vendor's new balance would be calculated and entered in the Balance column of the ledger card.
6. The cheque number would be entered in the appropriate column.
7. Both the cheque and the ledger card would be removed from the board.
8. With the cheque removed from the board, the amount of the cheque would be written in words. In some systems, a cheque-write machine may be used to imprint the cheque amount.
9. If the cheque is to be mailed, the payee's address is entered to complete the cheque.
10. The cheque is signed and inserted in a double-window envelope for mailing.

A cheque may also be issued for a general disbursement; that is, no vendor's accounts payable ledger card would be used. In this case, after the cheque form is aligned on the journal sheet, the cheque would be made out in the normal manner, except that the amount of payment would not be entered in the Accts. Payable block. Instead, the amount would be entered in the Check Amount column (the Credit column) and in an appropriate distribution column on the journal sheet.

Observe that the Cash Disbursements journal sheet has special columns to record a bank deposit and to maintain the current bank balance in a column headed "(Memo) Bank Balance."

When the journal sheet becomes full, the journal totals are proved so that the Cheque Amount total plus the Discount total minus the Accounts Payable total will equal the grand total of all Distribution columns. Of course, these totals are carried forward to the top line of the next journal sheet. At the end of the month, totals can be posted to appropriate accounts filed in the general ledger.

Identifying Main One-Write System Advantages   A one-write system for the accounts payable application has three main advantages over the traditional manual system:

- When recording purchases of all types on account, subsidiary records are always current and clerical time is reduced by at least 50%, because the vendor's accounts payable account and the Accounts Payable account in the G/L are recorded in one writing.
- On the disbursements side of the accounts payable application, the cheque, vendor's account, and journal are completed in one writing. Clerical time is therefore reduced by at least 50%.
- One-writing avoids transposition errors that are quite common under the traditional system.

TOPIC 3   Problems

Answering questions on the journalizing of batch totals and direct postings in an accounts payable application.

8.10 Answer the following questions about the journalizing of batch totals and direct postings in processing purchases on credit.
  a   How many copies of each purchase invoice are required?
  b   What would be done with copy 1 of the invoice?
  c   What data would be posted to the general ledger? From where would this data be obtained? What account would be debited? Credited?
  d   Briefly explain one method of paying an invoice under the journalizing of batch totals method.

Answering questions on journalless bookkeeping in an accounts payable application.

8.11 Answer the following questions about the processing of purchases on credit in journalless bookkeeping.
  a   How many copies of each purchase invoice are required?
  b   Explain how posting is achieved to the individual creditor's account filed in the accounts payable ledger.
  c   What journal is eliminated under the journalless bookkeeping method of processing credit invoices?
  d   What data is posted to the general ledger? From where is it obtained? What account is debited? Credited?
  e   Where can the total amount owed to any one creditor be found?
  f   How can the accounting clerk know which invoices to pay on a given day?
  g   What is done with the original invoices after they are paid?
  h   After an invoice is paid, how is this data posted to the Accounts Payable account in the general ledger? To the creditor's account in the subsidiary ledger?
  i   Are all journals eliminated under the journalless method of processing credit purchases? Explain your answer.

Answering questions on the combination journal.

8.12 Answer the following questions about the combination journal shown in Figures 8-32 to 8-35.
  a   Why was the October cash balance not entered in the Cash Debit column?

    b How many special money columns have been provided for general ledger accounts?
    c What type of transaction is recorded in the Sales Credit column?
    d On what date was the first credit sale of the month made? To whom was it made?
    e Why does the transaction of October 7 take two lines?
    f In the transaction for October 7, explain why the account Sales Tax Payable is entered in the Account Title column when a special money column has been provided for this account?
    g What was the amount of cash paid on October 9?
    h Explain briefly the procedure to be followed when a new page of the combination journal is required.
    i How is the transaction to replenish the petty cash fund on October 22 recorded in the combination journal?
    j Describe the procedure followed in posting individual amounts and column totals of the combination journal.

Answering questions on the one-write system for the accounts payable application.

8.13 Answer the following questions on using the one-write system for the accounts payable application. (Refer to Figure 8-36.)
    a How many accounting boards are required to process the complete accounts payable application on Safeguard's one-write system? Explain your answer.
    b What forms are required to record credit purchases on Safeguard's one-write system? In what order would these forms be placed on the accounting board?
    c How is the one-write principle sustained in recording credit purchases under Safeguard's accounts payable system?
    d Briefly explain the debit and credit theory involved in recording a credit purchase under Safeguard's one-write system.
    e Briefly explain how purchases returns and allowances are recorded on Safeguard's one-write system for the accounts payable application.
    f What forms are required to record a cash payment involving a payment to a creditor's (vendor's) accounts payable account? In what order are these forms placed on the accounting board?
    g What forms are required to record a cash payment to a payee other than a vendor (creditor) in the accounts payable application?
    h Briefly explain the debit and credit theory involved in recording a cash disbursement to a vendor's account on Safeguard's one-write system for the accounts payable application.
    i When do postings occur to the accounts payable ledger under the one-write system? To the general ledger under the one-write system? Explain your answer.

Chapter Summary

In theory, the accounts payable application would include all activities related to the purchase of all types of goods and services from creditors, any returns and allowances to those purchases, and the subsequent payment of cash to eliminate amounts owing to creditors. Since the application includes the accounting of cash payments, it is logical to conclude that persons connected with accounts payable must also deal with internal measures to control and account for all types of cash payments.

Under the traditional manual system, the accounts payable application begins with the accounting of purchase invoices received from suppliers (vendors). In a small business, a one-column purchases journal may be used to record the purchases of goods on credit. In larger businesses, a multi-column purchases journal may be used to record all types of "purchases" on credit.

When a business deals with a fair number of creditors, the accounting system is expanded to account for all creditors (vendors) in a subsidiary ledger called the accounts payable ledger. Of course, a complementary controlling account, Accounts Payable, would be used in the general ledger to account for accounts payable transactions on a total basis only.

Posting to individual creditor accounts in the accounts payable ledger is usually done on a daily basis. However, posting to the Accounts Payable controlling account in the general ledger is normally done at the end of each month. Therefore, at the end of each month, trial balances are taken to prove that the balance of Accounts Payable in the G/L agrees with the total of individual creditor account balances listed in the schedule of accounts payable.

All businesses dealing with the accounting of accounts payable must establish internal control measures for cash payments. Although these measures will vary from firm to firm, ideally all businesses should adopt measures such as the following: (1) verify and approve all invoices before payment is made; (2) issue cheques for all payments of material amount; (3) use only serially prenumbered cheques to permit their full accountability; (4) prepare a cheque record for every issued cheque; (5) void and retain all spoiled cheques; (6) prepare cheques with care to prevent their fraudulent alteration; (7) submit all cheques for authorized signature; (8) cancel all bills paid by cheque; (9) mail a remittance advice with the cheque; (10) divide the responsibility where possible so that the person handling the cheques is separated from the person recording the payments made by cheque; (11) where possible, use a tickler file system to keep track of invoices which are due for payment; and (12) use a special journal to record all cash payment transactions.

Under the traditional manual system, the special journal to record all cash payment transactions is known as the cash payments journal or cash disbursements journal. Most systems will use special money columns in the cash payments journal to take advantage of posting the totals of each column to general ledger accounts at the end of each month. Of course, any amounts recorded in the Accounts Payable debit column would be posted on a daily basis to individual vendor accounts filed in the accounts payable ledger. The majority of the cash payments journals will include special columns to identify the name of the payee and the cheque number of the cheque issued.

One uncommon transaction that may come up under the accounts payable application is the accounting of cash short and over transactions. If the cash proof shows less cash in the drawer than there should have been, the cash is said to be short. Therefore, a special entry may be made in the cash payments journal showing a debit to Cash Short and Over and a credit to Cash. On the other hand, if there is more cash than there should have been, the cash is said to be over. This overage is accounted for by debiting Cash and crediting Cash Short and Over in the cash receipts journal. When a financial statement is required, any debit balance in Cash Short and Over would be reported as part of Miscellaneous Expenses or Other Expenses in the income statement. On the other hand, any credit balance would be reported as part of Miscellaneous Revenue or Other Revenue in the income statement.

Most businesses employ a petty cash *imprest* system to control minor or petty expenditures—that is, the procedure of borrowing a sum like $50 from the main Cash account to establish a petty cash fund. Therefore, a cheque would be issued in the name of the petty cashier to establish the fund and a double entry would be made showing a debit to Petty Cash and a credit to Cash.

To control petty cash, all petty cash disbursements would be made under the control of the petty cashier, who may use a petty cash book to record petty cash vouchers issued against the fund. The petty cash book is not a journal but simply a record for the convenience of the petty cashier.

When the petty cash fund becomes low, the petty cashier prepares a summary of the disbursements made and a request to replenish the fund. All petty cash vouchers would be turned over to accounts payable prior to a cheque being issued for the total amount of these vouchers. In turn, an accounting entry is made in the cash payments journal to account for all issued vouchers.

In preparing a balance sheet, it is customary to combine the amount of petty cash with Cash (in the bank) to report the Total Cash on Hand or simply Cash. To the reader, therefore, Cash means all sources of cash immediately available to pay for current liabilities and current operating activities. Of course, this Cash would consist of cash in the bank and the petty cash fund.

In processing the accounts payable application, businesses using the manual system may employ one or more shortcut measures. In general, the shortcuts are related to journalizing and posting procedures and may include the following: (1) journalizing batch totals and direct posting to accounts payable; (2) journalless bookkeeping procedures; (3) ledgerless bookkeeping procedures; (4) using a combination journal; (5) using the one-write system.

Many would acknowledge that the one-write system is the most efficient shortcut manual system in the accounting of accounts payable. Under such a one-write system, it is common to employ separate accounting boards to record purchases on account and to record cash disbursements of all kinds.

Chapter Questions

1. What procedures should be followed in posting entries from a one-column purchases journal?
2. What is a columnar purchases journal? What is the essential difference between this journal and the one-column purchases journal?
3. Under what circumstances is a diagonal line inserted in the posting reference column opposite an entry in the two-column general journal?
4. In accounting for merchandising transactions, who would create a debit memo? A credit memo? State the double entry required for each memo.
5. Explain how the use of a four-column cash payments journal simplifies journalizing and posting entries to the subsidiary and general ledgers.
6. Briefly explain what cycle billing is.
7. What is a tickler file system? Who would be assigned the task of maintaining such a system?
8. Explain how the Accounts Payable controlling account actually "controls."
9. In general, what measures should be included in any efficient system for controlling the outflow of cash in any business enterprise?
10. Name three advantages of paying by cheque for a business enterprise.
11. Explain how internal control over cash transactions is strengthened by supporting the following measure: "Deposit each day's cash receipts intact in the bank, and make all disbursements by cheque."
12. One important internal measure to control cash payments is to use only prenumbered cheques in order to ensure their full accountability. Briefly explain what is meant by "their full accountability."
13. Why should all bills paid by cheque be cancelled immediately after issuing the cheque?
14. Explain what is meant by the practice, in large businesses, of "countersigning" cheques.
15. What is a voucher cheque? Why would one be used?
16. What are the steps involved in completing the cash payments journal at the end of the month?
17. At the end of the accounting period, the Cash Short and Over account showed total debits of $14.80 and total credits of $13.90. Is the balance of this account considered revenue or expense?
18. For the month of August, the Cash Short and Over account has total debits of $297 and total credits of $3. The accountant feels that the procedures for handling shortages and overages should be investigated. Do you agree? Why?
19. What source documents serve as the basis of the entries in the cash payments journal?

20 What is the chief reason for introducing a petty cash system in a business?
21 How is the measure of dividing the responsibility maintained in a petty cash system?
22 Under what situation may the Petty Cash account be debited more than once?
23 Would the Petty Cash account ever be credited? Explain why or why not.
24 Mary's Stationery Shop has for years maintained a petty cash fund of $765, which is replenished twice a month.
   a How many debit entries would you expect to find in the Petty Cash account each year?
   b When would expenditures from the petty cash fund be entered in the ledger accounts?
   c Explain briefly how the balance in the Petty Cash account would be reported in the business's balance sheet at year-end.
25 Honest John's Store sells only for cash and records all sales on cash registers before delivering merchandise to the customers. On a given day the cash count at the close of business indicated $10.25 less cash than was shown by the totals on the cash register tapes. In what account would this cash shortage be recorded? Would the account be debited or credited? Explain.
26 Outline the main advantages and disadvantages of the journalless method in processing credit purchases under a manual system.
27 What is a combination journal? Briefly explain how an individual entry is recorded and posted in such a journal.
28 Briefly explain the procedures for posting the monthly totals in a combination journal.
29 Would a professional accountant support the use of a combination (synoptic) journal for all types of businesses? Explain.
30 Why are two accounting boards used in Safeguard's one-write system for accounts payable?
31 Briefly explain how returns and credits from vendors are recorded under Safeguard's one-write system for accounts payable.
32 Briefly identify three advantages of using the one-write system for accounts payable when the manual accounting system is supported by management.

Accounting Case Problems

CASE 8-1
Preparing a report on the basic measures for controlling cash of a medium-sized company.

A friend of yours, the owner of a medium-sized company, learns that you have studied the basic measures for controlling cash. You are invited to spend a few days studying the application of these control measures in her business. At the end of your study, you come across the following facts:

1. A petty cash fund of $1 000 was established to take care of small payments. Instead of a regular voucher form, the system permitted those using the petty cash to submit their own forms. Many of the forms were a variety of store receipts; some of the forms were mere short pieces of paper with some explanation by the user of the petty cash. A check of the petty cash book revealed that the fund was replenished weekly.
2. The petty cashier was permitted to issue the replenishing cheque, sign the cheque, and make the accounting record for all petty cash payments.
3. The petty cashier was permitted to approve payments of any amount up to and including $100.
4. Personal cheques of customers and employees were permitted to be cashed from the petty cash fund.
5. One person was given the responsibility to act as the cashier-bookkeeper. Among other duties, he handled cash receipts, deposited all cash in the bank, issued and signed all cheques, and maintained the accounting records for all cash transactions other than those of a petty cash nature.
6. A cheque for $855 issued in payment of an accounts payable was erroneously listed in the cash payments journal as $585. The error was not corrected until the next month when the cancelled cheque was received from the bank.

Required

a Assume that you were planning to present a written report of your findings, and identify the apparent cash control weaknesses for each disclosed fact.

b What changes in the overall cash control system would you recommend to eliminate the problem areas?

Note: If possible, prepare your report using a microcomputer and appropriate word processing software.

CASE 8-2

Analyzing one office manager's view on handling and controlling the petty cash fund.

Sophia Theodoropolus commenced a branch office some 200 km away from her main base of business operations. Before returning home, she instructed the office manager to establish a petty cash fund of $50 for making small payments. She also instructed the office manager to keep a close watch on the fund so that the petty cash expenditures could be controlled.

After three months of operations, the owner returned to the branch office to make an inspection of all internal control procedures. Among several inconsistencies, Sophia learned the following:

1. Five people within the organization were permitted to make payments from the petty cash fund.
2. Very few documents were available to substantiate the majority of payments.
3. When the money in the fund was low, the contents of the coin box in the office soft-drink machine were used to replenish the petty cash fund.

When criticized by the owner for loose control over the fund, the office manager casually shrugged his shoulders and replied, "Don't get excited, Sophia. After all, the most we can lose is $50."

a Do you agree or disagree with the office manager's view?
b Identify the main weaknesses in the operation of this petty cash system.
c If you were the owner, what measures would you take to control the system of petty cash?

CHAPTER 9 Banking Applications

After completing this chapter, you should be able to:

— Show an accounting analysis from a banker's point of view, of a selected number of transactions affecting the chequing (current) account of a depositor-enterprise.

— Rewrite the banker's analysis of transactions affecting the current account from the viewpoint of the depositor-enterprise's books.

— Analyze the entries made on a computerized bank statement.

— Construct a computerized bank statement from given data on a current account depositor.

— Prepare a bank reconciliation statement from given information.

— Record the necessary adjusting entries following the preparation of a bank reconciliation statement.

— Prepare a monthly statement of cash flows for unincorporated businesses.

— Prepare a 12-month statement of cash flows using electronic spreadsheet software.

— Define the following key terms used in this chapter: current account, depositors, demand deposits payable, demand deposit accounting, time deposit accounting, bank debit memo, bank credit memo, certified cheque, NSF cheque, clearing of cheques, MICR, cancelled cheques, bank statement, outstanding cheques, deposit in transit, discrepancy items, bank reconciliation statement, historical statement of cash flows, prospective statement of cash flows.

In the last two chapters, you learned of several important internal control measures for the effective control of cash receipts and cash payments. Two important measures should stand out above all others: that all cash receipts should be deposited intact and that all cash payments should be made by cheque. In actual fact, both measures identify the important role that a bank contributes to the overall system of any firm's attempt to control the inflow and outflow of its cash. This chapter, therefore, analyzes in more detail the relationship between a business and its banker. In particular, Topic 1 examines the type of accounting the bank offers the business so that cash may be more effectively controlled. Topic 2 introduces the

CHAPTER 9: Banking Applications **375**

important concept that, once a month, the cash balance reported by the bank must be made to agree with the cash balance reported by the person who handles the cash and the (separate) person who keeps an accounting record of the cash. With this monthly bank reconciliation and cash records, the firm is able to prepare its monthly statement of cash flows.

TOPIC 1 Bank Accounting Concepts

Many persons, unfamiliar with the fundamentals of accounting, often are heard to express the idea that bank accounting is "backwards" to the accounting practice followed by other profit-making businesses—that the rules for debiting and crediting accounts are opposite. This notion is completely wrong! What may confuse these persons (and many beginning accounting students) is the lack of understanding of the normal relationship between a business and its banker. Examine the following four points carefully; then apply this knowledge to the analysis of the banking transactions that follow.

Current account: a bank chequing account payable on demand.

1. In general, business enterprises open a bank **current account** as part of their overall system to control cash.

2. Businesses that deposit their cash receipts intact in a bank current account are actually lending this money to the bank for safekeeping; therefore, these businesses are known by the bank as **depositors**.

Depositors: persons and businesses that lend money to bankers.

3. In receipting cash receipts from any business, the banker acts as a custodian of the spendable funds of the depositor-enterprise. This means that the banker is responsible for safeguarding the most valuable asset of the depositor until such time as the depositor instructs the banker to pay some person or some business. As you know, the depositor gives such instructions each time a cheque is prepared and later presented for payment.

4. Since the funds of the enterprise on deposit in a bank current account are "lent" to the bank for safekeeping, these funds must represent a debit owing by the bank for the enterprise payable on demand. And, as you should know, any debt that is owing by any business is known in the language of accounting as a *liability*.

This last point must be understood to avoid any confusion in the debit and credit analysis of transactions from the banker's point of view. Consider, for example, the following fictitious transactions identified by one of Canada's chartered banks, Royal Bank of Canada, in relation to one depositor, Kelly's Office Services.

Transaction 1 Kelly's Office Services deposits intact receipts totalling $500.

From the opening chapter, you learned that the accounting equation stated that, at any particular point in time, assets must be equal to the claims against those assets, or A = L + OE. If the banker received $500 to hold for Kelly's Office Services, then the banker's equation to account for that cash must be stated as in Figure 9-1.

FIGURE 9-1

Assets	=	Liabilities	+	Owner's Equity
Cash		Kelly's Office Services		Banker's Capital
$500	=	$500	+	$0

In T-account form the analysis by the banker would be as in Figure 9-2.

FIGURE 9-2

Cash		Demand Deposits Payable/ Kelly's Office Services
(1) 500		(1) 500

Analysis   These points should be recalled as you analyze the banker's equation and T-account double entry labelled (1):

- The Cash account on the "books" of the banker would be a current asset. Since cash was received by the bank, the banker's Cash account must be increased; consequently, an accounting entry must be shown as a debit to record this increase to the asset.
- In the case of the credit entry, a type of "accounts payable" account known as **Demand Deposits Payable** is used to record the increase to a current liability. Demand deposits payable indicates that the depositor, by depositing cash in a current account, can withdraw his or her money on demand. In other words, when the depositor issues a cheque, he or she is actually ordering the bank to pay the funds to the payee identified on the cheque without delay. Since the banker must comply with the instructions of the depositor when the cheque is presented for payment, all demand deposit accounts would appear as the top item under the Liabilities section of any banker's balance sheet.

At this stage it is useful to point out that, in addition to current accounts, bank personal chequing accounts are classified as demand deposits also. In other words, a person having money on deposit in a personal chequing account may withdraw his or her money on demand. A third class of bank account, however, is quite different. You will be familiar with the pure savings account that generally earns interest for the depositor. Since the bank reserves the right in times of emergency to require 15 days' notice of withdrawal of all or any portion of the funds on deposit in such a savings account, these savings accounts are commonly known as *time deposits*. On a banker's balance sheet, therefore, time deposits would be classified as current liabilities, but they must be listed

Demand Deposits Payable: a current liability account in the ledger of a banker.

CHAPTER 9: Banking Applications **377**

Demand deposit accounting: the accounting of current and personal chequing accounts.

Time deposit accounting: the accounting of pure savings accounts.

after all demand deposits. In banking terminology, the accounting of current accounts and personal chequing accounts would be acknowledged as ***demand deposit accounting***, while pure savings accounts would fall under the special class of ***time deposit accounting***.

Transaction 2   The Royal Bank of Canada "cashes" cheques drawn by Kelly's Office Services to the amount of $300.

Examine carefully the T-account entry and analysis shown in Figure 9-3.

FIGURE **9-3**

Cash		Demand Deposits Payable/ Kelly's Office Services	
	(2) 300	(2) 300	

Analysis

- From the banker's point of view, cashing a depositor's cheque simply means that the bank will have less cash in its Cash account. Therefore, the bank's Cash account must be decreased by means of a credit entry.
- You should have little difficulty in understanding the debit entry if you remember that Kelly's Office Services' account is being decreased as a current liability account. In any banker's books, therefore, cheques issued and subsequently cancelled by the banker will be recorded as debits to the current liability account called Demand Deposits Payable. On the other hand, all deposits must be recorded as credits to record increases to this current liability account.

Transaction 3   The Royal Bank of Canada agrees to lend Kelly's Office Services $1 400 on the signature of a demand note. Kelly's Office Services in turn deposits the amount of the loan in its current account.

In account theory, three complete transactions may be analyzed. Examine carefully the T-account entries labelled (3a), (3b), and (3c) in Figures 9-4 to 9-6.

FIGURE **9-4**

Demand Loans Receivable/ Kelly's Office Services		Cash	
(3a) 1 400			(3a) 1 400

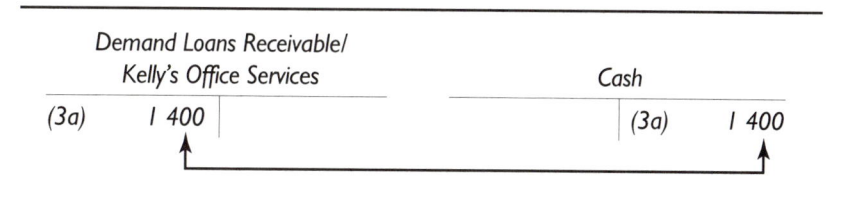

FIGURE **9-5**

Cash		Demand Deposits Payable/ Kelly's Office Services	
(3b) 1 400			(3b) 1 400

FIGURE 9-6

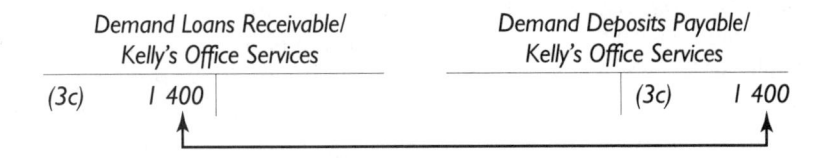

Demand Loans Receivable/ Kelly's Office Services	Demand Deposits Payable/ Kelly's Office Services
(3c) 1 400	(3c) 1 400

Analysis

- In (3a), Demand Loans Receivable/Kelly's Office Services must be analyzed as a type of accounts receivable on the books of the banker. Therefore, a debit entry is shown to record an increase to the current asset. Of course, the credit to the banker's Cash account reflects the accounting theory of recording a decrease to the current asset.

- In (3b), the theory of debits and credits for this second transaction should cause you no difficulty if you remember that, by depositing the loan in the depositor's current account, the depositor is returning the cash to the banker for safekeeping. Therefore, both the bank's Cash account and its liability to Kelly's Office Services will be increased.

- In actual practice, however, the two theoretical transactions in (3a) and (3b) are combined into one, as illustrated in (3c). Observe carefully that (3c) debits Demand Loans Receivable/Kelly's Office Services, and credits Demand Deposits Payable/Kelly's Office Services for the amount of the loan. In other words, the banker's Cash account is not used, because this account is cancelled out by the two related transactions (3a) and (3b). Therefore, in granting a loan which is deposited in the firm's chequing account, the banker's Cash account is not used. Of course, in depositing the funds, the depositor intends to issue cheques against his current account. In no way will the issuance of these cheques affect the banker's Demand Loans Receivable account. At some future time, however, Kelly's Office Services will be required to issue a cheque to the banker in order to pay part or all of the loan. The correct analysis of the next transaction should prove this point.

Transaction 4   The Royal Bank of Canada receives a cheque for $100 in part payment of the demand loan granted earlier to Kelly's Office Services.

This transaction may be a little tricky to analyze, because, in accounting theory, two events can be identified, as illustrated in the T-accounts labelled (4a) and (4b) in Figures 9-7 and 9-8.

FIGURE 9-7

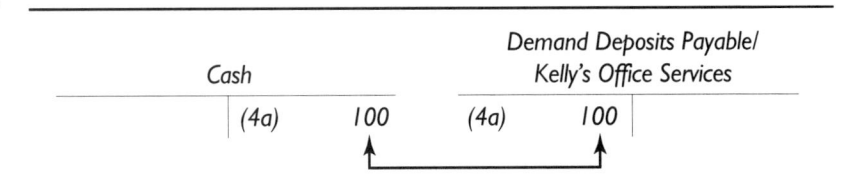

Cash	Demand Deposits Payable/ Kelly's Office Services
(4a) 100	(4a) 100

CHAPTER 9: Banking Applications **379**

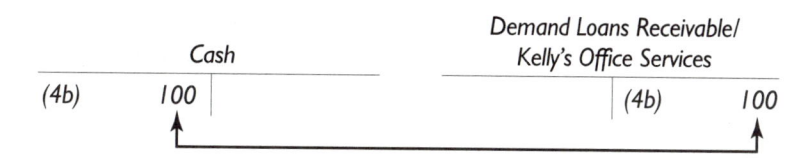

FIGURE **9-8**

	Cash		Demand Loans Receivable/ Kelly's Office Services	
(4b)	100	(4b)		100

Analysis

- In (4a), the banker cashes the cheque written by the current account depositor and accounts for this cancelled cheque in the normal way. The banker's liability account will be debited and the banker's Cash account will be credited.
- In (4b), the T-account supports the theory of the banker's receiving the cash amount disclosed on the cheque. Remember, the banker has been named as the payee on the cheque and, therefore, is entitled to the cash. In this case, the banker's Cash account must be debited, because an increase in assets is analyzed. Since the cash received is in part payment of the Demand Loans Receivable, this asset account must be credited on the banker's books to show a decrease in the amount owing by the borrower.
- In practice, however, the banker merely debits the Demand Deposits Payable account and credits Demand Loans Receivable, because the theoretical Cash account balances in (4a) and (4b) cancel each other out. The correct method of recording Transaction 4, therefore, is analyzed in T-account form as shown in Figure 9-9 as (4c).
- As a concluding point in the analysis of payments of loans to banks, it is worthwhile noting that the depositor may simply notify the bank by telephone to remove the amount from the firm's current account. When this practice is followed, the banker usually makes out an advice slip known as a *bank debit memorandum* for the amount of the demand loan to be reduced. This debit memorandum (*debit memo* for short) would be mailed to the depositor, or included with the bank's monthly statement to the depositor.

An example of the Royal Bank's debit memo is shown in Figure 9-10.

FIGURE **9-9**

Demand Deposits Payable/ Kelly's Office Services			
(4c)	100		

Demand Loans Receivable/ Kelly's Office Services			
		(4c)	100

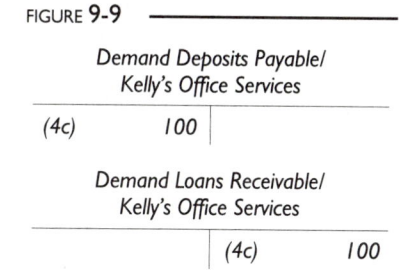

FIGURE **9-10**

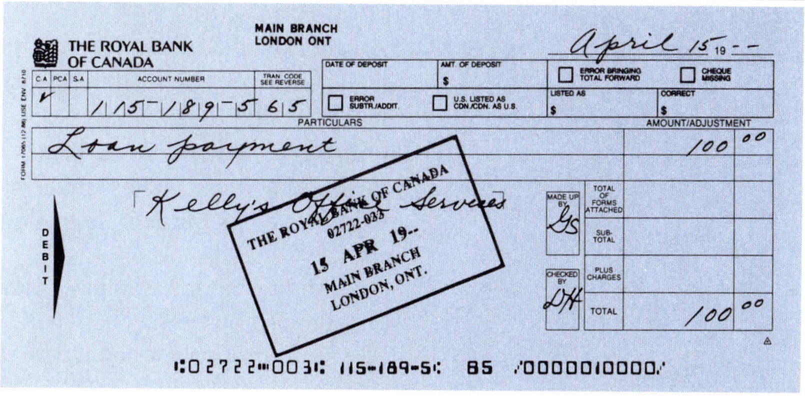

Observe the significance of the word "Debit." You should have little difficulty understanding that the depositor's current account (the liability) has been decreased by the amount shown on the memorandum.

Transaction 5 The Royal Bank of Canada calculates interest in the amount of $10 on the demand loan for one month and charges this amount to Kelly's Office Services.

Analysis In this transaction, labelled (5), the banker will issue a debit memo showing that $10 has been deducted from the depositor's current account. Since the interest is earned by the bank, this interest is recognized as revenue that causes an increase to the banker's equity. The banker's equity is claimed by many shareholders; therefore, the proper heading would be "Shareholders' Equity." The T-account analysis by the banker may be viewed as shown in the side margin.

When Kelly's Office Services receives the bank debit memo showing that the current account has been reduced by the amount of loan interest, some responsible person within the business must check the accuracy of the interest calculation. After the the accuracy has been verified, an entry must be made on the books of Kelly's Office Services to record the expense of the interest on the loan. The analysis of the debit and credit entry on the books of Kelly's Office Services may be made as shown in Figure 9-12.

Of course, no cheque is issued by Kelly's Office Services for the bank interest. Instead, an appropriate explanation in the cash payments journal may be entered, as shown in Figure 9-13.

FIGURE 9-11

Demand Deposits Payable/
Kelly's Office Services

(5)	10

Interest Revenue

	(5)	10

FIGURE 9-12

Interest Expense

10	

Cash

	10

FIGURE 9-13

| | CASH PAYMENTS JOURNAL | | | Page 5 |
Date	Account Debited	Explanation	Cheque No.	Post. Ref.	Amount
19—					
Apr. 15	Interest Expense	Bank debit memo for loan interest.	—		10 00

Transaction 6 The Royal Bank of Canada issues a debit memo to Kelly's Office Services showing that $27.50 has been deducted for the rental of a safety deposit box.

Analysis When a business firm uses a bank safety deposit box to store valuable documents, the banker generally will deduct the fee for the rental of the box through the issue of a debit memo as shown in Figure 9-14.

From the banker's point of view, the fee received for the rental of safety deposit boxes may be regarded as miscellaneous revenue or credited to an appropriate account with some such name as "Rental Revenue,"

CHAPTER 9: Banking Applications **381**

FIGURE 9-14

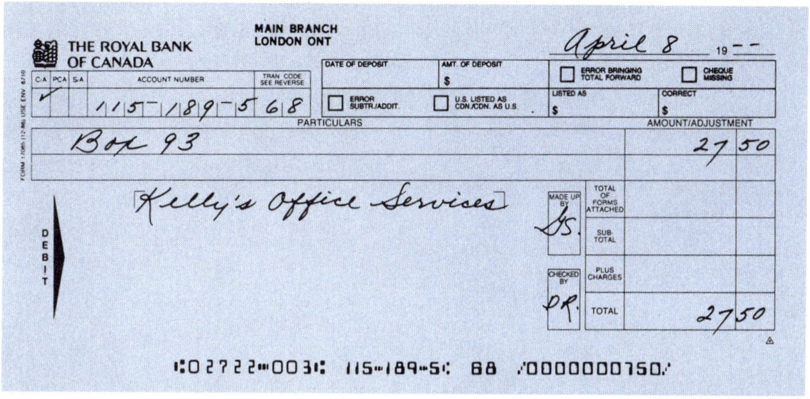

FIGURE 9-15

Demand Deposits Payable/
Kelly's Office Services

| (6) | 27.50 |

Miscellaneous Revenue

| | (6) | 27.50 |

Certified cheque: cheque carrying the guarantee of the drawee (the depositor's bank).

"Safety Deposit Box Rental Revenue," etc. The T-account analysis of the transaction may be viewed by the banker as shown in the side margin.

From the depositor's point of view, however, the receipt of the debit memo must be analyzed quite differently. An accounting entry would be recorded in the cash payments journal debiting an account named "Safety Deposit Box Rental Expense" or "Miscellaneous Expense," and crediting Cash. Of course, no cheque would be issued to pay for the rental of the safety deposit box; instead, the bank debit memo would be acknowledged in the Explanation column of the Cash Payments Journal.

Transaction 7   Kelly's Office Services has a cheque for $800 certified at the Royal Bank of Canada. The certified cheque is then mailed to the payee.

Analysis   Before the accounting side of this transaction is analyzed, some explanation is required about the nature of a certified cheque. Briefly, a ***certified cheque***, when granted, carries the guarantee of the drawee (the depositor's bank) that sufficient funds are available to pay the cheque when it is presented. To certify a cheque, the depositor issues the cheque in the usual manner and takes it to his or her bank. See Figure 9-16.

FIGURE 9-16

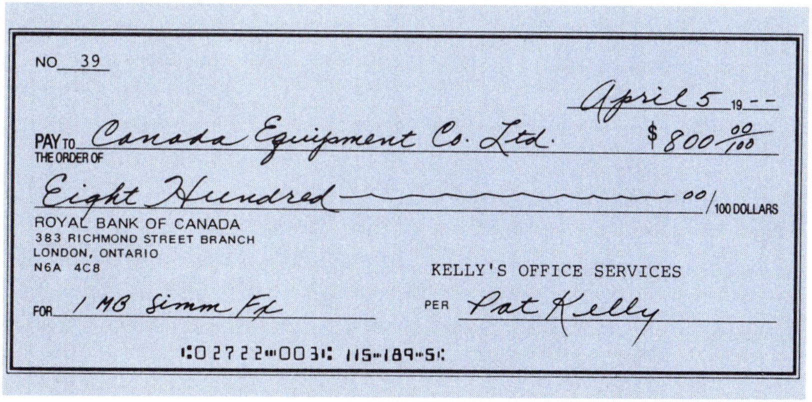

FIGURE 9-17

**Demand Deposits Payable/
Kelly's Office Services**

(7)	800		

Cash

		(7)	800

Before the teller stamps "Certified," together with the date and name and address of the bank, across the face of the cheque, he or she must check that sufficient funds are on deposit in the current account to cover the amount of the cheque. If there are sufficient funds, the cheque is "certified" and passed through a protectograph machine to impress the amount into the cheque to ensure greater safety.

Once the cheque is properly certified, the banker will deduct the amount of the cheque from the depositor's current account. It is important to remember that the banker does not wait for the cheque to be cancelled in order to make this deduction; the accounting entry is done immediately and may be viewed in T-account form as shown in the side margin.

The banker will also deduct $4 for providing the cheque certification service to the issuer. Some banks will deduct this amount immediately; other banks may choose to show this deduction on the monthly bank statement as a separate debit memo.

In the books of Kelly's Office Services, no additional entry is required to record a certified cheque. Some firms add the letters "CC" ("certified cheque") opposite the appropriate cheque number in the cheque record and in the cheque number column of the cash payments journal. You will learn later that the banker will also show either "CC" or "Certified" opposite the cheque amount listed on the banker's monthly statement to the depositor. As indicated earlier, most bankers now charge a service fee of $4 for each cheque that is certified. In the case of Kelly's Office Services, assume that a separate debit memo will be issued and is accounted for later when the depositor receives the monthly bank statement.

Transaction 8   The Royal Bank of Canada prepares a debit memo to inform Kelly's Office Services that its current account has been decreased by $50.75 as a result of an NSF cheque drawn by J. P. Sands, an accounts receivable customer of the depositor.

Analysis   In this transaction, it is important to learn the meaning of the term **NSF cheque**. Briefly, the depositor has deposited a cheque earlier received from a customer. The banker, in good faith, has credited the depositor's current account with the amount of the cheque. When the depositor's bank tries to collect the amount from the bank on which the cheque was drawn, it is learned that there are not sufficient funds to cover the payment of the cheque. In other words, the cheque is dishonoured and "bounces" back to the depositor's bank. Since the cheque has been returned and marked NSF, the depositor's bank will deduct the amount from the depositor's current account. At the same time, the banker will have to decrease his Cash account, because he has not been able to collect cash from the drawer's bank. The accounting entry for an NSF cheque, on the banker's books, may be viewed in T-account form as shown in the side margin.

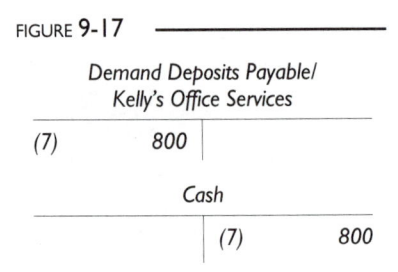

NSF cheque: a cheque previously deposited but returned because of insufficient funds.

FIGURE 9-18

**Demand Deposits Payable/
Kelly's Office Services**

(8)	50.75		

Cash

		(8)	50.75

Of course, Kelly's Office Services will not know of this returned item until the firm receives the debit memo and NSF cheque from its bank. When the depositor receives this information, an accounting entry will be required in Kelly's books to charge the amount back to the appropriate accounts receivable account and to credit Cash for the decrease to this asset account. This entry will be examined in more detail in the next Topic.

As a final note regarding an NSF cheque, keep in mind that Kelly's bank does not charge the firm for the returned item. At the time of writing, however, banks do charge the drawer of the cheque a fee of $17 each time the cheque becomes NSF. In this way, banks try to encourage all depositors to have sufficient funds to cover the issuance of cheques and thereby avoid NSF situations.

Transaction 9 The Royal Bank of Canada prepares a credit memo notifying the depositor that its current account has been credited for $37.50 interest on bank short-term deposit receipts held for the depositor.

Analysis It is common practice for many firms to invest some of their cash receipts in 30-, 60-, or 90-day term deposit receipts. For example, Kelly's Office Services has invested in 60-day deposit receipts with its banker and leaves instructions to credit its current account with interest earned on those deposits. When such practice is followed, the banker usually prepares a credit memo to notify the depositor that his or her account has been increased by the amount of the memo as illustrated below.

FIGURE 9-19

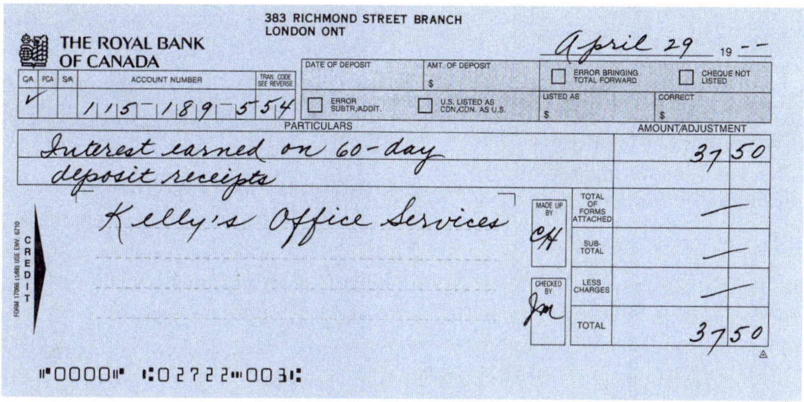
THE ROYAL BANK OF CANADA
383 RICHMOND STREET BRANCH
LONDON ONT
April 29 19 --
CA | PCA | SA | ACCOUNT NUMBER
✓ 115-189-554
DATE OF DEPOSIT | AMT. OF DEPOSIT $ | ERROR BRINGING TOTAL FORWARD | CHEQUE NOT LISTED
ERROR SUBTR./ADDIT. | U.S. LISTED AS CDN./CDN. AS U.S. | LISTED AS $ | CORRECT $
PARTICULARS | AMOUNT/ADJUSTMENT
Interest earned on 60-day deposit receipts | 37 50
Kelly's Office Services
MADE UP BY CH | TOTAL OF FORMS ATTACHED —
SUB-TOTAL —
CHECKED BY JM | LESS CHARGES —
TOTAL 37 50
CREDIT

FIGURE 9-20

Cash	
(9) 37.50	

Demand Deposits Payable/ Kelly's Office Services	
	(9) 37.50

The accounting entry on the books of the banker may be analyzed in T-account form as shown in Figure 9-20. Notice by this analysis that the banker's Cash account would have increased, since interest earned has been credited to the depositor's current account. The offsetting debit represents an additional amount of Cash on the banker's books until such time as the depositor issues additional cheques on its current account.

Once the depositor receives the bank's credit memo, an appropriate accounting entry must be made in the cash receipts journal showing a debit to Cash and a credit to an account named "Interest Earned on Bank Deposit Receipts" or simply "Interest Revenue."

Transaction 10   The Royal Bank of Canada deducts $8.95 from Kelly's Office Services' current account for monthly packaged banking services.

Analysis   In general, every month, banks calculate a service charge to cover the expense of handling the current account of depositors. Some banks offer packaged banking services which include servicing current and other accounts. Since the amount of this charge is based upon such considerations as the average balance of the account, the number of cheques and deposits processed, and other banking services rendered, it follows that this service charge will vary from bank to bank. The amount of the service charge shown in the side margin figure illustrates the concept of a monthly service charge. In some banking practice, a debit memo may be issued to explain this charge. In most cases, however, the charge is marked "S," "SC," or "Service Charges" before or after the amount on the monthly bank statement. Notice that the T-account analysis of this transaction in the margin represents the double entry on the banker's books.

Of course, from the depositor's viewpoint, the service charge would be regarded as an expense. This expense would be recorded in the cash payments journal or general journal under some account title such as "Miscellaneous Expense" or "Bank Charges Expense."

FIGURE 9-21

Demand Deposits Payable/ Kelly's Office Services	
(10) 8.95	

Miscellaneous Revenue	
	(10) 8.95

Clearing Bank Cheques

Clearing: a method adopted by banks for making an exchange of cheques held against the others and for settling the differences that remain.

At the time of writing, Canada's chartered banks operate a system known as ***clearing*** in order to return cheques and settle amounts among them, including amounts issued through other, non-chartered banks such as trust companies. In general, there are two types of clearing: (1) an internal system that returns cheques drawn on branches of the same bank; and (2) an external system to allow banks to make an exchange of cheques and settle the difference in the amounts exchanged.

To explain the entire clearing process would require a separate chapter of many pages. What you should learn here is only the basic idea of clearing. Generally, all cheques from a given bank's branches are first sent to the bank's main branch or to its regional data centre, where they are sorted and bundled for clearing. Cheques drawn on the same bank are then returned to the branches, while cheques drawn on other banks are exchanged at one of the banks which is designated as the *clearinghouse*. Once the cheques are exchanged and settlements are approved, they are returned to the bank's branches for further processing.

Processing Cheques and Bank Memos

In addition to the common use of a clearinghouse system, the chartered banks have also agreed to use a special code line on all cheques and bank memos known as ***magnetic ink character recognition (MICR) codes***. You may have come across this term in a data processing course. Briefly,

Magnetic ink character recognition (MICR) codes: machine-readable numbers placed at the bottom of cheques, deposit slips, and bank memos to allow the bank's computer system to process those documents.

the use of the code line at the bottom of cheques and bank memos permits the bank's computer to post the data to appropriate accounts. Of course, the computer is programmed to post MICR dollar amounts on cheques and debit memos as debits to the depositor's current account, while MICR amounts on credit memos would be posted as credits.

Processing the Depositor's Bank Statement

Once a month the banker processes a statement of account to the current account depositor. It is important to understand that this statement summarizes the current account's transactions from the banker's point of view. Another way to express this idea is to say that a monthly statement of account represents an exact summary of the banker's postings to the demand deposit liability account.

The statement shown in Figure 9-22 illustrates how the bank may report one month's transactions to a depositor. In this illustration, the transactions are for the one month ended April 30. In practice, banks differ on the one-month interval. Some will use a one-month period ended on the fourteenth of each month; others will use the end of the month. Regardless of the monthly period, the bank will prepare the statement of account so that it can be mailed or picked up in person a short time after the monthly period expires. It is also important to understand that banks usually prepare these monthly statements through their regional computer centre; therefore, a delay of one or two days can be expected before the statements are returned to the branch bank where the depositor has his or her account.

One other point must be considered before you study the illustrated bank statement. Enclosed with the bank statement will be the return of all ***cancelled cheques***, that is, those cheques issued by the depositor and paid by his or her bank. These cheques will be bundled in the same order as each cheque amount appears on the bank statement. In addition, enclosed will be any bank debit and credit memos not as yet mailed to the depositor. Now examine carefully the illustration and study the points of analysis given below.

Cancelled cheques: cheques paid by the bank.

- The top portion of the statement identifies the depositor by name and account number. In addition, this section indicates the month-end period for which the statement is prepared, and the number of enclosures returned with the statement.
- Observe that all letters of the alphabet printed on the statement are shown in uppercase, that is, there are no "small" or lowercase letters. The exclusive use of uppercase letters is quite common in computer printouts.
- Observe that the column headings follow the popular three-column account form: debits at the left, credits at the right, and a balance column to print a "running" balance after each set of postings. What

386 PART 2: COMMON ACCOUNTING APPLICATIONS

FIGURE 9-22

THE ROYAL BANK OF CANADA

ACCOUNT STATEMENT

PLEASE NOTIFY US OF ANY CHANGE IN YOUR ADDRESS

2722 KELLY'S OFFICE SERVICES
1263 COMMISSIONERS RD WEST
LONDON ONT
N6K 1C9

ACCOUNT NO. 115-189-5
STATEMENT DATE APR 30 --
ENCLOSURES 34

CURRENT ACCOUNT BALANCE FORWARD ▶ 3,115.48

DESCRIPTION - DEBITS / CHEQUES			DEPOSITS / CREDITS	DATE M D	NEW BALANCE
CHEQUE	032	200.00		4 01	2,915.48
CHEQUE	033	100.00		4 01	2,815.48
DEPOSIT			500.00	4 01	3,315.48
CHEQUE	034	71.80		4 03	3,243.68
DEMAND LOAN			1,400.00	4 03	4,643.68
CERTIFIED CHEQUE	035	800.00		4 05	3,843.68
CHEQUE	036	60.00		4 05	3,783.68
DEPOSIT			75.00	4 05	3,858.68
CHEQUE	037	50.00		4 05	3,808.68
DEBIT MEMO		27.50		4 08	3,781.18
CHEQUE	038	95.80		4 08	3,685.38
CHEQUE	039	1,500.00		4 08	2,185.38
DEPOSIT			100.00	4 08	2,285.38
DEPOSIT			78.75	4 10	2,364.13
CHEQUE	040	350.00		4 11	2,014.13
CHEQUE	041	67.90		4 11	1,946.23
DEPOSIT			300.00	4 11	2,246.23
DEBIT MEMO		100.00		4 15	2,146.23
CHEQUE	042	78.90		4 15	2,067.33
CHEQUE	044	16.70		4 15	3,050.63
CHEQUE	045	48.95		4 15	2,001.68
DEPOSIT			375.85	4 17	2,377.53
CHEQUE	047	88.90		4 19	2,288.63
CHEQUE	048	50.00		4 19	2,238.63
DEPOSIT			396.80	4 22	2,635.43
RETURNED ITEM		50.75		4 23	2,584.68
CHEQUE	049	48.75		4 23	2,535.93
DEPOSIT			178.50	4 24	2,714.43
CHEQUE	050	67.40		4 26	2,647.03
CHEQUE	051	19.37		4 26	2,627.66
CHEQUE	052	47.50		4 26	2,580.16
DEPOSIT			190.50	4 26	2,770.66
CREDIT MEMO			37.50	4 29	2,808.16
CHEQUE	054	65.00		4 30	2,743.16
SERVICE CHARGES		8.95		4 30	2,734.21
DEBIT MEMO		10.00		4 30	2,724.21

NO DEBITS	TOTAL AMOUNT - DEBIT	NO. CREDITS	TOTAL AMOUNT - CREDIT
25	4,024.17	11	3,632.90

PLEASE CHECK THIS STATEMENT WITHOUT DELAY
THE BANK MUST BE NOTIFIED IN WRITING OF ANY ERROR WITHIN 45 DAYS AFTER THE ABOVE STATEMENT DATE

Note: At the time of writing, the Royal Bank of Canada had not considered the introduction of the International System of Units (SI); consequently, the comma appears in the above printout of dollar amounts exactly as programmed by the Bank's computer.

is quite different, however, is the fact that a concise description is shown for each debit and each credit item listed on the bank statement. It is worth noting that some of the other chartered banks may vary their method of describing debit and credit items posted on their statements.

- Since a current account represents a demand deposit liability account, it follows that debits must be deducted from the previous balance. Similarly, any credit entry will increase the liability account and, therefore, it must be added to a previous balance.
- Notice also that the running balance is unqualified; that is, there is no DR. or CR. placed after each running balance. Obviously, each running balance must be regarded as a credit balance unless the amount is qualified. If a minus sign appears after any running balance, it would be regarded as an overdrawn amount, and, therefore, a debit balance on the banker's books to account for a current liability.
- The first dollar amount shown is the balance forward from the previous statement. It is important, therefore, to keep a file of all past bank statements so that the previous month's balance can be verified on the next month's statement.
- Checking the accuracy of any "running" balance is a simple procedure. Simply follow the horizontal line to total all debits. Next, deduct the total debits from the last balance; then, add any credits to this figure. Of course, the total debits and total credits may be matched on one line and the resulting answer may be deducted or added to the previous balance as the case may be.
- Notice that the statement shows the date of each line's transactions according to the *banker's* records. In other words, the individual dates are the banker's dates for debiting and crediting the depositor's account.
- Observe how the bank statement explains by various descriptive words the nature of each posted debit and credit entry. For example the computer has printed the words CHEQUE 032 to identify the first cheque appearing under the Debits/Cheques column. On other banker's statements, symbols or a full translation of the transaction may be found. When symbols are used, the banker will provide a translation either on the front or on the back of the statement form.
- The bottom of the statement provides a number of valuable proofs. The depositor should check each proof listed. For example, the total amount of debit, the number of debit items, the total amount of credit, and the number of credits should be verified. Any discrepancy should be reported to the bank immediately. In actual practice, the total debits and total credits may be verified by using an adding machine. Of course, the final balance reported by the bank statement should also be verified.

TOPIC 1 Problems

Journalizing selected transactions from the banker's point of view and from the depositor's point of view.

9.1 For the separate transactions below, show an accounting analysis from the *banker's* point of view. Use a T-account form of analysis, or show a record of the double entries in a two-column journal. Make up appropriate account titles for each transaction.

1. Dolly's Flowers, a current account depositor, deposits cash receipts totalling $500.
2. The bank cashes cheques drawn by Dolly's Flowers to the amount of $200.
3. The bank agrees to a demand loan for Dolly's Flowers in the amount of $1 000. In turn, Dolly's Flowers deposits the amount of the loan in its current account.
4. The bank receives a cheque for $200 from Dolly's Flowers in part payment of the demand loan.
5. The bank issues a debit memo to Dolly's Flowers showing that $8 interest has been charged on the demand loan for one month.
6. The bank issues a debit memo to Dolly's Flowers showing that $27.50 has been charged against the depositor's account for the rental of a safety deposit box.
7. Dolly's Flowers has a cheque for $1 200 certified at the bank. The certified cheque is promptly mailed to the payee.
8. The bank prepares a debit memo informing Dolly's Flowers that its current account has been decreased by $100 as a result of an NSF cheque drawn by H. Hunt, an accounts receivable customer of the depositor.
9. The bank prepares a credit memo notifying Dolly's Flowers that its current account has been credited for $46.50 interest on 60-day term deposits held for the depositor.
10. The bank deducts $23.50 from Dolly's Flowers' current account for monthly bank service charges.

Note: Save your solution for use in the next problem.

Analyzing the transactions in Problem 9.1 from the viewpoint of the depositor's records.

9.2 Rewrite the accounting entries for each transaction in Problem 9.1, but in this case analyze each transaction from the viewpoint of the *depositor's* records. Use the T-account form or two-column journal form. Suggest appropriate accounting titles for each accounting entry.

CHAPTER 9: Banking Applications

Journalizing selected transactions from the banker's point of view and from the depositor's point of view.

9.3 A banker identified the set of transactions below as affecting one of its current account depositors.

1. Posted to the depositor's current account a deposit slip showing $750 of cash receipts.
2. Approved a demand loan for $2 500. Approved the deposit slip showing that the loan was deposited to the depositor's current account.
3. Cashed $1 000 of cheque issued by the current account depositor.
4. Received in the mail cheques totalling $1 200 and a correctly prepared deposit booklet. All cheques stapled together and marked "For Deposit Only." Mailed Part 2 of the deposit slip showing that the receipts were received and posted to the depositor's account.
5. Received a telephone call from the depositor instructing the bank to deduct $100 in part payment of the demand loan. Mailed a debit memo to acknowledge this part payment.
6. Certified a cheque signed by the depositor for $1 600.
7. Received an NSF cheque signed by T. Wilks, an accounts receivable customer of the depositor. Issued an appropriate memo for $200.
8. Enclosed with the bank statement of account a debit memo showing that $28 has been charged to the depositor's account for the rental of a safety deposit box.
9. Mailed a credit memo notifying the depositor that interest earned on 90-day deposit receipts in the amount of $75.80 has been credited to the depositor's current account.
10. Deducted $21.80 from the depositor's current account for monthly bank service charges.
11. Issued a debit memo charging the depositor's current account for $20.80 for one month's interest on the demand loan.

Required

a Use a T-account form or the two-column journal form to show an accounting analysis of each of the banker's transactions summarized above. Devise appropriate account titles for each transaction.

b Provide an accounting analysis of each transaction from the viewpoint of the depositor's records. Suggest appropriate accounting titles for each accounting entry.

Constructing a computerized monthly bank statement of account from selected transactions for one depositor.

9.4 You are employed at a commercial bank called Dominion Bank. You are responsible for preparing through a computer a printout of a monthly statement of account for each current account depositor identified at your bank. From the information provided below, prepare a monthly statement of account similar to the one in Figure 9-22. Be sure to use symbols after appropriate amounts or printed words similar to the ones in the figure. And be sure to complete the various box sections at the bottom of the statement. *Note*: Construct your statement to look like a computer printout.

Information

1. Current account depositor: E. Blake Refrigeration Co. Ltd., 738 Main Street (your town and province).
2. Current account number: 110-134-4.
3. Period ended June 30 (current year).
4. Balance forward from previous statement, $895.75.
5. The depositor's transactions are identified as follows:

June 3 Cheques cashed: #215, $25.80; #216, $75.40; #219, $30.90.
4 Cheque #217 cashed for $75.80. Demand loan for $1 000 granted; the loan amount was immediately deposited.
5 Cheques cashed: #218, $18.95; #220, $150.70. Deposit slip showed total cash receipts for $189.50.
6 Certified cheque #221 for $675.
7 Deposit slip showed a total deposit of $267.50.
10 Cheques cashed: #224, $17.40; #225, $157.80; #226, $190.70. Deposit slip showed a total deposit of $228.70.
12 Debit memo showed a charge of $27.50 for rental of safety deposit box. Cheques cashed: #222, $27.50; #230, $14.90; #231, $85.70; and #232, $49.50.
14 Depositor telephoned instructing the bank to deduct $200 in part payment of the demand loan. Issued an appropriate bank memo to acknowledge that part payment. A deposit slip showed that cash amounting to $587.50 had been deposited.
17 A cheque for $76.80, issued by Frank Joyce and deposited earlier by Blake Refrigeration, was returned and marked NSF. Issued an appropriate bank memo.
19 Cheques cashed: #227, $116.90; #228, $40.70; and #233, $80.95. Deposit slip showed $189.55 correctly deposited by the company.
20 Cheques cancelled: #234, $98.75; #235, $48.90; #237, $55.00; #238, $76.45; and #240, $38.98.
21 Deposit slip showed a deposit of $432.70.
24 Cheques cancelled: #236, $16.90; #239, $45.80; and #241, $17.50.
25 Issued credit memo for $118.70 showing deposit of interest earned on 60-day bank deposit receipts.
26 Cheques cancelled: #242, $173.40; #243, $18.90; #244, $37.40. Deposit slip showed a cash deposit totalling $147.60.
28 Cheques cancelled: #223, $14.90; #245, $17.60; #248, $87.50. Charged depositor $22.40 for monthly service charges. Issued a debit memo for $12 for one month's interest on bank loan.

TOPIC 2   Preparing a Bank Reconciliation and the Statement of Cash Flows

From Topic 1, you learned that the banker provides the current account depositor with a monthly statement showing an accounting of the depositor's inflow of cash, outflow of cash, and cash balance in the current account as at a certain month-end date. As you have also learned, this month-end cash balance is a dollar amount calculated from the banker's knowledge of debiting and crediting transactions affecting the depositor's account. And from earlier work, you have learned that the depositor maintains his or her own record of cash transactions on a cheque record such as a cheque stub, and in the general ledger on the Cash account. In theory, therefore, it is logical to assume that, at any given time, an identical amount should appear for the cash balance in the banker's books and in the depositor's books. In practice, however, the bank seldom agrees with the month-end cash balance calculated by the depositor's records. Three factors explain why the two cash balances seldom agree.

> Outstanding cheques: cheques issued by the depositor but not as yet cancelled by the depositor's bank.

1. The depositor may have issued one or more cheques that have yet to be cancelled by the bank. In the language of business, these are known as **outstanding cheques**. In issuing these cheques, the depositor has credited his or her Cash account in the general ledger and he or she has decreased the cash balance on the cheque stub. But since the banker has yet to account for these cheques, the banker's records will show a greater figure for the cash balance than that calculated in the depositor's records.

> Deposit in transit: a late deposit not as yet recorded by the depositor's bank.

2. The depositor deposits his or her cash receipts intact on a regular basis. In all probability, then, a late deposit at the end of the month has not been recorded by the banker; this **deposit in transit** will cause the cash balance according to the banker's records to be understated.

3. The banker may have issued one or more bank debit or credit memos and may have enclosed these with the bank statement rather than mailing them separately to the depositor. These memos have decreased or increased the current account in the banker's books, but they have yet to affect the depositor's books.

> Discrepancy items: various items which help to explain why the cash balance reported by the bank does not agree with the depositor's records.

Obviously, the above **discrepancy items** and others will cause a disagreement in the reported cash balance between the banker's and the depositor's books.

Obviously, from the depositor's viewpoint, it is essential that all discrepancy items be located so that the two balances can be brought into agreement as at a particular date. The procedure for doing this is known as *preparing a bank reconciliation*.

Preparing the Bank Reconciliation

In studying the important steps that follow, keep in mind that the procedure for reconciling the cash balances is performed within the depositor's accounting system.

STEP 1. VERIFYING THE INTERNAL CASH BALANCES

Before a reconciliation of the bank statement balance and the depositor's cash balance can be made, it is important that the cash records within the firm be in agreement. As you will recall, two internal records of the cash balance are generally kept, as follows: (1) the person who is given the responsibility to issue cheques usually keeps a record of the "running" cash balance on a cheque record like the stub; and (2) a second person is responsible to maintain an up-to-date record of cash in the asset account. Ideally, a cash proof between the cheque book and the Cash account should reveal the same dollar amount at the end of each month. Obviously, no reconciliation of the bank balance may begin until the internal cash balances agree. As an example to illustrate bank reconciliation, assume that the balance on the final cheque stub in April kept for Kelly's Office Services does agree with the updated general ledger account for Cash at the end of April, as shown in Figure 9-23.

With the internal cash balances verified, attention may now turn to the receipt of the April bank balance. If the bank statement illustrated in Figure 9-22 is used, it should be obvious that a reconciliation is required to bring the two balances shown in the side margin into agreement.

FIGURE 9-23

Cash   Account No. 101

Date		Explanation	Post. Ref.	Debit	Credit	Balance
19—						
April	1	Balance.	√			4 755 80
	30	Total cash receipts.	CR4	6 950 75		11 706 55
	30	Total cash payments.	CP4		8 882 85	2 823 70

NO. 55   DATE April 30, 19—
ORDER OF Eastown Furniture Ltd.
In full payment of account.

April 30/ — $ 127.50

	DEPOSITS		JOURNAL	
	295	14	BALANCE	$ 2 656.06
			ADD DEPOSIT(S)	295.14
			BALANCE	$ 2 951.20
			DEDUCT CHEQUE	127.50
TOTAL	295	14	BALANCE	$ 2 823.70

STEP 2. LOCATING AND LISTING DISCREPANCY ITEMS

FIGURE 9-24

Bank statement balance:
$2 724.21
2 751.16

Depositor's internal cash balance:
$2 843.70

As mentioned earlier, the depositor receives monthly a bank statement together with the return of all cancelled cheques and any enclosed bank debit and credit memos not as yet mailed to his or her office. Ideally, a responsible person other than the employee who handles the cash or who keeps the cash records should prepare the bank reconciliation. Of course, in a small business, this task may be performed by a bookkeeper-cashier or even the owner-manager. In any preparation of a bank reconciliation, it is important to compare closely the information reported by the bank with similar information reported by the firm's records of maintaining cash. Through such an examination, the various discrepancy items between the bank and the depositor can be located and listed on a "rough" sheet before an actual bank reconciliation is prepared. The following steps, in the order given, may be used to locate and list discrepancy items.

i. **Compare the returned items with the listing of those items on the bank statement** The majority of banks will enclose cancelled cheques and any bank debit and credit memos carefully bundled in the same order as each returned item is listed on the bank statement. Begin with the top item of the enclosed bundle and check each amount against the listing on the bank statement. Make sure that the number of enclosures agrees with the stated number at the bottom of the bank statement. And make sure that the returned items are related to your account and not to someone else's. If a bank error is discovered, it should be listed as a dis-crepancy item in order to reconcile the bank's reporting of the depositor's current account balance. Of course, all bank errors and omissions of enclosures should be reported promptly to the bank's accounting department.

ii. **Check all reported calculations on the bank statement**   In particular, check the various proof totals indicated at the bottom of the bank statement. This means making a careful check of the total amount of reported debit, the number of debits, the total amount of reported credit, and the number of credits. Of course, the most important amount to check is the final balance reported by the bank. In many offices, these calculations may be double-checked with the aid of an adding machine or electronic calculator. If any bank errors are discovered at this checking stage, these too would be listed and then reported to the bank's accounting department. To simplify matters, assume that the bank statement illustrated for Kelly's Office Services has been checked and that no bank errors are disclosed.

iii. **Compare deposits reported by the bank with the receipts and deposits shown in the firm's records**   To do an effective comparison, place check marks in the company's cash records and on the bank statement beside the items that agree. This would mean that check marks should be made beside each Cash debit amount in the cash receipts journal and beside each bank credit entry that is in agreement. (Since the cheque record balance of cash has already been verified with the ledger account, it is not necessary to check the items with both the cheque stub and the accounting records.) One more point: do not forget to check also last month's reconciliation statement to make sure that any deposits then in transit have been recorded on this month's statement.

Unchecked items in the cash receipts journal may consist of errors made by the depositor or by the bank, or may be deposits which are in transit at the end of the month. Errors should be listed and properly identified so that they can later be applied to the reconciliation of the bank statement or the firm's cash balance, as the case may be. On the other hand, deposits in transit are items unknown by the bank; consequently, they must be related to the adjustment of the bank's reported balance as shown by the bank statement.

Unchecked items in the credit column of the bank statement will mean that the bank has credited the depositor's current account with an amount or amounts unknown to the depositor. Of course, such items are discrepancy items and will have to be listed in order to adjust the Cash account (and chequebook) balance.

To provide examples for this point, assume that the deposits on Kelly's bank statement were checked against the firm's cash receipts journal, and that two discrepancy items were identified: the late deposit of April 30 for $295.14 not as yet recorded by the bank, and the credit memo showing that interest of $37.50 on 60-day deposit receipts has been credited by the bank but not as yet treated by the cash records of the firm. To assist with the later preparation of the formal bank reconciliation statement, both discrepancy items may be listed on a "rough" sheet as in Figure 9-25.

FIGURE 9-25

List of Discrepancy Items
As at April 30, 19—

Items Unknown by the Bank	Items Unknown by the Depositor
Deposit of April 30 in transit .. $295.14	Interest from 60-day deposit receipt $37.50

iv. Compare payments made by the bank with payments shown in the firm's cash records First, rearrange the cancelled cheques in numerical order and compare each cheque with the corresponding entry in the cash payments journal. Be sure to place a check mark in the depositor's cash payments journal opposite each entry for which a paid cheque has been returned to the bank. Of course, amounts and names of payees on the cancelled cheques should agree with the firm's cash payments records, and the cheques should be currently endorsed by the payees. And do not forget to examine the bank statement of the previous month to determine whether any unchecked items have been paid and whether they were recorded properly by the bank in the current month's statement. After this detailed examination, unchecked items in the depositor's records may be identified as follows:

- Cheques issued by the business but not paid by the bank. These items are outstanding cheques and would have to be listed as items unknown by the bank.
- An error or errors made in recording the cheque amount in the cash records. It may be discovered that the cheque amount recorded in the cash records (on the cheque record and in the cash payments journal) does not agree with the amount shown on the actual cancelled cheque. When this error occurs it is usually when the cheque is issued prior to the cheque amount being recorded (in error) in the cash records. When such an error is disclosed, list

it as such under "Items Unknown by the Depositor," since the error must be reconciled against the cash balance reported by the depositor's books. One other point here: since the Cash account has received the error amount from the cash payments journal, it is important that the check of the amount take place from the journal and not just from the chequebook stub or voucher. For this reason, some businesses will require a verification of the cash payments journal and not require checking amounts with the chequebook record.

Other unchecked items that will be disclosed by this comparison will appear on the bank statement. These items will be debits made to the depositor's current account but not recorded on the depositor's books. In general, these differences will be items such as bank debit memos for bank interest on a demand loan and for the fee to rent a safety deposit box. In addition, a returned NSF cheque may not yet have been recorded in the depositor's books. And, finally, the bank statement may show a monthly service charge debited to the current account but not as yet recorded in the depositor's records. Of course, all these discrepancy items should be listed under "Items Unknown by the Depositor" in any prior preparation of a bank statement.

For Kelly's Office Services, assume that the discrepancy items added to the list in Figure 9-26 were identified as a result of comparing payments made by the bank with payments shown in the firm's cash records.

FIGURE 9-26

List of Discrepancy Items
As at April 30, 19—

Items Unknown by the Bank		Items Unknown by the Depositor	
Deposit of April 30 in transit	$295.14	Interest from 60-day deposit receipt	$37.50
Outstanding cheques:		Debit memo for safety deposit box	27.50
No. 042	46.70	NSF cheque of J. P. Sands	50.75
No. 046	75.80	Debit memo for bank interest on demand loan	10.00
No. 053	68.30	Monthly service charge	8.95
No. 055	127.50	Error on Cheque Stub No. 038:	
		Correct cheque amount $95.80	
		Incorrect cheque stub 59.80	
		Additional amount to be deducted	36.00

Two important observations should be made before the actual reconciliation is examined:

- Notice in the list of outstanding cheques that no listing is shown for a certified cheque. Although this cheque may be outstanding, it is an item known by both the bank and the depositor, that is, both parties have made the correct cash entry for the cheque. Therefore, do not show a certified cheque as a discrepancy item in any problem you tackle later.
- Secondly, notice under "Items Unknown by the Depositor" that an error has been made in recording the cheque amount on Stub No. 038. In this case, assume that the cheque amount has been made out correctly for $95.80, but that the cheque record and the cash payments journal showed only $59.80. If the cheque was issued in payment of an accounts payable (Hay Stationery), the transposition error of $36 must be later adjusted to bring this item into agreement with the bank statement.

STEP 3. PREPARING THE BANK RECONCILIATION Once all of the discrepancy items have been identified and listed, an actual reconciliation of the bank statement balance and the cash account balance can be made. As an aid to help you to understand which items must be added to or subtracted from these reported balances, it is useful first to do an analysis of each discrepancy item listed on the "rough" sheet. The following two guides may help you to make a reconciliation of each item:

i. Except for discovered errors, treat each discrepancy item according to the way in which the known party has recorded the item in his or her own records.

ii. Treat all discovered errors according to their effect on the appropriate cash balance to be adjusted.

For example, if an insufficient cheque amount were recorded in the depositor's books, the error must be reconciled as a further decrease to the Cash account. On the other hand, if the listing showed that the bank had debited erroneously a cheque belonging to some other depositor, this amount would have to be added to the bank statement balance. Examine closely the pluses and minuses opposite each discrepancy item shown in Figure 9-27; then read carefully the analysis that follows.

Analysis You should have little difficulty in the correct analysis of each discrepancy item to be reconciled. Consider, for example, the two major items unknown by the bank. Since the depositor has already increased his or her cash by the amount of the deposit of April 30, to reconcile this amount the late deposit must likewise be acknowledged as an addition to the bank statement balance. Similarly, since the known

FIGURE 9-27

List of Discrepancy Items
As at April 30, 19—

Items Unknown by the Bank	Items Unknown by the Depositor
Deposit of April 30 in transit ..$295.14 (+)	Interest from 60-day deposit receipt .... $37.50 (+)
Outstanding cheques:	Debit memo for safety deposit box .... 27.50 (−)
No. 042 .... 46.70 (−)	NSF cheque of J. P. Sands .... 50.75 (−)
No. 046 .... 75.80 (−)	Debit memo for bank interest on demand loan .... 10.00 (−)
No. 053 .... 68.30 (−)	Monthly service charge ...... 8.95 (−)
No. 055 .... 127.50 (−)	Error on Cheque Stub No. 038:
	Correct cheque amount $95.80
	Incorrect cheque stub 59.80
	Additional amount to be deducted .... 36.00 (−)

party—the depositor—has decreased his or her cash balance for each outstanding cheque, each outstanding cheque must be shown as a deduction from the bank statement balance. On the other hand, each discrepancy item listed under the ones unknown by the depositor—except for the error—must be treated in the same way that the bank has recorded the item in its records. For example, the bank has increased the depositor's account balance as a result of the credit memo for interest earned on 60-day deposit receipts. Therefore, a plus sign must be shown after the amount so that the depositor's cash balance can be made to agree with what was done by the bank. Similarly, each deduction by the bank for the rental fee of the safety deposit box, the NSF cheque, the debit memo for the loan interest, and the monthly service charge must be treated as a deduction from the depositor's Cash account. Finally, the depositor's error in recording an insufficient cheque amount must be treated as a deduction by the amount of the error. On this last point, keep in mind that the bank has deducted the full amount of the cheque. Therefore, the error must be reconciled against the depositor's cash balance.

After one has analyzed each item correctly for reconciliation, the formal bank reconciliation statement can easily be prepared. In some businesses, this is done on the reverse side of the bank statement, because some banks do provide the necessary format there. In other businesses, however, the bank statement received may not show a reconciliation form; consequently, the reconciliation statement may be prepared as in Figure 9-28.

FIGURE 9-28

Kelly's Office Services
Bank Reconciliation Statement
April 30, 19—

Balance as per bank statement, April 30		$2 724.21 ~~$2 724.21~~ 2751.16
Add: Deposit of April 30 not recorded by bank		295.14
		$3 046.30
Deduct: Outstanding cheques:		
No. 042	$ 46.70	
No. 046	75.80	
No. 053	68.30	
No. 055	127.50	318.30
Adjusted bank balance of cash		$2 728.00
Balance as per Cash account, April 30		$2 823.70
Add: Interest earned on 60-day deposit receipts		37.50
		$2 861.20
Deduct:		
Debit memo for safety deposit box	$ 27.50	
NSF cheque of J. P. Sands	50.75	
Bank interest on demand loan	10.00	
Monthly service charge	8.95	
Error on Cheque Stub No. 038	36.00	~~132.20~~ 133.20
Adjusted book balance of cash		$2 728.00

(Annotation: "GL" written next to "Balance as per Cash account, April 30")

These amounts must agree.

Here are the important points to remember when preparing a formal bank reconciliation statement:

- Begin with the traditional three-line heading: line 1 shows the name of the firm; line 2, the name of the statement; and line 3, the date of bringing the two cash balances into agreement. Since the balance shown by the bank statement is the balance on April 30, it is important to remember that reconciliation occurs as of this date and not the date of actually preparing the bank reconciliation statement.

- Observe that the body of the statement consists of two sections: one section reconciles discrepancy items that affect the bank statement balance; the other section reconciles discrepancy items that affect the depositor's records of the month-end cash balance. Do not be concerned over which section to begin with. Although the illustration shows the reconciliation of the bank statement balance first, it is just as correct to begin with the section that shows the reconciliation of the depositor's cash balance. The important point to remember is that discrepancy items must be related to the correct section in reconciliation; otherwise, the two cash balances cannot possibly be brought into agreement.

- Each section begins with the acknowledgement of the cash balance reported by its records. From here, it is just a simple matter of reconciling each group of discrepancy items. Notice that in the illustration the additions are shown before the deductions; it is just as correct, however, to begin with the deductions.
- Notice that each section is shown as being completed by means of a double line.
- And, finally, notice that the two adjusted balances must agree. In simple terms, this figure represents the "true" or "correct" balance of cash on April 30—that is, the one both bank and depositor would have arrived at had they had complete knowledge of all items.

STEP 4. ADJUSTING THE CASH RECORDS AFTER RECONCILIATION

From the depositor's point of view, two cash records must be adjusted after the bank reconciliation: (1) the balance on the latest cheque stub must be brought into agreement with the adjusted book balance of cash on the reconciliation statement; and (2) the Cash account in the general ledger must be updated by journalizing and posting appropriate entries to bring the ledger account into agreement with the adjusted book balance of cash on the reconciliation statement. Each of these adjustments will be examined in the separate sections that follow.

1. Adjusting the Latest Cheque Stub   As you know, the balance of cash calculated at the bottom line of each cheque stub is carried forward as the new balance on the next cheque stub. After a bank reconciliation is prepared, the latest cheque stub should be adjusted to reflect the changes shown by the reconciliation of the depositor's discrepancy items. For Kelly's Office Services, Cheque Stub No. 056 would show a net deduction of $94.70 ($132.20 less $37.50) in order to bring the former cash balance into agreement with the adjusted book balance of cash on the reconciliation statement. This adjustment may be made on the latest stub as illustrated in the side margin.

FIGURE 9-29

2. Adjusting the Cash Account in the General Ledger   To update the Cash account, appropriate journal entries must first be made. The source of these entries is the section of the bank reconciliation statement that reconciles the cash balance of the depositor and not of the bank. For Kelly's Office Services, this would mean two sets of journal entries: one set to debit Cash for the amount of interest earned from 60-day deposit receipts, and a second set to credit Cash for each deduction shown by the bank reconciliation statement. These two sets of entries would suggest that the cash receipts journal is to be used to debit the Cash, and the cash payments journal is to be used to credit the Cash. And such would be the case if the reconciliation was prepared for a "month-end" that really fell in the middle of the month. In the case of Kelly's, however, the month-end for reconciliation was the calendar month-end. Since both special journals have been previously closed for the month of April, the adjusting entries to update the Cash account as a result of bank reconciliation have to be recorded in the general journal as shown in Figure 9-30. Note that, in some accounting systems, all adjusting entries will be recorded in the general journal regardless of the date of preparing the bank reconciliation.

The first entry illustrated in the general journal should be self-evident. Since interest earned increases Cash, a debit must be recorded to the Cash account. And since this interest is earned by the business, an appropriate revenue account is credited to record the increase to owner's equity.

FIGURE 9-30

GENERAL JOURNAL — Page 3

DATE 19--	ACCOUNT TITLE AND EXPLANATION	POST. REF.	DEBIT	CREDIT
Apr. 30	Cash		37 50	
	Interest Revenue			37 50
	To record interest earned on 60-day deposit receipts.			
30	Safety Deposit Box Expense		27 50	
	Cash			27 50
	To record deduction for rental of safety deposit box.			
30	Bank Service Charges Expense		8 95	
	Cash			8 95
	To record deduction for monthly service charge.			
30	Interest Expense		10 00	
	Cash			10 00
	To record deduction made by bank for interest on bank loan.			
30	Accts. Pay./Hay Stationery		36 00	
	Cash			36 00
	To record the correction on Cheque No. 038, issued as $95.80, but recorded as $59.80.			
30	Accts. Rec./J. P. Sands		50 75	
	Cash			50 75
	To record the NSF cheque of J. P. Sands, not as yet recorded on the books.			

Notice that the second and third adjusting entries reflect the deductions to Cash for the bank fee for the safety deposit box, and the monthly service charges. Although two separate entries are shown, some accountants may prefer to combine the two debits into one debit for Miscellaneous Expense. On the other hand, using separate debits permits the depositor to account for the safety deposit box rental fee so that this amount can be reported on the depositor's yearly income tax return.

The fourth general journal entry should, again, be self-evident. The bank has charged the business with a monthly interest amount on the bank loan; consequently, Interest Expense (or Bank Interest Expense) must be debited, while the Cash account must be credited for the decrease.

Notice the error correction entry in the fifth general journal entry. You should try to remember that, so far, the general journal has been used to record the opening entry, adjusting entries at year-end, adjusting entries as a result of bank reconciliation, and error correction entries.

The final adjusting entry in the general journal may cause some confusion. To understand why Accounts Receivable/J. P. Sands must be debited for the NSF cheque, it is useful to review the background of all the transactions that led to the NSF cheque. In the first place, the firm must have rendered office services on credit to J. P. Sands. This would suggest that Accounts Receivable/J. P. Sands was debited for $50.75 and that Fees Earned was credited for a similar amount. Next, the customer remitted his cheque for $50.75 in full payment of his account. As you know, the dollar result of this transaction would have debited Cash and credited Accounts Receivable/J. P. Sands for $50.75. Of course, the cheque would have been endorsed "For Deposit Only" and Kelly's banker would have credited the current account with the amount of the cheque. However, when the cheque was returned NSF to Kelly's banker, the banker promptly deducted the amount from the current account. The adjusting entry on Kelly's books, therefore, must debit the customer's account and credit Cash. Kelly will have to wait for another cheque from J. P. Sands before the customer's account will be cleared.

Once the adjusting and correcting entries have been posted to the appropriate general ledger accounts, the Cash account balance will be in agreement with the adjusted book balance of Cash shown on the bank reconciliation statement. Thus, the business has gained one more effective control over its most valuable asset.

FIGURE 9-31

Cash			
Apr. 30 Bal.	2 823.70	Apr. 30	27.50
30 GJ 3	37.50	30 GJ 3	8.95
		30 GJ 3	10.00
		30 GJ 3	36.00
		30 GJ 3	50.75
Apr. 30 Adj. bal.	2 728.00		

Preparing the Statement of Cash Flows

In Topic 2 of Chapter 6, the statement of cash flows was prepared for a business corporation in support of Section 1540 of the *CICA Handbook*. A similar statement is also recommended for single proprietorships and partnerships. Many accountants would agree that these forms of business organizations should prepare this statement at least once a month and especially after completing a bank reconciliation.

Why is a monthly statement of cash flows recommended? The answer is to provide useful information to owner-managers so that they can effectively manage their business's most valuable asset. In addition, bank managers may request such a statement before granting a loan.

To be useful, the statement should report the details of how cash was collected (cash inflows) and how cash was spent (cash outflows) during the month that has just ended. Some accountants would even suggest that a separate statement of cash flows be prepared on what cash the business hopes to receive and anticipates what will be paid out for an accounting period in the future. In this text, only cash flow statements based on a period that has ended will be covered. Such statements are known as **historical statements**, because the sources of cash inflows and cash outflows have been accounted for. On the other hand, those cash flow statements based on a future time period are **prospective**.

> Historical statements: ones that report on periods that have ended.
>
> Prospective statements: ones that report on future time periods.

As explained in Chapter 6, the statement of cash flows can be prepared directly from the analysis of the Cash account, and from the cash receipts journal and cash payments journal if these journals are in use. As you learned, corporations prefer to report their historical cash flows under headings such as "Cash Provided By (Used In) Operating Activities," "Cash Provided By (Used In) Financing Activities," "Cash Provided By (Used In) Investing Activities," "Increase (Decrease) in Cash During the Period," "Cash at the Beginning of the Period," and "Cash at the End of the Period."

A similar arrangement can be used for single proprietorship and partnership forms of business. However, management may prefer a simpler arrangement along the lines of the illustration reported for Kelly's Office Services in Figure 9-32.

Analysis

- As in all financial statements, two main parts are the heading and the body.
- The heading consists of three lines. In the date line, the time period is for the month ended April 30, 19—.
- The sources of cash are reported under "Cash Was Provided By:"; these sources would be obtained by examining the Cash account and the cash receipts journal and general journal.
- The applications or uses of cash are reported under "Cash Was Used For:"; the main uses of cash for the month would be taken from examining the Cash account and cash payments journal and general journal for the month being reported.
- Since more cash was used than received, the statement shows a net decrease in cash flow during the month. This decrease is reported in parentheses to indicate a negative figure.
- A cash proof is shown by adding the cash balance at the beginning of the month to the net increase (decrease) in cash during the month. Obviously, the cash at the end of the month must agree with the balance reported in

the Cash account following the preparation of the bank reconciliation and journalizing and posting all adjusting entries.

FIGURE 9-32

Kelly's Office Services
Statement of Cash Flows
For the Month Ended April 30, 19—

Cash Was Provided By:
Remittances from accounts receivable	$5 550.75	
Proceeds from demand loan	1 400.00	
Interest from 60-day bank deposit receipts	37.50	
Total sources of cash		$6 988.25

Cash Was Used For:
Monthly office rent	$1 500.00	
Telephone calls	67.40	
Personal withdrawals	650.00	
Part payment of bank demand loan	100.00	
Salaries	2 450.00	
New office equipment	800.00	
Monthly interest on bank loan	10.00	
Safety deposit box charge	27.50	
Monthly bank service charges	8.95	
Payment to creditors for utilities, service of office equipment, and office supplies	3 402.20	
Total uses of cash		9 016.05
Net increase (decrease) in cash for April		(2 027.80)
Cash balance at beginning of April		4 755.80
Cash balance at end of April		$2 728.00

General Ledger

Cash   Account No. 101

Date	Explanation	Post. Ref.	Debit	Credit	Balance
19—					
Apr. 30	Adjusted balance forward.	√			2 728.00

These amounts must agree.

TOPIC 2 Problems

Preparing a simplified bank reconciliation statement; recording the resulting adjusting entry.

9.5 At the end of January, current year, Southview Cleaning Shop reports a balance of $1 987.55 in its Cash account and cheque record. The bankstatement for January 31, however, shows a balance of $2 369.66. The following were found to be the discrepancy items.
  1. The bank statement contains a deduction of $21.89 for service charges.
  2. A comparison of the cheques issued in the cash payments journal and the cheques cashed on the statement indicates that these cheques were outstanding: No. 0510 for $78.90; No. 0512 for $250; and No. 0517 for $75.10.

Required **a** Prepare a bank reconciliation statement as at January 31.

b Record the necessary adjusting entry to bring the Cash account into agreement with the reconciliation statement. Assume that the cash payments journal has been ruled off for the month of January.

Preparing a bank reconciliation statement which includes one error in the depositor's cash records; recording the resulting adjusting entries.

9.6 The information below resulted from identifying and listing discrepancy items for Kraus Novelty Company as of the February 28 bank statement.
1. Final bank balance as shown on the bank statement, $3 241.82.
2. Cash account balance on February 28, $3 544.22. (The chequebook balance on February 28 also agreed with this amount.)
3. Cheques outstanding: No. 140, $51.40; No. 144, $40; and No. 147, $7.15.
4. Deposit put in night depository on last day of February, recorded in the chequebook and in the cash receipts journal but not shown on the bank statement, $234.00.
5. Dishonoured cheque (NSF of J. W. Krestel), $144, was included with the bank statement.
6. Bank service charge shown on the bank statement, $22.75.
7. The paid cheques returned with the February bank statement disclosed one error in the cash records of Kraus Novelty Company. Cheque No. 141 for $14.40 had been erroneously recorded as $14.20 on the cheque stub and in the journal. The cheque was issued in payment of the Telephone Expense account.

Required
a Prepare a bank reconciliation statement for the current account depositor as of February 28.
b Prepare in general journal form any entries that the depositor should make as a result of his having prepared the bank reconciliation.

Preparing a bank reconciliation statement involving a certified cheque and an error entry in the cash payments journal; recording the resulting adjusting entries.

9.7 Parkside Shop deposits all receipts intact on the day received and makes all payments by cheque. On October 31, after all postings were completed, the Cash account in the general ledger showed a $1 510 debit balance. On the other hand, the October 31 bank statement showed only $1 299 on deposit in the current account on that day.

a Prepare a bank reconciliation for the depositor-enterprise, using the following information:
1. The October 31 cash receipts for $425 were placed in the bank's night depository after banking hours on that date and were unrecorded by the bank at the time the October bank statement was mailed.
2. Outstanding cheques: No. 12, $70; No. 13, $65; No. 17, certified for $100; and No. 19, $85.
3. Included with the October cancelled cheques returned by the bank was a $24 debit memo for bank service charges for maintaining the current account during October.
4. Cheque No. 18, returned with the cancelled cheques, was correctly drawn for $24 in payment of the telephone bill. On identifying discrepancy items, Parkside Shop found that this cheque had been erroneously entered in the cash payments journal and debited to the Telephone Expense account as though it were for $42.

b Prepare in general journal form any entries that the depositor should make a result of his having prepared the bank reconciliation statement.

Preparing a bank reconciliation statement from a given bank statement and the depositor's cash records; recording the resulting adjusting entries.

9.8 Martin Flowers Ltd. has a current account with Northern Bank of Canada. The Company last reconciled its book and bank statement balances on July 31 with two cheques outstanding, No. 310 for $118 and No. 311 for $265. Also, the bank reconciliation on July 31 showed that a deposit in transit on July 31 for $298.75 had not been recorded by the bank. The information

FIGURE **9-33**

MARTIN FLOWERS LTD
5 ALGONQUIN AVE N
THUNDER BAY ONT P7A 6E1

STATEMENT OF ACCOUNT WITH
THE NORTHERN BANK OF CANADA

CURRENT ACCT NO 107-247-6

EXPLANATION OF SYMBOLS

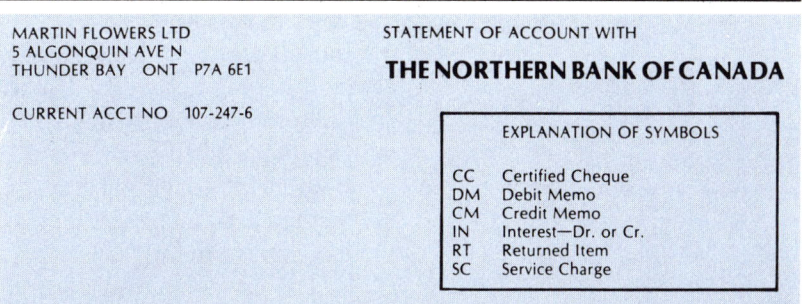

CC	Certified Cheque
DM	Debit Memo
CM	Credit Memo
IN	Interest—Dr. or Cr.
RT	Returned Item
SC	Service Charge

DATE	DEBITS		CREDITS	BALANCE
AUG 1	BALANCE BROUGHT FORWARD			1 572.15
1			298.75	1 870.90
2	265.00		600.00	2 205.90
3	195.70	216.85	375.40	2 168.75
5	402.00			1 766.75
9	89.40			1 677.35
12	60.00		412.75	2 030.10
14	417.65	375.10	1 000.00	2 237.35
18	500.00CC			1 737.35
21			296.25	2 033.60
22	28.75		78.90	2 083.75
26	9.80DM		53.75	2 127.70
30	53.75RT			2 073.95
31	5.00IN	3.50SC	174.70CM	2 240.15

NO. ENCLOSURES	FULL PAGE	TOTAL AMOUNT- DEBIT	NO. DEBITS	TOTAL AMOUNT- CREDIT	NO. CREDITS	TOTAL SERVICE CHARGE
13		2 622.50	14	3 290.50	9	3.50

FIGURE **9-34**

CASH RECEIPTS JOURNAL Page 16

Date		Post. Ref.	Amount
Aug.	2	201	600 00
	3	401	375 40
	12	401	412 75
	14	301	1 000 00
	21	401	296 25
	22	103	78 90
	26	105	53 75
	31	401	448 95
	31	101	3 266 00

FIGURE **9-35**

CASH PAYMENTS JOURNAL Page 21

Cheque No.	Post. Ref.	Amount
315	202	195 70
316	519	216 85
317	203	89 40
318	112	420 00
319	520	217 40
320	302	60 00
321	104	127 90
322	516	417 65
323	107	500 00
324	110	375 10
325	205	59 40
326	505	28 75
327	502	17 90
	101	2 726 05

FIGURE 9-36

Cash						Account No. 101
Date	Explanation	Post. Ref.	Debit	Credit	Balance	
Aug. 1	Balance.	√			1 487 90	
31	Total cash receipts.	CR 16	3 266 00			
31	Total cash payments.	CP 21		2 726 05	2 027 85	

below and in Figures 9-33 to 9-36 has been supplied in order to do the August 31 reconciliation.

- Included with the bank statement was an NSF cheque drawn by a customer, Peter Gruhn. The cheque was charged back to the depositor's account on August 30. Its return is unrecorded.
- Cheque No. 318 was correctly issued for $402 in payment of Office Equipment. An examination of the cash records, however, showed that the accounting clerk misread the amount and entered it as though it were for $420.
- The credit memo resulted from the banker's clipping of bond interest coupons on Canada Savings Bonds held for the depositor at the bank.
- Two debit memos were included with the bank statement: one for the monthly interest charged on the bank loan of August 2 and one for the annual fee for renting a safety deposit box.

Required
a Compare the bank statement with the depositor's cash records; then locate and list all discrepancy items.
b Prepare an August 31 bank reconciliation for the company.
c Prepare the general journal entries needed to adjust the book balance of cash to the reconciled balance.

Preparing a historical statement of cash flows as illustrated in this chapter as well as the one used in Topic 2 of Chapter 6.

9.9 The cash receipts and cash payments journals, together with general ledger information for Hutton Farm Supply Company, revealed the following data for January, 19-1:

1. Total cash received from customers during January, $6 875.80.
2. Cash received from interest earned on 30-day bank deposit receipts, $100.
3. Total cash paid to creditors for purchases of farm supplies, $1 968.70.
4. Total cash paid for rent of building, $600.
5. Total cash paid for telephone, $50.08.
6. Total cash paid for utilities, $72.80.
7. Total cash paid for heating, $64.90.
8. Total cash paid for truck repairs, $84.50.
9. Total cash paid for salaries and wages, $3 120.40.
10. Total cash paid for interest on bank demand loan for one month, $50.
11. Total cash paid for miscellaneous expenses, $12.50.
12. Beginning month's balance (January 1, 19-1) in Cash account, $3 870.00.

13. Ending month's balance (January 31, 19-1) after a bank reconciliation, $4 886.82.

Required a Prepare a statement of cash flows for Hutton Farm Supply Company for January along the lines of the statement illustrated in this chapter.

b Assume that the firm in **a** is incorporated as Hutton Farm Supply Inc. Prepare a statement of cash flows for Hutton Farm Supply Inc. for January in support of Section 1540 of the *CICA Handbook* as presented in Topic 2 of Chapter 6.

9.10 Use your school's electronic spreadsheet software, or one to which you have access, to do the following spreadsheet application:

a Repeat the format you used for the solution of part **a** of Problem 9.9 only this time by using electronic spreadsheet software.

b Add additional columns for the remaining months in the current year, 19-1.

c Complete a 12-month spreadsheet by applying the following "what if" situations:
- That the cash received from customers increased over January by 5% per month
- That the interest earned on bank deposit receipts increased over January by 10% per month
- That the cash paid to creditors for farm supplies increased by 5% per month
- That the cash paid for the rent of building, telephone, utilities, interest on the bank loan, and miscellaneous expenses remained the same
- That the cash paid for heating in February and March increased by 10% per month over January; in April and May, decreased by 5% per month over March's amount; in June, July, and August, decreased by 10% per month over March's amount; in September and October, increased by 5% over the amount for August; in November and December, increased by 5% over the amount for October
- That the cash paid for truck repairs increased by 5% per month over January's amount
- That the cash paid for salaries and wages increased by 5% per month to the end of June and remained constant after June to the end of December

Chapter Summary

All profit-seeking businesses open a bank chequing account, usually called a *current account*, as one important measure to control the safety of its most valuable asset, Cash.

From the viewpoint of the banker, any deposit made to a current account represents a current liability payable on demand. Thus, any increases to this account, called "Demand Deposits Payable," must be credited, and any decreases must be debited. On the other hand, that same current account, on the books of the depositor-enterprise, is the current asset called "Cash" or "Cash in Bank." As you know, to increase and decrease this current asset, amounts must be debited and credited respectively.

For example, every time the Cash account (or Cash in Bank account) is debited, the amount debited is assumed to be deposited intact. Therefore, on the banker's books, the amount deposited will be credited to support the theory of increasing the banker's current liability to the depositor-enterprise. Similarly, every time the Cash account (or Cash in Bank account) on the depositor-enterprise's books is credited for the issuance of a cheque, the cheque amount is not accounted for by the banker until that cheque is cashed (cancelled). Once it is cancelled (marked as paid), the banker will debit the depositor's current account to support the theory that this current liability is being decreased.

Most of the transactions affecting the current account on the banker's books are straightforward. However, a few require a complete analysis to understand the shortcut involved. For example, when the bank agrees to lend money on a demand loan to the depositor-enterprise, in theory two transactions may be analyzed on the banker's books. First, a debit is made to a current asset Demand Loans Receivable/Depositor-Enterprise, and a credit is made to Cash. Second, the deposit of this loan to the depositor's current account is made by debiting Cash and crediting Demand Deposits Payable. In practice, however, the Cash credit in the first transaction and the Cash debit in the second transaction cancel each other out. Therefore, only one entry is made on the banker's books as a debit to Demand Loans Receivable (a current asset) and a corresponding credit to Demand Deposits Payable (a current liability). Of course, on the depositor-enterprise's books, the accounting of the demand loan would be made by debiting Cash (Cash in Bank) and crediting Bank Loan Payable.

In theory, at any particular time, the balance in the banker's current account and the balance in the depositor's Cash in Bank account should always agree. However, the two balances rarely agree, because of timing differences. For example, the depositor-enterprise will credit its Cash in Bank account every time a cheque is issued; but the banker will not account for this issued cheque until such time as the cheque is cashed and cancelled. Thus, a delay occurs between the time that transaction is recorded by the business and the bank.

A similar timing difference occurs when the banker debits the current account for any bank debit memos and credits the current account for any credit memos. For example, the banker may issue a debit memo for the monthly interest charged on the outstanding demand loan. The amount is immediately debited to the current account. However, it may be several days before the depositor-enterprise receives the debit memo in order to credit its Cash in Bank account for the amount of bank interest expense.

Once a month, bankers supply the depositor-enterprise with a bank statement showing the details of posting amounts to the current account. Because of timing differences, the balance reported by the bank statement will not agree with the balance of Cash in Bank shown on the depositor's books. As a measure of internal control, it is essential to bring the balances into agreement. The procedure for removing all timing differences so that the two balances can agree is called *bank reconciliation*.

The initial step in bank reconciliation is to compare items on the bank statement with items on the cash records of the depositor. All discrepancy items—whether unknown by the banker or unknown by the depositor-enterprise—should be noted. A bank reconciliation statement can only be prepared after all discrepancy items have been located.

The actual preparation of the bank reconciliation statement can be made on the reverse side of the bank statement if a reconciliation form has been provided there. Many businesses, however, prefer to prepare their own, separate bank reconciliation. One common format has a three-line title and the body of the statement below.

The heading identifies the name of the business, the name of the statement, and the date of reconciliation. In most cases, this date must correspond to that of the bank statement, because reconciliation must occur between statements as of the same date.

The body of the statement consists of adjusting the ending balances of both the banker and the depositor-enterprise. It does not matter which one is used to begin the reconciliation. For example, you can begin with the ending balance as reported by the bank statement. Adjustments are made by adding any amounts made by the depositor-enterprise but unknown by the banker. For example, a late deposit made at the end of the month will not appear on the bank statement. Since the depositor has added (debited) the amount to its Cash in Bank, you must add all late deposits to the ending balance as reported by the bank statement. Similarly, all outstanding cheques have already been deducted from the depositor's Cash in Bank account. Therefore, all such outstanding cheques must also be deducted in reconciling the bank statement balance to an adjusted bank statement balance. The only exception is an outstanding certified cheque, since both banker and depositor-enterprise will have accounted for this cheque.

After reconciling the bank statement balance, you can begin to reconcile the Cash in Bank's ending balance as reported in the depositor's books. Discrepancy items such as bank credit memos would be added to the Cash in Bank's balance, because the amounts have been added in the banker's books. Similarly, all debit memos would be deducted, because the banker has debited (decreased) its current account. After all unknown items have been listed, the final amount must be the Adjusted Balance of Cash in Bank. This adjusted amount must agree with the Adjusted Bank Statement Balance.

Two cash records of the depositor-enterprise must be adjusted following the preparation of the bank reconciliation statement. First, the latest cheque stub, showing the balance of cash in bank forward, should be adjusted to reflect the adjustments made in the depositor's section of the bank reconciliation statement. Second, adjusting entries are made in the general journal to account for all adjustments made to the Cash in Bank account in the depositor's books.

Most bank reconciliations are prepared on a monthly basis, usually at the end of each month. As an additional measure of cash control, accountants support the preparation of a monthly statement of cash flows even for unincorporated businesses. The statement of cash flows can take several forms, because it is prepared for different reasons. One form, described as the *historical statement of cash flows*, is prepared to show how cash was spent or collected during a specific accounting period that has ended. A second form, called the *prospective statement of cash flows*, is prepared to report what cash the business hopes to receive and anticipates paying out for an accounting period in the future.

In this text, only the historic statement of cash flows is treated. Although the format used by corporations in support of Section 1540 of the *CICA Handbook* may be used, many unincorporated businesses use a simple format that includes a three-line title, and a body with the following headings and calculations: (1) "Cash Was Provided By:," (2) "Cash Was Used For:," (3) "Net Increase (Decrease) in Cash," (4) adding the Cash at the beginning of the period, and (5) reporting the Cash balance at the end of the period. Obviously, the Cash balance at the end of the period must be the same as that reported by the Cash in Bank account for the same end-of-period date.

Chapter Questions

1. Name the two important internal control measures which stand out above all others for an effective control of cash receipts and cash payments.
2. "In receiving cash receipts from any business, the banker acts as a custodian of the spendable funds of the depositor-enterprise." Explain this statement in simple terms.
3. From the viewpoint of the banker, how must one analyze deposits on the banker's books?
4. In simple terms, distinguish between demand deposit accounting and time deposit accounting.
5. Explain the difference between a bank debit memo and a bank credit memo.
6. Name three common transactions that would appear on a bank debit memo.
7. How often will the bank calculate interest on a demand loan?
8. Give one reason why a business would rent a bank safety deposit box.
9. Explain how a cheque becomes certified.
10. Explain how a cheque becomes an NSF cheque.
11. How much does a bank charge each time a cheque becomes NSF? Who is charged this amount?
12. In general terms, explain why chartered banks operate a clearinghouse system.
13. What does a monthly bank statement represent?
14. Explain the differences and similarities between a bank statement and the traditional three-column ledger account.
15. Name five proofs that commonly appear on a monthly bank statement.
16. Name five discrepancy items that would cause disagreement between the balance of cash reported by the monthly bank statement and the depositor's cash records.
17. Explain why an outstanding cheque that has been certified is *not* an item of discrepancy in any bank reconciliation procedure.
18. In what order will the banker return cancelled cheques and bank memos enclosed with the bank statement?

19 After all discrepancy items have been identified, what two guides (rules) may be of help to reconcile each item? Give one example to explain how each rule may be applied.
20 What date must appear in the heading of the bank reconciliation statement?
21 With what section should one begin the body of the bank reconciliation statement?
22 What two cash records of the depositor must be adjusted after the preparation of the bank reconciliation statement?
23 In what journal would adjusting entries be recorded to update the Cash account after bank reconciliation? Explain your answer.
24 When a customer's cheque is received, recorded, and deposited, but later returned by the bank as NSF, what accounting entry is required to record this transaction?
25 Why is the preparation of monthly bank reconciliation statements essential to any business?
26 Why is it important for sole proprietorships and partnerships to prepare a monthly statement of cash flows?
27 What simple format is used in the preparation of a monthly statement of cash flows for sole proprietorships and partnerships? How does this format differ from ones used by business corporations?

Accounting Case Problems

CASE 9-1

Using the case method to solve a problem involving a large number of outstanding cheques.

The Moncton Manufacturing Company, Limited, processes approximately 1 400 cheques each month, most of which are paycheques issued to 830 employees. Under a union agreement, the employees are paid by cheque every two weeks. At month-end, many of these cheques are not cashed immediately; consequently, the large number of outstanding cheques makes the preparation of the bank reconciliation a difficult and time-consuming task.

    a Identify the true problem.
    b What are the important facts to be considered in the problem?
    c List several possible solutions.
    d Evaluate the possible results of each solution.
    e Which solution do you recommend? Why?

CASE 9-2

Using the case method to solve problems related to the recording and posting of adjusting entries resulting from a year-end reconciliation of the bank statement.

The year-end for Everything Goes Company is December 31. Both the cash receipts and the cash payments journal have been posted and ruled off as of December 31. Some of the key figures from the financial statements prepared on December 31 were: Cash, $1 275; Revenue, $75 000; Expenses, $65 000; Net Income, $10 000.

The depositor's bank statement was received on January 3, in the next accounting period. A bank reconciliation statement was prepared on January 3. Adjusting entries were journalized and posted on January 3 as follows:

FIGURE 9-37

(i)	Cash	1 000	
	Interest Revenue		1 000
	To record interest earned on 60-day deposit receipts.		
(ii)	Accounts Receivable/B. Sanger	500	
	Cash		500
	To record the NSF cheque of B. Sanger.		
(iii)	Miscellaneous Expenses	20	
	Cash		20
	To record bank monthly service charges.		
(iv)	Interest Expense	50	
	Cash		50
	To record bank interest on outstanding demand loan.		

a Identify the true problem in this case.
b What are the important facts to be considered in this case?
c State the effects of journalizing and posting the adjusting entries from the bank reconciliation on January 3.
d What should be done to avoid a similar problem in the future?

CHAPTER 10 Payroll Application

After completing this chapter, you should be able to:

— From given data, compute the gross earnings, the common payroll deductions, and the net pay for hourly-rated employees, salaried employees, and employees paid on a commission and piece-rate basis.

— From given data, compute the employer's contribution to the Canada Pension Plan and the employer's premium for UI.

— From given data, prepare an hourly payroll register, a salary payroll register, a combined hourly/salary payroll register; prove each payroll register; and record in general journal form the payroll summary and additional employer's expense resulting from each payroll summary.

— From given payroll data, complete the final month's individual earnings record for one employee.

— From given payroll data, record in general journal form payroll disbursements for amounts owing to employees, to the federal government, to a provincial government, and to other agencies affected by the data.

— From given payroll data, prepare a payroll voucher cheque for an employee.

— From given payroll data, prepare a T4 Supplementary slip for one employee.

— Identify and briefly discuss two shortcuts that may be applied to the payroll application under a manual system.

— Define the following key terms used in this chapter: gross earnings; hourly-rated plan; salary plan; commission plan; salary-commission plan; piece-rate plan; timekeeping; CPP; UI; insurable earnings; CPI; remuneration subject to tax withholding at source; garnishment; government demand; payroll register; employee's individual earnings record; accumulated earnings; payroll ledger; payroll journal; payroll clearing account; payroll taxes expense; employer health tax; payroll bank account; T4 Supplementary; T4 Summary; T4A Supplementary; T4A Summary.

In general, the payroll application includes such activities as computing gross earnings and calculating deductions from those gross earnings, recording the payroll and maintaining detailed payroll records, disbursing the various cash payments to employees, governments, and other agencies, and, finally, preparing annual tax statements and returns. In a small business, these activities or payroll functions are usually performed by one person—an accounting clerk or bookkeeper. In large companies, however, management will organize a separate payroll department or office to ensure a proper division of responsibility among the various payroll functions. Hence, a separate, timekeeping function may be organized to be responsible for keeping all time records; a payroll accounting section may be organized to compute and prepare the payroll, record the payroll, and maintain all payroll records; and a separate paymaster's function may be created to disburse the payroll. This chapter will cover these important functions.

TOPIC 1 Computing Gross Earnings and Deductions

It is useful to begin the study of the payroll accounting application with a basic view of hiring employees for any profit-seeking enterprise. In a small business, the applicants for a job are usually interviewed and hired by the owner-manager. The large enterprise generally leaves the duty of interviewing and hiring new employees to a department known as "Personnel," "Industrial Relations," or simply "Employment Office." Regardless of who, or which department, hires a new employee, it is important to understand that payroll accounting must be furnished with at least four important pieces of information from the personnel department or the owner-manager before the employee can be paid:

1. The official list of employees who are on the payroll. Briefly, employees of the payroll department or any clerk assigned to payroll accounting activities would be forbidden to enter a new name on the payroll without a formal notification from the personnel department or the owner manager.

2. A *social insurance number* for each employee as illustrated in the side margin. Under the Income Tax Act, all employees are required to have this number, commonly called the *SIN*, before any payroll is processed for them.

3. An income tax form known as the *TD1* (Personal Tax Credit Return) form. Under Canadian tax law, all employees must complete the TD1, which becomes the employer's authorization to deduct income tax. The front of the form is illustrated in Figure 10-2; details on the front and back are treated later on in this Topic.

4. The fourth important area of information required is the particular salary or wage plan under which the employee was hired. Some of the more common salary or wage plans may be identified as the *hourly-rate plan* (employee's gross earnings are based on the number of hours worked at a set rate per hour); the *salary plan* (employee's gross earnings are stated as so many dollars for a certain time period);

FIGURE 10-1

the *commission plan* (employee's gross earnings are based on a stated percentage of his or her output of sales); the *salary-commission plan* (a combination of salary and commission); and the *piece-rate plan* (employee's gross earnings are related to a stated amount for each item he or she produces). In all of these plans, observe closely that the plan will determine only the **gross earnings** of the employee, that is, his or her earnings before payroll deductions are applied.

Gross earnings: the amount of an employee's wage before deductions are applied.

Hours of Work and Wages

People engaged in payroll accounting generally agree that three factors will influence an employee's hours of work and his or her wages: (1) labour legislation of provincial and federal governments; (2) the contract of employment between employer and employee; and, where applicable, (3) the basic agreement between the employee's union and management. Of course, payroll accounting personnel must be well informed on the details of these factors before a payroll is processed.

EMPLOYMENT STANDARDS ACTS

Under Canada's constitution, the power to enact labour legislation is largely the prerogative of the provinces. Laws (statutes) exist in all provinces establishing the standards on the hours of work, minimum wages, public holidays, premium pay for working on the public holiday, overtime pay, vacation pay, and equal pay for equal work. In addition, the Canadian government has enacted similar legislation for employees hired to work for the federal government. While the details of the legislation vary with each province, employers generally are required to pay *overtime* at the rate of at least "time-and-a-half"—that is, one-and-one-half times the regular rate for hours worked in excess of 40 or 44 per week. In addition, some of the provinces include a provision that overtime be paid on a daily basis when an employee is required to work in excess of eight hours a day. Thus, an employee who is paid a regular rate of $12 per hour is paid an overtime rate of $18 (1.5 × $12) per hour for all hours worked in excess of 40 or 44 in any week, and in excess of eight hours during the day where such provisions are enacted in the provincial statute.

CONTRACT OF EMPLOYMENT

You should note that the laws in the provinces set only the maximum hours of work and minimum wage levels. For example, the Ontario Employment Standards Act, at the time of writing, provides for a minimum general hourly rate of $5.40 per hour, excludes provision for overtime pay on a daily basis, and stipulates that an employee shall not work more than eight hours a day or 48 hours a week without a permit issued by the Ministry of Labour to do so. On the other hand, an employer may offer a contract of employment with fewer hours, a higher minimum wage rate, and overtime pay for work in excess of eight hours during the day.

416 PART 2: COMMON ACCOUNTING APPLICATIONS

FIGURE 10-2

Revenue Canada / Revenu Canada	page 1
Taxation / Impôt	TD1 (E) Rev.91

1991 PERSONAL TAX CREDIT RETURN

FAMILY NAME (Please print): **BLAIR**
USUAL FIRST NAME AND INITIALS: **JOHN**
EMPLOYEE NUMBER: **3**
ADDRESS: **843 DRIFTWOOD RD.**
For NON-RESIDENTS ONLY — Country of permanent residence:
SOCIAL INSURANCE NUMBER: **143 413 663**
LONDON, ONTARIO   Postal code: **N6H 4H9**
DATE OF BIRTH: Day **14** / Month **JAN** / Year **1965**

Instructions

- Please fill out this form so your employer or payer will know how much tax to deduct regularly from your pay. Otherwise, you will be allowed **only** the basic personal amount of $6,280. Regular deductions will help you avoid having to pay when you file your income tax return.
- **You must complete this form if you receive**
  - salary, wages, commissions or any other remuneration;
  - superannuation or pension benefits including an annuity payment made under a superannuation or pension fund or plan;
  - Unemployment Insurance benefits including training allowances.
- You may also complete this form if you receive payments under registered retirement income funds and/or registered retirement savings plans.
- Give the completed form to your employer or payer. Pensioners who receive Canada Pension Plan benefits, Old Age Security or Guaranteed Income Supplements should send the completed form to the Regional Office of Health and Welfare Canada.
- **Need help?** If you need help to complete this form, you may ask your employer or payer, or call the Source Deductions section of your local Revenue Canada district taxation office. Before you do this, see the additional information on page 2 under "Notes to Employees and Payees."

1. **Are you a non-resident of Canada?** (see note 1 on page 2). If so, and **less than** 90 per cent of your 1991 total world income will be included when calculating taxable income earned in Canada, enter claim code 0 in the box on line 17 and sign the form. If you are a resident of Canada, go to item 2.

2. **Basic personal amount.** (everyone may claim $6,280.) ▶ $6,280. 2.

3. (a) **Are you married and supporting your spouse?** (see notes 4 and 5 on page 2).
   or
   (b) **Are you single, divorced, separated or widowed and supporting a relative who lives with you who is either your parent or grandparent, OR who is under 19 at the end of 1991, OR 19 or older and infirm?** (see notes 2, 3 and 4 on page 2).
   Note: A spouse or dependant claimed here cannot be claimed again on lines 4 or 5.
   If you answered yes to either (a) or (b) and your spouse's or dependant's 1991 net income will be
   - under $524, CLAIM $5,233
   - between $524 and $5,757, CLAIM (e)
   - over $5,757, CLAIM $0

   $5,757 (c)
   Minus: spouse or dependant's net income _____ (d)
   Claim (c minus d) _____ (e) ▶ **5233** 3.

4. **Do you have any dependants who will be under 19 at the end of 1991?** (see notes 2 and 4 on page 2). If so, and your 1991 net income will be **higher** than your spouse's, calculate the amount to claim for **each** dependant. If you are not married, please see notes 2, 3 and 4 on page 2.
   Note: If you have three or more dependants who will be under 19 at the end of the year, you do not have to claim them in the order they were born. You may claim them in the **most beneficial** order. For example, a dependant who is 16 with a net income of $3,500 could be claimed as the first dependant (claim 0) while the other two, with no income, could be claimed as second and third dependants.

   First and second dependant:
   If your dependant's 1991 net income will be
   - under $2,617, CLAIM $406
   - between $2,617 and $3,023, CLAIM (e)
   - over $3,023, CLAIM $0

   $3,023 (c)
   Minus: dependant's net income _____ (d)
   Claim (c minus d) _____ (e)

   dependants
   1st **406**
   2nd _____
   3rd _____
   4th _____

   Third and each additional dependant:
   If your dependant's 1991 net income will be
   - under $2,617, CLAIM $812
   - between $2,617 and $3,429, CLAIM (e)
   - over $3,429, CLAIM $0.

   $3,429 (c)
   Minus: dependant's net income _____ (d)
   Claim (c minus d) _____ (e)

   5th _____
   6th _____
   Total **406** ▶ **406** 4.

5. **Do you have any infirm dependants who will be 19 or older at the end of 1991?** (see notes 2 and 4 on page 2). If so, and your dependant's net income will be
   - under $2,617, CLAIM $1,540
   - between $2,617 and $4,157, CLAIM (e)
   - over $4,157, CLAIM $0

   $4,157 (c)
   Minus: dependant's net income _____ (d)
   Claim (c minus d) _____ (e)

   dependants
   1st _____
   2nd _____
   3rd _____
   Total _____ ▶ _____ 5.

6. **Do you receive eligible pension income?** (see note 6 on page 2). If so, claim your pension income amount or $1,000, whichever is less. ▶ _____ 6.

7. **Will you be 65 or older at the end of 1991?** If so, claim $3,387. ▶ _____ 7.

8. **Are you disabled?** (see note 7 on page 2). If so, claim $3,387. ▶ _____ 8.

9. **Are you a student?** If so, claim
   - **tuition fees** paid for courses you take in 1991 to attend either a university, college or a certified educational institution. If you receive any scholarships, fellowships or bursaries in 1991, subtract the amount over $500 from your tuition fees before you claim them. _____
   - $60 for each month in 1991 that you will be enrolled in a qualifying program, full-time, at either a university, college or a school offering job retraining courses or correspondence courses. Total _____ ▶ _____ 9.

10. Total (add 2 to 9 – please enter this amount on line 11 on page 2) **$11919.** 10.

(See reverse)

BASIC AGREEMENT In businesses employing many workers, there is commonly a basic agreement between the employer and a union that covers wages, hours of work, and other terms and conditions of employment. The basic agreement becomes the contract of employment, and must be followed by both employer and employee. Of course, the terms of this agreement must not be in violation of the Employment Standards Act of the province or federal government; otherwise, the agreement would be invalid. In general, the basic agreement usually provides for higher wages than those stated in the various provincial acts.

One other point regarding hours of work and wages is very important. Under the law of each province and the federal government, every employer is required to keep wage records, including the name and address of the worker, the hours worked each week, and the wage rates and actual earnings of each employee. In some provinces, and for industries under federal jurisdiction, a record must also be kept of each employee's work time in excess of eight hours a day or 48 hours in a week. As indicated earlier, permits are required to allow employees to work for more than eight hours per day and more than 48 hours per week. In order to conform to legislation, it is important that every accounting system keep accurate and reliable records.

Timekeeping

Timekeeping: the accounting of time spent on the job with each employee.

As has been stated, an employer is required by law to keep a complete record of hours worked by each employee. In many firms, a separate timekeeper or ***timekeeping*** department is given the responsibility of preparing daily records of time worked by each employee. Of course, the type of record will vary with the type of employee wage plan. For example, for hourly-rated employees the daily time record generally is kept with the aid of a time clock and clock cards. Where timekeeping is separated from the payroll department, it is important that one copy of the timekeeping record be forwarded to the payroll department or office in order to process the payroll.

FIGURE 10-3

Name ____________ Employee No. ____
Social Insurance No. ____________
Week Ending ____________

WESTERN SALES COMPANY
CLOCK CARD

	Regular				Extra		
Days	In	Out	In	Out	In	Out	Hours
Thur.							
Fri.							
Sat.							
Sun.							
Mon.							
Tue.							
Wed.							

	Hours	Rate	Earnings
Regular			
Overtime			
Total Hours		Gross Earnings	

An important internal measure to control daily time records must be mentioned here. In general, all employees paid under the hourly-rate plan will be required to punch in and out on clock cards. To control the hours punched in and out on these cards, an accounting system usually requires an independent record of this time. In the majority of cases, the person in charge of the hourly-rated employees—the supervisor—will be required to complete a *daily report of time* form. The supervisor is required to show on this form the number of hours that each employee has worked, based upon observation of the employees on their job. When completed, a copy of the supervisor's report must be submitted to the payroll department, where it will be checked against the clock card records.

A similar internal check on the time worked by salaried employees will be required of heads of the various operating departments. For example, the sales manager and office manager may be required to sign the attendance time record kept for their respective salaried personnel before the record is submitted for payroll processing. Where a piece-work basis of pay is in operation, the departmental report must show all details for remunerating employees on this payroll plan. Of course, such a piece-work report must also be signed by a responsible department head before the form is forwarded to the payroll department.

Computation of Gross Earnings

As stated earlier, it is important in the preparation of a payroll for a large firm (say with 50 or more employees) that the activities involved be divided among different persons to ensure strong internal control over each payroll. Ideally, therefore, a clerk assigned to the payroll department should receive the various reports of time worked by employees. One important responsibility of the payroll clerk would be to calculate the gross earnings of each employee for each pay period.

FOR HOURLY-RATED EMPLOYEES   As has been stated, the majority of firms having many hourly-rated employees will use a time clock to keep the record of time worked for each employee. Under this system, every employee has a clock card which he or she inserts in the time clock upon arrival and again upon leaving. The clock automatically punches these times on the card. After the cards are collected at the end of the pay period, the first responsibility of the payroll clerk is to check the time recorded on the card against the supervisor's daily report of time and reconcile any discrepancy. If an employee failed to ring "in" and "out" on the same day, the payroll clerk is required to obtain in writing on the back of the clock card the supervisor's authorization to give pay. Once other discrepancies are reconciled, the payroll clerk can begin to compute on the card the number of hours worked, the regular earnings, the overtime earnings, and the total earnings of each employee.

It is worth mentioning here that, under a computer method of processing the payroll, the various calculations to arrive at the total gross earnings of each employee would not be done by the payroll clerk. Briefly, when clock cards are used to record the time worked for each employee, the payroll clerk's job ends at the point where he or she has reconciled all the cards with the supervisor's daily report of time. Once the cards are checked, they (or special payroll forms showing employee time data) may be submitted to the data processing department, where the gross pay of each employee is calculated automatically by the computer. Of course, in the smaller businesses where time cards or time books are used, the payroll clerk may be required to perform the calculations by hand or with an office calculator.

To begin the calculation of an hourly-rated employee's gross earnings, it is first important to check the contract of employment regarding working hours. For example, hourly-rated employees may be required to work

CHAPTER 10: Payroll Application **419**

from 8:00 a.m. to 12:00 noon in the morning and from 1:00 p.m. to 5:00 p.m. in the afternoon. Some rules must be made regarding tardiness and the computation of time. The rules followed by some employers that are shown below will be used for the illustration of calculating the gross earnings for one employee:

- Time before 8:00 a.m. and 1:00 p.m. is not counted.
- Daily time is computed in hours and quarter-hours. Fractions of an hour less than 15 minutes are not counted when calculating either the regular or the overtime hours.
- For lateness, the employee loses 15 minutes for every 15 minutes or portion thereof of lateness in the morning or afternoon. In the clock card for John Blair, illustrated in the side margin, a penalty of 15 minutes is charged on Thursday and Tuesday mornings for clocking in at 8:01 and 8:05 respectively, and a penalty of 30 minutes is charged on Wednesday afternoon for clocking in at 1:16 p.m.
- The same penalties apply for clocking out early. On Friday, Blair is penalized 15 minutes for clocking out at 11:59 a.m.
- Overtime is calculated only in quarter-hours. The employee must work a full quarter-hour (15, 30, 45 minutes, etc.) as clocked in the extra-time section of the card, headed "Extra."
- In computing the total hours for an employee's pay period, the regular hours are calculated separately from the overtime period.

FIGURE 10-4

Name: John Blair Employee No. 3
Social Insurance No. 143-413-663
Week Ending June 30, 19—

WESTERN SALES COMPANY CLOCK CARD

Days	Regular In	Out	In	Out	Extra In	Out	Hours
Thur.	8:01	12:00	1:00	5:01			7¾
Fri.	7:59	11:59	1:00	5:00			7¾
Sat.							
Sun.							
Mon.	7:55	12:02	12:58	5:05	6:00	8:00	8+2
Tue.	8:05	12:03	12:59	5:01	6:00	7:01	7¾+1
Wed.	7:59	12:01	1:16	5:02	5:57	8:01	7½+2

	Hours	Rate	Earnings
Regular	38¾	$12.00	$465.00
Overtime	5	$18.00	$ 90.00
Total Hours	43¾	Gross Earnings	$555.00

Completed clock card. At the time of writing, the majority of Canadian industries using a time clock system do not use the 24-hour clock.

FOR SALARIED EMPLOYEES   Employers are also required by most provincial statutes to keep some form of attendance record for salaried employees. One form of attendance record used by business is illustrated in Figure 10-5.

Although attendance records for salaried personnel vary in form from one type of business to another, the following details are commonly shown: department name and/or number, the pay period ending date, and the name and social insurance number of each employee. In general, the attendance record is operated on the *exception principle*. If no details are entered opposite the name of an employee, this indicates that the employee will receive

FIGURE 10-5

PAYROLL AND ABSENTEE REPORT

Department: Gregg
Completed by: L. Taylor

From: Monday 26 April
To: Friday 30 April

NAME	MONDAY absent	TUESDAY absent	WEDNESDAY absent	THURSDAY absent	FRIDAY absent	SATURDAY absent	TOTAL DAYS ABSENT	EXPLANATIONS Reasons for absence, vacations etc.
Scott Aplin	x						1	Virus cold
Ray Butler								
Henry Conway								
John Davis	x	x	x	x	x		5	Vacation

his or her regular pay. On the other hand, if exceptions are noted for items such as absences, overtime, etc., these would be explained in the appropriate column. For unauthorized absences, management may instruct the payroll department to deduct an amount from the regular employee's salary.

FOR OTHER EMPLOYEES Of course, some appropriate timekeeping record will be kept for employees hired on a piece-rate plan or on a commission basis. In these cases, the record forwarded to the payroll clerk or department must include the necessary details so that the employee's gross earnings can be calculated correctly.

Calculating Public Holiday Pay, Premium Holiday Pay, and Vacation Pay

Many firms follow the employment standards of their respective province in calculating pay for a public holiday, the premium pay for working on a public holiday, and vacation pay. For example, the Ontario Employment Standards Act, at the time of writing, sets forth the following provisions:

- **Public holiday pay** As a general rule, employees are entitled to eight public holidays with pay: New Year's Day, Good Friday, Victoria Day, Canada Day, Labour Day, Thanksgiving Day, Christmas Day, and Boxing Day. When a public holiday falls upon a day when an employee must work, an employer may, with the agreement of the employee or employee's agent, substitute another working day for the public holiday. This day must occur no later than the next annual vacation of the employee, and the day so substituted must be treated as the public holiday. On the other hand, if the holiday falls on a day that is normally non-working, such as a Saturday, the employee shall be given another, regular working day off with pay or, if the employee agrees, the employer will pay the employee the regular wage for the public holiday.

- **Premium holiday pay** In general, if a qualified employee does not have a substitute arrangement and works on a public holiday, the employee must be paid a "premium" for those hours worked, in addition to the employee's regular day's pay for that public holiday. In Ontario, the premium must be at least one-and-one-half times the regular rate for those hours worked—time-and-a-half. Suppose, for example, Monday is a public holiday, the regular rate is $14 per hour, and the employee worked the week as follows: Monday, 8 hours; Tuesday, 8 hours; Wednesday, 8 hours; Thursday, 8 hours; and Friday, 8 hours. If the employee qualified for holiday pay, the calculation of his or her gross earnings would be calculated as in Figure 10-6.

- **Vacation pay** In Ontario, after one year's service, employees are entitled two weeks' vacation with pay. The vacation pay must be at least four percent of the total wages for the year for which the vacation is given. Remember again the fact that this provision is only the minimum standard for vacation pay. In practice, the contract of employment may stipulate other terms, terms above the minimum standard.

FIGURE 10-6

Regular pay	32 × $14.00 =	$448.00
Public holiday pay (Monday)	8 × $14.00 =	112.00
Premium holiday pay	8 × $21.00 =	168.00
Employee's gross earnings		$728.00

Deductions from Gross Earnings

As you are aware, the actual amount of "take-home" or net pay is not the same as the amount calculated from gross earnings. The reason is that a number of payroll deductions must be considered. In general, these deductions include *deductions required by law*, such as the Canada Pension Plan contributions, unemployment insurance premiums, and income taxes; *deductions required by collective bargaining agreements*, such as union dues; and *voluntary deductions*, for items such as life insurance premiums and Canada Savings Bonds payments. For large industrial plants, accountants generally assign priority to each type of authorized deduction that may be made from an employee's pay. Here is one such plan.

Priority of Payroll Deductions

The following is the order of priority assigned to the types of authorized deductions that may be made from an employee's paycheque:

- **Required by law**
    1. Canada Pension Plan
    2. Unemployment insurance
    3. Federal and provincial income taxes
    4. Garnishments and government demands
- **Required by collective bargaining agreements**
    5. Union initiation fees
    6. Union dues
- **Voluntary**
    7. Company pension plan (if available)
    8. Group insurance
    9. Canada Savings Bonds
    10. Credit union
    11. Community services (United Way, etc.)
    12. Miscellaneous deductions: for safety shoes, glasses, badges, tools, etc.

Canada Pension Plan

Canada Pension Plan (CPP): a compulsory employee's pension plan administered by the federal government in all provinces except Quebec, which has its own Quebec Pension Plan.

For most types of employment, the employer must deduct the required *Canada Pension Plan (CPP)* contributions from the remuneration of every employee who meets all three of the following criteria:

- The employee is 18 years old and has not reached 70 years of age.
- The employee is employed in pensionable employment during the year.
- The employee is not receiving a Canada or Quebec Pension Plan retirement or disability pension.

EMPLOYEES' CONTRIBUTIONS   The employer must deduct employees' contributions from salary, wages, or any other remuneration, including any taxable benefits the employer pays or provides. The amount of the CPP contribution to be deducted from gross earnings is determined by the federal government before the start of each new calendar year. For example, the following schedule in Figure 10-7 took effect on January 1, 1991.

FIGURE 10-7

Year's maximum pensionable earnings	$30 500
Year's basic exemption	3 000
Maximum earnings on which contributions are based	$27 500
Maximum employee contribution:	
2.3% of $27 500	$632.50

[handwritten annotations: 1992 → 696.00; 1993 → 752.50]

Therefore, the maximum amount any employer may deduct from an employee for the 1991 CPP contribution is $632.50. Obviously, if the employee makes more than $30 500 in the year, say $40 000, the maximum that can be deducted for CPP is $632.50. Although the "calculating" method shown in the above schedule may be used, Revenue Canada—Taxation publishes a booklet that combines tables not only for CPP, but also for unemployment insurance and income tax deductions. These booklets are published annually for release in January of each new calendar year. Currently, CPP contribution tables are provided for weekly, biweekly, semimonthly, and monthly pay periods. An example of a partial weekly pay period table is given in Figure 10-8.

To illustrate the use of the contribution table, consider the earlier example of John Blair's weekly gross earnings which showed $555. The amount of contribution to be deducted from this employee, and from every other employee, may be determined as follows:

1. Refer to the page in the table corresponding to the pay period. For example, if the employee is paid weekly, refer to the page headed "Weekly Pay Period."

2. Look down the appropriate remuneration column for the bracket containing the amount of the employee's pay. (In the table method, it is not necessary to deduct the employee's prorated exemption, because this calculation has already been reflected in the amounts shown in adjoining columns.)

3. The amount in the adjoining column is the amount of contribution to be withheld from the employee's remuneration. (The employer is required to match this contribution.)

    In the case of John Blair, one would look down the Remuneration column of the Weekly Pay Period table until the bracket

FIGURE 10-8

18   CANADA PENSION PLAN CONTRIBUTIONS   COTISATIONS AU RÉGIME DE PENSIONS DU CANADA

WEEKLY PAY PERIOD — *PÉRIODE HEBDOMADAIRE DE PAIE*

433.13—558.34

Remuneration Rémunération From-de — To-à	C.P.P. R.P.C.	Remuneration Rémunération From-de — To-à	C.P.P. R.P.C.	Remuneration Rémunération From-de — To-à	C.P.P. R.P.C.	Remuneration Rémunération From-de — To-à	C.P.P. R.P.C.
433.13 - 433.55	8.64	464.43 - 464.86	9.36	495.74 - 496.16	10.08	527.04 - 527.47	10.80
433.56 - 433.99	8.65	464.87 - 465.29	9.37	496.17 - 496.60	10.09	527.48 - 527.90	10.81
434.00 - 434.42	8.66	465.30 - 465.73	9.38	496.61 - 497.03	10.10	527.91 - 528.34	10.82
434.43 - 434.86	8.67	465.74 - 466.16	9.39	497.04 - 497.47	10.11	528.35 - 528.77	10.83
434.87 - 435.29	8.68	466.17 - 466.60	9.40	497.48 - 497.90	10.12	528.78 - 529.21	10.84
435.30 - 435.73	8.69	466.61 - 467.03	9.41	497.91 - 498.34	10.13	529.22 - 529.64	10.85
435.74 - 436.16	8.70	467.04 - 467.47	9.42	498.35 - 498.77	10.14	529.65 - 530.08	10.86
436.17 - 436.60	8.71	467.48 - 467.90	9.43	498.78 - 499.21	10.15	530.09 - 530.51	10.87
436.61 - 437.03	8.72	467.91 - 468.34	9.44	499.22 - 499.64	10.16	530.52 - 530.95	10.88
437.04 - 437.47	8.73	468.35 - 468.77	9.45	499.65 - 500.08	10.17	530.96 - 531.38	10.89
437.48 - 437.90	8.74	468.78 - 469.21	9.46	500.09 - 500.51	10.18	531.39 - 531.82	10.90
437.91 - 438.34	8.75	469.22 - 469.64	9.47	500.52 - 500.95	10.19	531.83 - 532.25	10.91
438.35 - 438.77	8.76	469.65 - 470.08	9.48	500.96 - 501.38	10.20	532.26 - 532.68	10.92
438.78 - 439.21	8.77	470.09 - 470.51	9.49	501.39 - 501.82	10.21	532.69 - 533.12	10.93
439.22 - 439.64	8.78	470.52 - 470.95	9.50	501.83 - 502.25	10.22	533.13 - 533.55	10.94
439.65 - 440.08	8.79	470.96 - 471.38	9.51	502.26 - 502.68	10.23	533.56 - 533.99	10.95
440.09 - 440.51	8.80	471.39 - 471.82	9.52	502.69 - 503.12	10.24	534.00 - 534.42	10.96
440.52 - 440.95	8.81	471.83 - 472.25	9.53	503.13 - 503.55	10.25	534.43 - 534.86	10.97
440.96 - 441.38	8.82	472.26 - 472.68	9.54	503.56 - 503.99	10.26	534.87 - 535.29	10.98
441.39 - 441.82	8.83	472.69 - 473.12	9.55	504.00 - 504.42	10.27	535.30 - 535.73	10.99
441.83 - 442.25	8.84	473.13 - 473.55	9.56	504.43 - 504.86	10.28	535.74 - 536.16	11.00
442.26 - 442.68	8.85	473.56 - 473.99	9.57	504.87 - 505.29	10.29	536.17 - 536.60	11.01
442.69 - 443.12	8.86	474.00 - 474.42	9.58	505.30 - 505.73	10.30	536.61 - 537.03	11.02
443.13 - 443.55	8.87	474.43 - 474.86	9.59	505.74 - 506.16	10.31	537.04 - 537.47	11.03
443.56 - 443.99	8.88	474.87 - 475.29	9.60	506.17 - 506.60	10.32	537.48 - 537.90	11.04
444.00 - 444.42	8.89	475.30 - 475.73	9.61	506.61 - 507.03	10.33	537.91 - 538.34	11.05
444.43 - 444.86	8.90	475.74 - 476.16	9.62	507.04 - 507.47	10.34	538.35 - 538.77	11.06
444.87 - 445.29	8.91	476.17 - 476.60	9.63	507.48 - 507.90	10.35	538.78 - 539.21	11.07
445.30 - 445.73	8.92	476.61 - 477.03	9.64	507.91 - 508.34	10.36	539.22 - 539.64	11.08
445.74 - 446.16	8.93	477.04 - 477.47	9.65	508.35 - 508.77	10.37	539.65 - 540.08	11.09
446.17 - 446.60	8.94	477.48 - 477.90	9.66	508.78 - 509.21	10.38	540.09 - 540.51	11.10
446.61 - 447.03	8.95	477.91 - 478.34	9.67	509.22 - 509.64	10.39	540.52 - 540.95	11.11
447.04 - 447.47	8.96	478.35 - 478.77	9.68	509.65 - 510.08	10.40	540.96 - 541.38	11.12
447.48 - 447.90	8.97	478.78 - 479.21	9.69	510.09 - 510.51	10.41	541.39 - 541.82	11.13
447.91 - 448.34	8.98	479.22 - 479.64	9.70	510.52 - 510.95	10.42	541.83 - 542.25	11.14
448.35 - 448.77	8.99	479.65 - 480.08	9.71	510.96 - 511.38	10.43	542.26 - 542.68	11.15
448.78 - 449.21	9.00	480.09 - 480.51	9.72	511.39 - 511.82	10.44	542.69 - 543.12	11.16
449.22 - 449.64	9.01	480.52 - 480.95	9.73	511.83 - 512.25	10.45	543.13 - 543.55	11.17
449.65 - 450.08	9.02	480.96 - 481.38	9.74	512.26 - 512.68	10.46	543.56 - 543.99	11.18
450.09 - 450.51	9.03	481.39 - 481.82	9.75	512.69 - 513.12	10.47	544.00 - 544.42	11.19
450.52 - 450.95	9.04	481.83 - 482.25	9.76	513.13 - 513.55	10.48	544.43 - 544.86	11.20
450.96 - 451.38	9.05	482.26 - 482.68	9.77	513.56 - 513.99	10.49	544.87 - 545.29	11.21
451.39 - 451.82	9.06	482.69 - 483.12	9.78	514.00 - 514.42	10.50	545.30 - 545.73	11.22
451.83 - 452.25	9.07	483.13 - 483.55	9.79	514.43 - 514.86	10.51	545.74 - 546.16	11.23
452.26 - 452.68	9.08	483.56 - 483.99	9.80	514.87 - 515.29	10.52	546.17 - 546.60	11.24
452.69 - 453.12	9.09	484.00 - 484.42	9.81	515.30 - 515.73	10.53	546.61 - 547.03	11.25
453.13 - 453.55	9.10	484.43 - 484.86	9.82	515.74 - 516.16	10.54	547.04 - 547.47	11.26
453.56 - 453.99	9.11	484.87 - 485.29	9.83	516.17 - 516.60	10.55	547.48 - 547.90	11.27
454.00 - 454.42	9.12	485.30 - 485.73	9.84	516.61 - 517.03	10.56	547.91 - 548.34	11.28
454.43 - 454.86	9.13	485.74 - 486.16	9.85	517.04 - 517.47	10.57	548.35 - 548.77	11.29
454.87 - 455.29	9.14	486.17 - 486.60	9.86	517.48 - 517.90	10.58	548.78 - 549.21	11.30
455.30 - 455.73	9.15	486.61 - 487.03	9.87	517.91 - 518.34	10.59	549.22 - 549.64	11.31
455.74 - 456.16	9.16	487.04 - 487.47	9.88	518.35 - 518.77	10.60	549.65 - 550.08	11.32
456.17 - 456.60	9.17	487.48 - 487.90	9.89	518.78 - 519.21	10.61	550.09 - 550.51	11.33
456.61 - 457.03	9.18	487.91 - 488.34	9.90	519.22 - 519.64	10.62	550.52 - 550.95	11.34
457.04 - 457.47	9.19	488.35 - 488.77	9.91	519.65 - 520.08	10.63	550.96 - 551.38	11.35
457.48 - 457.90	9.20	488.78 - 489.21	9.92	520.09 - 520.51	10.64	551.39 - 551.82	11.36
457.91 - 458.34	9.21	489.22 - 489.64	9.93	520.52 - 520.95	10.65	551.83 - 552.25	11.37
458.35 - 458.77	9.22	489.65 - 490.08	9.94	520.96 - 521.38	10.66	552.26 - 552.68	11.38
458.78 - 459.21	9.23	490.09 - 490.51	9.95	521.39 - 521.82	10.67	552.69 - 553.12	11.39
459.22 - 459.64	9.24	490.52 - 490.95	9.96	521.83 - 522.25	10.68	553.13 - 553.55	11.40
459.65 - 460.08	9.25	490.96 - 491.38	9.97	522.26 - 522.68	10.69	553.56 - 553.99	11.41
460.09 - 460.51	9.26	491.39 - 491.82	9.98	522.69 - 523.12	10.70	554.00 - 554.42	11.42
460.52 - 460.95	9.27	491.83 - 492.25	9.99	523.13 - 523.55	10.71	554.43 - 554.86	11.43
460.96 - 461.38	9.28	492.26 - 492.68	10.00	523.56 - 523.99	10.72	554.87 - 555.29	11.44
461.39 - 461.82	9.29	492.69 - 493.12	10.01	524.00 - 524.42	10.73	555.30 - 555.73	11.45
461.83 - 462.25	9.30	493.13 - 493.55	10.02	524.43 - 524.86	10.74	555.74 - 556.16	11.46
462.26 - 462.68	9.31	493.56 - 493.99	10.03	524.87 - 525.29	10.75	556.17 - 556.60	11.47
462.69 - 463.12	9.32	494.00 - 494.42	10.04	525.30 - 525.73	10.76	556.61 - 557.03	11.48
463.13 - 463.55	9.33	494.43 - 494.86	10.05	525.74 - 526.16	10.77	557.04 - 557.47	11.49
463.56 - 463.99	9.34	494.87 - 495.29	10.06	526.17 - 526.60	10.78	557.48 - 557.90	11.50
464.00 - 464.42	9.35	495.30 - 495.73	10.07	526.61 - 527.03	10.79	557.91 - 558.34	11.51

424   PART 2: COMMON ACCOUNTING APPLICATIONS

FIGURE 10-9

John Blair's CPP Contribution (calculation method)

1. Prorated basic exemption (calculating the basic exemption on the basis of one week):

   $1/52 \times \$3\ 000 = \$57.69$

2. Amount of contribution:

   2.3% of ($555.00 less $57.69)
   $= 0.023 \times \$497.31$
   $= \$11.44$

$554.87–$555.29 was found. The contribution is located by simply identifying the amount on the same line in the CPP column which, for Blair, is $11.44. Of course, Blair's weekly contribution may also be found by the calculation method, shown in the side margin.

CALCULATING THE EMPLOYER'S CONTRIBUTION
By law, the employer must *match*, dollar for dollar, every employee's contribution to the Canada Pension Plan. These amounts will obviously become an additional payroll expense for the employer. You should keep this point in mind when the accounting entries to record the employee's share and the employer's share are treated in the next Topic.

EMPLOYEES' CONTRIBUTIONS ARE TAX-DEDUCTIBLE
Under the Income Tax Act, all contributions made by an employee to CPP are deductible from the employee's income tax. Therefore, if John Blair contributed the maximum CPP in 1991, this would mean that he could use $632.50 as one of his non-refundable tax credits for the 1991 tax year.

Unemployment Insurance

Unemployment insurance (UI): a federal government plan protecting workers against loss of income due to unemployment.

Insurable earnings: the amount of earnings upon which UI premiums are calculated.

With a few exceptions, all persons employed under a contract of service (contract of employment) are required by the Unemployment Insurance Act of 1971 (a federal law) to contribute an **unemployment insurance (UI)** premium. It is important to understand that unemployment insurance is not a savings account. The premium pays for protection against unemployment and, whether or not there has been a loss of job, there is no refund of the amount paid into the fund. For purposes of learning payroll accounting, it is also important to remember that the law requires the employer as well as the insured employee to make a contribution.

EMPLOYEE'S PREMIUM
In general, the employee's premium is a certain percentage on every $100 of **insurable earnings** that fall within the range of a certain minimum and maximum limit of such earnings. This certain percentage is a rate published at the beginning of each calendar year by the Department of National Revenue—Taxation, which is the federal government department responsible for administering the coverage and collection of unemployment insurance premiums. For 1991, the rate established is 2.25% on every $100 of insurable earnings. This means that $2.25 must be deducted on every $100 of the employee's gross earnings that fall between the range of minimum and maximum insurable earnings. See Figure 10-10, which gives a table published by Revenue Canada—Taxation for payroll periods in 1991.

At times, an employee may question having to pay the UI premium on the grounds that he or she is simply a part-time employee. In general, under Regulation 13 of the Unemployment Insurance Act, an employee is in insurable employment if either of the following conditions is met:

FIGURE 10-10

Schedule 2 — Unemployment Insurance

Pay Period (PP)	MINIMUM Hours	MINIMUM Earnings ($)	Maximum Insurable Earnings ($)	MAXIMUM PREMIUM Per Period @ 2.25% ($)	MAXIMUM PREMIUM Per Year ($)
Weekly (52 PP)	15	136.00	680.00	15.30	795.60
Biweekly (26 PP)	30	272.00	1 360.00	30.60	795.60
Semimonthly (24 PP)	33	294.66	1 473.33	33.15	795.60
Monthly (12 PP)	65	589.33	2 946.66	66.30	795.60
10 pay periods per year	78	707.20	3 536.00	79.56	795.60
13 pay periods per year	60	544.00	2 720.00	61.20	795.60
22 pay periods per year	35	321.45	1 607.27	36.16	795.52
Yearly (commission)		7 072.00	35 360.00		795.60

- The employee has cash earnings of at least 20% of the maximum weekly insurable earnings.
- The employee has worked at least 15 hours in a week.

Therefore, as long as an employee has worked in each week or part-week of the pay period, and the cash earnings or hours worked in the pay period are equal to or more than the minimum for the pay period, as shown in Figure 10-10, earnings for the whole pay period are insurable. To be excepted employment for UI purposes, it is necessary to fall below *both* of the minimum requirements specified in Regulation 13 above.

In the case of John Blair, for example, the employer is obliged to deduct $12.49 from the employee's weekly gross earnings of $555 (2.25% of $555). If, however, this employee had earned $800 in the week, the employer would deduct only $15.30 and not $18, since $15.30 is the maximum premium that can be deducted for a weekly pay period. At the other extreme, if John had the misfortune to earn only $60 in a work week of five hours, the law exempts him from making a contribution for that week, because his gross earnings are below the minimum amount of insurable earnings (below $136, which is below 20% of the maximum insurable earnings of $680).

To help payroll clerks calculate the correct amount of employee contributions, the Department of National Revenue—Taxation includes in its booklet tables of unemployment insurance premiums as shown in Figure 10-11. Check the table shown to verify that, in the case of John Blair's weekly gross earnings of $555, the employer is required to deduct a UI premium of $12.49.

CALCULATING THE EMPLOYER'S PREMIUM

By law, employers are required to contribute a premium to the unemployment insurance fund. At the time of writing, the employer's premium is to be calculated

426 PART 2: COMMON ACCOUNTING APPLICATIONS

FIGURE 10-11

| UNEMPLOYMENT INSURANCE PREMIUMS | | | COTISATIONS À L'ASSURANCE-CHÔMAGE | | | 65 |

For minimum and maximum insurable earnings amounts for various pay periods see Schedule II. For the maximum premium deduction for various pay periods see bottom of this page.

Les montants minimum et maximum des gains assurables pour diverses périodes de paie figurent en annexe II. La déduction maximale de primes pour diverses périodes de paie figure au bas de la présente page.

Remuneration Rémunération From-de — To-à	U.I. Premium Cotisation d'a.-c.	Remuneration Rémunération From-de — To-à	U.I. Premium Cotisation d'a.-c.	Remuneration Rémunération From-de — To-à	U.I. Premium Cotisation d'a.-c.	Remuneration Rémunération From-de — To-à	U.I. Premium Cotisation d'a.-c.
512.23 - 512.66	11.53	544.23 - 544.66	12.25	576.23 - 576.66	12.97	608.23 - 608.66	13.69
512.67 - 513.11	11.54	544.67 - 545.11	12.26	576.67 - 577.11	12.98	608.67 - 609.11	13.70
513.12 - 513.55	11.55	545.12 - 545.55	12.27	577.12 - 577.55	12.99	609.12 - 609.55	13.71
513.56 - 513.99	11.56	545.56 - 545.99	12.28	577.56 - 577.99	13.00	609.56 - 609.99	13.72
514.00 - 514.44	11.57	546.00 - 546.44	12.29	578.00 - 578.44	13.01	610.00 - 610.44	13.73
514.45 - 514.88	11.58	546.45 - 546.88	12.30	578.45 - 578.88	13.02	610.45 - 610.88	13.74
514.89 - 515.33	11.59	546.89 - 547.33	12.31	578.89 - 579.33	13.03	610.89 - 611.33	13.75
515.34 - 515.77	11.60	547.34 - 547.77	12.32	579.34 - 579.77	13.04	611.34 - 611.77	13.76
515.78 - 516.22	11.61	547.78 - 548.22	12.33	579.78 - 580.22	13.05	611.78 - 612.22	13.77
516.23 - 516.66	11.62	548.23 - 548.66	12.34	580.23 - 580.66	13.06	612.23 - 612.66	13.78
516.67 - 517.11	11.63	548.67 - 549.11	12.35	580.67 - 581.11	13.07	612.67 - 613.11	13.79
517.12 - 517.55	11.64	549.12 - 549.55	12.36	581.12 - 581.55	13.08	613.12 - 613.55	13.80
517.56 - 517.99	11.65	549.56 - 549.99	12.37	581.56 - 581.99	13.09	613.56 - 613.99	13.81
518.00 - 518.44	11.66	550.00 - 550.44	12.38	582.00 - 582.44	13.10	614.00 - 614.44	13.82
518.45 - 518.88	11.67	550.45 - 550.88	12.39	582.45 - 582.88	13.11	614.45 - 614.88	13.83
518.89 - 519.33	11.68	550.89 - 551.33	12.40	582.89 - 583.33	13.12	614.89 - 615.33	13.84
519.34 - 519.77	11.69	551.34 - 551.77	12.41	583.34 - 583.77	13.13	615.34 - 615.77	13.85
519.78 - 520.22	11.70	551.78 - 552.22	12.42	583.78 - 584.22	13.14	615.78 - 616.22	13.86
520.23 - 520.66	11.71	552.23 - 552.66	12.43	584.23 - 584.66	13.15	616.23 - 616.66	13.87
520.67 - 521.11	11.72	552.67 - 553.11	12.44	584.67 - 585.11	13.16	616.67 - 617.11	13.88
521.12 - 521.55	11.73	553.12 - 553.55	12.45	585.12 - 585.55	13.17	617.12 - 617.55	13.89
521.56 - 521.99	11.74	553.56 - 553.99	12.46	585.56 - 585.99	13.18	617.56 - 617.99	13.90
522.00 - 522.44	11.75	554.00 - 554.44	12.47	586.00 - 586.44	13.19	618.00 - 618.44	13.91
522.45 - 522.88	11.76	554.45 - 554.88	12.48	586.45 - 586.88	13.20	618.45 - 618.88	13.92
522.89 - 523.33	11.77	554.89 - 555.33	12.49	586.89 - 587.33	13.21	618.89 - 619.33	13.93
523.34 - 523.77	11.78	555.34 - 555.77	12.50	587.34 - 587.77	13.22	619.34 - 619.77	13.94
523.78 - 524.22	11.79	555.78 - 556.22	12.51	587.78 - 588.22	13.23	619.78 - 620.22	13.95
524.23 - 524.66	11.80	556.23 - 556.66	12.52	588.23 - 588.66	13.24	620.23 - 620.66	13.96
524.67 - 525.11	11.81	556.67 - 557.11	12.53	588.67 - 589.11	13.25	620.67 - 621.11	13.97
525.12 - 525.55	11.82	557.12 - 557.55	12.54	589.12 - 589.55	13.26	621.12 - 621.55	13.98
525.56 - 525.99	11.83	557.56 - 557.99	12.55	589.56 - 589.99	13.27	621.56 - 621.99	13.99
526.00 - 526.44	11.84	558.00 - 558.44	12.56	590.00 - 590.44	13.28	622.00 - 622.44	14.00
526.45 - 526.88	11.85	558.45 - 558.88	12.57	590.45 - 590.88	13.29	622.45 - 622.88	14.01
526.89 - 527.33	11.86	558.89 - 559.33	12.58	590.89 - 591.33	13.30	622.89 - 623.33	14.02
527.34 - 527.77	11.87	559.34 - 559.77	12.59	591.34 - 591.77	13.31	623.34 - 623.77	14.03
527.78 - 528.22	11.88	559.78 - 560.22	12.60	591.78 - 592.22	13.32	623.78 - 624.22	14.04
528.23 - 528.66	11.89	560.23 - 560.66	12.61	592.23 - 592.66	13.33	624.23 - 624.66	14.05
528.67 - 529.11	11.90	560.67 - 561.11	12.62	592.67 - 593.11	13.34	624.67 - 625.11	14.06
529.12 - 529.55	11.91	561.12 - 561.55	12.63	593.12 - 593.55	13.35	625.12 - 625.55	14.07
529.56 - 529.99	11.92	561.56 - 561.99	12.64	593.56 - 593.99	13.36	625.56 - 625.99	14.08
530.00 - 530.44	11.93	562.00 - 562.44	12.65	594.00 - 594.44	13.37	626.00 - 626.44	14.09
530.45 - 530.88	11.94	562.45 - 562.88	12.66	594.45 - 594.88	13.38	626.45 - 626.88	14.10
530.89 - 531.33	11.95	562.89 - 563.33	12.67	594.89 - 595.33	13.39	626.89 - 627.33	14.11
531.34 - 531.77	11.96	563.34 - 563.77	12.68	595.34 - 595.77	13.40	627.34 - 627.77	14.12
531.78 - 532.22	11.97	563.78 - 564.22	12.69	595.78 - 596.22	13.41	627.78 - 628.22	14.13
532.23 - 532.66	11.98	564.23 - 564.66	12.70	596.23 - 596.66	13.42	628.23 - 628.66	14.14
532.67 - 533.11	11.99	564.67 - 565.11	12.71	596.67 - 597.11	13.43	628.67 - 629.11	14.15
533.12 - 533.55	12.00	565.12 - 565.55	12.72	597.12 - 597.55	13.44	629.12 - 629.55	14.16
533.56 - 533.99	12.01	565.56 - 565.99	12.73	597.56 - 597.99	13.45	629.56 - 629.99	14.17
534.00 - 534.44	12.02	566.00 - 566.44	12.74	598.00 - 598.44	13.46	630.00 - 630.44	14.18
534.45 - 534.88	12.03	566.45 - 566.88	12.75	598.45 - 598.88	13.47	630.45 - 630.88	14.19
534.89 - 535.33	12.04	566.89 - 567.33	12.76	598.89 - 599.33	13.48	630.89 - 631.33	14.20
535.34 - 535.77	12.05	567.34 - 567.77	12.77	599.34 - 599.77	13.49	631.34 - 631.77	14.21
535.78 - 536.22	12.06	567.78 - 568.22	12.78	599.78 - 600.22	13.50	631.78 - 632.22	14.22
536.23 - 536.66	12.07	568.23 - 568.66	12.79	600.23 - 600.66	13.51	632.23 - 632.66	14.23
536.67 - 537.11	12.08	568.67 - 569.11	12.80	600.67 - 601.11	13.52	632.67 - 633.11	14.24
537.12 - 537.55	12.09	569.12 - 569.55	12.81	601.12 - 601.55	13.53	633.12 - 633.55	14.25
537.56 - 537.99	12.10	569.56 - 569.99	12.82	601.56 - 601.99	13.54	633.56 - 633.99	14.26
538.00 - 538.44	12.11	570.00 - 570.44	12.83	602.00 - 602.44	13.55	634.00 - 634.44	14.27
538.45 - 538.88	12.12	570.45 - 570.88	12.84	602.45 - 602.88	13.56	634.45 - 634.88	14.28
538.89 - 539.33	12.13	570.89 - 571.33	12.85	602.89 - 603.33	13.57	634.89 - 635.33	14.29
539.34 - 539.77	12.14	571.34 - 571.77	12.86	603.34 - 603.77	13.58	635.34 - 635.77	14.30
539.78 - 540.22	12.15	571.78 - 572.22	12.87	603.78 - 604.22	13.59	635.78 - 636.22	14.31
540.23 - 540.66	12.16	572.23 - 572.66	12.88	604.23 - 604.66	13.60	636.23 - 636.66	14.32
540.67 - 541.11	12.17	572.67 - 573.11	12.89	604.67 - 605.11	13.61	636.67 - 637.11	14.33
541.12 - 541.55	12.18	573.12 - 573.55	12.90	605.12 - 605.55	13.62	637.12 - 637.55	14.34
541.56 - 541.99	12.19	573.56 - 573.99	12.91	605.56 - 605.99	13.63	637.56 - 637.99	14.35
542.00 - 542.44	12.20	574.00 - 574.44	12.92	606.00 - 606.44	13.64	638.00 - 638.44	14.36
542.45 - 542.88	12.21	574.45 - 574.88	12.93	606.45 - 606.88	13.65	638.45 - 638.88	14.37
542.89 - 543.33	12.22	574.89 - 575.33	12.94	606.89 - 607.33	13.66	638.89 - 639.33	14.38
543.34 - 543.77	12.23	575.34 - 575.77	12.95	607.34 - 607.77	13.67	639.34 - 639.77	14.39
543.78 - 544.22	12.24	575.78 - 576.22	12.96	607.78 - 608.22	13.68	639.78 - 640.22	14.40

Maximum Premium Deduction for a Pay Period of the stated frequency.
Déduction maximale de prime pour une période de paie d'une durée donnée.

Weekly - Hebdomadaire	15.30	
Bi-Weekly - Deux semaines	30.60	
Semi-Monthly - Bi-mensuel	33.15	
Monthly - Mensuellement	66.30	
10 pp per year - 10 pp par année	79.56	
13 pp per year - 13 pp par année	61.20	
22 pp per year - 22 pp par année	36.16	

at *1.4 times the employee's premium*. It is important to remember that the employer's share is thus always slightly *more* than the employee's contribution. Consider, for example, the case of John Blair's calculated premium of $12.49 on weekly gross earnings of $555. On the basis of this employee's amount, the employer would have to contribute $17.49 (1.4 × $12.49). As you will learn in the next Topic, the employer's share becomes a payroll expense and must be accounted for accordingly.

EMPLOYER'S ACCOUNTING RESPONSIBILITIES

By federal law, the employer is responsible for maintaining books and records of account sufficient to determine correct premiums for both employee and employer. This would mean that payroll accounting must keep records of each employee's gross earnings and his or her insurable earnings. In addition, the law requires a record of the total premiums paid for the year. The accounting treatment of maintaining these records will not be covered here; it is examined in detail in the next two Topics.

EMPLOYEES' PREMIUMS ARE TAX-DEDUCTIBLE

Under the Income Tax Act, all premiums paid by an employee to UI are deductible from the employee's amount of income tax. Therefore, if John Blair paid the maximum UI in 1991, this would mean that he could use $795.60 as one of his non-refundable tax credits for the 1991 tax year.

Federal and Provincial Income Tax Deductions

The federal government and the provincial governments all levy taxes on the income of wage earners within their territories. By law, employers are required to withhold a portion of their employees' earnings for income taxes and periodically to make payments to the proper governments.

The amount of income tax withheld at source depends upon the amount of an employee's earnings, upon the net claim amount claimed for calculating the taxpayer's personal non-refundable tax credits, as shown on back of the TD1 form (see Figure 10-12), and upon the province in which he or she resides.

EMPLOYEE'S PERSONAL TAX CREDIT RETURN (FORM TD1)

In the figure, notice that employee's net claim amount is converted to a *Net Claim Code*. If the employee has not completed the TD1 form, Revenue Canada—Taxation requires that he or she be treated as having Net Claim Code 1 (the code for deducting the highest possible amount of income taxes from the employee's pay). Also observe that no deductions are made if the employee certifies that the total remuneration received, and also receivable, during the calendar year will not exceed the total of personal tax credits claimed, in which case Net Claim Code E will be used. This means that, for example, in the 1991 taxation year if an employee is only eligible for the basic personal amount and certifies that he or she will earn less than $6 280, he or she will not pay any income tax for that calendar year.

PART 2: COMMON ACCOUNTING APPLICATIONS

FIGURE 10-12

page 2

11. Total (from line 10 on page 1) ▶ $11919. **11.**

12. Are you claiming any transfers of unused pension income, age, disability, tuition fees and education amounts from your **spouse and/or dependants?** (see note 10 below).

- If your **spouse receives eligible pension income**, you may claim any unused balance to a maximum of $1,000 (see note 6 below).
- If your **spouse will be 65 or older** in 1991, you may claim any unused balance to a maximum of $3,387.
- If your **spouse and/or dependants are disabled**, you may claim any unused balance to a maximum of $3,387 for each (see note 7 below).
- If you are supporting a **spouse and/or dependants who are attending either a university, college or a certified educational institution**, you may be entitled to claim the unused balance to a maximum of $3,529 for each (see item 9 on page 1). Total ▶ NIL **12.**

13. Total claim amount – Add lines 11 and 12. ▶ 11 919. **13.**

14. Will you or your spouse receive family allowance (baby bonus) payments in 1991? If so, and your 1991 net income will be **higher** than your spouse's, enter the amount of family allowance payments you will receive in 1991. If you are not married, see note 3 below. ▶ 407.16 **14.**

Voluntary: If your 1991 taxable income will be **more than $28,784**, and you have **reported family allowance** income, not enough tax will be withheld by your employer. If you wish to have this additional tax withheld, use the following table to calculate the amount and enter the result on line 18. If you already have additional tax withheld, only show the total of both amounts on line 18.

Pay period		Number of children		Enter this amount on line 18
Weekly	$1 X	_____	=	$ _____
Bi-weekly or semi-monthly	$2 X	_____	=	$ _____
Monthly	$5 X	_____	=	$ _____

15. NET CLAIM AMOUNT – Line 13 minus line 14. ▶ 11 511.84 **15.**

16. Is your estimated total income for 1991 (excluding family allowance payments) less than your net claim amount on line 15? If so, enter E in the box on line 17 and tax will **not** be deducted from your pay. Otherwise, go to line 17.

17. NET CLAIM CODE – Match your net claim amount from line 15 with the table below to determine your net claim code, and enter this code in the box. If you already have a code in the box, go to line 18. ▶ 5 **17.**

18. Do you want to increase the amount of tax to be deducted from your salary or from other amounts paid to you such as pensions, commissions etc.? (see note 8 below). If so, state the amount of additional tax you wish to have deducted from each payment. ▶ _____ **18.**

19. Will you be living in the Yukon, Northwest Territories or another prescribed area for more than six months in a row beginning or ending in 1991? If so, claim $225 for each 30-day period that you live in a prescribed area, **or** if you maintain a "self-contained domestic establishment" in a prescribed area and you are the only person within that establishment claiming this deduction, claim $450 for each 30-day period. You **cannot claim** more than 20 per cent of your net income for 1991 (see note 9 below). ▶ _____ **19.**

I HEREBY CERTIFY that the information given in this return is correct and complete.

Signature *John Blair*   Date *January 2, 1991*

Complete a new return within seven days of any change in your claim. It is an offence to make a false return.

NOTES TO EMPLOYEES AND PAYEES

1. If you are in doubt about your **non-resident** status, please contact the Source Deductions section of your local district taxation office. If you are a **non-resident and 90 per cent or more** of your 1991 total world income will be included in determining your taxable income earned in Canada, you are entitled to claim certain personal amounts. Again for more information contact your district taxation office.
2. A **dependant** is an individual who is dependent on you for support and is either under 19, OR 19 or older and physically or mentally infirm. This includes a child, grandchild, parent, grandparent, brother, sister, aunt, uncle, niece or nephew (including in-laws). Except in the case of a child or grandchild, this individual must also be living in Canada.
3. Except for married individuals, the person who receives the **family allowance** must report the benefits and claim the amount for dependent children. Whoever claims the dependant for an equivalent-to-married amount must report the family allowance for that dependant regardless of who receives the family allowance benefits.
4. Your spouse's or dependant's **net income**, for tax withholding purposes, is the total annual income from all sources including salary, pensions, Old Age Security, UI benefits, workers' compensation and social assistance (welfare) payments minus annual deductions for registered pension plan and registered retirement savings plan contributions.
5. If you **marry** during the year, your spouse's net income will include the income before and during marriage.
6. **Eligible pension income** includes pension payments received from a pension plan or fund as a life annuity and foreign pension payments. It does not include payments from Canada or Quebec Pension plans, Old Age Security, guaranteed income supplement and lump-sum withdrawals from a pension fund.
7. To claim a **disability**, you must be severely impaired (mentally or physically) in 1991 and have a Disability Credit Certificate. Such an impairment must markedly restrict you in your daily living activites. The impairment must have lasted or be expected to last for a continuous period of at least 12 months.
8. You may find it convenient to deduct additional tax on line 18 for other income you receive that has little or no tax deducted from it. For example, UI benefits, Old Age Security, investment or rental income.
9. "**Self-contained domestic establishment**" means the dwelling house, apartment or similar place where you sleep and eat. It does not include a bunkhouse, dormitory, hotel room or rooms in a boarding house. For more information, including the list of prescribed areas, see the *Northern Residents Deductions Tax Guide*, available at any district taxation office.
10. Your spouse and/or dependants must first use their pension income, age, disability, tuition fees and education amounts as applicable to reduce their federal tax to zero before they can **transfer** any **unused balance** of these amounts to you.

Cette formule est disponible en français.

1991 NET CLAIM CODES

Net claim amount over – not over	claim code
NO claim amount	0
$0 – $6,280	1
6,280 – 7,818	2
7,818 – 9,357	3
9,357 – 10,897	4
10,897 – 12,435	(5)
12,435 – 13,973	6
13,973 – 15,512	7
15,512 – 17,050	8
17,050 – 18,589	9
18,589 – 20,129	10
20,129 and over	X
NO tax withholding required	E

> Consumer Price Index (CPI): one index used by the federal government to measure the movement from month to month in retail prices of goods and services bought by a representative cross-section of Canadians.

Under the present income tax law, it is important to note that the amounts claimed for non-refundable tax credits will change yearly to reflect the yearly change in the **Consumer Price Index (CPI)**. If the Index goes up during the year, this means that inflation has occurred and that your former dollar will not buy as much as before the rise in prices. To offset some of this loss in the purchasing power of the dollar, in each new calendar year the federal government increases non-refundable credits such as the basic personal amount. For payroll accounting, it is important that the latest non-refundable tax credits be acquired for each employee at the beginning of every calendar year. As you will learn, the increase in non-refundable tax credits to which an employee is entitled due to increases in the CPI is taken into account in the calculation of the tax deduction in the body of the tax tables. For the most part, the information on increased non-refundable tax credits is obtained by having each employee complete form TD1.

TAX DEDUCTION TABLES The income tax to be withheld from the earnings of an employee is determined by using the tax deduction tables provided by the Department of National Revenue—Taxation. In the province of Quebec a provincial tax deduction table must be used in addition to the special table supplied by the federal government. In all other provinces, a combined table is used, since the federal government acts as the collecting agent on behalf of those provinces. However, it is important to observe that special tables are also supplied by the federal government for the various provinces. These tables take into account the fact that not all provinces set the same tax rates. At the time of writing, a separate booklet of tables is used for each of the ten provinces, and an additional one covers the Northwest Territories, the Yukon Territory, and areas outside of Canada.

To simplify the employer's calculations of tax deductions at source, the tables are provided for weekly, biweekly, semimonthly, and monthly payroll periods. In addition, Revenue Canada—Taxation offers separate publications: *Supplementary Source Deductions Tables* for employers who require pay periods such as daily, 10 monthly, 13 pay periods, or 22 pay periods; and *Machine Computation of Income Tax Deductions, Canada Pension Plan Contributions, and Unemployment Insurance Premiums (MC Tables)* for employers who use computer systems to process payrolls.

Figure 10-13 has been reproduced from the booklet *Ontario Source Deduction Tables*, January 1991, effective at the time of writing for employees who report for work in the province of Ontario. The page reproduced gives the weekly tax deductions to be made when there are 52 pay periods a year.

It is important to remember that these tables are revised every year. The latest, correct forms and tables can be obtained from the local district

PART 2: COMMON ACCOUNTING APPLICATIONS

FIGURE 10-13

ONTARIO
TABLE 1
WEEKLY TAX DEDUCTIONS
Basis — 52 Pay Periods per Year

ONTARIO
RETENUES D'IMPÔT PAR SEMAINE
Base — 52 périodes de paie par année

WEEKLY PAY Use appropriate bracket / PAIE PAR SEMAINE Utilisez le palier approprié		0	1	2	3	4	5	6	7	8	9	10
From- De	Less than Mains que				DEDUCT FROM EACH PAY – RETENEZ SUR CHAQUE PAIE							
453.-	461.	117.50	85.10	81.10	73.15	65.20	57.25	49.30	41.35	33.40	25.50	17.50
461.-	469.	119.55	87.15	83.15	75.20	67.25	59.30	51.35	43.40	35.45	27.55	19.60
469.-	477.	121.60	89.20	85.20	77.25	69.30	61.35	53.40	45.45	37.55	29.60	21.65
477.-	485.	123.65	91.25	87.25	79.30	71.35	63.40	55.45	47.50	39.60	31.65	23.70
485.-	493.	125.75	93.30	89.30	81.35	73.40	65.45	57.50	49.55	41.65	33.70	25.75
493.-	501.	127.80	95.35	91.35	83.40	75.45	67.50	59.55	51.65	43.70	35.75	27.80
501.-	509.	129.85	97.40	93.40	85.45	77.50	69.55	61.60	53.70	45.75	37.80	29.85
509.-	517.	131.90	99.45	95.45	87.50	79.55	71.60	63.65	55.75	47.80	39.85	31.90
517.-	525.	133.95	101.50	97.50	89.55	81.60	73.65	65.75	57.80	49.85	41.90	33.95
525.-	533.	136.00	103.55	99.55	91.60	83.65	75.70	67.80	59.85	51.90	43.95	36.00
533.-	541.	138.05	105.60	101.60	93.65	85.70	77.75	69.85	61.90	53.95	46.00	38.05
541.-	549.	140.10	107.65	103.65	95.70	87.75	79.80	71.90	63.95	56.00	48.05	40.10
549.-	557.	142.15	109.70	105.70	97.80	89.80	81.85	73.95	66.00	58.05	50.10	42.15
557.-	565.	145.25	112.80	108.80	100.85	92.90	84.95	77.05	69.10	61.15	53.20	45.25
565.-	573.	148.40	116.00	112.00	104.05	96.10	88.15	80.20	72.25	64.30	56.40	48.40
573.-	581.	151.60	119.15	115.20	107.25	99.30	91.35	83.40	75.45	67.50	59.55	51.60
581.-	589.	154.80	122.35	118.40	110.45	102.50	94.55	86.60	78.65	70.70	62.75	54.80
589.-	597.	158.05	125.60	121.60	113.65	105.70	97.75	89.80	81.90	73.95	66.00	58.05
597.-	605.	161.25	128.85	124.85	116.90	108.95	101.00	93.05	85.10	77.15	69.20	61.25
605.-	613.	164.50	132.05	128.10	120.15	112.20	104.25	96.30	88.35	80.40	72.45	64.50
613.-	621.	167.75	135.30	131.35	123.40	115.45	107.50	99.55	91.60	83.65	75.70	67.75
621.-	629.	171.00	138.55	134.55	126.60	118.65	110.70	102.80	94.85	86.90	78.95	71.00
629.-	637.	174.20	141.80	137.80	129.85	121.90	113.95	106.00	98.05	90.10	82.15	74.20
637.-	645.	177.45	145.00	141.05	133.10	125.15	117.20	109.25	101.30	93.35	85.40	77.45
645.-	653.	180.70	148.25	144.30	136.35	128.40	120.45	112.50	104.55	96.60	88.65	80.70
653.-	661.	183.95	151.50	147.50	139.55	131.60	123.65	115.75	107.80	99.85	91.90	83.95
661.-	669.	187.15	154.75	150.75	142.80	134.85	126.90	118.95	111.00	103.05	95.10	87.15
669.-	677.	190.40	157.95	154.00	146.05	138.10	130.15	122.20	114.25	106.30	98.35	90.40
677.-	685.	193.65	161.20	157.25	149.30	141.35	133.40	125.45	117.50	109.55	101.60	93.65
685.-	693.	196.95	164.50	160.55	152.60	144.65	136.70	128.75	120.80	112.85	104.90	96.95
693.-	701.	200.20	167.80	163.80	155.85	147.90	139.95	132.00	124.05	116.15	108.20	100.25
701.-	709.	203.50	171.05	167.10	159.15	151.20	143.25	135.30	127.35	119.40	111.45	103.50
709.-	717.	206.80	174.35	170.40	162.45	154.50	146.55	138.60	130.65	122.70	114.75	106.80
717.-	725.	210.10	177.65	173.65	165.75	157.75	149.80	141.90	133.95	126.00	118.05	110.10
725.-	733.	213.35	180.95	176.95	169.00	161.05	153.10	145.15	137.20	129.25	121.35	113.35
733.-	741.	216.65	184.20	180.25	172.30	164.35	156.40	148.45	140.50	132.55	124.60	116.65
741.-	749.	219.95	187.50	183.55	175.60	167.65	159.70	151.75	143.80	135.85	127.90	119.95
749.-	757.	223.25	190.80	186.80	178.85	170.90	162.95	155.05	147.10	139.15	131.20	123.25
757.-	765.	226.50	194.10	190.10	182.15	174.20	166.25	158.30	150.35	142.40	134.45	126.50
765.-	773.	229.80	197.35	193.40	185.45	177.50	169.55	161.60	153.65	145.70	137.75	129.80
773.-	781.	233.10	200.65	196.70	188.75	180.80	172.85	164.90	156.95	149.00	141.05	133.10
781.-	789.	236.35	203.95	199.95	192.00	184.05	176.10	168.15	160.20	152.30	144.35	136.40
789.-	797.	239.65	207.20	203.25	195.30	187.35	179.40	171.45	163.50	155.55	147.60	139.65
797.-	805.	242.95	210.50	206.55	198.60	190.65	182.70	174.75	166.80	158.85	150.90	142.95
805.-	813.	246.25	213.80	209.80	201.90	193.90	185.95	178.05	170.10	162.15	154.20	146.25
813.-	821.	249.50	217.10	213.10	205.15	197.20	189.25	181.30	173.35	165.40	157.50	149.50
821.-	829.	252.80	220.35	216.40	208.45	200.50	192.55	184.60	176.65	168.70	160.75	152.80
829.-	837.	256.10	223.65	219.70	211.75	203.80	195.85	187.90	179.95	172.00	164.05	156.10
837.-	845.	259.40	226.95	222.95	215.00	207.05	199.10	191.20	183.25	175.30	167.35	159.40
845.-	853.	262.65	230.25	226.25	218.30	210.35	202.40	194.45	186.50	178.55	170.60	162.65
853.-	861.	265.95	233.50	229.55	221.60	213.65	205.70	197.75	189.80	181.85	173.90	165.95
861.-	869.	269.25	236.80	232.85	224.90	216.95	209.00	201.05	193.10	185.15	177.20	169.25
869.-	877.	272.55	240.10	236.10	228.15	220.20	212.25	204.30	196.35	188.45	180.50	172.55
877.-	885.	275.80	243.35	239.40	231.45	223.50	215.55	207.60	199.65	191.70	183.75	175.80
885.-	893.	279.10	246.65	242.70	234.75	226.80	218.85	210.90	202.95	195.00	187.05	179.10

office of the Department of National Revenue—Taxation. It is also recommended that a separate publication, *Employer's Guide to Source Deductions*, be obtained for the latest calendar year.

HOW TO USE THE TAX DEDUCTION TABLE

Once the gross remuneration, including any taxable benefits, for the employee's pay period has been determined, the employer must subtract the following amounts before determining the tax to withhold at source:

- The employee's contributions to a registered pension fund or plan
- Union dues (not initiation fees)
- A deduction for living in a prescribed area as calculated on the TD1 form
- Deductions authorized by the district taxation office (for example, alimony payments)

Under the present Income Tax Act, employee contributions to a registered pension fund or plan, deductions for union dues, deductions for living in a prescribed area (from the TD1 form), and deductions authorized by the district tax office are tax-deductible. This means that an employee can claim contributions to these areas on his or her income tax return. In fact, Revenue Canada—Taxation instructs employers specifically to make this prior calculation in the booklet *Employer's Guide to Source Deductions* in order to arrive at an amount called **remuneration subject to tax withholding at source**. Failure to do so would simply mean that approximately ten million Canadians would have paid too much income tax and costly refunds would have to be processed to individual taxpayers each year.

Special Note: Before 1989, the payroll clerk had to deduct also CPP contributions and UI premiums from the employee's gross earnings to arrive at the employee's taxable earnings. However, in 1989, 1990, and to the time of writing, the employee deductions for CPP and UI have been reflected in the tax deduction tables. Therefore, while the clerk is still required to deduct CPP contributions and UI premiums, these amounts need no longer be subtracted from the gross remuneration when determining the amount of income tax to deduct.

To illustrate how the tax tables should be used, the case of John Blair and his weekly pay of $555 is analyzed below.

- First, deduct any amounts the employee contributed to a registered pension plan and union dues from the employee's gross earnings. In this case, assume that $27.75 is the amount that the employee contributes to his registered company pension plan and that union dues and other tax-deductible items are not involved at this time. The result—that is, the amount subject to income tax—is $527.25. *Note*: Again, amounts contributed as employee's CPP and UI, although tax-deductible, have already been reflected in the tax deduction tables.

Remuneration subject to tax withholding at source: the employee's taxable earnings—that is, earnings subject to income tax.

Therefore, do not deduct these amounts from gross earnings to arrive at the employee's earnings subject to tax.
- Second, refer to the pages of the table appropriate to the pay period. In this case, you would have to refer to "Weekly Tax Deductions," since the employee's earnings are based on a weekly period.
- Next, on those pages look down the appropriate "Pay" column for the bracket listing the employee's remuneration subject to tax withholding (taxable earnings). For John Blair, you would locate the bracket shown as 525–533. This bracket appears on the page reproduced as Figure 10-13.
- Next, follow the line across to the appropriate "Net Claim Code" column which you obtained from the employee's TD1 form. In John Blair's case, assume that he has asserted Net Claim Code 5; the amount shown under "5" is $75.70. This then is the amount of income tax to be withheld.

Provincial Health Insurance Plan

In general, some of the provinces have legislated compulsory payroll deductions to cover the payment of the premium for their respective provincial health insurance plans. When such legislation exists, the employer is required to deduct an amount from the gross earnings of the employee and remit the total amount to the provincial treasurer at intervals stated by provincial regulations.

However, at the time of writing, the trend in the majority of provinces is to impose an employer's health tax on the employer. For example, Ontario introduced in January 1990 its new Employer Health Tax Act, which replaces the former OHIP premiums with such a tax. Under the EHT, no deduction is required from the gross earnings of employees. Instead, the employer must pay a payroll tax rate based on the total calendar-year gross payroll of the employer. The accounting of the employer's health tax as a payroll tax will be treated in Topic 2.

Garnishments and Government Demands

Deductions for the Canada Pension Plan, unemployment insurance, income taxes, and provincial health insurance plans where applicable are required by law. In addition to these compulsory deductions, the employer must be aware of two other deductions that may be ordered by law.

GARNISHMENTS   In all Canadian provinces, to recover money owed to him or her a creditor may obtain a court order from the small claims court called a **garnishment**. Briefly, this court order requires an employer to retain a portion of the debtor's wages on payday and to surrender the withheld sum to the court. This action is called *garnisheeing* an employee's wages. In general, most provinces have regulations that limit the percentage of the wages that may be garnisheed (usually a maxi-

Garnishment: a court order requiring an employer to deduct a portion of the debtor-employee wages on payday.

mum of 30%). On the other hand, the creditor can continue to request the court to issue a fresh "Direction of Garnishee" until the debt is satisfied. Only one garnishment, however, may be made against any one pay of an employee.

GOVERNMENT DEMANDS ON EMPLOYEES' EARNINGS An order in writing from the Department of National Revenue or the Quebec Income Tax Service requiring the payment of a lump sum or designated payments in settlement of income tax arrears is known as a *tax demand* or *government demand*. In addition, demands may be made for withheld payments to recover an overpayment of benefits under the Unemployment Insurance Act and the Canada Pension Plan.

<small>Tax demand/government demand: a written order requiring the payment of a lump sum or designated payments in settlement of income tax arrears or overpayments of unemployment insurance and Canada Pension Plan benefits.</small>

Other Deductions

Other common deductions in computing the net pay of employees are amounts for union initiation fees and annual union dues, amounts contributed to a company registered pension plan, and a number of other voluntary deductions.

UNION INITIATION FEES AND UNION DUES Generally, the payment of an initiation fee and of union dues is a condition of employment for all employees who are members of a union. As part of the basic agreement, the employer is obliged to withhold from an employee's gross earnings an amount for union dues.

Because deductions for union dues are not covered by law, the employer is required to have a written authorization from the employee before making any such deduction. However, as part of the basic agreement between the union and employer, all employees covered by the agreement are generally required, as a condition of employment, to sign an authorized payment for deduction of their annual union dues. As stated earlier, only annual union dues are tax-deductible on the employee's income tax return.

COMPANY PENSION PLAN Although the company pension plan is shown in the earlier priority chart under the "voluntary" class of deductions, it is treated separately to help you understand this important deduction. The term *voluntary deduction* simply refers to the idea that the employee agrees, usually in writing, to have a certain amount deducted from his or her gross earnings; in this case, the employee agrees to contribute to a company pension plan.

In general, the federal government permits employers to offer a pension plan so that employees may build up an overall pension plan for themselves. It is important to remember these points about any company pension plan:

- The plan is not a substitute for the required contributions to the Canada Pension Plan. Any company pension plan is maintained *in addition to* the Canada Pension Plan.

- Most company pension plans are *registered*, because the Income Tax Act provides for such registration. This means that the employer has first submitted the plan for approval by the Department of National Revenue—Taxation. Once approval has been given, the plan is registered and the employer must abide by the provisions of the Department. In general, most company pension plans are registered, because they offer the best security for the employees' savings invested in such plans.
- As in the Canada Pension Plan, contributions must be made by both employee and employer. At the time of writing, the employer's share is an amount equal to the employee's contribution. Of course, the employer's share will be identified as an additional payroll expense and must be accounted for as such.
- Also as in the Canada Pension Plan, contributions by the employee are deductible from the employee's income tax.

In following John Blair's calculation for net pay, we have assumed that this employee has agreed to a deduction of $27.75 as his contribution to a registered company pension plan.

OTHER VOLUNTARY DEDUCTIONS

In addition to the compulsory deductions required by law, and those voluntary ones covered in a basic agreement, the employee may request his or her employer to make special deductions for such items as safety shoes, group life insurance, Canada Savings Bonds, donations to community services, and savings in a credit union. These optional deductions are computed individually for each employee and are handled in the same manner as compulsory deductions.

Computation of Net Pay

Once the various compulsory and voluntary deductions have been calculated, their total can be subtracted from the employee's gross earnings to identify the employee's net pay—his or her "take-home pay."

The net pay for John Blair for the weekly pay period ending June 30 may be computed as shown in Figure 10-14.

FIGURE 10-14

Gross Earnings	−	Total Deductions	=	Net Pay
Regular: 38 3/4 hours × $12 . $465.00		CPP $11.44		
Overtime: 5 hours × $18 ... 90.00		UI 12.49		
		Income tax 75.70		
		Company pension plan . 27.75		
		Group insurance 6.00		
Gross earnings $555.00	−	Total deductions $133.38	=	$421.62

TOPIC I Problems

Timekeeping and computing gross earnings, deductions, and net pay for two hourly-rated employees.

10.1 Clock cards for two employees are given in Figures 10-15 and 10-16.

FIGURE 10-15

Name: Diane Logan Employee No. 47
Social Insurance No. 378-143-478
Week Ending DECEMBER 22, 19—

CLOCK CARD

Days	Regular In	Out	In	Out	Extra In	Out	Hours
Thur.	7:58	12:01	1:00	5:02			
Fri.	7:59	12:00	12:59	5:01			
Sat.	7:59	12:01					
Sun.							
Mon.	7:59	12:00	1:00	5:02			
Tue.	8:04	12:01	12:59	4:59			
Wed.	7:58	12:00	12:59	5:03			

	Hours	Rate	Earnings
Regular			
Overtime			
Total		Gross	
Hours		Earnings	

FIGURE 10-16

Name: Dennis Lunau Employee No. 73
Social Insurance No. 532-890-345
Week Ending DECEMBER 22, 19—

CLOCK CARD

Days	Regular In	Out	In	Out	Extra In	Out	Hours
Thur.	7:55	11:56	1:00	5:01	6:00	8:02	
Fri.	7:51	12:00	12:59	5:01			
Sat.							
Sun.							
Mon.	7:59	12:02	12:59	5:02			
Tue.	7:58	11:59	1:01	4:59			
Wed.	7:59	12:02	12:59	5:14	5:59	8:03	

	Hours	Rate	Earnings
Regular			
Overtime			
Total		Gross	
Hours		Earnings	

Required

a Determine the total number of hours worked each day. Compute the daily time in hours and quarter hours. Regular hours are 8:00 a.m. to 12:00 noon and 1:00 p.m. to 5:00 p.m. daily, 40 hours per week. For lateness, the employee is docked 15 minutes for each 15 minutes or portion thereof of lateness in the morning or afternoon, or of clocking out early.

b Determine the total number of hours worked during the week.

c Compute the regular, overtime, and total gross pay. Logan's regular rate is $13.50 an hour, and Lunau's is $13 an hour. Consider all hours in excess of eight per day and on Saturdays and Sundays as overtime. Overtime is calculated only in quarter-hours and is paid at one-and-one-half times the regular rate.

d Refer to the partial tables of Canada Pension Plan contributions and unemployment insurance premiums, Figures 10-8 and 10-11 respectively; then report what Logan and Lunau must contribute to CPP and UI. *Note*: If the partial tables do not supply the data, use the calculation method described in the chapter.

e Assume that both employees contribute to their registered company pension plan on the basis of 5% of their weekly gross earnings. Assume also that Logan's Net Claim Code is 5 and Lunau's is 1. Refer to the tax deduction table in Figure 10-13; then report the amount of income tax to be withheld from each of the two employees.

f Assume that Logan and Lunau both contribute to a group life insurance plan through a weekly deduction of $6. Construct separate tables for the two employees to report calculations leading to their respective net pays.

Timekeeping and computing gross earnings, deductions, and net pay for three hourly-rated employees.

10.2

a Prepare clock cards for the following employees of the Canada Lumber Company for the week ending June 20. After completing each clock card, compute the regular, overtime, and total gross pay. Regular hours are from 8:00 a.m. to 12:00 noon, and from 1:00 p.m. to 5:00 p.m. daily, based on a 40-hour week. Time-and-a-half is paid for overtime for periods of over 15 minutes after 5:00 p.m., and on Saturdays; double time is paid for work performed on Sundays. For lateness, the employee is docked 15 minutes for each 15 minutes or portion thereof of lateness in the morning or afternoon, or of clocking out early.

- Employee No. 14; Paul Sage, SIN 457-878-433; rate of $13.75 per hour. Net Claim Code of 1.
    Monday: 7:58–12:01; 1:01–5:00; 5:00–6:00
    Tuesday: 7:59–11:55; 1:15–5:00
    Wednesday: 8:00–12:00; 1:00–5:00; 6:00–8:00
    Thursday: 8:00–12:01; 12:55–5:05
    Friday: 8:02–12:02; 12:57–5:01

- Employee No. 15; Joe Fabiani, SIN 768-328-103; rate of $14.50 per hour. Net Claim Code of 1.
    Monday: 8:00–12:01; 1:00–5:00
    Tuesday: 7:59–12:00; 1:01–5:00
    Wednesday: 8:02–12:01; 1:01–5:03
    Thursday: 7:59–12:00; 1:00–5:02
    Saturday: 7:58–12:01; 1:00–5:04
    Sunday: 1:00–5:05

- Employee No. 16; Penny Coates, SIN 583-123-382; rate of $15 per hour. Net Claim Code of 2.
    Monday: 8:00–12:00; 1:01–5:00
    Tuesday: 7:55–12:00; 1:00–4:55
    Wednesday: 7:56–12:00; 1:00–5:05; 5:30–7:00
    Thursday: 7:57–12:00; 1:00–5:01
    Friday: 12:59–5:05
    Saturday: 7:59–12:02

b Refer to Figures 10-8 and 10-11, and report what each employee is required to contribute to CPP and UI. Use the calculation method described in the chapter if the partial table does not supply the data.

c Refer to the table "Weekly Tax Deductions" (Figure 10-13), and report for each employee the taxable earnings and the amount of tax to be withheld.

d Assume that each employee has agreed to have deducted weekly the following additional amounts: $6 for group insurance; $5 to the local credit union. Construct separate tables for the employees to report the calculations leading to their respective net pays.

CHAPTER 10: Payroll Application **437**

Timekeeping and computing gross earnings, deductions, and net pay for one employee on a piece-rate basis.

10.3 Clinton Speaker Company pays different piece rates in its stereo speaker assembly plant. The daily rates are as follows:

Speakers Assembled per Day	Rate per Speaker
Up to 20	$2.00
21 to 25	2.50
26 to 30	3.00
31 to 35	3.50
36 and over	4.00

During the week ended February 7, Judy McEwen assembled the following pieces: Monday, 25; Tuesday, 30; Wednesday, 32; Thursday, 35; and Friday, 40.

a Calculate the gross wages earned by the employee.
b Use the table method (illustrated in this chapter) or the calculation method to record the amount of CPP and UI for this employee.
c Use the income tax table in this chapter to identify the amount of income tax that will be withheld from this employee. Assume a Net Claim Code of 1.
d Assume the following additional deductions: group insurance, $6; and credit union, $5. Construct a table to report this employee's gross earnings, deductions, and net pay.

Timekeeping and computing gross earnings, deductions, and net pay for six employees on a fixed salary plus commission basis. FIGURE 10-17

10.4 Halifax Auto Sales Limited pays its sales representative a base salary of $1 200 per month plus a 5% commission on their sales. The following salespersons had the sales as reported below.

Pierre Belliveau	$30 000
Frank Dillon	31 400
William Ryan	30 800
Linda Crawford	28 800
Helen Greenwood	30 600
Jane Westwood	42 750

a Calculate the monthly gross earnings for each salesperson.
b Calculate each employee's contribution to the Canada Pension Plan for the month. Use the calculation method described in the text. Remember that the year's basic exemption is $3 000 and that the calculation required is for only one month.
c Calculate each employee's unemployment insurance premium, assuming that the minimum monthly insurable earnings are $589.33 and that the maximum monthly insurable earnings are $2 946.66. Use the calculation method described in the text.
d Assume the following monthly income tax deductions for each employee: Belliveau, $595.44; Dillon, $618.60; Ryan, $622.05; Crawford, $460.20; Greenwood, $591.10; Westwood, $858.40. Construct a sepa-

rate table for each employee to report the calculations leading to the respective net pays.

Timekeeping and computing gross earnings, deductions, and net pay for two employees on a commission-scale basis.

10.5 William Murphy and Paulette Moore are on the sales staff of the Toronto Widget Company. Under a contract of service, both are paid commissions of 5% on sales up to and including $1 000; 7.5% on sales over $1 000 up to and including $1 500; and 9% on sales over $1 500.

a If Murphy's weekly sales amounted to $6 340 and Moore's weekly sales amounted to $6 485, how much did each employee earn?

b Use the calculation method to report each employee's contribution to CPP and the UI premium.

c Assume the following additional information: both contributed to a registered company pension plan at the weekly rate of $10; Murphy's Net Claim Code is 5 and Moore's is 1. Use the income tax table in the text to report the calculation of each employee's withholding of income tax.

d Assume that each employee contributes $6.50 weekly to group insurance premiums. Construct a schedule reporting each employee's net pay.

Computing employee deductions for UI, employer payroll tax to UI, and the total premium to be paid for UI.

10.6 Using a table with headings as illustrated in Figure 10-18, record the following employees' names and their weekly gross earnings in columns 1 and 2 respectively: Gerald Butler, $493.10; Robert Bulloch, $575.80; Carl Cunningham, $605; Trevor Davies, $545.32; Ed Holowchuk, $573; Michael Shinagawa, $573; Robert Strople, $556.70.

FIGURE 10-18

Employee's Name	Weekly Gross Earnings	Employee Deduction for UI	Employer Payroll Tax to UI	Total Premium to Be Paid for UI
(1)	(2)	(3)	(4)	(5)
Gerald Butler	$493.10			

Then calculate and record the unemployment insurance contribution for each employee in column 3, for the employer in column 4, and the total premium to be paid in column 5. Assume that the employees report for work in your province. You may use the premium rates quoted in this chapter if applicable or the latest figures supplied by the Department of National Revenue—Taxation. Complete the table by totalling the columns.

Note: Save your solution for use in the next three problems.

CHAPTER 10: Payroll Application **439**

10.7 Using the information in Problem 10.6 above and a similar table, calculate the employee's deduction for CPP, the employer's contribution to CPP, and the total contribution to be remitted for CPP. For all calculations, use the date given in this chapter, or, if you prefer, use the latest information supplied by Revenue Canada—Taxation.

Note: Save your solution for use in the next two problems.

Continuing the problem solved for Problem 10.6 with solutions for CPP deductions.

10.8 Assume that all the employees named in Problems 10.6 and 10.7 have agreed to contribute to a registered company pension plan. Assume further that the plan calls for deductions of 5% of the employee's gross earnings and that the employer has agreed to contribute an equal share. Construct a table with the following numbered column headings: (1) Name of Employee; (2) Weekly Gross Earnings; (3) Employee Contribution; (4) Employer Contribution; and (5) Total Amount to Be Remitted. Complete the table by totalling all money columns.

Note: Save your solution for use in the next problem.

Continuing the problem solved for Problems 10.6 and 10.7 with solutions for contributions to a company registered pension plan.

10.9 Construct a table with headings similar to those illustrated in Figure 10-19 and use the following information to complete columns 1 and 2: Butler, 2; Bulloch, 3; Cunningham, 5; Davies, 1; Holowchuk, 2; Shinagawa, 7; Strople, 4. Complete the table by recording the information obtained from the previous three problems and calculations and recording the amount of the income tax to be withheld from each employee's earnings.

Completing the problems solved for Problems 10.6, 10.7, and 10.8.

FIGURE 10-19

Calculation of Employees' Income Taxes								
Employee's Name (1)	Net Claim Code (2)	Weekly Gross Earnings (3)	DEDUCTIONS			Taxable Earnings (Cols. 3–6) (7)	Income Tax Deduction (8)
^	^	^	CPP (4)	UI (5)	Co. P.P. (6)	^	^
Gerald Butler	2	$493.10					

TOPIC 2 Accounting for the Payroll

By the federal Income Tax Act and provincial law, every employer and payer who is required to withhold or deduct taxes, CPP contributions, or UI premiums must keep records and books of account and allow officers of Revenue Canada to verify these books and records on request. Normally, books and records of account must be kept for at least six years from the end of the year to which they relate. However, if the employer wishes to destroy any payroll books and records, he or she must apply in

440 PART 2: COMMON ACCOUNTING APPLICATIONS

[Handwritten margin notes: #1 & 2 is in deans pay roll book. #3 end of month int accounts records]

writing to the director of the district office in the area in which the business is located. Before permission to destroy any payroll documents will be granted, all returns for the taxation years concerned must have been filed and assessed. Consequently, it is the responsibility of a payroll department to ensure that a complete recording of every payroll be made. A complete recording of payroll involves at least three activities: (1) preparing a payroll summary known as the "payroll register"; (2) preparing a summary of the details of each employee's earnings in an employee's individual earnings record; and (3) journalizing and posting the payroll so that ledger accounts affected by the payroll may be updated.

Preparing the Payroll Register

Payroll summary/payroll register: a payroll record summarizing the names of employees and amounts payable to them as salaries or wages at a given time, with particulars as to rate of pay and deductions.

After calculating the details of gross earnings, deductions, and the net pay for each employee for a particular payroll period, the complete payroll is usually summarized in a record known as the ***payroll summary*** or ***payroll register***. In some accounting systems, a payroll register is prepared for each different payroll plan. Thus, a separate hourly payroll register may be prepared to summarize the payroll for hourly-rated employees; and a separate salary payroll register may be used to summarize a particular pay period for salaried employees. On the other hand, some accounting systems, especially those with computer facilities, may combine the payroll summaries for hourly-rated employees and salaried personnel.

Of course, the actual design and format of payroll registers will vary from one business to another and with the actual method of processing the payroll. For example, the preparation of the summary by hand will require a forms design quite different from that required by a payroll register prepared by computer. Regardless of how the payroll summary is prepared, however, every payroll register will contain at least the names and identification numbers of employees, the details of the employees' gross earnings, the details of the employees' payroll deductions, and the calculation of the employees' net pay. In Figures 10-20 and 10-21, assume that the Summerhill Sales Company prepares two payroll summaries: one for hourly-rated employees and one for salaried employees. Figure 10-22, combining the salaried and the hourly-rated employees, offers a comparison. Study all three illustrations closely; then examine the analysis which follows.

ANALYSIS OF PAYROLL REGISTERS Here are the main points to remember when analyzing the contents and the preparation of any payroll register:

- Notice that each payroll summary identifies the type of payroll and the pay ending period. In the hourly payroll register, the employees are paid on a weekly basis, while the salary payroll register informs the reader that salaried personnel are paid biweekly (once every two weeks). It is common practice in many businesses that hourly-employed personnel are paid on a basis quite different from that used for salaried personnel.

- In the payroll register combined for hourly/salary workers, notice that all employees are listed in order of their employee number. In addition, observe that each employee is given an employee-type code: HW stands for "hourly worker" and SW "salaried worker."
- Although payroll periods end on June 30 on all three registers, the employees may not be paid until one, two, or even three days after the pay ending period, to give the accounting department time to prepare the payroll. For this reason, the actual payment date is not identified on the register until the cheques are prepared. As you will see in the next Topic, the payment date will be the date of the employee's cheque. In other accounting systems, especially with salaried personnel, the payroll may be processed one or two days before the pay ending period, but cheques will be dated for the pay ending period. Should adjustments be required for employees' absences or overtime on those one or two days, these would be reflected on the next payroll period.

FIGURE 10-20

Hourly Payroll Register
For the Week Beginning June 24 19— **and Ending** June 30 19— **Paid** _____ 19—

No.	SIN	Name	Net Claim Code	Hours	Rate of Pay	Regular	Overtime	Gross Pay	CPP	UI	Income Tax	Co. P.P.	Group Insur.	Other	Total	Net Pay	Chq. No.
1	387-430-193	Adams, Joe	3	40	15 00	600 00		600 00	12 52	13 50	104 05	30 00	6 00		166 07	433 93	
2	214-617-119	Adler, Ron	5	40	15 75	630 00		630 00	13 21	14 18	101 00	31 50	6 00		165 89	464 11	
3	143-413-663	Blair, John	5	43.75	12 00	465 00	90 00	555 00	11 44	12 49	75 70	27 75	6 00		133 38	421 62	
4	391-715-110	Calvert, Linda	1	42	15 00	600 00	45 00	645 00	13 44	14 51	132 05	32 25	6 00		198 25	446 75	
5	617-417-385	Gavreluk, Rob	2	44	13 00	520 00	78 00	598 00	12 52	13 46	112 00	29 90	6 00		173 88	424 12	
6	233-128-387	Granum, Lorri	1	40	11 50	460 00		460 00	9 25	10 35	79 45	23 00	6 00		128 05	331 95	
7	425-127-511	Janzen, John	4	39	12 00	468 00		468 00	9 44	10 53	61 60	23 40	6 00		110 97	357 03	
8	456-897-343	Martin, Lynn	2	40	10 50	420 00		420 00	8 33	9 45	66 25	21 00	6 00		111 03	308 97	
						4 163 00	213 00	4 376 00	90 15	98 47	732 10	218 80	48 00	0 00	1 187 52	3 188 48	

FIGURE 10-21

Salary Payroll Register
For the Two Weeks Ending June 30 19— **Paid** _____ 19—

No.	SIN	Name	Net Claim Code	Base Salary per Wk.	Regular	Overtime	Gross Pay	CPP	UI	Income Tax	Co. P.P.	Group Insur.	Other	Total	Net Pay	Chq. No.
21	425-187-873	Barzo, Ann	1	400 00	800 00		800 00	15 75	18 00	130 15	40 00	12 00		215 90	584 10	
22	127-345-876	Bugno, Julia	1	450 00	900 00	100 00	1 000 00	20 35	22 50	178 35	50 00	12 00		283 20	716 80	
23	458-214-489	Chan, Audrey	4	500 00	1 000 00		1 000 00	20 35	22 50	138 65	50 00	12 00		243 50	756 50	
24	763-092-982	Gander, Donna	1	350 00	700 00	50 00	750 00	15 97	16 88	117 85	37 50	12 00		200 20	549 80	
25	231-344-779	Long, Henry	2	425 00	850 00	150 00	1 000 00	20 35	22 50	170 45	50 00	12 00		275 30	724 70	
26	654-345-980	Price, Deborah	1	600 00	1 200 00		1 200 00	24 91	27 00	231 95	60 00	12 00		355 86	844 14	
					5 450 00	300 00	5 750 00	117 68	129 38	967 40	287 50	72 00		1 573 96	4 176 04	

FIGURE 10-22

Combined Hourly/Salary Payroll Register

As of _June 30_ 19— for Pay Period _26_   Paid ____ 19—

No.	SIN	Name	Type Code	Net Claim Code	Hours or Weeks	Regular	Over-time	Gross Pay	CPP	UI	Income Tax	Co. P.P.	Group Insur.	Other	Total	Net Pay	Chq. No.
1	387-430-193	Adams, Joe	HW	3	40 hr.	600 00		600 00	12 52	13 50	104 05	30 00	6 00		166 07	433 93	
2	214-617-119	Adler, Ron	HW	5	40 hr.	630 00		630 00	13 21	14 18	101 00	31 50	6 00		165 89	464 11	
3	143-413-663	Blair, John	HW	5	43.75 hr.	465 00	90 00	555 00	11 44	12 49	75 70	27 75	6 00		133 38	421 62	
4	391-715-110	Calvert, Linda	HW	1	42 hr.	600 00	45 00	645 00	13 44	14 51	132 05	32 25	6 00		198 25	446 75	
5	617-417-385	Gavreluk, Rob	HW	2	44 hr.	520 00	78 00	598 00	12 52	13 46	112 00	29 90	6 00		173 88	424 12	
6	233-128-387	Granum, Lorri	HW	1	40 hr.	460 00		460 00	9 25	10 35	79 45	23 00	6 00		128 05	331 95	
7	425-127-511	Janzen, John	HW	4	39 hr.	468 00		468 00	9 44	10 53	61 60	23 40	6 00		110 97	357 03	
8	456-897-343	Martin, Lynn	HW	2	40 hr.	420 00		420 00	8 33	9 45	66 25	21 00	6 00		111 03	308 97	
21	425-187-873	Barzo, Ann	SW	1	2 wk.	800 00		800 00	15 75	18 00	130 15	40 00	12 00		215 90	584 10	
22	127-345-876	Bugno, Julia	SW	1	2 wk.	900 00	100 00	1 000 00	20 35	22 50	178 35	50 00	12 00		283 20	716 80	
23	458-214-489	Chan, Audrey	SW	4	2 wk.	1 000 00		1 000 00	20 35	22 50	138 65	50 00	12 00		243 50	756 50	
24	763-092-982	Gander, Donna	SW	1	2 wk.	700 00	50 00	750 00	15 97	16 88	117 85	37 50	12 00		200 20	549 80	
25	231-344-779	Long, Henry	SW	2	2 wk.	850 00	150 00	1 000 00	20 35	22 50	170 45	50 00	12 00		275 30	724 70	
26	654-345-980	Price, Deborah	SW	1	2 wk.	1 200 00		1 200 00	24 91	27 00	231 95	60 00	12 00		355 86	844 14	
						9 613 00	513 00	10 126 00	207 83	227 85	1 699 50	506 30	120 00		2 761 48	7 364 52	

FIGURE 10-23

Proof of Hourly Payroll Register

Earnings:
- Regular $4 163.00
- Overtime 213.00
- Total $4 376.00

Deductions:
- CPP .... $ 90.15
- UI 98.47
- Income tax 732.10
- Co. P. P. 218.80
- Group insur. 48.00
- Other 0.00
- Total 1 187.52

Net pay $3 188.48

FIGURE 10-24

Proof of Salary Payroll Register

Earnings:
- Regular $5 450.00
- Overtime 300.00
- Total $5 750.00

Deductions:
- CPP $117.68
- UI 129.38
- Income tax 967.40
- Co. P. P. 287.50
- Group insur. 72.00
- Other 0.00
- Total 1 573.96

Net pay $4 176.04

- In the hourly payroll register, you will observe that much of the information for figuring the individual employee's gross earnings has been taken from the clock card. You will recall the important measure that, as part of timekeeping, the accounting of all time must be reconciled with the supervisor's report of daily time. Similarly, in the case of salaried employees, the supervisor or manager's signature will appear on all attendance reports so that the salaried payroll register may be prepared with authorized additions for overtime or authorized deductions for being absent without permission.

- After each employee's gross pay is entered, observe the method of recording the various deductions. In particular, remember the point that any registered company pension plan figures must be deducted from the employee's gross earnings *before* the income tax tables are used to enter the amount of income tax withheld. As you recall, the calculation of income taxes was performed on taxable earnings and not on gross earnings.

- In all payroll registers, the amounts of the deductions are added and the total is entered in the Total column of the Deductions section. Obviously, this step is important for calculating the net pay for each employee.

- Observe in all registers how the payroll is proved. After all the data for each employee is entered and *before the payroll is paid*, the various columns must be totalled. The proof of any payroll register is done by adding and subtracting the appropriate column totals across the register. In some methods of data processing, the register proof is obtained automatically with the use of computers. In your classroom, use an adding machine or electronic calculator to prove the payroll register similarly to the proofs shown in Figures 10-23, 10-24, and 10-25. As you will see later, all payroll registers must be proved before payment is made to employees and before journal entries are made to record the dollar results of each payroll.

Preparing the Employee's Individual Earnings Record

After a payroll register is prepared and proved, the details of each employee's earnings may be posted to the **employee's individual earnings record**. This individual record of the employee's earnings is especially important, for the following reasons:

- It provides for each employee in one record a full year's summary of his or her pay periods, gross earnings, deductions, and net pay.
- It serves as a basis for preparing important tax slips so that the employee may complete an income tax return.
- It helps the employer to tell when the employee has reached the maximum points of contributions to the Canada Pension Plan and the UI premium.

Figure 10-26 gives an example of how the employee's individual earnings record may be prepared for John Blair. In actual practice, keep in mind that the form will probably vary directly with the method of processing the record. Also remember that the individual earnings record for a given pay period must agree with the payroll register for the same period and, as you will see later, with the employee's payroll statement issued on paying the employee.

Three final points are worth noting:

- From the illustration, observe that the Earnings, Deductions, and Net Pay sections are in the same order as on the payroll register. This is so that the amounts can be efficiently posted to the employee's individual earnings record. Under some manual shortcut methods of processing the payroll, this order is important, because the payroll register and individual employee's earnings record are prepared in one writing. The one-write system of processing the payroll is treated in Topic 4.
- Observe that a column has been added to the earnings record that does not appear on the payroll register: **accumulated earnings** or "year-to-date earnings." This column provides a current total of the gross earnings so that the payroll clerk can easily notice when the employee has earned his or her maximum amount for the Canada Pension Plan and for the year-end reporting of gross earnings. In some accounting systems, the accumulated earnings column is titled "Year-to-Date Earnings."
- Note that the employee's individual earnings record is actually a payroll subsidiary ledger account. In payroll accounting, the **payroll ledger** becomes the subsidiary ledger, disclosing the details of individual employees' wages, deductions, and net pay. Obviously, it would be most inefficient to list all of the individual employees' gross earnings (an expense to the business) in the general ledger. Instead, a general

FIGURE 10-25

Proof of Combined Hourly/Salary Payroll Register

Earnings:
Regular $9 613.00
Overtime 513.00
   Total $10 126.00
Deductions:
CPP .... $ 207.83
UI 227.85
Income tax 1 699.50
Co. P. P. 506.30
Group insur. 120.00
Other 0.00
   Total 2 761.48
Net pay $7 364.52

Employee's individual earnings record: an accounting record reporting the details of an individual employee's payroll, usually for a complete calendar year.

Accumulated earnings (year-to-date earnings): the total to date of gross earnings for an individual employee.

Payroll ledger: a subsidiary ledger containing employee individual earnings records.

444 PART 2: COMMON ACCOUNTING APPLICATIONS

FIGURE 10-26

Employee's Individual Earnings Record for the Year 19—

Employee's Name Blair, John **SIN** 143-413-663 **Employee No.** 3

Address 843 Driftwood Rd. London, Ontario N6H 4H9 **Phone No.** 471-8622

Date of Birth January 14, 1965 **Date of Reaching 65** January 14, 2030

Date Employed January 2, 1991 **Date of Termination** _____ **Reason** _____

Position Stockroom Clerk **Salary or Wage Plan** Hourly-Rate Plan **Rate of Pay** $12.00 per hour

Net Claim Code per TD1 5 **UI Insurable Earnings** Minimum: $136.00 per wk.; Maximum: $680.00 per wk. **Maximum UI Yearly Premium:** $795

CPP Year's Maximum Pensionable Earnings $30 500.00 **Year's Basic CPP Exemption** $3 000.00 **Maximum Earnings for Contributions** $27 500.00 **Maximum Yearly CPP** $632.50

Pay Period	Rate per Hour	Hours	Regular	Over-time	Gross Pay	CPP	UI	Income Tax	Co. P.P.	Group Insur.	Other	Total	Net Pay	Accumulated Earnings
														10 987 75
June 2	12 00	40	480 00	0 00	480 00	9 71	10 80	57 25	24 00	6 00	0 00	107 76	372 24	11 467 50
June 9	12 00	41	480 00	18 00	498 00	10 13	11 21	61 35	24 90	6 00	0 00	113 59	384 41	11 965 50
June 16	12 00	43.5	480 00	63 00	543 00	11 16	12 22	71 60	27 15	6 00	0 00	128 13	414 87	12 508 50
June 23	12 00	38	456 00	0 00	456 00	9 16	10 26	43 70	22 80	6 00	0 00	91 92	364 08	12 964 50
June 30	12 00	43.75	465 00	90 00	555 00	11 44	12 49	75 70	27 75	6 00	0 00	133 38	421 62	13 519 50

account called "Wages Expense," "Salaries Expense," or "Wages and Salaries Expense" is used to "control" by total the individual gross earnings of each employee.

Journalizing and Posting the Payroll to the General Ledger

When the totals of the payroll register have been proved and posting has been completed to each employee's individual earnings record, the payroll data is ready to be recorded and posted to appropriate accounts in the general ledger. In some accounting systems, the totals of each individual payroll register are posted directly to the general ledger. In this case, the payroll register becomes the book of original entry and may now be called a ***payroll journal***. In many other systems, like the one used in the Summerhill Sales Company example, the totals of each payroll register are usually summarized in the form of a compound entry and recorded in the general journal. Regardless of the system followed, two distinct classes of entries must be considered: (1) the entry to record the dollar results of the payroll register; and (2) the entry to record the employer's additional

Payroll journal: the payroll register used as a book of original entry.

expenses resulting from each payroll. Each of these classes will now be analyzed separately.

1. RECORDING THE PAYROLL REGISTER TOTALS   It is useful to return to the proof of the hourly payroll register, the salary payroll register, and the combined hourly/salary payroll register and analyze the key figures reported in each proof. Examine the proof of the hourly payroll register in Figure 10-27, and analyze carefully the explanation that follows.

FIGURE 10-27

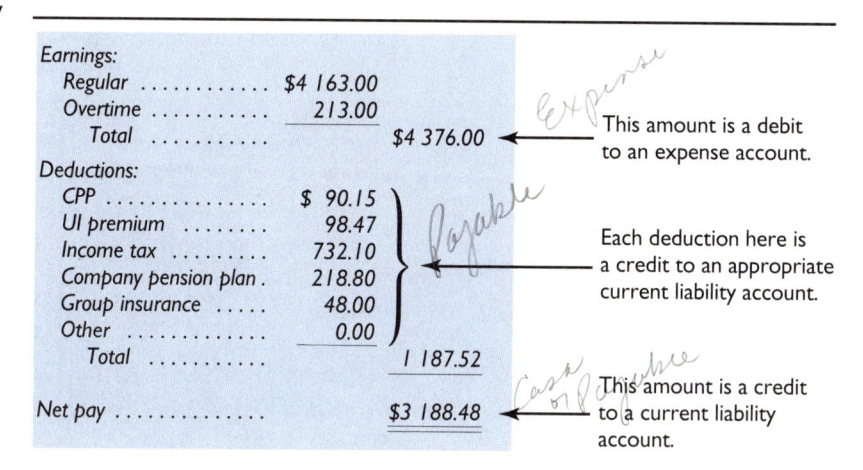

Earnings:		
Regular	$4 163.00	
Overtime	213.00	
Total		$4 376.00
Deductions:		
CPP	$ 90.15	
UI premium	98.47	
Income tax	732.10	
Company pension plan	218.80	
Group insurance	48.00	
Other	0.00	
Total		1 187.52
Net pay		$3 188.48

Expense — This amount is a debit to an expense account.

Payable — Each deduction here is a credit to an appropriate current liability account.

Cash or due — This amount is a credit to a current liability account.

- Observe that the total of the Gross Pay column of the hourly payroll register may be debited to the expense account Wages Expense or a combination account Wages and Salaries Expense. Similarly, the total of the Gross Pay column of the salary payroll register may be debited to Salaries Expense or Wages and Salaries Expense. Of course, if a combined hourly/salary payroll register is used, the total of the Gross Pay column would normally be debited to the combination account Wages and Salaries Expense. However, when a distribution of this Gross Pay column is required to separate accounts, a change is required in the accounting; this change will be discussed later.

- For each payroll deduction, an appropriate current liability account must be credited, because the amounts withheld do not belong to the employer; they must be paid to the federal government, the provincial government, or to the insurance agency as the case may be. It is helpful to remember that the employer acts as the collecting agent for these parties. In the example of Summerhill Sales Company, the employer withholds from each employee's pay the contribution to the Canada Pension Plan, the unemployment insurance premium, income taxes, the company pension plan contribution, and the group insurance premium. At specified dates, the employer must remit the

FIGURE 10-28

**Summerhill Sales Company
Chart of Accounts**

Current Liabilities
210 Wages Payable
211 Salaries Payable
212 CPP Contributions Payable
213 UI Premium Payable
214 Income Tax Deductions Payable
215 Company Pension Plan Payable
216 Group Insurance Payable

Expenses
515 Wages Expense
516 Salaries Expense
517 Payroll Taxes Expense

amounts withheld to the federal government (CPP, UI, and income taxes), the trust company or other agency which looks after the company pension plan, and the insurance company designated for the group insurance coverage. Until these amounts are paid, they must be treated as current liabilities on the books of the employer.

- As for the Net Pay column of the payroll register, the total amount is also a current liability until the employees are paid. An appropriate liability account, therefore, will be credited for the total of each Net Pay column of the payroll register. For example, Wages Payable would be an appropriate credit for the total of Net Pay of the hourly payroll register. Similarly, Salaries Payable would be appropriate for the Net Pay column of the salary payroll register. And if a combined hourly/salary payroll register were used, a combined current liability account like Wages and Salaries Payable could be used.

The chart of accounts illustrated in the side margin for Summerhill Sales Company identifies the payroll accounts preferred for this business. The meaning of all accounts should be self-evident, with the exception of the special expense account called Payroll Taxes Expense. This account will be explained later.

The entries made to record the payroll for Summerhill Sales Company for the pay period ended June 30 are analyzed in general journal form in Figure 10-29. You should observe that a compound entry may be made to record the combined totals of each payroll register; however, the entries in the figure are as shown to simplify the presentation of the payroll entry as it is related to each payroll register. After these entries are posted to the general ledger, the various liability accounts will show the amounts owed to the federal government, the trust company, the insurance company, and the employees. Of course, the gross earnings of each payroll register will be shown in suitable wage and salary expense accounts.

FIGURE 10-29

June 30	Wages Expense	4 376.00	
	CPP Deductions Payable		90.15
	UI Premium Payable		98.47
	Income Tax Deductions Payable		732.10
	Company Pension Plan Payable		218.80
	Group Insurance Payable		48.00
	Wages Payable		3 188.48
	To record the payroll of hourly-rated employees for the week ended June 30.		
June 30	Salaries Expense	5 750.00	
	CPP Deductions Payable		117.68
	UI Premium Payable		129.38
	Income Tax Deductions Payable		967.40
	Company Pension Plan Payable		287.50
	Group Insurance Payable		72.00
	Wages Payable		4 176.04
	To record the payroll of salaried employees for the two weeks ended June 30.		

CHAPTER 10: Payroll Application **447**

Using a Special Payroll Clearing Account When a payroll register is used combining different payroll plans such as for wages and salaries, many accounting systems will record the gross earnings to a special ***Payroll Clearing Account***. For example, if Summerhill Sales Company had used the combined hourly/salary payroll register, the general journal entry to record the combined payroll may be made as shown in Figure 10-30.

Payroll Clearing Account: a special account used to distribute the combined gross earnings of different payroll plans to appropriate expense accounts.

FIGURE 10-30

June 30 Payroll Clearing Account	10 126.00	
CPP Deductions Payable		207.83
UI Premium Payable		227.85
Income Tax Deductions Payable		1 699.50
Company Pension Plan Payable		506.30
Group Insurance Payable		120.00
Wages and Salaries Payable		7 364.52
To record the payroll of hourly-rated and salaried employees for the payroll period ended June 30.		

Periodically, the payroll clearing account must be analyzed and be distributed to appropriate expense accounts. In the case of Summerhill Sales Company, the entry to bring about this distribution may be made as follows:

FIGURE 10-31

June 30 Wages Expense	4 376.00	
Salaries Expense	5 750.00	
Payroll Clearing Account		10 126.00
To distribute the amount in Payroll Clearing to separate Wages and Salaries Expense accounts in accordance with the Employee Type Code identified in the Combined Hourly/Salary Payroll Register.		

When a payroll clearing account is used, it is normal to list it as an account in the expenses section of the company's chart of accounts. However, the use of this clearing account is strictly optional. Many companies distribute their labour costs when the payroll is analyzed in the payroll register.

2. RECORDING THE EMPLOYER'S ADDITIONAL PAYROLL EXPENSES

As you will recall from the opening Topic of this chapter, the employer is obliged by law to contribute 1.4 times the employee's share of unemployment insurance, and an equal dollar amount to the Canada Pension Plan and to any company registered pension plan. In addition and where applicable, the employer may be required by provincial law to contribute to a provincial health insurance plan. The amounts contributed by the employer represent additional expenses resulting from each payroll and must be journalized and posted to appropriate general ledger accounts.

Payroll Taxes Expense: an account used to record the additional employer's expense resulting from the payroll.

In practice, an account called ***Payroll Taxes Expense*** is commonly used to record the total debit of the various employer's additional payroll expenses. The use of the word "taxes" should not be confused with that of "income taxes"; income taxes are withheld from the employees and accounted for in the current liability account. Instead, the word is used as part of the Payroll Taxes Expense account to suggest that the additional amounts are levied against the employer by the government in much the same way as in the case of property taxes or licence fees required for doing business. Since the employer had no choice but to contribute, in the language of business these additional levies may be regarded as taxes related to payroll expense.

To complete the double entry, separate current liability accounts are used to show the dollar amounts that must be paid on behalf of the employer for the Canada Pension Plan, unemployment insurance, the company pension plan, and the employer's health tax for the premium payable to the Ontario Health Insurance Plan. For Summerhill Sales Company, separate general journal entries are illustrated in Figure 10-32 so that they can be related to the appropriate payroll register. Of course, a compound journal entry may also be used to combine similar accounts from both payroll registers.

FIGURE 10-32

June 30 Payroll Taxes Expense	489.69	
CPP Contributions Payable		90.15
UI Premium Payable		137.86
Company Pension Plan Payable		218.80
EHT Payable		42.88
To record the employer's payroll taxes resulting from the hourly-rated payroll of the week ended June 30.		
June 30 Payroll Taxes Expense	642.66	
CPP Contributions Payable		117.68
UI Premium Payable		181.13
Company Pension Plan Payable		287.50
EHT Payable		56.35
To record the employer's payroll taxes resulting from the salary payroll of the two weeks ended June 30.		

Individual computations in the above double entries may be analyzed as follows:

- The amount of CPP Contributions Payable, by federal law, is equal to the amount contributed by the employees from each payroll. Therefore, the employer's payroll taxes will always be related to CPP in a 1:1 ratio.
- The amount of UI Premium Payable, by federal law, is calculated by multiplying 1.4 times the amount deducted from the employees' gross earnings.
- The amount of Company Pension Plan Payable, by federal law, is equal to the amount contributed by the employees from each payroll to their

CHAPTER 10: Payroll Application **449**

company registered pension plan. Therefore, the employer's payroll taxes will always be related to the registered company pension plan in a 1:1 ratio.

- When employers are required to pay the total premium to a provincial health insurance plan, the amount payable will be based on the regulations of individual provinces. Where such provincial legislation exists, residents will continue to receive health care coverage, but will no longer have to pay provincial health insurance premiums through payroll deductions. Instead, all employers with permanent establishments in a particular province must pay the total premium.

Employer Health Tax (EHT): a provincial tax imposed on employers to cover the health care coverage of all citizens of the province.

For example, in Ontario, the **Employer Health Tax (EHT)** replaces the former OHIP premiums. Under the new legislation, the rate of EHT which Ontario employers must pay is based on the total calendar-year gross payroll. For those who pay up to $200 000 annually the rate is 0.98%, and for those who pay more than $400 000 annually the rate is 1.95%. There are graduations in this rate for all remuneration totals between these two amounts; tax tables are available from the Ontario Ministry of Revenue. Employers with a gross annual payroll exceeding $400 000 must make EHT installment payments on a monthly basis. If the employer's gross annual payroll is less than $400 000, EHT installment payments must be made quarterly, with payments due on the 15th of April, of July, of October, and of January. Following the end of each calendar year, employers must file an annual tax return which will include a declaration of the total Ontario remuneration paid for the prior calendar year, the calculation of the difference between installment payments and the tax due, and the balance of tax payable. Similar regulations exist in all provinces where there is a legislated employer health tax.

For Summerhill Sales Company, assume that the estimated total calendar-year gross payroll will be under $200 000. Therefore, the payroll clerk will simply multiply the total gross earnings of each payroll by 0.98%. For example, from the hourly payroll register, the total gross pay is $4 376. Consequently, the EHT Payable is $42.88 ($4 376 × 0.98%). Similarly, from the Salary Payroll Register, the total gross pay is $5 750. Thus, the EHT Payable is $56.35. Obviously, after posting the amounts from each double entry, the balance in EHT Payable will be the sum of $42.88 and $56.35, or $99.23. According to provincial regulations, this balance account is due by the 15th of July.

TOPIC 2 Problems

Preparing an hourly payroll register; proving the payroll register; analyzing the resulting payroll entries in general journal form.

10.10 You will require the information of Problems 10.6, 10.7, 10.8, and 10.9 for this problem. Figure 10-33 presents some additional information for the payroll period beginning July 6 and ending July 12.

FIGURE 10-33

Employee No.	SIN	Name	Group Insurance	Other Deductions (United Way)
1	485-234-987	G. Butler	$6.00	$20.00
2	328-876-323	R. Bulloch	6.00	10.00
3	138-989-340	C. Cunningham	6.00	15.00
4	128-987-342	T. Davies	6.00	10.00
5	480-009-123	E. Holowchuk	6.00	10.00
6	237-900-236	M. Shinagawa	6.00	10.00
7	808-320-289	R. Strople	6.00	10.00

Required

a Using the information obtained in Problems 10.6, 10.7, 10.8, and 10.9 and the added information above, prepare an hourly payroll register.

b Total and prove the payroll register. (If possible, show your proof on an adding-machine tape.)

c Show how the payroll entries would appear in general journal form. Ignore additional employer's expense entries in this problem.

Note: Save your solution for use in Problems 10.16 and 10.17 of this chapter.

Preparing an hourly payroll register; proving the payroll register; recording the payroll summary and additional employer's expenses resulting from the payroll.

10.11 The payroll data in Figure 10-34 covers the week beginning April 1 and ending April 7.

a Record the payroll in an hourly payroll register. Use the tables for contributions to CPP, UI, and the weekly tax deductions as found in this chapter (or obtain the latest available tables for your province). Each employee has agreed to contribute to a registered company pension plan on the basis of 2% of weekly gross earnings. The employer has agreed to match this contribution. In addition, each employee has a weekly deduction of $2.50 for group insurance and of $2 for annual union dues.

b Show a separate schedule of calculations for taxable earnings and the resulting income tax withheld for each employee. *Hint:* Two deductions stated in **a** are tax-deductible.

c Total and prove the hourly payroll register.

d Show accounting entries to record the payroll summary and the additional employer's expenses resulting from the payroll. Ignore any provincial health tax insurance premium in this part of the problem.

e Assume that the employer's business is located in a province like Ontario, where the employer is required to pay an employer's health tax. Assume also that the employer's annual gross payroll earnings are estimated to be under $200 000. Record the additional payroll expense resulting from a required provincial employer's health tax.

Note: Save this solution for use in Problem 10.17 of the next Topic.

CHAPTER 10: Payroll Application 451

FIGURE 10-34

No.	Name	SIN	Net Claim Code	Hours	Regular	Overtime
1	Tom Allan	480-763-487	2	40	$480.00	
2	Barbara Cook	328-890-321	1	40 + 2	520.00	$39.00
3	Mike Farlow	321-908-380	3	40 + 4	480.00	72.00
4	Andrea Hart	876-234-098	2	40	520.00	
5	Sandra Lambe	332-387-348	2	41	540.00	20.25
6	Suzanne McLurg	675-843-982	1	38	484.50	
7	Laima Pecs	545-687-345	2	40 + 4	480.00	72.00

Preparing a salaried payroll register; proving the payroll register; recording the payroll summary and additional employer's expenses resulting from the payroll.

10.12 The salaried payroll information for the Central Medical Clinic for the one week ending April 7 is shown in Figure 10-35. The only deductions from gross earnings are for CPP, UI, and income tax.

a Record the payroll in a salary payroll register suitable for the deductions required for this business. Use the tables for Canada Pension Plan contributions, unemployment insurance premiums, and the weekly tax deductions as found in this chapter (or obtain the latest available tables for your province).

b Total and prove the salaried payroll register.

c Show accounting entries to record the payroll summary and the additional employer's expenses resulting from the payroll. Ignore any provincial health tax insurance premium in this part of the problem.

d Assume that the employer's place of business is located in a province like Ontario where the employer is required to pay an employer's health tax. Assume also that the employer's annual gross payroll earnings is estimated to be under $200 000. Record the additional payroll expense resulting from a required provincial employer's health tax.

FIGURE 10-35

Employee No.	SIN	Name	Net Claim Code	Base Salary per Week
1	489-778-932	Armstrong, Jane	1	$485.00
2	321-348-892	Circelli, Sue	1	500.00
3	672-342-348	Dallaire, Dorothy	2	550.00
4	223-387-348	Finnie, Lenore	1	500.00
5	141-678-876	Hammond, Abbey	1	490.00
6	332-345-788	Mascarin, Treva	2	600.00
7	335-778-444	Shurget, Janet	1	575.00
8	554-443-668	Wodwud, Julie	1	470.00

Preparing a combined hourly/salaried payroll register; proving the payroll register; recording the payroll summary and additional employer's expenses resulting from the payroll.

10.13 The payroll data in Figure 10-36 covers the final week ending June 30, current year, of hourly-rated and salaried workers who work under a contract of employment for Peel Engines Ltd.

FIGURE 10-36

No.	Name	SIN	Net Claim Code	Hours/ Weeks	Type Code	Regular	Overtime
1	Ralph Bailey	425-876-230	2	40 + 1 hr.	HW	$640.00	$ 16.00
2	Couse, Merv	477-666-555	2	40 + 2 hr.	HW	680.00	51.00
3	Edwards, Bob	490-333-444	2	40 + 5 hr.	HW	620.00	115.25
4	Foster, Eileen	430-555-222	2	39 + 6 hr.	HW	663.00	153.00
5	Groleau, Freida	430-680-121	1	40 hr.	HW	600.00	
6	Laxton, John	463-280-140	1	40 + 2 hr.	HW	560.00	42.00
21	Anderson, Peggy	418-668-423	1	1 wk. + 5 hr.	SW	500.00	93.75
22	Beattie, Nora	408-345-980	1	1 wk.	SW	550.00	
23	Bisset, Vicki	424-125-680	1	1 wk. + 8 hr.	SW	600.00	180.00
24	Domszky, Cathy	408-789-367	1	1 wk.	SW	750.00	
25	Hewett, Peggy	418-198-380	1	1 wk.	SW	600.00	
26	Hostetler, Howard	449-380-178	4	1 wk. + 6 hr.	SW	800.00	180.00

a   Record the above payroll data in a combined hourly/salary payroll register. Use the tables for contributions to the Canada Pension Plan, unemployment insurance, and the weekly tax deductions as found in this chapter (or obtain the latest available tables for your province). Each employee has agreed to contribute to a registered company pension plan on the basis of 3% of weekly gross earnings. The employer has agreed to match this amount. In addition, each employee has a weekly deduction of $5 for group insurance.

b   Total and prove the hourly payroll register.

c   Show accounting entries to record the totals of the combined payroll register with the assumption that management prefers the use of a payroll clearing account to distribute the payroll expense to separate the accounts Wages Expense and Salaries Expense.

d   Prepare the general journal entry to record the additional employer's expenses resulting from the payroll. Ignore any provincial health tax insurance premium in this part of the problem.

e   Assume that the employer's business is located in a province like Ontario where the employer is required to pay an employer's health tax. Assume also that the employer's annual gross payroll earnings are estimated to be under $200 000. Record the additional payroll expense resulting from a required provincial employer's health tax.

Note: Save this solution for use in Problem 10.20 of the next Topic.

Completing an employee's individual earnings record for an hourly-rated employee.

10.14   Charles J. Molyneaux has worked at the Windsor Machine Company since January 2 of this year as a machinist, second class. His personal data for the employee's individual earnings record is as follows: address, 1800 Liberty Street, Windsor, Ontario N9E 1J2; telephone no., 969-2530; SIN, 426-126-510; employee no., 170; date of birth, June 1, 1964; marital status, married with one child aged 5; Net Claim Code as per TD1, 5; hourly-rate plan at

$16.25 per hour; time-and-a-half is paid for all overtime; UI insurable earnings, minimum $136 per week, maximum $630 per week. His individual earnings record card shows accumulated (year-to-date) totals to the end of November 30 as follows:

- Earnings: regular, $30 080.00; overtime, $1 170.24; gross pay, $31 250.24
- Deductions: CPP, $632.50 (maximum in 1991 is $632.50); UI, $695.52 (maximum in 1991 is $795.60); income taxes, $5 935.20; company pension plan (registered), $1 562.51; group insurance ($5 per week), $240; union dues ($2 per week), $96; total deductions, $9 161.73
- Net pay, $22 088.51; accumulated earnings, $31 250.24

Required

a Set up an employee's individual earnings record for Charles J. Molyneaux on a form similar to the one illustrated in this chapter; then record the balances accumulated as of November 30.

b Assume that the employee worked the remaining five weeks in the calendar year as follows: week ending December 7, 40 regular hours; week ending December 14, 40 regular and 4 overtime hours; week ending December 21, 39 regular and 4 overtime hours; week ending December 28, 40 regular hours. For each week, calculate the payroll data required and post this data to the employee's individual earnings record. Use the tables illustrated in the chapter, and be sure to check that the employee does not contribute more than the maximum to the Canada Pension Plan and the total UI premium.

c After posting the final week's payroll data, total all columns under "Earnings," "Deductions," and "Net Pay." How much money did the employee make during the year? How much income tax was withheld during the year?

TOPIC 3 Accounting for Payroll Disbursements and Preparing Annual Tax Statements and Returns

As a result of journalizing and posting the payroll, a number of current liabilities have been recorded in appropriate ledger accounts. In the main, these current liabilities represent amounts owing to the employees, federal and provincial governments, trust or insurance companies, trade unions, and any other agency identified by the journalizing of the complete payroll. Of course, these various liabilities must be discharged by a series of individual cash payments.

In addition to the accounting of payroll disbursements, those associated with payroll accounting will also be responsible for the preparation of annual tax statements and returns, as stipulated by government regulations. The main ones will be identified and briefly discussed after treating the accounting of payroll disbursements.

Paying the Employees

Many employers establish a certain day in the week or month as the normal payday; for example, for hourly-rated employees, Friday of each week. Similarly, salaried employees paid on a regular semimonthly system may find that their payday is established on the fifteenth and the last day of each month. In general, employers may pay their employees in any one of three ways: by cash, by cheque, or by bank deposit. Regardless of the method used, it is important to remember that all methods represent a large cash payment; therefore, each must be carefully controlled.

PAYMENT OF SALARIES AND WAGES IN CASH

Cash payrolls were once common, but they are becoming a rarity in modern accounting practice. From the company's standpoint, the payment of salaries and wages in cash is the least desirable method, because (1) it requires additional work in the preparation of payrolls, (2) it increases the possibility of errors in pay, and (3) it involves a significant risk, because large amounts of cash must be transported and kept at the company. Since most well-managed business concerns pay their employees by cheque or by bank transfer to an employee's bank account, the treatment of the payment of salaries and wages in cash ends here.

PAYMENT OF SALARIES AND WAGES BY CHEQUE

As a measure of greater control over cash payments, many employers prefer to issue special "payroll cheques" to pay their employees. The general procedure leading up to the issuance of these payroll cheques may be outlined as follows:

1. After the payroll register or registers are verified, the paymaster requests approval of the treasurer or some other responsible person to have a cheque issued to transfer the amount required by the net pay sections of the registers to a separate **payroll bank account**. This account is just like other demand deposit accounts, except that it is given a special account number. Suppose, for example, Summerhill Sales Company decided to pay both their hourly-rated and their salaried employees by cheque. A regular cheque, dated as of the pay date, would be made out payable to the payroll bank account for the net amount of all payroll cheques to be issued in the pay period. The journal entry would be recorded in the cash payments journal and would be analyzed as shown in Figure 10-37. Observe in the entry that both Wages Payable and Salaries Payable are debited in order to eliminate the current liabilities set up previously by the payroll journal entry.

Payroll bank account: a special bank account to clear only payroll cheques.

FIGURE 10-37

July 2	Wages Payable	3 188.48	
	Salaries Payable	4 176.04	
	Cash (in bank)		7 364.52
	To transfer the total amount of net pay owing to employees to the special payroll bank account.		

2. Next, the paymaster issues individual payroll cheques against the payroll bank account. In most cases, these cheques will be in the form of a voucher cheque, so that the employee may keep the detachable part as a record of the gross earnings, deductions, and net pay. In point of fact, the detachable voucher becomes the employee's earnings statement. A typical voucher payroll cheque is illustrated in Figure 10-38.

FIGURE 10-38

Period Ending	Hours Worked	Regular	Over-time	Gross Pay	CPP	UI	Income Tax	Co. P.P.	Group Insur.	Other	Total	Amount	Cheque No.
—06 30	43 3/4	465.00	90.00	555.00	11.44	12.49	75.70	27.75	6.00	0.00	133.38	421.62	503
		EARNINGS					DEDUCTIONS					NET PAY	

Employee's Statement of Earnings
Detach and retain for your records.

Summerhill Sales Company
London, Ontario

- -

Summerhill Sales Company
22 Adelaide St. North
London, Ontario N6B 3G6

Payroll Cheque No. 503

Date July 2, 19—

Pay to the Order of   John Blair $421.62

Four Hundred Twenty-One .... 62/100 Dollars

THE ROYAL BANK OF CANADA
BYRON VILLAGE CENTRE BRANCH
1240 COMMISSIONERS ROAD
LONDON, ONT. N6K 1C7

SUMMERHILL SALES COMPANY

George C. Brown

⑆02732⑆003⑈519⑈238⑊011⑊

One very important observation should be made about the employee's statement of earnings. Note the similarity in the arrangement of columns for "Earnings," "Deductions," and "Net Pay" to that of the form shown on both the payroll register (journal) and the employee's individual earnings record. Since the order is identical, it follows that the preparation of all three payroll forms might be done in one writing. This feature will be treated again in the next Topic, where the one-write system is featured for the payroll application.

3. As each payroll cheque is issued and signed by an authorized person or persons, the cheque number is entered in the payroll register for a

FIGURE 10-39

Total	Net Pay	Cheque No.
166 07	433 93	
165 89	464 11	
133 38	421 62	503
198 25	446 75	
173 88	424 12	
128 05	331 95	
110 97	357 03	
111 03	308 97	
1 187 52	3 188 48	

Paid July 2 19—

permanent record. Of course, to sign a great number of payroll cheques, many large firms will use signature plates containing a signature facsimile.

4. When these payroll cheques are all presented for payment, the amounts are debited by the bank against the firm's payroll bank account, and no balance should remain in that account. It is important to remember that the general current account of the employer's firm is not affected, since the payroll cheques were issued against the payroll bank account. Separating the payroll bank account from the general current account allows the employer to simplify month-end bank reconciliations of both accounts. Cancelled payroll cheques can be checked against the cheque listings in the payroll register, while cheques issued against the current account can be checked against their listings in the cash payments journal. A separate bank reconciliation can then follow for each bank account. The most efficient time to reconcile is immediately prior to each payroll, when most of the cheques issued for the preceding payroll should have been presented. A typical reconciliation of the payroll bank account may be prepared as in Figure 10-40.

FIGURE 10-40

Summerhill Sales Company
Reconciliation of Payroll Bank Account
As at July 6, 19—

Balance of payroll bank account as per bank statement		$1 090.12
Less: Outstanding payroll cheques:		
No. 505	$424.12	
No. 507	357.03	
No. 508	308.97	
Total outstanding payroll cheques		1 090.12
Balance of payroll bank account (if any) per our ledger		Nil

PAYING OF SALARIES AND WAGES BY BANK DEPOSIT   There is a growing trend among many firms to pay their employees by means of a deposit to the credit of an employee in his or her account in a chartered bank located near the employer's place of business. Some of the very large firms may make arrangements to transfer the employee's deposit to a chartered bank, trust company, or credit union of his or her choice. While the exact mechanics of processing such deposits may vary from firm to firm, some businesses contract a "package deal" with their bank. In general terms, the employer provides the bank with the necessary payroll data, while the bank processes the entire payroll through its computer. In return for a processing fee, the bank provides the employer with a payroll summary and takes care of the employees' payment by bank deposit as well. Regardless of the method used, it is important to understand that the laws of each province require that employees paid by bank deposit be provided with a statement to explain their earnings. To meet the legal requirements, employees' statement of earnings, such as the one illustrated in Figure 10-41, are usually given to each employee at work on payday.

FIGURE 10-41

STATEMENT OF EARNINGS AND DEDUCTIONS	DESCRIPTION	AMOUNT	TO DATE	DESCRIPTION	AMOUNT	TO DATE
	00 BASE PAY	1109 38	19968 84	DEDUCTIONS		
NOT NEGOTIABLE				13 G.P.P.	22 64	407 61
				14 U.I.	31 06	485 97
				15 FED. TAX	201 35	3644 79
				31 DENTAL	20 31	210 63
				44 LI INS TB		3 06—
				46 LTD	6 66	59 94
				50 PENSION	44 38	798 84
(–): REVERSAL	869 1 0250 030041436			51 PEN EMPR	55 48	998 64

JOHN G. TAGGART
367 ATLANTIS DR.
UREY, ONTARIO
M4T 2K8

PAYEE: JOHN CONWAY & CO. LTD.
PLEASE PAY FROM TO ISSUE DATE
RETAIN 18 30 09 —
THIS BANK BRANCH ACCOUNT NO GROSS PAY TOTAL DEDS NET PAY
PORTION 1653 24362 2907380 1109.38 326.40 ***782.98

Analyzing Other Payroll Disbursements

The paying of employees represents only one important disbursement of the payroll. Before other payroll disbursements are examined, it is useful to study the liability accounts created by the payroll in order to determine how much should be paid. Consider, for example, the general ledger in T-account form of Summerhill Sales Company immediately after the payment of wages and salaries to employees, shown in Figure 10-42.

FIGURE 10-42

```
         Cash            101              Wages Payable         210              Salaries Payable      211
    July 2   7 364.52         July 2  3 188.48 | June 30  3 188.48    July 2  4 176.04 | June 30  4 176.04

      CPP Contributions                                                         Income Tax Deductions
           Payable         212              UI Premium Payable       213               Payable         214
             | June 30    90.15                      | June 30     98.47                   | June 30    732.10
             | June 30   117.68                      | June 30    129.38                   | June 30    967.40
             | June 30    90.15                      | June 30    137.86
             | June 30   117.68                      | June 30    181.13                   | Balance   1 699.50
             | Balance   415.66                      | Balance    546.84

       Company Pension
         Plan Payable     215            Group Insurance Payable    216              EHT Payable       217
             | June 30   218.80                      | June 30     48.00                   | June 30    732.10
             | June 30   287.50                      | June 30     72.00                   | June 30    967.40
             | June 30   218.80
             | June 30   287.50                      | Balance    120.00                   | Balance   1 699.50
             | Balance   1 013.20
                         1012.60

         Wages Expense    515              Salaries Expense         516            Payroll Taxes Expense  517
  June 30  4 376.00               June 30  5 750.00                       June 30    489.69
                                                                          June 30    642.66
                                                                          Balance  1 132.35
```

From the illustration of ledger accounts related to the payrolls, observe that each liability account shows exactly the amount to be paid to the governments and others identified by the deductions section of the payroll registers. What remains now is to issue cheques to disburse the various payroll returns in accordance with the wishes of those requiring payment.

RETURN OF CPP, UI, AND INCOME TAXES Under federal law, the amount of income tax withheld from employees' earnings, together with the employee's and employer's contributions to the Canada Pension Plan and the employees' and employer's unemployment insurance premiums, must be remitted on a special form called the PD7AR form. This form is divided into four parts: Parts 1 and 2 are illustrated in Figure 10-43; Part 3 is a statement of account from Revenue Canada—Taxation; and Part 4 will be completed by the employer, though only when no more deductions are forthcoming, because the business is permanently or temporarily discontinued.

This form, along with a cheque or money order made payable to the Receiver General for Canada, must be paid at the bank at which the business has an account, or mailed to the appropriate Taxation Centre by the fifteenth of the month following that in which the payrolls are recorded.

From Figure 10-43, observe that the data to complete the necessary blocks is obtained from the balances of general ledger accounts for CPP Contributions Payable (employer's and employees' combined), UI Premium Payable

FIGURE 10-43

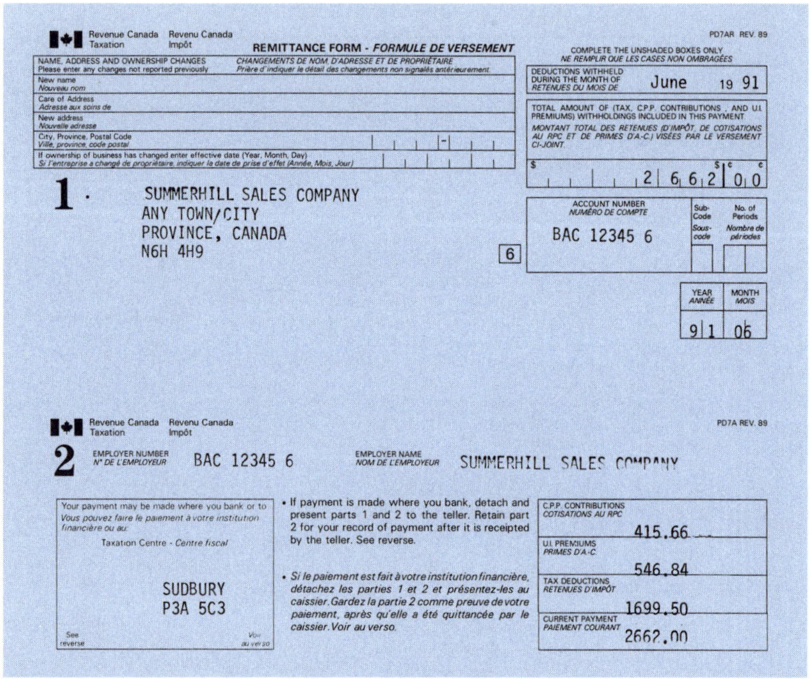
Revenue Canada Taxation / Revenu Canada Impôt

REMITTANCE FORM - *FORMULE DE VERSEMENT*

PD7AR REV. 89

NAME, ADDRESS AND OWNERSHIP CHANGES — *CHANGEMENTS DE NOM, D'ADRESSE ET DE PROPRIÉTAIRE*
Please enter any changes not reported previously — *Prière d'indiquer le détail des changements non signalés antérieurement*

New name / *Nouveau nom*

Care of Address / *Adresse aux soins de*

New address / *Nouvelle adresse*

City, Province, Postal Code / *Ville, province, code postal*

If ownership of business has changed enter effective date (Year, Month, Day) / *Si l'entreprise a changé de propriétaire, indiquer la date de prise d'effet (Année, Mois, Jour)*

COMPLETE THE UNSHADED BOXES ONLY / *NE REMPLIR QUE LES CASES NON OMBRAGÉES*

DEDUCTIONS WITHHELD DURING THE MONTH OF / *RETENUES DU MOIS DE* June 19 91

TOTAL AMOUNT OF (TAX, C.P.P. CONTRIBUTIONS, AND U.I. PREMIUMS) WITHHOLDINGS INCLUDED IN THIS PAYMENT / *MONTANT TOTAL DES RETENUES (D'IMPÔT, DE COTISATIONS AU RPC ET DE PRIMES D'A-C.) VISÉES PAR LE VERSEMENT CI-JOINT.*

$ 2 662 ¢ 00

1. SUMMERHILL SALES COMPANY
ANY TOWN/CITY
PROVINCE, CANADA
N6H 4H9

6

ACCOUNT NUMBER / *NUMÉRO DE COMPTE* BAC 12345 6

Sub-Code / *Sous-code*

No. of Periods / *Nombre de périodes*

YEAR / *ANNÉE* 91 — MONTH / *MOIS* 06

Revenue Canada Taxation / Revenu Canada Impôt

PD7A REV. 89

2 EMPLOYER NUMBER / *N° DE L'EMPLOYEUR* BAC 12345 6 — EMPLOYER NAME / *NOM DE L'EMPLOYEUR* SUMMERHILL SALES COMPANY

Your payment may be made where you bank or to / *Vous pouvez faire le paiement à votre institution financière ou au:*
Taxation Centre - *Centre fiscal*
SUDBURY
P3A 5C3
See reverse / *Voir au verso*

- If payment is made where you bank, detach and present parts 1 and 2 to the teller. Retain part 2 for your record of payment after it is receipted by the teller. See reverse.
- *Si le paiement est fait à votre institution financière, détachez les parties 1 et 2 et présentez-les au caissier. Gardez la partie 2 comme preuve de votre paiement, après qu'elle a été quittancée par le caissier. Voir au verso.*

C.P.P. CONTRIBUTIONS / *COTISATIONS AU RPC*	415.66
U.I. PREMIUMS / *PRIMES D'A-C*	546.84
TAX DEDUCTIONS / *RETENUES D'IMPÔT*	1699.50
CURRENT PAYMENT / *PAIEMENT COURANT*	2662.00

(employer's and employees' combined), and Income Tax Deductions Payable. Of course, the total of all these account balances represents the total amount to be remitted to the federal government. In the case of Summerhill Sales Company, a certified cheque for $2 662.00 would be issued, recorded, and analyzed as shown in Figure 10-44.

FIGURE 10-44

July 15	CPP Contributions Payable	415.66	
	UI Premium Payable	546.84	
	Income Tax Deductions Payable	1 699.50	
	Cash		2 662.00
	To record cheque issued to Receiver General for Canada as per form PD7AR.		

After the remittance is received, the bank teller or the Taxation Centre returns Part 2 of form PD7AR as a receipt. A blank remittance form to process next month's returns is mailed by Revenue Canada once the payment reaches the Taxation Centre.

RETURN OF COMPANY PENSION PLAN CONTRIBUTIONS
At designated monthly periods following the payroll, a cheque will be issued to the trust company, insurance company, or other agent handling the investment of money contributed to the company pension plan. Of course, an appropriate journal entry would be made to record this disbursement.

RETURN OF PROVINCIAL EMPLOYER HEALTH TAX
By a certain monthly date, each province will require the amounts imposed as the employer's health tax to be paid on an appropriate remittance form. In this case, a cheque for the correct amount would be made payable to the treasurer of the province. Payment of this liability is recorded in the same manner as payment of any other liability.

RETURN OF OTHER AMOUNTS OWING
For all other liabilities created by the payroll, a cheque must be issued to eliminate each liability. For example, a cheque would be issued to a life insurance company to eliminate Group Insurance Payable. Similarly, a cheque would be issued to the trade union for amounts collected as union initiation fees and union dues.

Preparing Annual Payroll Tax Statements and Returns

T4 Supplementary: the statement of remuneration paid, prepared by the employer for reporting salary, wages and taxable benefits paid, and deductions made from an employee during a specified calendar year.

On or before the last day of February of each year, employers are required to report returns to Revenue Canada—Taxation depending on the nature of their individual payrolls. For the 1990 taxation year, ten such returns were available to cover employers with different payroll plans. Only four of the most common returns will be treated in the sections that follow.

T4 SUPPLEMENTARY
Employers are required to give their employees their yearly earnings and deductions on the **T4 Supplementary** form, also known as the "Statement of Remuneration Paid," or simply the "T4

FIGURE 10-45

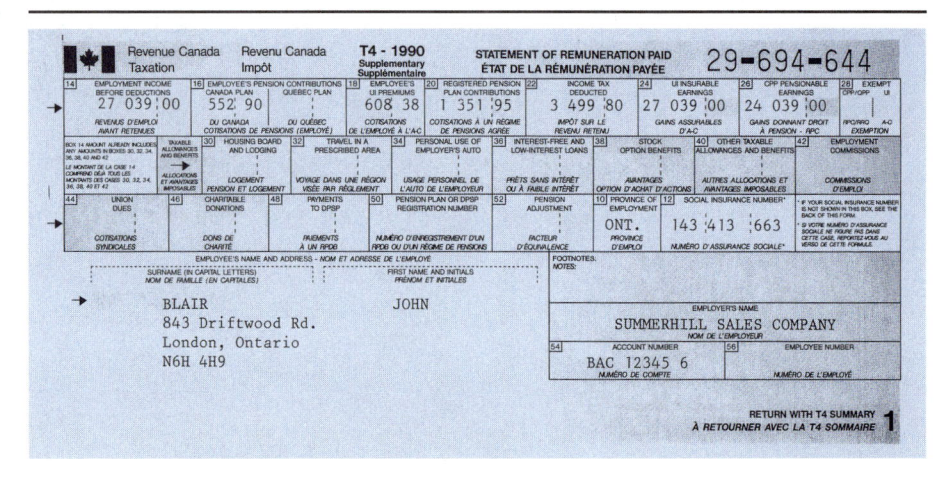

slip." A typical T4 slip, made out on behalf of John Blair for the 1990 tax year, is shown in Figure 10-45.

Notice that the employer must fill out important boxes headed "Employment Income Before Deductions," "Employee's Pension Contributions to Canada Plan," "Employee's UI Premiums," "Registered Pension Plan Contributions," "Income Tax Deducted," and "UI Insurable Earnings." Again, the information for completing these boxes is obtained from accounting ledgers. However, for the details on individual employees one would refer to the payroll ledger, where the employee's individual earnings record cards are filed.

After completing the four-copy set of T4 slips for all employees, the employer must mail or deliver copy 1 of each T4 Supplementary to Revenue Canada—Taxation by no later than February 28 of each year. Copies 2 and 3 must be given to the employee, also by no later than February 28, while copy 4 is retained by the employer for future reference. Copy 2 is attached to the employee's income tax return, which must be mailed by no later than April 30.

T4A SUPPLEMENTARY This tax "slip" is similar to the T4, except that the ***T4A Supplementary*** is a statement that reports a retired employee's pension income, retirement income, annuity paid by a trust or insurance company, or income earned other than through normal wages and salaries under a contract of employment. The T4A Supplementary is prepared in four parts and transmitted essentially as explained for the T4 Supplementary.

T4 AND T4A SUMMARIES (SUMMARY OF REMUNERATION PAID) Prior to 1990, the employer was required to report the totals of remuneration paid to workers on a combined T4-T4A Return. Beginning with the 1990 tax year, however, the T4 and T4A have been separated on individual forms. Briefly, the ***T4 Summary*** is completed by

---

T4A Supplementary: a statement of pension, retirement, annuity, and income other than normal wages and salaries under a contract of employment.

T4 Summary: a summary of remuneration paid, prepared by the employer, reporting the totals of all amounts recorded on T4 slips during a specified calendar year.

CHAPTER 10: Payroll Application

the employer to report the totals of all amounts recorded on the T4 Supplementaries, and the ***T4A Summary*** is completed by the employer to report the totals of all amounts recorded on T4A Supplementaries. The T4A Supplementary is used for reporting other amounts paid to an employee or retired employee such as pensions, annuities, etc. Obviously, the totals for completing both the T4 Supplementary and the T4A Supplementary would be obtained from appropriate accounts in the general ledger.

The payroll clerk should always refer to the latest issue of the *Employer's Guide to Source Deductions* or of *T4001(E)*, available on request from the nearest office of Revenue Canada—Taxation.

In addition to annual statements required by the federal government, clerks involved with payroll accounting may be required to complete a report for an individual province. For example, the Ontario Ministry of Revenue requires every employer to file an annual "Employer Health Tax Return," which will include a declaration of the total Ontario remuneration paid for the prior calendar year, the calculation of the difference between any installment payments made on behalf of the Employer Health Tax and the tax due, and the balance of EHT payable. Obviously, the purpose of this annual return is to reconcile the in-year installments (payments made during the year) to the annual tax due. Any tax then due must be remitted. Conversely, credits are either refunded or applied to future tax owing.

> T4A Summary: a summary of remuneration paid, prepared by the employer, reporting the totals of all amounts recorded on T4A slips (other amounts such as pensions or annuities paid to employees or retired employees).

TOPIC 3 Problems

> Recording totals for a weekly payroll for hourly-rated employees; recording the payment to employees through a payroll bank account; and recording remittances to the federal and provincial governments, trust companies, and insurance companies.

10.15 The payroll register for the Cambridge Printing Company showed the following totals for the hourly payroll for the week beginning June 24 and ending June 28.
- Earnings: regular, $4 706; overtime, $160; gross pay, $4 866
- Deductions: CPP, $110.50; UI, $79.56; income tax, $1 805.60; company pension plan (registered), $243.30; group insurance, $60; total, $2 298.96
- Net pay, $2 567.04

Required

a Record the payroll in the general journal. Assume that the employer is required by agreement to contribute equally to the employees' company pension plan. Also assume that the employer is required by provincial law to pay the employer's health tax in support of the provincial health insurance plan on the basis of 0.98% of gross earnings. All other expenses resulting from the payroll are in accordance with current legal requirements.

b Record the payment of the employees in the cash payments journal. (Assume that Cheque 151, dated June 9, was issued to transfer the necessary amount to the payroll bank account and that payroll cheques 630 numbered through 648 were issued on that date.)

c Record the following remittances in the cash payments journal: July 15, Cheque 160 for the required payment to the Receiver General for Canada; Cheque 161 to Canada Trust for the contributions to the registered company pension plan; July 15, Cheque 162 to the Treasurer—Province of Ontario for the Employer's Health Tax; July 17, Cheque 163 to the Ontario Insurance Company for the group insurance premium.

Preparing entries in general journal form to record payroll disbursements to the Receiver General for Canada, a trust company, an insurance company, and a charitable agency.

10.16 Refer back to the solution for Problem 10.10 of this chapter. Using the information of Problem 10.10, prepare entries in general journal form for the transactions summarized below. Show a brief explanation for each entry.

a July 12: Issued employees' earnings statements informing the employees that their net pays have been deposited by bank transfer in the bank account of their choice.

b August 15: Issued certified cheque to the Receiver General for Canada and enclosed form PD7AR to return the required amount for Canada Pension Plan, unemployment insurance, and income taxes. *Note:* Reference to subsequent weekly payrolls in July has been omitted to simplify the problem.

c August 15: Issued cheque to Canada Trust for contributions received on behalf of the registered company pension plan.

d August 16: Issued a cheque to North American Life Assurance Company covering the premiums for the group insurance plan.

e August 16: Issued a cheque to the United Way in remittance of payroll deductions for donations to the United Way.

Preparing entries in general journal form to record payroll disbursements arrived at in Problem 10.11 of Topic 2.

10.17 Refer back to the solution for Problem 10.11 of this chapter; then prepare entries in general journal form for the transactions identified below. Show a brief explanation for each entry.

a April 7: Issued Cheque 301 to transfer the necessary amount to the payroll bank account. Also issued payroll cheques P1001 to P1007.

b April 15: Issued the following cheques: No. 310 to the Receiver General for Canada in compliance with remittance form PD7AR; No. 311 to Canada Trust in payment of the required contributions to the registered company pension plan; No. 312 to Canada Life Assurance Company for the premium to the group insurance plan; and No. 313 to Local 1000, United Employees' Union, for the total union dues collected.

c April 15: Issued Cheque 314 to the Treasurer—Province of Ontario for the amount of EHT payable. (Refer to part **e** of Problem 10.11.)

Preparing entries in general journal form to record payroll disbursements arrived at in Problem 10.12 of Topic 2.

10.18 Refer back to the solution for Problem 10.12 of this chapter; then record in general journal form all disbursements resulting from the salaried payroll for the week ending April 7. Assume that the employees are paid by payroll cheques issued against the payroll bank account and that the date of such cheques is April 7. Assume also that all other remittances are made on April 15.

Preparing payroll cheques for two employees.

10.19 Return to the hourly payroll register solved for Problem 10.10. From the information it contains prepare payroll cheques P1006 and P1007 for M. Shinagawa and R. Strople respectively. Use a payroll voucher cheque form similar to the one illustrated in this chapter. Check to see that the details of the employee's statement of earnings (the voucher) correspond with the details recorded in the payroll register.

Preparing the required payroll disbursements for Problem 10.13.

10.20 Refer back to the solution for Problem 10.13 and prepare entries in general journal form for the transactions identified below. Show a brief explanation for each entry.
  a June 30: Issued Cheque 401 to transfer the necessary amount to the payroll bank account. Also issued payroll cheques P101 to P112.
  b July 15: Issued the following cheques: No. 402 to the Receiver General for Canada in compliance with remittance form PD7AR; No. 403 to Canada Trust in payment of the required contributions to the registered company pension plan; and No. 404 to London Life Assurance Company for the premium to the group insurance plan.
  c July 15: Issued Cheque 405 to the Treasurer—Province of Ontario for the amount of EHT Payable. (Refer to part **e** of Problem 10.13.)

Preparing a T4 Supplementary for one employee.

10.21 Return to Problem 10.14. From the information given, prepare the yearly T4 slip for Charles J. Molyneaux on a T4 slip similar to the one illustrated in this chapter.

TOPIC 4 Applying Manual Shortcuts to Payroll Accounting

In businesses with fewer than ten employees, two manual shortcuts are quite popular in payroll accounting. One is to take advantage of commercially prepared forms that are widely available through leading bookstores and stationery shops; another is to use a one-write system like the one developed by Safeguard Business Systems Inc.

Using Commercially Prepared Payroll Forms

Instead of designing their own payroll forms, owner-managers of small businesses may prefer simply to purchase commercially prepared ones that are widely available through leading bookstores and stationery shops.

For example, for timekeeping, Brownline (published by Esselte Pendaflex Canada Inc.) offers a variety of timekeeping books for different pay periods. Figure 10-46 illustrates a blank page from Brownline's Weekly Time Book; Figure 10-47 is a page from the payroll report.

As you can see, the Time Book may be used to account for time for both hourly and salaried workers. The columns are self-explanatory. In addition to timekeeping books, Brownline also offers a booklet of payroll

464 PART 2: COMMON ACCOUNTING APPLICATIONS

FIGURE 10-46

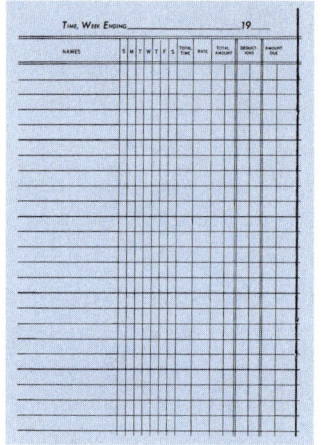

FIGURE 10-47

FIGURE 10-48

reports in duplicate forms, as illustrated in the side margin. Obviously, this payroll report would serve as a statement of earnings for an employee.

A second enterprise worth noting in commercially prepared forms and books for manual payroll systems is Dean et Fils Inc. This business specializes in the publication of the Dean Payroll Book and the Dean Employee's Payroll Statement. The two publications complement each other.

Briefly, the Dean Payroll Book is designed for small and medium-size businesses which prefer a manual payroll application. The book includes a payroll recapitulation, a record of remittances to governments, and a list of all employees for quick reference. In addition, the book offers a set of easily followed instructions, as shown in Figure 10-49. Obviously, the payroll clerk would also have for use the latest copy of Revenue Canada's *Employer's Guide to Source Deductions* and the book outlining source deductions for the province in which the business is located.

In addition to the Dean Payroll Book, the publisher provides employee's payroll statements in booklets containing 100 sheets. As you learned earlier, government regulations stipulate that the employer must provide every employee with a statement of earnings and deductions with each pay. The Dean payroll statements provide that information for businesses in which the number of employees does not justify the use of special payroll voucher cheques. A typical Dean employee's payroll statement is shown in Figure 10-48.

From the illustration one can conclude that the Dean employee payroll statement is easy to us, since the payroll clerk merely copies entries from the Dean Payroll Book in the same sequence. The statement can then be enclosed with a regular cheque or cash when the employee is paid.

Using the One-Write System

Safeguard Business Systems Inc. offers a payroll one-write system tailored to the needs of small and medium-sized payrolls. Like the one-write systems applied earlier for accounts receivable and accounts payable, Safeguard's One-Write Payroll System offers advantages over the traditional manual system. The three main advantages are:

FIGURE 10-49a

EMPLOYEE'S EARNINGS

SOCIAL INSURANCE NUMBER: 2 2 2 3 3 3 4 4 4

NAME: Dolittle, John

ADDRESS: 3rd Avenue

TOWN: Anytown

PROVINCE / POSTAL CODE:

TELEPHONE: (777) 999-3333

FORMER EMPLOYER:

FORMER OCCUPATION:

DATE OF BIRTH: YEAR 55 / MONTH 12 / DAY 04

WILL REACH 18 ☐ OR 70 ☐ YEARS

MALE ☑ FEMALE ☐

SINGLE ☐ MARRIED ☑

DIVORCED ☐ WIDOW(ER) ☐

NUMBER OF DEPENDENTS: 2

EXEMPTION CODES — TD1 FEDERAL: 5

TYPE OF WORK: Mechanic

JOB CODE: Class 2   **UNION:** C.P.A.

DATE OF EMPLOYMENT: YEAR 78 / MONTH 01 / DAY 04

RATE OF WAGES AND REVISIONS:

DATE	HOURLY	WEEKLY	OTHER
89/10/10	8.44		

Empl. terminated / Date notice given:

REASON:

VACATION PERIODS: FROM July 15th TO July 31st

SECTIONS IDENTIFIED WITH A CAPITAL LETTER OR ASTERISK(*) ARE TO BE TRANSFERRED TO EMPLOYEE'S PAYROLL STATEMENT

ALL RIGHTS RESERVED © DEAN ET FILS INC.

JANUARY

Line	Week Ending	S	M	T	W	T	F	S	C Reg.	D x1½	E x2	(f) Hours Paid	G Wages	H Other Earnings (Bonus)	I Total Earnings	J Taxable Benefits	(k) Total Taxable
1	6		8	8	8	8	8		40			40	337.60	500.00	837.60		837.60
2	13		9	9	8	8	8		40	2		43	362.92		362.92		362.92
3	20		8	8	8	8	8		40			40	337.60		337.60		337.60
4	27		8	10	10	10	8		40	6		49	413.56		413.56		413.56

MONTHLY TOTALS ▶

INSTRUCTIONS

The following instructions will help you with the use of the Dean Payroll Book. This book has been designed for general use by small and medium size businesses in all provinces of Canada, except Quebec. The example shown is purely fictitious, amounts and entries may differ from one province to another.

For specific cases, please see your accountant.

EMPLOYEE'S FILE

At the far left of the payroll sheet is the employee's personal file. Indicate relevant information in the appropriate sections.

The following sections require some explanation:

Will reach 18 or 70: This section is only important for the purpose of calculating the number of months the employee is subject to a Government Pension Plan.
(See the appropriate guide. ‡°).

Exemption codes: As per forms TD1 and TPD 1 completed annually by the employee or following any change in status, fill in the appropriate code. This code is used to determine the amount of tax to be deducted at source.

Job code: As per collective agreement or job classification.

Information in sections marked with an asterisk (*) is to be brought forward to the "Employee's Payroll Statement."

EMPLOYEE'S EARNINGS / EMPLOYEE'S DEDUCTIONS

All columns and lines are respectively identified by a letter and a number to facilitate transfer to the "Payroll Recapitulation" at the back of the book.

Columns identified with a capital letter are to be transferred to the "Employee's Payroll Statement."

COLUMNS

A   Week ending: Fill in date indicating end of week.

(b) Daily hours worked: Indicate the number of hours worked each day.
NOTE: Statutory paid holidays or their replacement date can be indicated by a distinctive mark in the proper daily entry. E.g. "PH" for "Paid Holiday" and add number of regular hours for this day to "hours paid", column (f). (See example above). For further information, communicate with your provincial department of labour about paid statutory holidays.

C   Regular: Total hours paid at regular rate.

D   × 1½: Overtime hours paid at time-and-a-half.

E   × 2: Overtime hours paid at double time.

(f) Hours paid: Total of columns C, D multiplied by 1½, and E multiplied by 2.

G   Wages: Column (f) multiplied by the hourly rate. If employee is paid weekly or on any other regular basis, fill in the corresponding amount in this column.

H   Other earnings: Bonuses, commissions, vacation pay, etc.

I   Total earnings: Total of columns G and H.

J   Taxable benefits: Value of benefits received — such as company car, free lodging or others. (See guides concerning deductions at source ‡).

(k) Total taxable: Total of columns I and J.

Continued on next page

ANNUAL TOTALS ▶

FIGURE 10-49b

L REG'D PENSION PLAN	M UNION DUES	(n) TAXABLE EARNINGS FEDERAL	GOVERNMENT PENSION PLAN O DED.	(p) CUMUL.	UNEMPLOYMENT INSURANCE Q INS. EARN.	R DED.	(s)	T FEDERAL INCOME TAX	U	V HEALTH INS.	W GROUP INS.	X OTHER DEDUCTIONS	Y TOTAL DEDUCTIONS	Z AMOUNT PAID	AA CHEQUE NO. OR DATE
	2 93	834 67	16 51	16 51	605 00	11 80		214 05					245 29	592 31	
	1 45	361 47	6 53	23 04	362 92	7 08		40 35					55 41	307 51	
	1 27	336 33	6 00	29 04	337 60	6 58		28 85					42 70	294 90	
	1 65	411 91	7 56	36 60	413 56	8 06		54 45					71 72	341 84	

INSTRUCTIONS
Continued from previous page

L Registered pension plan: Amount deducted for employee's contribution to a registered pension plan.

M Union dues: Amount deducted for employee's union dues.

(n) Taxable earnings — Federal: Column K minus L and M.

O Government Pension Plan — Deduction: Amount deducted for employee's contributions. (For amounts and exclusions, see guides ‡ °).

(p) Government Pension Plan — Cumulative: Cumulative contributions of employee up to maximum amount allowable. (See guides ‡ °).

Q Unemployment Insurance — Insurable earnings: Indicate insurable earnings. (See guide°).

R Unemployment Insurance — Deduction: Amount deducted for employee's contribution. (See guide°).

(s) For other deductions where applicable.

T Income tax — Federal: The deduction at source is determined using the amount appearing in column (n). (See guide for tax tables ‡).

U For other deductions where applicable.

V Health insurance: Amount deducted for employee's contribution to health insurance plan.

W Group insurance: Amount deducted for employee's contribution to a group insurance plan.

X Other deductions: These two columns remain available for any additional deductions.

Y Total deductions: Total of columns L, M, O, R, T, U, V, W and X.

Z Amount paid: Column I minus column Y.

‡ *Income tax deductions at source — Revenue Canada-Taxation.*
° *Canada pension plan contribution and unemployment insurance premium tables — Revenue Canada-Taxation.*

Additional instructions on last page.

- **It saves time** The payroll register, individual employee's ledger card, and payroll cheque are completed simultaneously—in one writing.
- **It improves accuracy** Since the essential payroll records are completed in one writing, transposition errors are completely eliminated.
- **Payroll tax reporting is made easy** Essential payroll records are always up to date and in balance. Therefore, individual employee earnings records are readily available for tax reporting.

PAYROLL LAYOUT A typical payroll layout in Safeguard's system is illustrated in Figure 10-50. Although the illustration shows an American payroll application, similar payroll forms are available for Canadian practice. The step-by-step procedures are identical regardless of the payroll forms used.

1. First, the Payroll Summary (Register) (Journal) is loaded, by placing its holes over the metal pegs of the accounting board.
2. Second, carbon or NCR paper is placed on the Payroll Summary.
3. Next, a set of "shingled" cheques is loaded onto the metal pegs with the carbon strip of the first cheque just covering the first blank line of the Payroll Summary. Note that each cheque contains a layer of carbon along the top edge on the reverse side of that cheque.
4. Finally, the employee's individual earnings card (payroll ledger card) is inserted below the set of shingled cheques so that the

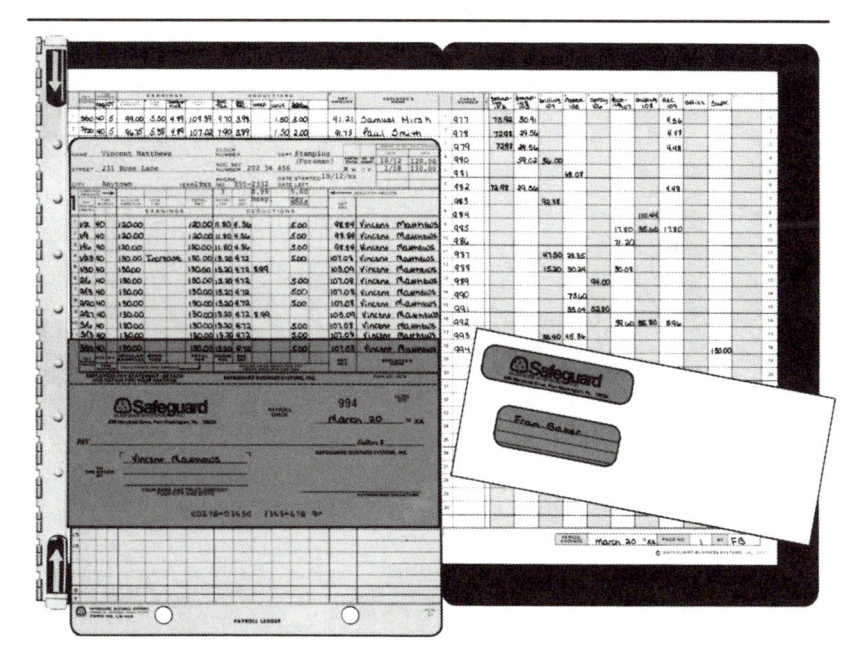

FIGURE 10-50

468 PART 2: COMMON ACCOUNTING APPLICATIONS

carbon strip of the statement section of the cheque covers the appropriate blank line of the card.

WRITING THE PAYROLL CHEQUE
As you can observe from the illustration, the payroll cheque consists of two sections: the cheque and the employee's pay statement. The statement section is located above the perforations at the top of the cheque. The recommended sequence for completing the payroll cheque and payroll summary sheet is as follows:

1. Begin at the extreme left and complete the blocks for "Pay Period Ending," "Time Worked," "Regular Earnings," any "Overtime," "Total Pay," the appropriate deductions earlier computed for the employee, the "Net Pay," and "Employee's Name."

2. On the journal sheet, complete the box for "Cheque Number"; then enter the amount(s) in the appropriate distribution column(s). For example, in the case of Vincent Matthews, the amount of his gross earnings is placed in the "Supv." (supervisor) column, as shown in Figure 10-51.

3. After the one-write entry is completed—that is, the employee's pay statement (upper part of the cheque form), the employee's individual earnings record (payroll ledger card), and the payroll register (payroll summary)—the cheque and ledger card are re-

FIGURE 10-51

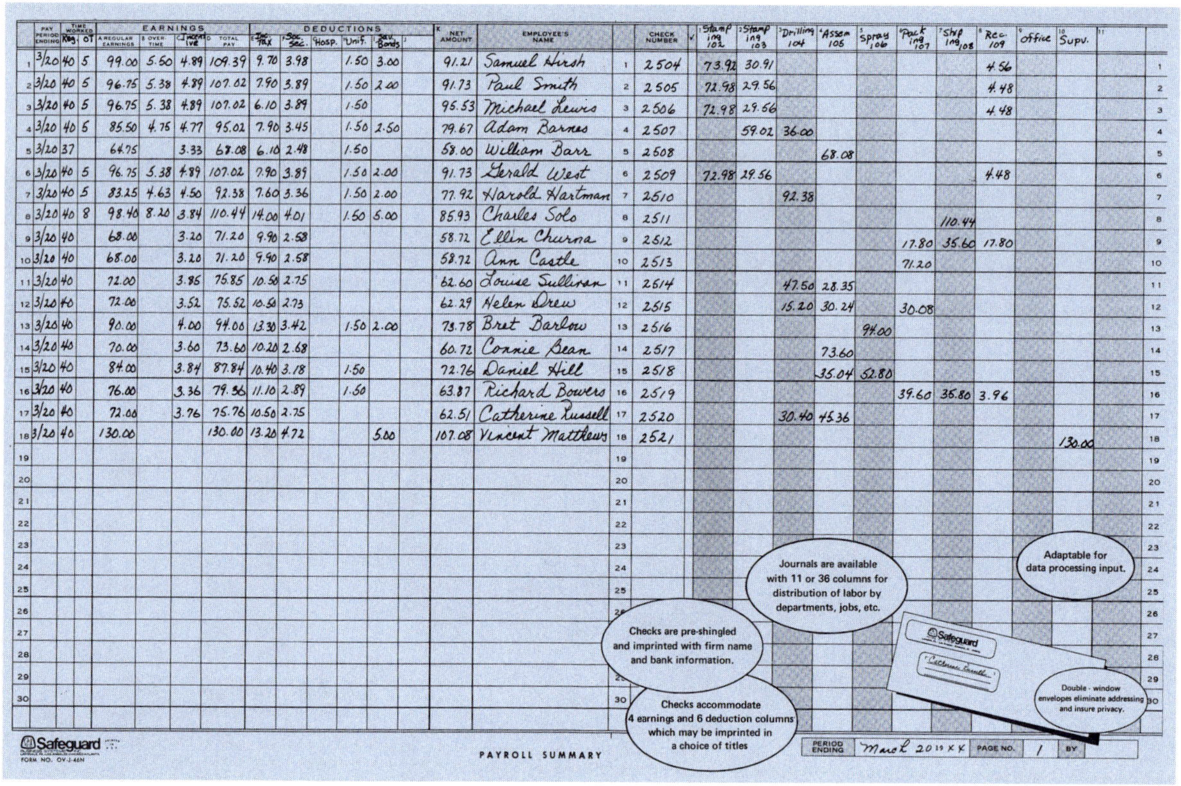

moved from the board. A perforated edge is at the left edge of the cheque so that it can be removed easily.
4. On the cheque itself, removed from the board, the payroll clerk would write the amount of the employee's net pay on the "Pay" line. As with any cheque, the net pay amount is written in words and figures in the appropriate sections. Then, the employee's name would be entered opposite "To the Order of."
5. If the cheque is to be mailed, the employee's address would be entered below the name.
6. The cheque and employee's pay statement can then be inserted in a double-window envelope for mailing or for privacy during payroll distribution.
7. The next employee's individual earnings card can now be inserted and the process repeated.

MONTHLY ACCOUNTING PROCEDURES In a small payroll system, the accounting of the column totals as disclosed by the payroll journal (register) sheets, as well as the additional employer's payroll taxes, may be delayed until the end of the month when the hired accountant arrives to do the month-end accounting. On the other hand, in some practices, these entries may be treated immediately after each payroll run. Regardless of timing, you will recall from the study of Topic 2 that the payroll summary should be proved before journal entries are made of the journals and posting occurs to appropriate general ledger accounts.

Because of the one-write feature of the system, proving the Payroll Summary assures the accuracy of all entries on all forms. The following formulae can be used on the Safeguard system for line proof and/or page proof. Of course, the Payroll Summary should always be proved before the information is written on the cheque:

1. Regular Earnings column total *plus* Overtime column total *plus* any other earnings = Total Pay column total.
2. Total Pay column *minus* grand total of all Deduction columns = Net Amount column total.
3. If the pay is distributed, Total Pay column total = grand total of all Distribution columns.

Once the Payroll Summary is proved successfully, general journal entries may be made and posting can occur to all accounts affected by the payroll. Subsequently, appropriate disbursements may be made as discussed in Topic 3.

TOPIC 4   Problems

Completing a weekly time sheet and payroll record for one employee, using Brownline's payroll forms.

10.22 Joan Mader has just completed her first work week at Nairn Road Farm Supply. The contract of employment required her signing in and out each day for a six-day work week at rate of $10 per hour with time-and-a-half for working after 5:00 p.m. Regular hours are from 8:00 a.m. to 5:00 p.m. with an hour off for lunch. An analysis of the sign-in register showed the following data for the week ending March 31, current year: Monday, 8 hours; Tuesday, 7 hours; Wednesday, 8 hours plus 1 hour overtime; Thursday, 8 hours; Friday, 8 hours; Saturday, 4 hours. Assume the following payroll data for Joan Mader: employee no., 425-865-798; Net Claim Code as per TD1, 1; and deductions for only income tax, unemployment insurance, and Canada Pension Plan.

Required

a Assume that the employer uses Brownline's Weekly Time Book to account for the work time of all employees. As the payroll clerk, record Joan Mader's work time for the week ending March 31 on a Brownline Weekly Time Sheet as illustrated in this chapter.

b On a Brownline Payroll Record form similar to the one illustrated in this chapter, complete the payroll record for Joan Mader's work week ending March 31. Use the deduction tables illustrated in this chapter or ones available from the latest source deduction tables for your province.

Completing a payroll register based on the Dean Payroll Book; completing Dean payroll statements for four employees.

10.23 William Brintnell, D.D.S. prefers to use the Dean Payroll Book and Dean payroll statements to process his dental practice's weekly salary payroll. The data below is a summary taken from time sheets accounting for the time worked for four salaried employees for the week ending May 31:

- Shirley Buckborough: SIN, 345-789-123; Net Claim Code, 1; dental receptionist at a weekly salary of $450. No overtime, no absences recorded.
- Gail Elgie: SIN, 445-889-665; Net Claim Code, 2; dental assistant at a weekly salary of $500. No overtime, no absences recorded.
- Rosa Meyerhoffer: SIN, 679-234-908; Net Claim Code, 2; dental hygienist at a weekly salary of $600. Four hours' overtime at $22.50 per hour.
- Marilyn Oneschuk: SIN, 214-338-993; Net Claim Code, 1; office manager at a weekly salary of $700. No absences recorded.

Required

a Record the payroll for the week ending May 31 on forms simulating the Dean Payroll Book illustrated in this chapter.

b Prepare the employee's payroll statements on a Dean simulated statement for the four salaried employees. Make up appropriate data to complete the boxes on this form where necessary.

Listing and explaining payroll pegboard system components.

10.24 List the individual components that make up the payroll pegboard system treated in this chapter; then offer a brief explanation of the main function of each item.

Answering questions on the one-write payroll system.

10.25 Answer the following questions about the processing of the payroll application on the Safeguard one-write system. (Refer to the illustrations in this chapter.)

a In what order should the accounting forms that make up the accounting set for processing a payroll be placed on the writing board?

CHAPTER 10: Payroll Application   471

b When is the employee's individual earnings record placed on the board? Explain your answer.

c Briefly explain how the one-write principle is achieved for a payroll application.

Processing a payroll run from given information.

10.26 Assume that you have been engaged as the payroll clerk for the dental office of Lillian Thompson, D.D.S. of your town/city and province. For the weekly payroll, assume the following data:

- Receptionist-clerk: your own name; Net Claim Code, 1; weekly salary, $490
- Dental assistant: Helen Soderquest; Net Claim Code, 1; weekly salary, $500
- Hygienist: Heidi Potvin; Net Claim Code, 2; weekly salary, $650

Required

a On a separate form prior to entering the data on a pay statement, show the deductions for each employee for CPP, UI, and the health insurance premium of your province, if applicable. Use the latest booklet of tables for CPP, UI, and income tax or the tables illustrated in this chapter.

b On separate pay statements similar to the ones illustrated in this chapter, simulate the one-write payroll application by completing a pay statement for each employee. Assume that the pay period is for the weekly period ending June 30.

c In general journal form, show the double entry to record the dollar results of the weekly payroll.

d In general journal form, show the double entry to record the employer's additional expenses resulting from the weekly payroll. (If you are located in a province like Ontario, account for the employer's health tax on the basis of 0.98% of total gross earnings.)

e Set up a T-account general ledger for all accounts related to the payroll; then post all data to the appropriate accounts.

f From the T-account ledger in **e**, how much must be remitted to the federal government on form PD7AR? (Refer back to Topic 3 if you have forgotten the details of form PD7AR.)

Chapter Summary

Payroll accounting would include the following activities: timekeeping; computing gross earnings, deductions, and the net pay for each employee; recording the payroll and maintaining detailed payroll records; disbursing the various cash payments to employees, governments, and other agencies; and preparing annual tax statements and returns.

All payroll applications begin with the timekeeping of employees who are authorized by management for payroll purposes. The actual accounting of time spent on the job with each employee may be done under an elaborate clock card system or a simple time book which keeps track of each employee's daily work time and/or absentees. In the majority of cases, the person in charge of employees should authorize the correctness of all timekeeping before any payroll is processed.

Once the gross earnings of employees have been computed and authorized for payroll processing, a payroll clerk under a manual system would compute deductions such as for the Canada Pension Plan, unemployment insurance, and income taxes. For purposes of determining each deduction, Revenue Canada—Taxation annually publishes booklets titled *Source Deductions* for each province. In addition, the Taxation Centre publishes annually *Employer's Guide to Source Deductions*, which gives specific information on each deduction required by federal law. All payroll clerks should use both publications to process any payroll.

After gross earnings, deductions from gross earnings and the net pay for each employee are computed, the payroll application normally requires the recording of the payroll in a summary record called the payroll register. Payroll registers may be prepared separately for each type of payroll plan. Therefore, management may prefer to summarize the payroll of hourly-rated employees in a separate hourly payroll register, of salaried employees in a separate salary payroll register, etc.; or the employer may prefer to use a combined payroll register summarizing the payroll for all types of employees.

Every payroll register should be proved before any disbursement is made. In general, proving a payroll register requires the totalling of all columns and cross-checking of those columns to prove that the total gross earnings less the total deductions is equal to the total of the net pay column.

Once the payroll register is proved, individual amounts may be posted from the register to appropriate employee's individual earning record. In general, these individual earnings records form the basis of a subsidiary payroll register which stores all of the employees' files.

In addition to posting individual amounts, the totals of the payroll register must be journalized or directly posted to appropriate accounts in the general ledger. The total gross earnings would be debited to a payroll expense account such as Wages Expense, Salaries Expense, or Wages and Salaries Expense. Each deduction would be credited to an appropriate current liability account. For example, the contribution to the Canada Pension Plan and the employee's UI premium may be credited to CPP Contributions Payable and UI Premium Payable respectively. The total net pay would also be credited to a current liability such as Wages Payable, Salaries Payable, or Wages and Salaries Payable.

Payroll accounting is also responsible for accounting for the extra employer's expenses resulting from each payroll. For example, the employer's required contribution to CPP, the required UI premium, and any amount required as an employer's health tax to a provincial government may be recorded in separate current liability accounts with the total being debited to an account called Payroll Taxes Expense.

Payroll disbursements involve the control and accounting of cash payments to clear the current liability accounts resulting from payroll summaries. One major cash disbursement involves the payment of employees, who may be paid by cash, by cheque, or by deposit transfer. Many businesses use a special payroll bank account to clear payroll cheques issued to many employees.

A second important payroll disbursement involves the regular payment made to the Receiver General for Canada for the total of three current liability accounts: CPP Payable, UI Premium Payable, and Employees' Income Tax Deductions Payable. In general, this payment must be accompanied by the completion of form PD7AR.

Other payroll disbursements may include the clearance of amounts owing to registered company pension plans, employer's health tax, group insurance, etc. A debit would be made to the appropriate current liability account and a credit would be shown for the cheque issued.

The final payroll function is to prepare annual tax summaries and statements in accordance with federal and provincial government regulations. The federal government requires the completion of a number of tax statements and summaries to be processed by no later than February 28 of which four important ones are the T4 Supplementary, T4A Supplementary, T4 Summary, and T4A Summary.

In general, the T4 Supplementary is prepared as a statement of remuneration paid to each employee. Two copies would be mailed or submitted to each employee. One copy would be mailed to a designated taxation centre and another would be kept by the employer for filing. The T4A Supplementary is a similar form but prepared as a statement of pension, retirement, annuity, and other income paid by employer and appropriate business concerns. On the other hand, the T4 Summary and T4A Summary are summaries reporting the totals of all amounts reported by individual T4 and T4A Supplementaries.

Two important shortcuts are available to businesses using a manual accounting system to process regular payrolls for a small number of employees. One popular one is to use commercially prepared payroll forms from leading bookstores and stationery shops. Among these are time books, time sheets, and payroll reports produced by Brownline (Esselte Pendaflex Canada Inc.), and the Dean Payroll Book and Dean Payroll Statements produced by Dean et Fils Inc.

A second popular manual shortcut is to use a one-write system such as the one produced by Safeguard Business Systems Inc. Under a one-write system, the employee's cheque, the employee's individual earnings record, and the payroll register are processed in one writing, thus saving record-keeping time and eliminating errors made in copying data and figures from one individual payroll form to another. Of course, serious limitations occur when any manual system is used to process the payroll for hundreds of employees. In this case, a computerized system is normally used.

Chapter Questions

1. From an accounting viewpoint, why are employees hired in most profit-seeking enterprises?
2. State two reasons why large and small firms alike must organize an efficient payroll accounting system.

3. In general, state six important activities that make up an efficient payroll accounting system.
4. Name three pieces of information that are important for the processing of any employee's payroll.
5. Describe the various plans used to pay employees.
6. Mary Best has weekly gross earnings of $600, yet her take-home pay is only $410. List several possible reasons for the difference.
7. Explain briefly how legislation affects hours of work and wages.
8. What internal control measure is usually supported to account for an employee's working time under the hourly-rate plan? Under the salary plan?
9. Do deductions for unemployment insurance represent credits to an employee's savings account? Explain why or why not.
10. By federal law, the employer is required to contribute a premium to the unemployment insurance fund. How is this employer's contribution calculated?
11. Under the Canada Pension Plan Act, what contribution is required by employers on behalf of their employees' contribution?
12. "Employee's contributions to the Canada Pension Plan and deductions for their UI premium are tax-deductible." Explain the meaning of this statement.
13. Most company pension plans are registered pension plans. Explain the meaning of such a plan.
14. On what two factors does the amount of income tax withheld from an employee's earnings depend?
15. Under the present Income Tax Act, the amount of personal non-refundable tax credits changes every year. Explain why.
16. What is form TD1, and when must it be completed by an employee?
17. What is an employee's Net Claim Code, and why is this code important in payroll accounting?
18. Does a high Net Claim Code mean that the amount of tax withheld will also be high? Explain why or why not.
19. In general terms, outline the steps to be followed for the correct use of the income tax deduction tables which are supplied by the Department of National Revenue—Taxation.
20. Use an example to explain the difference between a garnishment and a government demand on employee's earnings.
21. Are payroll deductions for union dues covered by law? Explain why or why not.
22. Name five "voluntary" deductions that may be found in many payroll accounting applications.
23. What information does the employee's individual earnings record contain? Why are both a payroll register and an employee's individual earnings record used in an accounting application?

24 What are the source documents for computing an employee's gross pay? An employee's deductions?

25 Two types of entries are required each pay period to record the payroll. What is the purpose of each entry, and what accounts are affected?

26 Explain the difference between payroll journal, payroll register, and payroll summary.

27 Explain the meaning of the account called "Payroll Taxes Expense" in payroll accounting.

28 Explain the advantages of using a special payroll bank account in a large payroll accounting system.

29 How must an employer remit contributions for the Canada Pension Plan? Employees' deductions for income taxes? Premiums to unemployment insurance?

30 Explain briefly the employer's responsibilities in preparing and remitting the annual T4 slip. Explain the use of each copy and identify the due date by which this tax slip must be mailed or delivered.

31 Explain the similarity between the payroll journal (summary), the employee's individual earnings record, and the employee's pay statement under a one-write payroll system.

32 Summarize the main advantages and limitations of a one-write payroll system.

Accounting Case Problems

CASE 10-1

Calculating the CPP for one employee hired on a commission basis only; calculating the amount of the employer's contribution.

Vera Nisbet is continuously employed by Richardson Sales Company strictly on a commission basis. According to the contract of employment, the commission is paid only when a sale is completed, which does not occur at regular intervals. Assume that Vera Nisbet is paid $700 commission 73 days after being paid the last commission.

As the payroll clerk, you are required to calculate the amount of this employee's contribution to the Canada Pension Plan. You discover that the CPP contribution tables cannot be used, because the salesperson works on an irregular basis. However, you have checked the government booklet under "Schedule 1—Canada Pension Plan" to learn the following facts for the current year: year's maximum pensionable earnings, $30 500; year's basic exemption, $3 000; maximum earnings on which contributions are based, $27 500; maximum employee contribution, 2.3% of $27 500; and maximum employer contribution, 2.3% of $27 500.

What calculations would you make to prorate the employee's contribution to the Canada Pension Plan? How much would the employer contribute in this case? Show calculations.

CASE 10-2

Analyzing the payment of a payroll to employees in cash only.

X Company Limited is required by a basic agreement to pay wages to construction workers in cash. Tom Estay, a payroll clerk, completes carefully the change sheet for payroll and the currency requisition. A cheque for $250 000 is issued to Tom, who cashes the cheque at a nearby bank. At the bank, Tom also prepares each employee's pay envelope with the correct change.

On his return from the bank, Tom is held at gunpoint by two robbers. Fortunately, the gunmen are frightened away by a passing police car which, in turn, escorts Tom safely to his employer's place of business. Tom promptly hands the bags containing the pay envelopes to Jack Jones, the paymaster, who quickly locks the cash in his desk drawer for overnight safekeeping.

The next day, all pay envelopes are claimed by the employees except one marked for Ed Hurst. A few hours later, a woman claiming to be Mrs. Ed Hurst appears at the paymaster's office to claim her husband's pay. After receiving an identification card, the paymaster gives the pay envelope to the woman, who later turns out to be an imposter.

If you were the chief accounting officer for the company, what protective steps would you include to cover: (a) delivering funds to the company; (b) filling pay envelopes; (c) safekeeping of funds prior to payment; (d) issuing pay envelopes; and (e) handling unclaimed pay envelopes?

CHAPTER **11** Using Microcomputer Software to Process Common Accounting Applications

After completing this chapter, you should be able to:

— Identify three characteristics that support the concept that general accounting packages for microcomputers differ.
— Distinguish clearly between real-time accounting and batch processing accounting.
— Present an overview of Bedford's Accounting System and identify the main characteristics of each accounting module under this system.
— Present an overview of AccPac Plus's Accounting System and identify the main characteristics of each accounting module under this system.
— Present an overview of Summation's Accounting System and identify the main characteristics of each accounting module under this system.
— Present an overview of Easypay's Payroll System and explain how this Canadian system may be interfaced with another microcomputer's general accounting package.
— Answer specific questions on the DYNA Dental Office Management System, identify DYNA menus for processing dental transactions, explain how posting to the G/L is achieved under DYNA, and prepare a memo to explain DYNA and its main advantages over the traditional one-write system.
— Define the following key terms used in this chapter: menu bar, company window, fully integrated accounting package, integration accounts, vendors, open-item accounting, average cost method, modular-type accounting software, batch-operated system, posting journal, source journal, Easypay, \EASYPAY, \EASYPAY\OLAS, vertical accounting package, DYNA, Xenix, xenix286!login.

The main objective of this final chapter is to expose you to a few microcomputer accounting packages that are programmed to process common accounting applications like the general ledger, accounts receivable, accounts payable, and payroll.

As stated earlier, microcomputer accounting packages may be classified into two groups: those accounting packages that are general in nature and are available through dealers as "off-the-shelf" packages; and those

477

"customized" accounting packages that are specifically written for specialized businesses such as dental and medical practices.

Topic 1 presents an introduction to five general accounting packages in Canadian use; Topic 2 examines one customized accounting package that is in popular use in Canadian dental practices.

TOPIC 1 — Examining General Accounting Packages

As stated in Chapter 5, all microcomputer accounting packages have characteristics that must be considered before a user considers adopting one. Three are worth reemphasizing.

- All accounting packages must be written to run under a specific operating system. Therefore, AccPac Bedford, written for the MS-DOS, will not run under the Macintosh Finder Operating System. Similarly AccPac Bedford, written for the Macintosh Finder Operating System, will not run under the MS-DOS.

- General accounting packages may be classified into two groups: (1) those that support real-time accounting; and (2) those that support batch processing. For example, AccPac Bedford and Summation support real-time accounting, while AccPac Plus is written for the traditional batch processing of accounting data. Often, help-wanted ads, such as the two in the side margin, refer to this distinction. Note that when AccPac alone is mentioned in the ad, the employer normally wants someone with a knowledge of batch processing, since earlier versions of AccPac have been associated with the traditional batch processing of accounting data.

- All general accounting packages are created under an original version, usually called "Version 1.0." Subsequent versions may differ greatly from Version 1.0. For example, Summation's current 2.40 version differs markedly from Summation 1.0.

An introductory overview of four accounting packages—AccPac Bedford, AccPac Plus, Easypay, and Summation—will be treated in the subsections that follow. When studying this overview, it should be noted that:

- Newer versions of the software may have been released since the printing of this text. As stated earlier, software developers are constantly making changes to meet the needs of their particular markets.

- Since each package offers attractions to meet the accounting needs of some (but not all) small and medium-sized businesses, no comparisons will be made between any of the accounting packages. Therefore, most of the better packages on the market must be evaluated in the light of a company's needs. A general accounting package may work very well for one business but have limitations for a competitor's business. In searching for the right accounting package, many accountants have

FIGURE 11-1

ACCOUNTS. Person required with knowledge of accounts payable, deposits & reconciliation a must. Real Time computer experience preferred. Non smoking office located Don Mills-Eglinton. Fax resume

FIGURE 11-2

ACCOUNTING Clerk. Previous exper. required in A/R and A/P. Good knowledge of Lotus and ACC PAC. Must have good communication skills. Excel. opportunity for responsible individual with a growing co. Qualified person please fax resume to

CHAPTER 11: Using Microcomputer Software to Process Common Accounting Applications

urged management to identify its business "needs" first, then to shop around and actually test demonstration versions of the software before actually making a decision. In the final analysis, management usually makes a decision on the basis of cost, immediate accounting needs, and projected growth potential for future accounting needs.

AccPac Bedford Package

The original version of Bedford was developed by Bedford Software Ltd. in the mid-1980s under the name "Bedford Integrated Accounting®," "Bedford Accounting®," or simply "Bedford®." The first version was programmed to run under MS-DOS-based microcomputers. In 1987, an Apple Macintosh version called "Bedford Simply Accounting®" was released to meet the demands of a growing Macintosh business market. Soon after, however, Computer Associates Canada, Ltd., developers of AccPac Easy® and AccPac Plus®, acquired full rights to Bedford's PC and Mac versions. Consequently, Bedford is now marketed as "AccPac Bedford®," and should not be confused with the other accounting packages which make up the AccPac family of products.

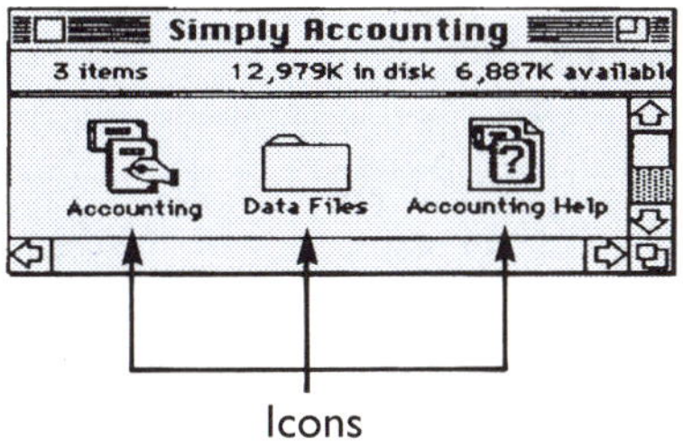

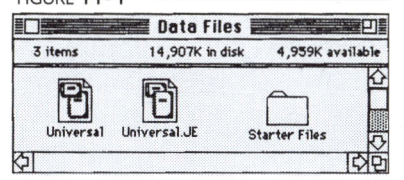

OVERVIEW One way to check the extent of accounting modules supported by any accounting package is to test that package's main or master menu. Suppose, for example, you had access to Bedford's Simply Accounting® for the Apple Macintosh and then successfully opened the demo data files, called "Universal Construction," from the Data Files folder (see Figures 11-3 and 11-4). Bedford's menu bar and Company Window would display an overview of the accounting modules as in Figure 11-5. (Figures 11-3 to 11-6 offer exact reproductions of the screen displays; most other figures are simplified.)

FIGURE 11-3

FIGURE 11-4

FIGURE 11-5

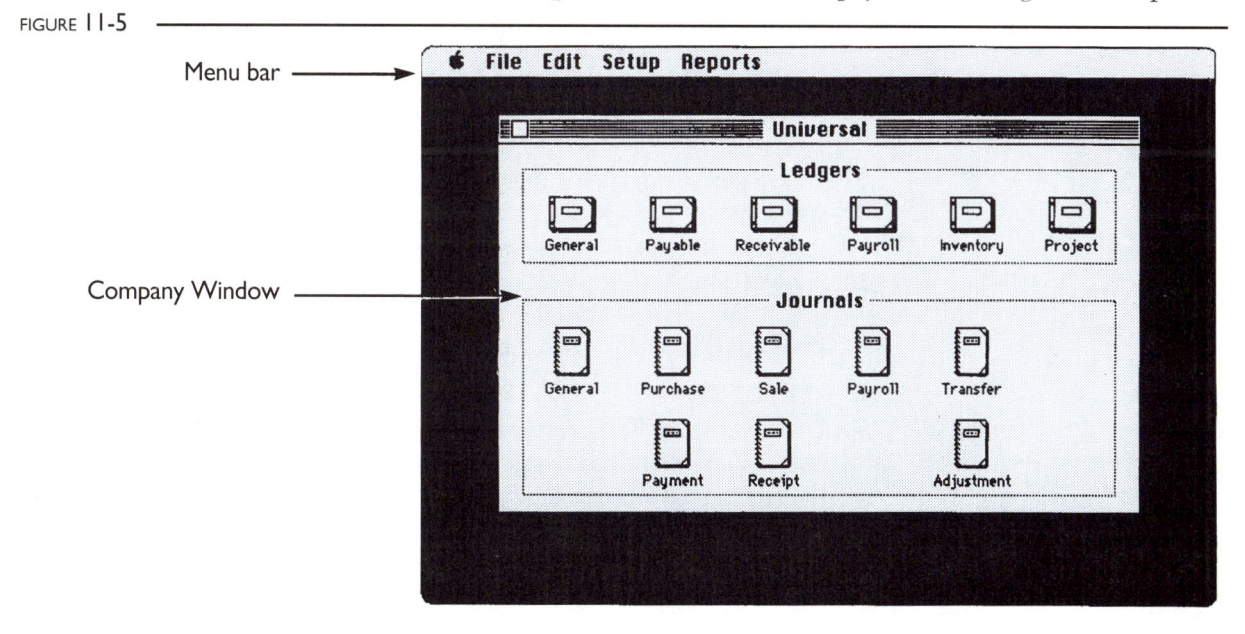

PART 2: COMMON ACCOUNTING APPLICATIONS

Menu bar: a horizontal strip at the top of the screen containing menu titles for a designated program.

FIGURE 11-6

```
Reports
 Display...                    ⌘D
 ─────────────────────────────────
 Balance Sheet...
 Income Statement...
 Trial Balance...
 General Ledger...
 ─────────────────────────────────
 Vendor Aged...
 ─────────────────────────────────
 Customer Aged...
 Print Customer Statements...
 ─────────────────────────────────
 Employee Summary...
 Print T4 Slips...
 Print Relevé 1 Slips...
 ─────────────────────────────────
 Inventory...
 ─────────────────────────────────
 Project...
```

Company Window: Bedford's main menu showing the accounting modules in the form of ledgers and related journals for a specific company.

Fully integrated accounting package: a package in which all accounting sub-modules, such as Accounts Receivable and Accounts Payable, are integrated with the G/L so that real-time accounting of transactions is supported.

Analysis   As Figure 11-5 shows, when any records created under Bedford have been loaded into memory and are ready to use, the screen will display the program's menu bar and the main window identifying a specific company name.

Under the Macintosh system, the **menu bar** is the horizontal strip at the top of the screen. As the illustration shows, the menu bar contains an icon and menu titles from left to right called The Apple (icon), File, Edit, Setup, and Reports. Each title designates one menu. Therefore, by "pulling down" a menu title with the mouse you can display the menu of items directly below the title. For example, by pulling down the Reports menu, you can see the commands that are used for accessing all the reports that can be displayed or printed, as the side margin illustration shows.

Obviously, the **Company Window** displays the icons that represent the company's accounting books that have been loaded into the computer's working memory. In the illustration, the Company Window displays the ledgers and journals for the Universal Company. As you can see, under Bedford Accounting, there are six ledgers; therefore, you can say that there are six accounting modules, namely, from left to right, the General Ledger System, the Accounts Payable System, the Accounts Receivable System, the Payroll System, the Inventory System, and the Project (Job Cost) System. Briefly, the ledgers contain current information on G/L accounts, vendors, customers, employees, and inventory items; and projects in the G/L, accounts payable, accounts receivable, payroll, inventory, and job cost ledgers—respectively. A more detailed explanation of each accounting module will be presented later.

Notice the relationship between the first five of these ledgers and the "Journals" directly below them. For example, the "General" journal would contain the listing of all respective journal transactions related to the "General" ledger. Similarly, the "Purchase" and (Cash) "Payment" journals would contain transactions that would be posted to the accounts payable system.

Special Note: Those who prefer the IBM PC or compatible using MS-DOS will find the same format of accounting ledgers and journals. The only visible difference between the two is the presence of icons under the Macintosh system; in contrast, Bedford under MS-DOS displays the accounting modules in the form of a large menu bar at the top of the screen, as shown in Figure 11-7. Except for this, and the differences in the operating system, Bedford will operate much the same on PC microcomputers.

MAIN CHARACTERISTICS   The Bedford Accounting System may be classified as a ***fully integrated accounting package*** aimed primarily at small merchandising businesses. The term *integrated* simply refers to the fact that once a particular business transaction is recorded, all files related to that transaction are updated immediately. For example, if you record a sale through the accounts receivable system, the accounts in the general ledger and accounts receivable ledger will be updated automatically

CHAPTER 11: Using Microcomputer Software to Process Common Accounting Applications **481**

FIGURE 11-7

| GENERAL | PAYABLE | RECEIVABLE | PAYROLL | INVENTORY | JOBCOST | SYSTEM |

Company: ....   d: \[path]

V3.24bR (C) Copyright 1986-1989 Bedford Software
All rights reserved.

to reflect the sale, and the inventory will be adjusted automatically to reflect the sale as well. Since financial statements can be prepared immediately after entering the last transaction, we can say that Bedford Accounting supports the concept of real-time accounting.

GENERAL LEDGER SYSTEM The following points should be considered when analyzing an overview of Bedford's General Ledger System:

- If you try to use the General Journal without setting up a G/L chart of accounts for a specific business, Bedford's program will display the following message: "The Ledger must be Set Ready before this Journal can be opened." What this means is simply that the user must set up a chart of accounts in the general ledger before using this module. Without going into details, the user can define a chart of accounts with flexible four-digit design in the Mac version with numbers limited from 1000 to 5999 (three-digit design in the PC version must use numbers from 100 to 599), or choose from six starter companies and modify any one of those six "demo" companies. As with most other microcomputerized G/L systems, an account number must be assigned in numerical order to every item that will be printed on the financial statements.

- Since Bedford supports a totally integrated accounting system, it naturally follows that ***integration*** (controlling) ***accounts*** must be set up in the G/L, namely Accounts Payable, Accounts Receivable, Wages (Salaries) Expense, Payroll Bank Account, Inventory, and so on. In general terms, the allocation of the integration accounts is done automatically when you set up a default chart of accounts. This means that there is no need to make another entry into the general ledger or to manually make a transfer of any entry from the other accounting modules. Under any real-time accounting system, when an entry is made in one of the sub-modules, the G/L is updated automatically.

- Accounting entries affecting only the G/L are made through the General Journal. As you are aware, the general journal is commonly used to record the opening entry (or the opening balances from an

Integration accounts: the term used in Bedford accounting for controlling accounts.

established company that has decided to computerize its manual accounting records), adjusting entries, or reversing entries.
- Under Bedford's system of journalizing, you can only make an entry to one account at a time. Thus, if you have two entries to make, each affecting the same account, you must make a complete, separate entry for each account.
- Furthermore, the General Journal is used to make all entries that cannot be made in the subsidiary ledgers. This means that you can make journal entries affecting all postable G/L accounts except those set up as controlling (integration) accounts. The integration accounts can only be changed through the use of the appropriate journal related to the subsidiary ledger. For example, Accounts Payable will be updated through entries made in the Purchases and Cash Payments journals.
- Bedford relies heavily on a system of pluses and minuses to support the theory of debits and credits. Therefore, under Bedford Accounting, a sale on account is analyzed (1) as a debit to Accounts Receivable with a positive amount, because that asset account is being increased on the left (debit) hand side of the ledger; and as a credit to Sales with a positive amount, because that revenue account is being increased on the right (credit) hand side of the ledger. The chart shown as Figure 11-8 may be useful when analyzing debits and credits under Bedford Accounting.

FIGURE 11-8

Debit and Credit Analysis Chart

1. Entering a positive amount will increase the specified account's balance; entering a negative amount will decrease the specified account's balance.

2. Increases in asset and expense accounts will be increased with positive amounts while those accounts will be decreased with negative amounts.

3. Liabilities, owner's equity, and revenue accounts will be increased with positive amounts, because those accounts originate on the right (credit) side of the ledger. Conversely, these accounts are decreased with negative amounts as debits.

- At the end of each accounting year, the user is required to make adjusting entries where necessary, print annual financial statements and other reports, make a backup copy of the company's files, and then enter a *using date* which is in a new accounting year. Bedford's program will then automatically close revenue and expense account balances into retained earnings and reset the "Start" and "Finish" dates for the new accounting year.
- As you may have observed from the study of Figure 11-6, Bedford supports the printing or screen-displaying of the two most common financial statements: the balance sheet and income statement.

- Other reports that are produced by the General Ledger System are the trial balance, the general ledger detail report, and the printout of the general journal, by posting date or by journal number.

To illustrate how one aspect of the General Ledger System under Bedford works, study the steps below for recording and posting the opening entry for the Universal Company. Assume that the General Ledger has been made ready and that an opening investment is to be recorded from an approved journal voucher form that shows $100 000 cash being received from the issuing of common shares and the fact that the proceeds were deposited into the company's chequing account. The 11 steps to record this opening entry would be as follows:

- **Step 1** On gaining access to Bedford, enter the using date for this session as 01-10-91; then click "OK."
- **Step 2** From the Company Window, select the icon for General Journal; then open this icon from the file menu or double-click the selected icon with the mouse.
- **Step 3** A General Journal grid appears, as in Figure 11-9.

FIGURE 11-9

```
┌─────────────────────────────────────────────────────────┐
│                     General Journal                      │
│                                                          │
│   Source    [          ]           Date    [ 01-10-91 ]  │
│                                                          │
│   Comment   [                                        ]   │
│                                                          │
│   Total Debits:    $0.00                                 │
│   Total Credits:   $0.00                                 │
│                                                          │
│        Account                      Amount               │
│   ┌──────────────────────┬──────────────────────┐        │
│   │                      │                      │        │
│   │                      │                      │        │
│   │                      │                      │        │
│   │                      │                      │        │
│   │                      │                      │        │
│   └──────────────────────┴──────────────────────┘        │
│                                                          │
│                      [ Distribute ]      [ Post ]        │
└─────────────────────────────────────────────────────────┘
```

Analysis of Preceding Steps

- Observe that the date entered for the "using date" on opening Bedford appears automatically in the Date box of the grid.
- A flashing vertical cursor is displayed in the first field (box), Source. Here, the source of the journal entry will be entered, in accordance with the concept that all transactions entered should have an audit trail.

- The next blank field, Comment, is where a short explanation of the journal entry will be made.
- Note that the Total Debits and Total Credits will be displayed as amounts are entered. As in the majority of G/L computer systems, no posting of any entry can be made until total debits is equal to total credits.
- Below the Total Debits and Total Credits indicators is the large field where account numbers and the amounts of entries will be entered. Along the right side of this field is the common Apple Macintosh elevator rectangle, which allows the user to "scroll" to accounts located above and below those displayed in the window.
- And, finally, two oval boxes are displayed. One, called "Distribute," can be used to distribute amounts to job costing projects. The other, "Post," will be darkened when the journal entry is completed and balances.
- **Step 4** In the Source box, type "JV#1", which stands for Journal Voucher 1. We will assume that the opening entry has been authorized on a journal voucher form. Press <Return> to enter the information.
- **Step 5** Since no change has to be made to the date, press <Return>.
- **Step 6** The cursor is now in the Comment field. Type "Opening entry" and then press <Return>.
- **Step 7** The cursor rests on the first line below the Account field. Type "1090" and press <Return>. The G/L account title "Cash in Royal Bank" and a zero amount automatically appear to complete the first line.
- **Step 8** Move the cursor to the zero amount and enter "100000" (for $100 000). Press <Return>. The amount is entered in the Amount column as well as being shown opposite Total Debits, as illustrated in Figure 11-10.
- **Step 9** Below the debit entry, that is, on the next line, type "3100", the account code for Common Shares. Press <Return>. The account title and zero amounts appear automatically.
- **Step 10** Place the cursor at the zero amount and change it to read "100000". Press <Return>.
- **Step 11** Since the total debits, $100,000, is equal to the total credits, as shown in Figure 11-11, the entry can be posted by simply clicking on the Post rectangle.

It is important to note that both debit and credit amounts are positive values, in accordance with Bedford's system of debits and credits. In this case, Cash in Royal Bank is positive, since the asset is being increased. Similarly, Common Shares is positive, since this equity account is being increased also.

The user can print the opening entry by simply going to the Reports menu, selecting "Display General Journal," and clicking "OK"; a screen

CHAPTER 11: Using Microcomputer Software to Process Common Accounting Applications **485**

FIGURE 11-10

```
┌─────────────────────────────────────────────────────────┐
│ ▤                    General Journal                    │
├─────────────────────────────────────────────────────────┤
│  Source    │ JV#1              │   Date   │ 01-10-91 │  │
│                                                         │
│  Comment   │ Opening entry                           │  │
│                                                         │
│  Total Debits:    $100,000.00                           │
│  Total Credits:   $0.00                                 │
│  ┌──────────────────────────────┬────────────────────┐  │
│  │ Account                      │ Amount             │  │
│  ├──────────────────────────────┼────────────────────┤  │
│  │ 1090 Cash in Royal Bank      │       100,000.00   │  │
│  │                              │                    │  │
│  └──────────────────────────────┴────────────────────┘  │
│                          [ Distribute ]   [ Post ]      │
└─────────────────────────────────────────────────────────┘
```

FIGURE 11-11

```
┌─────────────────────────────────────────────────────────┐
│ ▤                    General Journal                    │
├─────────────────────────────────────────────────────────┤
│  Source    │ JV#1              │   Date   │ 01-10-91 │  │
│                                                         │
│  Comment   │ Opening entry                           │  │
│                                                         │
│  Total Debits:    $100,000.00                           │
│  Total Credits:   $100,000.00                           │
│  ┌──────────────────────────────┬────────────────────┐  │
│  │ Account                      │ Amount             │  │
│  ├──────────────────────────────┼────────────────────┤  │
│  │ 1090 Cash in Royal Bank      │       100,000.00   │  │
│  │ 3100 Common Shares           │       100,000.00   │  │
│  └──────────────────────────────┴────────────────────┘  │
│                          [ Distribute ]   [ Post ]      │
└─────────────────────────────────────────────────────────┘
```

display of the general journal entry automatically appears. To print a hard copy, the user simply selects the Print command from the pull-down menu under File. Under the Macintosh system, it is important to see a screen display before the Print command is used to print hard copies.

ACCOUNTS PAYABLE SYSTEM

The following points are useful when examining an overview of Bedford's accounts payable module:

- As the main menus in Figures 11-5 and 11-7 show, Accounts Payable is the first of the sub-ledgers in the Bedford Accounting System.
- If you try to use the Purchases Journal or the Cash Payments Journal without setting up a complete list of **vendors** (creditors) with whom the company has an account on converting from a manual system to Bedford, the program will display the usual message "The Ledger must be Set Ready before this Journal can be opened."

  Therefore, it is important to create vendor accounts before the Accounts Payable System can be used. In general, this means entering important information such as the vendor's name, street address, city, province, postal code, and telephone number.

  Above all else, it is important that the outstanding balance of each vendor account be determined and that the total of these balances equals the Accounts Payable controlling account in the General Ledger. Under Bedford Accounting, you will not be able to "Set Ready" the Accounts Payable System until these are the same. An illustration of a completed vendor's account under Bedford is shown as Figure 11-12. (Exact reproduction of screen.)

- The Accounts Payable module is normally used to record all credit purchases made by the business. To record these credit purchases, a Purchases Journal icon is opened and a grid is displayed to receive important data such as the name of the supplier, the supplier's invoice, the date of the purchase invoice (and not present or using date), the amount of the purchase, and the account to which the purchase should be charged. A typical entry in the Purchases Journal is illustrated as Figure 11-13.

Vendors: the term preferred by Bedford Accounting instead of creditors.

FIGURE 11-12

Vendor Ledger

Vendor:	Harry's Lumber
Street:	7077 76th Avenue
City:	New Westminster
Province:	British Columbia
Postal Code:	V8F 3K7
Phone:	(604) 531-6732
Balance:	992.00

☐ Purge invoices when paid

FIGURE 11-13

Purchase Journal

PURCHASED FROM
Harry's Lumber
7077 76th Avenue
New Westminster, B.C.
V8F 3K7

Invoice: HL78891
Date: 10-15-91

Item	Quantity	Unit	Description	Unit Price	Amount	Acct	Project
D1010	5	Each	Doors: Exterior	55.160	275.80	1650	
D5020	6	Unit	Cabinets: Kitchen	147.640	885.84	1650	
H2510	10	Pound	Nails: Drywall	1.930	19.30	1570	

Freight:
Total: $1,180.94

Post

CHAPTER 11: Using Microcomputer Software to Process Common Accounting Applications **487**

Analysis These additional points should be considered in any analysis of journalizing credit purchases in Bedford's Accounts Payable application:

- The Item field is used to enter the inventory number or alphanumeric code of the item in question. If what is being purchased is not an inventory item, the program permits the user to click "Other" in a special dialogue box that is displayed.
- The number of units being invoiced is entered in the Quantity box.
- If the item is an inventory item, this field will be filled automatically by the program that reacts to what was entered in the Item field.
- Similarly, if the item is an inventory item, this field will be filled automatically in reaction to what was entered in the Item field.
- The Unit Price and Amount will be provided automatically if the Item field is used to enter an inventory item. If both the invoiced Unit Price and the Amount differ from those displayed by the program, the clerk must enter the correct unit price. The amount is calculated automatically by the program. If the item is not an inventory one, the clerk simply enters the unit price and the program calculates and displays the correct amount.
- If the inventory item being entered has previously been displayed by completing the Item field, the Account number will be shown automatically by the program. If the item is a non-inventory one, the clerk must enter the number of the account required.
- Any cost of freight included on the invoice which *cannot be directly allocated to a specific item* will be entered in the Freight field. Of course, this amount will be charged (debited) to a Freight Expense account and not to the cost of the inventory item being purchased.
- At any time during the preparation of the journal entry, the clerk can choose "Display Purchase Journal Entry" from the Reports menu so that the details of the entry can be reviewed or printed. See Figure 11-14 for the journal entry to support the Purchase Journal displayed as Figure 11-13 earlier.
- When all items on the purchase invoice have been entered, the clerk simply clicks "Post" in the Purchase Journal window. Of course, all entries will be posted automatically to the creditor's account in the Accounts Payable Ledger and the controlling (integration) accounts in the G/L.
- It is important to emphasize that, under Bedford Accounting, all credit purchase invoices must be accounted for on an individual basis to support the ***open-item method*** of accounting. As explained in Chapter 7, the open-item method keeps track of all individual invoices together with any payments made on behalf of that invoice. Under this method, management can learn which specific invoices

FIGURE 11-14

Universal Company Purchase Journal Entry	debits	credits
2200 Accounts Payable	-	1,180.94
1650 Doors & Cabinets	1,161.64	-
1570 Hardware	19.30	-
	1,180.94	1,180.94

Open-item method: method whereby invoices and payments to invoices are accounted for on an individual basis.

are unpaid or owing. As explained in Chapter 7, the open-item method is in direct contrast to the balance-forward method, which simply accounts for the balance in any creditor's account. Of course, the open-item method is also commonly used in the Accounts Receivable System.

- The Accounts Payable module is also used to record all cheques issued by the company. This would include both cheques made as payments to the separate purchase invoices and cash disbursements made to suppliers of other goods and services.

- To make a journal entry to account for an issued cheque, the clerk simply selects the Payment Journal icon in the Company Window, then chooses "Open" from the File menu or double-clicks on this icon. A simulated cheque and stub from the payment journal will then appear. To illustrate, assume that the clerk records the cheque in payment of the purchase invoice earlier illustrated for Harry's Lumber. The completed cash disbursement may be recorded as in Figure 11-15.

FIGURE 11-15

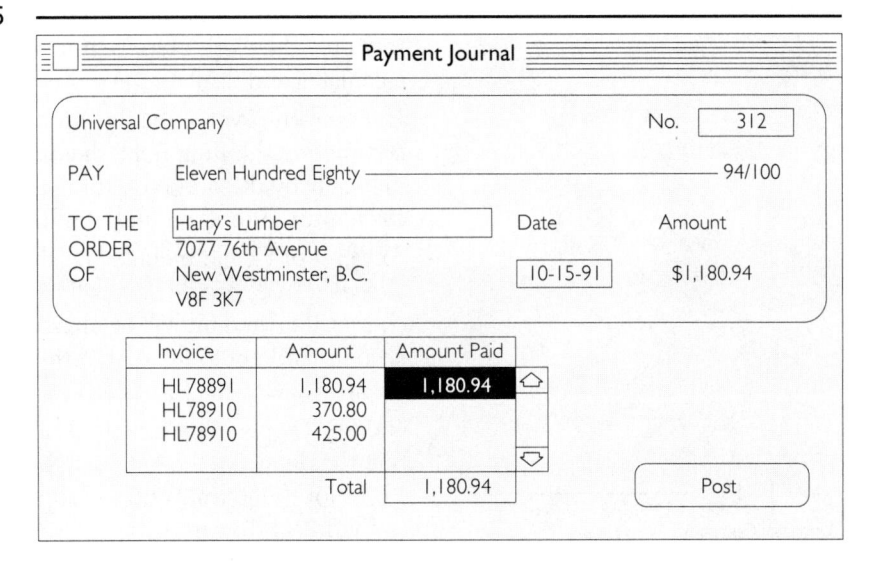

Payment Journal

Universal Company   No. 312

PAY   Eleven Hundred Eighty   94/100

TO THE ORDER OF: Harry's Lumber, 7077 76th Avenue, New Westminster, B.C. V8F 3K7

Date: 10-15-91   Amount: $1,180.94

Invoice	Amount	Amount Paid
HL78891	1,180.94	1,180.94
HL78910	370.80	
HL78910	425.00	
Total		1,180.94

Post

Analysis

- Notice that the journal simulates the preparation of an actual cheque and then accounts for it against one specific invoice. For actual payments, the firm may use either computer-generated cheques or its own cheque form. If the firm wishes to print cheques, it can purchase Bedford accounts payable/payroll cheques with its company name and address imprinted. In any case, the cheque form within the journal becomes a valuable "stub" to identify the issued cheque.

- In keeping with the open-item method, the information at the bottom of the screen displays how much the firm owes against each

invoice. As the illustration shows, only the oldest invoice, HL78891, is being paid, since the amount owing is selected and is shown as the total.
- When the clerk clicks on the Post field, Bedford's program will debit the vendor's account in the Accounts Payable Ledger, debit the integration account (Accounts Payable), and credit Cash in Royal Bank in the G/L. Verification of the double entry to the G/L can be displayed for printing either before or after posting by simply pulling down the Reports menu, selecting Display, and selecting the Print command under the file menu. The screen display of the payment entry is shown as Figure 11-16.

FIGURE 11-16

Universal Company Payment Journal Entry	debits	credits
2200 Accounts Payable	1,180.94	-
1090 Cash in Royal Bank	-	1,180.94
	1,180.94	1,180.94

ACCOUNTS RECEIVABLE SYSTEM
The following points are useful when examining an overview of Bedford's accounts receivable module:

- Obviously, Bedford's Accounts Receivable System will be used to account for credit sales and customer payments.
- If you try to use the Sales Journal or the Cash Receipts Journal without setting up a complete list of customers with whom the company has an account on converting from a manual system to Bedford, the program will display the usual message, "The Ledger must be Set Ready before this Journal can be opened." Therefore, it is important to create customer accounts before the Accounts Receivable System can be used. In addition, it is most important that the outstanding balance of each customer's account be determined and that the total of these balances equals that of the Accounts Receivable controlling account in the general ledger. Under Bedford Accounting, you will not be able to "Set Ready" the Accounts Receivable System until these are the same.
- Bedford uses the open-item method to account for individual sales invoices as well as the customer payments made on those invoices. Therefore, this method permits management to identify how much is owing from a specific customer and which invoices are still unpaid.
- The user has the option of either recording the sale of items from inventory or recording sales for services. Of course, the G/L chart of accounts must be organized to support appropriately entitled revenue accounts.
- If a sale is made from inventory, Bedford permits integration among the accounts receivable, inventory, and general ledger systems. Therefore, the program will account not only for the sales revenue, but also for the cost of goods sold. It is important to recognize that Bedford supports only the perpetual inventory method to account for cost of goods sold. And where cost prices differ for items purchased during the accounting period, Bedford supports the ***average cost method*** to account for the cost of goods sold. For example, if item X were purchased during the

Average cost method: one acceptable method of costing the cost of goods sold when purchase prices vary during the accounting period.

accounting period at three cost prices, say at $10, $12, and $14 per item, this good sold during the period would be costed at $12. In accounting theory, firms may prefer to use other costing methods. These other methods are best examined in more-advanced levels of accounting study.

To illustrate how a sale of inventory is journalized, assume that the following items were sold by the Universal Company to R. Thomas Stanhope, an approved credit customer: one D1010 exterior door at $66; and one D5020 kitchen cabinet at $185. To simplify matters, only the British Columbia sales tax will be considered. (As indicated in earlier chapters, the accounting of the federal GST is treated in the Appendix.)

To make a journal entry to account for this sale, the clerk will find the Sale Journal icon in the Company Window and open it either by double-clicking the mouse on it or by choosing the Open command from the File menu. A simulated invoice will then appear for completion by the clerk. An invoice properly completed on-screen is illustrated in Figure 11-17.

FIGURE 11-17

```
                           Sale Journal

SOLD TO                    SHIP TO
Stanhope, R. Thomas        Stanhope, R. Thomas        Invoice   1
12 Stratford Street        12 Stratford Street
Vancouver, B.C.            Vancouver, B.C.            Date      10-15-91
V2D 9T7                    V2D 9T7
```

Item	Quantity	Unit	Description	GST	PST	Unit Price	Amount	Acct	Project
D1010	1	Each	Doors: Exterior		6.000	66.000	66.00	4060	
D5020	1	Unit	Cabinets: Kitchen		6.000	185.000	185.00	4520	

Comments	Net 30 days	GST		
		PST	15.06	
		Freight		
		Total	$266.06	Post

Analysis Completing the simulated invoice is straightforward. These points should be studied:

- The Invoice field automatically shows the first number in the current series if no previous invoice has been prepared in that series. Bedford allows the clerk to change this number to suit any number corresponding to a manually prepared system. In addition, the number can be changed to suit a sequence for printing computer-generated invoices under the program.
- To complete the Sold To field, the clerk simply places the cursor on the first line and enters the first three letters of the customer's surname. A

Select Customer window appears, allowing the clerk to select and "OK" the correct customer. The program enters the full name and address automatically from information created for the customer in the Accounts Receivable Ledger. Also, the program automatically repeats the customer's name and address in the Ship To field. If changes are necessary, they can be made by selecting the correct field and typing the correction.

- The Date field is completed automatically by the program and corresponds to the using (current system) date. Of course, this date can also be changed in the normal manner.
- The clerk then places the cursor on the first line in the Item field and types in the item number of the good sold. The program automatically completes the line by showing under Quantity the remaining quantity in stock and filling in the remaining columns also. Of course, since only one item of D1010 was sold, the clerk must change the quantity shown to 1. The program then applies the change where necessary across the line.
- The same procedure is followed for the next item. Notice that Bedford's program shows the PST percentage and automatically computes the total PST. The total amount of the sale is shown just as for the printed invoice.
- Once all items have been entered correctly, the clerk simply clicks the mouse on the Post field and the program automatically journalizes and posts the entry to the customer's account in the Accounts Receivable Ledger and the appropriate double entry in the General Ledger. As was the case with all other modules, this double entry to the G/L can be displayed or printed by drawing down the Reports menu. In this case, the double entry might be displayed as shown in Figure 11-18.

FIGURE 11-18

Universal Company Sale Journal Entry	debits	credits
1200 Accounts Receivable	266.06	-
1650 Inventory	-	202.80
5090 Cost of Goods Sold	202.80	-
4600 Sales	-	251.00
2480 PST Payable	-	15.06
	468.86	468.86

Note that the compound entry has to be analyzed into two parts. One part deals with the revenue entry by debiting Accounts Receivable (for the total sale plus PST) and crediting two accounts: Sales for the total less PST, and PST Payable for the amount of provincial sales tax to be paid. The second part is the costing entry. As stated earlier, under the perpetual inventory system, the expense Cost of Goods Sold is debited under Bedford for the average cost price of the items sold while the Inventory account is reduced by the same average cost price. Of course, all calculations and the costing entry are done automatically once the accounts have been "Set Ready" in the General and Inventory Ledgers.

Accounting for cash receipts from credit customers is done by selecting the Receipt Journal icon in the Company Window and then opening this icon in the normal manner. A simulated receipt and stub grid will appear on which the clerk completes the various fields. For example, assume that R. Thomas

Stanhope mailed a cheque in full payment of Invoice 1. The entry would be made in the Receipt Journal as illustrated in Figure 11-19.

FIGURE 11-19

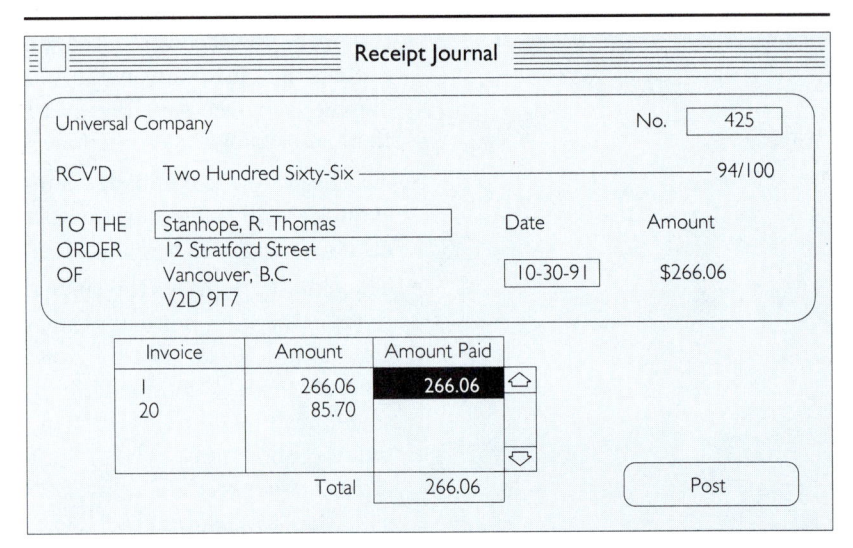

Receipt Journal

Universal Company No. 425

RCV'D Two Hundred Sixty-Six — 94/100

TO THE ORDER OF: Stanhope, R. Thomas, 12 Stratford Street, Vancouver, B.C. V2D 9T7

Date: 10-30-91 Amount: $266.06

Invoice	Amount	Amount Paid
1	266.06	266.06
20	85.70	
	Total	266.06

Post

Notice that the top portion of the Receipt Journal is a simulated receipt and stub. Therefore, the No. field will receive the customer's cheque number. Also notice that the journal supports the open-item method by displaying all of the outstanding invoices to be paid by the customer. Under the open-item method, the clerk must always allocate a payment to a specific invoice. When the clerk clicks on the Post field, the program will update the customer's account in the Accounts Receivable Ledger for the payment, debit the Cash account in the G/L that is used to deposit the customer's cheque in the firm's bank account, and credit the Accounts Receivable controlling account, also in the G/L. As in the case of all other modules, the double entry can be reviewed by simply choosing "Display Receipt Journal" under the Report menu, as shown in Figure 11-20.

In addition to displaying and printing a sales journal and cash receipts journal, the Accounts Receivable module can generate useful reports such as an Aged Customer Report, Customer Statements, Customer Address Listing, Customer Summary, and Customer Detail. The program can also print customer address labels.

FIGURE 11-20

Universal Company
Receipt Journal Entry

		debits	credits
1090	Cash in Royal Bank	266.06	-
1200	Accounts Receivable	-	266.06
		266.06	266.06

OTHER BEDFORD MODULES Lack of space in this edition prevents a detailed overview Bedford's other accounting modules for payroll, inventory, and job costing. The following is a short overview.

Payroll One of the features of Bedford Integrated Accounting is its Canadian payroll module. Bedford requires significantly less time to process a small business's regular pay period than any other manual system. Of course, all payroll journal entries are made through the Payroll Journal

icon. In summary, the Bedford Payroll module is programmed to:
- Perform both automatic and manual calculations to determine an individual employee's gross pay
- Calculate automatically common payroll deductions
- Display and print the payroll journal
- Post automatically all payroll entries to individual employee accounts and to controlling accounts in the G/L
- Print paycheques on computer form stock, or support manually prepared cheques
- Display or print employee summary reports and year-end T4 slips

It is important to note that Bedford's payroll module, like any other payroll program, must be updated every year so that the latest rates for CPP, UI, and income tax deductions can be applied. These changes are usually available early in the new year in the form of an updated diskette.

Inventory Bedford's Inventory module is aimed at the small merchandising business which prefers to use the perpetual inventory system and the average cost method to account for the cost of goods sold. The program can also be used for small manufacturers and small wholesaler-type businesses. The main features of this module are as follows:

- Additions to and reductions of inventory are made automatically as the clerk enters purchases through the Accounts Payable module and sales through the Accounts Receivable module.
- Under the perpetual inventory method, the laid-down cost is debited to the asset Inventory. For each sale, revenue is recognized as well as the cost of goods sold. As stated earlier, costing of the goods sold is done by using the average cost method. The program will automatically calculate the cost of the good sold and make the necessary entry to record the expense called Cost of Goods Sold and reduce the asset Inventory on the basis of the average cost.
- When the Inventory module is used, any cash purchase and cash sale of inventory items must be processed through the Accounts Payable and Accounts Receivable systems respectively. First, "dummy" accounts would be set up for "Cash Purchases" in the payable ledger and "Cash Sales" in the receivable ledger. Then, it is necessary to follow a two-step procedure to account for all cash purchases and cash sales of inventory. For example, a cash sale would be recorded through the Receivable Journal to a hypothetical customer called "Cash Sales." Next, you would enter the same amount as the "customer's" payment through the Payment Journal. Posting both entries results in a zero balance in the "Cash Sales" account and correctly updates the inventory item sold in the Inventory ledger.

494 PART 2: COMMON ACCOUNTING APPLICATIONS

- The program generates useful reports such as the Quantity Report, the Inventory Summary Report, and the Inventory Report Based on Margin or Markup.

Job Costing This area of accounting is generally treated in more-advanced levels of accounting. Briefly, this module permits the user to track revenues and expenses by project or department. Therefore, revenues or expenses can be allocated to projects whenever journal entries are made to record revenues or expenses in the other modules. This is possible because all of the program's relevant journals have a Project Distribution dialogue. It is important to emphasize that only revenues and expenses can be allocated to projects. The job costing program can produce summary and detail reports on revenue and expenses for any project or department. In this way, management is able to analyze specific costs associated with a particular job or department. Job costing, therefore, is essential to managers who need to plan and control costs so that the company can maximize its profits on any job.

AccPac Plus Package

As stated at the beginning of this chapter, accounting under batch processing in Canada is usually associated with the AccPac name. Since the AccPac family of accounting products now includes a variety of accounting packages, it is essential to identify those packages that do emphasize batch processing. The top-of-the-line batch processing package is called AccPac Plus (not to be confused with AccPac Easy).

At the time of writing, AccPac Plus is marketed under Version 6.00 with versions specifically written for MS-DOS and the IBM OS/2 system. Unlike the integrated AccPac Bedford package, AccPac Plus is classified as **modular-type accounting software**, because the individual modules, such as General Ledger, Accounts Receivable, Accounts Payable, Payroll, etc., are marketed separately. A business can obtain one module at a time according to its priority need. According to Computer Associates, developers of all Plus modules, the software is designed for medium-sized businesses and divisions of large corporations with specialized accounting requirements and large transaction volumes. At the time of writing, AccPac Plus includes applications for the modules summarized in Figure 11-21. In addition, over 100 add-ins and industry-specific applications are available such as the accounting of fixed assets, an Auto Dealership Management System, and an interface with Easypay for those who prefer to use that Canadian payroll package.

Although AccPac Plus software is designed so that each module may be used as an individual unit, it is important to realize that several modules can be integrated to work together. For example, a business usually begins with the General Ledger module, because it is central to the operation of an integrated AccPac Plus accounting system when other modules such as Accounts Receivable and Accounts Payable are added.

Modular-type accounting software: accounting programs in which the entire accounting system is divided into separate modules such as G/L, A/R, A/P, etc.

FIGURE 11-21

AccPac Plus Accounting Modules

General Ledger and Financial Reporter
Accounts Receivable
Accounts Payable
U.S. Payroll
Canadian Payroll
Inventory Control and Analysis
Order Entry
Retail Invoicing
Sales Analysis
Time, Billing & Client Receivables
Job Costing

CHAPTER 11: Using Microcomputer Software to Process Common Accounting Applications **495**

Batch-operated/oriented system: accounting system in which entries are first saved in groups called batches, enabling the user to verify and correct entries before posting them to accounts.

It is also important to remember that AccPac Plus is a ***batch-operated*** or ***-oriented system***. As mentioned earlier, this means that transactions entered into, say, the general ledger must be saved in groups called transaction batches. To illustrate how batch processing works under AccPac Plus, study the overview of the General Ledger module in the separate sections that follow. Once a user learns the batch-oriented system for the General Ledger module, the concept of batch processing can be applied to other modules such as Accounts Receivable and Accounts Payable.

GENERAL LEDGER MODULE

After installing the General Ledger and Financial Reporter module on the company's hard disk, the program requires that the company name be added to the Start list. In simple terms, this is a list of all companies for which accounts are maintained, with information on where AccPac Plus can find their data files.

For illustrative purposes, assume that the Universal Corporation has been added correctly to the Start list. Once this company name is selected, it will appear in the Start list screen as shown in Figure 11-22.

FIGURE 11-22

```
Computer Associates International, Inc.
ACCPAC PLUS
┌─ Start ─────────────────────────────────────┐
│                                             │
│     Accounts Payable  ABC Company           │
│     Accounts Payable  Sample Company        │
│     Accounts Receivable  ABC Company        │
│     General Ledger  ABC Company             │
│     General Ledger  Universal Corporation   │
│     Inventory Control  Sample Co.           │
│     Job Costing  Sample Company             │
│     Order Entry  ABC Company                │
│     Payroll  Sample Company                 │
│     Printer Configuration                   │
│                                             │
└─────────────────────────────────────────────┘
```

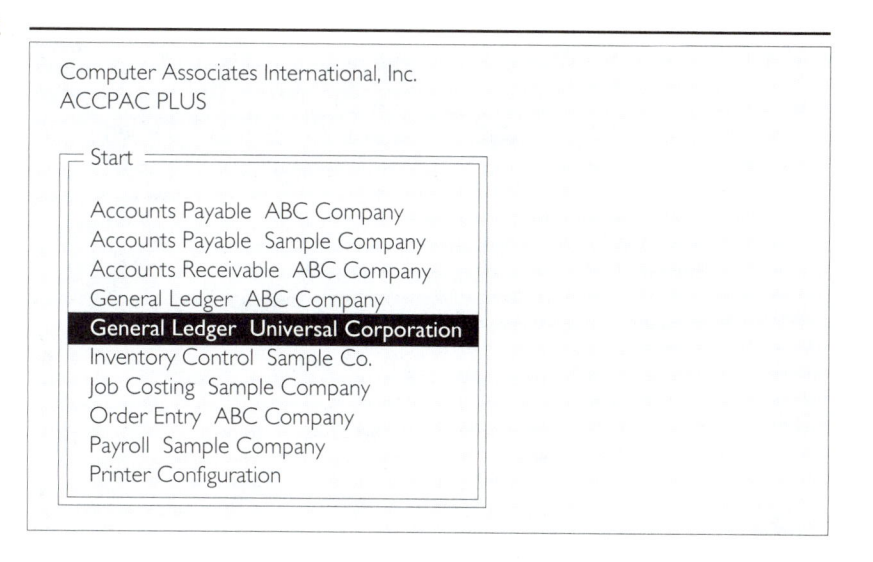

FIGURE 11-23

```
┌─────────────────────────────────────────┐
│ UNIVERSAL CORPORATION  Sept 30 91       │
│                                         │
│ General Ledger and Financial Reporter   │
│ Version 6.0A                            │
│                                         │
│   Last access date:      Sept 30 91     │
│                                         │
│   New date      [ Sept 30 91 ]          │
│                                         │
└─────────────────────────────────────────┘
```

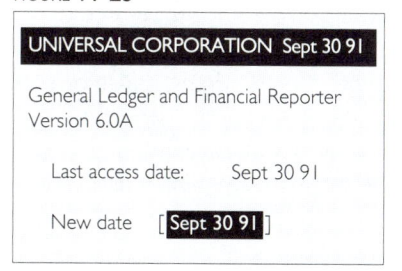

From the above illustration, you can conclude that the Start screen becomes AccPac Plus's first menu for those modules that have been installed and for which company names have been entered correctly. To select the General Ledger module, the user simply types the first character (such as "G" for General Ledger), or scrolls through the list using the arrow cursors to select the module, and then presses <Enter>. A title screen will then be displayed as in Figure 11-23. Obviously, the main function of this title screen is to set the date for the user's work session. Once "today's" date is confirmed, AccPac Plus's General Ledger Master Menu will be displayed, as illustrated in Figure 11-24.

PART 2: COMMON ACCOUNTING APPLICATIONS

FIGURE 11-24

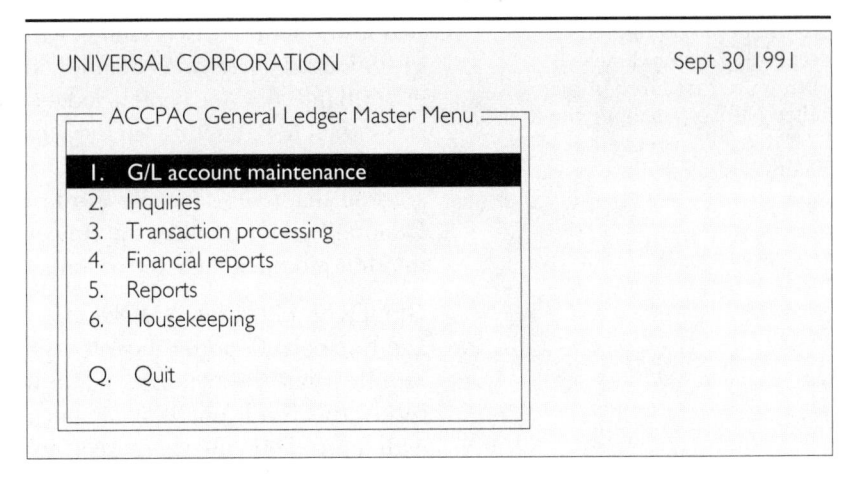

```
UNIVERSAL CORPORATION                          Sept 30 1991
┌─ ACCPAC General Ledger Master Menu ─┐
│                                      │
│  1.  G/L account maintenance         │
│  2.  Inquiries                       │
│  3.  Transaction processing          │
│  4.  Financial reports               │
│  5.  Reports                         │
│  6.  Housekeeping                    │
│                                      │
│  Q.  Quit                            │
│                                      │
└──────────────────────────────────────┘
```

Analysis All AccPac Plus programs have similar menu structures so that learning several modules is as easy as learning the one for the General Ledger Master Menu.

- Program 1 at the top of this menu, "G/L account maintenance," is used for adding and modifying account and transaction information. As with the majority of G/L packages, it is essential that a chart of accounts be well organized, with a system of account codes, department codes if necessary, account names, and in the case of AccPac Plus the "Type," which refers to whether an account is a balance sheet item (B), an income statement account (I), or a retained earnings account (R). Obviously, a good knowledge of accounting and financial reporting setup is essential to create a good G/L chart of accounts under AccPac Plus. Under the program, account codes can be created up to six digits. For example, the chart of accounts for the Universal Corporation may consist of a four-digit plan as shown in the side margin as Figure 11-25. The chart of accounts may be printed by selecting the "Reports" option from the G/L Master Menu.

  In addition to creating new accounts, Program 1 permits the user to delete accounts and perform other maintenance functions, as shown in Figure 11-26. Of course, these functions are displayed when the user selects the G/L account maintenance menu and presses <Enter>. Under AccPac Plus, when you select a menu item, the sub-menu is displayed below the previous menu so that you cannot get lost in the program's "tree."

- Program 2 on this menu, "Inquiries," allows the user to display information about one or more accounts, such as the data entered to define the account and its current balance, details posted to the account in the specified period, and budget figures and comparative percentages. In addition, this sub-menu displays batches, enabling the user to review on-screen the entries in current unposted batches.

FIGURE 11-25

1000-2999	Current Assets
3000-3299	Fixed Assets
3300-3999	Accumulated Dep'n, Fixed Assets
4000-4999	Current Liabilities
5000-5499	Long-Term Liabilities
5500-5999	Shareholders' Equity
6000-6499	Sales
6500-6999	Cost of Goods Sold
7000-7999	Operating Expenses
8000-8499	Other Revenue
8500-8999	Other Expenses

FIGURE 11-26

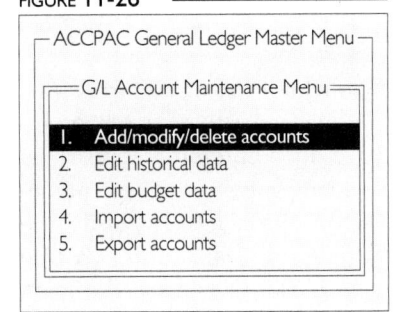

```
┌─ ACCPAC General Ledger Master Menu ─┐
│ ┌─ G/L Account Maintenance Menu ──┐ │
│ │                                  │ │
│ │  1.  Add/modify/delete accounts  │ │
│ │  2.  Edit historical data        │ │
│ │  3.  Edit budget data            │ │
│ │  4.  Import accounts             │ │
│ │  5.  Export accounts             │ │
│ │                                  │ │
│ └──────────────────────────────────┘ │
└──────────────────────────────────────┘
```

- The third option, "Transaction processing," contains programs to initiate batch processing, to print batches, to post batches, and to print the posting journal. As you will learn, once a batch has been created and printed, this batch must then be posted to G/L accounts.
- Program 4, "Financial reports," contains programs to print the financial statements. In addition, this sub-menu allows the user to create quick financial report specifications which can be used when printing balance sheets and income statements.
- Program 5, "Reports," leads to sub-menus that allow the user to print important reports such as the chart of accounts, trial balance, G/L listing, source journals, a batch status report, and the company profile.
- Program 6, "Housekeeping," contains a number of important functions. In Program 6 the user can edit the company profile and maintain specifications. In addition, the program contains sub-menus: the department maintenance menu, source code maintenance menu, source journal maintenance menu, account group maintenance menu, and periodic processing menu.
- Program Q, "Quit," permits the user to leave the General Ledger Master Menu.

ANALYZING SIMPLE BATCHING ENTRIES   Before proceeding to the next section, "Entering Transactions in the General Ledger," it is important that you analyze simple batching entries so that you can identify basic batching entry terminology and relate the traditional accounting double entry with a batching entry. Study the two transactions given below.

Transaction 1   A cheque is issued to pay rent. Under the traditional method, this transaction would be analyzed as shown in Figure 11-27.

FIGURE 11-27

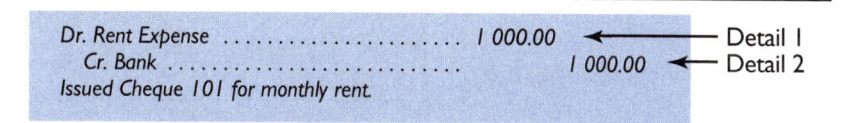

```
Dr. Rent Expense .....................  1 000.00   ← Detail 1
    Cr. Bank ..........................            1 000.00   ← Detail 2
Issued Cheque 101 for monthly rent.
```

Under batch processing, this double entry would be identified as one batch entry with two details.

Transaction 2   A cheque is issued to pay for one invoice. The traditional compound entry may be analyzed as in Figure 11-28.

FIGURE 11-28

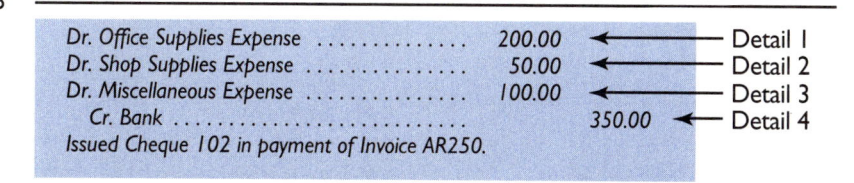

```
Dr. Office Supplies Expense .............   200.00   ← Detail 1
Dr. Shop Supplies Expense ...............    50.00   ← Detail 2
Dr. Miscellaneous Expense ...............   100.00   ← Detail 3
    Cr. Bank ..........................              350.00   ← Detail 4
Issued Cheque 102 in payment of Invoice AR250.
```

Under batch processing, this would be treated as one batch entry with four details. In other words, under batch processing each line in the traditional double entry becomes a detail line. As you will learn, the program assigns a number to each detail line you enter. You can use the number to recall the line for editing and to trace it from a printed batch listing report.

ENTERING TRANSACTIONS IN THE GENERAL LEDGER

As stated earlier, under AccPac Plus, transaction information must first be entered into transaction batches, which then can be posted to the G/L. To illustrate, assume that Universal Corporation commenced business on October 1, 1991 with cash in the Royal Bank, $300 000, Inventory at Cost, $100 000, Office Equipment, $150 000, Accounts Payable, $50 000, and an investment of common shares being issued to five original shareholders contributing $100 000 each. The steps to journalize and post this opening entry under AccPac Plus may be analyzed as follows:

- Using digits only, enter October 1, 1991 as the system date, because you want this date as the transaction date.
- Enter the usual commands required to display the AccPac Plus start menu.
- Select "Universal Corporation" from the start menu.
- Respond to the prompts displayed on the first screen, making sure that the date to be used is the transaction date and that the fiscal period is number 12 (that is, you want to program to accept 12 fiscal periods).
- You must now record the opening entry as at October 1, 1991. Assume that the chart of accounts has been created so that you can confirm the account codes. Some accountants also suggest that you print a hard copy of this chart as well as writing down the entry or entries in general journal form before entering them through the batching process.
- Make sure that the General Ledger Master Menu is displayed as shown earlier in Figure 11-24. Then select Program 3, for "Transaction processing," whose menu will be displayed as shown in Figure 11-29.

FIGURE 11-29

```
UNIVERSAL CORPORATION                          Oct 01 1991
┌─ ACCPAC General Ledger Master Menu ─┐
    ┌─ Transaction Processing Menu ─┐
    │ 1.  Batch processing           │
    │ 2.  Print batches              │
    │ 3.  Post batches               │
    │ 4.  Print posting journal      │
    └────────────────────────────────┘

    Q.  Quit
```

CHAPTER 11: Using Microcomputer Software to Process Common Accounting Applications **499**

Analysis A close study of Figure 11-29 is important, because the Transaction Processing Menu may be called the "heart" of the batch-oriented system under AccPac Plus.

- Option 1, "Batch processing," permits the user to add, modify, or delete batches; retrieve sub-ledger batches; create a reallocation batch; create, archive, or delete recurring batches; and import batches.
- Option 2, "Print batches," is used to print lists of unposted batches and identify errors for use in verifying the batches before posting.
- Option 3, "Post batches," contains the programs to post batches to current-year accounts and, if necessary, to previous-year accounts.
- Option 4, "Print posting journal," is not to be confused with the traditional "book" of original entry. Under batch processing, a ***posting journal*** is used to print an audit trail report of details posted in one or more posting runs or by the Close Year function, and to allow the file to be cleared. This option is important, because if errors are found during posting an Error Report is printed at the end of the journal, indicating where the errors were found and the number of the new batch in which the incorrect entries were placed.

> Posting journal: under batch processing, an audit trail of what was posted.

CREATING A NEW BATCH FILE THROUGH OPTION 1
Follow these steps to enter the opening entry through the "Batch processing" function:

- **Step 1** Since option 1 is already selected, simply press <Enter>. A Batch Processing Menu will appear as shown in Figure 11-30.

FIGURE 11-30

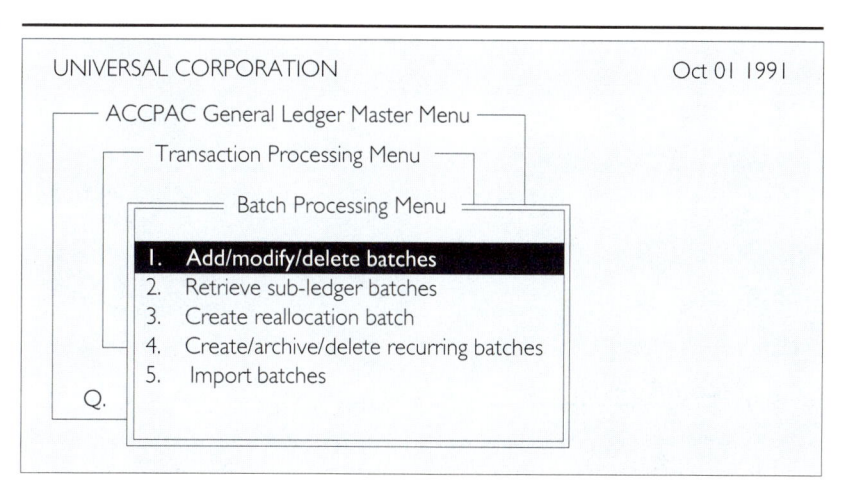

```
UNIVERSAL CORPORATION                          Oct 01 1991
    ACCPAC General Ledger Master Menu
        Transaction Processing Menu
            Batch Processing Menu
            1.  Add/modify/delete batches
            2.  Retrieve sub-ledger batches
            3.  Create reallocation batch
            4.  Create/archive/delete recurring batches
            5.  Import batches
            Q.
```

Analysis A close study of Figure 11-30 is important, because the Batch Processing Menu may be called the "heart" of the batch-oriented system. As can be observed, the menu shows five options. Since we want to add a new batch to record the opening entry and option 1 is already highlighted (selected), simply press <Enter>. A screen appears as illustrated in Figure 11-31.

500 PART 2: COMMON ACCOUNTING APPLICATIONS

FIGURE 11-31

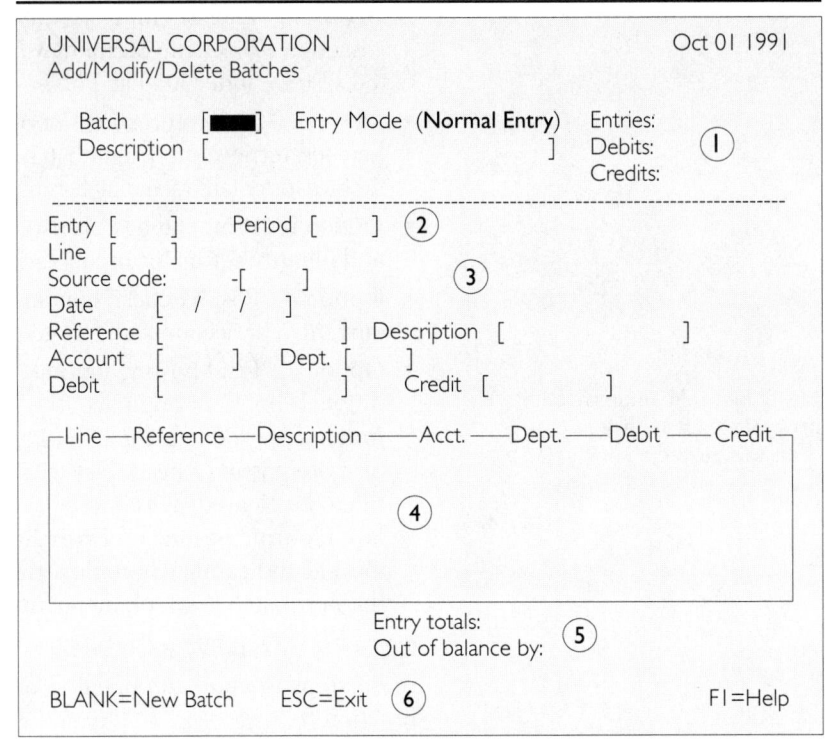

```
┌─────────────────────────────────────────────────────────────────────┐
│  UNIVERSAL CORPORATION                              Oct 01 1991     │
│  Add/Modify/Delete Batches                                          │
│                                                                     │
│     Batch        [■]     Entry Mode (Normal Entry)  Entries:        │
│     Description  [                              ]   Debits:    (1)  │
│                                                     Credits:        │
│     -------------------------------------------------------------   │
│     Entry  [    ]      Period [    ]  (2)                           │
│     Line   [    ]                                                   │
│     Source code:      -[    ]           (3)                         │
│     Date       [   /   /   ]                                        │
│     Reference  [            ]  Description [              ]         │
│     Account    [       ]  Dept. [    ]                              │
│     Debit      [        ]      Credit [         ]                   │
│                                                                     │
│    ┌─Line──Reference──Description───Acct.──Dept.──Debit──Credit─┐   │
│    │                                                            │   │
│    │                         (4)                                │   │
│    │                                                            │   │
│    │                                                            │   │
│    └────────────────────────────────────────────────────────────┘   │
│                              Entry totals:                          │
│                              Out of balance by:  (5)                │
│                                                                     │
│    BLANK=New Batch     ESC=Exit  (6)                     F1=Help    │
└─────────────────────────────────────────────────────────────────────┘
```

(1) Information that applies to all entries in a batch, and the batch debit and credit totals which are updated when each new or modified entry is saved.

(2) The number assigned to an entry, and the fiscal period that is common to all details in the entry.

(3) Information that can be entered for each detail.

(4) Display area which can list up to five of the details being added for the current entry.

(5) Debit and credit totals of details entered for the current entry, and the amount, if any, by which the entry is out of balance.

(6) "Chat line" list of activities and keystrokes that are possible from the current cursor position. This line tells you to leave the Batch (number) field blank if you are creating a new batch, or to press <Esc> if you want to exit the function.

FIGURE 11-32

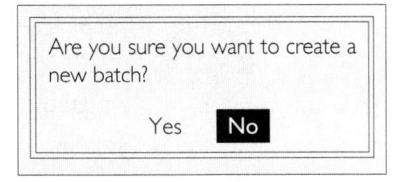

```
┌──────────────────────────────────────┐
│                                      │
│  Are you sure you want to create a   │
│  new batch?                          │
│                                      │
│              Yes    ▌No▐             │
│                                      │
└──────────────────────────────────────┘
```

- **Step 2** To create a new batch, press <Enter> in the Batch field without making an entry. You will see a dialogue box as shown in Figure 11-32. Type <Y> (or use the <right arrow> key) to move the highlight to Yes; then press <Enter> to create the new batch.

  Note that 1 appears in the Batch field, because no previous batch has been processed. When working with the user's own source data, for example, journal vouchers, it is recommended that you note the batch number on the source document used for transaction entry.

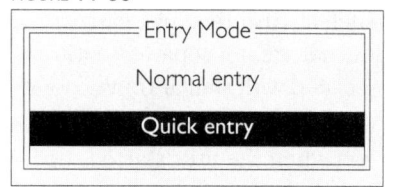

CHAPTER 11: Using Microcomputer Software to Process Common Accounting Applications **501**

The batch number will be included with the batch entries on the posting journal that is printed under option 4 of the Transaction Processing Menu (Figure 11-29).

- **Step 3** A small "Entry Mode" window is displayed at the top of the new batch grid as in Figure 11-33. Use <downward arrow> to select "Quick entry" and press <Enter>.

  Briefly, the Quick Entry mode is used for entries whose detail lines use the same date, source code, reference description, and comment lines. On the other hand, the Normal Entry mode is used when you want to vary the information included with detail lines. Since we are creating a batch for the opening entry whose detail lines will use the same date, source code, and reference description, we want the Quick mode.

- **Step 4** A large block cursor is displayed opposite the batch description field. Here, simply type "Opening entry" and press <Enter>.

- **Step 5** The cursor moves down to the Entry field. Briefly, entry numbers are assigned sequentially by the program and you must use the number that appears. In this case, the number 1 appears automatically and it will apply to all the detail lines in the entry. This number is important, because it will appear with the entry on the batch listing and the posting journal as a means of tracing transactions back to their source documents. Press <Enter> to accept number 1 in the Entry field.

- **Step 6** The cursor moves to the Period field. AccPac Plus automatically supplies the fiscal period number that is associated with the date you entered when you started the program and data. Since we assume that 12 was entered as the number of the current fiscal period during the setting up of the company, we will assume that 12 has appeared in the Period field. Press <Enter> to accept this displayed fiscal period.

- **Step 7** The Line field automatically shows number 1 and is skipped. Briefly, the Line field is used when you are modifying details. The cursor moves to the Source Code field.

  Under the program, every detail line entered into the G/L must have a source code associated with it. Under AccPac Plus, the code must be in two parts and consist of three or four characters. For example, in the code GL-CD, the first two characters identify the ledger or program where the transaction originated (GL = general ledger); the final one or two characters describe the type of transaction (CD = cash disbursement).

  To simplify matters, the user simply presses <F5> at the Source Code field to display the finder list of the source codes defined for the company in the Source Code Maintenance Menu. In our example, we assume a finder list of source codes for Universal Corporation as shown in Figure 11-34. Since the opening entry is a journal entry for

FIGURE 11-33

```
┌─────── Entry Mode ───────┐
│      Normal entry        │
│      Quick entry         │
└──────────────────────────┘
```

FIGURE 11-34

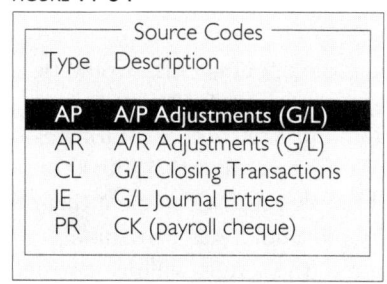

```
┌────── Source Codes ──────┐
│ Type   Description       │
│ AP     A/P Adjustments (G/L) │
│ AR     A/R Adjustments (G/L) │
│ CL     G/L Closing Transactions │
│ JE     G/L Journal Entries │
│ PR     CK (payroll cheque) │
└──────────────────────────┘
```

Source journal: under AccPac Plus, a listing of transactions of a specific type, such as sales, cash receipts, or cash disbursements.

the G/L, the user would use the <downward arrow> key to highlight source code JE, for G/L Journal Entries, then press <Enter> to select it.

Note that the ***source journal*** is not the same as the journal under a manual system. Instead, each source journal is equivalent to a subsidiary ledger. Thus, source journals such as cash receipts, cash disbursements, payroll, and general journal are not separate entities. They merely represent names to be associated with similar transactions.

- **Step 8** The cursor moves down to the Date field which displays the date that was entered on the title screen when the user started the G/L program. Press <Enter> to accept the displayed date.
- **Step 9** The cursor moves to the Reference field. Although you are not required to enter a reference, we will assume that the opening entry was approved on JV#1 (journal voucher number 1). We will assume that the user is requested to enter this reference as a further means of tracing this transaction back to its source documents.
- **Step 10** Type "Opening entry" and press <Enter> for the Description field.
- **Step 11** The cursor moves to the Account field. You can enter 1020 for Cash in Royal Bank or press <F5> to select the proper account from the Finder. In both cases, after pressing <Enter> the correct account number and account title will be displayed in their correct fields. In our example, the Dept. field has been skipped, because no departments were identified in the setup of the chart of accounts.
- **Step 12** The cursor moves to the Debit field. Here, the correct amount, 300000.00, would be entered without the currency sign or comma. Under AccPac Plus, you can enter an amount with or without the decimal point. If you do not include a decimal point, the program automatically inserts one, allowing for the number of decimal places you use. After pressing <Enter> for the Debit amount, the program displays the first line reference as shown in Figure 11-35.

    Observe below the line reference section that the entry totals correspond to the debit of $300 000. Of course, the program shows that the batch file is out of balance by that amount, since only one line detail has been entered. As stated earlier, you cannot post a batch file of entries to accounts unless the file shows that debits equal credits.
- **Step 13** The remaining detail lines of the opening entry would be entered in consecutive order; that is, account 1300 for Inventory at Cost, $100 000; 1520 for Office Equipment, $150 000; 2010 for Accounts Payable, $50 000; and 3000 for Common Shares, $500 000. For the two credit entries, you would simply press <Enter> at the Debit field to move the cursor to the Credit field. After the final detail line of the opening entry is entered, the screen will display the batch file as in Figure 11-36.

CHAPTER 11: Using Microcomputer Software to Process Common Accounting Applications   **503**

FIGURE 11-35

```
UNIVERSAL CORPORATION                                      Oct 01 1991
Add/Modify/Delete Batches

   Batch          [  1  ]   Entry Mode  (Quick Entry)   Entries:  0
   Description    [ Opening entry                   ]   Debits:   0.00
                                                        Credits:  0.00
   ------------------------------------------------------------------------
   Entry  [  1  ]      Period  [ 12 ]
   Line   [  2  ]
   Source code:   GL  -[ JE  ]   G/L Journal Entries
   Date         [ 10 / 01 / 91 ]
   Reference    [ JV#1          ]    Description  [ Opening entry  ]
   Account      [ ■■■■ ]    Dept. [        ]
   Debit        [              ]    Credit       [                 ]

   ┌─Line──Reference──Description──────Acct.──Dept.──Debit──────Credit─┐
   │  1     JV#1       Opening entry    1020         300,000.00        │
   │                                                                    │
   │                                                                    │
   │                                                                    │
   └────────────────────────────────────────────────────────────────────┘

                                   Entry totals:       300,000.00
                                   Out of balance by:  300,000.00

   ESC=Re-enter                                              F1=Help
```

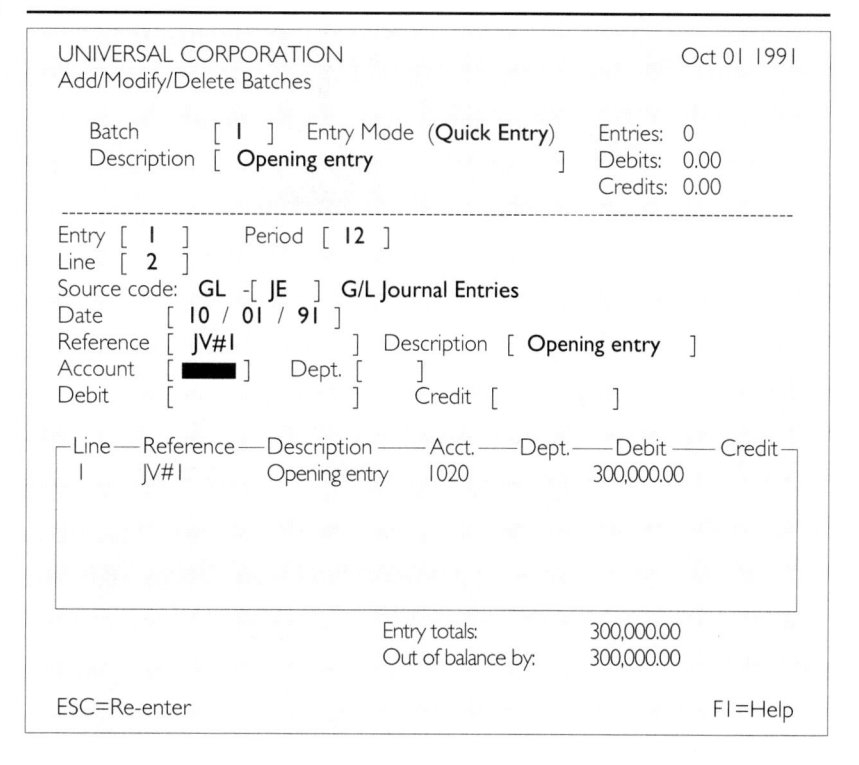

FIGURE 11-36

```
UNIVERSAL CORPORATION                                      Oct 01 1991
Add/Modify/Delete Batches

   Batch          [  1  ]   Entry Mode  (Quick Entry)   Entries:  0
   Description    [ Opening entry                   ]   Debits:   0.00
                                                        Credits:  0.00
   ------------------------------------------------------------------------
   Entry  [  1  ]      Period  [ 12 ]
   Line   [  2  ]
   Source code:   GL  -[ JE  ]   G/L Journal Entries
   Date         [ 10 / 01 / 91 ]
   Reference    [ JV#1          ]    Description  [ Opening entry  ]
   Account      [ ■■■■ ]    Dept. [        ]
   Debit        [              ]    Credit       [                 ]

   ┌─Line──Reference──Description──────Acct.──Dept.──Debit──────Credit─┐
   │  1     JV#1       Opening entry    1020         300,000.00        │
   │  2     JV#1       Opening entry    1300         100,000.00        │
   │  3     JV#1       Opening entry    1520         150,000.00        │
   │  4     JV#1       Opening entry    2010                    50,000.00│
   │  5     JV#1       Opening entry    3000                   500,000.00│
   └────────────────────────────────────────────────────────────────────┘

                                   Entry totals:       550,000.00  550,000.00
                                   Out of balance by:       0.00

   ESC=Re-enter                                              F1=Help
```

- **Step 14** When the cursor is again in the Account field, you would press <Esc> to call up the dialogue box at the bottom of the screen as shown in Figure 11-37.

FIGURE 11-37

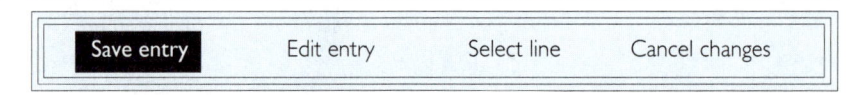

| Save entry | Edit entry | Select line | Cancel changes |

After checking the contents of Batch 1 to ensure that all details are accurate, you would press <Enter> to save the file. If any changes were to be made, you would move the cursor to "Edit entry" and press <Enter>. Of course, you could cancel all entries by using the "Cancel changes" section of the dialogue box.

After saving Batch 1, the cursor returns to the Entry field and the next entry number is displayed. Also, the program displays in the upper right corner the summary of entries made as well as the total debits and total credits entered in the first batch file, as shown in Figure 11-38.

FIGURE 11-38

Entries	1
Debits	550,000.00
Credits	500,000.00

PRINTING A BATCH LISTING Under batch processing, it is important to print a batch listing before posting of accounts is done to the G/L. Refer back to the Transaction Processing Menu, Figure 11-29. AccPac

FIGURE 11-39

```
Date: Oct 01 91        9:40am         UNIVERSAL CORPORATION
Batch Listing

Batch number      from   [  1  ] to [  1  ]
Source ledger     from   [     ] to [  ZZ ]
Creation date     from   [Oct 01 91] to [Dec 31 91]
Status(es) selected: Open, Printed

Batch number:     1  Opening entry           Creation date: Oct 01 91   Status: Open

Entry      Line
Number     No.     Pd.         Acct.     Dept.      Account Description
           Srce.   Date                  Reference  Description                 Debits        Credits       Errors

  1         1       12          1020                Cash in Royal Bank
           GL-JE  Oct 01 91  JV#1                   Opening entry              300,000.00
            2       12          1300                Inventory at Cost
           GL-JE  Oct 01 91  JV#1                   Opening entry              100,000.00
  1         3       12          1520                Office Equipment
           GL-JE  Oct 01 91  JV#1                   Opening entry              150,000.00
  1         4       12          2010                Accounts Payable
           GL-JE  Oct 01 91  JV#1                   Opening entry                            50,000.00
  1         5       12          3000                Common Stock
           GL-JE  Oct 01 91  JV#1                   Opening entry                           500,000.00
                                                                               ──────────   ──────────
                                                                               550,000.00   550,000.00      *
                                                                               550,000.00   550,000.00
                                                                               ══════════   ══════════

1 entry printed.       0 errors found.
1 batch printed.
```

CHAPTER 11: Using Microcomputer Software to Process Common Accounting Applications **505**

Plus deliberately sets the order so that the user is forced to "Print batches" before option 3, "Post batches," is selected.

The steps to print a batch listing are easy to follow. From the Transaction Processing Menu, you would select 2 to "Print batches." From a dialogue box, you would simply select "Print" to print the listings as specified on the screen. The printout would appear as shown in Figure 11-39.

Of course, after printing the batch listing, you would review the information. If the listing reports errors in the batch, you would correct the mistakes before posting the contents to the G/L.

POSTING THE BATCH TO THE G/L

Under AccPac Plus, when a batch or batches have been listed and are error-free, a clerk can post them to the appropriate accounts in the G/L.

As Figure 11-29 shows, posting is done through option 3 of the Transaction Processing Menu. When option 3 is selected, a "Post Batches Menu" appears similar to the one shown in Figure 11-40. In the majority of cases, the user will want to post the batch to the current year. Since this option is highlighted, the user would simply press <Enter>. An important message is displayed as shown in Figure 11-41.

FIGURE 11-40

Post Batches Menu
1. Post batches to current year.
2. Post batches to previous year.

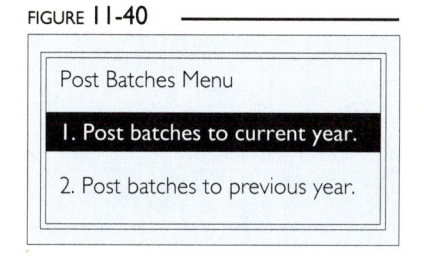

FIGURE 11-41

UNIVERSAL CORPORATION   Oct 01 1991
Post Batches to Current Year

    Starting Batch   [1]
    Ending Batch   [1]

    Warning! Back up data before proceeding.
    This function will post batch entries in the range of
    batches selected, and update account information.

                    Post   Edit   Cancel

                                                        F1=Help

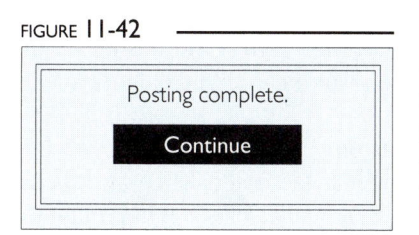

FIGURE 11-42

Posting complete.
Continue

Obviously, the message warns you to make a backup copy of the data disk containing the Universal Corporation files before proceeding. As the screen indicates, you would move the cursor to the Post field to select it. The posting process begins. You will see the message displayed in Figure 11-42. To return to the Post Batches Menu, press <Enter> or type C for "Continue." Press <Esc> to return to the Transaction Processing Menu.

PRINTING THE POSTING JOURNAL

The final procedure in AccPac Plus's Transaction Processing Menu is to print the posting journal (option 4 in Figure 11-29). To print this journal, you would select 4 from the Transaction Processing Menu and simply follow the screen display to specify the posting sequence number of the journal you want to print or to select "Print" to print all the journals specified on the screen. As indicated previously, the posting sequence number was assigned to the journal when you posted the batch. This number is also attached to each of the posted details, and can be used to track the details from the G/L listing and source journals. A facsimile of the G/L Posting Journal printout is shown as Figure 11-43.

FIGURE 11-43

```
Date: Oct 01 91      12:18pm           UNIVERSAL CORPORATION                                    Page: 1
G/L Posting Journal

Posting sequence number:  1

Posting Batch Entry
Entry   No.     No.    Pd.
        Date    Srce.        Description       Reference    Acct.    Dept.    Debits       Credits

  1      1       1      12
        Oct 01 91  GL-JE     Opening entry      JV#1        1020              300,000.00
        Oct 01 91  GL-JE     Opening entry      JV#1        1300              100,000.00
        Oct 01 91  GL-JE     Opening entry      JV#1        1520              150,000.00
        Oct 01 91  GL-JE     Opening entry      JV#1        2010                            50,000.00
        Oct 01 91  GL-JE     Opening entry      JV#1        3000                           500,000.00
                                                                                                      *
                                                                              550,000.00   550,000.00

                                                                Posted Total  550,000.00   550,000.00

1 posting entry printed.
```

As you can see, the posting journal is the sequential record of each entry that is posted to the general ledger accounts during the fiscal year. Under AccPac's batch processing system, it forms an essential part of the audit trail, linking the batch listings to the general ledger listing. Under the program, you must print the posting journal before you can close the ledger at year-end.

Other useful follow-up procedures to posting would be to print the General Ledger Listing, Source Journals, and Batch Status Report under the Reports Menu, which occurs under option 5 of the G/L Master Menu (Figure 11-24). Of course, you could also print the opening balance sheet under option 4, "Financial reports."

Limited space in this chapter prevents our examining other important AccPac Plus General Ledger functions such as the trial balance worksheet and closing the ledger. To end this overview of AccPac Plus, it is important to emphasize that the batching process would also be used in other modules such as Accounts Receivable (through sales invoice batching) and Accounts Payable (through purchase invoice batching). Furthermore, these modules would be integrated with the general ledger, since the G/L program will accept transaction batches from other modules such as Accounts Receivable and Accounts Payable. Since batch processing is an essential characteristic of AccPac Plus, it is now useful to examine the controversy about batch processing versus real-time accounting as summarized in the next section.

Batch Processing Versus Real-Time Accounting

Supporters of batch transaction processing (the batch-oriented system) may be called traditionalists, because of the long history associated with this method of processing transactions. For example, when mainframe computers first emerged to process accounting data in the 1960s, it was normal to separate the function of accounting from central data processing, where that accounting data would be processed. Consequently, accounting personnel insisted on submitting accounting transactions in batches with instructions to data processing to process those transactions in batches. Subsequently, a batch listing of transactions would be submitted to accounting to check that all transactions were accounted for. Only after checking that all transactions were there and accurately processed did accounting give permission to data processing to post these batches to the G/L and other subsidiary ledgers. Thus emerged to central idea that accounting needed strong internal control over accounting transactions because accounting did not have hands-on control over those early computers.

When microcomputers emerged in the late 1970s, it was logical to extend the idea of batch processing in areas where strong accounting control was essential. In some large businesses, for example, microcomputers may still be removed from the direct control of accounting personnel. Furthermore, a business may assign one data entry clerk to processing payables, another to processing receivables, and still another to the G/L. In this case, batch processing may be the answer to control transactions entered by data entry clerks with little or no knowledge of accounting.

In summary, supporters of batch transaction processing claim these advantages:

- Batch processing gives the user strong accounting control, because, within each batch, transaction is assigned a number so that the user can audit the system easily.
- Under batch processing, the user must print the Transaction Batch List to show that all the transactions in the batch have been accounted for.
- Under batch processing, the user is normally required to print the Batch Listing and Batch Status Report so that the user can review all up-to-date information on all unposted batches.
- Under batch processing, posting to the G/L and other accounting modules will be prevented if errors are found in any batch. Consequently corrections can be made before posting the transactions to the G/L and other modules.

- Batch processing does support an integration of accounting modules, because the G/L will accept batches directly from other modules such as accounts receivable and accounts payable.
- Under batch processing, you can assign a data entry clerk to enter transaction batches; these transaction batches would be approved by the accountant, who then posts them directly or authorizes clerks to post them to the G/L and other ledgers.

On the other hand, supporters of real-time accounting of transactions emerged when computers to process accounting data were brought under the direct control of accounting personnel. This trend was most evident when microcomputers became widely accepted in accounting departments rather than being separated in a central data processing department. Therefore, accounting had strong control over accounting data as well as the processing of that data.

In summary, supporters of real-time processing (sometimes called direct on-line entry processing) claim these advantages:

- All reports and summaries are available and are as current as the last posted transactions. Therefore, up-to-the-minute financial information is always available to management. On the other hand, batch processing usually limits this type of reporting to month-ends and year-ends, thus making the information too late for many management-type decisions on financial matters.
- Direct entry allows the operator to enter transactions into the accounts without first entering them into a batch. Thus, valuable time is saved.
- Most real-time accounting packages prevent any posting of double entries that do not balance; therefore, there is no need for the extra step of preparing batch files of all transactions.
- Real-time accounting is easier to use, because data entry clerks do not have to be trained in the setting up of batch files.
- Real-time accounting is much quicker, since the effects of the transactions are immediately reflected in the account balances. On the other hand, batch processing is time-consuming because of the extra steps required between entry and posting of transactions.
- Batch processing can be cumbersome, especially when a data entry clerk with little or no knowledge of accounting records the same transaction in more than one batch. Thus, added steps, such as the recording of transactions on manually prepared batch data entry forms, are often required before entering transactions via the computer.
- Real-time accounting works well in an environment in which accounting has strong control over computer systems and in which clerks have a good knowledge of accounting theory and application.

CHAPTER 11: Using Microcomputer Software to Process Common Accounting Applications

From the student's viewpoint, it is logical to conclude that some exposure to real-time and batch processing packages should be obtained, since both systems exist in accounting practice where computers are required.

Easypay Accounting Package

The majority of small businesses employing fewer than 20 employees process their payroll application by using one of the manual shortcuts described in the previous chapter. However, as the business grows and adds employees, management must consider a more efficient method to process and account for its regular payroll. In general, one of four alternatives is considered:

- Hire the services of a banker which has computer facilities to provide efficient and cost-saving payroll services. In this case, the employer would simply provide the banker with payroll data completed manually on the banker's standard payroll input forms. In return for a processing service fee, the banker returns payroll printouts that would include payroll cheques or bank deposit transfer slips and accompanying employee earnings stubs (vouchers), updated individual employee's earnings records, and payroll registers. Of course, the employer would still have to make manual payroll journal entries to post totals from the payroll register to the G/L. In February, the banker would also provide the extra service of printing annual tax slips and tax statements as described in Chapter 10.
- Engage the services of a professional accountant who has computer facilities and payroll software to do what the banker described above would perform.
- Replace the entire manual accounting system with a microcomputer and software which includes a Canadian payroll package.
- Add a Canadian payroll package to complement the business's present computer system and accounting package that presently lacks payroll.

Easypay: a Canadian payroll package produced by Vukusic Consulting Services Inc.

One Canadian company produces a powerful stand-alone payroll program called **Easypay** to service the needs of bookkeepers and professional accountants who require a Canadian payroll package to do their clients' payroll or to add such software to complement a business's present accounting package which lacks the payroll module.

MAIN CHARACTERISTICS

The following points may be regarded as the essential characteristics of the Easypay package, Version 6.05.

- It assumes that the user is familiar with the workings of an IBM PC (or compatible) and MS-DOS or PC-DOS, Version 2.1 or higher.
- It assumes that the user has a basic knowledge of payroll accounting.
- The program is of real value to businesses with a payroll of between 5 and 200 employees.

510 PART 2: COMMON ACCOUNTING APPLICATIONS

- The program requires a minimum of 2 megabytes of hard disk space and a working memory of at least 512K.
- For each pay period, the program allows time card entry and prints a time card journal; calculates payroll deductions automatically; allows for manual adjustments to calculated amounts; prints a payroll register; prints payroll cheques and a cheque register; and updates all year-to-date amounts automatically.
- The program maintains useful historical records by keeping year-to-date amounts for employees; by keeping details of every cheque issued indefinitely; and by keeping departmental costing history.
- The program has special features; for example, it permits the user to print cheques on demand, and it supports the printing of multiple cheques in the same period for an employee, of prior-period cheques, or of future cheques.
- Easypay produces T4s and Relevé 1s at year-end; it prints the Record of Employment upon employee termination; it produces a remittance report monthly or semimonthly; and it creates and prints general ledger entries.
- The program exports payroll journal entries to general ledger packages such as AccPac Plus, Business Vision II, Flex, Great Plains, Macola, Mibar, NewViews, Orchard, Platinum, Premier, SBT, Solomon III, and Summation.
- And, finally, for a nominal yearly cost, Easypay provides a support program that includes upgrades, the incorporation of any changes from the Department of National Revenue, and free telephone support.

OVERVIEW A fair overview of Easypay's program is to follow a payroll run. To simplify matters, assume a company, O. Laschuk, Inc., which has decided to use Easypay to process its weekly payroll of five salaried personnel and then to export the payroll summary to a compatible general ledger package such as Summation 2.40. Follow the steps below to see how one week's payroll run would be processed and accounted for.

- **Step 1. Installing Easypay** This is quite straightforward, since the first diskette of two contains the INSTALL program to install the entire payroll program into a main directory called **\EASYPAY**. What is important to remember, however, is that before you can start Easypay, you must create a directory called \EASYDATA to hold your company's data files. Under this directory subdirectories can then be created for your company or others. For example, if "O. Laschuk, Inc." were to be used, a subdirectory **\EASYDATA\OLAS** could be created. As you will learn, Easypay asks for a company directory every time you start the program. For purposes of following a payroll run, assume that O. Laschuk, Inc. has installed Easypay successfully and has created the directory and subdirectory called \EASYDATA\OLAS to process its weekly payroll for five salaried personnel.

\EASYPAY: under MS-DOS, the backslash character (\) is the symbol for the *root directory*; therefore, the directory \EASYDATA will be located in the root directory.

\EASYPAY\OLAS: the subdirectory, \OLAS, will be located under the main directory, \EASYDATA.

CHAPTER 11: Using Microcomputer Software to Process Common Accounting Applications **511**

- **Step 2. Starting and stopping the program** This too is quite straightforward. You must be in the root directory to start the program; for example, if the program were installed in drive C, then at the C prompt you would simply type EASYPAY and press <Enter>. When the program starts, the screen shown in Figure 11-44 appears.

FIGURE 11-44

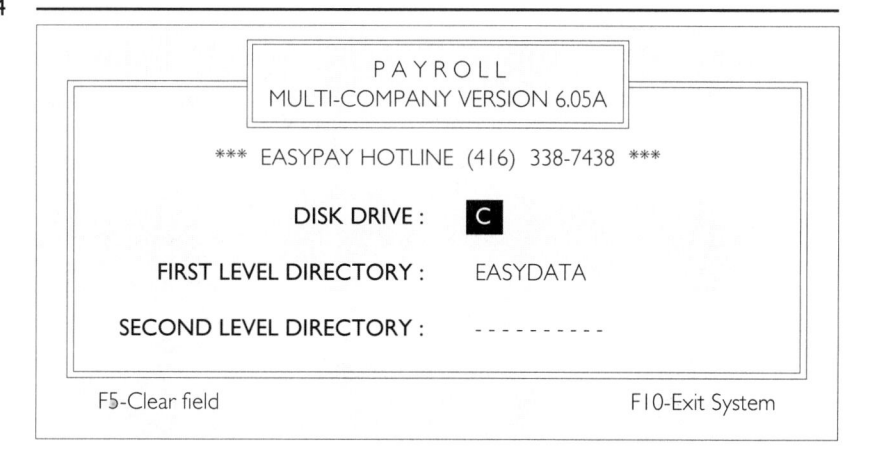

```
                    P A Y R O L L
              MULTI-COMPANY VERSION 6.05A

              *** EASYPAY HOTLINE (416) 338-7438 ***

                       DISK DRIVE :     C

                  FIRST LEVEL DIRECTORY :    EASYDATA

                 SECOND LEVEL DIRECTORY :    ----------

    F5-Clear field                                  F10-Exit System
```

FIGURE 11-45

```
              DISK DRIVE : C

    FIRST LEVEL DIRECTORY:  EASYDATA

    SECOND LEVEL DIRECTORY: OLAS

    Is the above information correct (Y, N)?  ▮

    data file path = C:\EASYDATA\OLAS\

    F5-Clear field          F10-Exit System
```

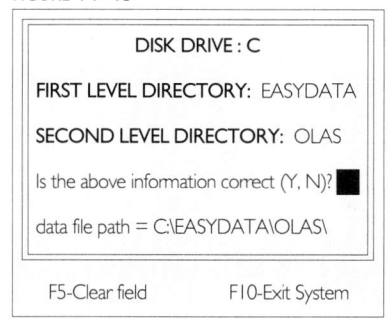

FIGURE 11-46

```
                EASYPAY
             CANADIAN PAYROLL

    PLEASE ENTER THE DATE  — / — / —
                            (dd mm yy)

         PASSWORD  ------------------------

    IS THIS A NEW COMPANY (Y,N)?  ▮

    data file path = C:\EASYDATA\OLAS\

    F1-Convention             F10-Exit
```

Analysis of Figure 11-44   The Multi-Company screen is where you tell Easypay which company you want to work on. You enter the disk drive letter and path for the company. In our case, we would simply leave disk drive C by pressing <Enter> and also press <Enter> to leave the first-level directory for EASYDATA. At the second-level directory, you would type the name of the company—in this case, OLAS—and press <Enter>. A verification message appears as shown in Figure 11-45. If the above information is correct, you would simply press <Y>. On the other hand, if an error were made, you would press <N> and start again.

If <Y> were pressed, a follow-up Date and Password screen appears as shown in Figure 11-46. This screen usually displays the name of the company you chose on the Multi-Company screen. If the company name appears, you would enter the date in the Date field. However, when it is a new company, the name is *not* displayed until you finish the setup and restart the program. Also, if it is a new company, there is no password to enter until you assign passwords in the setup procedure and restart the program.

O. Laschuk, Inc. is a new company; therefore, we would type Y and press <Enter>. The Company File Update screen appears and would be completed as shown in Figure 11-47.

Analysis   In general terms, the Update screen is where you enter the basic information for a company, set up default values, and assign passwords. Since fields that you complete on this screen appear on other screens as defaults (for example, on Timecard Entry and Employee Update screens), care

FIGURE 11-47

```
                        COMPANY FILE UPDATE

                Company name:   O. LASCHUK, INC. _____
                      Address:  300 Water Street _____
                                Whitby, ON _____
                                L1N 9B6 _____

    Employer Acct. # : ON123456789    Quebec Reg. # : _____
    Passwords : General - _____   Master - _____

    Cheque Date      Last Cheque    Pay Period    Employer: UIC      EHT
     28/06/91         000000          01           ____1.4%        0.000%

    Vacation Paid On    Reg Pay [Y]   Over Pay [Y]   Oth Pay [Y]   Each Pay [N]

                      (1)         (2)         (3)         (4)         (5)
    Deductions       [   ]       [   ]       [   ]       [   ]       [   ]
       Flags         (_)[_]      (_)[_]      (_)[_]      (_)[_]      (_)[_]

    Benefits         [   ]       [   ]       [   ]       [   ]       [   ]
       Flags         (_)[_]      (_)[_]      (_)[_]      (_)[_]      (_)[_]

    F1-Help       F2-Save & Exit          F8-Timecard Defaults       F10-Exit
```

should be taken to enter accurate data. Note that the fields at the bottom define the benefits and extra deductions for the company. Such deductions are in addition to the usual UI, CPP, and income tax ones. Easypay automatically calculates deductions for UI, CPP, and tax according to the conditions you set in each Employee Profile. In Figure 11-47, no extra deductions and benefits were set up in order to simplify a computerized payroll application.

The bottom of the screen identifies a function key as "F8-Timecard Defaults." Briefly, this program would be used as the last step in setting up the company file when hourly employees are involved. Since only salaried personnel with no changes to their regular pay are assumed for O. Laschuk, Inc., no timecards are required in the payroll system.

As the bottom of the screen directs, when the company file update is completed, you would press <F2> to save and exit this program. Easypay then returns to the Date and Password screen, where you can press <F10> to exit the entire program and return to the DOS prompt.

- **Step 3. Calling up the main menu** Another straightforward step. Start the program from the root directory by typing **EASYPAY**. On the title screen, complete the second-level directory with OLAS (as per Figure 11-45) and press <Enter>. Type <Y> to affirm the accuracy of the subdirectory. The Date and Password screen will be

CHAPTER 11: Using Microcomputer Software to Process Common Accounting Applications 513

displayed. Since the date for the payroll week ending 28/06/91 has been previously acknowledged, press <Enter> to accept it. Since no password has been entered, press <Enter> to skip this field. Easypay's main menu will be displayed as in Figure 11-48.

FIGURE 11-48

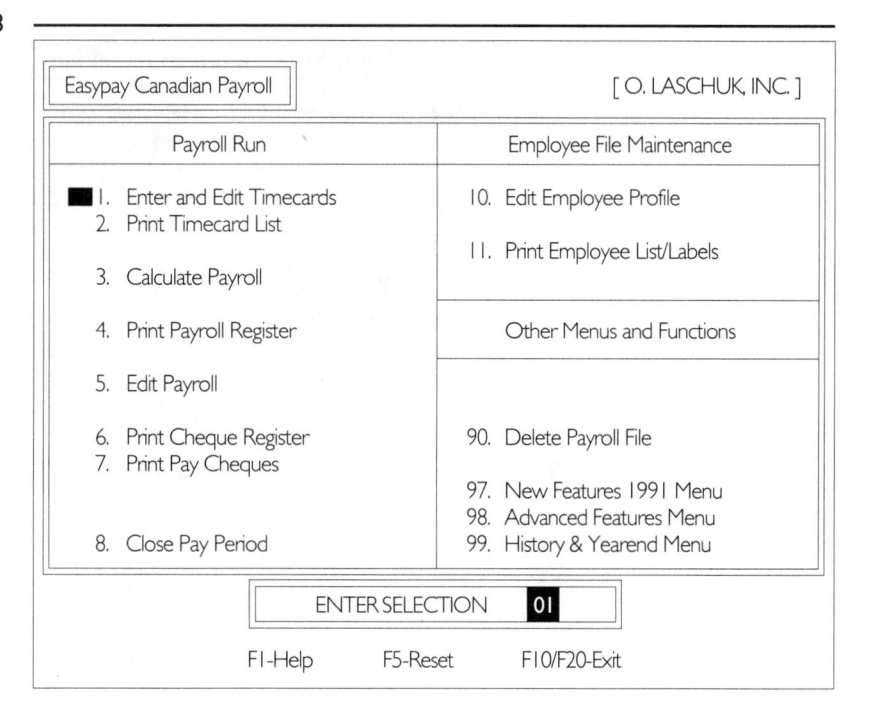

```
┌─────────────────────────────────────────────────────────────────┐
│  Easypay Canadian Payroll                    [ O. LASCHUK, INC. ] │
│  ┌──────────────────────────────┬──────────────────────────────┐ │
│  │        Payroll Run           │   Employee File Maintenance  │ │
│  ├──────────────────────────────┼──────────────────────────────┤ │
│  │ ■1.  Enter and Edit Timecards│  10.  Edit Employee Profile  │ │
│  │  2.  Print Timecard List     │                              │ │
│  │                              │  11.  Print Employee List/Labels │
│  │  3.  Calculate Payroll       │                              │ │
│  │                              ├──────────────────────────────┤ │
│  │  4.  Print Payroll Register  │  Other Menus and Functions   │ │
│  │                              │                              │ │
│  │  5.  Edit Payroll            │                              │ │
│  │                              │                              │ │
│  │  6.  Print Cheque Register   │  90.  Delete Payroll File    │ │
│  │  7.  Print Pay Cheques       │                              │ │
│  │                              │  97.  New Features 1991 Menu │ │
│  │                              │  98.  Advanced Features Menu │ │
│  │  8.  Close Pay Period        │  99.  History & Yearend Menu │ │
│  └──────────────────────────────┴──────────────────────────────┘ │
│                     ENTER SELECTION    [01]                      │
│                                                                  │
│              F1-Help     F5-Reset     F10/F20-Exit               │
└─────────────────────────────────────────────────────────────────┘
```

Analysis of Figure 11-48   The Easypay Canadian Payroll screen is regarded as the main menu. As you can see, this menu is divided into three sections: Payroll Run, Employee File Maintenance, and Other Menus and Functions. The different sections and functions of the main menu are briefly described below.

- **Payroll Run**   Steps 1 through 8 are executed in sequence to perform a regular payroll run. Therefore, even a relatively inexperienced computer clerk with accounting background will be able to complete the payroll run, because the program requires that all eight steps be done in sequence.
- **Employee File Maintenance**   Contains two options. Option 10, Edit Employee Profile, is where you enter individual employee records. In addition you can adjust the defaults you set up in the Company File Update for each employee. Option 11 allows the printing of employee lists or labels.
- **Other Menus and Functions**   This section contains special menu options, numbered 90, and then 97, 98, 99. For example, if you selected

99, History & Yearend Menu, the program will display a secondary menu as shown in Figure 11-49.

As you can observe, this menu is divided into two sections, headed History and Y-T-D Section and Yearend Functions Section, each of which offers a number of options. As you will learn, the option "51. Edit Department Codes" is important to run before you can create individual employee profiles.

FIGURE 11-49

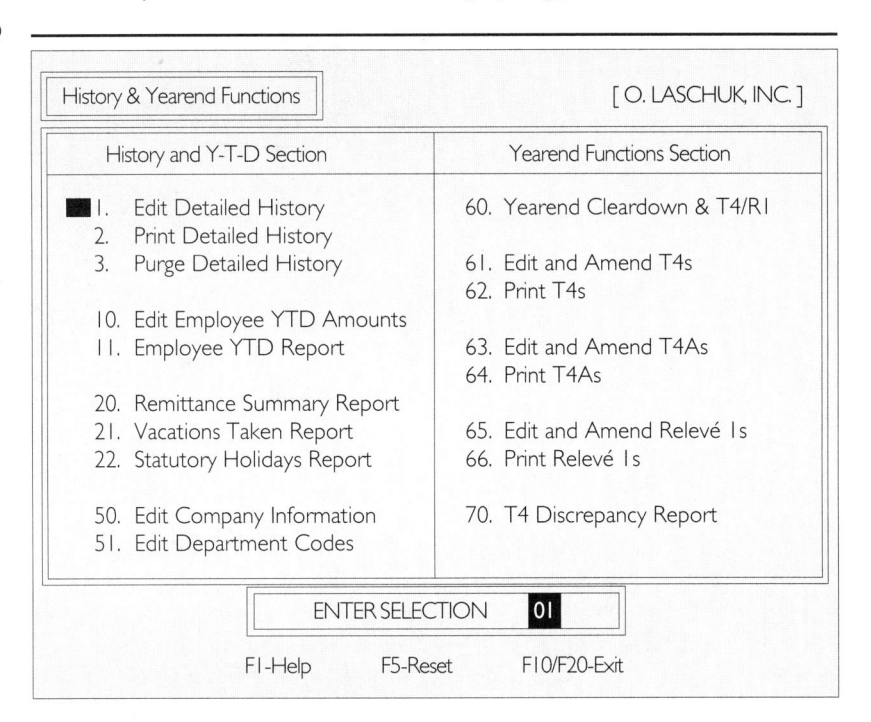

```
┌──────────────────────────────────────────────────────────────────┐
│ History & Yearend Functions                    [ O. LASCHUK, INC. ] │
├──────────────────────────────────┬───────────────────────────────┤
│   History and Y-T-D Section      │   Yearend Functions Section   │
│                                  │                               │
│  ■ 1.  Edit Detailed History     │  60. Yearend Cleardown & T4/R1│
│    2.  Print Detailed History    │                               │
│    3.  Purge Detailed History    │  61. Edit and Amend T4s       │
│                                  │  62. Print T4s                │
│   10.  Edit Employee YTD Amounts │                               │
│   11.  Employee YTD Report       │  63. Edit and Amend T4As      │
│                                  │  64. Print T4As               │
│   20.  Remittance Summary Report │                               │
│   21.  Vacations Taken Report    │  65. Edit and Amend Relevé 1s │
│   22.  Statutory Holidays Report │  66. Print Relevé 1s          │
│                                  │                               │
│   50.  Edit Company Information  │  70. T4 Discrepancy Report    │
│   51.  Edit Department Codes     │                               │
├──────────────────────────────────┴───────────────────────────────┤
│               ENTER SELECTION       01                           │
│                                                                  │
│       F1-Help         F5-Reset        F10/F20-Exit               │
└──────────────────────────────────────────────────────────────────┘
```

- **Step 4. Creating department codes** Under Easypay, you must create a department code before you can enter it on the Employee Profile even though the company may not be departmentalized. The reason is to offer management the ability to track the costs of individual employees. For example, in a restaurant business, the owner may wish to track the cost of waiters, chefs, bartenders, and other staff. Therefore, appropriate codes can be created such as WAITER, CHEFS, BAR, and OTHER. In the case of O. Laschuk, Inc., assume that the code OFFICE was set up through option 51 of Figure 11-49 to describe office personnel.
- **Step 5. Setting up the employee file** Once you have set up the Company File and created department codes, you must create a profile for each employee. In general, you would select "10. Edit Employee Profile" from the main menu (Figure 11-48). The screen that appears, called Employee Update/Profile, would be completed

CHAPTER 11: Using Microcomputer Software to Process Common Accounting Applications   **515**

for each employee. For example, the profile for the first employee for O. Laschuk, Inc. is completed as in Figure 11-50.

FIGURE 11-50

```
┌─ < Add > ─────────── EMPLOYEE UPDATE / PROFILE ─────────── 01.10 ─┐
│                                                                    │
│  Emp. No      Name              Address              City          │
│   0001    Chu Sam          1. 5789 Coopers Avenue    Mississauga   │
│                            2.                        Prov's  Pst cd│
│  Status  Dept  Type  Sex     Phone        SIN      Bank    ON ON L4Z 1R9│
│    A    OFFICE  SW   M   (416) 890-2400  425-127-511  Royal 519-238-0 │
│                                                                    │
│  Birth dt : 20/01/67    Reg rate : __600.00   Est inc.  : ____0.00   Exempt (Y/N)│
│  Hire dt  : 21/06/91    OT rate  : ___20.00   TD1 amt : __6489.00   UIC : N│
│  Term dt : 00/00/00     oth rate : _____.00   TD3 amt : _____.00   CPP/QPP : N│
│  Vac E/T : ____/____    Vac Flags : Y Y Y N   Vac Rt% : _____0     TAX : N│
│  TD1 L6 : _____.00      TD1 L9 : _____.00     TD1 L19 : _____.00   EHT : Y│
│  UIC rate : ___1.4      TPD-1V : _____.00     TPD-3V : _____.00    QHIP : __│
│                                                                    │
│  Deductions Name    [_]        [_]        [_]        [_]        [_]│
│             Amt    .00 (_)    .00 (_)    .00 (_)    .00 (_)    .00 (_)│
│             Ytd    .00        .00        .00        .00        .00│
│             Max    .00        .00        .00        .00        .00│
│  Benefits   Name    [_]        [_]        [_]        [_]        [_]│
│             Amt    .00 (_)    .00 (_)    .00 (_)    .00 (_)    .00 (_)│
│             Ytd    .00        .00        .00        .00        .00│
│             Max    .00        .00        .00        .00        .00│
│                                                                    │
│  F1-Help  F2-Save  F4-Print  F7-Windows  F8-YTD  F9-Hist  F15-Delete  F10/F20-Exit│
└────────────────────────────────────────────────────────────────────┘
```

Analysis   The program to complete the Employee Update/Profile covers all payroll requirements both in Quebec and in the remaining provinces.

- The screen is identified not only by its name, but also by its number as shown in the upper right corner. Here, the number 01.10 indicates that the screen originates from the main payroll menu (the first program screen, shown as Figure 11-48) from which program 10, Edit Employee Profile, was selected.
- Easypay requires that for every employee, a unique number between 1 and 9999 be chosen. In this way, you can always gain access to a given employee's payroll files by simply entering the correct number.
- In the spaces for the complete name and address of the employee, note that Easypay requires a recognized abbreviation for the province. Under the program, provinces are coded as shown in Figure 11-51.
- The letter A under Status means "active." L would be used for unpaid leave of absence, while T would disclose a terminated status. Obviously, only active employees can be paid; Easypay rejects payments by cheque or bank transfer for all others.

FIGURE 11-51

Valid Provincial Codes
Easypay Canadian Payroll

AL	Alberta
BC	British Columbia
MN	Manitoba
NB	New Brunswick
NF	Newfoundland
NS	Nova Scotia
NW	Northwest Territories
OC	Outside Canada
ON	Ontario
PI	Prince Edward Island
PQ	Quebec
SK	Saskatchewan
YK	Yukon

FIGURE 11-52

**Valid Employee Type Codes
Easypay Canadian Payroll**

HW	Hourly weekly
HB	Hourly twice weekly
H2	Hourly biweekly
HM	Hourly monthly
SW	Salaried weekly
SB	Salaried twice weekly
S2	Salaried biweekly
SM	Salaried monthly
CW	Commissioned weekly
CB	Commissioned twice monthly
C2	Commissioned biweekly
CM	Commissioned monthly

- As stated earlier, the classification of employees by department is required. Here, OFFICE is disclosed, since it was created in the Company File Update program.
- The Type field requires a two-digit code designating the type of payroll plan for each employee. As Figure 11-52 shows, Easypay covers payroll plans for the majority of situations for hourly, salaried, and commissioned personnel.
- The proper completion of the Sex, Phone, and SIN fields is self-evident. Note that the Bank field is used for direct deposits only; it can be left blank when employees are paid by cheque.
- The completion of the employee's birth date is required for CPP purposes. CPP begins immediately after the employee's eighteenth birthday and stops at 65.
- In the Reg Rate field a dollar value of the rate per unit of work as defined by the Type field must be shown. Therefore, for salaried personnel, the rate would be translated as the amount paid per pay period. If an hourly-rated employee were shown, the field would be completed as the rate per hour. For commissioned personnel, the rate would be the salary or draw per pay period.
- The next field, Est Inc, is to be filled out for commissioned employees only.
- The date the employee was hired is completed in the Hire Dt field.
- An overtime rate (OT Rate) of an amount per hour is to be completed for salaried, commissioned, or hourly employees.
- The TD1 amount is the actual dollar value on the employee's TD1 form (not the code).
- The Exempt (Y/N) column in the middle right corner shows fields for UIC, CPP/QPP, TAX, EHT (Employer's Health Tax), and QHIP (Quebec Health Insurance Plan). In Figure 11-50, UIC, CPP, and TAX are completed for Sam Chu with an N, because the employee is not exempt from these deductible items. However, a Y is shown opposite EHT, because employees in Ontario are no longer deducted for their provincial health insurance premium. As stated in Chapter 10, the premium must now be paid completely by the employer.
- Notice that there are four vacation flags, which are carried forward from responses on the Company Profile. The first flag is in answer to the question "Should vacation pay be paid on regular wages?" The answer must always be yes, because provincial pay regulations say so. If an employee does not receive vacation pay at all, you can code the Vac Rt% as zero. The second flag deals with the question "Should vacation pay be paid on overtime wages?" The third flag deals with the question "Should vacation pay be paid on other pay?" And, finally, the fourth flag answers the question "Should vacation pay be paid out on every cheque?"

- Notice that the UIC rate is fixed at 1.4, since that is the present rate (at the time of writing) at which the employer multiplies the employee's UI contributions to determine the employer's portion.
- The lower third of the Profile is used to complete extra deductions and benefits. These would have been set up in the Company Profile. For example, if a group insurance plan with a weekly deduction of $3 were in effect, the coded deduction GRINSU would be entered opposite "Name" and the amount directly below. The Ytd (year-to-date) amount is kept automatically by the system. An annual maximum can be put on a benefit or deduction. When the value specified in the Max field is reached in the Ytd field, the deduction or benefit is discontinued for the current year. For Sam Chu, no extra deductions or benefits were completed, since they were not acknowledged previously.
- Below the screen eight functions are made available. For example, to print a copy of the entire screen, you would simply press <F4>.
- **Step 6. Setting up general ledger accounts** Before a regular payroll run is processed, management must decide whether to interface Easypay with its computer system. As stated earlier, Easypay interfaces with many different general ledger packages. If the decision is made to integrate, G/L codes must be set up by someone familiar with how a general ledger works. On the other hand, if the company's G/L does not interface with Easypay, the G/L accounts cannot be set up. Instead, it is necessary to determine the journal entries from the monthly remittance summary report and then record and post them to the G/L manually. Since we assume that O. Laschuk, Inc. is using Summation 2.40 and since Summation's G/L does interface with Easypay, the following steps should be taken to set up G/L accounts:
  - From the main menu shown in Figure 11-48, select and enter 98 (the Advanced Features Menu). This menu contains several important functions under Other Reports and Functions, as shown in Figure 11-53.
  - From the Advanced Features Menu, select 40 (G/L Accounts Profile). A legend of codes for the available G/L interfaces is displayed, from which the user must enter the appropriate interface code. Once this code is entered, a Payroll G/L Accounts screen for the appropriate G/L software will be displayed, on which will be entered account code numbers for G/L accounts such as Wages or Salaries Expense, UI Payable, CPP Payable, Income Taxes Payable, other deductions payable, and Wages or Salaries Payable. Limited space prevents our illustrating the Payroll G/L Accounts screen and follow-up procedures. At this point, let us assume that G/L accounts have been set up by O. Laschuk, Inc. for the interface with Summation's general ledger package.

FIGURE 11-53

Other Reports and Functions
20. Printing of Separation Forms
30. Employee by Department Report
31. Departmental Costing Report
40. G/L Accounts Profile
41. Create G/L Journal Entries
42. Print G/L Journal Entries
50. Issue Automatic Advances
51. Recover Outstanding Advances
90. Delete Quick Cheque Payroll

FIGURE 11-54

Easypay Canadian Payroll
Payroll Run
1. Enter and Edit Timecards ✓
2. Print Timecard List ✓
3. Calculate Payroll ✓
4. Print Payroll Register
5. Edit Payroll
6. Print Cheque Register
7. Print Pay Cheques
8. Close Pay Period

- **Step 7. Processing the regular payroll run** As stated earlier, to run a regular payroll under Easypay, you would follow sequentially the options 1 through 8 on the main menu, shown sectionally in Figure 11-54. As each step is completed, the program places a check mark beside the option. This is a great feature, since it allows you to keep track of the pay period process. When you close a pay period, which is option 8, the check marks disappear. Again, limited space prevents our detailing each of the payroll run steps. Instead, a brief explanation of each function follows.

  - **Enter and Edit Timecards** Timecards are entered for hourly employees only. Salaried employees with no change to their standard rate of pay do not need to have timecards entered.

  - **Print Timecard List** After all of the timecards are entered for hourly-rated employees, an audit list of timecards is printed so that you can check all entries. At the end of the Timecard List, Easypay prints a list of all salaried employees available for payment.

  - **Calculate Payroll** Once you have printed the timecard list and have no further changes, you use this function to calculate automatically the payroll. Of course, the results of this automation are printed in the payroll register.

  - **Print Payroll Register** Under Easypay, the payroll register is a very important report, for it shows you the results of the previous step, "Calculate Payroll." A summary for each home department as well as a grand total is also printed. You should check this report carefully, and, if you catch any errors at this point, the program offers a simple way to correct the payroll before you print cheques or initiate bank deposit transfers. If this step were completed for O. Laschuk, Inc., the printout would look like Figure 11-55.

Analysis of Figures 11-55 and 11-56 These two figures represent printout pages 1 and 2 of the Payroll Register. Obviously, the concepts inherent in this printout are the same as those of a payroll register prepared under a manual system; only the format changes. Notice that on page 2, right-hand column, totals are provided for gross pay, minus the total deductions, to equal the total net pay. Obviously, these totals may be used to journalize and post the payroll to the G/L.

  - **Edit Payroll** Once you have calculated the payroll and printed the Payroll Register, the Edit Payroll function gives you access to the calculations of an employee's pay. If changes are required after checking the Payroll Register, you can edit the details of the payroll on a special edit screen. If no changes are required, you do not have to use this function.

  - **Print Cheque Register** The Cheque Register can be used for reconciliation of payroll cheques or to do direct deposits instead of issuing cheques. The printout will show a listing of employees by

FIGURE 11-55

```
O. LASCHUK, INC.                    PAYROLL REGISTER                        PAGE : 1

                        AS OF : JUN 30, 1991    FOR PAY PERIOD 01

  0001    Chu Sam                      SW      Cheque Date : 30/06/91         Cheque No. : 000001

  REG. HRS  :         .00      REG. PAY  :    600.00    OT. HRS  :       .00    OT. PAY   :       .00
  UIC INS   :      600.00      UIC DED   :     13.50    CPP/QPP  :     12.47    FED. TAX  :    127.34
                                                        GROSS    :    600.00    NET       :    446.69

  0002    Granum Lorri                 SW      Cheque Date : 30/06/91         Cheque No. . 000002

  REG. HRS  :         .00      REG. PAY  :    500.00    OT. HRS  :       .00    OT. PAY   :       .00
  UIC INS   :      500.00      UIC DED   :     11.25    CPP/QPP  :     10.17    FED. TAX  :     95.59
                                                        GROSS    :    500.00    NET       :    382.99

  0003    Macht Bernie                 SW      Cheque Date : 30/06/91         Cheque No. : 000003

  REG. HRS  :         .00      REG. PAY  :    450.00    OT. HRS  :       .00    OT. PAY   :       .00
  UIC INS   :      450.00      UIC DED   :     10.13    CPP/QPP  :      9.02    FED. TAX  :     83.44
                                                        GROSS    :    450.00    NET       :    347.41

  0004    McLean Sandra                SW      Cheque Date : 30/06/91         Cheque No. : 000004

  REG. HRS  :         .00      REG. PAY  :    650.00    OT. HRS  :       .00    OT. PAY   :       .00
  UIC INS   :      650.00      UIC DED   :     14.63    CPP/QPP  :     13.62    FED. TAX  :    147.62
                                                        GROSS    :    650.00    NET       :    474.13

  0005    Wright Sheelagh              SW      Cheque Date : 30/06/91         Cheque No. : 000005

  REG. HRS  :         .00      REG. PAY  :    550.00    OT. HRS  :       .00    OT. PAY   :       .00
  UIC INS   :      550.00      UIC DED   :     12.38    CPP/QPP  :     11.32    FED. TAX  :    108.72
                                                        GROSS    :    550.00    NET       :    417.58
```

employee number, their bank identification if bank deposit transfers are supported, cheque numbers, individual cheque amounts, and the total of the cheques (bank deposits) to be made.

- **Print Pay Cheques** This option lets you print payroll cheques and/or statements of earnings for each employee. Obviously, the information for printing cheques or statements is taken from the payroll transactions. You can preview these transactions by using the Edit Payroll function. If you discover an error once you print cheques and/or statements, you can use the Edit Payroll function to make adjustments and then reprint a cheque or issue a manual cheque.

- **Close Pay Period** Once all of the cheques are printed and all adjustments are made, Easypay requires the final step of closing the pay period. However, the program suggests that you do not close a pay period until you are ready to run the next payroll. This precaution allows for easy corrections, reprinting of cheques, etc. before the next payroll run. Once you close the pay period, you cannot reprint

FIGURE 11-56

```
O. LASCHUK, INC.                    PAYROLL REGISTER                              PAGE : 2

                  AS OF : JUN 30, 1991    FOR PAY PERIOD 01

GRAND REGULAR HOURS :           .00
GRAND OVERTIME HOURS:           .00

        GRAND HOURS             .00

                              GRAND TOTALS

GRAND REGULAR       - 1)        .00         REGULAR              2750.00
DEDUCTIONS            2)        .00         OVERTIME                 .00
                      3)        .00         OTHER PAY                .00
                      4)        .00         OTHER DED                .00
                      5)        .00

                  GRAND TOTAL (1)  .00      GRAND TOTAL (2)      2750.00

GRAND REGULAR       - 1)        .00         GRAND FED. TAX        562.71
BENEFITS              2)        .00         QUE. TAX                 .00
                      3)        .00         U.I.C.                 61.89
                      4)        .00         C.P.P                  56.60
                      5)        .00         Q.P.P.                   .00
                      *)        .00         DEDUCT'S                 .00
                                            SP. EARNINGS             .00
                                            SP. DEDUCTIONS           .00

                  GRAND TOTAL (3)  .00      GRAND NET            2068.80

                  SPECIAL EARNINGS          SPECIAL DEDUCTIONS

                  1. SPPAY 1      .00       1. SPDED 1               .00
                  1. SPPAY 1      .00       1. SPDED 1               .00
                  1. SPPAY 1      .00       1. SPDED 1               .00
                  1. SPPAY 1      .00       1. SPDED 1               .00
                  1. SPPAY 1      .00       1. SPDED 1               .00

                  GRAND TOTAL (4)  .00      GRAND TOTAL  (5)         .00

GRAND COST  :  TOTAL (2) + TOTAL (3) + TOTAL (4) - TOTAL (5) =      2750.00
```

reports or cheques, or make timecard changes. Therefore, it is important to make sure that the pay period is complete before closing. Of course, you should always back up your data files before running the Close Pay Period program.

Under the program, the closing of a pay period accomplishes these important functions:

- All of the year-to-date history and detailed history information is updated.

- Payroll costs are allocated to the appropriate departments if multi-departmental costing is followed.
- The files are prepared for a new pay period. Hence, the time-card and payroll fields are cleared and the pay period number is incremented by one.
- **Step 8. Exporting journal entries to the G/L** If you have set up G/L accounts in Easypay and your accounting G/L software supports an interface, you can export journal entries to your G/L package. Briefly, the pay period must first be closed. Then, from the Advanced Features Menu, the user would select 41 (Create G/L Journal Entries). A special General Payroll General Ledger Entries screen will appear. The screen simply prompts the user to press <F2> to create the G/L journal entries together with their total debit and total credit amounts. Easypay creates a file on your hard disk for your general ledger package to import. In turn, your G/L accounts will be automatically updated.

Summation Accounting Package

Since Summation's General Ledger package was introduced in Chapter 5 and will also be applied to account for the new federal government's goods and services tax in the Appendix, only a brief description of Summation's main features will be presented here.

- Summation is a real-time accounting package which offers a variety of small businesses modules not only for the general ledger, but also for accounts receivable, accounts payable, inventory management, and order entry/invoicing. In general, all modules consist of a series of menu-driven programs that support a user-friendly approach to process accounting data through microcomputers using MS-DOS or PC-DOS, Version 3.0 or later.
- The Accounts Receivable System interacts with the G/L System and uses the open-item invoice method to account for all aspects of accounts receivable. The system features well-defined reports to print user-definable customer statements, customer listings, customer purchases, customer details, detailed aged receivables, 30/60/90 aged receivables, the cash receipts journal, and the credit on account report.
- The Accounts Payable System interacts with the G/L System and also supports the open-item method to account for all purchase invoices. The system prints the following reports: vendor listing, vendor purchases, vendor details, general aged payables report, cash disbursements journal, open credit-on-account, vendor account activity, and discount availability. In addition, the program prints vendor cheques on user-defined forms.
- The General Ledger System is a menu-driven package designed to be interactive with all other Summation modules. See Chapter 5, Topic 4 for details on its reporting functions.

- The Inventory Management System is designed to interact with the Order Entry, Point-of-Sale and/or Invoicing functions. Easily obtainable, well-defined reports include item listing, sales, costing, stock levels, physical inventory worksheets, and a transaction journal. A variety of inventory item records—organized by category, product line, and minimum order quantities, etc.—can be printed. The system supports both perpetual and periodic inventory methods.

- The Order Entry/Point-of-Sale/Invoicing module integrates information processed by the Accounts Receivable, G/L, and Inventory systems. Under the Point-of-Sale system, the user has complete command of the sale, including the ability to look up prices and inventories instantly. All invoices are completely user-formattable, thereby allowing the user to print the invoice on virtually any preprinted invoice form. Cash receipt printers are also supported for those users with numerous small-item sales. The program includes printouts for an order entry detail report, general invoice statistics report by customer, detailed invoice statistics report by invoice, and sorted invoice statistics report either by customer or by item.

- The package includes a Systems Utilities Menu that allows the user to edit the company name, enter system attributes such as setting the data file locations, edit the passwords, print customer/vendor mailing labels, and run the system diagnostics.

- Summation 2.40 integrates with the Easypay payroll program.

- The package includes an on-line text editor which is available at any time simply by pressing <F10>. The text editor allows the user to view the majority of reports on the screen before they are printed as hard copy.

- Summation includes a built-in math function on any line where a number will be entered. Thus, whenever you edit a numerical input line, pressing <+>, <->, </>, or <°> will cause the program to transfer control to the bottom line of the screen where a math problem may be solved. Pressing <Enter> or <=> will cause the operation to be performed with the new total being displayed on the numerical input line.

- Summation has an On-Line Help System. The Help index may be accessed from anywhere within the program at any time by pressing <F1>.

- Summation includes a public-domain Menu program which is included when installing the complete package. Briefly, the Menu allows the user to define menu options so that the user's most frequently used programs can be started by pressing one key only.

TOPIC 1 Problems

Analyzing debits and credits of transactions entered under Bedford's system of accounting; identifying the Bedford module for recording each entry; and briefly explaining the debits and credits for each entry.

11.1 Susan Smart established the Thunder Bay Retail Supply Company on June 1 of the current year. Assume that the company uses AccPac Bedford to process all of its accounting data. Selected data for June are summarized below.

1. The owner invested $100 000 cash in the Royal Bank to begin business operations.
2. The company purchased land and building for a total cost of $125 000, of which $50 000 was applicable to the land and the remainder to the building. Paid $25 000 cash for part of the amount, and signed a 20-year 10% per annum mortgage payable for the balance.
3. Purchased merchandise on credit from Winnipeg Wholesale Ltd., $40 000. Terms, 2/10, n/30. (The company uses the perpetual inventory method under AccPac Bedford's package.)
4. Acquired office equipment for cash, $5 000.
5. Borrowed $20 000 on a demand note from the bank.
6. Paid City Transport $77 for delivery of goods purchased from Winnipeg Wholesale Ltd.
7. Cash sales for the month totalled $24 000 plus PST of $1 920. (GST accounting has been eliminated to simplify matters.) Average cost of sales totalled $14 400.
8. Sales on credit for the month totalled $30 000 plus PST of $2 400. Terms on all credit sales, n/30. Average cost of sales totalled $18 000.
9. A cheque issued to Winnipeg Wholesale Ltd. was issued within the discount period in full payment of the invoice described in (3) above.
10. Cheques received from credit customers totalled 80% of the amount owing in (8) above.
11. Cheques to pay operating expenses during the month were issued as follows: Salaries, $10 000; Advertising, $500; Telephone, $60; Repairs, $150; Utilities, $110; Supplies, $250.
12. The owner withdrew $500 cash for personal use.
13. Issued cheque for $1 000 in payment of the mortgage as follows: $800 to mortgage interest and $200 to the principal (mortgage payable).
14. The bank notified the firm that $150 cash was deducted from its bank account as a payment for the month's interest on the demand loan.

Required **a** Show an analysis of all transactions in general journal form to support the theory of using debits and credits under the Bedford Accounting System. Make up appropriate account titles and show a plus sign or a minus sign in front of each amount to support Bedford's debit and credit theory. Refer to Figure 11-57.

b For each entry, show a brief explanation and indicate in which Bedford module the entry would be recorded.
c Also for each entry, briefly explain why a plus or minus sign is used to support Bedford's theory of debiting and crediting amounts.

FIGURE 11-57

Example for Transaction 1

Dr. Cash in Royal Bank	+100 000	
Cr. Susan Smart, Capital		+100 000
To record the opening entry. (General ledger module.)		

Note: In the figure, a plus sign is used for the debit amount because the asset Cash in Royal Bank is being increased. Similarly, a plus sign is shown for the credit amount because the owner's Capital account is being increased.

Analyzing an accounting entry under AccPac Plus; simulating the preparation of a batching entry; explaining the procedures for posting the completed double entry.

11.2 Craig Leverman Inc. has decided to use the general ledger package of AccPac Plus, Version 6.0. After installing the program and taking care of all preliminaries, an accounting clerk received the first approved journal voucher to record the opening entry of the company. The journal voucher identified the following data: Cash in Bank, $50 000; Equipment, $60 000; Accounts Payable, $30 000; and Common Share Capital, $80 000.

Required
a Analyze the contents of Journal Voucher 1 in general journal form and briefly explain how this double entry would be identified under a batch-oriented system.
b Use a batching form similar to that shown in Figure 11-36 to simulate how AccPac Plus would complete Batch 1 for the opening entry. Make up appropriate details to complete the form.
c Explain the follow-up procedures required to post the opening entry to the G/L.

Simulating the completion of an employee's update/profile under Easypay for a newly hired hourly-rated employee.

11.3 Laura Shaw, Inc. uses Easypay to process the company's hourly-rated and salary-rated weekly payroll. Assume that you have been employed to create employee profiles and on this day you are to add a new hourly-rated employee as follows: employee number, 0076; Schuck, Saskia; 401 Nelson St., your town/city/postal code; warehouse department (make up a short form); phone (make one up for your town/city); SIN (use your own number); bank (use your bank and deposit number); birth date (use your birth date); regular rate, $15 per hour; hiring date (use today's date); overtime rate is time-and-a-half; TD1 amount (use your TD1 amount); deductions for UI, CPP, and tax are compulsory; EHT (check your province's regulations before entering Y or N); and two extra deductions as follows: company pension plan (use a five-letter code) with a deduction of $5 per week; a group insurance plan (use a six-letter code) with a deduction of $2 per week.

Required

a On a form similar to that in Figure 11-50, complete the Employee Update/Profile for Saskia Schuck. Make up appropriate data for any required portion.

b Briefly explain the method of processing a payroll run under Easypay.

TOPIC 2 Examining a Customized Accounting Package

Not all businesses can use accounting packages that are general in nature and which are available from dealers as "off-the-shelf" packages. Instead, many legal, medical, and dental offices have turned to software companies to customize accounting programs so that they include special functions. Examples of special functions are insurance forms and client recall in medical and dental packages, and client billing modules in packages designed for lawyers. Since packages directed toward a more generalized user group are called general accounting packages, those packages with a specific group in mind may be called ***vertical accounting packages***. From a student viewpoint, it is essential that at least an overview of one vertical package be examined so that a fair comparison may be made with a general accounting package and with the traditional manual system employing shortcuts to process accounts receivable.

Although there are several vertical accounting packages that can be presented, a package called ***DYNA® Dental Office Management System*** has been chosen, because it is regarded by many as the most comprehensive and easy-to-use dental software package available in Canada. (Reproduction of portions of the DYNA System is done by permission of Abel Computers Ltd.)

> Vertical accounting packages: programs that are individualized (customized) for a particular market such as dental, medical, and legal offices.

> DYNA® Dental Office Management System: a vertical accounting package developed by Abel Computers Ltd. to perform functions specific to a dental office. (DYNA is short for *dynamic*.)

Main Features of DYNA®

The main features of the DYNA® Dental Office Management System may be summarized under four subheadings as follows:

TIME SAVINGS

- Patient receipts, insurance claim forms, and patient statements are prepared quickly and are easy to print.
- The automated recall function eliminates a manual search through patient records.
- The user can quickly display any patient's accounting records or history.
- Daily journal reports expedite the task of balancing payments and deposits.
- The integrated word processing program speeds the preparation and printing of standard practice letters such as welcome, referral, or balance-overdue letters.

- The system is user-friendly, thus reducing the training time required for new staff members.

INCREASED CASH FLOW
- Insurance and patient charges are calculated while the patient is still in the office. Patients will know their portion of the charge immediately, thus reducing the possibility of bad debts.
- Patient account statements with customized messages can be generated automatically at any time, not just at month-end.
- The accounts receivable system will produce reports in minutes, complete with outstanding-account aging.
- The program includes aged accounts receivable statements for insurance companies.

IMPROVED CONTROL
- The system offers complete procedure analysis by provider and practice.
- Management reporting provides the information needed to make accurate business decisions.

EFFICIENT PATIENT COMMUNICATION
- Itemized patient statements with relevant messages are instantly produced.
- Questions regarding past or future services and charges can be answered promptly.
- The word processing function can easily be used to generate welcome letters, thank-you-for-referral letters, newsletters, service letters, etc.
- The recall system is timely, accurate, and personalized. It will not "lose" patients.

Hardware/Operating System Requirements

The DYNA Dental System has the following hardware/operating system requirements:

- An IBM AT or PS/2 computer, or compatible computer
- At least 512K of RAM with 1.5 megabytes of extended RAM
- At least a 40 megabyte hard drive with at least 1.5 megabytes free to receive DYNA
- The operating system called **Xenix**, Version 2.2.3 or later

Xenix: a registered trademark of the Microsoft Corporation. It is the multi-user, multi-tasking operating system instructing the computer how to read information, how to write information, and where to store information.

Overview

DYNA is a menu-driven system. This means that everything you will want to do in the DYNA system is selected from a menu. After correct installation of the system, the first menu presented is the DYNA Main Menu, as in Figure 11-58.

FIGURE 11-58

```
┌─────── DYNA Main Menu ───────┐
│                              │
│  B    Billing Transactions Menu │
│  A    Appointments Menu      │
│  T    Treatment Planning Menu│
│  P    Patient Information Menu│
│  R    Reports Menu           │
│  W    Word Processing Menu   │
│  D    Day End Menu           │
│  S    System Maintenance Menu│
│  C    Change Accounting Date │
│  X    Exit Menu              │
│                              │
│  Enter Choice        : B :   │
└──────────────────────────────┘
```

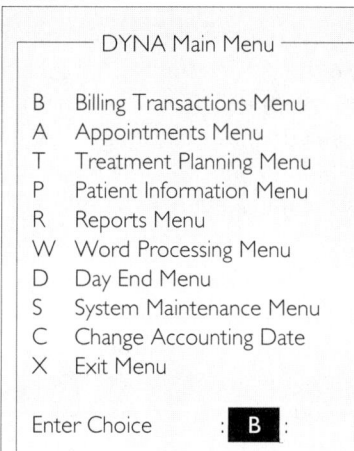

The following is a brief description of each of the functions identified on DYNA's Main Menu.

- **B: Billing Transactions Menu** From this menu, you can select all functions dealing with the financial status of a patient. Functions on this menu allow you to bill patients, enter payments, make adjustments, and check the financial status of any patient on file.

- **A: Appointments Menu** From this menu you can book, modify, cancel, and delete appointments for patients. Through this menu you can also block unavailable time on the appointment scheduler, print an appointment schedule, print a worksheet, and print an appointment confirmation telephone list.

- **T: Treatment Planning Menu** Functions on this menu allow you to set up a patient treatment plan and to add, generate, modify, and delete patient contacts. Through this menu you can also print contact reports.

- **P: Patient Information Menu** This menu will contain detailed information on the patient, including full name, address, home telephone number, work telephone number, health insurance number, birthdate, etc.

- **R: Reports Menu** Through this menu you can print a number of patient reports and financial reports and are able to create and print customized reports. Also, you can print the fee schedule, insurance plan lists, and a city list.

- **W: Word Processing Menu** This menu allows you to create, modify, and print letters. You can also send a chosen letter to a selected group of patients.

- **D: Day End Menu** From this menu you can print out all financial reports required at the end of the day—cash summary, cash receipts, missed appointments, etc. You can also change the accounting date through this menu.

- **S: System Maintenance Menu** From this menu you can add, modify, and delete insurance plans, insurance company names, procedure codes, cities, and special schedules. Also, through this menu you can set up your system and initialize your laser printer.

- **C: Change Accounting Date** This function allows you to change your accounting date. However, you will not be able to change the date until the day-end report, Print Cash Summary, has been run for the overall financial practice.

- **X: Exit Menu** Through this menu you can do a daily or weekly backup, verify backups, format diskettes, and exit the DYNA system.

As you can observe, all of the DYNA Main Menu selections are very general titles for different groups of jobs that are performed in a dental office. Upward and downward arrow keys may be used to select any title.

Or you may press the letter beside the selection you want to move the bar quickly to the selection you want. Selecting any of the DYNA Main Menu selections and pressing <Enter> will cause the sub-menu for that group of jobs to appear. Most sub-menu selections are specific tasks that may be performed. In some cases a sub-menu selection will cause a sub-sub-menu to appear with more-specific tasks listed. To illustrate, the following two applications of adding a new patient and billing a patient are offered.

Adding a New Patient

- **Step 1. Turning on the computer system**   Obviously you would turn your computer system on; that is, you would turn on all terminals, all printers, and the main console. Within a few minutes the computer will automatically load the operating system called Xenix and display several lines of information on the screen of the main console.

- **Step 2. Logging in**   Under the Xenix operating system, your screen will display a prompt as in Figure 11-59. This *login prompt* requires that you instruct the operating system to load DYNA into the working memory of the computer. Simply type the word "dental" in lowercase letters and then press <Enter>. The DYNA copyright screen will appear as in Figure 11-60. This screen contains the version number of the system you are currently using, the total disk space of your system, the total disk space that is still free, and the percentage of the available disk space that has been used. Also on this screen you can select the level of help that will be provided when using the system.

FIGURE 11-59

```
xenix286!login:  ▮
```

FIGURE 11-60

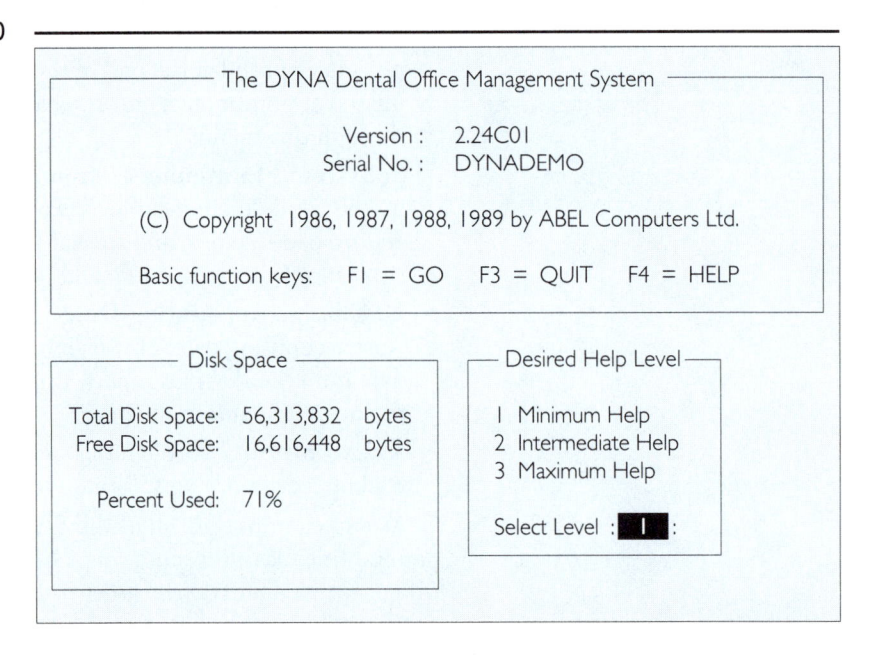

```
┌──────────── The DYNA Dental Office Management System ────────────┐
│                                                                   │
│                        Version :    2.24C01                       │
│                        Serial No. : DYNADEMO                      │
│                                                                   │
│        (C) Copyright  1986, 1987, 1988, 1989 by ABEL Computers Ltd.│
│                                                                   │
│        Basic function keys:   F1 = GO    F3 = QUIT    F4 = HELP   │
└───────────────────────────────────────────────────────────────────┘

┌──────── Disk Space ────────┐    ┌──── Desired Help Level ────┐
│                             │    │                             │
│  Total Disk Space:  56,313,832  bytes │    │  1  Minimum Help            │
│  Free Disk Space:   16,616,448  bytes │    │  2  Intermediate Help       │
│                             │    │  3  Maximum Help            │
│  Percent Used:  71%         │    │                             │
│                             │    │  Select Level :  ▮  :       │
└─────────────────────────────┘    └─────────────────────────────┘
```

CHAPTER 11: Using Microcomputer Software to Process Common Accounting Applications **529**

- **Step 3. Selecting help level**   Enter the number that corresponds to the level of help you desire. The DYNA Main Menu will then appear as shown earlier in Figure 11-76. At this point you are in the DYNA Dental Office Management System.
- **Step 4. Running option P**   From the DYNA Main Menu select option P for the Patient Information Menu and press <Enter>. The menu will appear on the screen as a sub-menu to the right of the Main Menu as shown in Fig. 11-61.

FIGURE 11-61

```
┌──────── DYNA Main Menu ─────────┐  ┌──── Patient Information Menu ────┐
│                                 │  │                                  │
│   B   Billing Transactions Menu │  │   U   Update Patient Information │
│   A   Appointments Menu         │  │   A   Add a Patient              │
│   T   Treatment Planning Menu   │  │   F   Financial Status           │
│   P   Patient Information Menu  │  │   H   Patient History            │
│   R   Reports Menu              │  │   Q   Return to Main Menu        │
│   W   Word Processing Menu      │  │                                  │
│   D   Day End Menu              │  │   Enter Choice : ███ :           │
│   S   System Maintenance Menu   │  │                                  │
│   C   Change Accounting Date    │  │                                  │
│   X   Exit Menu                 │  │                                  │
└─────────────────────────────────┘  └──────────────────────────────────┘
```

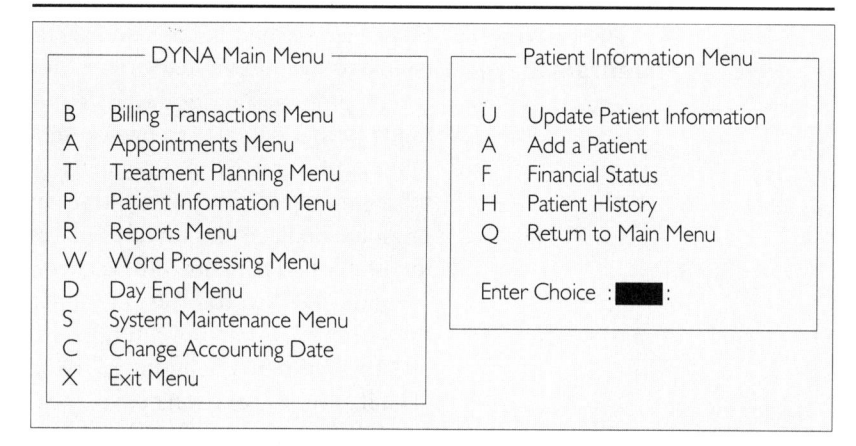

- **Step 5. Running option A**   Press <A> or move the selection bar to option A, Add a Patient. Then press <Enter> to run this program. The first of five screens to complete a new patient file would appear as shown in Figure 11-62.

FIGURE 11-62

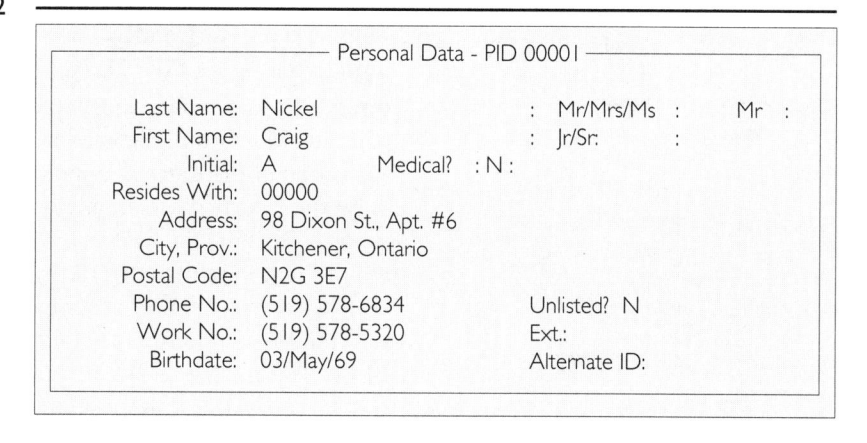

```
┌──────────────── Personal Data - PID 00001 ─────────────────┐
│                                                            │
│       Last Name:  Nickel           : Mr/Mrs/Ms :    Mr  :  │
│      First Name:  Craig            : Jr/Sr:     :          │
│         Initial:  A      Medical?  : N :                   │
│    Resides With:  00000                                    │
│         Address:  98 Dixon St., Apt. #6                    │
│      City, Prov.: Kitchener, Ontario                       │
│     Postal Code:  N2G 3E7                                  │
│       Phone No.:  (519) 578-6834       Unlisted?  N        │
│        Work No.:  (519) 578-5320       Ext.:               │
│       Birthdate:  03/May/69            Alternate ID:       │
│                                                            │
└────────────────────────────────────────────────────────────┘
```

Analysis   Much of this screen is self-explanatory. PID is short for "Patient ID." A unique number is assigned so that it can be used to access patients once they are registered on the system. DYNA also gives you the option of accessing patients by name. Y would be entered in the

Medical field if the patient has a medical condition; otherwise, N would be typed. After completing the Personal Data window, separate windows will be displayed: the Treatment Items window, the Insurance Plans window, the Insurance Plans File Update window, and the Extra Information window. When these are completed, the dental office will have a complete data file on the new patient before the first dental service is administered. Note that under the DYNA system, every person will have his or her own patient file.

Processing a Dental Charge

Before any accounting of a dental charge can be processed, it is essential to complete such preliminaries as setting the current accounting date; running certain programs under the System Maintenance Menu—for example, setting up the dental practice system, setting up options such as for a multi-dental practice, setting up the printer to print receipts and statements, setting up the laser printer, and setting up the master fee schedule with appropriate dental codes for all dental services; and entering opening balances for established patients with balances on the old one-write system.

Under DYNA, you can enter bills for patients through two functions in the system. You can bill through either "Billing Non-Scheduled Patients" or "Appointments Scheduler." Patient billing involves three main steps: (1) bill entry; (2) entering payments; and (3) receipt/insurance form printing. To illustrate, assume that Craig Nickel (the example used in Figure 11-62) has made an appointment to see Dr. J. Barnicke of the Kitchener Dental Centre. Assume also that the patient does have dental insurance with the Mutual Company and that the Appointment Scheduler lists him to appear at 9:00 a.m. on December 1, 19— to restore one tooth.

- **Step 1** From DYNA's Main Menu, select option A, Appointments Menu, and press <Enter>. The screen will display the Appointments Menu to the right of the DYNA Main Menu.

- **Step 2** From the Appointments Menu, select option S, Appointment Scheduler, and press <Enter>. Briefly, the screen will request verification of the dates of appointments that have been entered. To accept the information already on the screen, press <GO> on the keyboard. Briefly, the <GO> key will cause the system to "go ahead" to the next step in the current procedure. (This key is actually a function key that has been programmed to act as required.) The screen will fill in the appointment schedule for today's date (the accounting date) for each provider (dentist and hygienist).

- **Step 3** From the Appointment Scheduler, select the patient, Nickel, Mr. Craig, and then press <Enter>. A billing screen will appear as in Figure 11-64.

    As you can observe, the patient's PID, name, address, and insurance plan ID will appear at the top of the billing screen. The cursor will appear under Type.

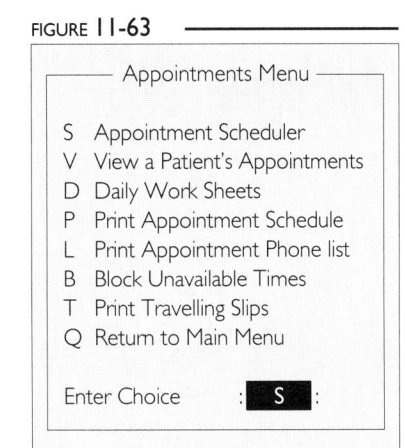

FIGURE 11-63

```
┌─── Appointments Menu ────┐
│                          │
│  S  Appointment Scheduler │
│  V  View a Patient's Appointments │
│  D  Daily Work Sheets    │
│  P  Print Appointment Schedule │
│  L  Print Appointment Phone list │
│  B  Block Unavailable Times │
│  T  Print Travelling Slips │
│  Q  Return to Main Menu  │
│                          │
│  Enter Choice     : S :  │
│                          │
└──────────────────────────┘
```

FIGURE 11-64

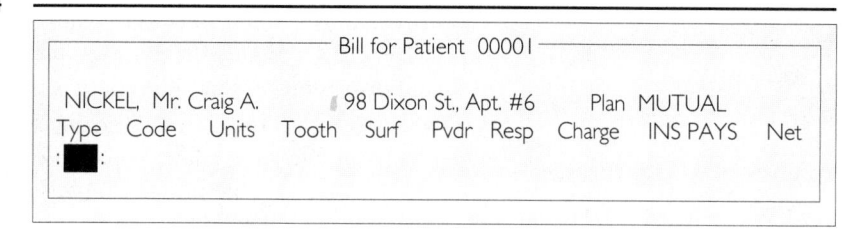

```
┌─────────────── Bill for Patient  00001 ───────────────┐
│                                                        │
│  NICKEL, Mr. Craig A.     98 Dixon St., Apt. #6    Plan  MUTUAL    │
│  Type   Code   Units   Tooth   Surf   Pvdr  Resp   Charge   INS PAYS   Net │
│  : ■ :                                                 │
│                                                        │
└────────────────────────────────────────────────────────┘
```

- **Step 4**   Leave the Type field blank. This indicates that this charge is to be billed on the current system date. Simply press <Enter> to move to the next field.
- **Step 5**   In the Code field, enter the five-digit code for the procedure performed on the patient as identified in the Master Fee Schedule, a schedule that would have been completed according to official codes supplied by the Ontario Dental Association. In this case, assume procedure code 21224 signifying amalgam used on four tooth surfaces.
- **Step 6**   At this point, after you have entered procedure code 21224, the program will have filled in several of the fields as shown in Figure 11-65.

FIGURE 11-65

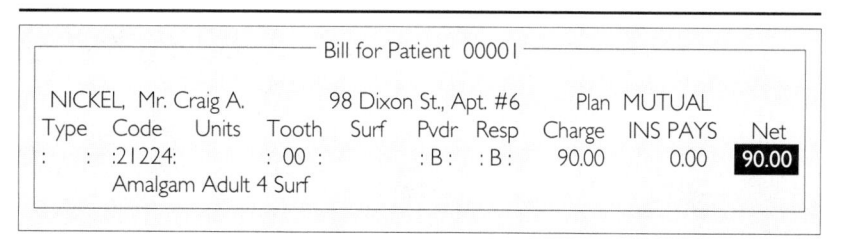

```
┌─────────────── Bill for Patient  00001 ───────────────┐
│                                                        │
│  NICKEL, Mr. Craig A.      98 Dixon St., Apt. #6    Plan  MUTUAL   │
│  Type   Code   Units   Tooth   Surf   Pvdr  Resp   Charge   INS PAYS   Net │
│  :    :21224:          : 00 :         : B :  : B :  90.00      0.00   90.00 │
│         Amalgam Adult 4 Surf                           │
│                                                        │
└────────────────────────────────────────────────────────┘
```

- **Step 7**   The cursor is now waiting under Tooth, indicating that the procedure signified by the code is associated with some tooth; the appropriate tooth number must now be entered. Assume that the dentist has identified tooth 46.
- **Step 8**   In the Surf (surface) field, enter one of the tooth surface codes appropriate to the procedure code for an amalgam. Assume that you will enter the surface code M, indicating the Mesial surface. (Obviously, the clerk entering data would benefit from a knowledge of common terms used in dental work.)
- **Step 9**   The Pvdr (provider of service) field has already been filled in. Briefly, this field shows the code of the provider who performed the actual service; in this case, B stands for Dr. Barnicke. The provider code will default to the correct provider if billing is done via the Appointment Scheduler.
- **Step 10**   The "Resp" (responsible provider) field receives the code representing the provider whose name will be on the insurance form

when this item is printed. Again, the code B is shown, because the program will default the responsible provider if the procedure was performed by a provider who is responsible for his or her own billing.

- **Step 11** The Charge field shows $90, the amount which will be charged to the patient as per the schedule of fees completed by the Master Fee Schedule. Though the amount charged may be modified, in most cases it will be consistent with the fees established by the Ontario Dental Association's fee schedule.
- **Step 12** The Ins Pays field displays the amount expected to be covered by the patient's dental insurance. This amount varies, but it may not exceed the total charge for the item. In our case, let us leave this field with zeros.
- **Step 13** The final field, Net, is for reference only. Obviously, the net amount will be charged to the patient as displayed here.
- **Step 14** Once you have finished entering a procedure code, you would press <Enter> to enter another procedure code. Assume that X-rays were required as shown in the completed screen in Figure 11-66.

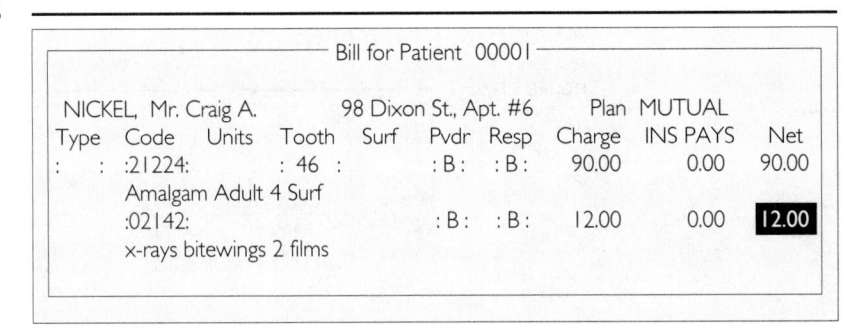

FIGURE 11-66

```
─────────── Bill for Patient 00001 ───────────

NICKEL, Mr. Craig A.      98 Dixon St., Apt. #6      Plan MUTUAL
Type   Code     Units    Tooth   Surf   Pvdr  Resp   Charge   INS PAYS    Net
  :   :21224:           : 46 :         : B :  : B :   90.00      0.00    90.00
       Amalgam Adult 4 Surf
      :02142:                          : B :  : B :   12.00      0.00    12.00
       x-rays bitewings 2 films
```

- **Step 15** After all codes are entered, you have the option of pressing <GO> to proceed to enter patient payments or pressing <Quit> (another example of a programmed key) to enter the bill and return to the Appointment Scheduler/Billing Transactions menu.
- **Step 16** From the Billing Transactions Menu, you would press <R> to print the receipt/insurance forms. A typical printout of the official receipt for our example of Craig Nickel appears as in Figure 11-67.

Financial Menus Space limitations prevent a detailed, step-by-step analysis of four other important DYNA financial menus: the Financial Transactions Menu (including the Financial Adjustments Menu), the Financial Reports Menu, and the Day End Menu. In the brief descriptions that follow, keep in mind that once financial data has been captured by one menu, that data may be used by other menus. For example, the fee charged to patients

FIGURE 11-67

```
┌─────────────────────────────────────────────────────────────────────────────┐
│   ┌─────────────────────┐      PATIENT RECEIPT        ┌──────────────────┐  │
│   │   ACCOUNT NO.       │                              │      DATE        │  │
│   │      00001          │   KITCHENER DENTAL CENTRE    │    01/DEC/—      │  │
│   └─────────────────────┘                              └──────────────────┘  │
│                                                                              │
│        Mr. Craig A. Nickel                  Dr. J. Barnicke                  │
│        98 Dixon St., Apt. #6                1150 Main Street West            │
│        Kitchener, Ontario                   Kitchener, Ontario               │
│        N2G 3E7                              N2G 2N9                          │
│                                                                              │
│                                    PLEASE RETURN THIS PORTION WITH YOUR PAYMENT │
│                                    ┌────────────────────────────┬──────────┐ │
│                                    │      AMOUNT DUE:           │  102.00  │ │
│   ┌─────────┬──────┬──┬──┬──┐      ├────────────────────────────┼──────────┤ │
│   │Days Owed│ Curr │  │  │  │      │      AMOUNT ENCLOSED:      │          │ │
│   │ Amount: │102.00│  │  │  │      └────────────────────────────┴──────────┘ │
│   └─────────┴──────┴──┴──┴──┘                                                │
│ - - - - - - - - - - - - - - - - - - - - - - - - - - - - - - - - - - - - - -│
│  PATIENT RECEIPT:  NICKEL, Mr. Craig A.          PRINTED:    01/DEC/—       │
│  PID NO.:  00001                                 TRANS. NO.: 000001         │
│                                                  DATE:       01/DEC/—       │
│  ┌────────────────────┬──────────┬──────────┬──────────────────────────┐    │
│  │ DESCRIPTION        │ CHARGE   │ LAB. FEE │    CHARGE SUMMARY        │    │
│  ├────────────────────┼──────────┼──────────┼──────────────────────────┤    │
│  │ Amalgam Adult 4 Surf│  90.00  │          │                          │    │
│  │ x-rays bitewings 2 films│ 12.00│         │ Total Acct. Charges Today:  102.00 │
│  │                    │          │          │ Balance Before Today:    0.00 │
│  │                    │          │          │       Subtotal:        102.00 │
│  │                    │          │          │ Today's Payment:         0.00 │
│  │                    │          │          │ NEW BALANCE:           102.00 │
│  │                    │          │          │                          │    │
│  │                    │          │          │ Inquiries: (519) 580-7600│    │
│  ├────────────────────┴──────────┼──────────┴──────────────────────────┤    │
│  │ Clean teeth mean better health.│ No appointment has been made for you.│  │
│  │ Have a great day!              │ We will contact you to arrange your next visit. │
│  └────────────────────────────────┴──────────────────────────────────────┘  │
│                     RETAIN THIS PORTION FOR YOUR RECORDS                     │
└─────────────────────────────────────────────────────────────────────────────┘
```

and cash payments made by patients under the Billing Transactions Menu will be used automatically in the Financial Reports Menu and the Day End Menu to print several reports.

FINANCIAL TRANSACTIONS MENU This menu is a branch or sub-menu of the Billing Transactions Menu. Obviously, you would select T to bring up the Financial Transactions Menu, shown in Figure 11-68. A discussion follows of each option title shown.

- **P: Postdated Cheques** This function allows the collection of a postdated cheque to be entered against a patient's account. Of course, a

FIGURE 11-68

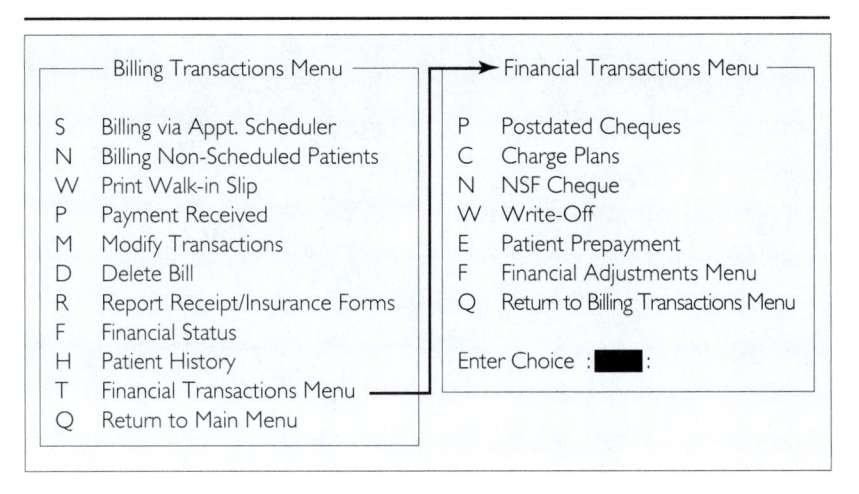

```
┌─ Billing Transactions Menu ──────┐   ┌─► Financial Transactions Menu ──────┐
│                                  │   │                                     │
│  S   Billing via Appt. Scheduler │   │  P   Postdated Cheques              │
│  N   Billing Non-Scheduled Patients│ │  C   Charge Plans                   │
│  W   Print Walk-in Slip          │   │  N   NSF Cheque                     │
│  P   Payment Received            │   │  W   Write-Off                      │
│  M   Modify Transactions         │   │  E   Patient Prepayment             │
│  D   Delete Bill                 │   │  F   Financial Adjustments Menu     │
│  R   Report Receipt/Insurance Forms│ │  Q   Return to Billing Transactions Menu│
│  F   Financial Status            │   │                                     │
│  H   Patient History             │   │  Enter Choice  :  ▓▓▓ :             │
│  T   Financial Transactions Menu─┼───┘                                     │
│  Q   Return to Main Menu         │
└──────────────────────────────────┘
```

Postdated Cheques menu would appear to direct the user to the correct method of handling such a cheque.

- **C: Charge Plans** This function allows the setup of a patient charge plan. It would be used when procedural services are not billed directly but charges (of a predetermined amount) are levied to the account periodically. This function is ideal for orthodontic billing.

- **N: NSF Cheque** This function allows the entry of a transaction representing a "not-sufficient funds" cheque along with the corresponding bank charge. Of course, this function is used when an entry is required for each NSF cheque received.

- **W: Write-Off** This function allows the entry of charge write-offs. Briefly, charge write-offs are required when fees for services cannot be collected.

- **E: Patient Prepayment** This function allows the entry of a payment onto an account that has a zero balance or a credit balance. A patient prepayment is necessary if the account balance is zero or the patient has a credit balance. The Payment Received entry screens do not allow payments to be posted on accounts having a zero balance or a credit balance.

- **F: Financial Adjustments Menu** From this menu you can enter fee or payment adjustments, create opening balances for patients, and display the financial status of a patient. These are on a separate menu because they are not normally required. See Figure 11-69 for a breakdown of this menu.

FIGURE 11-69

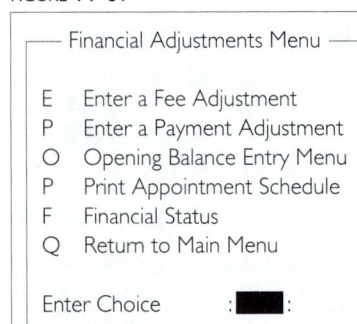

```
┌─ Financial Adjustments Menu ──┐
│                               │
│  E   Enter a Fee Adjustment   │
│  P   Enter a Payment Adjustment│
│  O   Opening Balance Entry Menu│
│  P   Print Appointment Schedule│
│  F   Financial Status         │
│  Q   Return to Main Menu      │
│                               │
│  Enter Choice     :  ▓▓▓ :    │
└───────────────────────────────┘
```

FINANCIAL REPORTS MENU

This menu is a sub-menu of the Reports Menu. Obviously, you would select F to bring up the Financial Reports Menu as in Figure 11-70.

FIGURE 11-70

Reports Menu

P	Patient Reports Menu
F	Financial Reports Menu
R	Report Generator Menu
M	Master Fee Schedule List
S	Supercode List
L	Special Schedule List
N	Names of Insurance Plans
I	Insurance Plan Information List
C	City List
Q	Return to Main Menu

Financial Reports Menu

S	Statement Printing
R	Aged Receivables Report
I	Aged Patient Insurance
P	Production Report
D	Summarized Daily Totals
T	Insurance Transactions
F	Fee Summary
E	Eliminate Notations
M	Cash Summary - Multiple Days
Q	Return to Reports Menu

Enter Choice : :

- **S: Statement Printing** This function allows you to print statements for patients who have owed the practice money for a certain period of time. This function only prints statements for subscribers, not dependents.
- **R: Aged Receivables Report** This important function prints an accounts receivable report of outstanding patient accounts only. It is not intended for insurance purposes.
- **I: Aged Patient Insurance** This function prints a report of what is owed by insurance companies for each patient. The report lists all patients in alphabetical order that have outstanding insurance amounts on their Financial Status report.
- **P: Production Report** This option produces a report of all procedures performed by each provider, for a specified date range. This report can be used to analyze the practice by showing how often procedures are performed and the revenue generated by each procedure, for the time period specified.
- **D: Summarized Daily Totals** The summarized daily totals report list the number of transactions in a given date range. You run this report for a specified provider and a specified date range.
- **T: Insurance Transactions** This report generates a list of insurance postings for a specified range of insurance companies by patient account.
- **F: Fee Summary** The fee summary is a list of all fees charged to each patient with a specified PID range. This list may be requested by a patient for income tax purposes. A fee summary is only printed for subscribers, not dependents. A separate fee summary page is printed for each subscriber.

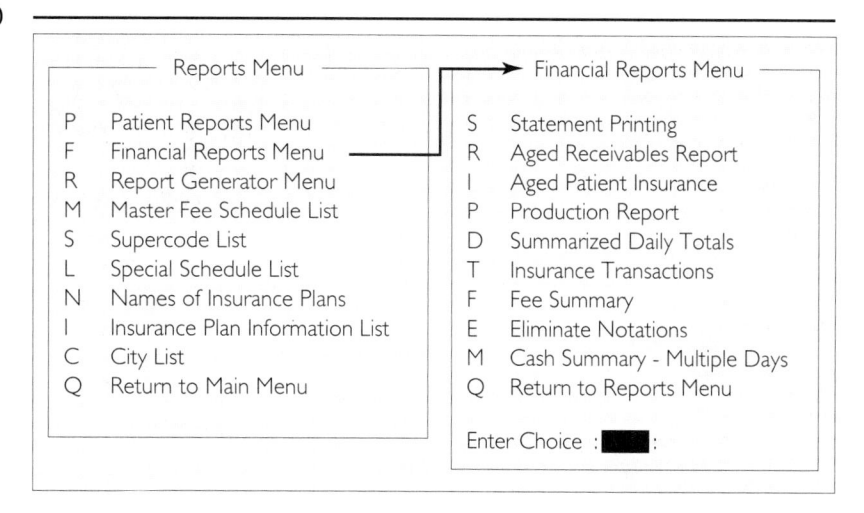

- **E: Eliminate Notations** This option allows you to eliminate outdated notations made on a patient's financial status—for example, "Statement Sent," "Interest Charge," etc.
- **M: Cash Summary—Multiple Days** This option allows you to print Cash Summaries, for a range of dates, for a specific provider. This system will ask you for a specific provider only if you are a multi-practice office.

DAY END MENU

This menu is a branch or sub-menu of the DYNA Main Menu. Obviously, you would select D from the Main Menu to bring up the Day End Menu, shown in Figure 11-71.

- **S: Print Cash Summary** From an accounting viewpoint, the Cash Summary is probably one of the most important reports of the dental practice. This report is actually made up of three separate reports generated at the same time: the Cash Summary proper, the Insurance Postings, and the Accounts Receivable. The Cash Summary is a summary of all fees charged, adjustments made, payments received, insurance postings, and other transactions for the day. It also includes on a separate page the Insurance Postings list, and on a third page the Aged Receivables Summary. A Cash Summary report has to be printed for each responsible provider (practice) at the end of every working day. An abbreviated sample of a Cash Summary appears as Figure 11-72.
- **D: Cash Summary—All Practices** This report would be similar to that of option S except that the Cash Summary would be broken down by individual practices.

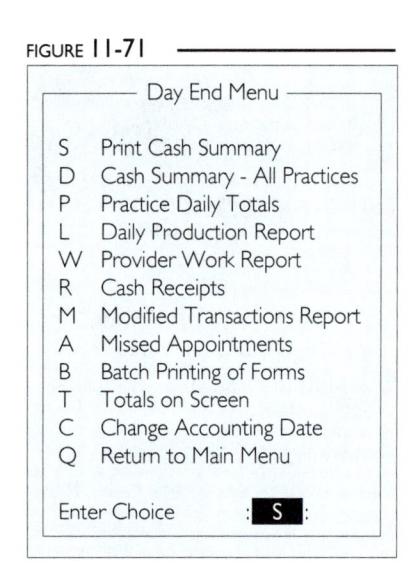

FIGURE 11-71

```
┌─────── Day End Menu ───────┐
│                            │
│  S    Print Cash Summary   │
│  D    Cash Summary - All Practices │
│  P    Practice Daily Totals │
│  L    Daily Production Report │
│  W    Provider Work Report │
│  R    Cash Receipts        │
│  M    Modified Transactions Report │
│  A    Missed Appointments  │
│  B    Batch Printing of Forms │
│  T    Totals on Screen     │
│  C    Change Accounting Date │
│  Q    Return to Main Menu  │
│                            │
│  Enter Choice       : S :  │
└────────────────────────────┘
```

FIGURE 11-72

CASH SUMMARY

For: 13/JUN/91
Printed: 06/MAR/92 09:48
ACCOUNTING DATE: 11/MAY/91

Patient Name	Account PID	Reference	Overall Prev Bal	Fees Chgd	Exp. Ins.	Lamont & Assoc. NSF/ Returns	Write Offs	Credit Adj.	Payment	Ins Paid	New Bal	Pat Dr.	Tm Pvd	Tm Pnt
SMALL Gera	13412	Bill/Visit	3.00	472.01	332.80			100.00		42.21	L	L	Y
TREMBLAY Roger	10567	Bill/Visit	4.00	554.09				200.00		358.09	L	L	
PRICE John	12728	Bill/Visit	0.00	130.02						130.02	L	L	
SMALLMAN Matthew	13397	Bill/Visit	30.10	97.60						127.70	L	M	
CAMERON Dianna	14945	Bill/Visit	0.00	519.43						519.43	L	M	
HANSEN Ella	12126	Bill/Visit	0.00	107.52	98.00					9.52	L	S	
WHITE Doug	11013	Bill/Visit	119.40	71.00						190.40	L	M	
BRADSHAW Vera	11695	Bill/Visit	0.00	70.00						70.00	L	L	
CAMERON Dianna	14945	Payment	519.43	0.00					500.00	19.43	L	L	
CAMERON Dianna	14945	ChargePlan	19.43	500.00						519.43	L	L	
				2521.67	430.80			300.00	500.00				
MONTH TO DATE:				19605.21	5811.49		258.00	2425.54	13504.45	5368.05				

- **P: Practice Daily Totals** This report gives a one-line summary for each provider of the total fees charged, expected insurance, returns (NSF payments), write-offs, credit adjustments, and patient and insurance payments received for the current accounting date. A sample of this report is given in Figure 11-73.

FIGURE 11-73

```
                                    PRACTICE DAILY TOTALS

                                                                       For:  11/MAY/91
                                                                   Printed:  12/MAY/91  12:26
                                          Dr. Jim Lamont

Pvdr   Pvdr                   Fees      Exp.    NSF/    Write   Credit                              Ins
ID     Name                   Chgd      Ins.    Returns Offs    Adj.    Cheque   Cash     Other    Paid

L      Dr. Jim Lamont        3199.21   1019.40                  782.00  1679.46  330.36           981.00
G      Dr. Mary Grainger     2594.29    903.75          52.60            675.87  557.90           947.60


       TOTALS - ALL PROVIDERS 5793.50  1923.15          52.60   782.00  2355.33  888.26          1928.60
```

- **L: Daily Production Report** This option prints a report of the work done, by each provider, on the current system accounting date. The report includes procedure codes, number of times a procedure was performed, time units used, responsibility factor, additional fees, total fees, and any lab fees for procedures performed. This report automatically prints a "work done" page for each provider in the provider file.
- **W: Provider Work Report** This report provides an itemized summary of the work performed on each patient over a given date range. The report consists of one page for each provider for each day. The work is described by procedure code and description. The time units, charged fees, and lab fees are printed and totalled.
- **R: Cash Receipts** The cash receipts report lists all the cash receipts for the day. As you can observe in Figure 11-74, the receipts are broken down by payment type. This report includes the overall amounts of each type of payment received by the practice as a whole or a separate report can be printed for each responsible provider. This report can be used as a bank deposit slip.
- **M: Modified Transactions Report** This option produces a report on any of the day's transactions which have been deleted or modified or for which you have issued a duplicate receipt. The modified transactions report also lists all transactions that were modified during the

FIGURE 11-74

CASH RECEIPTS

Printed: 06/MAR/91 09:54
Accounting Date: 07/MAY/90

Dr. Jim Lamont

Payment Type	Trans. No.	Patient PID	Name	Amount
Cheque	030396	10073	BAINBRIDGE, Mr. Reg	81.00
Cheque	030397	10239	CRANE, Mrs. Maureen	70.00
Cheque	030402	14039	MOULTON, Miss Connie	56.00
Cheque	030392	12844	SHKOPIAK, Mrs. Antoinette	178.00
Insurance	030367	10607	MILLER, Mrs. Barbara	34.00
Insurance	030405	10629	MUNDT, Mr. Bruce	77.00
Insurance	030371	11223	REINARTZ, Mrs. Gerda	82.00

Total Cheques: 2056.46

Visa	030427	10335	CAIN, Mr. Steven L.	240.85

240.85

Type	030364	10112	BAER, Ms. Mary	5.00

5.00

DEPOSIT SUMMARY

Total Cash: 407.00
Total Cheques: 2056.46
Total Visa: 240.85
Total Other Payments:: 5.00

TOTAL DEPOSIT ~~2463.46~~
2709.31 (handwritten)

day but were originally created on a previous day. The date of each of these transactions is also listed.

- **A: Missed Appointments** This report lists all the appointments on the Appointment Scheduler that were not billed.
- **B: Batch Printing of Forms** This option allows you to print patient receipts and/or insurance forms in groups (batches) based on a specified date range.
- **T: Totals on Screen** This option will give you a summary of all fees charged, adjustments made, payments received, and insurance postings entered on the current system accounting date. If you are a multi-practice office, you can specify for which practice.

CHAPTER 11: Using Microcomputer Software to Process Common Accounting Applications

- **C: Change Accounting Date** This function allows you to change the current accounting date. You must print Cash Summaries for each responsible provider before you can change the date. All transactions put through the system will be dated with this date.

Posting to the General Ledger

The DYNA Dental Office Management System does not include programs to post the dental transactions to appropriate accounts in the general ledger. Therefore, a dental practice must either journalize and post manually totals printed from appropriate reports, or consider adopting a General Ledger Package that is capable of interfacing its programs with DYNA. Abel Computers Ltd. does provide a DYNA General Ledger, Version 3.0, for those practices wishing such an interface.

OVERVIEW Space limitations prevent our presenting a detailed overview of this G/L system. Instead, the following short outline will be presented in conjunction with the analysis of DYNA's G/L main menu.

Since DYNA's G/L System has also been programmed to run under Xenix, you must login with the code "gl" (all lowercase letters) and then press <Enter>. A screen of information will appear which indicates that the system is loading; then the G/L main menu will appear as shown in Figure 11-75.

The option titles are discussed below.

- **1: Reports** From this menu you can print a trial balance, an income statement, a balance sheet, two special reports, a journal entries report, and a general ledger entry report. These reports can be printed out with specifications set up by you.
- **2: Postings** From this menu you can do manual entries and bring over the totals from your dental or medical system.
- **3: Payables** From this menu you can enter all cheques that have been written and print out a cheque register.
- **4: Payroll** From this menu you can print financial information on each employee and an employee list.
- **9: File Maintenance** From this menu you can set up your chart of accounts, set up your system, set up receivable accounts, enter your supplier and employees, print a supplier list, and print your chart of accounts.
- **S: Special Functions** From this menu you can format your diskettes, do backups, check the status and environment of your system, and check the speed of your system.
- **X: Exit GL** This menu option allows you to exit the general ledger program.
- **D: Date Change** This menu option allows you to enter the current transaction date.

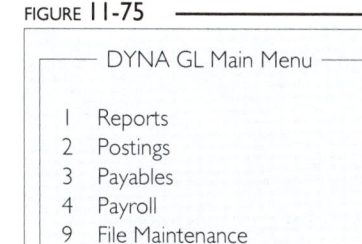

FIGURE 11-75

```
┌──── DYNA GL Main Menu ────┐
│                            │
│  1   Reports               │
│  2   Postings              │
│  3   Payables              │
│  4   Payroll               │
│  9   File Maintenance      │
│  S   Special Functions     │
│  X   Exit GL               │
│  D   Date Change           │
│                            │
│  Enter Choice      : 1 :   │
│                            │
└────────────────────────────┘
```

Obviously, option 2 will allow you to post all transactions from your dental system. Of course, the G/L chart of accounts must be set up before this option is run. In general, you enter the date range of the transactions you want posted from your dental system; then you simply press <Y> to begin posting the totals.

TOPIC 2 Problems

Answering specific questions on the DYNA Dental Office Management System.

11.4 Answer the following questions on the DYNA Dental Office Management System as presented in this chapter.
   a Why is DYNA classified as a vertical accounting package?
   b What hardware and operating system are required to run DYNA?
   c What common accounting application does DYNA support?
   d Use one example to support the statement "DYNA is a menu-driven system."
   e What is required when you see a display prompt such as "xenix286!login:"?
   f In general, what preliminaries must be completed before a dental charge can be processed under DYNA?
   g Summarize the steps required to bill a patient for a dental charge.
   h Briefly explain how you would print a patient's monthly statement of account.
   i What is the Day End Menu and why would it be used under DYNA?
   j Does DYNA include programs to post dental transactions to the general ledger? Explain your answer.

Identifying DYNA menus for processing dental transactions; analyzing those transactions in general journal form.

11.5 Arrange your answer paper into three columns as follows: column 1, Dental Transactions; column 2, DYNA Menu for Processing Transactions; column 3, Accounting Analysis in General Journal Form. Place the following transactions in column 1:
   1. A dental charge with no cash payment
   2. A patient's cheque issued on the same day on which dental services were completed
   3. A patient's postdated cheque
   4. A patient's NSF cheque
   5. A patient's account considered uncollectible and, therefore, authorized by management to be written off
   6. A dental charge and a partial payment on account

Required Complete columns 2 and 3.

Explaining how posting to the G/L is achieved under DYNA.

11.6 Assume that a dental practice uses DYNA to process its dental transactions. Briefly explain how these dental transactions would be posted to the G/L under each of the following conditions:
   1. The dental office uses a manual G/L system.

CHAPTER 11: Using Microcomputer Software to Process Common Accounting Applications   **541**

2. The dental office uses a G/L package like AccPac Plus or Summation.
3. The dental office wishes an interface between the present DYNA Dental Office Management System and an appropriate G/L package.

Preparing a memo to explain DYNA and its main advantages over the traditional one-write system.

11.7 Penny Thornton, D.D.S. is considering a move from her present one-write system to a computerized dental package. Use an interoffice memo format to identify the package called DYNA Dental Office Management System and summarize the main advantages of DYNA over the traditional one-write system. To begin your memo, use subheadings as follows: TO:, FROM:, DATE:, and SUBJECT:.

Note: If possible, use a microcomputer and appropriate word processing software to print a solution to this problem.

Chapter Summary

Accounting packages for the microcomputer may be classified in two ways. One classification divides them into real-time accounting packages and batch-processing packages. All real-time accounting software updates appropriate ledger accounts immediately after entering and posting individual transactions. Therefore, financial statements and other reports may be printed immediately after posted transactions. On the other hand, batch-processing software requires that entries be first saved in groups (batches) before posting them to appropriate ledgers. In practice, there are strong supporters of each classification.

A second way to classify accounting software is between horizontal packages and vertical packages. Horizontal packages are general in nature, because they can be used by a variety of businesses. Common examples of general accounting packages are AccPac Bedford, AccPac Plus, and Summation. On the other hand, a vertical package is aimed at a specific business such as a dental or medical practice. One vertical package in wide Canadian use is the DYNA Office Management System.

AccPac Bedford is a real-time, menu-driven package designed primarily for the small merchandising business with a variety of accounting needs. The package consists of integrated modules for the general ledger, accounts payable, accounts receivable, payroll, inventory, and job costing. Each module consists of a ledger and one or more related journals, and each ledger must be "set ready" before entries can be recorded through the related journal. Bedford relies heavily on a system of pluses (increases to accounts) and minuses (decreases to accounts) to analyze all debit and credit entries. The package is available in separate versions for computers using MS-DOS and the Apple Macintosh operating system.

AccPac Plus is regarded as the industry leader in batch-processing accounting packages. Its current version, 6.0, is designed for medium-sized businesses and divisions of large corporations with specific accounting requirements and large transaction volumes. AccPac Plus offers separate modules for the general ledger, accounts receivable, accounts payable, payroll, inventory control, order entry, retail invoicing, sales analysis, and job costing. All modules are menu-driven and use the same format of menus. Batch files of entries are required in each module before posting to accounts is allowed. The G/L module is capable of receiving batch files from other modules; therefore, the modules can be integrated through the transfer of batch files. The G/L module requires the creation of a chart of accounts, while debits and credits to those accounts are based on the theory of the accounting equation. Versions are available for MS-DOS and the IBM OS/2 system.

The Easypay accounting package is a Canadian payroll package, menu-driven, and intended for use by a variety of businesses with employees ranging from 5 to 200. Basically, the program consists of three main menu types: the payroll run menu, the employee file maintenance menu, and other menus and functions. The payroll run menu features eight consecutive programs with a check-off system so that payroll clerks may follow each step in order. The program supports a variety of payroll plans, and can print multiple cheques and all of the essential payroll remittances and year-end payroll tax slips and reports. The program now exports data to several general ledger packages that use MS-DOS.

Summation is a real-time accounting package intended for use by a variety of small to medium-sized businesses. Accounting modules consist of the General Ledger, Accounts Receivable, Accounts Payable, Inventory Management, and Order Entry/Invoicing. All modules may be used independently; however, the developers have emphasized the need to integrate them for maximum efficiency. The G/L requires an organized chart of accounts and supports both the periodic and the perpetual inventory method. Summation 2.40 integrates with the Easypay program and includes both an on-line text editor and a built-in math function to solve basic math problems on any line where a number will be entered. The current version supports computers with MS-DOS.

A Canadian package known as the DYNA Dental Office Management System may be classified as a vertical accounting package, because the programs are customized for dental offices that plan to move from the traditional one-write system to a computerized one. Basically, the program covers all aspects of the accounts receivable application for either a dental office operated by one doctor or a multi-user office in which several dentists and other providers (hygienists) offer services. DYNA features a system of layered menus, beginning with the main menu and proceeding to related branches or sub-menus. All menus appear on the screen so that the user can easily return to the original one without difficulty. Although all aspects of the accounts receivable are covered, the program does not post totals or individual dental entries to the general ledger. The user must post these manually to a traditional manual G/L, enter entries via a keyboard and journal grid into a G/L package, or acquire DYNA's separate G/L module which is interfaced with the Receivable package to receive separate or total entries. Currently, DYNA is available on computers which use the Xenix operating system.

Chapter Questions

1. Name and briefly explain three characteristics that are common to all microcomputer accounting packages.
2. Can fair comparisons be made between general accounting packages? Explain why or why not.
3. Bedford's accounting package consists of six ledgers and related journals. Identify each ledger and briefly explain the relationship between the ledger and its related journals.
4. Why is the Bedford accounting package known as a fully integrated accounting package?
5. An inexperienced user of Bedford accounting may encounter this screen message: "The Ledger must be Set Ready before this Journal can be opened." Briefly explain the meaning of this message.
6. Present a simple example to explain the average cost method of accounting for the cost of goods sold in any accounting system.
7. Briefly explain how cash sales and cash purchases are accounted for under the Bedford system.
8. What is the main function of a job costing module in any general accounting package? Why is this module important to management?
9. Why is AccPac Plus classified as a modular-type accounting package?
10. Why is AccPac Plus also classified as a batch-operated system?
11. Briefly explain how you would gain access to AccPac Plus's General Ledger Master Menu. Assume that the module has been installed correctly.
12. What is meant by the statement "All AccPac Plus programs have similar menu structures"?
13. In general terms, list in correct order the steps to record and post transactions to AccPac Plus's G/L System.
14. Why is it important to print a batch listing under the AccPac Plus accounting system?
15. Why is it important for accounting students to have exposure to real-time and batch-processing packages?
16. Outline the main characteristics of the Canadian payroll package called Easypay.
17. Assume that you have installed Easypay in drive D. Briefly explain how you would set up a company called TEST so that Easypay can be tested.
18. List the steps in correct sequence to process a payroll run under Easypay.
19. XYZ Company uses Easypay to process the company's weekly payroll. However, the company still employs the manual system to process its G/L. What

steps are required to update the appropriate accounts resulting from the weekly payroll?

20 Briefly explain how a company that uses Easypay and Summation may update its G/L after processing its regular payroll.

21 Is there a limitation to the use of any computerized payroll package? Explain your answer.

22 What is required to run Summation 2.40?

23 Briefly explain the built-in math function in Summation 2.40.

24 Distinguish between a vertical accounting package and a horizontal accounting package.

Accounting Case Problems

CASE 11-1

Preparing a report on the controversy of real-time versus batch-processing systems.

T. Story owns and operates a mid-sized merchandising business and is considering a microcomputer system and appropriate accounting software to replace the business's traditional manual system. In considering an accounting package, the owner expresses ignorance over the controversy of real-time versus batch processing accounting packages. The owner approaches you for help to clarify the controversy.

Write a short report to T. Story summarizing the views made by supporters of batch processing and real-time packages. End the memo by offering your personal view.

Note: If possible, use a microcomputer and appropriate word processing software to complete the report.

CASE 11-2

Analyzing rules for debiting and crediting accounts under Bedford's accounting package.

After completing an introductory course in accounting at the college level, two students exchanged views over the merits of the Bedford accounting package. Student A expressed some confusion over Bedford's system of debits and credits in relation to increases and decreases to accounts. In particular, the student believed that transactions such as owner's personal withdrawals and expense transactions contradicted the theory of applying increases and decreases based on the accounting model, A = L + OE.

On the other hand, Student B believed that Bedford's theory of using increases and decreases was acceptable, because all debits and credits result in a double entry which balances. Accordingly, the student saw no flaws in applying Bedford's system of pluses and minuses to the elements of the accounting equation.

Required Which student's view would you support? Justify your position by testing Bedford's theory on common transactions applied to the accounting equation.

APPENDIX

Accounting for the Goods and Services Tax (GST)

After studying this material, you should be able to:

— Prepare a sketch showing how the GST works through a marketing chain.
— Analyze in general journal form basic GST transactions and post these transactions to one GST Payable account.
— Compute GST and PST where the GST is included in the selling price of a product and analyze in general journal form the entry resulting from the sale.
— Record selected transactions affecting GST and PST in a sales journal, cash receipts journal, and general journal; post entries affecting GST Payable and PST Payable; and record and post GST remittance entries.
— Record selected GST transactions and post these transactions to two GST ledger accounts; prepare Section Two of the GST remittance form; account for the balance of GST at month-end.
— Explain what general ledger changes would be required to maximize the efficiency of accounting and reporting of GST in a microcomputer package like Summation, Version 2.4.
— Use an accounting package like Summation, Version 2.4 to account for selected transactions affecting GST and print the required reports to complete Section Two of the "Goods and Services Tax Return for Registrants" form.
— Define the following key accounting terms presented in this Appendix: Bill C-62, input tax credit, supplies, small suppliers, registrants, taxable supplies, zero-rated supplies, tax-exempt supplies, laid-down cost principle, capital property, fair market value, quick method of GST accounting, streamlined accounting, GST Payable, Goods and Services Tax Return for Registrants, GST Refund Receivable, GST Payable, GST Adjustments, Input Tax Credit (ITC), ITC Adjustments, GST Installments, GST Rebates.

Bill C-62: the bill that gave birth to the federal government's new Goods and Services Tax (GST).

At the time of developing the manuscript for this edition, the federal government had passed **Bill C-62**—the Goods and Services Tax (GST) Act—through the House of Commons but not through the Senate. Consequently, a decision was made to present the accounting of the GST in the form of an appendix. In November 1990, the Senate did pass Bill C-62, by a narrow margin, and the GST became law on January 1, 1991.

545

An examination of Bill C-62 is beyond the scope of this text, since there are many complex rules and regulations embodied in the GST. Even at the time of this writing, administrative policies and changes to what items would be exempt from the new tax were still under formulation. Therefore, the two topics in this Appendix give only an introduction to the basics of GST accounting. For more details on how the GST affects business enterprises, interested readers are referred to *The Complete Guide to the Goods and Services Tax for Accounting Professionals and Financial Executives*, Ernst & Young, published by the Canadian Institute of Chartered Accountants. Also available are numerous pamphlets and booklets from the nearest office of Revenue Canada—Customs and Excise.

TOPIC I Examining the Basics of the GST and GST Accounting

Examining a Few Introductory GST Concepts

The following points provide background that is necessary before any attempt is made to account for the GST.

- The GST, fixed at 7%, replaces the outdated federal sales tax (FST) which has been in effect since 1924 and which was imposed and hidden at the manufacturer's level only at a rate of 13.5%.

- The GST is actually a value-added tax like the one used by 48 countries around the world. As such, it is applied to all business levels in the marketing supply chain—from manufacturing to wholesaling to retailing to the end user, the consumer. Each business that collects the GST is entitled to subtract the GST paid on the purchase, commonly known as the ***input tax credit***, from the GST collected on the sale. If the tax paid on the purchase is greater than that collected on the sale, the government will refund the difference. On the other hand, if the tax paid on the purchase is less than that collected on the sale, the business will remit the difference. To illustrate, study Figure A-1.

  Input tax credit: a refundable credit awarded to those registered under the GST for GST paid or payable on purchases that relate to a commercial activity.

  From the illustration, you should conclude that taxpayers carrying on business will be able to recover all of the GST they pay on supplies they have to buy to provide their goods and services to customers. This recovery is achieved by allowing suppliers a credit for the GST they have paid against the GST they must collect and remit on sales. The actual accounting of the sale and recovery will be treated later.

- In general, the GST is calculated at the rate of 7% on the sales of the majority of goods and services sold or provided in Canada. Collectively, these goods and services are called ***supplies***. Only a limited number would be tax-exempt; for example, residential rent, most health and dental services, basic groceries, most education, day care, and most bank services.

Supplies: goods and services on which the 7% GST must be paid.

FIGURE A-1

How the Goods and Services Tax Works

Example: Purchase of a Wooden Chair at $1 000

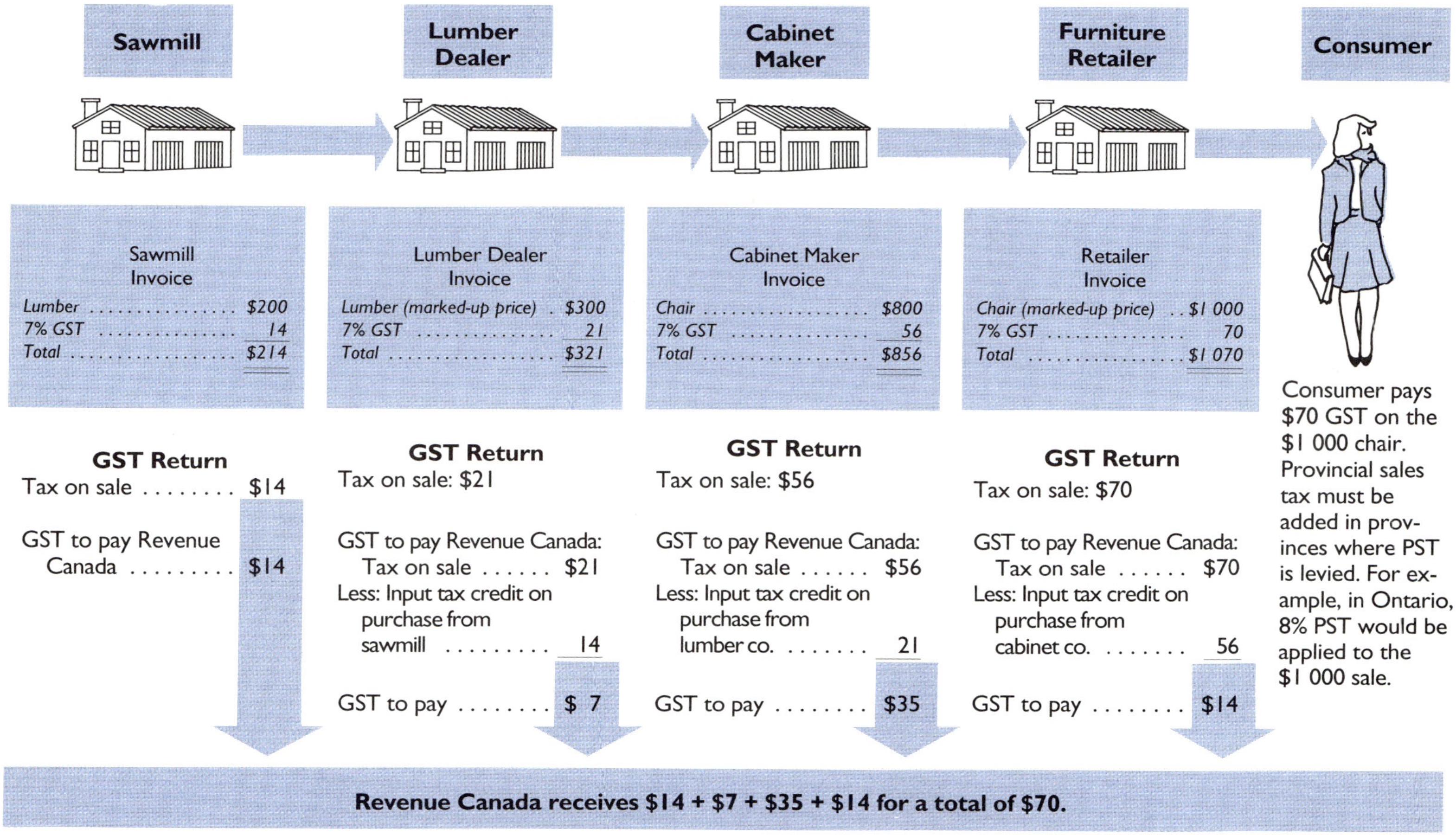

Sawmill

Sawmill Invoice
Lumber $200
7% GST 14
Total $214

GST Return
Tax on sale $14

GST to pay Revenue Canada $14

Lumber Dealer

Lumber Dealer Invoice
Lumber (marked-up price) .. $300
7% GST 21
Total $321

GST Return
Tax on sale: $21

GST to pay Revenue Canada:
Tax on sale $21
Less: Input tax credit on purchase from sawmill 14
GST to pay $7

Cabinet Maker

Cabinet Maker Invoice
Chair $800
7% GST 56
Total $856

GST Return
Tax on sale: $56

GST to pay Revenue Canada:
Tax on sale $56
Less: Input tax credit on purchase from lumber co. 21
GST to pay $35

Furniture Retailer

Retailer Invoice
Chair (marked-up price) .. $1 000
7% GST 70
Total $1 070

GST Return
Tax on sale: $70

GST to pay Revenue Canada:
Tax on sale $70
Less: Input tax credit on purchase from cabinet co. 56
GST to pay $14

Consumer

Consumer pays $70 GST on the $1 000 chair. Provincial sales tax must be added in provinces where PST is levied. For example, in Ontario, 8% PST would be applied to the $1 000 sale.

Revenue Canada receives $14 + $7 + $35 + $14 for a total of $70.

Small suppliers: businesses with annual sales under $30 000.

Total sales below 30,000 do not pay GST

Registrants: those who are registered under the GST system.

- Subject to a small-supplier exemption, any person engaged in a commercial (business) activity is required to register.
- Businesses with annual sales under $30 000 are classified as **small suppliers** or small traders, and they may choose to be exempted from the GST system. If they do so, they cannot charge GST on sales, nor can they claim any of the GST paid on their purchases. However, they may choose to register and thus will charge GST on sales and then deduct input tax credits. In general, it may be advantageous for small suppliers, particularly who supply goods and services to **registrants**, to elect to register and collect the GST.
- Businesses with annual sales over $30 000 must register and must collect GST on sales. They are required to file the "Goods and Services Tax Return for Registrants." The frequency of filing such a return and calculating GST collected and paid depends on their annual sales volumes. For example, if annual sales are less than $500 000, the business may calculate the GST yearly and make estimated quarterly installments. Those businesses with sales between $500 000 and $6 million will calculate and also remit GST on a quarterly basis. Finally, businesses with annual sales greater than $6 million must calculate and remit taxes monthly.
- In provinces where a provincial sales tax must also be collected, the GST applies "first" and PST (provincial sales tax) will have no effect on the computation for GST.
- Retail businesses must be careful to check on what base to charge customers for the PST, if applicable. For example, Ontario has announced that it will not stack its 8% PST on top of the GST. However, some provinces, such as Prince Edward Island, require the retailer to calculate its 10% PST on the total sale plus the 7% GST. To make matters more complicated, at the time of this writing two provinces—Quebec and Saskatchewan—have announced that they will integrate their PST with the GST within two years.

Identifying the Tax Base

Taxable supplies: the majority of goods and services consumed in Canada and on which 7% GST is applied.

Zero-rated supplies: a select list on which the GST rate is 0%; registrants will be able to claim input tax credits.

Tax-exempt supplies: a select list on which no GST is applied; businesses will not be able to recover GST paid on purchases.

As stated earlier, the GST will affect the vast majority of goods and services consumed in Canada. There are three basic categories of goods and services:

- *Taxable supplies*—most goods and services
- *Zero-rated supplies*—basic groceries, prescription drugs, medical services
- *Tax-exempt supplies*—health and dental care, education services, daycare services, legal aid services, residential rents, financial services, municipal transit and passenger ferries, etc.

Although zero-rated and tax-exempt items seem similar, there is a substantial difference between them. On zero-rated goods and services, the business will not charge GST on sales, but they may still claim input tax credits for any tax paid on purchases. On tax-exempt sales, the business will not charge GST on sales, but it will *not* be able to claim any input tax credits on purchases.

Under the GST, it is a fact that most goods and services are taxable. However, the Act does provide for exceptions that often defy comprehension. For example, salted peanuts are considered taxable foods whereas unsalted nuts are not. Similarly, the purchase from a bakery shop of fewer than six muffins is subject to GST while the purchase of six or more is exempt. To be sure, businesses must refer to the specific schedules under the GST to determine which items are taxable, zero-rated, and exempt.

Identifying Accounting Anomalies

Laid-down cost principle: original invoice price plus all other costs directly related to acquire the goods (invoice cost plus customs and excise duties, freight-in, and cartage).

For the most part, registrants will continue to use generally accepted accounting principles and procedures to do their accounting. However, the following departures from GAAPs should be noted:

- In acquiring goods (services), the **laid-down cost principle** must not include the amount computed for GST paid or payable. For example, if a registrant purchased goods for resale costing $10 000 and paid $700 for GST, the laid-down cost principle requires that the debit to Inventory (or Purchases under the periodic inventory method) be debited for $10 700 (the original cost plus the tax). Under GST accounting, however, the $700 paid for GST is regarded an input tax credit. As such, registrants are entitled to deduct this amount from the GST collected or collectible on taxable supplies made during the accounting period. Consequently, Inventory (or Purchases) will be debited for $10 000 while a separate debit must be identified for the $700. The proper GST accounting for this transaction will be treated later.

- The registrant does not have to wait until finished goods inventory is sold before claiming the input tax credit related to the purchase of the goods or their raw material. Thus, the matching principle used to determine the net income under GAAPs (matching revenues with *related* expired costs) is not followed under GST rules.

Capital property: another name for a fixed asset.

- Under GST accounting, there is no requirement to spread the cost of the input tax credit over the life of acquired **capital property**. Thus, the matching principle is not followed to spread the cost of GST paid over the useful life of, say, newly acquired equipment. Once again, the matching principle is not used under GST accounting.

- Registrants are required to collect and remit tax on the full invoiced price, regardless of whether any cash discount is subsequently taken by a purchaser. For example, assume a registrant receives an invoice showing the invoice amount before tax at $1 000 and GST of $70, with invoice terms of 2/10, n/30. The cash discount of 2% must be applied to the $1 000 and not to $1 070. Under GST accounting, the $70 of GST is always based on the full invoiced price and must still be remitted, because an input tax credit equal to that amount may be claimed.

- The withdrawal of business assets for personal use requires special attention. For example, if the owner of a sole proprietorship withdraws a computer or an inventory item for personal use, under GST accounting, the owner is said to have acquired the asset at *fair market value (FMV)*, and must collect GST on that item. The owner is viewed as a person who had purchased the asset in the regular manner. For example, suppose the owner operates a TV and radio store and takes home a colour TV that has a fair market value of $800, for which the business paid only $500. Under GAAPs, the owner's Drawing account would be debited for $500 and the Inventory (or Purchases) account would be credited for $500. Under GST accounting, the owner's Drawing account would be debited for $556, the Inventory (or Purchases) would be credited for $500, and GST Payable would be credited for 7% of $800 or $56.

Fair market value (FMV): that price for which the goods could be sold in normal business activity—that is, the price that would be agreed upon between the seller and potential buyer.

Introducing Simplified Accounting Methods

Quick method (of GST accounting): method whereby some businesses are permitted to apply a fixed percentage on total sales; eliminates accounting for GST on sales and accounting for input tax credits.

To help "small" business account for the GST, the federal government allows certain businesses to use one of three simplified account methods: the "quick method" and one of two streamlined accounting methods.

The **quick method** is limited to: (1) businesses with annual revenues up to $200 000, and (2) grocery and convenience stores with annual sales up to $500 000 if basic (zero-rated) groceries make up at least 25% of sales. Using this method, the business would still charge 7% on taxable goods when calculating GST owing. However, instead of tracking GST charged on sales, and then subtracting input tax credits, the business simply multiplies total sales by a specified percentage which is set by the government according to the type of business. The business does not receive specific input tax credits; it is presumed that the specified lower percentage applied to total sales takes into account the approximate amount of tax paid on purchases. There are special provisions for claiming input tax credits for major capital purchases, to ensure that the business is not at a disadvantage because of using this method. Note that this method does not apply to some types of businesses such as law, accounting, or financial consulting practices.

Streamlined accounting: one of two short methods available to some businesses in computing the amount of GST owing.

Streamlined accounting is available for businesses with annual revenues of up to $2 million that sell a combination of taxable and zero-rated groceries at the retail level. These businesses may elect to use one of two streamlined accounting methods, as follows:

- Under method 1, retailers will calculate GST owing on the basis of the retail selling price of purchases of taxable goods for resale. The input tax credits as recorded would be deducted from the calculated tax owing.
- Under method 2, retailers must rely on a prescribed standard markup for basic groceries instead of using retail selling prices. First,

the retailer estimates sales of zero-rated basic groceries by multiplying grocery purchases by a prescribed markup. The retailer then subtracts the estimated zero-rated sales from total sales for the period. The difference is the estimated total taxable sales, which is then multiplied by 7/107 (a government formula) to determine the tax on sales for the period. Finally, the value of any input tax credits is subtracted from the tax on sales to determine the tax owing.

Although these simplified accounting methods do eliminate much of the required tracking of the GST, many accountants point out these two shortcomings:

- Using simplified accounting methods may result in the registrant being in a more unfavourable position than would otherwise be the case under a system of tracking fully the GST.
- Using simplified accounting methods defeats the main objective of using accounting software capable of tracking all aspects of the GST and producing useful reports through the computer to facilitate the easy and efficient preparation of the GST remittance form.

Filing GST Returns and Keeping Accounting Records

- A form called the "Goods and Services Tax Return for Registrants" must be filed for each reporting period. See margin illustration. When no taxable supplies have been made during a reporting period, the registrant must nonetheless file a GST return for the period.
- When the registrant's reporting period is the fiscal year, the return is to be filed within three months after the end of the fiscal year; in every other case, the return is to be filed within one month after the end of the reporting period of the registrant.
- Every GST return is to be completed in the prescribed form, and must contain the prescribed information, and be filed in the prescribed manner.
- The Goods and Services Tax Return for Registrants is to be used by registered suppliers to: (1) declare tax collectible; (2) claim input tax credits; and (3) calculate the net tax for a reporting period.
- A draft copy of the Return appears in Figure A-3. Detailed instructions for completing this return will be provided to all businesses once they are registered with the Customs and Excise branch, which is the branch of Revenue Canada responsible for administration of the GST.
- Registrants will receive personalized GST returns in the mail well in advance of the return due date. Non-personalized returns will be available in Revenue Canada—Customs and Excise offices and major post offices.
- GST returns must be signed by an individual authorized to do so—by the governing person or body of the company.

FIGURE A-2

Summary of GST Reporting Periods (based on sales volume)

Annual sales of under $500 000:
Registrants must file at least annually, and must make quarterly installments.

Annual sales of between $500 000 and $6 million:
Registrants must file at least quarterly.

Annual sales of over $6 million:
Registrants must file at least monthly.

All registrants may file monthly.

552 APPENDIX: Accounting for the GST

FIGURE A-3

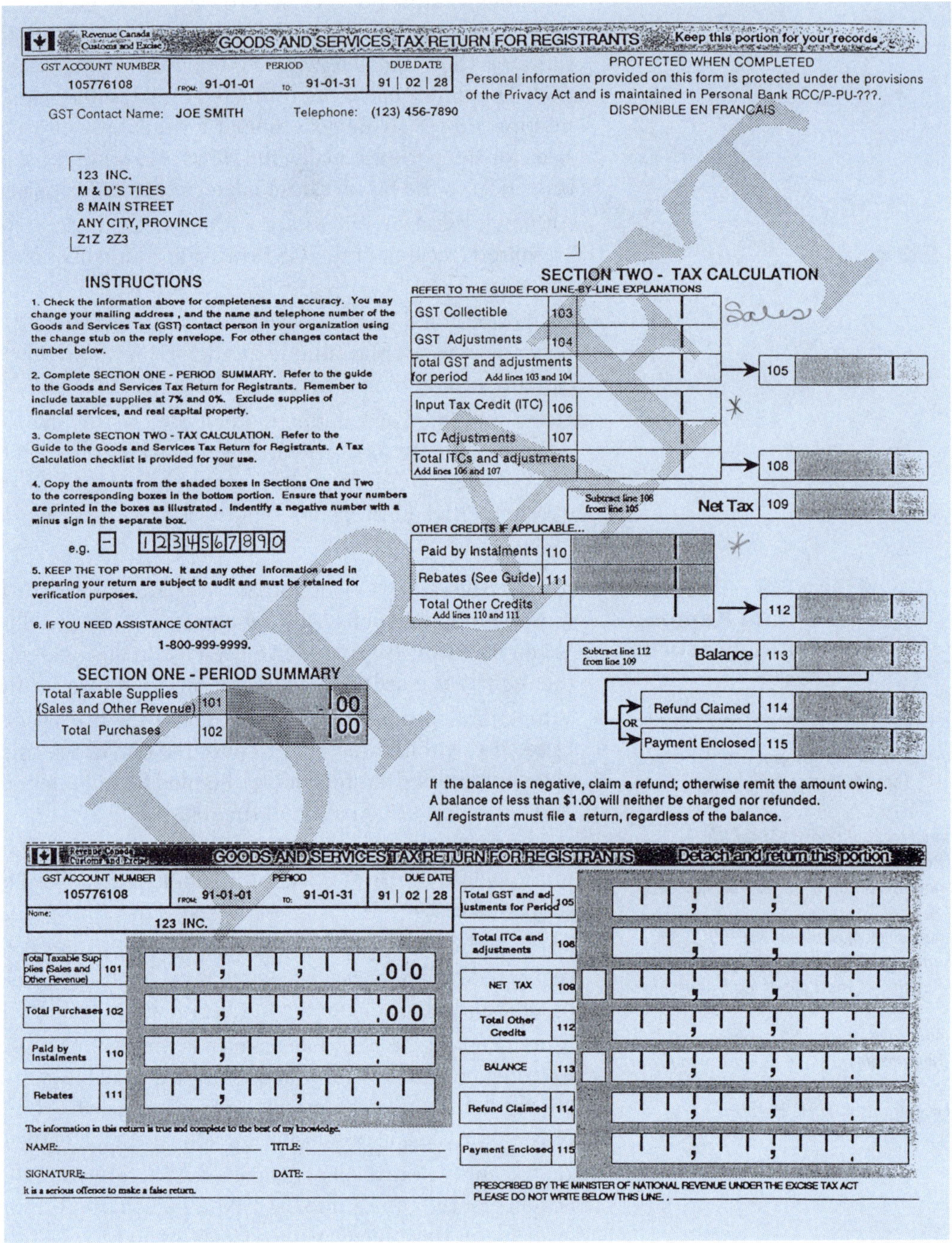

- On the matter of keeping books and records, Section 286(1) of the Bill C-62 states: "Every person who carries on a business or is engaged in a commercial activity in Canada, every person who is required under this Part to file a return and every person who makes an application for a rebate or refund shall keep records in English or in French in Canada, or at such other place and on such terms and conditions as the Minister may specify in writing, in such form and containing such information as will enable the determination of the person's liabilities and obligations under this Part or the amount of any rebate or refund to which the person is entitled."

Furthermore, Section 286(2) states: "Where a person fails to keep adequate records for the purposes of this Part, the Minister may require the person to keep such records as the Minister may specify and the person shall thereafter keep the records so specified."

As for the period for retaining such books and records, Section 286(3) states: "Every person required under this section to keep records shall retain them until the expiration of six years after the end of the year to which they relate or for such other period as may be prescribed."

In simple terms, the law applying to the GST requires businesses to keep accounting records and "books of accounts" for audit purposes. If the registrant uses electronic data processing, he or she must make all relevant software available for review. Finally, these accounting records must be retained for a period of six years from the end of the calendar year to which they relate—a rule similar to the one required for income tax reporting.

Tracking (Accounting for) the GST

In a simplified business with few transactions, it is possible to use only one account, GST Payable, a current liability account, to record all aspects of the GST. Although there are serious limitations to the use of only one account, it is useful in this opening Topic to simplify the examples that follow in originating GST accounting data, journalizing GST accounting data, and posting GST accounting data to the general ledger. With this background, you can then proceed to Topic 2, where alternative methods of accounting for the GST will be analyzed.

ORIGINATING GST ACCOUNTING DATA From earlier work, you learned that all transactions must originate on some form of source document. When the GST is involved, this means that source documents such as invoices and credit invoices must either indicate the computed amount of GST or indicate by a statement that the GST has been included in the final price. For an illustration, follow closely the examples below.

Example 1 Scarborough Wholesale Hardware sold merchandise to Eglinton Hardware Centre on Invoice 101, as illustrated in Figure A-4.

FIGURE A-4

SCARBOROUGH WHOLESALE HARDWARE

330 Progress Avenue
Scarborough, Ontario M1P 2Z5

INVOICE NO. 101

SOLD TO: Eglinton Hardware Centre
1975 Eglinton Avenue East
Scarborough, Ontario M1L 2N1

GST Reg. No. 112458989

INVOICE DATE: 19— 05 02
TERMS: 2/10, n/30

SHIP TO: Same

Purchase Order No.	Date	Shipped Via	FOB	No. of Packages
645839	19— 05 01	Barr Transport	Scarborough	3

QUANTITY	STOCK NO.	DESCRIPTION	UNIT PRICE	AMOUNT
30 sets	53Y5197	Wrench Set	3.59	107.70
20 sets	53Y1883	Socket Wrench Set	6.49	129.80
30 only	53-R1755	Tool Boxes	14.89	446.70
10 only	58-4628	Heavily Insulated Pliers	2.10	21.00
10 only	57-4121	450 g Deluxe Claw Hammer	3.79	37.90
		TOTAL INVOICE PRICE		743.10
		GST 7.00%		52.02
		TOTAL PAYABLE		795.12

COPY 2 - ACCOUNTING

Analysis Notice that Scarborough Wholesale Hardware, the seller, is required to show its GST Registration Number on the invoice. In addition, it is assumed that all goods sold are subject to the GST at the rate of 7%, since there is no indication that goods have been exempt or are zero-rated. Notice too that the calculation of the 7% GST is shown on the invoice, since the total invoice price is over $150. This disclosure is in accordance with GST regulations. In general, the regulations state that invoices with totals of $150 or more should disclose the amount of GST payable; and invoices with totals of less that $150 may disclose the GST as a separate amount or indicate by a statement that the GST has been included in the total price.

It is useful to do an accounting analysis of this invoice, in general journal form, first from the standpoint of the seller's books and then from the buyer's accounting records. Study the journal entries shown in Figures A-5 and A-6.

Further Analysis The double entry on the seller's books offers no complications. The debit for $795.12 shows the total amount that must be

FIGURE A-5

Accounting Records of Scarborough Wholesale Hardware (Seller)

```
19—
May 2   Acct. Rec./Eglinton Hardware Centre .........  795.12
           Sales ...........................................           743.10
           GST Payable ...............................            52.02
        Issued Invoice 101; terms 2/10, n/30.
```

FIGURE A-6

Accounting Records of Eglinton Hardware Centre (Buyer)

```
19—
May 2   Purchases (or Inventory) ....................  743.10
        GST Payable ..............................       52.02
           Acct. Pay./Scarborough Wholesale Hardware        795.12
        Purchased goods on Scarborough's Invoice 101;
        terms 2/10, n/30 from May 2.
```

paid by Eglinton Hardware within 30 days of the invoice date. Sales is credited for $743.10 to recognize revenue from the sale of goods on credit. And GST Payable for $52.02 is a current liability showing what amount is owing to Revenue Canada—Customs and Excise for the GST.

However, the double entry on the buyer's books may cause some confusion, since there is a departure from accounting under generally accepted accounting principles. First, the debit to Purchases (or Inventory under a perpetual inventory method) for $743.10 is the total invoice price without the GST added. The reason for avoiding the laid-down cost principle (invoice price plus additional amounts required to obtain the goods) is the federal government's ruling that any GST paid on purchases will be a deduction from the GST Payable on sales. Therefore, the next debit, to GST Payable for $52.02, must be analyzed as a deduction from the future amounts of GST Payable that Eglinton Hardware Centre will receive from customers who are sold goods. Of course, the credit to Acct. Pay./Scarborough Wholesale Hardware represents the total amount owing to the credit in accordance with the terms of the invoice.

Example 2   Scarborough Wholesale Hardware issued a credit memo to Eglinton Hardware Centre as illustrated in Figure A-7.

Analysis   Notice again that any document involving the calculation of GST must show the GST Registration Number of the business that has issued the document. In this case, the credit memo shows the registration number of Scarborough Wholesale Hardware. Notice too that the applicable credit for the GST portion is based on the original invoice price of

FIGURE A-7

SCARBOROUGH WHOLESALE HARDWARE

330 Progress Avenue
Scarborough, Ontario M1P 2Z5

CREDIT MEMO
NO. CM-01

TO: Eglinton Hardware Centre
1975 Eglinton Avenue East
Scarborough, Ontario M1L 2N1

GST Reg. No. 112458989

DATE: 19— 05 25

| Your Order No. 645839 | Our Invoice No. 101 |

We have credited your account as follows:

Return of eight No. 53Y5197 wrench sets received in damaged condition:

8 sets at $3.59		$28.72
Applicable GST at 7.00%		2.01
Total credit		$30.73

the goods returned. The total credit can then be analyzed on the books of the seller and the buyer as in Figures A-8 and A-9.

Further Analysis The double entry on the seller's books shows a debit to Sales Returns and Allowances to record the decrease in sales revenue which was caused by the return of goods sold on Invoice 101. The second debit is the decrease to GST Payable for the applicable portion of GST calculated originally on the goods sold but now returned. The only

FIGURE A-8

Accounting Records of Scarborough Wholesale Hardware (Seller)

```
19—
May 5   Sales Returns and Allowances  ..............   28.72
        GST Payable  ..........................    2.01
            Acct. Rec./Eglinton Hardware Centre .......        30.73
        Issued Credit Invoice CM-01 to Eglinton Hardware
        Centre.
```

FIGURE A-9

Accounting Records of Eglinton Hardware Centre (Buyer)

```
19—
May 5   Acct. Pay./Scarborough Wholesale Hardware  ...   30.73
            GST Payable  .........................         2.01
            Purchases Returns and Allowances (or Inventory) .   28.72
        Credit Invoice CM-01 received from Scarborough
        Wholesale Hardware.
```

credit entry has the effect of decreasing the customer's account by the total credit.

The double entry on the buyer's books requires careful analysis. The debit for $30.73 is to record the total decrease to the accounts payable account for the total credit issued by the seller. The credit to GST Payable for $2.01 is to reverse the original debit made as an input tax credit on the original purchase. The second credit entry is to record the decrease to Purchases under a periodic inventory system (or Inventory under the perpetual inventory system) for the total invoice price of the goods returned.

Example 3 Scarborough Wholesale Hardware receives a cheque dated on May 10 and issued by Eglinton Hardware Centre for $750.10 in full payment of Invoice 101, less the allowable 2% discount. The journal entry to record the cheque received by the seller and issued by the buyer may be shown as illustrated in Figures A-11 and A-12.

FIGURE A-10

Cheque No. 045	May 10, 19—
Pay to the order of Scarborough Wholesale Hardware	$750.10
Seven Hundred Fifty .... 10/100 DOLLARS	
	Eglinton Hardware Centre

FIGURE A-11

Accounting Records of Scarborough Wholesale Hardware (Seller)

19—
May 10   Cash 750.10
           Sales Discounts 14.29
              Acct. Rec./Eglinton Hardware Centre 764.39
         To record cheque in full payment of Invoice 101, less
         the return, and less the 2% sales discount on $714.38.

FIGURE A-12

Accounting Records of Eglinton Hardware Centre (Buyer)

19—
May 10   Acct. Pay./Scarborough Wholesale Hardware ... 764.39
              Purchases Discounts 14.29
              Cash 750.10
         Issued Cheque 045 in payment of Scarborough's
         Invoice 101, less return and less the 2% discount.

FIGURE A-13

Acct. Rec./Eglinton Hardware Centre

May 2 inv.	795.12	May 5 return	30.73
Amount owing on May 5 is	764.39		

Supporting Computations

Invoice 101 .... $743.10
GST at 7% 52.02
Amount owing $795.12
Less: Return 30.73
Amount owing after return 764.39
Less: Cash discount
   (2% on $714.38) 14.29
Cheque amount $750.10

Analysis The problem in both journal entries is to analyze the correct figure for the sales/purchases discount. On what amount would the 2% discount rate be applied? On the original invoice of $743.10? On $795.12 (the original invoice of $743.10 plus the $52.02 GST)? On the original invoice of $743.10 less the sales return of $28.72? Or on the amount owing in the customer's account of $764.39?

The answer is on $714.38, because the federal government has stated that vendors (sellers) will collect and remit the GST on the invoiced price, irrespective of any cash discounts. In this case, the original invoice amount of $743.10 was reduced by the amount of sales return of $28.72. Hence, the 2% cash discount will be applied to the net invoice amount of

$714.38. The correct analysis of the cheque received may be shown as in Figure A-14.

FIGURE A-14

	Invoice	+	7% GST	=	Amount Owing	
	$743.10	+	$52.02	=	$795.12	
Less:	−28.72	+	−2.01	=	−30.73	
	$714.38	+	$50.01	=	$764.39	← Cr. to Acct. Rec.
Less: 2% on $714.38				=	−14.29	← Dr. to Sales Discount
Cheque amount				=	$750.10	← Dr. to Cash

Example 4 Scarborough Wholesale Hardware purchases goods as shown in Figure A-15 on the illustrated invoice received from Small Tools Limited.

FIGURE A-15

Small Tools Limited
229 Kearney Sreet
Winnipeg, Manitoba R2M 4B5

Invoice No. **0387**

Sold To: Scarborough Wholesale Hardware
330 Progress Avenue
Scarborough, Ontario M1P 2Z5

GST Registration No. 110280955

Ship To: Same as above

Invoice Date: 19— 05 09
Terms: 2/10, n/30

Purchase Order No.	Date	Shipped Via	FOB	No. of Cartons
PO-0078	19— 05 03	Inter-City Express	Winnipeg	3

QUANTITY	STOCK NO.	DESCRIPTION	UNIT PRICE	AMOUNT
90 sets	53Y5197	Wrench Set	2.59	233.10
80 sets	53Y1883	Socket Wrench Set	4.25	340.00
50 only	53-R1650	Tool Boxes	8.75	437.50
		TOTAL PAYABLE		1 010.60
		GST 7.00%		70.74
		TOTAL PAYABLE		1 081.34

APPROVED
QUANTITIES RECEIVED
PRICES CHARGED
EXTENSIONS & TOTALS
DATE PAID
CHEQUE NO.

DATE 5/10 G. Morrison
G. Morrison
S. Davies

Analysis As you recall from Chapter 5, the invoice in the hands of Scarborough Wholesale Hardware is a purchase invoice. Notice that the supplier of the goods, Small Tools Limited, must show its GST Registration Number and the computed GST at 7%, since the total invoice price is greater than $150. Follow closely the analysis of the double entries on the buyer's and the seller's books shown in Figures A-16 and A-17.

FIGURE A-16

Accounting Records of Scarborough Wholesale Hardware (Buyer)

```
19—
May 10   Purchases (or Inventory) ..................  1 010.60
           GST Payable ..........................      70.74
             Acct. Pay./Small Tools Limited .........           1 081.34
         To record goods purchased from Small Tools
         Limited on their Invoice 0387 dated May 9, 19—
         with terms of 2/10, n/30.
```

FIGURE A-17

Accounting Records of Small Tools Limited (Seller)

```
19—
May 9    Acct. Rec./Scarborough Wholesale Hardware .. 1 081.34
           Sales ................................           1 010.60
           GST Payable ..........................             70.74
         Issued Invoice 0387 to Scarborough Wholesale
         Hardware on terms of 2/10, n/30.
```

Further Analysis The double entry on the seller's books requires no further explanation, since a similar entry was analyzed earlier. However, the double entry on the buyer's books should be reemphasized. Note that the debit amount is the total invoice price and not the laid-down cost. Also, note that the debit must be made to Purchases if the periodic inventory system is used and to Inventory if the perpetual inventory system is used. The second debit to GST Payable recognizes an input tax credit under the GST system of accounting. As explained earlier, an input tax credit is a deduction from future GST Payable amounts when collected on sales transactions. And, finally, the credit to Acct. Pay./Small Tools Limited recognizes the total amount owing to this supplier in accordance with invoice terms.

Example 5 Eglinton Hardware Centre sold for cash one toolbox at its retail price of $20.87 with GST included, plus the Ontario 8% PST as shown on the sales slip shown in Figure A-18.

Analysis Retailers selling goods/services totalling under $150 may choose to include the GST calculation as part of the selling price, as shown in the sales slip illustrated for Eglinton Hardware Centre. When such a

FIGURE A-18

```
EGLINTON HARDWARE CENTRE                         SALES SLIP NO. 150
1975 Eglinton Avenue East
Scarborough, Ont. M1L 2N1                        Date: May 15, 19—

GST Reg. No. 123456789                           Terms: Cash Only

One #53-R1755 Tool Box ....................      $20.87   GST Included
Plus Ontario 8% Provincial Sales Tax ..........    1.56

Total Cash Received ........................     $22.43
```

FIGURE A-19

Computation of GST on Basis of Tax-Included Price

Formula: Price with GST included × 7/107

(a) $20.87 × 7/107 = $1.37

(b) Original sales price:
    $20.87 − $1.37 = $19.50

Proof: $19.50 × 7% = $1.37

practice is followed, purchasers and accounting clerks may determine the amount of tax included in the price on the basis of the tax-included price, using the formula 7/107 times the total selling price but excluding any PST. As you can see from the side-margin calculation, the GST would be $1.37 and the original retail price without the GST would be $19.50.

In provinces where PST must be added, note that the GST computation must always be made *before* the PST. As stated earlier, some provinces, such as Ontario, prefer to apply their PST rate (8% in Ontario at the time of writing) to the selling price without the GST included. (Hence, the Ontario PST would be computed by multiplying the selling price without the GST, $19.50, by 8%.)

On the other hand, some provinces, such as Prince Edward Island, have levied their PST on top of the GST. Therefore, if the above sales slip were transacted in Prince Edward Island, the PST rate (10% at the time of writing) would be applied to the total of the selling price plus the GST.

And as indicated earlier, two provinces, Quebec and Saskatchewan, have announced their intention to integrate the GST with their respective PSTs over a two-year period. At that time, invoices will simply show GST plus PST at a rate of 14% being applied to the total selling price. It is anticipated that other provinces may follow; therefore, invoice forms and accounting procedures will probably change.

Further Analysis   Examine carefully the double entry that may be analyzed on the books of the retailer in support of the illustrated sales slip, as shown in Figure A-20.

FIGURE A-20

```
         Accounting Records of Eglinton Hardware Centre (Seller)

19—
May 15   Cash ....................................  22.43
             Sales ...............................          19.50
             GST Payable .........................           1.37
             PST Payable .........................           1.56
         To record cash sale on Sales Slip 150.
```

APPENDIX: Accounting for the GST   **561**

From the figure, one should conclude that separate liabilities are required for the GST Payable and PST Payable accounts. For this reason, many businesses will show both calculations on every source document to ensure accurate tracking of the GST and PST.

Example 6   The sole proprietor of Eglinton Hardware Centre, Mary Phills, issued the interoffice memo illustrated in Figure A-21.

FIGURE A-21

EGLINTON HARDWARE CENTRE	INTEROFFICE MEMO
1975 Eglinton Avenue East	
Scarborough, Ont. M1L 2N1	Date: May 31, 19—

TO: Head of Accounting

SUBJECT: Withdrawal of goods for personal use, as below.

Two #53-R1755 Tool Boxes costing $14.89 each	$29.78
Applicable GST: 7% of fair market value:	
7% × (2 × $19.50)	2.73
Total to be charged to Drawing account	$32.51

Analysis   In general terms, Section 172(1) of Bill C-62 states that when a sole proprietor who is a registrant withdraws property from inventory for his or her own use, the owner is deemed to have supplied it at fair market value and must remit GST on the withdrawal in the same manner as if the proprietor had sold the property to a customer of the business. Assuming that the data in the illustrated memo can be verified, the analysis shown in Figure A-22 may be made in general journal form.

FIGURE A-22

Accounting Records of Eglinton Hardware Centre (Seller)

19—			
May 31	M. Phills, Drawing	32.51	
	Purchases (or Inventory)		29.78
	GST Payable		2.73
	To record the withdrawal of merchandise for		
	personal use, as per proprietor's memo of May 31.		

Further Analysis   The debit to the owner's Drawing account is for the cost of the inventory items withdrawn plus the GST Payable in accordance with Section 172(1) of Bill C-62. The first credit entry is to recognize the decrease to inventory. Under a periodic inventory system, this decrease would be made to the Purchases account, since the Inventory account would not be updated until the end of the accounting period; or, if the business used a perpetual inventory system, the credit would be to the Inventory account. The second credit is to recognize the amount of GST Payable in accordance with the GST Act.

There are numerous other accounting data that would affect GST accounting. However, some of these are delayed for study in Topic 2.

JOURNALIZING GST ACCOUNTING DATA

In the analysis of previous examples, only general journal entries were used, to simplify GST accounting. However, in practice, when manual systems are employed special journals must be considered along with the general journal.

When special journals are used, it makes sense to add special money columns to track GST Payable, since transactions affecting GST are numerous. Special columns should be considered as listed below:

- **Sales Journal** A GST Payable Cr. money column to account for the GST on credit sales as the tax is computed on each invoice.
- **Cash Receipts Journal** A GST Payable Cr. money column to account for the GST on cash sales as evidenced on sales slips and/or cash register tapes.
- **Purchases Journal** A GST Payable Dr. money column to account for the GST input tax credit as shown on purchase invoices negotiated on a credit basis.
- **Cash Payments Journal** A GST Payable Dr. money column if there are numerous purchases made for cash and for which GST has been paid as an input tax credit.
- **General Journal** No special column is required, since this journal would record infrequent GST transactions such as sales returns and purchase returns.

To illustrate, examine Figure A-23, which shows a sales journal with three money columns.

FIGURE A-23

SALES JOURNAL (REXDALE WHOLESALERS)   Page 10

Date	Invoice No.	Account Debited	Terms	Post. Ref.	Accounts Receivable Dr.	Sales Cr.	GST Payable Cr.
19—							
June 2	510	Energy Control Inc.	2/10, n/30	√	1 070 00	1 000 00	70 00
3	511	CT Appliance Service	2/10, n/30	√	1 284 00	1 200 00	84 00
8	512	Mike's Auto Parts	2/10, n/30	√	3 076 79	2 875 50	201 29
10	513	Lakeshore Inn	2/10, n/30	√	510 50	477 10	33 40
12	514	Holmes Bindery Inc.	2/10, n/30	√	957 97	895 30	62 67
15	515	Acme Electronics	2/10, n/30	√	3 093 10	2 890 75	202 35
20	516	Impact Business Forms	2/10, n/30	√	2 022 30	1 890 00	132 30
25	517	Art Construction Ltd.	2/10, n/30	√	598 88	559 70	39 18
30	518	NEI Service	2/10, n/30	√	1 592 70	1 488 50	104 20
30		Totals			14 206 24	13 276 85	929 39
					(103)	(401)	(205)

From this illustration, one can conclude that the special money column GST Payable Cr. permits the accounting clerk to post the total of the column to the current liability account at the end of the month. Of course, if the business were a retailer located in a province requiring the collection of the provincial retail sales tax, an extra money column would be provided for PST Payable Cr.

POSTING GST ACCOUNTING DATA

From what has been analyzed so far, one can conclude that the general ledger will contain only one GST account, a current liability called GST Payable. When posting information to this one account, it is most important that detailed explanations be included in the ledger account so that an accounting clerk can track the source of GST data. To illustrate, examine the GST Payable account for Rexdale Wholesalers shown in Figure A-24.

FIGURE A-24

GST Payable   Account No. 205

Date		Explanation	Post. Ref.	Debit	Credit	Balance	Dr./Cr.
19—							
June	30	Total GST collectible on credit sales.	SJ 10		929 39	929 39	Cr.
	30	Total GST collected on cash sales.	CRJ 15		210 04	1 139 43	Cr.
	30	Total GST payable on credit purchases.	P 20	840 00		299 43	Cr.
	30	Total GST paid on cash purchases.	CPJ 18	84 00		215 43	Cr.
	30	Totals		924 00	1 139 43	215 43	Cr.
July	5	Cheque 130 to Receiver General.	CPJ 16	215 43		0 00	—

Analysis From the illustration, it is obvious that all posted debits represent input tax credits paid or still payable to suppliers for purchases of goods and/or services requiring the GST. On the other hand, the amounts posted in the Credit column represent the GST paid or still payable by customers who were sold goods and/or services during June.

Notice that final totals are shown at the end of the month, to facilitate the completion of the Goods and Services Tax Return for Registrants (refer back to the illustration of this return in Figure A-3). The total of the Credit column would be entered on Line 103, "GST Collectible," while the total of the Debit column would be entered on Line 106, "Input Tax Credit (ITC)." Of course, the difference between the GST Collectible and the Input Tax Credit (ITC) is the "Balance." In this case, there is a credit balance in the GST Payable account; therefore, this amount must be remitted to the Receiver General for Canada and would be shown in box 115 on the Return when the cheque is enclosed. Of course, a double entry would be made in the cash payments journal to record the cheque. The results of posting this cheque would eliminate the amount owing to the federal government.

On the other hand, if the total input tax credits (total of the Debit money column) were greater than the total of GST Collectible for the period, a debit balance would be shown in the GST Payable account. This debit balance would be entered in box 114 to claim a refund from the federal government. To account for this refund, a general journal entry would be made by debiting a current asset such as GST Refund Receivable and crediting GST Payable. When the refund is received, Cash can be debited and GST Refund Receivable can be credited.

It is important to end this Topic by emphasizing that the use of one account only to track GST data for most businesses of reasonable size is seriously limited. For example, there may be GST adjustments and ITC adjustments, payments by installment, and rebates to track as required by the Goods and Services Tax Return for Registrants. In this case, more than one account is required to track all aspects of the GST for an accounting period. Topic 2 will examine the use of alternatives for GST accounting.

TOPIC 1 Problems

Sketching how the GST works through a marketing chain; analyzing basic accounting entries; computing GST amounts.

A.1 Assume that a manufacturer buys on account $1 000 of material to produce shirts and subsequently sells finished shirts to a retailer for $3 000. Assume further that the retailer sells all of these shirts at a 100% markup on cost to consumers in a province where the 10% PST is "stacked" on top of the GST.

Required
a Produce a sketch showing how the GST works through the marketing chain—from manufacturer to retailer to consumer.
b Show in general journal form the double entries on the manufacturer's books for the purchase of raw materials and subsequent sale of finished shirts to the retailer. Assume that the sale occurred on credit.
c Show in general journal form the double entries on the retailer's books for the purchase of goods from the manufacturer and the sale of shirts to consumers. Assume that all sales occurred for cash only.
d How much GST should be paid by the manufacturer? By the retailer? By the consumer? Explain your answer.
e How much will the Receiver General for Canada receive in the form of GST? Explain your answer.

Computing GST and PST from a shoe sale where GST is included in the sales price; analyzing the resulting entry from the sale.

A.2 A retail shoe dealer has advertised that all sales would be sold with GST included. Suppose that a pair of shoes were sold for $120 cash with GST included in a province where the PST is 8% and which is applied on the selling price without GST.

Required
a Show computations to track the GST and PST from this sale.
b In general journal form, show the vendor's double entry resulting from the cash sale.

Recording selected transactions affecting GST and PST in a sales journal, cash receipts journal, and general journal; posting amounts affecting GST Payable; posting other data affecting GST Payable; totalling and ruling off GST Payable at month-end; analyzing the double entry for the month-end balance of GST Payable.

A.3 Central Wholesale/Retail Plumbing & Heating Supply accounts for its sales as follows: wholesale sales to registered retailers on the basis of credit terms of n/30; retail sales on a cash basis only. Assume that the business is located in a province where PST must be applied to all retail sales. (If you are located in Alberta, use the Ontario 8% PST tax system in this problem.) Also assume that all goods sold are taxable under the 7% GST rules.

To account for all sales transactions, assume that the business uses a sales journal to account for all credit sales; a cash receipts journal to account for all cash sales; and a general journal to account for all credit invoices. Assume that management has adopted the periodic inventory method of accounting.

The following transactions affecting sales for March of the current year are summarized as follows:

Mar. 5 Issued the following sales invoices to retailers: #101 to AC Plumbers, $2 000; #102 to Hicks Plumbing & Drains, $1 200; and 103 to AMS Plumbing Ltd., $3 000. Applicable GST must be applied to all invoices.
7 Cash sales to consumers totalled $2 800. Applicable GST and PST must be applied.
9 Issued Credit Invoice CM-10 for $200 to AMS Plumbing Ltd. for goods returned on Invoice #103. Applicable GST must be applied.
10 Issued the following sales invoices to retailers: #104 to Aardvark Plumbing & Heating, $4 800; #105 to Abony Plumbing & Heating, $2 700; #106 to Apple Plumbing & Heating, $3 600. GST must be applied to all invoices.
12 Cash sales to consumers totalled $5 500. Applicable GST and PST must be applied.
15 Issued the following sales invoices to retailers: #107 to Accord Plumbers, $4 000; #108 to Aqua-Flow Plumbing & Drains, $3 200; and 109 to AMS Plumbing Ltd., $2 400. Applicable GST must be applied to all invoices.
16 Cash sales to consumers totalled $3 800. Applicable GST and PST must be applied.
17 Issued Credit Invoice CM-11 for $400 to Accord Plumbers for goods returned on Invoice #107. Applicable GST must be applied.
25 Issued the following sales invoices to retailers: #110 to ARC Plumbing & Heating, $3 000; #111 to Hicks Plumbing & Drains, $2 200; and 112 to AMS Plumbing Ltd., $1 000. Applicable GST must be applied to all invoices.
27 Cash sales to consumers totalled $3 800. Applicable GST and PST must be applied.
31 Issued sales invoice #113 to Camgran Plumbing & Heating, a registered retailer, for $1 850. GST must be applied.
31 Cash sales to consumers totalled $1 250. Applicable GST and PST must be applied.

566 APPENDIX: Accounting for the GST

Required
a Record the above transactions in a sales journal, Page 12, a cash receipts journal, Page 18, and a general journal, Page 5 where applicable. Create a special money column for GST and PST where applicable.
b Total, prove, and rule off both special journals for the month. Post the appropriate total for GST to a GST Payable account (No. 210).
c Suppose month-end totals were proved from other special journals and showed totals from purchases journal as follows: Purchases Debit, $12 000; GST Payable Debit, $840; and Accounts Payable Credit, ~~$12~~ $12 840; from the cash payments journal affecting GST: Purchases Debit, $750; GST Payable Debit, $52.50; Cash Credit, $802.50. Post all amounts affecting GST to the general ledger account.
d Total and rule off the GST Payable account for March. Suppose a GST remittance form is prepared on April 4. Show the double entry in general journal form to account for the balance and post the result.

Recording selected transactions for a small stationery/book shop in a general journal; posting entries affecting GST Payable and PST Payable; recording and posting entries affecting GST and PST remittances.

A.4 Katherine Dittrich operates a small stationery and book shop in a province where the GST and PST must be collected on all sales. The owner uses the periodic inventory method of accounting and records all transactions in the general journal. The following transactions occurred in June of the current year. *Important Note:* At the time of writing, the sale of books was classified as a taxable item under the GST.

June 30 Purchases of merchandise on credit terms of n/30 for June totalled $18 000. GST must be applied to this total.
30 Merchandise returned for credit on purchases during June totalled $1 200. Applicable GST must be accounted for.
30 Domestic freight-in charges on account on merchandise purchased during June totalled $2 000. *Note:* Generally, domestic freight services are taxable under the GST and must be applied to this transaction.
30 Cash sales for June totalled $21 600. GST and your province's PST must be applied on this total. (Ontario residents are charged 8% PST on the sale price excluding GST.)
30 Returns of books sold during June totalled $500. Cash refunds on these book returns totalled $500 plus applicable GST and PST.
30 Issued cheque in payment of business gas heating bill which showed $60 natural gas consumption plus 7% GST charge of $4.20. (Natural gas consumption is subject to the GST.)
30 Issued cheque in payment of business telephone bill which showed $56 of telephone services plus $3.92 GST charges. (Telephone service is subject to the GST.)
30 Paid $7.44 cash for mailing a parcel via Priority Post. The bill of lading showed a total fee of $6.95 plus $0.49 for GST.
30 Purchased office supplies for cash totalling $30.99 plus $2.17 GST. (Use Office Supplies Expense in the double entry.)
30 Office equipment was purchased on 30 days' credit costing $19 500 plus 7% GST.

30 The owner withdrew for personal use books costing $32.80. The books sell at retail for $39.36.

Required

a Record all transactions in a general journal. Show applicable GST and PST entries.

b Post those entries that affect GST and PST to general ledger accounts for GST Payable (210) and PST Payable (211).

c Assume that separate remittance forms are required for GST and PST on July 15. Show the appropriate entries in the general journal to support each remittance. Include supporting computations in the journal narrative. Post the results of each remittance entry.

TOPIC 2 Analyzing Alternative Methods of Accounting for the GST

In a simplified business with few transactions, it is possible to use only one account—GST Payable—to record all aspects of the GST. In practice, however, several accounts are usually required when the volume of monthly transactions is large and especially when computer software is used to track the GST.

In general, separate accounts may be created for the key parts required to complete "Section Two—Tax Calculation" of the GST Return for Registrants as illustrated in Figure A-3. The key parts of this remittance form are numbered boxes as follows:

- "GST Collectible" (box 103)
- "GST Adjustments" (box 104)
- "Input Tax Credit" (ITC) (box 106)
- "ITC Adjustments" (box 107)
- "Paid by Instalments" (box 110)
- "Rebates" (box 111)

With separate account data for these six boxes, the registrant can complete Section Two to account for any "Refund Claimed" (114) or "Payment Enclosed" (115).

In the simple cases that follow, separate accounts will be shown to complete only the GST Collectible and Input Tax Credit boxes of the remittance form. The accounting of GST Adjustments, ITC Adjustments, Paid by Instalments, and Rebates will be examined under the section on using Summation, Version 2.4.

Case 1. Manual Method with a Balance Owing Assume a wholesale business called Oakville Wholesale Hardware. Assume also that the summary data below is supported by source documents for the month ended June 30, in a current GST year and that the registrant has elected to report the GST on a monthly basis.

i. Total purchases of merchandise for June, $100 000. GST charged on all purchase invoices totalled $7 000. Assume terms of net 30 days on all invoices. Assume that the accounting system uses the periodic inventory method.

ii. Total purchases of equipment for June, $20 000. GST charged on all invoices totalled $1 400. Assume terms of n/30 days on all invoices.
iii. Total freight-in charges for June, $1 000. GST charged on all freight bills totalled $70. Assume terms of n/30 days on all freight bills.
iv. Operating expense bills paid by cheque for which GST was charged totalled $1 800 plus $126 for the GST.
v. Total credit invoices received from creditors in June for goods returned, $2 500. Applicable GST on these credit invoices totalled $175.
vi. Total sales for June, $300 000. Applicable GST on these invoices totalled $21 000. Assume terms of n/30 on all sales invoices.
vii. Credit invoices issued to customers for June totalled $3 000. Applicable GST on these credit invoices totalled $210.

FIGURE A-25

Oakville Wholesale Hardware
Partial Chart of Accounts

Current Assets	Current Liabilities
101 Petty Cash	201 Bank Loan Payable
102 Cash in Bank	202 Accounts Payable
103 Accounts Receivable	203 GST Payable
105 GST Refund Receivable	204 Input Tax Credit (ITC)

To track the GST in the above transactions, assume that Oakville Wholesale Hardware includes G/L accounts as in Figure A-25. Note the following points when analyzing this chart:

- Three G/L accounts have been created to track the GST: 105 GST Refund Receivable, 203 GST Payable, and 204 Input Tax Credit.
- GST Refund Receivable is listed under Current Assets. This account will be used whenever the registrant completes the GST Return for Registrants remittance form and concludes that a refund is claimed.
- GST Payable is listed under Current Liabilities. This account will be credited each time a sale is made on which the GST must be collected. The account will be debited for the GST portion of credit invoices issued to customers. Also, the account will be debited each time a cheque is issued to pay any balance owing for GST. As you will learn, the posting of this cheque entry will result in a zero balance to this account.
- Input Tax Credit is listed under Current Liabilities. Since it is shown immediately after GST Payable, the ITC may be analyzed as being "contra" to the current liability. As a current liability contra account, it will be debited for all GST amounts charged on all types of invoices: purchase invoices of merchandise, invoices showing the purchase of equipment, freight-in bills, and bills for which an expense account will be debited. Conversely, the Input Tax Credit (ITC) account will be credited for all GST amounts quoted on credit invoices received for

APPENDIX: Accounting for the GST **569**

returned goods and similar adjustments on "purchase" invoices. And as you will learn, the Input Tax Credit (ITC) account will be closed out at the end of each month to support the preparation of the GST Return for Registrants remittance form.

Important Note: In practice, some accountants may choose to classify the Input Tax Credit (ITC) account as a current asset. In doing so, they are supporting the theory that a debit amount on a purchase invoice for the GST represents an unexpired cost. However, other accountants may argue that no current asset is possible under GST until the balance of the Input Tax Credit account is matched with the current liability GST Payable at the time the GST Return for Registrants remittance form is completed. In other words, no current asset for GST Refund Receivable can be identified until the Input Tax Credit account balance is subtracted from the balance in the GST Payable account. In this Appendix, Input Tax Credit (ITC) will be classified as a contra account to the current liability GST Payable.

To analyze the tracking of the GST, examine carefully the partial G/L in T-account form in Figure A-26, which shows the summary of debits and credits posted for transactions (i) through (vii).

FIGURE **A-26**

T-Account G/L Summary of Transactions (i) Through (vii)

	Cash in Bank	102			Accounts Receivable	103
	(iv)	1 926	(vi)	321 000	(vii)	3 210

	Accounts Payable		202			GST Payable	203
(v)	2 675	(i)	107 000	(vii)	210	(vi)	21 000
		(ii)	21 400				
		(iii)	1 070				

	Equipment	120			Input Tax Credit (ITC)	204
(ii)	20 000		(i)	7 000	(v)	175
			(ii)	1 400		
			(iii)	70		
			(iv)	126		

	Purchases	501			Freight-in	502
(i)	100 000		(iii)	1 000		

	Sales	401			Sales Ret. & Allow.	402
	(vi)	300 000	(vii)	3 000		

	Pur. Ret. & Allow.	503			Operating Expenses	515
	(v)	2 500	(iv)	1 800		

570 APPENDIX: Accounting for the GST

Analysis You can easily recreate the double entry for any transaction by identifying the transaction number in each T-account. For example, the first transaction would be analyzed in general journal form as in Figure A-27. As you check each numbered transaction, note that each individual double entry must balance, because the total debit or debits must equal the total credit or credits.

FIGURE **A-27**

(i) Purchases 100 000
    Input Tax Credit (ITC) 7 000
        Accounts Payable 107 000
    To record the total purchases of merchandise for June on account, plus the GST charged on all purchase invoices.

At month-end, the balances of the two GST accounts, Input Tax Credit (ITC) and GST Payable, can be used to complete Section Two of the GST Return for Registrants. The two T-accounts may be illustrated as in Figure A-28. Section Two of the Return is simulated in Figure A-29.

FIGURE **A-28**

	GST Payable	203		Input Tax Credit (ITC)	204
(vii)	210	(vi) 21 000	(i) 7 000	(v)	175
			(ii) 1 400		
	Bal.	20 790	(iii) 70		
			(iv) 126		
			Bal. 8 421		

FIGURE **A-29**

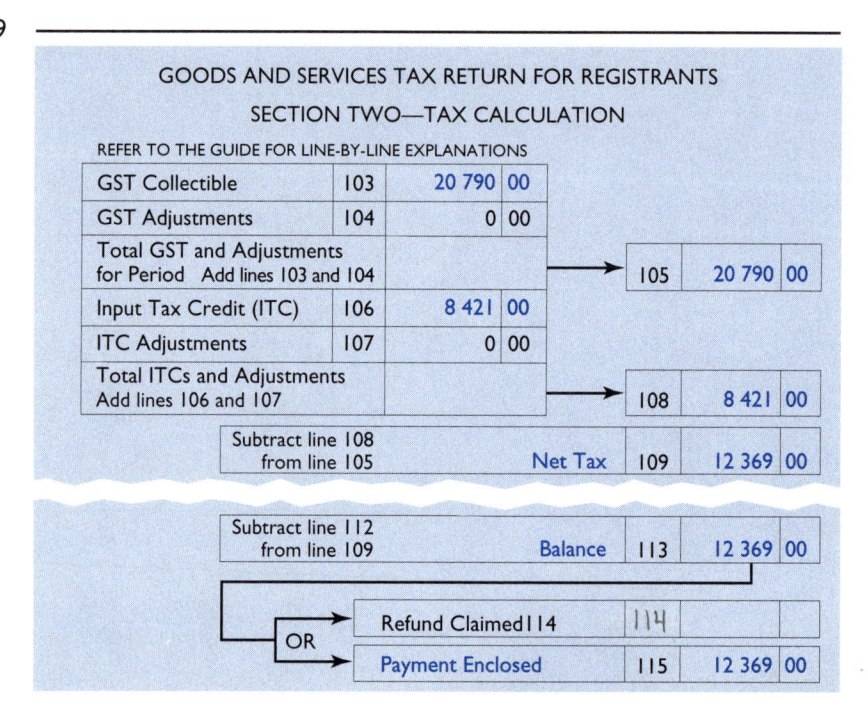

GOODS AND SERVICES TAX RETURN FOR REGISTRANTS

SECTION TWO—TAX CALCULATION

REFER TO THE GUIDE FOR LINE-BY-LINE EXPLANATIONS

GST Collectible	103	20 790 00			
GST Adjustments	104	0 00			
Total GST and Adjustments for Period Add lines 103 and 104			→	105	20 790 00
Input Tax Credit (ITC)	106	8 421 00			
ITC Adjustments	107	0 00			
Total ITCs and Adjustments Add lines 106 and 107			→	108	8 421 00
Subtract line 108 from line 105		Net Tax		109	12 369 00

Subtract line 112 from line 109		Balance	113	12 369 00
	Refund Claimed	114	114	
OR	Payment Enclosed		115	12 369 00

APPENDIX: Accounting for the GST   **571**

To account for the balance owing, assume that a cheque is made out to the Receiver General for Canada for $12 369. Under a manual system, the cheque would be recorded in the cash payments journal and may be analyzed in general journal form as transaction (viii) as in Figure A-30.

FIGURE A-30

> (viii) GST Payable 20 790
>   Input Tax Credit (ITC) 8 421
>   Cash in Bank 12 369
>   To record Cheque 319 in payment of the GST
>   payable at month-end.

Obviously, the result of posting the above entry will show that both the GST Payable and Input Tax Credit (ITC) accounts will have zero balances as shown in Figure A-31.

FIGURE A-31

	GST Payable	203			Input Tax Credit (ITC)	204
(vii)	210	(vi) 21 000	(i)	7 000	(v)	175
			(ii)	1 400	(viii)	8 421
(viii)	20 790		(iii)	70		
			(iv)	126		
	—0—				—0—	

Case 2. Manual Method with a Refund Claimed In this case, we will use the same data as outlined under Case 1 except that, in transaction (vi), we will assume that the sales for June totalled only $100 000 and the applicable GST on these sales totalled only $7 000. With this change, the two GST accounts may be viewed at month-end as illustrated in Figure A-32.

FIGURE A-32

	GST Payable	203			Input Tax Credit (ITC)	204
(vii)	210	(vi) 7 000	(i)	7 000	(v)	175
			(ii)	1 400		
		Bal. 6 790	(iii)	70		
			(iv)	126		
			Bal.	8 421		

Obviously, the difference between the balances in the two GST accounts shows that a refund of $1 671 ($8 421 − $6 850) will be claimed on the GST remittance form. To account for this claimed refund, a general journal entry would be made as in Figure A-33.

FIGURE A-33

> (viii) GST Payable 6 790
>   GST Refund Receivable 1 631
>   Input Tax Credit (ITC) 8 421
>   To record the refund claimed on the GST Return for
>   Registrants remittance form for June.

The results of posting the double entry may be analyzed in T-account form as in Figure A-34.

FIGURE A-34

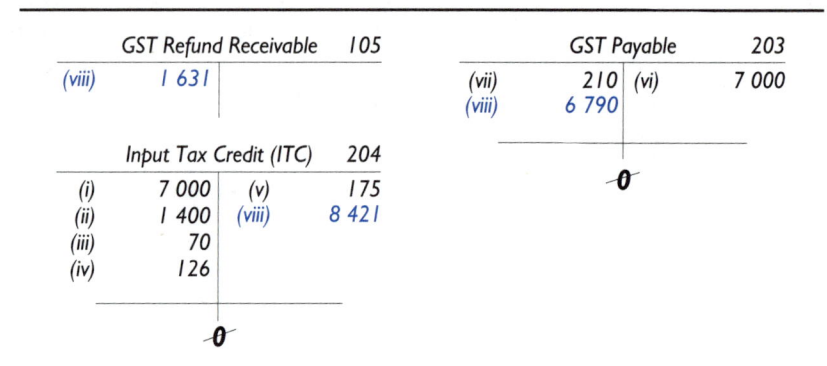

GST Refund Receivable 105		GST Payable 203
(viii) 1 631	(vii) 210	(vi) 7 000
	(viii) 6 790	

Input Tax Credit (ITC) 204	
(i) 7 000	(v) 175
(ii) 1 400	(viii) 8 421
(iii) 70	
(iv) 126	

Analysis Obviously, both the GST Payable and the Input Tax Credit (ITC) accounts show zero balances. However, the current asset GST Refund Receivable reports that a cheque for $1 631 is expected from the Receiver General for Canada's office. When the refund is received, a journal entry would be made by debiting Cash in Bank and crediting GST Refund Receivable. However, if a balance sheet were prepared before the cheque is received, the current assets section would report GST Refund Receivable for $1 631.

Case 3. Using Microcomputer Software Accounting software developers have modified their existing programs to permit the tracking of all data required to complete the GST Return for Registrants. Although each developer offers its own unique approach, the following general points may be applied to all microcomputer software programmed to track the GST:

- The G/L chart of accounts will be expanded to include additional accounts to track the data required to complete the boxes on the Goods and Services Tax Return for Registrants. Therefore, additional accounts may be created to track the GST collectible, the GST adjustments, the input tax credit (ITC), ITC adjustments, GST installments, GST rebates, and, if applicable, the GST refund claimed.
- Exact account titles to track all boxes on the remittance form will vary from one software package to another. However, these titles will usually be related to the function identified in the boxes of the GST Return for Registrants.
- The account title related to "GST Collectible" will probably be a current liability such as "GST Payable." However, one can expect different titles to support the data required for Input Tax Credit (ITC). As stated earlier, some accountants favour the use of a current asset account while others will recommend the use of a contra current liability account.

APPENDIX: Accounting for the GST   **573**

- With sufficient accounts to track and complete all required boxes on the GST Return for Registrants, one could expect to see the availability of a special printed report or schedule summarizing the account data for any accounting period. Obviously, such a report will be designed to facilitate the easy completion of the GST remittance form.
- The usual shortcuts over a manual system will be available. For example, in printing a sales invoice, the software may allow for the automatic accounting of the sale with GST and PST to the G/L and subsidiary ledgers. In other words, the invoicing program will be interfaced with the general ledger, accounts receivable ledger, and inventory ledger so that the resulting journal entry is posted automatically and correctly to all accounts.
- Above all, the theory of using more than one account to track the GST will be based on what was presented in the two cases under the manual method. Therefore, on completion of the GST Return for Registrants, if a refund is claimed, an entry would be made through the general ledger system to close out all GST accounts and debit a current asset such as GST Refund Receivable. On the other hand, if a payment is required to pay a balance owing, an entry would be made to close out all GST accounts and credit a current asset such as Cash in Bank.

Using Summation, Version 2.4

The Summation 2.4 program offers the GST registrant-user features to maximize the efficiency of accounting and reporting of the Goods and Services Tax. The following features are included in this latest version:

- **An open general ledger chart of accounts** to permit the user to add the maximum number of accounts required to track all aspects of GST transactions.
- **A supporting GST schedule** to facilitate the easy completion of Section Two of the Goods and Services Tax Return for Registrants. This feature reports the balances in all G/L GST accounts and discloses the amount of GST payable or receivable.
- **A general ledger detail report of only GST accounts**   The result of printing a G/L Detail Report of only GST accounts will verify the amount of GST payable or receivable as reported by the GST Schedule.
- **Modifications to the invoicing system** to allow the user to print an invoice showing separate money columns for the GST as applied to the exempt, zero-rated, and 7% categories on an item-by-item basis. Four totals are available on all invoices: the amount before taxes, GST at 7%, PST at the designated provincial rate, and the total amount owing. The GST at 7% is applied to the amount before taxes, enabling a cross-check against the separate items totalled in the GST Amount column. Where both GST and PST apply, users can include GST in the tax base for the PST or exclude the GST as the case may be.

- **Use of macro keys** to facilitate efficient updating of all customer files in the Accounts Receivable System, of all vendor accounts in the Accounts Payable System, and of all inventory items in the Inventory Management System to comply with GST requirements.

GST CHANGES REQUIRED IN SUMMATION'S GENERAL LEDGER SYSTEM

After installing Version 2.4, and after verifying that your latest data files are located in the Main Data Files section, these procedures are suggested:

Step 1. If applicable, delete FST payable from your G/L Chart of Accounts—that is, delete the old Federal Sales Tax Payable account.

Step 2. Enter the following new G/L accounts through Summation's General Ledger Update Program. Note that the four-digit account numbers illustrated are suggested account codes only. Use your own numbering system based on your chart of accounts. Also note that Summation recommends following this simple GST accounting theory: (1) that there be created only one current asset account, called GST Refund Receivable; and (2) that there be created a number of related accounts under Current Liabilities to account for GST Payable, Adjustments, Input Tax Credits, GST Installments, and GST Rebates. As you will discover, the new accounts under Current Liabilities will be the GST Payable and those accounts that are contra to it. Also observe carefully that these new accounts are given different levels to support the printout of the GST Schedule.

- The first new account is called *GST Refund Receivable*. (See Figure A-35.)

FIGURE A-35

Account number: 1220	General Ledger Account Update
Account Description	GST Refund Receivable
Account Type (H/R/T/S)	Regular
Report Print Type (A/C/D)	All Statements
Normal Balance (D/C)	Debit
Normal/Sales/Payment Account	Normal Account
Extra Lines (0 - 5 or Page)	No extra lines
Total Level (0 - 8)	1

FIGURE A-36

Kim Hall, Inc.
Partial Chart of Accounts

Current Assets	1100
Receivables	1200
Accounts Receivable—Trade	1200
Allowance—Doubtful Accounts	1210
Net Realizable Value	1215
GST Refund Receivable	1220
Total—Receivables	1230

Analysis   Ideally, this new account should be numbered after Accounts Receivable—Trade and its contra account Less Allowance for Doubtful Accounts, as shown in the partial chart of accounts illustrated in the side margin.

Debit GST Refund Receivable only if, after printing the GST Schedule, you discover you are in a GST Refund Receivable position; that is, you must have paid more GST than you collected through sales during

FIGURE A-37

Kim Hall, Inc.
Partial Chart of Accounts

Current Liabilities	2100
Bank Loan Payable (on demand)	2110
Accounts Payable	2120
GST Schedule #1	2200
GST Payable	2210
GST Adjustments	2215
Input Tax Credit (ITC)	2220
ITC Adjustments	2225
GST Installments	2230
GST Rebates	2235
GST Payable/(Receivable)	2240
GST Payable/(Receivable)	2245
PST Payable	2310

the current reporting period. The debit will be made as part of one large general ledger compound entry to close out all GST regular accounts for the reporting period.

The next series of accounts will be classified under Current Liabilities. As suggested earlier, the main account is GST Payable while all remaining ones will be contra to this current liability account. Additional accounts are also suggested to support the printout of the future GST Schedule. Once again, the account numbers are suggested codes only. However, it is recommended that you begin with a set of numbers that precede your PST Payable account. In tax theory, GST Payable is given priority over PST Payable.

- Create a heading account called *GST Schedule #1* as shown in Figure A-38.

FIGURE A-38

Account number: 2200	General Ledger Account Update
Account Description	GST Schedule #1
Account Type (H/R/T/S)	Heading
Report Print Type (A/C/D)	All Statements
Normal Balance (D/C)	Credit
Normal/Sales/Payment Account	Normal Account
Extra Lines (0 - 5 or Page)	No extra lines
Total Level (0 - 8)	0

Analysis   Obviously, the new account is simply a heading for the GST Schedule #1. Under Summation's program, note that the Total Level must be 0 to create any schedule related to a financial statement.

- Create a regular account called *GST Payable* as shown in Figure A-39.

FIGURE A-39

Account number: 2210	General Ledger Account Update
Account Description	GST Payable
Account Type (H/R/T/S)	Regular
Report Print Type (A/C/D)	All Statements
Normal Balance (D/C)	Credit
Normal/Sales/Payment Account	Normal Account
Extra Lines (0 - 5 or Page)	No extra lines
Total Level (0 - 8)	0

Analysis   The new account is a regular current liability account. It is given Total Level 0 so that the balance in this account can be reported only on the GST Schedule #1.

Credit GST Payable for every transaction requiring the collection of GST from customers during the current accounting period. In the majority of cases, the accounting of this GST Payable will be part of the double entry created through the invoicing system.

Debit GST Payable for the GST amount on every credit invoice issued during the current reporting period. Do not use the GST Adjustments account for credit invoices issued. As will be explained below, the GST Adjustments account must be used to record adjustments to GST Payable for *past* reporting periods. If Summation's Invoicing System is used to process a credit invoice, the debit to GST Payable for the GST amount is automatically calculated and correctly posted to G/L accounts.

- Create a regular account called *GST Adjustments* as shown in Figure A-40.

FIGURE A-40

Account number: 210152	General Ledger Account Update
Account Description	GST Adjustments
Account Type (H/R/T/S)	Regular
Report Print Type (A/C/D)	All Statements
Normal Balance (D/C)	Credit
Normal/Sales/Payment Account	Normal Account
Extra Lines (0 - 5 or Page)	No extra lines
Total Level (0 - 8)	0

Analysis   The above new account, GST Adjustments, is a regular Current Liability account. It is given Total Level 0 so that the balance in this account can be reported only on the GST Schedule.

In general, this account will be used to make adjustments to GST Payable for transactions that have occurred in different reporting periods. For example, suppose in the current reporting period you discovered that you sold goods but failed to apply the GST. In recognition that the federal government has the legal right to audit your books for at least the past six years, a responsible registrant would issue an adjustment invoice notifying the customer that the GST amount would be debited to the customer's account. The credit in this case would be made to GST Adjustments and not to GST Payable. The reason for using the GST Adjustments account is to recognize the fact that the GST remittance form makes a distinction between current reporting periods (for which the GST Payable account is used) and past reporting periods (for which the GST Adjustments account is used). You can verify this fact by reexamining the remittance form.

Consider this second example. If your business has sold taxable goods or services on credit, remitted the GST, and subsequently had written off a debit as a bad debt, your business can recover the GST that was remitted. As the GST is included in the amount of the bad debt, the tax adjustment would be 7/107 of the amount written off. For example, if you sold a $300 item, the debit owing would be $321. When this debit is written off, your business would claim an adjustment equal to $321 × 7/107 or $21. This value would be entered on the GST Return for Registrants on the line for adjustments. The general ledger entry may be analyzed as follows:

FIGURE A-41

```
Dr. Allowance for Doubtful Accounts ................   300
Dr. GST Adjustments .............................    21
    Cr. Accounts Receivable/Customer ...............            321
```

If subsequently the customer pays part of the debt that was previously written, say $100, your business must calculate and remit the GST that was included in that payment. The GST to be remitted would be $100 × 7/107 or $6.54. Thus, an adjusting entry would be made in the general ledger as follows, given that the write-off has already been reversed:

FIGURE A-42

```
Dr. Cash in Bank ................................  100.00
    Cr. Accounts Receivable/Customer ...............           93.46
    Cr. GST Adjustments ..........................            6.54
```

For more information on adjustments, refer to the CICA's *Complete Guide to the Goods and Services Tax* or contact the nearest office of Revenue Canada—Customs and Excise for brochures and answers to specific questions.

- Create a regular account called *Input Tax Credit (ITC)* as shown in Figure A-43.

FIGURE A-43

Account number: 2220	General Ledger Account Update
Account Description	Input Tax Credit (ITC)
Account Type (H/R/T/S)	Regular
Report Print Type (A/C/D)	All Statements
Normal Balance (D/C)	Debit
Normal/Sales/Payment Account	Normal Account
Extra Lines (0 - 5 or Page)	No extra lines
Total Level (0 - 8)	0

Analysis   The new account is a regular contra account to the current liability GST Payable. It is given Total Level 0 so that the balance in this account can be reported only on the GST Schedule.

An "input tax credit" is defined as "a credit claimed by a registrant for the GST paid or payable on any taxable input used in the course of a commercial activity." Therefore, this account will be debited every time the registrant purchases taxable goods and services during the current reporting period and receives an invoice to prove that GST has been paid or is payable. Conversely, this account will be credited every time the registrant receives a credit invoice during the current reporting period and on which is shown the computation for GST.

- Create a regular account called *ITC Adjustments* as in Figure A-44.

FIGURE A-44

Account number: 2225	General Ledger Account Update
Account Description	ITC Adjustments
Account Type (H/R/T/S)	Regular
Report Print Type (A/C/D)	All Statements
Normal Balance (D/C)	Debit
Normal/Sales/Payment Account	Normal Account
Extra Lines (0 - 5 or Page)	No extra lines
Total Level (0 - 8)	0

Analysis   The new account is a regular contra account to the current liability GST Payable. It is given Total Level 0 so that the balance in this account can be reported only on the GST Schedule.

Adjustments to ITC are not common. In general, this account will be debited each time the registrant receives an invoice charging GST on goods/services purchased in a *preceding* reporting period. Similarly, the registrant may receive an invoice charging GST for an error made on a invoice of a preceding reporting period.

- Create a regular account called *GST Installments* as in Figure A-45.

FIGURE A-45

Account number: 2230	General Ledger Account Update
Account Description	GST Installments
Account Type (H/R/T/S)	Regular
Report Print Type (A/C/D)	All Statements
Normal Balance (D/C)	Debit
Normal/Sales/Payment Account	Normal Account
Extra Lines (0 - 5 or Page)	No extra lines
Total Level (0 - 8)	0

Analysis   The new account is a regular contra account to the current liability GST Payable. It is given Total Level 0 so that the balance in this account can be reported only on the GST Schedule.

As stated earlier, if your annual taxable sales are over $6 million, you must pay GST on a monthly basis. However, if your annual taxable sales are $500 000 or less, you may file annually, with quarterly installments. Calculation of the installment base involves the application of a complex formula. Check the CICA's *Complete Guide to the Goods and Services Tax* or contact the nearest office of Revenue Canada—Customs and Excise for details. For example, if the net tax estimated on an annual basis totalled $12 000, quarterly installments of $3 000 are required. For each installment, make a G/L entry by debiting GST Installments and crediting your bank account.

- Create a regular account called *GST Rebates* as in Figure A-46.

FIGURE A-46

Account number: 2235	General Ledger Account Update
Account Description	GST Rebates
Account Type (H/R/T/S)	Regular
Report Print Type (A/C/D)	All Statements
Normal Balance (D/C)	Debit
Normal/Sales/Payment Account	Normal Account
Extra Lines (0 - 5 or Page)	2 lines
Total Level (0 - 8)	0

Analysis The new account is a regular contra account to the current liability GST Payable. It is given Total Level 0 so that the balance in this account can be reported only on the GST Schedule. Note that two extra lines are recommended, since this account completes the number of accounts required for printing the future GST Schedule.

GST Rebates should not be confused with FST (Federal Sales Tax) Rebates. In general, the GST Act provides for a rebate of GST paid on purchases in a variety of circumstances. Again, check references such as the CICA's *Complete Guide to the Goods and Services Tax* or contact the nearest office of Revenue Canada—Customs and Excise for details.

For example, assume that employees of a registrant's business incurred business-related expenses (travel and entertainment) in the course of their employment totalling $5 500 on which GST has been paid, the employee may claim a rebate equal to 7/107 of $5 500, or $360. Assume that no allowances or reimbursements were received by the employee. In this case, make a journal entry debiting GST Rebates and crediting the bank account for $360. Note that any such rebate also has income tax consequences. The amount of rebate paid is included in the employee's income from either office or employment.

- Create a "Total" type of account called *GST Payable/(Receivable)* as in Figure A-47.

FIGURE A-47

Account number: 2240	General Ledger Account Update
Account Description	GST Payable/(Receivable)
Account Type (H/R/T/S)	Total
Report Print Type (A/C/D)	All Statements
Normal Balance (D/C)	Credit
Normal/Sales/Payment Account	Normal Account
Extra Lines (0 - 5 or Page)	Page
Total Level (0 - 8)	0

Analysis The new account completes the accounts required for printing the GST Schedule. It is given "Total" status so that the total of all GST accounts reported appears on the GST Schedule. The Total Level is 0, because you want this account to appear on the GST Schedule. Since the normal balance is disclosed as a credit, any amount not enclosed in parentheses on the report will be treated as a credit balance—that is, as the amount of GST Payable for the reporting period. On the other hand, any amount appearing in parentheses will mean "opposite" and therefore will be interpreted as a GST Receivable. An explanation of how to print the GST Schedule appears after the instructions for creating the final G/L account.

- Create a "Subtotal" account called *GST Payable/(Receivable)* as in Figure A-48.

FIGURE A-48

Account number: 2245	General Ledger Account Update
Account Description	GST Payable/(Receivable)
Account Type (H/R/T/S)	Subtotal
Report Print Type (A/C/D)	All Statements
Normal Balance (D/C)	Credit
Normal/Sales/Payment Account	Normal Account
Extra Lines (0 - 5 or Page)	No extra lines
Total Level (0 - 8)	3

Analysis The new account is required so that the total reported by the GST Schedule is reported on the balance sheet under Current Liabilities. Accordingly, it is given "Subtotal" status with a Total Level of 3. If the balance in this account is a credit (as normally), it represents the GST Payable for the current period. On the other hand, if the amount appears in parentheses, it is interpreted as being receivable. In that case, the receivable will be transferred to GST Refund Receivable when the remittance form is completed and the entry is posted to close all GST accounts for the period.

Step 3. A Test   This might be a good place to test the printout of the GST Schedule. From the General Ledger Master Menu, press <5> and then <Enter> to print the Balance Sheet. Enter and verify the desired period. A new line appears in Summation's 2.4 version:

FIGURE A-49

```
Print supporting schedules ONLY?   (Y/N)   N
```

Answer Yes by pressing <Y>. Complete the remaining print instructions. The printout will be shown as in Figure A-50.

FIGURE A-50

```
                    Name of Business Enterprise
                        Supporting Schedules
                          U N A U D I T E D

         GST Schedule #1

    GST Payable                            0.00   cr
    GST Adjustments                        0.00   cr
    Input Tax Credit (ITC)                 0.00   dr
    ITC Adjustments                        0.00   dr
    GST Installments                       0.00   dr
    GST Rebates                            0.00   dr

    GST Payable/(Receivable)             $ 0.00
```

Analysis   The above schedule (report) should be run before you complete the Goods and Services Tax Return for Registrants remittance form. Obviously, all of the data exists to complete Section Two of this form.

In addition, it is recommended that a General Ledger Detail Report be printed for all GST regular accounts appearing on this Schedule: GST Payable; GST Adjustments; Input Tax Credit (ITC); ITC Adjustments; GST Installments; and GST Rebates. This report will show a balance identical to that of the final line printed on the GST Schedule.

If the final amount is a Credit balance, there must be a balance of GST to be paid. Therefore, you would issue a cheque for the amount owing and record this cheque in the form of one compound entry as in Figure A-51.

FIGURE A-51

Dr. GST Payable	xxx	
Dr. GST Adjustments	xxx	
Cr. Input Tax Credit (ITC)		xxx
Cr. ITC Adjustments		xxx
Cr. GST Installments		xxx
Cr. GST Rebates		xxx
Cr. Cash in Bank		xxx

To record cheque issued to Receiver General for Canada for the balance owing to GST Payable, as per GST Return for Registrants, dated xxxx.

On the other hand if the final amount is a debit balance, there must be recognition that a GST Refund is receivable. The compound entry shown in Figure A-52 should be made.

FIGURE A-52

Dr. GST Refund Receivable	xxx	
Dr. GST Payable	xxx	
Dr. GST Adjustments	xxx	
Cr. Input Tax Credit (ITC)		xxx
Cr. ITC Adjustments		xxx
Cr. GST Installments		xxx
Cr. GST Rebates		xxx

To record the GST Refund Receivable, as per GST Return for Registrants, dated xxxx.

This refund is payable by the Minister to the registrant within 21 days after filing the Return. According to the information received, interest on unpaid refunds will begin accruing 21 days after the return claiming the particular refund has been filed, provided that all required returns have been filed up to that time.

Step 4. Updating the Special Accounts List   From the G/L Master Menu, press <1> and then <2> to update the special account list. Delete any existing FST Payable account and replace it with the regular GST Payable account. In the case of earlier examples, this account would be 2210 GST Payable.

OTHER GST CHANGES REQUIRED IN SUMMATION, VERSION 2.4

Lack of space in this Appendix prevents our examining step-by-step procedures to make other GST changes in Summation's latest version. In general, these other changes would accommodate the new GST system in the Accounts Receivable System, the Inventory Management System, and the Invoicing System. When changes are made to these other systems, the accounting of GST carried out in any one of these would be integrated with the changes made in the General Ledger System.

TOPIC 2 Problems

Recording selected GST transactions in a general journal; posting transactions to two GST general ledger accounts; preparing Section Two of the GST remittance form; and accounting for the balance of GST at month-end.

A.5 The data below represents a summarized account of selected transactions for X Wholesale Company. Assume that all transactions are supported by source documents in a current GST year and that the registrant has elected to report the GST on a monthly basis.

i. Total purchases of merchandise for September, $250 000. GST charged on all purchase invoices totalled $17 500. All vendor invoices quoted terms of net 30 days. Assume that X Wholesale Company uses the periodic inventory system and the following G/L accounts to track GST: 105 GST Refund Receivable, 203 GST Payable, and 204 Input Tax Credit (ITC).

ii. Total purchases of equipment for September, $50 000. GST charged on all invoices totalled $3 500. Assume terms of n/30 days on all invoices.

iii. Total freight-in charges for September, $2 500. GST charged on all freight bills totalled $175. Assume terms of n/30 days on all freight bills.

iv. Operating expense bills paid by cheque for which GST was charged totalled $4 500 plus $315 for the GST.

v. Total credit invoices received from creditors in September for goods returned, $6 250. Applicable GST on these credit invoices totalled $437.50.

vi. Total sales for September, $750 000. Applicable GST on these invoices totalled $52 500. Assume terms of n/30 on all sales invoices.

vii. Credit invoices issued to customers for September totalled $7 500. Applicable GST on these credit invoices totalled $525.

Required

a Record all transactions summarized above in a general journal, Page 20. Date all transactions as at September 30.

b From the general journal, post only those entries that affect 203 GST Payable and 204 Input Tax Credit (ITC).

c From the two posted G/L accounts, prepare Section Two of the GST Return for Registrants for September, current year.

d If a balance on GST Payable is owing, record the issuance of the cheque in the general journal; then post the result of this remittance entry to the GST accounts. Use October 15 as the date of the remittance entry.

Repeating Problem A.5 with a change in the amounts for monthly sales and GST collected on those sales.

A.6 Assume the same data as in Problem A.5 except for the following change in transaction (vi): sales for September totalled only $300 000 and the applicable GST on these sales totalled only $21 000.

Required

a Recreate the two GST accounts 203 GST Payable and 204 Input Tax Credit (ITC) in T-account form. Show how these two T-accounts would appear after all journal entries have been posted for September. Use transaction numbers to identify each posting.

b From the two posted G/L accounts, prepare Section Two of the GST Return for Registrants for September, current year.

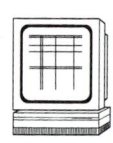

c Prepare a general journal entry to account for the balance reported in **b**; then post the result of this entry to the GST accounts. Use transaction (viii).

A.7 The purpose of this final problem is to simulate the accounting of GST transactions through a general ledger microcomputer package. However, the transactions may be done manually with the aid of a calculator.

Note: For users of Summation 2.4, data files have been created to support the chart of accounts for this problem. See your instructor for a copy of the data files for the file named KIMHALL and the supplementary notes for the step-by-step procedures to begin the problem.

Background Information

Assume a small retailer selling microcomputer hardware/software products and consulting services called Kim Hall, Inc., operating in a province where the collection of GST and PST are mandatory. Before accounting for the GST transactions summarized below, the following points should be considered:

- Kim Hall, Inc. uses the perpetual inventory system to account for the sale of computer hardware and software goods and their related cost of goods sold.
- For purposes of accounting for GST, assume that all products sold and all consulting services rendered are subject to the 7% GST.
- For purposes of accounting for PST, assume a provincial rate of 8% being applied only to the invoice price without the GST.
- For purposes of reporting periods, assume that Kim Hall, Inc. has selected an annual period with quarterly installment since gross annual sales are estimated to be under $500 000.

Selected Account Balances

- At the beginning of the second GST reporting period, January of the current calendar year, assume that Kim Hall, Inc. had the following assets, liabilities, and shareholders' equity: Petty Cash, $100; Cash in Royal Bank, $45 000; Cash in Bank of Montreal, $15 000; Bank Term Deposits, $50 000; Accounts Receivable—Trade, $4 000; Allowance—Doubtful Accounts, $1 000 Cr.; Inventory at Cost, $20 000; Prepaid Insurance, $3 600; Supplies on Hand, $400; Office Furniture & Fixtures, $12 000; Accumulated Depreciation (on Office Furniture & Fixtures), $1 200; Delivery Truck, $25 000; Accumulated Depreciation (on delivery truck), $5 000; Bank Loan Payable (on demand), $6 000; Accounts Payable, $3 000; Long-Term Notes Payable, $20 000; Common Stock Issued, $100 000; Retained Earnings, $38 900.

Selected Transaction Data

- At the beginning of the second GST reporting period, acquired office equipment costing $20 000 plus 7% GST of $1 400. Issued a cheque for $21 400 on the Cash in Royal Bank's account.

The following transactions, summarized in total form, occurred throughout the year. Use December 31 as the transaction date.

- Merchandise purchased for resale totalled $100 000 on 30 days' credit plus the 7% GST.

- Issued cheques on the Bank of Montreal to pay for freight-in charges on merchandise purchased. These transportation charges totalled $1 000 plus the 7% GST.
- Received additional vendor invoices indicating that GST totalling $70 had, in error, not been charged on purchases shipped in the previous GST reporting period. (Use ITC Adjustments account for this transaction.)
- Total sales of merchandise on 30 days' credit was divided between hardware sales, $130 000 and software sales, $70 000. GST and PST must be applied to these total sales. (Cost of hardware sold was $60 000 while the cost of software sold was $30 000.)
- During the year, rendered consulting services for cash totalling $7 000 plus GST plus PST. All cheques received were deposited in the Bank of Montreal. The cost of consulting fees involved the payment of a fee for services rendered totalling $2 500 through a cheque issued on the Bank of Montreal.
- Issued additional invoices to customers who were sold goods in the previous GST reporting period but, in error, the GST totalling $140 had not been charged. (Use GST Adjustments account. Assume that the applicable PST had been charged on the original sales.)
- Received cheques from customers totalling $189 300 in payment of their accounts. All cheques were deposited in the Royal Bank.
- Issued cheques against the Royal Bank totalling $80 951.60 as payments made to creditors on account.
- Issued cheques against the Royal Bank to the Receiver General for Canada totalling $16 000 in payment of quarterly installments under the GST system.
- Issued cheques against the Royal Bank in payment of the following operating expenses for which the 7% GST has been included: Rent Expense, $19 260 (GST included); Business and Promotion, $5 136 (GST included); Delivery Expense, $2 140 (GST included); Advertising Expense, $6 420 (GST included); Utilities Expense, $1 027.20 (GST included); and Telephone Expense, $706.20 (GST included).
- The annual payroll for salary and wages showed the following summary: Gross Earnings, $60 000; Employees' CPP Payable, $1 311; Employees' UI Payable, $1 350; Employees' Income Tax Payable, $19 176; net pay (payments made by cheques issued on the Royal Bank), $38 163. (No GST is involved in this transaction.)
- Payroll taxes, totalling $3 789, were distributed as follows: Employees' CPP Payable, $1 311 and Employees' UI Payable, $1 890; and EHT (Employer Health Tax) Payable, $588.
- Payroll remittances were made by cheque issued against the Royal Bank as follows: Receiver General for Canada, $25 038; provincial treasurer, $588.
- Issued cheques against the Royal Bank account totalling $210 for GST rebates granted to employees and non-residents under the GST system. (Use the account called GST Rebates.)

- Issued cheque on the Bank of Montreal's current account for the annual payment on the bank loan as follows: on principal, $4 000; on interest, $2 000; total cheque, $6 000.

Year-End Adjustments

The following year-end adjustments were authorized:

a. On December 31, the customer's account, Stuarts Cycle Shop, was written off as an uncollectible account for $1 200.
b. Under the aging method of accounts receivable, the allowance for doubtful accounts was increased by $2 000.
c. A bank credit memo from the Bank of Montreal stated that interest totalling $5 000 had been credited in the firm's current account. The interest had been earned on bank term deposits but had not as yet been recorded in Kim Hall, Inc.'s accounting records.
d. A bank debit memo from the Bank of Montreal was received as follows: for the annual fee on the safety deposit box, $85 plus 7% GST. The total, $90.95, had been debited against Kim Hall, Inc.'s current account, but had not as yet been recorded in the firm's accounting records. (Use Bank Charges Expense. Do not forget to account for the GST.)
e. A separate bank debit memo was received from the Royal Bank as follows: for interest charged on the bank loan, $660. This amount had been debited against the firm's current account but had not been recorded by Kim Hall, Inc.
f. Current portion of long-term debt is $4 000.
g. Unexpired insurance as at December 31 is $300; office supplies on hand as at December 31, $75.
h. Annual depreciation charges: on office furniture and fixtures, $1 200; on delivery truck, $5 000; on office equipment, $3 800.
i. A check of the inventory at cost, as at December 31, showed no disagreement with the book balance of Inventory at Cost under the perpetual inventory system used by Kim Hall, Inc.

Suggested Procedures

a Create a chart of accounts suitable for Kim Hall, Inc.'s general ledger system.
b Record and post all entries up to December 31 but excluding the year-end adjustments through a microcomputer G/L system.
c Print a preliminary year-end trial balance.
d Prepare the year-end adjusting entries, and record and post all entries through your microcomputer G/L system.
e Print the year-end financial statements.
f Do a year-end close through your G/L system.
g Print the year-end goods and services tax schedule if your microcomputer G/L software is programmed for such a schedule. (Summation users will find this printout as a separate schedule complementary to the Balance Sheet.)

h Prepare the annual GST Return for Registrants. Then account for the resulting balance either by issuing a cheque on January 15 of the new year or by accounting for the GST Refund Receivable.

Appendix Summary

The new Goods and Services Tax, GST for short, is embodied in a federal bill called Bill C-62, which became law when the Senate approved it in November 1990. The GST has replaced the former Federal Sales Tax of 13.5% with a tax on most goods and services consumed in Canada at a rate of 7%, effective January 1, 1991.

In conceptual form, the GST is a value-added tax that is applied to all levels of the marketing chain which supplies goods and services to Canadians. Only the consumer pays the entire 7% GST; suppliers in the marketing chain are entitled to subtract the GST paid on their purchases from that GST collected on their sales.

Many new terms are associated with the GST system. Among these are *supplies*, which is a collective term for all goods and services; *small suppliers*, which defines businesses with annual sales under $30 000; and *registrants*, which defines those who are registered under the GST system.

Identifying the tax base under the GST involves the study of three basic categories of supplies as follows: taxable (most goods and services); zero-rated (basic groceries, prescription drugs, medical services); and tax-exempt (health and dental care services, educational services, daycare services, etc.). Although no tax is collected on zero-rated and tax-exempt supplies, a distinction is made in that registrants are entitled to recover all GST paid on purchases related to the sale of zero-rated supplies while no such provision for recovery exists for tax-exempt supplies.

In the language of GST, the GST paid on purchases is called the *input tax credit*, and the GST collected on sales becomes the *GST payable*. Translated into accounting terms, GST Payable becomes a current liability, and Input Tax Credit may be considered as contra to GST Payable since any such credit reduces the GST Payable. It is worth mentioning that some accountants will treat the input tax credit as an unexpired cost and therefore treat any such amounts as a current asset.

Five important differences exist between GST accounting and accounting under generally accepted accounting principles. First, all GST amounts paid on taxable supplies are not treated as part of the laid-down cost of those supplies. As stated earlier, the GST paid is considered an input tax credit against all GST collected or payable through sales. Second, the GST registrant does not have to wait until goods purchased are sold before claiming the input tax credit related to those goods. Third, there is no requirement to spread the cost of the input tax credit over the life of acquired fixed assets. Fourth, any accounting of cash discounts must be applied to the invoice price excluding the GST. In other words, the full GST must still be remitted regardless of any cash discount taken. And, finally, any withdrawal of goods for personal use is subject to a GST at the fair market value of that withdrawn asset and not its cost.

Simplified accounting methods are available for certain "small" businesses. Under GST accounting, these are divided between the quick method and two streamlined methods. The quick method permits some businesses to apply a fixed percentage on total sales, thus eliminating the accounting for GST on sales and for input tax credits. Streamlined accounting is available to businesses that sell a combination of taxable and zero-rated groceries at the retail level to calculate the GST owing on the basis of the retail selling price of purchases of goods, or calculations based on a prescribed standard markup for basic groceries. Although these simplified methods do eliminate much of the required accounting of the GST, many accountants believe that these businesses are better off tracking all aspects of the GST, especially when computers and accounting software are employed.

The "Goods and Services Tax Return for Registrants" must be filed for each reporting period. In general, registrants with annual sales revenue under $500 000 are required to file this return on an annual basis with quarterly installments. On the other hand, large businesses with over $6 million of annual sales must file this return on a monthly basis. In all other cases where sales are between $500 000 and $6 million, registrants may file returns on a quarterly basis. All registrants have the option to file on an annual basis.

In a simplified business, it is possible to account for all GST transactions through one current liability account: GST Payable. When this practice is followed, GST Payable would be credited for all GST computed on sales and debited for all GST computed on purchases. Thus, at the end of any reporting period, the difference between the total debits and credits represents a balance owing if it is a credit balance, and a refund receivable if it is a debit balance.

A better alternative to the one GST account system is to use two general ledger accounts: one for GST Payable and one for Input Tax Credit (ITC). Under this system, GST Payable would receive posted entries to account for the GST computed on sales and sales returns, while Input Tax Credit (ITC) would receive posted entries to account for the GST computed on purchases and purchase returns. Thus, for any reporting period, the balances in each account may be used to complete Section Two of the GST remittance form. An accounting entry would then follow to account for the balance owing or refund receivable.

Businesses tracking GST transactions under a computerized accounting system will probably use separate general ledger accounts to account for individual boxes appearing on the GST remittance form. These would include separate accounts for GST Payable to complete box 103 (GST Collectible); GST Adjustments to complete box 104 (under the same name); Input Tax Credit (ITC) to complete box 106 (under the same name); ITC Adjustments to complete box 107 (under the same name); GST Installments to complete box 110 (Paid by Installments); and GST Rebates to complete box 111 (Rebates). Additional accounts would be created to account for any GST Refund Receivable, and for subtotals and totals appearing on a GST Schedule or Report that may be used to facilitate the preparation of the GST remittance form.

The theory of using several separate accounts to track GST is based on the requirements of completing the GST return. In general, the combination of GST Payable and GST Adjustments provides credit balances so that, when added, their total equals the Total GST and Adjustments for the period (box 105 on the return). On the other hand, the combination of Input Tax Credit (ITC) and ITC Adjustments will show debit balances so that, when added, their total equals the Total ITCs and Adjustments (box 108 on the return). The difference between the total credits and total debits results in the Net (GST) Tax for the period (box 109 on the return). If there are any payments of GST made by installments or through rebates, the total of these "Other Credits" will reduce the Net Tax to report the Balance of GST (box 113), which can then be disclosed as the Refund Claimed (box 114) or the Payment Enclosed (box 115). A compound entry can then be made to account for either the Refund Claimed or Payment Enclosed.

Appendix Questions

1. Use an example to explain why the new federal Goods and Services Tax is regarded as a value-added tax.
2. Are all businesses required to collect and account for the GST? Explain why or why not.
3. Under the GST system, what are taxable supplies and at what rate is the tax applied on them?
4. Give one example to distinguish between a zero-rated supply and a tax-exempt supply under the GST system.
5. Give two examples to prove that the accounting of GST does not follow generally accepted accounting principles.
6. In provinces where the provincial sales tax must be collected as well as the GST, which tax is computed before the other?
7. Give two examples to prove that the computation of a provincial sales tax is not uniformly applied across Canada.
8. Who is a registrant under the GST system? When must a registrant file a Goods and Services Tax Return?
9. Distinguish between GST Collectible (box 103) and Input Tax Credit (ITC) (box 106) on the Goods and Services Tax Return for Registrants.
10. The federal government allows certain businesses to use one of three simplified accounting methods to account for the GST. Identify and briefly explain each method.
11. What is the difference between the quick method and streamlined accounting under the GST system?
12. For how long must a registrant keep accounting books and records under the GST?

APPENDIX: Accounting for the GST

13. Briefly explain what postings would occur in an accounting system which uses only one account—GST Payable—to account for common transactions during a GST reporting period. What would a credit balance indicate in this account at the end of a reporting period? A debit balance at the end of a reporting period? Briefly explain what entry would be made to eliminate any credit balance or debit balance in this account at the end of a GST reporting period.

14. Briefly explain how GST accounting would be done during a GST reporting period in an system that uses the two accounts GST Payable and Input Tax Credit (ITC). What accounting is required at the end of a GST reporting period under this two-account system?

15. In accounting for the Input Tax Credit (ITC), one student indicated confusion over the word "Credit" in the account. "Why is the word 'Credit' used, when one would debit the account for all GST amounts paid on purchases?" asked the student.

16. A wholesale vendor issued an invoice with a total selling price on taxable goods of $1 000 and with credit terms of 2/10, n/30. GST has not been applied. Three days later, the same vendor issued a credit invoice against the original invoice of $100. GST has not been applied. The retail customer remits a cheque within the discount period in payment of the full invoice. Show the entry in general journal form to account for the receipt of this cheque. Explain each entry with supporting computations.

17. A retailer advertises all items at selling prices which include the GST. If the retailer sells a taxable item for $100 cash and the province requires PST at the rate of 10% "stacked" on top of GST, what entry would be made in the vendor's books? Show supporting computations.

18. Assume that the sole proprietor of an auto dealer withdraws for personal use a new car costing $18 000 but regularly sells in the range of $22 000 to $24 000. Show the accounting entry for this withdrawal and explain each amount that is made in this entry.

19. Briefly explain how a registrant using only the one account GST Payable would complete the required GST return at the end of a reporting period. What change would be made if the registrant used the two accounts GST Payable and Input Tax Credit (ITC) to complete the return?

20. What changes would be made in the accounting of GST if accounting software like Summation 2.4 is used?

21. What advantages are evident in the use of accounting software over the traditional manual system in the accounting of GST and preparing the GST return?

22. Some accountants would classify the account Input Tax Credit (ITC) as a current asset, while others would prefer to identify the account as a contra to the current liability GST Payable. Which classification would you prefer? Explain your answer.

Accounting Cases

CASE A-1

Analyzing one clerk's accounting of a new fixed asset acquisition.

During a GST reporting year, ABC Company acquired a new electronic printing press for operational use as follows: catalogue list price, $60 000; less 10% trade discount; plus 7% GST and 8% PST (not stacked); plus additional costs of freight, $300 (plus GST); insurance during shipment, $290.10 (exempt from GST); engineer's fee in testing the press before business use, $200 (plus GST); and materials used in testing, $70 (plus GST).

One accounting clerk used the laid-down cost principle and defended the debit to Plant Equipment for $63 000 with the supporting schedule shown in Figure A-53.

FIGURE A-53

Catalogue list price	$60 000.00
Less: 10% trade discount	6 000.00
True selling price	54 000.00
GST	3 780.00
PST	4 320.00
Invoice cost	$62 100.00
Additional costs:	
Freight plus GST	321.00
Insurance (no GST is levied on insurance)	290.10
Engineer's fee plus GST	214.00
Materials used in testing plus GST	74.90
Total laid-down cost	$63 000.00

Would you support the accounting clerk's accounting under current tax rules? Explain why or why not. Show a revised schedule if you do not agree. Also show an appropriate accounting entry in general journal form. Assume that all expenditures were made in cash.

CASE A-2

Analyzing transactions resulting in the write-off of a bad debt. Accounting for the write-off under GST rules.

During the first GST reporting year, XYZ Retailer sold merchandise in Alberta to a customer on account for $1 000 plus the GST. The retailer remitted the $70 GST on this sale to the government within one month of the end of the GST reporting year. However, the retailer has yet to receive payment from the customer.

Unfortunately, in the next GST reporting year, the customer fails to pay and, as a result, the retailer instructs you as the accounting clerk to write off the customer's account as a bad debt.

In analyzing the transaction, you conclude that the $1 000 must be written off against the Allowance for Bad Debts account, in accordance with generally accepted accounting principles. But you are confused over what to do with the $70 GST that has been remitted to the federal government. In effect, the retailer also has a bad debt for the $70 GST it remitted to the government on behalf of the customer.

Assume that you call the nearest office of Revenue Canada—Customs and Excise to obtain a ruling on the matter. From Customs and Excise you learn the following: (1) that the retailer can claim a recovery of the GST through a bad debt credit; (2) that the deduction may be claimed either in the reporting period in which the bad debt was written off, or in a reporting period that ends no later than four years from the end of the period in which the write-off was taken; that the bad debt deduction will be equal to 7/107 of the amount written off; and that it can be claimed as a deduction from the registrant's net tax amount for the period in which the bad debt was recognized.

a Show the accounting entry in general journal form to recognize revenue from the sale made in the first GST reporting period.

b Show the accounting entry in general journal form to write off the customer's account as a bad debt in the second GST reporting period. Explain each part of this entry with supporting computations.

c Explain how the recovery of GST in the write-off entry would be reported on the GST return for the second reporting period.

INDEX

Account form of balance sheet, *def.*, 23; *illus.*, 9; 21
Accounting, *def.*, 3; 76
  accrual basis of, *def.*, 260
  Bedford, *see* AccPac Bedford
  bookkeeping base of, 76; 146
  cash basis of, *def.*, 260
  equation, *see* Accounting equation
  for demand deposits, 375–384
  general (financial), *def.*, 77
  management (managerial), *def.*, 77
  for time deposits, 376–377
Accounting applications:
  accounts payable, 327–372
  accounts receivable, 271–326
  general ledger, *def.*, 272
  payroll, 413–476
Accounting boards, *see* Pegboards
Accounting clerk, *def.*, 64
  ads for, 478
Accounting concepts:
  going-concern, *def.*, 24
  separate entity, *def.*, 10
  time-period, *def.*, 22
  unit-of-measure, *def.*, 24
Accounting cycle, *def.*, 51
  with adjusting entries, 160–176
  for merchandising firm, 146–191
    step one, 148–153
    step two, 153–154
    step three, 154–155
    step four, 156
    step five, 161–178
    step six, 183–187
    step seven, 187
    step eight, 190
    step nine, 190–191
  for service firm, 51–76
    step one, 51
    step two, 53
    step three, 56
    step four, 62
    step five, 68
    step six, 70
    step seven, 73
    step eight, 75
Accounting equation, *def.*, 5; *illus.*, 5; 6; 7; 9; 17; 20; 24
  and balance sheet, 9
  cost of goods sold in, 123
  drawings in, 19
  elements of, 5–6
  expense section, 17; 20
  gross profit from sales in, 123
  within the ledger, 34
  net income in, 20
  net loss in, 20
  reporting, 9
  revenue section, 17; 20; 122–123
  solving, 6
Accounting model, *def.*, 24; *see also* Accounting equation
  completing, 16–24
  elementary form of, 24
  establishing, 4–14
Accounting packages:
  customized, *def.*, 525
  Easypay, 509–521
  fully integrated, *def.*, 480
  general, *def.*, 193
    AccPac Bedford, 479–494
    AccPac Plus, 494–507
    Summation, 194–219; 521–522
  vertical, *def.*, 525
  DYNA, 525–540
Accounting period, *def.*, 22
Accounting principles, *see* Generally Accepted Accounting Principles (GAAPs)
Accounting process, *see* Accounting
Accounting proofs:
  of account balance, 61
  of cash payments, 344
  of cash receipts, 291–292
  of general ledger, 62–63
  of journal, 285; 293; 296
  of petty cash, 351
  of posting, 306–307
  of subsidiary ledger, 280–281
  zero, *def.*, 62; 296; 344
Accounting year, *def.*, 22
Accounts:
  balance of, *def.*, 33–34; 61
    abnormal, 61
    finding, 40; 60–61
    integration, *def.*, 481
    opening, 33–34
    originating, 33
    T-account, 40
    transferring, 73–75
    zero, 61
  balance ledger form, 58
  chart of, *def.*, 57; *illus.*, 57; 147
    computerized, 195
  classes of, 57
  closing, *def.*, 73; *see also* Closing entries
  codes, computerized, 194
  contra, *def.*, 118
  controlling, 275; 331
  decreasing, 38–39; 116
  increasing, 35–37; 115
  ledger, *def.*, 34
  numbering, 57; 146–147
  opening, 33
  partners' drawing, 238–239

594 INDEX

payable, ***see*** Accounts payable
permanent, *def.*, 75
receivable, ***see*** Accounts receivable
Revenue and Expense Summary, 73
T-account, *def.*, 32; *illus.*, 33–34; 32–33
   calculating balance of, 40
temporary, *def.*, 76
uncollectible, 166–169
Accounts payable, *def.*, 8
   in accounting equation, 5–6; 7; 9; 17; 20
   applications, ***see*** Accounting applications
   on balance sheet, 9; 13
   controlling account, 331–332
   direct posting of, 358
   ledger, ***see*** Accounts payable ledger
   schedule of, 332
   tickler file, 342
   trial balance of, 332
Accounts payable application, ***see*** Accounting applications
Accounts payable clerk, *def.*, 328; 340
Accounts payable journal, *def.*, 332
Accounts payable ledger, *def.*, 331
   posting to, 329; 331
   trial balance of, 331–332
Accounts payable module, *def.*, 486; 521
Accounts receivable, *def.*, 8
   in accounting equation, 5–6; 7; 9; 17; 20
   accounts for, 274–285
   aging, 166; 298
   application, ***see*** Accounting applications
   balance-forward system, 311
   on balance sheet, 9; 13
   clerk for, 275–276
   controlling account, 275
   cycle billing, *def.*, 297
   direct posting of, *def.*, 276; 304–306
   layout for one-write system, 313
   ledger, ***see*** Accounts receivable ledger
   monthly summary, 281
   net, *def.*, 168
   open-item system, 310
   proof of, 280
   proof of posting, 59; 306–307
   schedule by age, 298
   schedule of, 281
   statement of account, 297–298
   trial balance of, 280–281
   uncollectible, ***see*** Bad debts
Accounts receivable application, ***see*** Accounting applications
Accounts receivable clerk, *def.*, 275–276
Accounts receivable department, *def.*, 275

Accounts receivable ledger, *def.*, 274; *illus.*, 277–278
   advantages of, 275
   need for, 274–275
   posting to, 277
      direct, 276; 304–306
Accounts receivable module, *def.*, 489; 521
Accounts receivable trial balance, ***see*** Schedule of accounts receivable
AccPac Bedford, 479–494; *def.*, 479
   accounts payable system, 486–489
      cash payments, 488–489
      credit purchases, 487
      payment journal, *illus.*, 488
      purchases journal, *illus.*, 486
   accounts receivable system, 489–492
      cash receipts, 491–429
      credit sales, 490–492
      receipt journal, *illus.*, 492
      sales journal, *illus.*, 490
   characteristics of, 480–481
   Company Window, *def.*, 480
   debit/credit analysis chart, 482
   general ledger system, 481–485
      chart of accounts, 481
      general journal, *illus.*, 483; 485
      journalizing, 481–482
      integration accounts, *def.*, 481
   inventory costing under, 489
   inventory module, 493–494
   job costing module, 494
   master (main) menu, *illus.*, 479
   menu bar, *def.*, 480; *illus.*, 479; 481
   opening entry under, 483–485
   overview of, 479–480
   payroll module, 492–493
   posting under, 484; 489; 491
   printing under, 485
   vendor's account, *illus.*, 486
AccPac Plus, 494–507; *def.*, 449
   accounting modules, 494
   characteristics of, 494–495
   general ledger module, 495–507
      batch processing, 497–507
         analyzing batch entries, 497–498
         creating batch files, 499–504
         posting batch files, 505
         printing batch files, 504–505
      chart of accounts for, 496
      posting journal, *def.*, 499
      source journal, *def.*, 502
      transaction posting menu, *illus.*, 498
      start screen, *illus.*, 495
Accumulated depreciation, *def.*, 170; ***see also*** Depreciation
   on balance sheet, 170; *illus.*, 186
   as a contra account, 170

on worksheet, 172–173
Adjusted trial balance, 174; *illus.*, 172–173
Adjusting entries, 188; ***see also*** Adjustments
Adjustments, 160–174; *def.*, 160
   bad debts, 166–169
   bank reconciliation, 399–401
   depreciation, 169–173
   journalizing, 188
   need for, 160–161
   prepaid insurance, 164
   supplies, 163
   unrecorded:
      bank interest expense, 171
      interest earned, 171
   worksheet section, 172; 174
After-closing trial balance, ***see*** Postclosing trial balance
Aged accounts receivable:
   schedule of, 167
   statement, *def.*, 298; *illus.*, 298
Aging accounts receivable, *def.*, 166
Allowance for bad debts, *def.*, 166
   on balance sheet, 166; 186
   entry for, 167; 188
   on worksheet, 172–173
   in write-off entry, 168
Analyzing transactions, 7–8; 16–19; 36–40; 116–127
Annual financial report, 254–255
   balance sheet in, 256–257
   contents of, 254–255
   income statement in, 255–256
   legal requirements, 254
   notes to financial statements in, 256
   retained earnings statement in, 256
   statement of changes in financial position in, 257–260
Asset accounts:
   balance of, 40; 61
   changes in, 35–40
   contra, 166; 170
   opening, 33
Assets, *def.*, 5
   in accounting equation, 5
   on balance sheet, 9; 13; 21
   buying:
      for cash, 8
      for credit, 8
   classification of, 10–11
   control of, 289–293; 337–342
   current, *def.*, 10; 165
   debit and credit rules, 35–40
   fixed, *def.*, 10
   liquidity order of, 10
   long-lived, *def.*, 10
   value of, *def.*, 11
Average cost method, *def.*, 489

INDEX

Authorized capital, *def.*, 247

Bad debts, 166–169; *def.*, 166
    adjusting entry for, 167; 188
    aging accounts receivable, 166–167
    allowance account, 166
        on balance sheet, 166
    expense on income statement, 185
        in closing, 189
    on worksheet, 172–173
    write-off entry, 168
Balance:
    of account, *def.*, 58; 60
        abnormal, *def.*, 60
    credit, 40; 60–61
    debit, 40; 60
Balance-forward system, *def.*, 311
Balance ledger form, *def.*, 58; *illus.*, 58
    disclosing balance in, 60–61
    posting to, 59–60
Balance sheet, *def.*, 9; *illus.*, 9; 13; 71; 107; 186; 233; 235; 238; 251
    account form, *def.*, 23; *illus.*, 13
    and accounting equation, 9
    accounts payable on, 9; 13
    accounts receivable on, 9; 13
    accumulated depreciation on, 186
    allowance for bad debts on, 186
    asset section, 10–11
    bank loan on, 12; 186
    body of, 10
    classified, 10
    corporation, 251; 257
    current assets on, 10; 166; 186
    current liabilities on, 12; 71; 107
    in debit and credit form, *def.*, 191
    dollar signs on, 12–14
    dummy printout of, 197
    fixed assets on, 10–11
    heading of, 10
    inventory on, 100; 107; 186
    liabilities section, 11–12
    long-term liabilities on, 13; 107; 186
    merchandising firm, 107
    other formats, 12–14
    owner's equity section, 12
    partnership, 233; 235; 238
    preparing, 10–14; 23
    report form, *def.*, 23; *illus.*, 21
    shareholders' equity on, 248–249; 251–252; 257
    as a source document, 51
    totalling and ruling, 12–14
    worksheet section, 68–70
Balance sheet equation, *see* Accounting equation
Balancing accounts, 40; 60–61

Bank accounting, 375–388
    basic concepts, 375
    clearing cheques, 384
    processing:
        cheques, 384–385
        depositor's statement, 385–388
        memos, 385
Bank charges, *def.*, 384
Bank cheques, *see* Cheques
Bank credit cards, 294
Bank debit cards, 294–295
Bank deposits, *see* Deposits, bank
Bank loan payable, *def.*, 8
    in accounting equation, 5–6; 9; 17; 20
    on balance sheet, 12–13
Bank memos:
    credit, *def.*, 383; *illus.*, 383
    debit, *def.*, 379; *illus.*, 379; 381
    processing, 384–385
Bank reconciliation, 390–401
    of payroll bank account, 456
Bank reconciliation statement, 391–399; *illus.*, 398
    entries from, 400
    preparing, 390–399
Bank statement, 385–388; *def.*, 385; *illus.*, 386; *see also* Bank reconciliation statement
Batches, *def.*, 304
Batch of invoices, *def.*, 304
Batch-operated/oriented system, *def.*, 495
Batch processing:
    versus real-time accounting, 507–509
Batch systems:
    computerized, 494–507
    manual, 304–308; 357–358
Batch totals, *def.*, 304
    journalizing, 304–308
    evaluation of, 306–308
Bedford accounting, *see* AccPac Bedford
Bill C-62, *def.*, 545
Bill of sale, *see* Invoice
Binders:
    purchase invoice, 358
    sales invoice, 308
Board of directors, *def.*, 245
Bond, *def.*, 245; *illus.*, 246
Bonds payable, *def.*, 245
    on balance sheet, 257
Book:
    of final entry, *def.*, 57
    of original entry, *def.*, 53
Bookkeeper, *def.*, 64; *see also* Accounting clerk
    ads for, *illus.*, 64
Bookkeeping, *def.*, 64
    aspects of, 51–64
    double-entry, *def.*, 44

    journalless, 308–310; 358
    ledgerless, 310–311; 358–359
Business corporation, *see* Corporation
Business ownership, forms of:
    corporation, 229
    partnership, 229
    sole proprietorship, 6
Business papers (forms), *see* Source documents
Business transaction, *def.*, 51

C.A., *def.*, 77
Canada Business Corporations Act, *def.*, 243
    and no-par-value shares, 248
Canada Pension Plan, *see* Payroll
Cancelled bill, *def.*, 341
Cancelled cheques, *def.*, 385
Capital, *def.*, 7; *see also* Owner's equity
    account, 34–36
    in accounting equation, 7
    authorized, 247
    on balance sheet, 71
    issued share, 247
    working, *def.*, 257
        computation of, 258
Capital assets, *see* Fixed assets
Capital property, *def.*, 549
Capital stock, *see* Share capital
Cash, *def.*, 290
    in accounting equation, 7; 9; 17; 20
    on balance sheet, 9; 13; 21
    as bank deposits, 292
    as credit cards, 290; 294
    daily proof of, 291–292
    as money currency, 290
    as negotiable instruments, 290
Cash account, verifying, 391
Cash control; *see also* Bank reconciliation
    for payments, 337–342
    for receipts, 290–293
Cash disbursements journal, *see* Cash payments journal
Cash discount, 119; 126–127; *see also* Purchases discounts; Sales discounts
Cash over, *see* Cash short and over
Cash payments:
    basic control measures, 338–342
    controlling, 337
    division of responsibility for, 342; 351
    invoice file, 342; 358
    journalizing, 343; *see also* Cash payments journal
    in one-write system, 364
    purchases discount, 343
Cash payments journal, *def.*, 342; *illus.*, 343

cash short in, 345
in one-write system, 363
posting from, 344
proof of, 344
purchases discounts in, 343
recording in, 343
totalling, 344
with special columns, 343
Cash, petty, *see* Petty cash
Cash proofs, *def.*, 291
of cash register, 291
of cash sales slips, 292
of petty cash, 351
of shortage, *illus.*, 345
Cash receipts:
controlling of, 290–293
deposit of, 292–293; *see also* Deposits, bank
division of responsibility for, 293
journalizing, 293; *see also* Cash receipts journal
in one-write system, 317–319
sales discounts, 296
sources of, 290
Cash receipts journal, *def.*, 293; *illus.*, 294–296
analyzed with credit cards, 294–295
cash over in, 347
posting from, 295–296
sales discounts in, 296
sales tax payable in, 294
totalling, 296–297
Cash short and over, 344–347
account, *def.*, 345
balance of, 347
classification of, 347
overage, 346
in cash receipts journal, 347
shortage, 345
Certificate, share, *def.*, 244; *illus.*, 244
Certified cheque, *def.*, 381; *illus.*, 381
on bank statement, 386
transaction analyzed, 381–382
C.G.A., *def.*, 78
Charter, *def.*, 244
Chart of accounts, *def.*, 57; *illus.*, 57
computerized, 148; 194–196
display window, *illus.*, 202
manual, 57; 147
need for, 146–148
Cheque protector, *def.*, 340
Cheque record (stub), *def.*, 52; *illus.*, 52
Cheques, *illus.*, 339
advantages of, 338
cancelled, 341; 385
certified, 381
clearing, 384
countersigned, 340

drawing of, 338; 340
endorsing, 292
mailing signed, 341
NSF, *def.*, 382
in one-write application, 363; 468
outstanding, 391
payroll, *illus.*, 455
prenumbered measure of, 338
processing, 384–385
record of, 338–339
signing, 340–341
voiding, *def.*, 340; *illus.*, 340
voucher, *def.*, 339; *illus.*, 339
CICA Handbook, *def.*, 255
Classifying:
accounts, 57
balance sheet, 10–11
income statement, 183–185
Clearing bank cheques, *def.*, 384
Clearinghouse, *def.*, 384
Closing, *def.*, 73
in computerized systems, 215–218
manual mechanics of, 73–74; *see also* Closing entries
Closing entries, 73; 189; *illus.*, 74; 189
in accounting cycle, 73; 189
bad debts, 189
for corporation, 252
depreciation, 189
drawing account, 75; 189
expense accounts, 74; 189
for partnership, 239
revenue accounts, 74; 189
summary account, 73–74. 189
C.M.A., *def.*, 78
Coding, in accounts, 57–58; 147–148; 194–196
Collating, *def.*, 314
in one-write applications, 314–315; 362
Combination journal, *def.*, 359; *illus.*, 360–361
advantages of, 359
designing, 359
in one-write system, 313
posting procedures, 359–360
proving, 359
Common stock, *see* Shares
Company pension plan, *see* Payroll
Compound entry, *def.*, 56
Computers:
customized accounting packages for, 525
electronic spreadsheets for, 80–90
general accounting packages for, 478
mainframe, *def.*, 80
micro, *def.*, 81
operating systems for, 83
Condensed income statement, *illus.*, 100
Consumer Price Index (CPI), *def.*, 429

Contra account, *def.*, 118
accumulated depreciation, 170
allowance for bad debts, 166
for current assets, 166
for expenses, 126
for fixed assets, 170
for GST accounting, 568–569; 575–581
purchases discount, 126–127
purchases returns and allowances, 126
for revenue, 117–118
sales returns and allowances, 118
sales discount, 119
Contract of employment, *def.*, 415; *see also* Payroll
Contra expense account, *see* Contra account
Contra revenue account, *see* Contra account
Controlling account, *def.*, 275
accounts payable, 331
accounts receivable, 275
Control measures:
for cash payments, 337–342
for cash receipts, 289–293
Corporation, *def.*, 243
annual report, 254–255
authorized capital of, *def.*, 247
board of directors, 245
bond, *illus.*, 246
characteristics of, 243–247
charter, 243
common stock of, 248
control of, 245
deficit, 252
dividends of, 245; 252–254
earnings of, 252
financial statements:
balance sheet, 256–257
income statement, 255–256
retained earnings, 254; 256
statement of changes in financial position, 257–260
income tax, 246–247
issued share capital of, 247
as legal entity, 243
limited liability of, 244
name of, 244
no-par-value shares of, 248
opening entries for, 249–250
outstanding shares of, 247
par value shares of, 247–248
perpetual existence, 245
preferred shares of, 248
pre-operating balance sheet, 251
retained earnings, 252; 254
share capital of, 249; 251
share certificate, *def.*, 244; *illus.*, 244

INDEX

shareholders' equity of, 229; 249; 251–252
working capital, 258
Cost of delivered goods, *def.*, 105
   on income statement, 106
Cost of goods available for sale, *def.*, 104; *illus.*, 102–103
   on income statement, 106
Cost of goods sold, *def.*, 100; 120
   in accounting equation, 123
   basic calculation of, 103
   factors affecting, 104–107
   on income statement, 100; 103; 108; 108; 121; 184–185
   ratio, *def.*, 109
Cost of goods unsold, *def.*, 102
Cost principle, *def.*, 11
Costs and expenses, *def.*, 183
Countersigned cheque, *def.*, 340
Cr., *see* Credit
Credit, *def.*, 32
   balance, *def.*, 33
Credit cards, 294
Credit memo, *def.*, 148; 277; *illus.*, 149
   for bank, *see* Bank memos
   for sales returns, 148–150
Creditors, *def.*, 4
Creditors' ledger, *see* Accounts payable ledger
Credits, debits must equal, 44
Credit terms, *def.*, 104–105
Cross-referencing, *def.*, 59
Current account, bank, *def.*, 375
Current assets, *def.*, 10
   on balance sheet, 9; 166
   redefined, 165
Current liabilities, *def.*, 12
   on balance sheet, 9
Customers' ledger, *see* Accounts receivable ledger
Customized accounting package, *def.*, 525
Cycle billing, *def.*, 297

Date of declaration, *def.*, 252
Date of payment, *def.*, 253
Date of record, *def.*, 253
Debit, *def.*, 32
   balance, *def.*, 33
Debit memo, *def.*, 152; *illus.*, 152
   for bank, *see* Bank memos
   for purchases returns and allowances, 152–153
Debits, credits must equal, 44
Debts, *see* Liabilities
Deficit, *def.*, 252
Demand deposit accounting, *def.*, 377

Demand deposits payable, *def.*, 376
Demand loan, *def.*, 6; *illus.*, 6
   on balance sheet, 9; 13; 21
   transactions analyzed, 22; 377–378
Demand note, bank, *def.*, 6; *illus.*, 6
Deposit in transit, *def.*, 391
Depositors, *def.*, 375
Deposits, bank:
   controlling, 291–293
   division of responsibility for, 293
   preparing, 292–293
   in transit, 391; 393
Deposit slip, *illus.*, 293
Depreciation, 169–170; *def.*, 169
   accumulated, 170
     on balance sheet, 186
   adjusting entry for, 188
   in closing, 189
   expense, 170
     on income statement, 184–185
   straight-line method, 170
   on worksheet, 172–173
Direct on-line entry processing, *def.*, 508; *see also* Real-time accounting
Direct posting, *def.*, 276; 304
   of accounts payable, 357–358
   of accounts receivable, 304–306
Discount:
   cash, *def.*, 104
   and GST accounting, 557–558
   purchases, *see* Purchases discounts
   sales, *see* Sales discounts
   terms, 104
Discrepancy items, *def.*, 391
   locating and listing, 394–397
Dishonoured cheques, *see* NSF cheque
Disposal value, *def.*, 104
Dividend, *def.*, 245
   date of payment, 253
   date of record for, 253
   declaring, 252
   ex-, *def.*, 253
   notice, *illus.*, 253
   payment of, 253
   on retained earnings statement, *illus.*, 254; 256
Division of responsibility:
   in accounts payable application, 341–342
   in accounts receivable application, 293; 351
Documentary ledger system, *def.*, 310
Dollar signs:
   on balance sheet, 12–14
   general rule for, 55
   on income statement, 22
Double-entry bookkeeping, *def.*, 44
Double-posting, *def.*, 279

Doubtful debts, *see* Bad debts
Dr., *see also* Debit
   letter *r* in, 48
Drawee of cheque, *def.*, 381
Drawer of cheque, *def.*, 338
Drawing, *def.*, 19
   on accounting equation, 20
   analysis of, 20; 23–24
   on balance sheet, 21
Drawing account, *def.*, 19
   in accounting equation, 17
   analysis of, 19; 23–24
   on balance sheet, 21
   closing of, 74–75
   redefined, 24
   on trial balance, 63
   on worksheet, 69
DYNA Dental Office Management System, 525–540; *def.*, 525
   adding a new patient, 528–530
   appointments menu, *illus.*, 530
   billing transactions menu, *illus.*, 534
   cash receipts report, *illus.*, 538
   cash summary, *illus.*, 536
   day-end menu, *illus.*, 536
   financial adjustments menu, *illus.*, 534
   financial reports menu, 534–536; *illus.*, 535
   financial transactions menu, 533–534; *illus.*, 534
   hardware/operating system requirements, 526
   logging in, 528
   main features of, 525–526
   main menu, *illus.*, 527
   overview, 526–528
   patient information menu, *illus.*, 529
   patient receipt, *illus.*, 533
   posting to G/L, 539–540
     G/L main menu, 539
   practice daily totals report, *illus.*, 537
   processing dental charges, 530–532

Earnings statement, *see* Income statement
Easypay package, 509–521; *def.*, 509
   company file update screen, 512
   creating department codes, 514
   employee update/profile screen, *illus.*, 515
     analysis of, 515–517
   exporting payroll entries, 521
   history and year-end functions menu, *illus.*, 514
   installing, 510
   main characteristics of, 509–510
   main menu, *illus.*, 513

INDEX

analysis of, 513–514
calling up, 512
other reports and functions menu, *illus.*, 517
overview, 510–521
payroll register, *illus.*, 519–520
payroll run menu, *illus.*, 518
analysis of, 518–519
processing regular payroll run, 518
setting up employee files, 514–515
setting up G/L accounts, 517
Economic resources, *def.*, 4
Electronic spreadsheet, *def.*, 80
advantages of, 89–90
common examples of, 81
common features of, 81–82
history of, 80–81
key differences of, 83–84
limitations of, 90
and projecting gross profit, 110–111
simple example of, 84–89
VisiCalc, *def.*, 81
Employee's individual earnings record, *def.*, 443; *illus.*, 444; *see also* Payroll
Employee's pay statement, *def.*, 455; *illus.*, 455; *see also* Payroll
Employee's taxable earnings, *def.*, 431; *see also* Payroll
Employer health tax (EHT), *def.*, 449; *see also* Payroll
Employment Standards Act, *def.*, 415; *see also* Payroll
End-of-year adjustments, *see* Adjustments
Endorsement:
restrictive, 291–292
Equation, accounting, *see* Accounting equation
Equity:
corporation, *def.*, 229
owner's, *def.*, 5
partners', *def.*, 229
Errors, by bank:
in cash balance, 396–397
in chequebook, 396–397
Estimate method (bad debts), 166–167
Ex-dividend, *def.*, 253
Expense accounts:
for bad debts, 166
classification, 57; 147
closing, 74; 189
for expired fixed assets, 169
for expired insurance, 164
for expired inventory, 175; 209–210
for expired supplies, 163
for payroll, 447
Expense recognition principle, *def.*, 19
Expenses, *def.*, 19

in accounting equation, 17; 20
in accounts, 43–44
in chart of accounts, 57
on income statement, 21; 71
operating, 101
other, *def.*, 183
on income statement, 184–185
payroll taxes, 447–448
prepaid, 163
in trial balance, 63
on worksheet, 69
Expense transactions, *def.*, 18
recording, 43–44
Expired costs, *def.*, 19; *see also* Expenses
Expired insurance, *def.*, 164

Fair market value, *def.*, 550
Federal income tax, *see* Payroll
Fees earned journal, *def.*, 284; *illus.*, 285
Fees earned register, *def.*, 284; *illus.*, 285
Final entry, book of, *def.*, 57
Financial accounting, *def.*, 77
Financial statements, *see also* entries for specific statements
in accounting cycle, 70–72; 183–187
notes to, *def.*, 256
Fiscal period (year), *def.*, 22
Fixed assets, *def.*, 10
on balance sheet, 9; 13; 21; 186
depreciation of, 169
FOB (free on board), *def.*, 151
destination, 151
shipping point, 151
Forms, business, *see* Source documents
tax, *see* Payroll
Fraud, 340
Freight-in, *see* Transportation-in
Fully integrated accounting package, *def.*, 480
Fund, petty cash, 348

GAAPs, *see* Generally accepted accounting principles (GAAPs)
Garnishments, *def.*, 432; *see also* Payroll
General accounting, *def.*, 77
General accounting packages, *def.*, 193
General journal, *def.*, 53; *illus.*, 54–55; 154–155; 188–189; 278
analysis of, 53–54
computerized, 205
double-posting from, 278; 334
entries:
adjusting, 188
bank reconciliation, 400
closing, 73–74; 189
compound, 56

GST, 555–557; 559–561; 570–572; 577; 582
opening, 56
payroll summary, 446–447
return of sales tax, 118
General ledger, *def.*, 35; 274; *see also* Ledger
basic function of, 35
under periodic inventory method, 131
under perpetual inventory method, 131
trial balance, 62
General ledger application, *def.*, 272
General ledger module, *def.*, 192
General ledger packages:
main characteristics of, 193–194
for microcomputers, 193; 481; 495
General ledger system:
manual, *see* Accounting cycle
microcomputer, 192–219; *see also* General ledger packages
Generally accepted accounting principles (GAAPs), *def.*, 11; 255
cost principle, 11
for defining current assets, 165
for defining depreciation, 169
expense recognition principle, 19
laid-down cost, *def.*, 549
matching principle, 20
objectivity principle, 51; 148
for reporting assets, 11
revenue recognition principle, 18
G/L, *see* General ledger
Going-concern concept, *def.*, 24
Goods and Services Tax (GST), *def.*, 545
and accounting anomalies, 549–550
accounts for:
GST Installments, *def.*, 578–579
GST Payable, *def.*, 575
GST Rebates, *def.*, 579
GST Refund Receivable, *def.*, 574
ITC Adjustments, *def.*, 578
alternative accounting methods, 567–572
computer accounting of, 572–582
advantages, 573
chart of accounts, 572; 574–575
creating accounts:
for GST Adjustments, 576
for GST Installments, 578
for GST Payable, 575
for GST Payable/Receivable, 579–580
for GST Rebates, 579
for GST Refund Receivable, 574
for Input Tax Credit (ITC), 577–578
detail report, *illus.*, 581

entries:
    for adjustments, 577
    for cheque issued, 582
    for refund claimed, 582
    schedule, 581
concepts, 546–548; *illus.*, 547
filing returns, 551
    reporting periods, 551
input tax credit, *def.*, 546;
    account for, 568
keeping accounting records, 552
manual accounting of, 553–564;
    567–572
    and cheques issued, 557
    and cheques received, 557
    and credit invoices, 555–556
    and journalizing GST data, 562
    and posting GST data, 563
    and purchase invoices, 558
    and sales discounts, 557–558
    and sales invoices, 553–554
        with GST included, 559–560
    with special journals, 562–563
        sales journal, *illus.*, 562
    and provincial sales tax, 560–561
registrants, *def.*, 548
return for registrants, *illus.*, 551; 570
schedule, *def.*, 581
simplified accounting, *def.*, 550–551
    quick method, *def.*, 550
    streamlined methods, *def.*, 550
small suppliers, *def.*, 548
supplies, *def.*, 546
    taxable, *def.*, 548
    tax-exempt, *def.*, 548
    zero-rated, *def.*, 548
tracking:
    with one G/L account, 553–564
    with three G/L accounts, 568–572
    with ten G/L accounts, 574–575
withdrawals for personal use, 561–562
Gross earnings, *def.*, 415; *see also* Payroll
Gross margin, *def.*, 101; *see also* Gross profit from sales
    ratio, *def.*, 109
Gross profit from sales, *def.*, 101
    in accounting equation, 123
    on income statement, 100; 106
Gross sales, *def.*, 104
    on income statement, 104; 106
GST, *see* Goods and Services Tax (GST)

Handwriting, importance of clear, 314; 318
Heading, on balance sheet, 10
    on bank reconciliation statement, 398
    on income statement, 22
    on statement of changes in financial position, 258
    on statement of owner's equity, 72
    on statement of retained earnings, 254
    on trial balance, 62
    on worksheet, 68
Historical statement, *def.*, 402
Holiday pay, 420–421

Imprest system, *def.*, 353; *see also* Petty cash
Income, *def.*, 20; *see also* Net income
    before taxes, 247; 255
    from operations, *def.*, 183
        on income statement, 184
Income statement, *def.*, 22; *illus.*, 21; 71; 100; 103; 106; 106; 108; 184–185; 237; 247; 255
    accounting period on, 22
    bad debts on, 184–185
    body of, 22
    cash short and over on, 347
    condensed, *illus.*, 100
    corporation, 255
    cost of delivered goods on, 106; 108; 184
    cost of goods sold on, 100; 108; 184–185
    depreciation expense on, 184–185
    dollar signs on, 22–23
    form of:
        multi-step, 184
        single-step, 185
    gross profit from sales on, 100; 106
    heading of, 22
    inventories on, 106
    of merchandising firm, 100
    net income on, 21
    of partnership, 237
    with percentage column, 108
    purchases discounts on, 105–106
    purchases returns and allowances on, 105–106
    sales discounts on, 104; 106
    sales returns and allowances on, 104; 106
    worksheet section, 69–70; 172–173; 177
Income tax, *see also* Payroll
    corporation, 246–247
    partnership, 246
    single proprietorship, 246
Input tax credit, *def.*, 546
    account, *def.*, 568–569
Insurable earnings, *def.*, 424; *see also* Payroll
Insurance, prepaid, adjustment for, 164

Integration accounts, *def.*, 481
Internal control measures, *see* Control measures
Inventory, *def.*, 100
    in accounting equation, 122–123
    on balance sheet, 108
    beginning, *def.*, 124; 175
    changes, 123–124
    ending, 176
    periodic method, *def.*, 101
    perpetual method, *def.*, 101
    physical, *def.*, 102
    on worksheet, 172–173; 175–176
Inventory accounting:
    AccPac Bedford, 492–493
    AccPac Plus, 494
    Summation, 522
Investment, owner's, *def.*, 4
    in accounting equation, 5; 7
    on balance sheet, 9
Invoice, *def.*, 51; *illus.*, 51; 149; 151; 330
    batch, *def.*, 304
    cancelling of, 341
    direct posting from, 304; 306
    with federal GST, 553
    with provincial sales tax, 283; 559–560
Issued share capital, *def.*, 247

Job costing, *def.*, 494
Journal, *def.*, 53; *illus.*, 54–55; *see also* General journal; Special journals
    in accounting cycle, 53; 153
    advantages of, 53
    combination, *def.*, 350
    synoptic, *def.*, 359
    voucher, *def.*, 200; *illus.*, 201
Journalizing, *def.*, 53
    batch totals, 304–308; 357–358; *def.*, 304
    under microcomputer method, 197–204
    shortcuts in, 304–320; 357–366
Journalless bookkeeping, 308–310; 358; *def.*, 308
    advantages of, 309
    binder in, 308–309
    disadvantages of, 310
    evaluation of, 308–310

Laid-down cost, *def.*, 549
Land:
    on balance sheet, 13; 186
    as fixed asset, 13; 169
Language of business, *def.*, 3
Ledger, *def.*, 34; *see also* General ledger; Subsidiary ledgers

INDEX

in accounting cycle, 56
accounts payable, 331–332
accounts receivable, 274–275
closing, 75–76
documentary, *def.*, 310
general, 35; 57
payroll, *def.*, 443
subsidiary, 275
trial balance of, 62–63
Ledger accounts, *see* Accounts
Ledgerless bookkeeping, *def.*, 310
for accounts payable, 358
for accounts receivable, 310–311
evaluation of, 311
Legal entity, *def.*, 243
Liabilities, *def.*, 5
in accounting equation, 5–6; 7; 9; 17; 20
on balance sheet, 11–12
current, *def.*, 12
long-term, *def.*, 12
Liability accounts:
balance of, 61
changes in, 35; 38
opening, 33
Limited company, *see* Corporation
Limited liability, *def.*, 244
Liquidity order, *def.*, 10
Long-term liabilities, *def.*, 12
on balance sheet, 13
bonds payable, 245
mortgage payable, 12
Lotus 1-2-3, *def.*, 81; *illus.*, 82
built-in functions in, 82; 87
cell cursor in, 82
cell cursor indicator, 82
cells in, 82
commands in, 83; *illus.*, 83
macros in, 83
scrolling in, 82
simple example of, 84–89

Macro, *def.*, 83
Magnetic ink character recognition (MICR), *def.*, 385
Mainframe computer, *def.*, 80
Management (managerial) accounting, *def.*, 77
Manual accounting systems:
combination journal in, 358–361
journalizing batch totals in, 304–307; 357
journalless bookkeeping in, 308; 358
journals in, 53–54
ledgerless bookkeeping in, 310–311; 358
ledgers in, 58; 274–275; 331
one-write system in, 311–320; 361–366; 464; 467–469

shortcuts in, 304; 357
source documents in, 51–52
special journals in, 272; 329
Marketable securities, *def.*, 165
on balance sheet, 166
Markups, *def.*, 109
examples of, 109
Matching principle, *def.*, 20
in accounting equation, 20
Menu bar, *def.*, 480; *illus.*, 479; 481
Merchandise inventory, *see* Inventory
Merchandise purchases, *see* Purchases account; Purchases discounts; Purchases journal; Purchases returns and allowances
Merchandising firm, *def.*, 99
transactions analyzed, 115–127
Microcomputer, *def.*, 81
electronic spreadsheet for, 81-90
general ledger system, 192–219; 481–485; 495–506
keyboard, *illus.*, 199
Modular-type accounting software, *def.*, 494
Mortgage, *def.*, 12
Mortgage payable, *def.*, 12
on balance sheet, 13; 107; 186
current portion of, 12
Multi-column purchases journal, 332–333
Multi-step income statement, *def.*, 184; *illus.*, 184

Negotiable instruments, *def.*, 290
Net earnings, *see* Net income
Net income, *def.*, 20; 23
in accounting equation, 20
in balance sheet, 21
in income statement, 21
ratio, *def.*, 109
on worksheet, 69; 177
Net loss, *def.*, 20; 23
in accounting equation, 20
in income statement, 23
on worksheet, 70; 177
Net pay, *see* Payroll
Net profit, *see* Net income
Net purchases, *def.*, 105
on income statement, 106
Net sales, *def.*, 104
on income statement, 106
No-par-value share, *def.*, 248
Notes to financial statements, 256
NSF cheque, *def.*, 382
on bank reconciliation statement, 298
on bank statement, 386
transaction analyzed, 400–401
Numbering of accounts, 57; 147; 195

Obsolescence in depreciation, 169
Off-shelf accounting packages, *def.*, 193
One-write applications:
accounts payable, 361–366
cash disbursements journal board, *def.*, 362; *illus.*, 363
cheque writing, 365
collating and assembling forms, 362; *illus.*, 363
double-window envelope, *def.*, 365
layout, 362; *illus.*, 363
posting distribution, 362–363
purchase register board, *def.*, 362; *illus.*, 363
recording:
cash disbursements, 364–365
credit purchases, 362
returns and credits, 364
accounts receivable, 311–320
advantages of, 320
ballpoint pen, *def.*, 314; *illus.*, 313
carbon sheet, *def.*, 314; *illus.*, 313
collating and assembling forms, 314–316; *illus.*, 316
combination journal, 313
common transactions analyzed, 315–319
entering zero balance, 315–316
envelopes, 319
layout, 313–314; *illus.*, 313
patient's ledger card, *def.*, 314; *illus.*, 316
patient transaction slip, *def.*, 314; *illus.*, 313; 319
receipt/fee bill section of, 314; *illus.*, 316
stub section of, 314; *illus.*, 316
function of, 316–317
pegboard, *def.*, 313; *illus.*, 313
recording charge and part payment, 317
payroll, 464; 467–469
advantages of, 467
carbon sheet, 467
cheque writing, 468
collating and assembling forms, 467; *illus.*, 467
employee's individual earnings record, *illus.*, 467
employee's pay statement, *illus.*, 467
journal, *illus.*, 468
layout, *illus.*, 467
monthly procedures, 469
paying the employees, 468
One-write boards, *see* Pegboards
One-write principle, *def.*, 311
One-write system, *def.*, 311

INDEX

for accounts payable, 361–366
for accounts receivable, 311–320
  advantages of, 320; 365–366
  ballpoint pen in, 314; *illus.*, 313
  evaluation of, 320
  manual equipment in, 311
  for payroll, 464; 467–496
Opening entry, *def.*, 56
Open-item system, *def.*, 310; 487
  compared with balance-forward system, 311
Operating cycle, *def.*, 165
Operating expenses, *def.*, 101
Operating income, **see** Income, from operations
Operating statement, **see** Income statement
Operating system software, *def.*, 83
  Macintosh Finder, 193
  MS-DOS, *def.*, 83
  OS/2, *def.*, 83; 193
  Unix, *def.*, 193
  Xenix, *def.*, 526
Original entry, book of, *def.*, 53
Originating transaction data, 51–53; 148–153
Outstanding cheques, *def.*, 391
Outstanding shares, *def.*, 247
Overtime, **see** Payroll
Owner's drawing redefined, 24
Owner's equity, *def.*, 5
  in accounting equation, 5–6; 7; 9; 17; 20
  accounts for, 32–33
  in balance sheet, 9; 13
  capital section, 12
  decreasing, 18–19; 38
  expense section, 17
  increasing, 16–17; 35
  opening, 9
  revenue section, 17
  statement of, 72
  total of, 21; 71
Ownership, types of, 228–229

Partners' equity, *def.*, 229
  on balance sheet, 233; 235; 238
  statement of, *def.*, 237; *illus.*, 238
Partnership, *def.*, 229
  accounting records for, 230–231
  balance sheet, 233; 235; 238
  capital accounts, 231
  characteristics of, 229–230
  division of profits (losses), 235-239
  equity of, 229
  formation, 231–235
  income statement, 237

investment:
  cash, 231
  cash and assets, 231–232
  opening entries for, 231–235
  postclosing trial balance, 239
  recording profits (losses) for, 235–239
  worksheet, 236
Par value share, *def.*, 247
Patient's ledger card, *def.*, 314; *illus.*, 313
Payables, *def.*, 11–12; **see also** Accounts payable
Payee of cheque, *def.*, 341
Payroll, 413–476
  accounting for, 439–449
  AccPac Bedford, 492–493
  accumulated earnings, *def.*, 443
  application, *def.*, 413–414
  attendance record for salaried employees, 419
  bank account, *def.*, 454
  basic agreement, 417
  book, *illus.*, 465–466
  Canada Pension Plan, 421–424; *def.*, 421
    calculation method, *illus.*, 424
    contribution tables, 423
    deduction criteria, 421
    employees' contribution, 422–424
    employer's contribution, 424
    pensionable earnings, 422
    year's basic exemption, 422
  clock card, *def.*, 417; *illus.*, 419
  commission plan, 415
  company pension plan, 433
  computerized, 492–493; 509–521
  and Consumer Price Index, 429
  contract of employment, 415
  daily report of time, *def.*, 417
  deductions from gross earnings, 421–434
  employee's individual earnings record, *def.*, 443; *illus.*, 444; 464
  employee's statement of earnings, *def.*, 455; *illus.*, 455
  employee's taxable earnings, *def.*, 431
  Employer Health Tax (EHT), *def.*, 449
  employer's responsibilities for, 439–440
  Employment Standards Act, 415
  entries for, 445–449
  garnishments, 432–433; *def.*, 432
  government demands, 433
  gross earnings, *def.*, 415
    computation of, 418–421
  holiday pay, 420–421; 516
  hourly-rate plan, 414
  hours of work and wages, 415–418

income tax deduction tables for, 429–432
journal, *def.*, 444
ledger, *def.*, 443
Net Claim Code, *def.*, 427
net pay, *def.*, 434
  computation of, 434
other deductions, 433–434
overtime, 415–416
paying, 454–457
  by bank deposit, 456–457
  by cash, 454
  by cheque, 454–456
personnel department, *def.*, 414
piece-rate plan, 415
premium holiday pay, 420, 421
priority of deductions, 421
provincial health insurance plan, 432
public holiday pay, 420–421
reconciliation of payroll bank account, 456
recording, 445–447
records, 439–440
register, *def.*, 441; *illus.*, 441
  analysis of, 440–441
  combined hourly/salary, 442
  hourly, *illus.*, 441
  proof of, 442–443
  recording totals, 445–446
  salary, *illus.*, 441
returns:
  Canada Pension Plan, 458
  form PD7AR, 458; *illus.*, 458
  income tax, 458
  other, 458
  unemployment insurance, 458
salary-commission plan, 415
salary plan, 414
social insurance number (SIN), *def.*, 414; *illus.*, 414
statement of remuneration paid, 455; 457
summary, *def.*, 440
supervisor's daily report of time, 418
take-home pay, *def.*, 434
taxes:
  expense (employer's), 447–449
  federal and provincial income, 427–431
  form TD1, 416; 428
  income, withholding, 427–431
  tax deduction tables, 429–431
  tax demands, 433
  T4 slip, 460
time clock, 418
timekeeping, 417–418; 463–464
  book, *illus.*, 464
unemployment insurance, *def.*, 424

602 INDEX

employee's premium, 424
employer responsibilities for, 427
employer's premium, 424
insurable earnings, *def.*, 424
    tables, 425
    Schedule 2, *illus.*, 425
    tables, *illus.*, 426
union dues, 435
union initiation fees, 433
vacation pay, 420; 516
voluntary deductions, 433–434
Payroll clearing account, *def.*, 447
  entries for, 447
Payroll journal, *def.*, 444; **see** *also* Payroll, register
  in one-write system, *def.*, 467
Payroll taxes expense, *def.*, 447
  journal entry for, 448
Payroll tax statements, 459–461
  T4 Supplementary, *def.*, 459; *illus.*, 460
  T4A Supplementary, 460
  T4 and T4A Summaries, 460–461; *illus.*, 461
PD7AR form, *def.*, 458; *illus.*, 458; **see** *also* Payroll
Pegboards, *def.*, 313; *illus.*, 313
  accounts payable, *def.*, 362; *illus.*, 363
  accounts receivable, *def.*, 313; *illus.*, 313
  one-write principle in, 311; 318
  payroll, *illus.*, 467
Pensionable earnings, *def.*, 422; **see** *also* Payroll
Period, accounting, *def.*, 22
Periodic inventory method, *def.*, 101; **see** *also* Inventory
  compared with perpetual, 127–134
  limitations of, 134
Permanent accounts, *def.*, 75
Perpetual existence, *def.*, 245
Perpetual inventory method, *def.*, 101; 127; **see** *also* Inventory
  advantages of, 133–134
  compared with periodic, 127–134
Petty cash, 347–353
  book, 352–353
    proof of, 353
  box, 349
  disbursements, 350
  establishing, 348–349
  flowchart of, 348
  imprest system, *def.*, 353
  journalizing entries for, 351
  proof of, 351
  replenishing, 350–351
  reporting of, 353
  requisition for, 350–351

system, *def.*, 348
voucher, 350; *illus.*, 350
Physical inventory, *def.*, 102
Postclosing trial balance, *def.*, 75; *illus.*, 78; 190; 239
  in accounting cycle, 75
  in computer system, 219
Posting, *def.*, 57; 154
  in accounting cycle, 56
  to accounts payable ledger, 329; 331
  to accounts receivable ledger, 276–277
  to balance ledger form, 59
  from cash payments journal, 329–331; 344
  from cash receipts journal, 295
  date of, 59
  direct, *def.*, 276; 304
  double, *def.*, 279
  from general journal, 59
  under microcomputer method, 204
  proof of accounts receivable, 280–281
  from purchases journal, 330; 333
  reference numbers, 59
  from sales journal, 277
  shortcuts in, 304–306; 357–358
Posting journal, *def.*, 499; *illus.*, 506
Preferred share, *def.*, 248
Pre-list, *def.*, 306; *illus.*, 306
Pre-operating balance sheet, *def.*, 9; *illus.*, 9; 13
Prepaid expenses, *def.*, 163; **see** *also* Adjustments
  on balance sheet, 186
  for insurance, 164
  other, 164–165
  for supplies, 163
  on worksheet, 172
Prepaid insurance, *def.*, 164
  adjustment for, 164
Profit, *def.*, 20; **see** *also* Income
Profit and loss statement, **see** Income statement
Proofs:
  of accounts payable ledger, 332
  of accounts receivable ledger, 281
  of cash, 291–292; 346
  of columnar purchases journal, 333
  of general ledger, 62–63
  of petty cash disbursements, 351
  of posting, 59; 306–307
  zero, of cash payments journal, 344
  zero, of cash receipts journal, 296
  zero, under microcomputer system, 207
  zero, of trial balance, 62–63
Proof tape, *def.*, 306; *illus.*, 306
Property, plant, and equipment, **see** Fixed assets

Proprietorship, **see** Owner's equity; Single proprietorship
Prospective statements, *def.*, 402
Provincial income tax, **see** Payroll
Provincial sales tax, 117–119; **see** *also* Sales tax, GST
Purchase allowances, *def.*, 126; **see** *also* Purchases returns and allowances
Purchase invoice, *def.*, 152; *illus.*, 151; **see** *also* Invoice
Purchase invoice binder, 358
Purchase order, *def.*, 150; *illus.*, 150
Purchase return, *def.*, 105; **see** *also* Purchases returns and allowances
Purchases account, *def.*, 124–125; *illus.*, 155
  cash, 124
  classification of, 125
  credit, 124
  net, *def.*, 105
Purchases discounts, *def.*, 105; **see** *also* Cash discount
  analysis of, 126; 176
  in cash payments journal, 343
  classification of, 126; 176
  on income statement, 106
Purchases journal, *def.*, 329; *illus.*, 329
  multi-column, 332–333
  posting from, 331
  proof of, 333
  totalling, 329; 333
Purchases returns and allowances, *def.*, 105
  analysis of, 126; 176; 333
  classification of, 126; 176
  credit memo received for, 153
  debit memo issued for, 152
  on income statement, 106; 184
  recording, 126; 334

Quick method, GST accounting, *def.*, 550
Quick trial balance, *def.*, 63

Real-time accounting, *def.*, 193
  compared with batch processing, 507–509
Receipt, *illus.*, 290
Receipt or statement of account form, *def.*, 297; *illus.*, 298; 319
Reconciling bank statement, **see** Bank reconciliation statement
Register, **see** Journal
Register, payroll, **see** Payroll
Registrants, GST, *def.*, 548
Remittance slip, *def.*, 52; *illus.*, 52; 290
Replenishing petty cash, 350–351

INDEX

Report form, of balance sheet, *def.*, 23; *illus.*, 21; 71; 107; 186
Responsibility, division of, 293; 341; 349
Restrictive endorsement, *def.*, 291; *illus.*, 292
Retailer, *def.*, 100
Retail sales tax, *def.*, 117
    returns analyzed, 118
Retained earnings, *def.*, 252
    on balance sheet, 252; 257
    deficit in, 252
    statement of, 254; 256
Returns and allowances:
    purchases, 126
    sales, 117–118
Revenue, *def.*, 17
    in accounting equation, 17
    in chart of accounts, 57
    describing, 22
    factors affecting sales, 104
    in income statement, 21–22; 184–185
    other, *def.*, 183
    rules of debit and credit, 42–43
Revenue and expense summary account, *def.*, 73
    in closing procedures, 73–74
Revenue and expense transactions, *def.*, 16
Revenue recognition principle, 18
Revenue transactions, *def.*, 16
    in accounting equation, 16–18
    recording, 42–43
Rounding of amounts, 256
Ruling:
    on balance sheet, 14; 21
    on income statement, 21
    on special journals, 277; 282; 285; 295–296; 329; 333; 343
    on trial balance, 63
    on worksheet, 69; 177

Salaries, *see also* Payroll
    in partnerships, 230
    in single proprietorship, 230
Sales, *def.*, 141; *see also* Sales journal
    analysis of, 116–120
    cash, 116–117
    classification of, 118
    credit, 117
    factors affecting, 104
    with GST, 553–555
    invoice, *see* Invoice
    net, *def.*, 104
    with provincial sales tax, 117–118
    revenue, *see* Revenue
    statement of account, 297–298
Sales allowance, *def.*, 104; *see also* Sales returns and allowances

Sales discounts, *def.*, 104
    analysis of, 104; 120
    in cash receipts journal, 296
    classification of, 120
    and GST, 557–558
    on income statement, 106
Sales invoice, *def.*, 51; *see also* Invoice
    batch, *def.*, 304
    binder, *def.*, 308
Sales journal, *def.*, 273; *see also* Special journals
    with federal GST, 562
    with provincial sales tax (PST), 281–284
Sales returns, *def.*, 104; *see also* Sales returns and allowances
Sales returns and allowances, *def.*, 104
    analysis of, 117–118
    classification of, 120
    credit memo for, 148; 277–278; *illus.*, 149
    and GST, 555–556
    on income statement, 106
    and provincial sales tax, 117–118; 282–284
Sales revenue, *see* Revenue
Sales slip, *def.*, 51
    cash proof of, 292
Sales tax, GST, *see* Goods and Services Tax (GST)
Sales tax, provincial (PST), *def.*, 117
    analysis of, 117–118
    on invoice, 283
    in sales journal, 282
    on sales returns and allowances, 118–119; 282–284
    table of, 117
Schedule of accounts payable, *def.*, 331; *illus.*, 332
Schedule of accounts receivable, *def.*, 280; *illus.*, 281
    by age, *illus.*, 167
Separate entity concept, *def.*, 10
Service charge, bank, 384
    adjustment, 400–401
    on bank reconciliation statement, 398
    on bank statement, 386
Share capital, *def.*, 247; *see also* Corporation
    on balance sheet, 251–252
    entries for, 249–250
Share certificate, *def.*, 244; *illus.*, 244
Shareholders, *def.*, 243
Shareholders' equity, *def.*, 229
    retained earnings in, 252
    share capital in, 251–252
Shares, *def.*, 244; *illus.*, 244
    authorized, 247
    common, 248

    issued for cash, 249
    issued for other assets, 249–250
    issued for services, 250
    no-par-value, 248
    outstanding, 247
    par value, 247
    preferred, 248
Shipping terms, *def.*, 151
SIN, *see* Payroll
Single proprietorship, *def.*, 6
    balance sheet for, 9
    income statement for, 21
    and income tax, 246
    and owner's equity, 12
Single-step income statement, *def.*, 185; *illus.*, 185
Six-column worksheet, *see* Worksheet
Small suppliers (re GST), *def.*, 548
Social insurance number, *see* Payroll
Sole proprietorship, *see* Single proprietorship
Source documents, *def.*, 51; *illus.*, 51–52
    in accounting cycle, 51
    direct posting from, 276; 304
    function of, 51
    journalizing from, 53–54
Source journal, *def.*, 502
Special journals, *def.*, 272
    cash payments, 342–344
    cash receipts, 294–296
    fees earned, 285
    payroll, 444
    purchases, 329; 333
    sales, 273; 277; 282; 562
    posting from, 276–277
Spreadsheet, *see* Electronic spreadsheet
Statement of account, *def.*, 297
    aged accounts receivable, 298
    descriptive, *illus.*, 298
    non-descriptive, *def.*, 297
Statement of changes in financial position, *def.*, 257
    direct method, 250
    financing activities in, *def.*, 259
    indirect format, *illus.*, 258
    investing activities in, *def.*, 259
    operating activities in, *def.*, 259
Statement of owner's equity, *def.*, 70; *illus.*, 72; 187
Statement of partners' equity, *def.*, 237; *illus.*, 238
Statement of remuneration paid, *see* Payroll
Statement of retained earnings, *illus.*, 254; 256
Stockholders, *def.*, 243
Straight-line depreciation, *def.*, 170
Streamlined accounting, GST, *def.*, 550

INDEX

Subsidiary ledgers, *def.*, 274
    for accounts payable, 329–330
    for accounts receivable, 274–275
Summary account, revenue and expense, 73
Summation, *def.*, 194; 521
    accounts payable system, 521
    accounts receivable system, 521
    backup procedures, 215–216; *def.*, 215
    balance sheet, 212; 215; *illus.*, 214
    built-in math function, 522
    chart of accounts, 195
        creating, 196
        display window, 202
        importance of, 202
    dummy balance sheet, *illus.*, 197
    G/L detail report, *illus.*, 206
    G/L journal, *illus.*, 205
    G/L master menu, *illus.*, 198
    G/L report generator, 205
    G/L transaction entry grid, 199–204
    G/L update program screen, 196
    and GST accounting, 573–582
    income statement, 211–212; *illus.*, 213
    inventory management system, 522
    journalizing and posting under, 197–206
    master system menu, 198
    menu program, 522
    month-end close, 216-217
    on-line help system, 522
    on-line text editor, 522
    opening entry under, 204
    order entry/point-of-sale/invoicing system, 522
    periodic inventory adjustment, 209–211
    schedule of owner's equity, 215
    system utilities menu, 522
    trial balance, *illus.*, 207
        postclosing, 219
    worksheet, 207–211; *illus.*, 208
    year-end close, 217–218
    zero proof under, 207
Supplies, GST, *def.*, 546
    taxable, *def.*, 548
    tax-exempt, *def.*, 548
    zero-rated, *def.*, 548
Supplies on hand, adjustment for, 164
Synoptic journal, *see* Combination journal

T-account, *def.*, 32; *illus.*, 33
    calculating balance of, 40
Take-home pay, *see* Payroll
Taxable supplies, GST, *def.*, 548
Taxes, *see* Income tax; Goods and Services Tax (GST); Payroll; Sales tax, provincial (PST)
Tax-exempt supplies, GST, *def.*, 548
TD1 form, *def.*, 414; *illus.*, 416; 428; *see also* Payroll
Temporary accounts, *def.*, 76
Ten-column worksheet, *see* Worksheet
Terms, discount, 104
T4 Supplementary (tax) slip, *def.*, 459; *illus.*, 460; *see also* Payroll
Tickler file, *def.*, 342; *illus.*, 342
Time clock, *see* Payroll
Time deposit accounting, *def.*, 377
Time deposits, *def.*, 376
Timekeeping, *def.*, 417; *see also* Payroll
Time-period concept, *def.*, 22
Total operating expense ratio, *def.*, 109
Transfer process, *def.*, 73–75
Transit, deposit in, *def.*, 391
Transportation-in, *def.*, 105
    analysis of, 125
    classification of, 126
    on income statement, 106
Transposition error, 363; 396
Travelling stub, *def.*, 314; *illus.*, 316
    advantages of, 317
Trial balance, *def.*, 62; *illus.*, 63
    in accounting cycle, 62; 156
    of accounts payable, 332
    of accounts receivable, 280
    analysis of, 62–63
    formal, 62
    of general ledger, 62
    postclosing, 75
    worksheet section, 69
    zero proof, 62; *illus.*, 63

Uncollectible accounts, *see* Bad debts
Unemployment insurance, *see* Payroll
Unexpired cost, *def.*, 163; *see also* Assets; Prepaid expenses
Union dues, *see* Payroll
Union initiation fees, *see* Payroll
Unit-of-measure concept, *def.*, 24
Unix, *def.*, 193
Unlimited liability, *def.*, 230
Unrecorded bank interest expense, 171
Unrecorded interest earned, 171

Value of assets, *def.*, 11
VisiCalc, *def.*, 81
Vendors, *def.*, 486
Vertical accounting package, *def.*, 525
Voided cheque, *def.*, 340; *illus.*, 340
Voucher cheque, *def.*, 339; *illus.*, 339
Voucher, journal, *def.*, 200; *illus.*, 201
Voucher, petty cash, *def.*, 350; *illus.*, 350

Wages, *see* Payroll
Wholesalers, *def.*, 99
Withdrawals, by owner, 19; 24; *def.*, 19
    in accounting equation, 24
    analysis of, 24
    on balance sheet, 21
    closing of, 74–75
    and GST accounting, 561–562
    on worksheet, 69
Withholding taxes, *see* Payroll
Working capital, *def.*, 257
    computation of, 258
Worksheet, *def.*, 68; *illus.*, 69; 172–173
    in accounting cycle, 68–70
    advantage of, 68
    computerized, 70;
    heading of, 68; 161
    under microcomputer system, 207–211
    net income in, 69; 177
    net loss in, 70; 177
    for partnership, 236
    six-column form, 68–70
    ten-column form, 161–178
Writing boards, *see* Pegboards
Writing dollar amounts, 318

Xenix, *def.*, 526

Year, accounting, *def.*, 22

Zero proof, *def.*, 62
    of cash payments, 344
    of cash receipts, 296
    under microcomputer system, 207
    of trial balance, 62–63
Zero-rated supplies, GST, *def.*, 548

— — — — — — — — — — — — — *CUT HERE* — — — — — — — — — — — — — —

STUDENT REPLY CARD

In order to improve future editions, we are seeking your comments on this text, INTRODUCTORY COLLEGE ACCOUNTING, Second Edition by Henry Kaluza.
   After you have used the book, please answer the following questions and return this form via Business Reply Mail. *Thanks in advance for your feedback!*

1. Name of your college or university: _____

2. Major program of study: _____

3. Your instructor for this course: _____

4. Are there any sections of this text which were not assigned as course reading?_____
   If so, please specify those chapters or portions:

5. How would you rate the overall accessibility of the content? Please feel free to comment on reading level, writing style, terminology, layout and design features, and such learning aids as chapter objectives, summaries, and appendices.

— — — — — — — — — — — — — *FOLD HERE* — — — — — — — — — — — — — —

6. What did you like *best* about this book?

7. What did you like *least*?

If you would like to say more, we'd love to hear from you. Please write to us at the address shown on the reverse of this card.

— — — CUT HERE — — —

681-
1232

— — — FOLD HERE — — —

**BUSINESS
REPLY MAIL**

No Postage Stamp
Necessary If Mailed
in Canada

Postage will be paid by

McGraw-Hill

7115

Attn.: Sponsoring Editor, Office Administration
The College Division
McGraw-Hill Ryerson Limited
300 Water Street
Whitby, Ontario
L1N 9Z9